Shakespeare's Religious Language

A Dictionary

ATHLONE SHAKESPEARE DICTIONARY SERIES

Shakespeare's Religious Language

A Dictionary

R. CHRIS HASSEL, JR

continuum
NEW YORK • LONDON

Continuum
The Tower Building   80 Maiden Lane
11 York Road   Suite 704
London SE1 7NX   New York, NY 10038

First published 2005
Reprinted 2006
Paperback edition 2007

British Library Cataloguing-in-Publication Data
A catalogue record for this book is available from the British Library.

ISBN-10: 0-8264-5890-4 (hardback)
0-8264-9332-7 (paperback)
ISBN-13: 978-0-8264-5890-2 (hardback)
978-0-8264-9332-3 (paperback)

Library of Congress Cataloging-in-Publication Data
Hassel, R. Chris (Rudolph Chris), 1939–
Shakespeare's relgious language: a dictionary / R. Chris Hassel, Jr.
p.   cm.—(Athlone Shakespeare dictionary series)
Includes bibliographical references and index.
ISBN 0–8264–5890–4
1. Shakespeare, William, 1564–1616—Language—Glossaries, etc.
2. Shakespeare, William, 1564–1616—Religion—Dictionaries.
3. English language—Early modern, 1500–1700—Dictionaries.   4. Religion
in literature—Dictionaries.   5. Religion—Dictionaries.
I. Title.   II. Series.
PR2892.H37.   2005
822.3′3—dc22   2004057978

Typeset by RefineCatch Limited, Bungay, Suffolk
Printed and bound in Great Britain by Antony Rowe Ltd., Chippenham, Wiltshire

To Sedley,
for her help and encouragement throughout the years
but especially on this project,
and for her faith, her hope, and her love.

Contents

List of Figures

Series Editor's Preface

The Athlone Shakespeare Dictionaries aim to provide the student of Shakespeare with a series of authoritative guides to the principal subject-areas covered by the plays and poems. They are produced by scholars who are experts both on Shakespeare and on the topic of the individual dictionary, based on the most recent scholarship, succinctly written and accessibly presented. They offer readers a self-contained body of information on the topic under discussion, its occurrence and significance in Shakespeare's works, and its contemporary meanings.

The topics are all vital ones for understanding the plays and poems; they have been selected for their importance in illuminating aspects of Shakespeare's writings where an informed understanding of the range of Shakespeare's usage, and of the contemporary literary, historical and cultural issues involved, will add to the reader's appreciation of his work. Because of the diversity of the topics covered in the series, individual dictionaries may vary in emphasis and approach, but the aim and basic format of the entries remain the same from volume to volume.

Sandra Clark
Birkbeck College
University of London

Acknowledgements

Thanks are due to Vanderbilt University for its continuing support of my research, including a sabbatical in the spring and summer of 2002 which was dedicated to this project; to the helpful and knowledgeable staff of the Vanderbilt Library, in particular Paula Covington, Dale Manning, Yvonne Boyer and Scott McDermott; to my colleagues in the Vanderbilt English Department and Divinity Schools, particularly Jack Forstman, Paul Elledge, Roy Gottfried and John Plummer; to the secretaries of the Vanderbilt English Department; to graduate assistants Jennifer Clement and Jason Lovvorn for their careful and insightful assistance on the bibliographies and the notes; to all the scholars and students who have taught me about Shakespeare and religion; to Sandra Clark, the editor of this series, for her consistent encouragement and good advice; to my good friends Layng Martine and Ben Curtis for their patient interest in and suggestions about this work; and last, and first, to my wife Sedley, without whose cheerful, thoughtful and conscientious editorial assistance the work would have taken much longer to finish, and been much less accurate as well. The faults, of course, 'I acknowledge mine'.

Abbreviations

1. *Often-cited works, primary and secondary*

Andrewes   Andrewes, Lancelot, *Ninety-Six Sermons*, 1843, 5 vols, 1967r. Andrewes, 3: 241, cites vol. 3 of this edition.

Arden   The individual volumes of *The Arden Shakespeare*, London: Methuen & Co.

BCP   *Book of Common Prayer, 1559: The Elizabethan Prayer Book*, ed. John E. Booty, Charlottesville: The University Press of Virginia, 1976.

Becon   The Parker Society edition of the works of Thomas Becon, '*Chaplain to Archbishop Cranmer, Prebendary of Canterbury, &c.*', 1843–44. Becon, 2: 463, cites vol. 2 of this edition.

BEV   *The Complete Works of Shakespeare*, ed. David Bevington, 4th edn, 1992.

Britannica   *Encyclopaedia Britannica*, 14th edn, London, 1929.

Bullinger   The Parker Society edition of '*The Decades of Henry Bullinger, Minister of the Church of Zurich*', 1849–52. Bullinger, 4: 287, cites vol. 4 of this edition.

Certaine Sermons   *Certaine Sermons or Homilies appointed to be read in Churches, In the Time of the late Queen Elizabeth*, 1623.

Donne   Donne, John, *The Sermons of John Donne*, ed. George R. Potter and Evelyn M. Simpson, 10 vols, 1953–62. Donne, 8: 324, cites vol. 8 of this edition.

Hooker   Hooker, Richard, *Of the Laws of Ecclesiastical Polity*. The Folger Library Edition (1977–81) which I cite is in 3 vols, containing Books 1–4, Book 5 and Books 6–8 respectively. Hooker, 4: 311, refers to Book 4 of the *Laws*, printed in the first vol. of this edn.

LW   *Luther's Works*, 55 vols, individually edited, St Louis: Concordia Press, 1955–86.

NDS   Bullough, Geoffrey, *Narrative and Dramatic Sources of Shakespeare*, 8 vols, 1957–75.

NewCathEncy   *New Catholic Encyclopedia*, 1967.

NV   The New Variorum editions of individual works of Shakespeare. NV *1H4* would refer to the edn of *1H4* in this series.

OED   *The Oxford English Dictionary*, 2nd edn, 1989.

OxfordEncyRef   *The Oxford Encyclopedia of the Reformation*, 1996.

PEL   *William Shakespeare: The Complete Works* ('The Complete Pelican Shakespeare'), ed. Alfred Harbage, 1969.

PL	*Paradise Lost*, in John Milton, *The Complete Poetical Works*, 1965.
RIV	*The Riverside Shakespeare*, ed. G. Blakemore Evans, 2nd edn, 1997.
ST	Aquinas, Thomas, St, *Summa Theologica*, English edn in 3 vols, trans. Fathers of the English Dominican Province, 1947–48. Citations are to the first, second and third parts of the *Summa*, however, and not to these three vols. *ST* II.2.146 would thus refer to part two of the second part, question 146.
Tilley	Tilley, Morris Palmer, *A Dictionary of the Proverbs in England in the Sixteenth and Seventeenth Centuries*, 1950.
Tyndale	The Parker Society edition of the works of William Tyndale, translator of an influential English New Testament and *'Martyr, 1536'*, 1848–50. Tyndale, 2: 311, cites vol. 2 of this edition.

2. *Books of the Bible*

Chron.	Chronicles
Col.	Colossians
Cor.	Corinthians
Dan.	Daniel
Deut.	Deuteronomy
Eccles.	Ecclesiastes
Ecclus.	Ecclesiasticus
Eph.	Ephesians
Ex.	Exodus
Gal.	Galatians
Gen.	Genesis
Heb.	Hebrews
Isa.	Isaiah
Jer.	Jeremiah
Lam.	Lamentations
Lev.	Leviticus
Matt.	Matthew
Num.	Numbers
Prov.	Proverbs
Ps.	Psalms
Rev.	Revelation
Rom.	Romans
Sam.	Samuel
Thess.	Thessalonians
Tim.	Timothy

3. *Shakespeare's Works*

ADO	*Much Ado About Nothing*
ANT	*The Tragedy of Antony and Cleopatra*
AWW	*All's Well That Ends Well*
AYL	*As You Like It*

COR	*The Tragedy of Coriolanus*
CYM	*Cymbeline*
ERR	*The Comedy of Errors*
HAM	*The Tragedy of Hamlet, Prince of Denmark*
1H4	*The First Part of Henry the Fourth*
2H4	*The Second Part of Henry the Fourth*
H5	*The Life of Henry the Fifth*
1H6	*The First Part of Henry the Sixth*
2H6	*The Second Part of Henry the Sixth*
3H6	*The Third Part of Henry the Sixth*
H8	*The Famous History of the Life of Henry the Eighth*
JC	*The Tragedy of Julius Caesar*
JN	*The Life and Death of King John*
LC	*A Lover's Complaint*
LLL	*Love's Labour's Lost*
LR	*The Tragedy of King Lear*
LUC	*The Rape of Lucrece*
MAC	*The Tragedy of Macbeth*
MM	*Measure for Measure*
MND	*A Midsummer Night's Dream*
MV	*The Merchant of Venice*
OTH	*The Tragedy of Othello, the Moor of Venice*
PER	*Pericles, Prince of Tyre*
PHT	*The Phoenix and the Turtle*
PP	*The Passionate Pilgrim*
R2	*The Tragedy of Richard the Second*
R3	*The Tragedy of Richard the Third*
ROM	*The Tragedy of Romeo and Juliet*
SHR	*The Taming of the Shrew*
SON	*Sonnets*
STM	*Sir Thomas More* (the additions ascribed to Shakespeare)
TGV	*The Two Gentlemen of Verona*
TIM	*The Life of Timon of Athens*
TIT	*The Tragedy of Titus Andronicus*
TMP	*The Tempest*
TN	*Twelfth Night*
TNK	*The Two Noble Kinsmen*
TRO	*The History of Troilus and Cressida*
VEN	*Venus and Adonis*
WIV	*The Merry Wives of Windsor*
WT	*The Winter's Tale*

4. *Others*

| ch. | chapter |
| Cho. | Chorus |

ed.	editor(s) or edited by
Epil.	Epilogue
esp.	especially
F1	the 'First Folio' edition of Shakespeare's collected plays, 1623
fig.	figurative
fol.	folio, for pagination of early texts
l. or ll.	line number(s) in poems
L.	Latin
Q	a quarto edition, usually of a single play by Shakespeare
Q1, Q2	first quarto edition, second quarto, etc.
qu.	question
refs	references
s.d.	stage directions
sig.	signature, for pagination of early texts
trans.	translated by
vol.	volume

Introduction

It should come as no surprise that the energies and the oddities of the Protestant Reformation would find their way into Shakespeare's richly absorptive works. Religious issues, religious discourse, were vastly more important in the sixteenth and seventeenth centuries than they are now. England just before and after Shakespeare's birth in 1564 experienced a jarring series of re-formations, from Henry the Eighth's differences with the Catholic Church, to the brief Protestantism that marked the reign of his son Edward the Sixth, to the martyrdom of many of Edward's Protestant advisors like Hugh Latimer, Nicholas Ridley and Thomas Cranmer at the hands of Edward's half-sister and Catholic successor Mary, to the final and also sometimes bloody establishment of the Church of England under the reign of Elizabeth. Puritans, Catholics, Protestants all died for their faith and their faction in sixteenth- and seventeenth-century England. *Henry VIII*, set just at the cutting edge of this political and religious turmoil, includes a reference to these 'new opinions, / Diverse and dangerous', these 'heresies', which, if 'not reform'd, may prove pernicious' (H8 5.2.52–5). The Catholic Bishop Gardiner says of the resultant 'commotions' and 'uproars' in 'upper Germany', 'Which Reformation must be sudden too' (H8 5.2.63). To these two Catholic prelates it is thus the Reformation which must be reformed, not Catholic Europe. But though their usage reverses the usual meaning of this explosive word, the great architect of the English Reformation, Thomas Cranmer, is emerging as Henry's most powerful counsellor even as the play concludes.

Beyond the topicality of one play, even beyond the general forms and pressures of the Protestant Reformation, Shakespeare's audience were very interested in religious matters. Sandra Clark (1983), 34, the editor of this dictionary series, mentions as one indication of 'the great popularity of sermons and moral philosophy' during Shakespeare's lifetime that the Sternhold-Hopkins Psalter, originally published in 1547, was in its forty-seventh edition by 1600. She also notes that 'half of all books extant between 1583 and 1623 were theological'. The amount and the range of Shakespeare's religious usage show him to be an unusually well-informed Christian layman even in the midst of this unusually well-informed Christian era. This dictionary contains over 1000 keywords which have some religious denotation or connotation. Dogberry's priceless 'Well, God's a good man' (ADO 3.5.36) is one of over 1300 references to some form of **God** in Shakespeare's works. His religious usage ranges elsewhere from over 750 references to **heaven** or a derivative and many references to some form of **damn**

(150), **sin** (240) and **devil** (280), to one usage each of more esoteric words like **pax**, **unanel'd**, and **unhousel'd**. Some of the usage, as with **angel**, **blessed**, **devil**, **grace**, **soul** and **spirit**, is so complex that there are from three to six discernable meanings for a word. Sometimes, as in the usage of **grace** in MM or **spirit** in HAM, these meanings are intricately interwoven. Shakespeare (or his characters) also cites the Bible so precisely that scholars have shown him alternating between the Bishops' and the Genevan versions. Shakespeare shows himself knowledge-able about the commonplaces as well as the controversies of his Christian era. He also populates his plays with quite a range of church figures, competent as well as bumbling ones, Machiavellian and benign. There are **cardinal**s and **archbishop**s, **priest**s and **hedge-priest**s, papal **legate**s and humble **friar**s, Anglicans, Puritans, and Catholics; there is also a famous Jew. Shakespeare's figurative language is also frequently derived from religious discourse. All of this energy finds its way into Shakespeare's works in the dazzling display of religious usage which is the topic of this dictionary.

When Lucio says, 'grace is grace, despite of all controversy' (MM 1.2.25), he is referring with uncharacteristic wisdom to what Baker (1985), 115, and many others have called the central doctrinal dispute of the Reformation, the issue of salvation by **merit** versus salvation by grace. The Catholic princess of France plays on the same issue when she complains to the forester who has just com-plimented her beauty, 'See, see my beauty will be saved by merit. / O heresy in fair, fit for these days!' (LLL 4.1.21). **Idolatry** was another flashpoint of Refor-mation controversy. The Roman Church was often accused by the more extreme Reformers of idolatrous excesses in its devotional rites and decorative practices, and the iconoclasts were breaking religious images all over northern Europe in their Talibanic zeal to eliminate the offending paintings, carvings and other objects of religious veneration. Thus when Juliet calls Romeo 'the god of my idolatry' (ROM 2.2.114) or when SON 105 begins, 'Let not my love be call'd idolatry', analogy connects excessive religious and romantic expres-sions of devotion. **Scripture**, that central issue of the Reformation and the **text** on which so many of its disputes and so much of its disputing hinges, also comes into controversial play in Shakespeare's usage. The Gravedigger makes a fool of himself by literally misinterpreting the Scripture which reads 'Adam digg'd' in arguing that Adam had arms and was therefore a gentleman (HAM 5.1.29–37). Antonio criticises Shylock's reference to a biblical passage about Jacob and Laban's spotted sheep as he attempts to justify usury, 'The devil can cite Scripture for his purpose' (MV 1.3.98). Among the many other religious words named and sometimes exploited for their controversial overtones in Shakespeare are **altar**, **beads**, **candle**, **canoniz'd**, **charity**, **chastity**, **confession**, **controversy** itself, **cross** as an object, **cross** as a gesture, **desert**, **equivocate**, **justifi-cation**, **fasting**, **hallow'd**, **intercessor**, **kneel**, **limbo**, **Mass**, **miracles**, **nun**, **organ**, **penance**, **Pope** and **papal**, **purgatory**, **Puritan**, **Rome**, **sacrament**, **saint**, **sister-hood**, **surplice**, and **zeal**.

Referring rather to religious commonplace than religious controversy, Clarence cites 'the **table** of his law', especially 'Thou shalt do no **murther**', in his futile effort to convince the murderers not to kill him (R3 1.4.196–7). The cynical Lucio similarly refers to the '**sanctimonious** pirate' who 'scrap'd' 'Thou shalt not steal' 'out of the' '**Ten Commandements**' before he set off for work (MM 1.2.7–10). As Richard II approaches spiritual despair in his final soliloquy, he misreads as contradictory the scriptural passages 'Come, little ones' and 'It is as hard to come as for a **camel** / To thread the postern of a small needle's eye' (R2 5.5.11–17). Othello refers to many of the traditional images of the **Last Judgement** – liquid **fire**, **sulphur**, **fiends** and **devils** – as he imagines himself condemned eternally to the **torments** of **hell**. Characters name major biblical figures like **Judas**, **Herod** and **Pilate**, **Job** and **Jezebel**, **Jesus**, **Mary**, and **Joseph**, as well as minor ones like **Jephthah** and his daughter. They speak of the stories of **Dives** and **Lazarus**, the **prodigal Son**, the **Slaughter** of the Innocents and the drowning of **Pharoah**'s soldiers. They refer to 'our **Saviour**'s birth' (HAM 1.1.157–61), betrayal, crucifixion and **resurrection**. We also hear of biblical place-names like **Golgotha** and **Egypt** and **Jerusalem**. **Holy baptism**, the **Mass** (also 'the **sacrament**'), **penance**, and extreme **unction** also find their explicit and sometimes controversial way into Shakespeare's words and works. Thirty-three individual saints and saints' days are also mentioned in Shakespeare, some, like St George, frequently, others only once. More churches than taverns are graced by their names.

So persistent and informed is this religious usage that various readers have tried to argue Shakespeare's faith as well as his position on Reformation controversies. Yet for all of the light that has been shed on Shakespeare's work and his time by such inquiries, most readers, myself included, still reserve judgement on just what and how Shakespeare believed. For one thing, Shakespeare never speaks in his own voice. Even in the sonnets there is an imagined speaker, and in the plays, characters and not Shakespeare speak out their own beliefs and disbeliefs, their Catholic and Protestant and Puritan leanings as well as their sceptical and irreligious ones. Their religious humour – malapropisms, jokes, light and serious metaphors – is usually good-humoured, but ill-humoured characters provide exceptions to that rule. Further, the religious issues in the plays, like the religious words that convey them, are almost always exploited for dramatic fun or dramatic tension rather than explicated to make a theological point or take a theological stance. When the Princess twits the Forester about merit and grace, her informed joke does not preach her Catholicism; indeed, her point, that it is **heresy** to take credit for a beauty that is God-given, runs quite counter to the stereotyped (and misleading) Catholic favouring of merit or **works** over grace or **faith**. On the other hand, she takes what could be called a firm Catholic stance when she subsequently insists that her suitor, the king of notoriously Protestant **Navarre**, prove his **amendment** of life by enacting a formally prescribed **penance**. Portia stresses the doctrine of **grace** as she preaches 'The quality of mercy' to Shylock, yet she can only defeat him (and save Antonio) by resorting to a legalistic strategy of **justice**. 'I stand here for the law' vividly marks Shylock's relationship to this issue as a Jew, and 'Is that the law?' is his stunned response to Portia's eventual victory (MV 4.1.184, 142, 314). Finally, a legion of Reformation issues undoubtedly swirl around Hamlet's attempt to determine if his father's Ghost is 'a spirit of health or goblin damn'd?' (HAM 1.4.40), or whether he is from heaven, purgatory or hell, but in a play as complex as *Hamlet*, who knows what finally to believe?

Some of Shakespeare's most informed and imaginative religious usage is figurative, and such usage is a prominent part of the dictionary. The comparison of religious and romantic experience has a rich heritage among such Christian humanists as Erasmus, and Shakespeare richly and playfully develops this tradition. Familiar examples include the metaphor of the **penitent** and the **saint**, the **palmer** and the **shrine**, that informs the first exchange between Romeo and Juliet. 'Lest faith turn to despair' is Romeo's ultimate argument for her to grant his '**prayer**', first for a touch, then for a kiss (ROM 1.5.93–110). In a similar speech, Valentine uses the theologically loaded words **humbled**, **confess**, **penance**, **fasts**, and **penitential** (TGV 2.4.128–37) to romantic effect. **Sacred** is also frequently used to describe the object of romantic worship. 'Impiety' can describe romantic faults, as when Claudio calls the Hero he imagines to be false but wants to be true, 'pure **impiety** and **impious** purity' (ADO 4.1.104). Benedick is similarly called 'ever an **obstinate heretic** in the despite of beauty' because of his sworn lack of faith in women (ADO 1.1.232–5). These metaphors range, however, far beyond the romantic. Characters are described, sardonically as well as devoutly, as **absolv'd** 'with an axe' and **sacrifice**d 't' **appease** an **angry** god'. There are **requiem**s and **anthem**s of grief, and people are **catechised** on matters of self-indulgence as well as romance. Empty winter trees are 'Bare ruin'd choirs, where late the sweet birds sang' (SON 73.4); wounds are '**graves** i' th' **holy churchyard**' (COR 3.3.51). 'The **worm** of **conscience** still begnaw thy soul' is among the most vivid of Margaret's curses for Richard of Gloucester (R3 1.3.221). **Angel**, **devil**, **heaven**, **hell**, **profane**, **worship**, **hymn**, **homily**, **penance** and **paradise**, **faith** and **despair** are also used metaphorically to many serious and silly ends in Shakespeare.

Omissions, Inclusions, and Conventions

Risking the danger of writing something like Quince's Prologue in MND, or exclaiming like Snout, 'You can never bring in a wall' (MND 3.1.65), I must hazard a few comments about my possible sins of inclusion and omission. I have attempted to include all of the words in Shakespeare with any religious nuance, but have tried not to dwell too long on the most obvious. I have been even more selective with Shakespeare's biblical and liturgical allusions, which are included only when a word to be glossed – like **mote** or **needle's eye** – takes on religious significance largely through that allusion. Shaheen (1999) offers a compre-hensive collection of such allusions. I also do not usually include Shakespeare's usage of words merely mythological, words merely moral, or words pertaining to popular superstition unless there is some compelling religious dimension to that usage. Rich discussions of such matters can similarly be found elsewhere, as in Gillespie (2001) and Walker (2002). This is also predominantly a dictionary of Shakespeare's Christian usage, though his references to other religious groups and persons are included if they contain something more than merely ethnic nuance. It is not a dictionary of historical persons who are characters in the plays.

I have usually identified the Reformed and Recusant voices I cite for context and definition only by prefixes like 'the Reformer Latimer' and 'the Recusant Persons'. In the more frequent references to John Donne, Lancelot Andrewes, and Richard Hooker, three of the most famous Anglican divines of Shakespeare's time, I thought it unnecessary to include even that much prefix. The two Protestant catechisms I most frequently cite are those by Alexander Nowell, Dean of St Paul's (1570) and the Cambridge Puritan William Perkins (1596); the Catholic one I repeatedly use is the often-republished catechism by Laurence Vaux. Recusants, of course, were the Catholics who not only declined the then-compulsory participation in the Anglican Church but who also wrote (or translated), often secretly, in defence of a repressed Roman Catholicism. Besides Vaux and Robert Persons, Richard Hopkins and Stephen Brinkley were, respectively, the English translators of the popular continental works of Fr Luis de Granada and Jaspar Loarte. John Rastell was the chief controversialist against Bishop John Jewel, and Gregory Martin was the Catholic who translated the Rheims New Testament into English in 1582. The Parker Society collection is a carefully edited and indexed 55-volume collection of 'the works of the fathers and early writers of the reformed English church' (1841–55). It includes writers like the influential Lutheran translator of the English New Testament William Tyndale, Nowell, Ridley, Cranmer, and the Swiss Reformer Bullinger. Southern (1950) and Roberts (1966) give useful information about the Recusants in their representative if much briefer collections and introductions. Readers interested in more information about any of these often fascinating authors might start in the edited editions of their works as well as Cross and Livingstone (1997), the *New Catholic Encyclopedia* or the *Oxford Encyclopedia of the Reformation.* Milward (1977 and 1978) usefully catalogues many of the religious controversies and controversialists of the Elizabethan and Jacobean periods.

The sermons of Donne and Andrewes are perhaps disproportionately represented here, not because their voices are Protestant but because their styles – not just their psychological insight but also their verbal wit – so consistently provide crisp definitions of these words and entertaining illustrations of parallel contextual usage. It is particularly interesting to see how their religious discourse draws upon secular analogies to make its points richer and clearer in much the same way that Shakespeare uses religious analogies to embellish, enrich and clarify his psychological, romantic and political insights. I have with less relish only occasionally included in my quotations of the theologians examples of the outrageously insulting language of religious controversy so characteristic of this period. Shakespeare's characters show in their sometimes alarming usage of such narrow and condescending terms as **Jew**, **Muslim** and **Turk**, as well as words like **irreligious, infidel** and **non-believer**, a similar tendency towards what Archbishop Rowan Williams has recently called such ethnic and religious 'branding' (2002), ch. 5. We have since September 11 had too many fresh experiences, from all sides, of the explosive effect of such language and such thinking to include it lightly, but of course it has to be included.

Quotations from Shakespeare come unchanged from *The Riverside Shakespeare*, ed. G. Blakemore Evans, 2nd edn, Boston: Houghton Mifflin, 1997. The standard concordance, Marvin Spevack's *Complete and Systematic Concordance to the Works of Shakespeare*, 9 vols, Hildesheim: George Olms, 1968–80, and his shorter *Harvard Concordance to Shakespeare*, Cambridge, MA: Harvard University Press, 1973, are keyed to this edition. The biblical and liturgical quotations come from many sources, including the frequently embedded biblical quotations or translations in the works of Donne, Andrewes and the other theologians. Biblical quotations, unless they pertain to unique parallels between Shakespeare's usage and a particular Bible, usually come from the King James version of 1611. The quotations of the *Book of Common Prayer* cite the Booty edition of 1976.

When quoting old-spelling editions, I have followed the convention of silently modernizing v for u, i for j, long s, and the many contractions in the *Geneva Bible*. Otherwise, I have kept the original spelling. When reliable nineteenth- and twentieth-century editions of these theologians are available, as with the sermons of Donne and Andrewes, the work of Hooker, Augustine and Aquinas, and the monumental and richly indexed Parker Society Collection of the works of the fathers of the English Church, I have usually cited those editions.

The dictionary is arranged alphabetically. Cross-references are boldfaced in the text; they are also sometimes indicated by a 'see also' reference. In some cases the cross-reference merely indicates the existence of the other, related word. In others it suggests that more information is available elsewhere about the topic under current discussion, or its context. In either event, I have tried to make each item as self-contained as possible. Words with several distinctive meanings like **bless**, **soul**, **spirit**, **devil**, **angel** or **faith** are indicated as **soul**^{1}, **soul**^{2}, **soul**^{3}, etc. Parts of speech are indicated by the common abbreviations *sb.*, *v.*, *adj.*, *adv.* only if an item is used in two or more of these ways. When the entries are marked (A), (B), and (C), (A) marks the section of definition and context, (B) the 'guided tour' through Shakespeare's usage of the word, and (C) the primary and secondary bibliography for that item. The (A), (B), (C) designation is not used unless an item has all three of these parts. With the exceptions listed in the Abbreviations section, the brief citations in the text of the dictionary give the author's last name, the date, and if necessary the page(s) of the reference, as in Bevington (1962), 21–2 or Frye (1979). In the rare case of two items by the same author with the same date, the date will be indicated as 1985a and 1985b in both the note and the relevant bibliography.

ABBESS

The female superior of a convent of nuns.

Because the Abbess will not relinquish Adriana's husband to her care, Adriana first threatens to 'take perforce my husband from the Abbess', then calls for 'Justice, most sacred Duke, against the Abbess' (ERR 5.1.117, 133).

ABBEY

Either a convent under the supervision of an abbess or a monastery under the supervision of an abbot.

Cardinal Wolsey is described after his fall from power (and into grace) as 'Lodg'd in the abbey' at Leicester, where, 'full of repentance, / Continual meditations, tears and sorrows, / He gave his honours to the world again, / His blessed part to heaven, and slept in peace' (H8 4.2.27–30). This abbey is both a sanctuary from the world and a place of spiritual preparation. On the other hand, 'the crowd i' th' abbey' in London (Westminster), where Anne Boleyn's coronation occurs, is described as bustling, 'broiling', 'wedg'd in' with a 'rich stream of lords and ladies' and 'a rankness', whether of smells or abundance the Gentleman does not specify (H8 4.1.56–9, 62–3). In ERR, the abbey is mentioned nine times as the **sanctuary** for the Abbess's son and Adriana's husband Antipholus (ERR 5.1.122, 129, 155, 165, 188, 264, 266, 279, 395). In the other plays the abbey seems to function mostly as a secular meeting-place (TGV 5.1.9; JN 5.3.8; ROM 2.4.187).

ABBOT

(A) The head or superior of a monastery.

(B) Shakespeare's characters reveal a wide range of attitudes towards 'abbot'. King John, no friend of the Roman Church, says to the Bastard before his return to England, 'And ere our coming see thou shake the bags / Of hoarding abbots, imprisoned angels / Set at liberty' (JN 3.3.7–9). John's slur, 'The fat ribs of peace / Must by the hungry now be fed upon' (JN 3.3.9–10), refers to the conventionally overfed monastics. The 'reverend abbot' and 'father abbot' whom Griffith speaks to is, in contrast, obviously a good man, and his abbey a useful place for Wolsey's spiritual retreat (H8 4.2.18–20). Cf. R2 5.6.19–21.

(C) On the alleged corruption of abbots, both their greed and their spiritual extortion, see Tyndale, 2: 288; 1: 249. For their 'imprisoned angels' as gold coins, see **angel**[3].

ABEL

(A) The second son of Adam and Eve, who was killed by his brother Cain in a fit of jealousy because God preferred Abel's sacrifice to Cain's. Damascus was thought to be the scene of the murder. Donne warns against seeking personal revenge on the basis of Gen. 4.10, '*That Abels blood cryes for revenge*'; indeed, Donne reminds his parishioners that God explicitly forbids such vengeance in Gen. 4.15 (1: 172).

(B) Gloucester, the Lord Protector, challenges the Bishop of Winchester for shutting him out of the Tower. Winchester responds, 'Nay, stand thou back, I will not budge a foot: / This be Damascus, be thou cursed Cain, / To slay thy brother Abel, if thou wilt' (1H6 1.3.38–40). Bolingbroke listens to only the first of the passages in Genesis when he says of Richard II's hand in his uncle Woodstock's death, 'Which blood, like sacrificing Abel's, cries, / Even from the tongueless caverns of the earth, / To me for justice and rough chastisement' (R2 1.1.104–6). Since both sets of relationships are uncle-to-nephew rather than brother-to-brother, Shakespeare obviously felt that the allusion could apply to any murdered relative. Claudius refers more precisely to this story of Cain's slaying of Abel when he says that his killing of his own brother, Old Hamlet, has 'the primal eldest curse upon't, / A brother's murther' (HAM 3.3.37–8).

(C) See Donne, 8: 189 and Andrewes, 3: 321. Stump (1985) argues that the Cain and Abel story is the archetype for HAM. For an interesting medieval woodcut of Cain slaying Abel with the jawbone of an ass, see *Mirror* (2002), fig. 72. See also **Cain**, below.

ABOVE

(A) Refers in both Christian and non-Christian contexts to God(s) and heaven. It can imply superior position, superior power or control, or both.

(B) Phrases like Gonzalo's 'The wills above be done!' (TMP 1.1.67), Quickly's 'all is in His hands above' (WIV 1.4.144), Cassio's 'well, God's above all' (OTH 2.3.102), and Albany's 'This shows you are above, / You justicers' (LR 4.2.78–9) refer to **divine** providence, sometimes ironically; prayerful petitions and promises contain phrases like Isabella's 'O, you blessed ministers above, / Keep me in patience' (MM 5.1.115–16) and Warwick's 'Here on my knee I vow to God above' (3H6 2.3.29).

(C) For similar usage among the theologians, see Donne, 4: 109 (on 2 Cor. 4.6); Andrewes, 4: 299; Jewel (1845–50), 2: 942 (on 2 Thes. 3.3–14); and Vaux (1590a), *sig.* B2[v].

ABRAHAM

(A) 'The bosom of Abraham', familiar today from the old spiritual, originates in Luke 16.22, where the beggar Lazarus is described as 'carried by the angels into Abraham's bosom'. The homily 'against the feare of Death' in *Certaine Sermons* also refers to this story. This was a controversial site during the Reformation because of its association with the Catholic doctrine of **purgatory**.

(B) Richard III, newly crowned but still gleefully expressing false piety, says of his two murdered nephews, 'The sons of Edward sleep in Abraham's bosom' (R3 4.3.38). Bolingbroke's comment about his sworn enemy Mowbray, who died in the Holy Lands, 'Sweet peace conduct his sweet soul to the bosom / Of good old Abraham' (R2 4.1.103–4), is likewise both perfunctory and hypocritical. A grieving Mistress Quickly tries to assign Falstaff to the same place, but her malapropism as well as Falstaff's checkered past both complicate her blessing: 'he's in Arthur's bosom, if even man went to Arthur's bosom' (H5 2.3.9–10). See **Lazarus**.

(C) The Reformer Fulke represents the Recusant Gregory Martin, translator of the Rheims New Testament, as saying against the Protestants, 'the patriarchs, and other just men of the Old Testament, were in some third place of rest, called "**Abraham's** bosom," or *limbus patrum*, till our Saviour Christ descended thither, and delivered them from thence' (1843), 1: 285. See also *Certaine Sermons*, 60; Andrewes, 2: 78; Donne, 5: 43, 99–100; 7: 257–8; Bullinger, 1: 138–9; and Shaheen (1999), 378. Nathan (1970) and Shaheen (1991) discuss the use of 'Abram' instead of 'Abraham' in MV.

ABSOLUTION

(A) Technically an affirmation in Protestant liturgy of the remission of sins through grace after the sacrament of **baptism** or communion; in Catholic terms it can also refer to the remission of sin effected by a **priest** in the **sacrament** of **confession** or **penance**. In 'Of Absolution of pœnitents', the great Anglican apologist Hooker complains,

> soe great a difference appeareth betweene the doctrine of Rome and ours, when wee teach **repentance** . . . . [W]ee stand cheifly upon the true inward conversion of the heart, they more upon **workes** of externall shew . . ., a sacramentall **pœnance** of their owne devising and shaping: wee labour to instruct men in such sort, that everie soule which is wounded with **sinne**, may learne the way how to cure itselfe; they cleane contrarie, would make all soares seeme incurable, unlesse the **Preist** have a hand in them.
>
> (VI.6.2)

(B) Tarquin's 'The blackest sin is clear'd with absolution' (LUC 354) is his futile attempt to assure himself that though the gods abhor rape, they will forgive his rape of Lucrece.

(C) See also Andrewes, 5: 94; Donne, 4: 83; 8: 295; and Tyndale, 1: 257. The Recusant Vaux's *Catechisme* says that 'The forme of the Sacrament of penaunce is the wordes of absolution, that the Priest speaketh over the sinner: by vertue of the whiche the Holy Ghost worketh remission and forgevenes of sinne' (1590a), *sig.* G6ᵛ.

ABSOLV'D

(A) Made free of sin or its punishment through confession, public or private, and either repentance or penance.

(B) In ROM Juliet tells the Nurse that she is, 'gone, / Having displeas'd my father, to Lawrence' cell, / To make confession and to be absolv'd' (ROM 3.5.231–3). When Queen Katherine of Aragon, the Spanish Catholic wife of Henry VIII, asks the English Catholic Cardinal Wolsey not to speak **Latin** in their conversation, Shakespeare connects their conversation to the **Reformation** issue of the vernacular liturgy: 'The willing'st sin I ever yet committed / May be absolv'd in English' (H8 3.1.49–50). In a sardonic metaphor, Surrey says to Cardinal Wolsey of his hand in the execution of 'noble Buckingham', 'your great goodness, out of holy pity, / Absolv'd him with an axe' (H8 3.2.263–4).

(C) See **absolution, sin-absolver**, and Vaux (1590a), *sigs.* I1ʳ⁻ᵛ.

ABSTINENCE

(A) The act or habit of delaying or denying the satisfaction of some appetite; the context sometimes suggests a religious impulse for this self-control. Andrewes calls abstinence 'an act or fruit of **repentance**' and 'an act of humiliation, to **humble** the **soul**' (1: 380; cf. 5: 341).

(B) When the Duke says of Angelo that 'He doth with holy abstinence subdue / That in himself which he spurs on his pow'r / To qualify in others' (MM 4.2.81–3), 'holy' probably defines the basis of the abstinence as severe religious **scruples**, though '**holy**' could also mean merely 'extreme' or 'absolute'. Angelo is also called 'A man of stricture and firm abstinence' (MM 1.3.12). Surrounding religious terms like '**devil**', '**angel**', '**grace**' and '**confess** yourself to **heaven**' give some religious nuance to Hamlet's advice to his mother that her refraining once from having sex with Claudius 'shall lend a kind of easiness / To the next abstinence' (HAM 3.4.144, 149, 162, 165–7).

(C) See ST II.2.146.

ACCIDENT

The word is usually associated with chance rather than divine causation, as when Lodovico speaks of 'The shot of accident nor dart of chance' (OTH 4.1.267), and Cleopatra of death as an event 'Which shackles accidents and bolts up change' (ANT 5.2.6). However, 'accident' sometimes contains a religious nuance. On the topic 'It seems chance, that is indeed destiny' (4: 139), Andrewes speaks explicitly of 'a high and wonderful disposition of God's heavenly providence': 'For God will have it out certainly; rather than not, by some mere accident.' And though Donne warns his parishioners to 'distinguish between naturall accidents, and immediate judgements of God; between ordinary declarations of his power, and extraordinary declarations of his anger' (3: 279), he also urges them not to mistake 'judgements uttered from God, but [as] naturall accidents, casuall occurrencies, emergent contingencies, which as the Atheist might think, would fall out though there were no God' (6: 217).

The Duke in MM says of the death of Ragozine just when they needed a head to prove that Claudio had been executed, 'O, 'tis an accident that heaven provides!' (MM 4.3.77). Queen Margaret is equally sure that apparent accidents, that is unexpected events, can manifest the hand of God when she curses many of her enemies, 'God, I pray him / That none of you may live his natural age, / But by some unlook'd accident cut off!' (R3 1.3.211–13).

ACCOUNT (also ACCOMPT)

(A) 'The rendering of a reckoning', specifically 'the final account at the judgement-seat of God, on "the great day of accounts" ' (OED *sb.* 8.b). Donne (3: 275; citing 1 Peter 1.17) says of the fear of God, 'The name of Father implyes a great power over you, therefore feare him; And, amongst other powers, a power of *judging* you, of calling you to an account, therefore feare him.'
(B) The Ghost of Hamlet's father complains of being 'sent to my account / With all my imperfections on my head' (HAM 1.5.76–9). As he is about to express his lust for her, Angelo tries to assure Isabella that 'our **compelled** sins / Stand more for number than for accompt' (MM 2.4.57). King John concedes that a death warrant he has signed seals his own damnation: 'O, when the last accompt 'twixt heaven and earth / Is to be made, then shall this hand and seal / Witness against us to damnation!' (JN 4.2.216–18). Such explicit, self-defining references reveal the verbal irony behind Lady Macbeth's desperate assurance in the sleepwalking scene, 'What need we fear who knows it, when none can call our pow'r to accompt?' (MAC 5.1.37–9).
(C) Cf. Donne, 6: 275; Andrewes, 5: 146 (from 1 Cor. 15.52).

ACCOMPTANT

Responsible for, accountable, sometimes theologically.

When Iago says he loves Desdemona 'Not out of absolute lust (though peradventure / I stand accomptant for as great a sin)' (OTH 2.1.292–3), to whom else would he stand accountable but God?

ACHERON

(A) A river in the Lower World, hence the infernal regions in many traditions, including the Christian (*OED*).
(B) In MAC Hecate's 'Meet me' 'at the pit of Acheron' (MAC 3.5.15–16) could suggest the Christian as well as the classical hell as Macbeth's destination.
(C) Battenhouse (1951), 190, observes that 'the purgatory of the Ancients, or their hell, or their vague afterworld, hades' are all 'hell from a Christian point of view'.

ACKNOWLEDGE

Publicly worship and recognise; profess (*OED v.* 2). Nowell's *Catechism* of 1570 says of the love of God that it is 'meet for God . . ., that we acknowledge him, both for our most mighty Lord, and our most loving Father, and most merciful Saviour' (1853), 137.

King Henry IV speaks of 'all the kingdoms that acknowledge Christ' (1H4, 3.2.111).

ACQUIT

Relieve from a charge or crime. Usually a legal term, acquit can also be used of God's **justice** and **mercy**.

Henry V, having charged Cambridge, Scroop and Grey with treason and condemned them to death, combines his severe earthly justice with the possibility of heaven's mercy when he says 'Their faults are open, / Arrest them to the answer of the law, / And God acquit them of their practices!' (H5 2.2.142–4).

ADAM

(A) As the first man in the Judaeo-Christian creation myth, 'Adam' is arguably next to 'Christ' the richest of Shakespeare's biblical names.

(B) For Adam as the progenitor of all subsequent persons, see Beatrice's rationalization for not marrying: 'Adam's sons are my brethren, and truly I hold it a sin to match in my kindred' (ADO 2.1.63–5). For Adam as the first gardener, see the Queen's words to the gardener in R2: 'Thou old Adam's likeness, set to dress this garden' (R2 3.4.72). The Gravedigger in HAM says that 'gard'ners, ditchers, and grave-makers' 'hold up Adam's profession', since 'The Scripture says that Adam digged' (HAM 5.1.29–37). In ERR Dromio puns about a pub when he mentions 'that Adam that kept the Paradise' (ERR 4.3.17); he also compares his master's quick change of clothing to 'old Adam new apparell'd' (ERR 4.3.13–14), referring to the original nakedness of the first couple. Berowne tweaks the legend when he says of Boyet's wit and his influence over women, 'Had he been Adam, he had tempted Eve' (LLL 5.2.322). Eve of course was usually represented as tempting Adam. In AYL the outrageously perfect servant Adam may suggest his namesake's prelapsarian perfection, and 'the penalty of Adam' (AYL 2.1.5) refers to the harsh weather that was considered one of the repercussions of the Fall. When Canterbury in H5 says of the apparent miracle of Hal's 'Reformation' that 'Consideration like an angel came, / And whipt th' offending Adam out of him' (H5 1.1.28–9), he refers to the persistence in all persons of Adam's 'original sin'. Falstaff uses the same ideas of prelapsarian perfection and original sin to rationalise his sinfulness in 1H4: 'Thou knowest in the state of innocency Adam fell, and what should poor Jack Falstaff do in the days of villainy?' (1H4 3.3.164–6). Holofernes' riddle, 'The moon was a month old when Adam was no more, / And raught not to five weeks when he came to five-score' (LLL 4.2.38–9), requires the biblical knowledge that Adam and the moon were created almost simultaneously, and the cosmological knowledge that the moon's age never reaches five weeks.

(C) Of the 'penalties of Adam', see Donne, 2: 59; of Adam's keeping the Paradise (from Gen. 2.15), Donne says, '*Adam* himself was commanded to *dresse* Paradise, and to *keep* Paradise' (7: 424). See also Andrewes, 2: 214; Perkins's popular catechism begins with the problem that 'All men are wholly corrupted with sinne through Adams fal: & so are become slaves of Sathan' (1591), *sig.* A4. 'Adam digs and Eve spins' is the subject of a medieval woodcut in *Mirrour* (1986), 48. See also Hankins (1964).

ADJUDG'D

(A) Usually condemned in a court of law; sometimes like 'acquit' referring to the court of God's **Judgement**.

(B) King Henry, condemning to death three of the four witches standing before him, calls witchcraft one of the 'sins / Such as by God's **book** are adjudg'd to death' (2H6 2.3.4).

(C) He probably refers to Ex. 22.18, 'Thou shalt not suffer a witch to live.'

ADORE

(A) Worship, sometimes idolatrously. While Donne concedes the occasionally inappropriate Roman Catholic adoration of religious **images**, he warns against excessive iconoclasm, 'That because pictures have been adored, we do not abhor a picture; Nor sit at the Sacrament, because Idolatry hath been committed in kneeling' (8: 331).

(B) Helena describes her love for Bertram to the Countess his mother: 'Thus, Indian-like, / Religious in mine error, I adore / The sun, that looks upon his worshipper, / But knows of him no more' (AWW 1.3.204–7). Presumably, to adore the right god is religious, but to adore the wrong one error. Silvia tells the adoring Proteus, who has asked for her picture, 'I am very loath to be your idol, sir; / But since your falsehood shall become you well / To worship shadows and adore false shapes, / Send to me in the morning, and I'll send it' (TGV 4.2.128–31).

(C) See **idolatry** for a fuller discussion of the theological issue and its relationship to romantic discourse. See also *ST* II.2.84; Donne, 8: 331; 10: 150–1; Ridley (1841), 106.

ADULTERY; ADULTEROUS

(A) Having sex with someone else's marriage partner; more generally, having sex outside of wedlock; guilty of that crime. This is one of the crimes biblically adjudged punishable by death, as in Lev. 20.10; Deut. 22.22. In John 8.4–5, the Scribes and Pharisees say of the 'woman . . . taken in adultery, in the very act', that 'Moses in the law commanded us, that such should be stoned'. Jesus, of course, famously responds, 'He that is without sin among you, let him first cast a stone at her' (John 8.7).

(B) Lear refers to a similar law when he says to the blinded Gloucester, 'What was thy cause? / Adultery? / Thou shalt not die. Die for adultery? No, / The wren goes to't, and the small gilded fly / Does lecher in my sight' (LR 4.6.109–13).

The novice Isabella takes the opposite position when she calls the death penalty for adultery a 'just but severe law' (MM 2.2.41). When she later calls Angelo 'adulterous' for trying to coerce her to have sex with him to save her brother's life, she may be taking a nun's vows of marriage to Christ more literally than usual (MM 5.1.40–1).

(C) The English Reformer Becon, 1: 450, cites many 'sentences out of' Scripture 'against fornication and adultery'; Vaux's Catholic *Catechism* (1590a), *sigs.* E2ᵛ–E3ʳ, discusses the many varieties of adultery. See also *Certaine Sermons*, pp. 78–89, for the sermons 'against whoredome and uncleannesse'. Parten (1984) looks at female characters' attitudes towards male adultery. For Posthumus's unique forgiveness of what he thinks is his wife's adultery in CYM, see Marshall (1991), 19–23; Blincoe (1997) discusses the precise nature of Gertrude's adultery in HAM. Garner (1989) describes imagined female adultery in ADO, OTH, CYM and WT, and Loomis (1999) briefly explains the relationship between an 'entire and perfect chrysolite' and adultery in OTH.

ADVANTAGE

Benefit, assistance (*OED sb.* 6), once used spiritually in reference to Christ's crucifixion.

In what is finally a self-serving speech, Bolingbroke promises to take a journey to the 'holy fields, / Over whose acres walk'd those blessed feet / Which fourteen hundred years ago were nail'd / For our advantage on the bitter cross' (1H4 1.1.24–7).

ADVOCATION

(A) Speaking in behalf of; usually a legal term (an advocate is a lawyer), this word can be used theologically as well, as of the Virgin's intercessions with Christ for forgiveness of sins. 'Advocate' and 'advocation' are words which the Reformers use to express their nervousness that Mary usurps Christ's traditional role of defence attorney, 'advocate with the Father' (from 1 John 2.1).

(B) Desdemona's puzzled words about her early failure to reconcile the fallen Cassio and his sternly judgemental master Othello could therefore suggest the Virgin's analogous role in reconciling sinners and Christ: 'My advocation is not now in tune' (OTH 3.4.123). However, Iago 'turn[s Desdemona's] virtue into pitch' by telling Othello that she pleads for the same man, Cassio, with whom she is committing adultery (OTH 2.3.355–60).

(C) Speaking against other advocates than Christ are Andrewes, 3: 158; Donne, 8: 330; Luther (LW 22: 37, 165; 23: 57, 59, 104, 123, 137); favouring them is the recusant Vaux (1590a), *sigs.* C2ᵛ–C3ʳ. On the religious suggestiveness of 'advocation', see also Hassel (2001a), 44–8; Milward (1987), 91, observes that 'Our Lady . . . is called "advocate" in the hymn "*Salve Regina*".' See **Jaques, Saint**.

AFFECTION(S)

(A) Sinful desire(s); often plural, as with **affects**. Donne speaks of 'our carnal affections, our concupiscencies' as 'those beasts, that is, those brutish affections, that are in us[;] . . . in sinning we lose this dominion over our selves, and forfeit our dominion over the creature too' (10: 186; 2: 100).

(B) Hector says that the law of marriage can be 'corrupted through affection', which he then calls 'raging appetites that are / Most disobedient and refractory' (TRO 2.2.181–2); Laertes urges Ophelia to 'Keep you in the rear of your affection, / Out of the shot and danger of desire' (HAM 1.3.34–5). Escalus tries to convince Angelo to be less severe in administering the law against fornication by recalling a moment when 'the working of your own affections' or 'the resolute acting of your blood' tempted you to err 'in this point which now you censure' (MM 2.1.10–15). Claudio is later surprised that this same Angelo has 'affections in him' (MM 3.108). The King urges his friends at the beginning of LLL to 'war against your own affections, / And the huge army of the world's desires' (LLL 1.1.9–10). Hal, just crowned Henry V, announces his 'Reformation' by saying 'My father is gone wild into his grave / For in his tomb lie my affections' (2H4 5.2.123–4); he later calls these affections 'the tide of blood in me [that] / Hath proudly flowed in **vanity** till now' (2H4 5.2.129–30). Emilia also asks Desdemona, 'have not we affections, / Desires for sport, and frailty, as men have?' (OTH 4.3.100–1).

(C) See also Donne, 7: 135; Bullinger, 1: 175.

AFFECTS

(A) Sinful desires (*OED sb.* 1.c).

(B) Berowne in LLL advises the other lords of the impossibility of their mutual vow 'Not to see ladies, study, fast, not sleep':

> Necessity will make us all forsworn
> Three thousand times within this three years' space;
> For every man with his affects is born,
> Not by **might** mast'red, but by special **grace**.
> (LLL 1.1.149–52)

The 'Necessity' here is both the inconvenient arrival of the ladies and human **nature**, original **sin**, 'affects' as 'the desires and devices of our own hearts', over which we do not have absolute or even moderate control.

(C) See *BCP*, 50.

AFFLICTION

(A) Though it can just mean infirmity, sometimes the word is associated with the tradition of Christian (and classical) **patience** and with the idea that God (or the gods) try people, like **Job**, with divinely inflicted sufferings. Donne speaks vividly of this tradition when he says 'God sends us a **purgatory** too in this life, **Crosses**, Afflictions, and Tribulations, and to burne out these infectious staines and impressions in our flesh, . . . to wash us, and to burne us cleane with afflictions from his own hand.' 'Affliction is a Christians daily bread' (7:183).

(B) Though Gloucester promises the 'mighty gods' to 'Shake patiently your great affliction off' (LR 4.6.34–6), he is so impatient in adversity that he soon resolves to leap from the cliff so that he will not 'fall / To quarrel with your great opposeless wills' (LR 4.6.37–8). Even after his son Edgar saves him once from this despair, leading Gloucester to resolve to 'bear / Affliction, till it do cry out itself / "Enough, enough", and die' (LR 4.6.75–7), the defeat of Lear's forces breaks his resolve again (LR 5.2.8–12). Othello mentions the same tradition of heaven-sent affliction, and conforms almost as poorly to it, when he proclaims 'Had it pleas'd heaven / To try me with affliction, had they rain'd / All kind of sores and shames on my bare head', 'I should have found in some place of my soul / A drop of patience' (OTH 4.2.47–9, 52–3).

(C) See Job 2.7–10 and James 5.11: 'Ye have heard of the patience of Job'. See also Andrewes, 5: 443; Donne, 2: 177; and Shaheen (1999), 593.

ALBONS, SAINT

(A) Saint Albans. A shrine and a town named for Saint Alban, traditionally the first Christian martyr of Britain, a Roman soldier executed under the Emperor Decius in 254 for protecting a Christian priest. Feast Day: 20 June. The town, earlier called Verulamium, was located on a busy road about twenty miles north of London, hence the line 'as common as the way between Saint Albons and London' (2H4 2.2.167–8). Its 'holy shrine' was associated with miracles of healing.

(B) The imposter Simpcox claims such a **miracle** when he testifies to being called 'A hundred times and oft'ner, in my sleep, / By good Saint Albon, who said, 'Simon, come; / Come offer at my shrine, and I will help thee.' Simpcox says of his pretended restoration of sight that he sees 'clear as day, I thank God and Saint Albon'. Gloucester mocks the imposter with 'Saint Albon here hath done a miracle', further twisting the knife by telling his quarry that if he, an actual rather than a pretended cripple, can now run away from his deserved whipping, a miracle will indeed have occurred (2H6 2.1.86, 88–90, 106, 129–31). Indeed, '*After the Beadle hath hit him once, he leaps over the stool and runs away, and they follow and cry "A miracle!"* ' (2H6 2.1. *s.d.* 150).

(C) Farmer (1978), 8–9. The early Reformer Tyndale cites this story as part of his argument against miracles (2: 298n). The great English Reformer Cranmer (1846), 2: 65 relates another imposture at St Albans.

ALL-ENDING DAY

Doomsday, the day of **judgement**, the end of time.

Prince Edward refers to 'the general all-ending day' (R3 3.1.78). See also **doomsday, promised end**.

ALL HAIL

(A) A common reverent greeting, but one that could carry theological nuance, since Shakespeare's characters say more than once that Judas said 'All-hail' to Christ on the night that he betrayed him.

(B) Richard II laments during his deposition scene: 'Did they not sometimes cry "All hail!" to me? / So Judas did to Christ; but He, in twelve, / Found truth in all but one; I, in twelve thousand none' (R2 4.1 169–71). Kissing the young prince he will eventually kill, Richard of Gloucester identifies himself with the betrayer rather than the betrayed as he exults, 'so Judas kissed his master, / And cried "All hail!" when as he meant all harm' (3H6 5.7.33–4). Though the reference is less direct, the witches repeatedly 'all hail' Macbeth as they begin to betray him to his own 'dark and deep desires' (MAC 1.3.48–50).

(C) Shaheen (1999), 380–1, points out that Judas actually said 'All hail' only in the York mystery play; in most of the English Bibles available to Shakespeare, he greeted Christ, 'Hail, Master'. See *The English Hexapla* (1841), Matt. 26.49; *The Agony and the Betrayal* (1963), 243.

ALL-HALLOND EVE
The evening before **all-hallowmass**; Halloween.

In MM Froth and Pompey quibble, to no apparent purpose, about whether Froth's father 'died at Hallowmas' or 'All-hallond eve' (MM 2.1.124–6).

ALL-HALLOWMASS
(A) All Saints' or All Hallows' Day, 1 November, sometimes called Hallowmass because a mass would usually mark this day sacred to all the saints of the Church, living and dead. On the eve of All Hallows, Halloween, the spirits of the dead, good and bad apparently, were most likely to walk abroad. **All Souls' Day**, on which one prays for the dead, is 2 November.

(B) When Simple refers to 'All-hallowmas last, a fortnight afore Michaelmas' (WIV 1.1.204–5), he errs about the calendar. Michaelmas is always September 29.

(C) See Donne, 10: 41, 64.

ALL-HALLOWN
(A) Also **all-hallond**. The season of All-hallows or All Saints.

(B) When Prince Hal bids Falstaff, 'Farewell, All-hallown summer' (1H4 1.2.158–9), he is likening him to the end of the summer season.

(C) *Summer's Last Will and Testament* is a popular earlier sixteenth-century pageant that attests to the prominence of this seasonal tradition in Shakespeare's England. See Barber (1967) on Shakespeare's use of such traditions.

ALL-SEEING
Omniscient.

Queen Elizabeth begins to reveal her scepticism about divine providence when she responds to the news of the death of Clarence, 'All-seeing heaven, what a world is this!' (R3 2.1.83).

ALL-SEER
The One who sees all; God.

Buckingham concedes the justice of God's hand in his political reversal: 'That high All-Seer, which I dallied with, / Hath turn'd my feigned prayer on my head,

11

/ And giv'n in earnest what I begg'd in jest' (R3 5.1.20–2). He refers to the promise he made to Queen Elizabeth earlier in the play, 'Whenever Buckingham doth turn his hate / Upon your Grace, . . . God punish me' (R3 2.1.32–4).

ALL-SOULS'
(A) All Souls' Day is 2 November, the day on which the Catholic Church prayed for the souls of the departed dead.
(B) Buckingham is so struck by the irony that this 'All-Souls' day is my body's doomsday' that he soon repeats the idea: 'This, this All-Souls' day to my fearful soul, / Is the determin'd respite of my wrongs' (R3 5.1.12, 18–19). Like his reference in the same speech to the 'high All-Seer' who has so justly punished him, this comment includes the (belatedly) faithful idea that this 'respite' or payback is predetermined, preordained by God.
(C) Marshall (1991), 27, briefly relates Posthumus's dream in CYM to this day.

ALMIGHTY *adj.*
All-powerful, often following 'God', as in Gen. 28.3: 'And God Almighty bless thee, and make thee fruitful.' This phrase is used both seriously and casually by Shakespeare's characters, as it is today. Vaux, echoing the Apostles' Creed, speaks of 'God the Father almighty, the first person in Trinitie, the Creator and maker of heaven and earth, and of al creatures therein, both visible and invisible' (1590a), *sigs.* A4^{r-v}.

Exeter accentuates Henry V's claim to France by telling the French that he comes to take their land, their 'borrowed glories', 'in the name of God Almighty' (H5 2.4.77, 79). Henry later heartens both himself and his cold and out-numbered leaders by using 'God Almighty' as an injunction (H5 4.1.3). A less heroic figure, Simpcox, tries but fails to authenticate his claim of a miraculous cure from blindness with a similar 'Ay, God Almighty help me!' (2H6 2.1.93). In this case, God apparently demurs.

ALMSHOUSES
(A) Poorhouses run by the Church, and apparently to the Church's benefit.
(B) The churchmen fear in H5 that 'a hundred almshouses right well supplied' (H5 1.1.17) might be closed, and their considerable revenues thus lost, unless it proves that 'The King is full of grace and fair regard. / And a true lover of the holy Church' (H5 1.1.22–3). If he is not, or more to the point, if he cannot be bribed by the Church's authorization of the invasion of France, he might seize these assets for himself.
(C) See *Certaine Sermons*, 2nd tome, pp. 154–66, for the sermons of 'Almes deedes, and mercifulnesse toward the poore and needy'. See also *ST* II.2.32.

ALMSMAN
One who begs for alms, thereby generously allowing Catholic parishioners to do their prescribed acts of charity. Beggars still congregate around Catholic churches. Though an almsman is not called a religious figure in *OED* 1, a

synonym cited there is bedesman; beadsman is called in *OED* beadsman 1 'a man of prayer' and in *OED* beadsman 2, 'One paid or endowed to pray for others'.

This definition works fairly well for Richard II, who, once deposed, would have lived, had he lived, at Bolingbroke's charge. He thus imagines an exchange of courtly extravagance for the religious poverty of a beadsman: 'I'll give my jewels for a set of beads, / My gorgeous palace for a hermitage, / My gay apparel for an almsman's gown' (R2 3.3.147–9).

ALTAR

(A) An elevated place or structure, often like a table, where religious rites are enacted. As the most traditional site for marriage in the Renaissance, 'the altar' could also be used as a synecdoche for marriage or funeral rites. Though 'altar' is often a controversial word among theologians, that tension is absent from Shakespeare's usage.

(B) There are both literal and figurative altars in Shakespeare; there are classical and Christian ones as well. The classical references include those to the altars of Diana (MND 1.1.89; AWW 2.3.74), Mars (1H4 4.1.116; TNK 1.1.62; 1.2.20), and Venus (TNK 5.4.105–6). In each of these cases the phrase combining the god(dess) and altar actually refers through eponym to the deity's predominant characteristic. As a result, swearing on Diana's altar means promising chastity, flying from it means committing to a sexual life. Mars, described by Hotspur as sitting on his own altar (1H4 4.1.116–17), promises imminent bloodshed; being 'by Mar's altar' (TNK 1.1.62) means being warlike or actually engaging in battle, while scorning it is preferring pacifism. Venus' gracing her altar means that she has 'given you your love' (PER 5.3.16–18). Emilia, loved by the two noble but rivalrous kinsmen, asks Diana why her own chastity should become, metaphorically, 'the altar where the lives of lovers' 'must be the sacrifice / To my unhappy beauty?' just after she had been styled Diana's 'priest', 'humbl'd 'fore thine altar' (TNK 5.1.143; 4.2.59–4).

More literal and more Christian altars appear in references to actual churches and events. Melune tells Salisbury that he has sworn upon 'the altar at Saint **Edmundsbury**' (JN 5.4.18) to revenge the revolt of many Englishmen against King John. In 1H6, Bedford's 'Let's to the altar' (1H6 1.1.45) means 'Let's get on with the funeral service for the dead King Henry V'; 'altar' is thus a synecdoche for both the Church and the service. On the other hand, 'the altar' in H8 is the actual site in Westminster Abbey where Anne Boleyn is crowned as the new and 'saint-like' queen of Henry VIII (H8 4.1.83).

(C) On the controversial Roman altar, see Bale (1849), 262; Pilkington (1842), 493; Ridley (1841), 320; and Jewel (1845–50), 2: 1109.

AMEN [1]

(A) Though 'amen' often means merely the secular 'so be it', it can also refer to a liturgical response. Donne plays with the mere 'yes', 'But *all the promises of God are yea, and Amen,* (2 Cor. 1.20) that is, surely, verily'. Andrewes says of the liturgical 'Amen', 'by it we acknowledge the truth of the prayer, and our desire that God would hear it' (5: 467). Whitaker (1849), 259–60, complains of 'the papists', 'they deny it to be requisite that the whole people should understand the prayers which the minister repeats; for they say it is sufficient if one only, whom they commonly cal the *clerk*, understand them; who is to answer *Amen* in behalf of the whole congregation'.

(B) Macbeth is deeply troubled that he cannot exchange liturgical greetings with the grooms after he has murdered Duncan:

> As they had seen me with these hangman's hands,
> List'ning their fear, I could not say 'Amen',
> When they did say 'God bless us!'

To Lady Macbeth's 'Consider it not so deeply', he responds again

> But wherefore could I not pronounce 'Amen'?
> I had most need of blessing, and 'Amen'
> Stuck in my throat.
>
> (MAC 2.2.25–30)

Desdemona and Othello enact a quasi-liturgical exchange like the one Macbeth missed, but the result is equally frustrating, largely because Othello assumes shriving and judgemental roles at which he is inadequately priest-like and Godlike:

> OTH   Thou art to die.
> DES.   Then Lord have mercy on me!
> OTH.   I say amen.
> DES.   And you have mercy too.
>
> (OTH 5.2.56–8)

In a lighter vein, when Gratiano, reprimanded for his levity, promises to 'Wear prayer-books in my pocket, look demurely, / Nay more, while grace is saying hood mine eyes / Thus with my hat, and sigh and say amen' (MV 2.2.192–4), he associates 'amen' with any act of formal piety, including the liturgical exchange. Another playful example occurs in the exchange between Balthasar and Margaret:

> MAR.   I say my prayers aloud.
> BAL.   I love you the better. The hearers may cry amen.
> MAR.   God match me with a good dancer!
> BAL.   Amen.
> MAR.   And God keep him out of my sight when the dance is done! Answer, clerk.
> BAL.   No more words; The clerk is answer'd.
>
> (ADO 2.1.104–11)

Cf. JN 2.1.287; 3.1.181; and R2 1.4.64–5.

(C) Targoff (2002) discusses 'amen' as a devotional practice and explores contemporary concerns over the word's efficacy.

14

AMEN²

When God is asked to say 'Amen', he is asked to second a human wish or prayer.

Victorious Richmond twice asks God to ratify his will as minister, with 'Great God of heaven, say amen to all' and 'That she may long live here, God say amen' (R3 5.5.8, 41). A similar request for God's benediction also occurs at the end of H5, where the French Queen asks of her prayer for a good marriage of these two countries and these two persons, Katherine and Henry, 'God speak this Amen!' (H5 5.2.368). The cynic Thersites, however, once asks 'devil Envy say amen' (TRO 2.3.21).

AMEND

(A) Change. Liturgically, the promise to amend one's life concludes the formal process of **repentance**, which includes **contrition**, **confession**, and the promise to change for the better. Andrewes says that 'a complete repentance' is 'reflecting and sorrowing for that which is past', and 'resolving to amend that which is to come' (1: 359).

(B) When Roderigo 'confess[es]' his weakness to Iago: 'that it is my shame to be so fond, but it is not in my virtue to amend it' (OTH 1.3.317–18), Iago responds with his famous Pelagian assertion that 'the power and corrigible authority of this lies in our wills' (OTH 1.3.325–6). In contrast, the theological need for grace lurks behind Berowne's flippant 'God amend us, God amend' (LLL 4.3.74) about what he considers their incapacity to amend their own faults, and Feste's stated philosophy of amendment as the 'botching' or patching of the tattered cloth of fallen humanity: 'bid the dishonest man mend himself: if he mend, he is no longer dishonest; if he cannot, let the botcher mend him. Anything that's mended is but patch'd; virtue that transgresses is but patch'd with sin, and sin that amends is but patch'd with virtue' (TN 1.5.45–9). Richard of Gloucester, flanked by two bishops, cynically plays out with Buckingham before the citizens of London a little ritual of repentance for the 'fault' of not accepting the crown:

> BUCK.   Would it might please your Grace,
> On our entreaties, to amend your fault.
> RICH.   Else wherefore breathe I in a Christian land?
> (R3 3.7.114–16; see also WT 5.2.151–5; AWW 3.4.4–7)

(C) See Hunter (1976), 129–33, and Battenhouse (1969), 380–4, on Iago's Pelagianism.

AMENDMENT

Change. Becon calls '**correction**' 'An **amendment** of our former evil life, taming of our carnal will, **mortifying** our flesh, applying of ourselves to the **commandment**, will, and example of Christ, to take away and banish the evil, to bring in and establish the good' (3: 619).

Three of Shakespeare's four uses of 'amendment' refer to improved health rather than improved character; the fourth, though sarcastic, is religious. Prince

Hal, testing one of Falstaff's promises to amend his life, asks 'Where shall we take a purse to-morrow?' When Falstaff eagerly agrees, Hal ironically says, 'I see a good amendment of life in thee, from praying to purse-taking' (1H4 1.2.98–103). See also **amend**.

ANGEL(S)[1]

(A) Supernatural being(s) thought in the Judaic, Christian and Mohammedan traditions to be messengers and attendants of God; also evil or ill angels, those who rebelled in heaven and who subsequently tempted humans on earth. To the question 'What are angels?' Andrewes answers, 'Surely, they are Spirits; – Glorious Spirits; – Heavenly Spirits; – Immortal Spirits. For their nature or substance, Spirits; for their quality or property, glorious; for their place or abode, Heavenly; for their durance or continuance, immortal' (1: 4). Becon distinguishes between good and evil angels: 'What is a good angel? The messenger of God, or whatsoever ye will, by which God worketh us, and in us that that is good, profitable, and commodious. What is Satan, or an evil angel? An adversary and enemy of God, a worker of all mischief and death unto us. Otherwhiles it is put only for the devil' (3: 605).

(B) Lennox prays, 'Some holy angel / Fly to the court of England, and unfold / His message' (MAC 3.6.45–6). Macduff in contrast refers sarcastically to Macbeth's trust in the witches as 'the angel whom thou still hast serv'd' (MAC 5.8.14), probably marking these supernatural solicitors as Macbeth's evil angels. Laertes angrily tells the 'churlish priest' who refuses to give Ophelia a proper burial, 'A minist'ring angel shall my sister be / When thou liest howling' (HAM 5.1.241–2). When Gratiano laments Othello's murder of Desdemona by saying of her father Brabantio, 'Did he live now, / This sight would make him do a desperate turn; / Yea, curse his better angel from his side, / And fall to reprobance' (OTH 5.2.206–9), he refers to the agency of good and evil angels. In desperation Richard II similarly asserts his belief that 'God for his Richard hath in heavenly pay / A glorious angel' to match each of Bolingbroke's rebels (R2 3.2.60–1). The young Arthur believes in angels as truth-tellers when he says 'And if an angel should have come to me / And told me Hubert should put out mine eyes, / I would not have believ'd him' (JN 4.1.68–70). Arthur keeps his eyes, but soon loses his life.

The plural usage evokes more often than the singular the angel as guardian. Richard II desperately asserts 'if angels fight, / Weak men must fall, for heaven still guards the right' (R2 3.2.61–2). Canterbury greets Henry V 'God and his angels guard your **sacred** throne' (H5 1.2.7). Hamlet prays, 'Angels and ministers of grace defend us' when he first sees his father's **ghost**, and Claudius prays 'Help angels' after the Mousetrap scourges his **soul**. Horatio prays, or hopes, after Hamlet dies, 'And flights of angels sing thee to thy **rest**' (HAM 1.4.39, 3.3.69, 5.2.360). R3 ends with many prayers to the 'good angels [that] fight on Richmond's side', asking that they 'guard thy battle', and 'guard thee from the boar's annoy' (R3 5.3.175, 139, 157). H8 is also frequented by references to good ministering angels, as well as a reminder of the ones who fell through ambition: 'By that sin fell the angels' (H8 3.2.441).

Other bits of angel lore are embedded in Shakespeare's usage. Berowne's phrase 'angel knowledge' (LLL 1.1.113) seems to mean rather 'that knowledge which you idolise' than 'the more perfect knowledge of angels', though both are possible since angels were thought 'superior to man in power and intelligence' (*OED sb.* 1.a). Hamlet once says of 'a man' in this vein, 'how like an angel in apprehension' (HAM 2.2.306). Lorenzo compares the music of the spheres to the songs of angels: 'There's not the smallest orb which thou behold'st / But in his motion like an angel sings' (MV 5.1.60–1). Arviragus also says of the disguised Imogen's voice, 'How angel-like he sings' (CYM 4.2.48).

(C) On good and evil angels, see also Donne, 10:45, 57, and *ST* I.50–64. On the traditional Dionysian hierarchy of angels, see Cross and Livingstone (1997), 'Angel', 61–3; and 'Angel', *NewCathEncy*, 1: 506–19, *esp.* 511–13. See **cherubin**.

ANGEL[2]

(A) Figurative, and often romantic.

(B) The Jailkeeper in ERR is 'like an evil angel' because 'he came behind you, sir, . . . and bid you forsake your liberty' (ERR 4.3.20–1). Prince Hal styles himself Falstaff's good angel for paying his bill to Mistress Quickly (1H4 3.3.176–7). SON 144 compares the speaker's internal conflict between comfort and despair to the battle of good and evil angels within him, then suggests that these are figurative angels, two persons in a very complicated love triangle, 'the better angel . . . a man right fair' and 'the worser spirit a woman coloured ill' (SON 144.3–4). Falstaff is also accused by the Lord Chief Justice of following Hal 'the young prince up and down, like his ill angel'. Falstaff responds 'Not so my lord. Your ill angel is light' (2H4 1.2.163–5), punning with **light** on both the brightness and incorporeality of the fallen angels and the great flesh of his own fallenness. The Friar calls Hero's purity 'angel whiteness' (ADO 4.1.160–2). The Ghost of Hamlet's father compares himself to 'a radiant angel' 'in a celestial bed', whom Gertrude left 'to prey on garbage' (HAM 1.5.55–7); Clarence even describes the figure in his dream as 'A shadow like an angel, with bright hair' (R3 1.4.53). In more romantic veins, Titania asks of Bottom 'What angel wakes me from my flowery bed?' (MND 3.1.129); Romeo calls Juliet a 'bright angel' for her radiant beauty (ROM 2.2.26); Morocco hopes to find 'an angel in a golden bed' when he opens the golden casket and finds Portia's picture (MV 2.7.58–9); and Henry V tries to flatter Katherine of France by saying 'An angel is like you, Kate, and you are like an angel' (H5 5.2.109–10). She responds, 'the tongues of men be full of the deceits' (H5 5.2.109–10).

(C) For another figurative usage of good and evil angels, see Donne on 'the Angels of the Church, the Minister, the Angels of the State, the Magistrate' (3: 182–3) and on 'the spirit of error, . . . slumber, and . . . fornication' (10: 57). Donne associates the phrase 'angel of light' with 2 Cor. 11.14 (3: 276).

ANGEL[3]

(A) Angel was also the name of an old gold coin in Renaissance England, originally called the Noble, which was inscribed with the angel Michael standing over the slain dragon.

(B) Morocco glosses this usage for us when he says 'They have in England / A coin that bears the figure of an angel / Stamp'd in gold' (MV 2.7.55–7). The Bastard promises King John to liberate from 'the bags / Of hoarding abbots, imprisoned angels / Set at liberty' (JN 3.3.7–9). The witty Benedick plays on the same meaning when he says of the only woman he would marry, 'noble, or not I for an angel' (ADO 2.3.33).

(C) For angelic songs, see also **angel**[1]. Reynolds (1996), 313–14, briefly explains a reference to these coins in WIV.

ANGRY

(A) Spoken both of God's and of the heavens' displeasure over human sinfulness. Andrewes says of such anthropomorphic conceptions of God, 'God forbid it should lie in the power of flesh to work any grief in God; or that we should once admit this conceit, the Deity to be subject to this or the like perturbations that we be. And yet both the passion of grief and divers other, as anger, repentance, jealousy, we read them ascribed to God in Scripture; and as ascribed in one place, so denied as flatly in another' (3: 213–14).

(B) The reference to God's anger is most frequent in WT, where Leontes' defiance of the oracle of Apollo leads to such comments as his own 'Apollo's angry, and the heavens themselves / Do strike at my injustice', the Mariner's 'The heavens that we have in hand are angry, / And frown upon's', and Leontes' 'I have done sin, / For which the heavens, taking angry note, / Have left me issueless' (WT 3.2.146–7; 3.3.5–6; 5.1.172–4). It also occurs in a more Christian context when Young Clifford says 'O war, thou son of hell, / Whom angry heavens do make their minister' (2H6 5.2.33–4). Malcolm uses the word metaphorically in comparing himself to 'a weak, poor, innocent lamb' who is sacrificed 'T' appease an angry god' (MAC 4.3.16–17).

(C) Andrewes cites 1 Sam. 15.11, 29; Gen. 6.6; and Ps. 16.11 as passages either denying or affirming God's anger, adding, '[W]hen they are denied, that is to set out unto us the perfect steadiness of the nature **Divine** . . . But when they are ascribed, it is for no other end but even . . . "for our infirmity" (Rom. 6.19), to speak to us our own language, and in our own terms, so to work with us the better' (3: 213–14). See **appease**.

ANOINTED

Consecrated with holy oil. Because oil was applied during the consecration of a priest or sovereign, a phrase like 'the Lord's anointed' came to be associated with a priest, a king, and at the top of this hierarchy of consecration and divine right, Christ. Andrewes, in a sermon on the Gunpowder Plot, says of 1 Chron. 16.22, 'Touch not Mine anointed', 'That God would not have His "anointed" touched'. His reason is that 'they did in some kind of measure partake *chrisma Christi*, even "such a chrism as wherewith Christ is anointed" ' (4: 56).

Richard II desperately proclaims in the midst of Bolingbroke's rebellion, 'Not all the water in the rough rude sea / Can wash the balm off from an anointed king' (R2 3.2.54–5). Later the Bishop of Carlisle, defending the **divine** right of

Richard's absolute sovereignty in the scene in which Richard will be deposed, asks,

> And shall the figure of God's majesty,
> His captain, steward, deputy elect,
> Anointed, crowned, planted many years,
> Be judg'd by subject and inferior breath?
> (R2 4.1.125–8)

Gaunt has earlier refused to avenge his brother's death on Richard because he is 'God's substitute, / His deputy anointed in His sight' (R2 1.2.37–8), implying that God attends the ceremony of investiture. Anointing a king, a priest like Carlisle, or Christ himself is also associated in Carlisle's images with things as permanent as planted trees and crowned monarchs, though Carlisle, like York and Richard before him, knows that in realpolitik as in the garden such permanence is not always guaranteed.

As Andrewes has shown, both Christ and Christian kings could be called 'the Lord's anointed'; sacrilege is therefore often associated with king-killing. Carlisle compares ousting Richard II with Christ's crucifixion on 'The field of Golgotha and dead men's skulls' (R2 4.1.144). Macduff compares the stolen life of the anointed king Duncan to the sacrilegious theft of something as precious as the elements of communion, or even faith itself: 'Confusion now hath made his masterpiece! / Most sacrilegious murther hath broke ope / The Lord's anointed temple and stole thence / The life o' th' building' (MAC 2.3.66–8; cf. R3 5.3.124–6). Gloucester's disgust that Lear's daughters would 'In his anointed flesh [stick] boarish fangs' (LR 3.7.58) expresses in natural imagery that same sense of enormity. Tyrants and usurpers can of course also use this potent word. Richard III tries to drown out the verbal assaults of the women aligned against him: 'A flourish, trumpets! Strike alarum, drums! / Let not the heavens hear these tell-tale women / Rail on the Lord's anointed' (R3 4.4.149–51). Armado shows in LLL that 'Anointed' can also serve as the king's name in formal address (LLL 5.2.522).

ANSWER[1]

To be responsible or accountable for. Andrewes calls Christ 'our "Advocate", to appear for us before God, there to answer the slanderous allegations of him that "is the accuser of" us and "our brethren" '(3: 158, of Rev. 12.10).

In challenging Mowbray with treason and other offences, Bolingbroke promises that 'what I speak / My body shall make good upon this earth, / Or my divine soul answer it in heaven' (R2 1.1.36–8).

ANSWER[2]

(A) To respond, as in a catechism.
(B) Celia says to Rosalind's barrage of questions about Orlando, and especially to her request that she 'Answer me in one word', 'To say ay and no to these

particulars is more than to answer in a catechism' (AYL 3.2.224–8). Since in a catechism like Nowell's popular one of 1570, the student's answers are usually longer than the master's questions about the 'Christian Religion', Celia's point must be that Rosalind's questions are not so predictable, and her expected answers not so pat, as catechistic exchanges. However, once in a while the expected answer is briefer, 'Yea forsooth maister' (1975r), *fols* 66b, 73b, or even just 'It is true' (1975r), *fols* 70b, 30b. Feste also teases Olivia when he is teaching her of her folly, 'I must catechise you for it, madonna. Good my mouse of virtue, answer me' (TN 1.5.62–3).

(C) Hassel (1980), 127–8, discusses Feste's catechizing of Olivia.

ANSWER[3]

To respond liturgically, as of a **clerk** or a **congregation**. Whitaker (1849), 259–60, speaks of the clerk, 'who is to answer *Amen* in behalf of the whole congregation'.

'Answer clerk' (ADO 2.1.110) is Margaret's sarcastic response to a Balthasar who has just merely answered 'Amen' to her attempt at witplay rather than engaging her with a challenging riposte.

ANSWER[4]

(A) To respond antiphonally, of musical responses. Donne defines 'Antiphones, and Responsaries in the Church of God, (when in that service, some things are said or sung by one side of the Congregation, and then answered by the other, or said by one man, and then answered by the whole Congregation)'. He also defends them in terms of biblical precedent: 'that this manner of serving God, hath a pattern from the practise of the Triumphant Church [i.e. heaven]. For there, the *Seraphim cryed to one another*, or (as it is in the Originall) *this Seraphim to this, Holy, Holy, Holy*; so that there was a voice given, and an answer made, and a reply returned in this service of God' (8: 56).

(B) Venus's grief for Adonis is metaphorically described, 'Her heavy anthem still concludes in woe / And still the choir of echoes answer so' (VEN 840).

(C) Hooker (V.39) also defends this liturgical practice. Donne is quoting the *Te Deum* (*BCP*, 53).

ANTHEM

Vocal religious music, usually based on scriptural texts and traditionally performed by choirs rather than congregations (*OED sb.* 2). Donne defends church singing when he says of 'The Quire, the Chancell of the Church, in which all the service of God is officiated and executed . . . we are made not onely hearers, and spectators, but actors in the service of God, when we come to beare a part in the Hymnes and Anthems of the Saints' (7: 165).

Falstaff tells the Lord Chief Justice that he has lost his voice 'with hallowing and singing of anthems' (2H4 1.2.190); earlier he has told Prince Hal, 'I would I were a weaver, I could sing psalms, or anything' (1H4 2.4.133–4). In Shakespeare, however, the anthem more often serves as a metaphor for romantic than religious expression. When Valentine asks Proteus to tell him no more of Silvia's suffering, he phrases the ironic request as though her story would be his requiem: 'I pray thee breathe it in mine ear, / As ending anthem of my endless dolor' (TGV 3.1.241–2). In PHT the song of lament is called both a 'requiem' and an 'anthem' (PHT 16, 21), and in VEN 835, 839, Venus's lament for Adonis is also compared to a requiem, a 'wailing note' whose 'heavy anthem still concludes in woe'.

APOSTLE

(A) One of the twelve original followers of **Christ**, or one of the early missionaries of the **Church**.

(B) Twice in Shakespeare this word refers to the chief of these missionaries, St Paul; however, the word is also used more generally. Shaken by his premonitory dream of the eleven ghosts, Richard III swears 'By the Apostle Paul' (R3 5.3.216). The character St Thomas More warns the crowd that rebellion is according to St Paul 'a sin / Which oft th' apostle did forewarn us of, urging obedience to authority, / And 'twere no error if I told you all you were in arms 'gainst God' (STM II.93–5). When Queen Margaret says scornfully of her husband King Henry VI that 'His champions are the prophets and apostles, / His weapons holy saws of sacred writ' (2H6 1.3.57–8), she is using the term more generally to include all of the writers of Scripture; the 'apostles' for the New Testament, the 'prophets' for the Old.

(C) More refers to Rom. 13.1–5 on obedience. Morris (1978) argues that Prince Hal acts as an apostle in the Henriad. See **Paul, Saint**.

APPARELL'D

(A) Dressed.

(B) Though Dromio knows that he is speaking 'Not [of] that **Adam** that kept the Paradise, but [of] that Adam that keeps the prison', his reference to 'The picture of old Adam new apparell'd' (ERR 4.3.14–18) still evokes the biblical story of Adam and **Eve**'s fall and subsequent need to cover their shame with a fig leaf.

(C) See Shaheen (1999), 112; *BCP*, 274.

APPEAL

Make a request of God.

When Henry V speaks of invading France after the incident of the tennis balls, he predicts victory but adds, with proper humility, the prayer-like 'But this lies all within the will of God, / To whom I do appeal' (H5 1.2.289–90). When the fallen Gloucester defends himself against the charges of both King Henry VI and his Queen Margaret that he is among 'the wicked ones', his response, 'to heaven I do appeal, / How I have lov'd my king and commonweal' (2H6 2.1.182, 186–7), casts heaven more as a superior judge who might reverse their worldly decision against him than as a power who might deliver him on earth.

APPEASE

(A) To pacify or propitiate, as of an **angry** god. In the Christian scheme, 'true repentance', deeply felt contrition and confession, faith in forgiveness, and amendment of life were crucial steps in the process of appeasing God's anger over human fallenness; both Catholics and Protestants would have agreed that only Christ the Lamb of God, could offer a 'full, perfect, and sufficient sacrifice, oblation, and satisfaction for the sins of the whole world' (*BCP*, 263). As Tyndale says, 'His blood, his death, his patience in suffering rebukes and wrongs, his prayers and fastings, his meekness and fulfilling of the uttermost point of the law, appeased the wrath of God: brought the favour of God to us again' (1: 18–19).

(B) Gloucester's brother Clarence is not sure of divine forgiveness when he prays, 'O God! if my deep pray'rs cannot appease thee, / But thou wilt be aveng'd on my misdeeds, / Yet execute thy wrath in me alone!' (R3 1.4.69–71). Proteus pleads for Valentine's human forgiveness with similar misgivings: 'if hearty sorrow / Be a sufficient ransom for offense, / I tender't here'. But Valentine forgives, citing the religious analogy: 'By penitence th' Eternal's wrath's appeased' (TGV 5.4.74–81). In MAC, Malcolm, using the religious word as an analogy for Macbeth's fearsome vengeance, compares Macduff's betrayal of him to a worshipper who might 'offer up a weak, poor, innocent lamb / T' appease an angry god' (4.3.16–17).

(C) See also Andrewes, 5: 259–60.

APPLE

(A) An instrument of the Fall, 'the fruit, / Of that forbidden tree'.

(B) In SON 93.13, the speaker says 'How like Eve's apple doth thy beauty grow', referring to her tempting outward appearance of love, sweetness and truth.

(C) See PL 1.2.

APPREHEND

(A) Though the *OED* aligns this word with 'comprehend', 'to lay hold of with the mind' (*OED v.* comprehend 5), theologians can use it as an antonym of 'comprehend' which suggests either transcendent knowing or transcendent foolishness. The Cambridge Puritan Perkins says that 'the essential property [of "justifying faith"] 'is to apprehend Christ with his benefites, and to assure the verie conscience thereof' (1597b), 249. Trapp ([1656], *Exp.* Rom, iii, 29) says that 'Men are said to be justified apprehensively by faith.'

(B) The best example of this usage in Shakespeare occurs in MND, where the rationalistic Duke Theseus twice in the same speech condescendingly prefers things comprehended to things apprehended. 'I never may believe' the lovers' stories, he says, because 'Lovers and madmen have such seething brains, / Such shaping fantasies, that apprehend / More than cool reason ever comprehends' (MND 5.1.2–6). He also attributes 'Such tricks' to 'strong imagination / That if it would but apprehend some joy, / It comprehends some bringer of that joy' (MND 5.1.18–20). Advocates of the imagination, like Erasmus in *The Praise of*

Folly or St Paul in his First Epistle to the Corinthians, might find praise in such blame; sometimes the hot imagination can shape and grasp 'more than cool reason ever comprehends', be it in matters of romantic or religious faith. Bottom's prominent allusion to St Paul's most famous passage to the Corinthians prefaces Theseus's speech, and puts it in its place: 'Eye hath not seen, nor ear heard, neither have entered into the heart of man, the things which God hath prepared for them that love him' (1 Cor. 2.9). When another duke, Vincentio, says of the reprobate Barnadine that because of his 'stubborn soul' he 'apprehends no further than this world' (MM 5.1.480–1), we see him preferring through the usage of 'apprehend' the grasping of transcendent over ephemeral things. Hamlet's 'How like an angel in apprehension' (HAM 2.2.306) is more ambiguous, but in either case the apprehension of angels or of gods would be considered superior to mere human understanding, or comprehension.

(C) Bottom's words are 'The eye of man hath not heard, the ear of man hath not seen, man's hand is not able to taste, his tongue to conceive, nor his heart to report, what my dream was' (MND 4.1.211–14). See Hassel (1980), ch. 1, on the Pauline and Erasmian contexts of the comedies. Trapp is quoted in *OED* apprehensively *adv.* 1. See also van Beek (1969), 62. F1 reads, 'in action, how like an Angel? in apprehension how like a God'.

ARCHBISHOP

(A) A bishop of the highest rank.

(B) Identified archbishops in the plays include several Archbishops of Canterbury, including Stephen Langton (JN 3.1.143), Arundel's brother (BEV – R2 2.1.282) and Thomas Cranmer (H8 3.2.401); Archbishops of York include Richard Scroop (1H4 1.3.268, 3.2.119; 2H4 1.2.205 etc., & *dramatis personae*), and Warwick's brother George Nevill (3H6 4.3.53). Adversaries of these churchmen are sometimes struck by the irony of their involvement in military and political affairs. The King's man Westmoreland upbraids Scroop, the rebellious Archbishop of York, 'You, Lord Archbishop', 'Wherefore do you so ill translate yourself / Out of the speech of peace which bears such grace, / Into the harsh and boist'rous tongue of war?' (2H4 4.1.41, 47–9). Prince John, King Henry IV's son, picks up the same theme to the 'gentle Archbishop' in the next scene (2H4 4.2.2–10).

(C) See Whitgift (1851–53), 2: 265 for a sceptical account of the relationship between ecclesiastical hierarchy and spiritual authority. See also **sword**.

ARCHDEACON

(A) In Anglicanism, this ecclesiastical figure serves as a bishop's assistant; in the Roman Church, the title can refer to a member of the cathedral chapter.

(B) In Shakespeare's only use of this title, the 'Archdeacon' (1H4 3.1.71) is the Archdeacon of Bangor, in whose house the rebels 'divided the realme amongst them' before the Battle of Shrewsbury.

(C) See *NDS*, 4: 185.

ARCH-HERETIC

(A) A chief heretic; someone charged with taking and/or asserting extreme doctrinal positions or sometimes merely resisting the authority of the Roman Catholic Church or the Pope.

(B) In JN, 'that arch-heretic' is the papal legate Pandulph's name for King John of England, who has refused to accept the authority of the Pope (JN 3.1.173, 191–2). Thomas Cromwell is also called an arch-heretic in H8 (5.1.45), again by a Roman Catholic sympathizer, Gardiner, Bishop of Winchester. Since both of these plays are set before the Reformation in England, all of the figures are still Catholic. But King John was widely considered in Reformation England a proto-reformer for his defiance of the Pope, and both Cromwell and Cranmer were instrumental in establishing Protestantism, or at least Anglicanism, as the official religion of Tudor England.

(C) On Cranmer as 'a chief architect of religious change', see 'Cranmer', *OxfordEncyRef*, 1: 449; see also *NewCathEncy*, 4: 413–14. See also MacCulloch (1996). Cromwell had a major hand in both early versions of *The Book of Common Prayer* (1549 and 1552), and in the Ordinal (1550); he also oversaw the publication of the first Book of Homilies (1547) and the work on the Forty-two Articles (1553). Cromwell supervised the complete dissolution of the monasteries (1536–40), promoted and supervised the production of the Great Bible (1539), cooperated with Cranmer's efforts at reform, and supported other Reformers like Latimer. On King John as a proto-reformer, see Saccio (1977), 204–5, and *NDS*, 3: 3. On 'Cromwell', see *OxfordEncyRef*, 1: 454; *NewCathEncy*, 4: 471.

ARM

By synecdoche, the intervening power of **heaven**. Andrewes says of the arm of **God**, 'His hand signifies his ordinary, His arm his special **providence**' (4:86–7; from Isa. 53.1).

In H5 Salisbury says 'God's arm strike with us' (H5 4.3.5). Henry V also celebrates God's victory (and his own ministry) at Agincourt, 'O God, thy arm was here! / And not to us, but to thy arm alone, / Ascribe we all' (H5 4.8.106–8; cf. H5 4.3.5).

ASCENSION-DAY

(A) The fortieth day after **Easter**, a Thursday, commemorating the ascension of Christ into heaven.

(B) In JN a prophet is said to have predicted that King John will deliver up his crown 'ere the next Ascension-day at noon' (JN 4.2.151). Ascension Day is mentioned three more times in the play (JN 5.1.22–6). Though the references seem merely calendrical, they do reveal how readily Shakespeare and his contemporaries, as well as these represented medieval princes, thought of their secular calendars in terms of the Church year.

(C) See Donne, 7: 450.

ASHES

(A) These remnants of fire are associated traditionally with **repentance**, with prescribed days of **penance** like **Ash Wednesday**, and with **death**. Becon says of the Ash Wednesday service, 'For when the priest layeth ashes on your heads he saith these words, "Remember, man, that thou art ashes, and unto ashes thou shalt return" ' (1: 110). The burial service similarly reads 'We therefore commit his body to the ground, earth to earth, ashes to ashes, dust to dust, in sure and certain hope of resurrection to eternal life' (*BCP*, 310). Matt. 9.21 speaks of 'penance in haircloth, or sackcloth, and ashes'.

(B) Falstaff refers to this tradition when he pretends before the Lord Chief Justice to have brought young Prince Hal to repentance: 'the young lion repents, [aside] marry, not in ashes and sackcloth, but in new silk and old sack' (2H4 1.2.197–8). Ashes of repentance are probably combined with the black garments of mourning when Richard II, lamenting his deposition to his wife, says of their former subjects, 'some will mourn in ashes, some coal-black, / For the deposing of a rightful king' (R2 5.1.49–50). Hubert, holding a glowing poker with which he planned to put out the eyes of Prince Arthur, says of changing his mind, and therefore of letting the poker cool, 'There is no malice in this burning coal; / The breath of heaven hath blown his spirit out, / And strew'd repentant ashes on his head' (JN 4.1.108–10).

(C) See also Andrewes, 1: 362.

AUDIT

(A) The Day of **Judgement** was sometimes called **compt** (as in OTH 5.2.273), the day of accounting (*OED sb.* count 4 *fig.*). Consonant with such usage, 'audit' could be used to describe the process of counting up virtues and sins, and weighing them in the balance at the Last Day (*OED sb.* 3 *fig.*).

(B) Hamlet says of Claudius at prayer, 'And how his audit stands, who knows save heaven?' (HAM 3.3.82). When Lady Macbeth tells Duncan, whom she has already decided to kill, that they hold 'what is theirs, in compt, / To make their audit at your Highness' pleasure' (MAC 1.6.26–7), 'compt' and 'audit' suggest the eternal consequences of acting out their dreadful desire.

(C) See Bevington (1985) on Just Judgement motifs in the dramatic tradition.

AVARICE

(A) Vaux defines this deadly sin as 'an inordinate desire of getting and keeping mony and other worldly goods'.

(B) Lying in order to test Macduff's loyalty, Malcolm proclaims himself possessed of 'a stanchless avarice' that would destroy even 'the good and loyal' 'for wealth' (MAC 4.3.78, 83–4).

(C) See Vaux's *A Brief Fourme of Confession*, (1590b), *sigs*. f6ʳ⁻ᵛ.

AVARICIOUS

Characterised by avarice.

Just before accusing himself of avarice, Malcolm accuses Macbeth, more justly, of the same sin: 'I grant him bloody, / Luxurious, avaricious, false, deceitful, / Sudden, malicious, smacking of every sin / That has a name' (MAC 4.3.57–60).

AVE-MARIES

(A) Hail Marys; reference to the famous (and by Shakespeare's time contro-versial) Catholic prayer to the Virgin, 'Hail Mary full of grace, the Lord is with thee, blessed art thou among women, and blessed is the fruit of thy womb; Holy Mary, Mother of God, pray for us sinners now and at the hour of our death.'

(B) Shakespeare has two explicit references to this prayer. Queen Margaret dis-approves of her pious husband King Henry VI, 'But all his mind is bent on holiness, / To number Ave-Maries on his beads' (2H6 1.3.55–6). Richard of Gloucester is similarly dismissive when he says of Henry's reputation for piety: 'Shall we go throw away our coats of steel, / And wrap our bodies in black mourning gowns, / Numb'ring our Ave-Maries with our beads?' (3H6 2.1.160–2).

(C) The prayer echoes Luke 1.28, 42. On the controversial devotion to the Virgin in fifteenth- and sixteenth-century Europe, see O'Connor (1983), 313–14; and Martz (1962), 96–101.

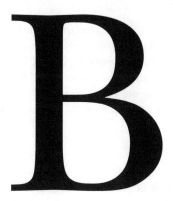

BABYLON

(A) This ancient city, located in southwest Asia, in the lower Euphrates valley, is the setting for several biblical stories, including the apocryphal legend of Susanna.

(B) Shakespeare refers to both of these associations. Toby Belch, drunk and singing, starts one of his songs 'There dwelt a man in Babylon' (TN 2.3.79); Falstaff, dying, is described by the Hostess as 'rheumatic, and talk'd of the whore of Babylon'. Since he also 'babbl'd of green fields' as he lay dying, and 'cried out, "God! God! God!" ' (H5 2.3.38–9, 17–19), Falstaff seems, however incongruously, to have been preoccupied with both physical and spiritual matters as he approached death.

(C) Shaheen (1999), 237; BEV, 339n; and RIV, 452n, all describe this as the first line of a popular song about the apocryphal story of Susanna. Shaheen (1999), 458, tells us that 'the majority of Shakespeare's audience would have associated "the Whore of Babylon" with the Roman Catholic Church', from a passage in Rev. 17.5: 'And upon her forehead *was* a name written, MYSTERY, BABYLON THE GREAT, THE *MOTHER* OF HARLOTS'. The *Geneva Bible*'s notes read, 'this woman is the Antichrist, that is, the Pope' and 'the whore of Rome' (*fol.* 200). See also Donne, 8: 104; 10: 176; Bale (1849), 498; Bradford (1848), 1: 390; Coverdale (1846), 2: 586. Kaula (1973) argues that Helen in TRO closely resembles the Protestant image of the Whore of Babylon. For a brief analysis of Cleopatra as the Whore of Babylon, see Davidson (1980), 38–9.

BALM

An oily substance used for religious or medicinal purposes; often in Shakespeare the word is used to describe the **holy oil** used during the coronation of the king.

Richard refers to the coronation oil during the scene of his deposition: 'Not all the water in the rough rude sea / Can wash the balm off from an anointed king'

(R2 3.2.54–5). Henry V refers to this same oil when he includes 'balm' as part of the 'tide of pomp' that can do nothing to ease the anxiety of a king (H5 4.1.260, 264). His own deposed son King Henry VI laments of his own deposition, 'Thy balm wash'd off wherewith thou was anointed' (3H6 3.1.17). The association of 'balm' with holy oil also informs King Henry IV's conceit to his son: 'Let all the tears that should bedew my hearse / Be drops of balm to sanctify thy head' (2H4 4.5.113–14).

BAN
Curse.

In 2H6 the Duchess of Gloucester, who consorts with conjurers, once advises Gloucester to 'ban thine enemies, both thine and mine' (2H6 2.4.25). Later in the same play, Suffolk tells the often-cursing Queen Margaret that 'every joint should seem to **curse** and ban' (2H6 3.2.308, 319) if only he believed in the efficacy of bans and curses. After her own formidable curses, Joan of Arc is also called 'Fell banning hag, enchantress' as York asks her to 'hold thy tongue' (1H6 5.3.42). See also HAM 3.2.258; LUC 1460; PP 18.32.

BANES
(A) Banns; the publication of an intention to marry, usually by proclamation during three consecutive worship services, sometimes by posted notice.
(B) In SHR, 'ask the banes' and 'proclaim the banes' (SHR 2.1.180; 3.2.16) both refer to the proposed marriage of Kate and Petruchio. Falstaff proposes to press only 'contracted bachelors, such as had been ask'd twice on the banes' (1H4 4.2.16–17), presumably because they would be so eager to marry that they would pay him anything to avoid military service. Albany, proclaiming an 'interlude' or comic interval, pretends to support his wife's marriage contract with Edmund against Regan's competing claim:

> For your claim, fair sister,
> I bar it in the interest of my wife;
> 'Tis she is sub-contracted to this lord,
> And I, her husband, contradict your banes.
> If you will marry, make your loves to me,
> My lady is bespoke.
>
> (LR 5.3.84–9)

(C) See 'banes' in Cross and Livingstone (1997) and *NewCathEncy*, 9: 274, under 'Marriage'.

BAPTISM
(A) One of the two **Christian sacraments** that survived the **Reformation**, baptism is the ritual cleansing from sin with water and the **Spirit** (through either immersion or sprinkling) that marks a communicant's new life in Christ. The Recusant Persons (1604b), 186, calls 'baptisme, the externall washinge by water', and says

it 'is the signe of the internall washing of the soule by grace'. In the *Book of Common Prayer*, this ritual is described both in the petition, 'Give thy Holy Spirit to these infants, that they may be born again, and be made heirs of everlasting salvation', and in the one which follows, 'to bless them, to release them of their sins, to give them the kingdom of heaven, and everlasting life'. In infant baptism, the godparents are asked to answer for the child such questions as 'Wilt thou be baptised in this faith?' and 'Dost thou forsake the devil, and all his works . . .?' (*BCP*, 272–3).

(B) Henry VIII asks Thomas Cranmer, Archbishop of Canterbury, if he will serve as the baby Elizabeth's godfather:

> My Lord of Canterbury,
> I have a suit which you must not deny me:
> That is, a fair young maid that yet wants baptism,
> You must be godfather, and answer for her.
> (H8 5.2. 194–7)

Since Cranmer will subsequently author the *Book of Common Prayer* as well as Queen Elizabeth's Protestantism, he is becoming godfather not only to Elizabeth but also to Anglican England. When King Henry V asks the Archbishop of Canterbury for absolute truthfulness in his assessment of the validity of his claims to the crown of France, he punctuates his seriousness by referring to this sacrament's association with purity: 'For we will hear, note, and believe in heart, / That what you speak is in your conscience wash'd / As pure as sin with baptism' (H5 1.2.30–2). In OTH, Iago imagines Desdemona's influence on Othello to be so great that she could even 'win the Moor, were't to renounce his baptism, / All seals and symbols of redeemed sins' (OTH 2.3.343–4).

(C) See *BCP*, 272–3. On the controversies concerning the style, timing and interpretation of baptism, see Donne, 5: 108–9; Perkins (1597a), 130–4 (ch. 33 – 'Of Baptisme'); Becon, 2: 203–4; *ST* III.66–71. Sexton (1994) notes allusions to the sacrament of **baptism** in AWW. See also **cross**[2].

BARBARIAN

Generally anyone not civilised; even anyone foreign (*OED sb.* 1). In Shakespeare it also refers to the non-Christian alien (*OED sb.* 2.a).

Iago may refer to several of these associations when he speaks of the marriage of Desdemona and Othello as one 'betwixt an erring barbarian and a supersubtle Venetian' (OTH 1.3.355–6). He prefaces this remark with sarcasm about their 'sanctimony and a frail vow', presumably speaking both of their marriage and of Othello's baptism (OTH 1.1.111–12).

BARABBAS

(A) The thief and revolutionary for whom Jesus was exchanged to be crucified.
(B) Shylock says of Jessica, who has recently married the Christian Lorenzo, 'I have a daughter – / Would any of the stock of Barabbas / Had been her husband

rather than a Christian!' (MV 4.1.294–7). Like the Jews who chose Barabbas over Christ, Shylock would exchange even a Barabbas, of whom he obviously disapproves, for these 'Christian husbands'.
(C) For the story, see Luke 23.18, 25, Matt. 27.21, Mark 15.7, John 18.39–40 and Acts 3.14.

BAYONNE
A French cathedral city.
The 'Bishop of Bayonne' is mentioned as a 'French ambassador' sent to England to debate 'A marriage 'twixt the Duke of Orleance and / Our [King Henry VIII's] daughter Mary' (H8 2.4.175–6).

BEADLE
(A) The beadle has the ecclesiastical role of keeping order during services in a parish church (*OED sb.* 4).
(B) In Shakespeare it is seldom clear that the beadle is a parish officer, though he is often a whipper of transgression. When Berowne says of his incongruously falling in love, 'O, and I, forsooth, in love! I, that hath been love's whip, / A very beadle to a humourous sigh' (LLL 3.1.174–5), his metaphor could refer to the beadle's role of punishing minor offences like a disruptive sigh during a church service. Henry V says metaphorically of God's corrective strokes, 'War is his beadle, war is his vengeance' (H5 4.1.169). The beadle thrice named in 2H6 as the person to whip Simpcox, the man caught in the false claim that his sight was restored by divine miracle (2H6 2.1.133–4, 137, 145–6), may be an officer of the Church or the state.
(C) Cf. BEV, 552n and RIV, 677.

BEADS
(A) The rosary, used to help the penitent count the requisite number of 'Hail Mary' and 'Our Father' prayers.
(B) Dromio, frightened, says 'O for my beads! I **cross** me for a sinner' (ERR 2.2.188). Among the many worldly things Richard II says he is willing to trade for religious objects are 'my jewels for a set of beads' (R2 3.3.147). Queen Margaret complains about her pious husband, 'But all his mind is bent to **holiness**, / To number **Ave-Maries** on his beads' (2H6 1.3.55–6). In contrast, she describes herself as always thinking about her confederate Suffolk, her 'alder-liefest sovereign', whether 'In courtly company, or at my beads' (2H6 1.1.27–8). Buckingham, lying, describes Richard as one of three 'devout **religious** men' who are 'at their beads' (R3 3.7.92–3). Constance may be punning on the 'heaven-moving pearls' of Arthur's tears as rosary beads when she says, 'with these crystal beads heaven shall be brib'd' (JN 2.1.169–71). If so, her words invite into the play the theological controversy about the efficacy and ethicality of rosaries.
(C) For complaints against rosaries, see Grindal (1843), 140; Hooper (1852), 2: 135–6; Latimer (1844–45), 1: 70; and Bale (1849), 262.

BEADSMAN
A religious **hermit**, sometimes employed to **pray** for someone else.

One of Shakespeare's direct verbal references is metaphoric and the other ironic. When Proteus promises 'I will be thy beadsman, Valentine', it is upon a 'love-book' rather than the Bible that he will pray (TGV 1.1.18). And when Scroop describes a whole nation rising up against Richard II, 'The very beadsmen learn to bend their bows' (R2 3.2.116) contributes to his list of the unlikeliest soldiers. When Henry V describes the 'five hundred poor I have in yearly pay' to pray for his father's fault (H5 4.1.298), he is speaking of such a vocation, though he does not name them beadsmen.

BEAM
(A) A large piece, distinguished from a mote or speck. Christ's familiar metaphor distinguishes large and small sins as the mote in the other's eye and the beam in one's own (Matt. 7:3–5).
(B) Berowne obviously alludes to this biblical usage when he says, 'You found his mote, the king your mote did see; / But I a beam do find in each of three' (LLL 4.3.159–60).
(C) See Shaheen (1999), 131; see also Luke 6.41–2.

BEGGAR; BEGGING
(A) One who asks for alms; the asking. Mendicants were **friars** whose occupation was to beg, for their soul's good and also for the good of the **almsman**.
(B) When Speed says that a lover will 'speak puling, like a beggar at **Hallowmas**' (TGV 2.1.25–6), he reminds us that beggars asked for special alms on 1 November. Titus also speaks of 'begging **hermits** in their holy **prayers**' (TIT 3.2.41).
(C) Carroll (1996), 127–57, 180–207 and 158–78, examines the portrayal of beggars in several plays, especially H6, LR, SHR and WT.

BELFRY
The bell-tower of a church.

When the First Fisherman mentions the whale which 'swallow'd . . . **church**, **steeple**, **bells** and all', the Third responds, 'if I had been the **sexton**, I would that day have been in the belfry'. His reason: 'in his belly, I would have kept such a jangling of the bells, that he should never have left till he cast bells, steeple, church, and **parish** up again' (PER 2.1.32–43).

BELIEVE (BELIEF)
(A) Though almost always used either as a formula of personal reassurance, like 'Believe me', or as a synonym for think or opine, 'believe' occasionally refers to an assertion of faith, though not literally the religious faith it would affirm in the creeds.
(B) Horatio responds to Marcellus' superstitious comment, 'Some say' the cock 'singeth all night long' during the 'season . . . Wherein our Saviour's birth is celebrated . . . And then they say no spirit dare stir abroad', 'So have I heard and

do in part believe it' (HAM 1.1.157–65). In the pre-Christian LR, the King of France says metaphorically that Lear's claim about Cordelia's 'offence': 'which to believe of her / Must be a faith that reason without miracle / Should never plant in me' (LR 1.1.218–23). Casca says 'I believe they are portentous things' about the 'prodigies' he has just described (JC 1.3.31).

(C) Lim (2001) argues that WT questions the nature of religious belief.

BELL[1]

(A) Church bells are associated in Shakespeare with funerals, times of rejoicing, and the summoning of the congregation to a church service.

(B) In PER, the Fisherman speaks of a whale which 'swallowed the whole parish, church, **steeple**, bells and all' (PER 2.1.33–4). The 'doleful knell' (PP 17.18) of funeral bells are frequently referred to, as in 'the bell rings and the widow weeps' (ADO 5.2.79), or 'No mournful bell shall ring her burial' (TIT 5.3.197). Even amidst Ophelia's 'maimed **rites**', the Priest allows 'the bringing home of bell and burial' (HAM 5.1.219, 233–4). Church bells also 'knolled to church' (AYL 2.7.114, 121) and marked times of rejoicing (JN 2.1.312; 2H4 4.5.111; 1H6 1.6.11; 2H6 5.1.3). Lady Capulet compares the 'sight of death' of Juliet and Romeo to 'a bell / That warns my old age to a sepulchre' (ROM 5.3.206–7). 'Bell, book and candle shall not drive me back' (JN 3.3.12) refers to the three instruments associated with the ritual of excommunication.

(C) See Cressy (1989); *OED sb.* 8 describes 'bell, book, and candle' as 'referring to a form of excommunication which closed with the words "Doe to the book, quench the candle, ring the bell!" '; *Britannica* (1929), 3: 376, says of these symbols that the bell would have called the participants together, the book would have symbolised the presiding bishop's authority, and the candle, thrown to the ground and extinguished, would have suggested the possibility of the individual's reversing the judgement by rekindling his faith. See also Tilley, B276.

BELL[2]

(A&B) The '**sacring** bell' or '**sanctus** bell' that startles 'when the brown wench / Lay kissing in your arms, Lord Cardinal' (H8 3.2.295–6) is the bell which is rung when the host is consecrated during the Eucharist.

(C) See Bradshaw (2002), 57.

BELOW

In a lower position, thus theologically either earth or hell in relation to heaven, or hell in relation to earth. 'Below the moon' signifies the sublunary world, which unlike the eternal heavens waxes and wanes.

Of the first, Claudius, after his failed attempt at prayer, says 'My words fly up, my thoughts remain below; / Words without thoughts never to heaven go' (HAM 3.3.97–8). Henry VIII says similarly of Cardinal Wolsey's worldliness,

> If we did think
> His contemplation were above the earth,

And fix'd on spiritual object, he should still
Dwell in his musings, but I am afraid
His thinkings are below the moon.
                              (H8 3.2.130–4)

In two classical references, the Stoic Brutus refers to 'some high powers / That govern us below' (JC 5.1.107), and Titus promises to 'dive into the burning lake below' (TIT 4.3.44), referring to **Acheron**, a river in **Hades**. See **beneath, above**.

BELZEBUB

Beelzebub is named 'prince of the devils' in Matt. 12.24. As the *OED* says, 'the word became at an early period one of the popular names of the Devil'.

Fluellen conflates 'Lucifer and Belzebub himself' (H5 4.7.137–9). Feste may speak of Malvolio's self-love, the devil's sin, when he says 'He holds Belzebub at the stave's end as well as a man in his case may do', since he has earlier styled Malvolio 'goodman Devil' and Olivia has called him 'sick of self-love' (TN 5.1.284–5; 4.2.131; 1.5.90). The self-styled 'porter of hell gate' in MAC swears 'i' th' name of Belzebub' at the knocking that awakens him (MAC 2.3.3–4).

BENEATH

(A) Can refer to earth as regards its physical (and theological) relationship to heaven or the moon. It can also refer to **hell**, which is in the Ptolemaic universe positioned below the earth as earth is **below** the **heavens**.

(B) Portia, speaking to Shylock about the godlike 'quality of mercy', says that 'It droppeth as the gentle rain from heaven / Upon the place beneath' (MV 4.1.185–6). In TIM 'this beneath world' (TIM 1.1.44) is probably more the world below the moon, the sublunary world therefore of chance and change, though it also refers to that which interests mortals rather than gods. Cleon's 'all the faults beneath the heavens' (PER 4.3.20) uses the same visual and moral orientation to locate sinfulness on earth and perfection in heaven. Lear's cynical 'But to the girdle do the gods inherit, / Beneath is all the fiends': there's hell, there's darkness, / There is the sulphurous pit' locates hell within rather than outside of the microcosm, the little world which is man (LR 4.6.126–8). Othello consigns himself to the deepest damnation if it turns out that he has killed Desdemona without just cause: 'O, I were damn'd beneath all depth in hell / But that I did proceed upon just grounds / To this extremity' (OTH 5.2.137–9). The two extremities, his killing and the place where it will be punished eternally, are conflated nicely in this pun.

(C) The English Reformer Coverdale (1846), 2: 212, says, 'In St Luke it is read, that Abraham's lap or bosom is above in the height, but the harbour or dwelling of the damned beneath in the depth.' The recusant Sander says of the vertical hierarchy of material being: 'as the angels occupie the highest place, so doe the heavens with the lights and starres in them occupie the second place, & the foure elements are beneth them' (1565), *sig.* F1^v.

BENEDICITE

Literally in Latin a good word, a blessing or benediction.

This is spoken in Shakespeare only by religious persons, or their impersonators. In ROM The Friar responds to Romeo's 'Good morrow' with '*Benedicite*' (ROM 2.3.31). Similarly, the Duke, disguised as a friar, says '*Benedicite*' (MM 2.3.39) in farewell to the contrite and shriven Juliet.

BENEDICTION

(A) Act of blessing, often involving a human gesture. This can be religious, fatherly, or a combination of the two in Shakespeare. Andrewes calls Heb. 13.20, 21 ('The God of peace . . . Make you perfect . . . through Jesus Christ') 'a benediction', saying, 'the use the Church doth make of it and such other like, is to pronounce them over the congregation by way of a blessing' (3: 81).

(B) In calling that 'miraculous work' of King Edward the Confessor his 'healing benediction', and in describing it as one which 'solicits heaven' 'with holy prayers' (MAC 4.3.147, 149, 154), Malcolm seems to describe not only a liturgical gesture but also its medical efficacy. Kent in LR refers to the returning warmth of the sun as a heavenly rather than a priestly or a fatherly gesture of blessing when he says that it comes 'out of heaven's benediction' (LR 2.2.161–2). When Lear's rash banishment of Cordelia is described later in the play as 'his own unkindness, / That stripp'd her from his benediction' (LR 4.3.42–3), the word refers merely to a father's blessing, but his subsequent request for her blessing and forgiveness, 'hold your hand in benediction o'er me' (LR 4.7.57), combines a father's request for his child's blessing with a priest's characteristic gesture. The cynical Autolycus says the large amounts paid for the valueless trinkets he sells at the feast makes it seem 'as if my trinkets had been **hallow'd** and brought a benediction to the buyer' (WT 4.4.601–2). Their adoptive father Belarius **blesses** Cymbeline's sons with a father's invocation of heaven's grace: 'The benediction of these covering heavens / Fall on their heads like dew!' (CYM 5.5.350–1).

(C) Chaucer's Pardoner, of course, memorialises the analogous (and notorious) selling of religious **relics** in the Roman Catholic Church.

BENEFICE

Ecclesiastical living (see *OED sb.* 6).

Mercutio describes a poor parson, who, when he 'lies asleep, / Then he dreams of another benefice' (ROM 1.4.79–81).

BENISON

Another word for **blessing** or **benediction** (*OED* 1).

Gloucester's blessing of the disguised Edgar with 'The bounty and the benison of heaven' (LR 4.6.225) simply expresses the wish that heaven would bless him for his kindnesses. More ambiguous is the Old Man's 'God's benison go with you, and with those / That would make good of bad, and friends of foes!' (MAC 2.4.40–1), since it seems to bless both the suspicious Macduff who has already decided not to attend Macbeth's coronation and those more cowardly or cynical thanes who will come to it regardless of their fears that Macbeth 'play'dst most foully' for the crown (MAC 3.1.3).

BENNET, SAINT
(A) St Benedict's 'rule', which stresses munificence to the poor, became the model **monastic** code of Western Europe. Feast Day: 21 March.
(B) When Feste, **begging** from Orsino, says that 'the bells of Saint Bennet', i.e. the Church of Saint Benedict, 'may put you in mind' of more charity, Orsino understands the allusion to St Benedict's munificence but declines to follow his model: 'You can fool no more money out of me at this throw' (TN 5.1.39–42). St Benedict's is also the church Feste refers to when he tells Viola 'I live by the church' (TN 3.1.3). If invoking St Benedict is Feste's most effective strategy, then he does indeed live, make his living, by a begging which is authorised by the Church.
(C) Farmer (1978), 35–6; Baring-Gould (1914), 3: 388–405.

BESTIAL
(A) Animalistic. The angel–beast, soul–body dichotomy usually carries some religious overtones in Shakespeare; usually this pertains to the uniquely human responsibility for thinking and acting morally.
(B) In R3, King Edward's notorious sexual indiscretions are described as 'his hateful luxury / And bestial appetite in change of lust' (R3 3.5.80–1). Cassio, in contrast, confuses moral responsibility with the reputation for probity that would result from its proper functioning when he laments, 'O, I have lost my reputation! I have lost the immortal part of myself, and what remains is bestial' (OTH 2.3.262–4). Finally, Hamlet, also confused, complains to himself that his failure to have killed Claudius sooner must manifest in him either 'Bestial oblivion, or some craven scruple / Of thinking too precisely on th' event' (HAM 4.4.40–1). In this lose-lose case, thinking so morally that he cannot avenge his father's murder is just as bad as not caring enough for his father to seek revenge.
(C) Whitaker (1969), ch. 11, speaks of the conflict between Senecan and Christian mandates in HAM.

BIBLE
See **Pible.**

BISHOP
(A) A prelate who oversees a diocese, and whose seat resides in a cathedral. Whitgift says, 'for order the bishop is above a priest, the archbishop above a bishop, and the Pope above them all' (1851–53), 2: 265.
(B) Since these figures were often politically active in English history, 'bishop' is usually just the way of referring to a character in one of Shakespeare's history plays. This usage is almost equally divided between a title like 'the Bishop of Carlisle' (R2 3.3.30) and 'Lord Bishop' as a form of address, as in 'With you, Lord Bishop, / It is even so' (2H4 4.2.15–16). The king's resolution in 2H6 to 'send

some holy bishop to entreat' (2H6 4.4.9) with Cade's rebels is an unusually generic use of the word, almost implying that bishops are a dime a dozen. The specifically named bishops in these histories include the English 'Bishop of Carlisle' (R2 3.3.30), 'Bishop Scroop' (2H4 4.4.84), 'Bishop of York' (3H6 4.4.11), 'Bishop of Exeter' (R3 4.4.501), 'Bishop of Winchester' (H8 5.2.158) and the French 'Bishop of Bayonne' (H8 2.4.173). References to the possessive form, 'Bishop's', which include 'the Bishop's deer', 'the Bishop's huntsmen', and 'the Bishop's palace' (3H6 4.5.17, 4.6.84, 5.1.45), reveal something of the splendour of their lifestyles, though, to be fair, one bishop, York, is the subject of all three comments. There are also three 'reverend bishops' and one 'well-learned bishop' (1H4 3.2.104; 2H6 1.1.8; H8 4.1.99; R3 3.5.100).

(C) The Reformer Fulke (1843), 1: 218, complains of their rich lifestyle; so does Whitgift (1851–53), 2: 382. Throughout Book VII, Hooker reveals a continuing controversy about the role of bishops in the Church of England when he defends them in 'What a Bishop is, what his name doth import, and what doth belong unto his Office as he is a Bishop'. Knapp (1993), 34–8, discusses possible satirical portraits of bishops in the plays.

BLACK MONDAY

(A) The Monday after Easter. On Easter Monday 1360, severe cold caused many deaths among the English forces of Edward III outside of Paris, thus the name.

(B) Lancelot Gobbo refers to this day in the midst of some Christian calendrical gibberish designed to distract Shylock from his suspicions about his daughter Jessica: 'my nose fell a-bleeding on Black Monday last at six a' clock i' th' morning, falling out that year on Ash We'n'sday was four year in th' afternoon' (MV 2.5.24–7). The fact that Easter is a 'movable feast' whose date comes on the first Sunday following the first full moon after the vernal equinox also lies behind Gobbo's confusing calendrical reference.

(C) See RIV, 298n, and NV R3, 89n., citing Stowe's *Chronicle* (1631), 264b.

BLACKFRIARS

(A) The Blackfriars were Dominicans. Their monastic building in London was surrendered to the crown in King Henry VIII's time. In 1576 a suite of rooms within the building was leased for the construction of a private theatre for children's performances.

(B) Henry VIII, apparently speaking to Cardinal Wolsey before the dissolution of the monasteries, describes Blackfriars as 'The most convenient place that I can think of / For such receipt of learning' (H8 2.2.137–8). He hopes the learning of religious persons will help him justify dissolving his marriage with Queen Katherine of Aragon.

(C) BEV, 788n; Campbell and Quinn (1966), 72. Irwin Smith (1964) discusses the use of the Blackfriars as both a **priory** and theatre; Gurr's discussion (1996) of early modern theatre culture includes much useful information about the Blackfriars.

BLASPHEME

(A) Speak **profanely** against God, religion, or the religious. The Swiss Reformer Bullinger says, 'we do especially blaspheme God, when we detract his glory, gainsay his grace, and of set purpose do stubbornly contemn and dispraise his truth revealed unto us and his evident works declared to all the world' (2: 421).

(B) Shakespeare either marks Isabella's extraordinary goodness or alerts us to her dangerously elevated self-image when he has her criticise Lucio's possibly mocking praise of her early in the play, 'You do blaspheme the good in mocking me'. Our reading depends in part on Lucio's tone when he calls her 'renounce-ment' 'a thing enskied and sainted', and her 'an immortal **spirit**' and 'a **saint**' (MM 1.4.34–8). Macduff cries out that Malcolm in his utter (if also feigned) sinfulness, 'By his own interdiction stands accus'd, / And does blaspheme his breed' (MAC 4.3.107–10). Only because Macduff will go on to style Malcolm's father as 'most **sainted**' and his mother as 'Oft'ner upon her **knees** than on her feet' do we catch a religious usage that is not merely metaphoric (MAC 4.3.110). King John claims that he is 'supreme head' of the Church of England, and the **Pope** merely an '**Italian** priest' and a '**mortal** hand', concluding, 'So tell the Pope, all **reverence** set apart / To him and his usurp'd authority' (JN 3.1.153–60). King Philip of France responds, 'Brother of England, you blaspheme in this' (JN 3.1.161). His use of 'blasphemy' depends upon two key questions, at least during the Reformation: is that authority absolute and does that authority derive from God? When Gonzalo calls the Boatswain by the name of 'blasphemy, / That swear'st grace overboard', he must refer to his scepticism in the first scene that prayer would calm the storm (TMP 1.1.20–2; 5.1.218–19).

(C) McAlindon (2001), 337–50, looks at cursing in TMP. See also **virgin**.

BLASPHEMING

(A) Speaking impiously of God or religious things.

(B) When we hear the Witches put the 'Liver of blaspheming Jew' into their charmed pot (MAC 4.1.26), we cannot be sure whether 'blaspheming' is meant to represent the denial of Christ by all Jews, i.e. their refusal to be converted to Christianity, or the more particular blasphemy of one organ donor. A 'grievous sickness' makes Cardinal Beauford 'gasp, and stare, and catch the air, / Blas-pheming God and cursing men on earth' (2H6 3.2.370–2) as he dies. This is the more traditional usage, one Donne amusingly glosses when he speaks of 'certaine formes of speech, certaine interjections, certaine suppletory phrases, which fall often upon their tongue, and which they repeat almost in every sentence. . . . And this . . . many men, God knowes, do out of impiety' (8: 292).

(C) See *ST* II.2.13–14, 90–91; Vaux (1590a), *sigs*. D1^{r-v}; Donne, 7: 367. See **Jew**.

BLASPHEMOUS *adj.*

(A) Spoken of the person or the words that blaspheme.

(B) The Boatswain of their sinking ship is called a 'bawling, blasphemous, incharitable dog' by a Sebastian who could more easily be describing himself than the shipman (TMP 1.1.40). All we have heard the accused say that sounds even remotely blasphemous is a little cursing of the storm, 'A plague upon this howling!' (TMP 1.1.36). Since even Lucy aboard the *Dawn Treader* knows 'that landsmen – and lands women – are a nuisance to the crew' in a storm, and must therefore 'Get below', the word must be misused in this instance, stemming from the blasphemous assumption of its speaker that the shipman is being irreligious to deny that kings and councillors can command storms to cease: 'What cares these roarers for the name of king?' (TMP 1.1.11–17). See, however, **blaspheme**. (C) Lewis (1952), 56–7.

BLASPHEMY
The act of blaspheming, usually by word rather than deed.

Isabella articulates a problematic hierarchy of blasphemy, where persons of rank are apparently permitted more freedom of expression than commoners: 'That in the captain's but a choleric word, / Which in the soldier is flat blasphemy' (MM 2.2.130–1). She does not illustrate, but one suspects that she means that a Captain's 'Goddamn', uttered in the heat of command, is less blasphemous than a mere soldier's uttered in the same circumstance. Her parallel comment is equally perplexing: 'Great men may jest with saints; 'tis wit in them, / But in the less foul profanation' (MM 2.2.127–8). Perhaps she is saying to Angelo that since great ones (like you and me) are judged by more lenient standards, so we should judge more leniently. Cf. 2H6 5.2.85.

BLESS[1]
(A) Protect, used in a serious invocation of divine assistance.
(B) The Old Lady says of Anne Boleyn at Princess Elizabeth's birth, 'The God of heaven / Both now and ever bless her: 'tis a girl' (H8 5.1.164–5). The Nurse twice asks that 'God in heaven bless' Juliet (ROM 2.4.194; 3.5.168). 'Bless thee, Bottom, bless thee! Thou art translated' (MND 3.1.118) is his friends' response to his metamorphosis into an ass. Claudio says 'God bless me from a challenge' just as Benedick issues it to him (ADO 5.1.144). The Traveller prays, 'Jesus bless us', as he is about to be robbed by Falstaff's people (1H4 2.2.82), and Dorcas asks, 'Bless me from marrying an usurer' (WT 4.4.268). Grey, frightened and angry as he goes to execution, says of young Edward, 'God bless the Prince from all the pack of you! / A knot you are of damned blood-suckers' (R3 3.3.5–6). Edgar's mad 'Bless thee from whirlwinds, star-blasting, and taking' and 'bless thy five wits' are interesting pagan versions of this invocation of divine protection (LR 3.4.58–9).

Macbeth seems to refer to a more formal liturgical exchange when he recalls of the sleeping grooms, 'One cried "God bless us!" and "Amen!" the other. . . . I could not say "Amen" when they did say "God bless us" '; later he adds similarly, 'I had most need of blessing, and "Amen" / Stuck in my throat' (MAC 2.2.24–30).
(C) In the Holy communion service, the final blessing and response read 'And the blessing of God Almighty, the Father, the Son, and the Holy Ghost, be amongst you, and remain with you always. Amen' (*BCP*, 265). See **Amen**[1], **benediction**.

BLESS²

The 'bless' in 'God bless you' is often essentially a casual greeting in Shakespeare, as in Feste's 'God bless thee, lady' (TN 1.5.36), Old Gobbo's 'God bless your **worship**' to Bassanio (MV 2.2.120), and Toby's '**Jove** bless thee, Master **Parson**' (TN 4.2.11).

BLESS³

Part of a casual blasphemy.

Flute's 'A paramour is (God bless us!) a thing of naught' (MND 4.2.13–14) and Gobbo's description of Shylock, 'who, God bless the mark, is a kind of devil' (MV 2.2.23–4) are good examples. Iago's 'God bless the mark!' (OTH 1.1.33) is more sinister because of his overt and gleeful opposition to things religious and **sacred**.

BLESS⁴

(A) **Consecrate**, signify as or make **holy**, spoken, for example, of the **sign** of the cross or of a priest's liturgical gestures.

(B) Shakespeare twice has characters pun on the association between crossing oneself and the word 'bless'. Don John says of Claudio, 'If I can cross him any way, I bless myself every way' (ADO 1.3.67–8). Dromio E. says of his equal fear of Adriana's blows and his master's, 'And he will bless that cross with other beating: / Between you, I shall have a holy head' (ERR 2.1.79–80). The shepherd may urge his son the Clown to cross himself after seeing the sailors die and discovering the infant Perdita: 'Now bless thyself: thou met'st with things dying, I with things new-born' (WT 3.3.113–14). Palamon plays metaphorically on the blessing of holy **ashes** when he says of the prospect of dying for love, 'If I fall from that mouth, I fall with favor, / And lovers yet unborn shall bless my ashes' (TNK 3.6.282–3).

(C) Andrewes speaks of 'the Cup of the New Testament, which we bless in His Name' (1: 113); Hooper speaks disparagingly of 'priests, that bless water, wax, bone, bread, ashes, candles' (1843), 1: 308.

BLESSED (BLEST)¹ *adj.*

(A) Holy or sacred; full of God's grace and favour. As a result, sometimes but not always without sin. Donne calls Christ 'our blessed Saviour himself' (10: 125); his 'Mother Mary is therefore most blessed by God, 'full of grace'. Gabriel says as the scene continues, 'blessed art thou among women, and blessed is the fruit of thy womb' (Luke 1.28, 42).

(B) King Henry IV refers both to Christ's 'blessed cross' and his 'blessed feet' (1H4 1.1.20, 25) as he tries, with mixed success, to bless his precarious new kingship with some **divine** authority. The Duke, disguised as a friar, describes himself to the pregnant and imprisoned Juliet as 'Bound by my charity and my blest order' to 'visit the afflicted spirits / Here in the prison' (MM 2.3.3–5). Gaunt speaks of 'the world's ransom, blessed Mary's Son' (R2 2.1.56). An association with the Blessed Virgin Mary may also inform the dispute between

Iago and Roderigo about Desdemona's blessedness. Refuting Iago's insinuation that she has already been unfaithful with Cassio, Roderigo says 'I cannot believe that in her; she's full of most bless'd condition.' Iago's cynical response, that she is all appetite, is rich in both biblical and bodily imagery: 'Bless'd fig's end! The wine she drinks is made of grapes. If she had been bless'd, she would never have lov'd the Moor. Bless'd pudding' (OTH 2.1.250–3). Mere bread and mere wine accompany his degraded images of sexual shame and sexual appetite, the fig leaf and the fig's end. See also 'God's blest mother!' (H8 5.1.153). Queen Elizabeth's withering denial of Richard III, 'My babes were destin'd to a fairer death, / If grace had blest thee with a fairer life' (R3 4.4.220–1) clearly proclaims her explicit conviction that he is a reprobate, divorced from God's grace.

Cordelia's blessing upon her father, 'All blest secrets, / All you unpublish'd virtues of the earth, / Spring with my tears; be aidant and remediate / In the good man's distress!' (LR 4.4.15–17), uses 'blest' in the sense of 'not cursed', 'not unholy', to distinguish the powers she invokes from the black arts, and darker forces. Her holy blessings are medicinal herbs and the curative forces that might be activated by her compassion and her prayer. Regan's exasperated 'O, the blest Gods!' (LR 2.4.168), on the other hand, simultaneously blasphemes the gods and dishonours her father.

(C) See Williams (1997), 123–4; Hassel (2001a).

BLESSED (BLEST)[2] *v., adj.*
Rewarded by God; made prosperous.

Winchester's 'He was a king blest of the King of kings' (1H6 1.1.28), spoken of Henry V, and Grey's comment to Queen Elizabeth, 'The heavens have blest you with a goodly son' (R3 1.3.9) are two good examples. A third occurs when Capulet, angry that Juliet will not obey him, says to his wife, 'Wife, we scarce thought us blest / That God had lent us but this only child' (ROM 3.5.164–5).

A 'blessed day' (JN 3.1.75) could be merely someone's response to a moment of success or carry theological meaning, and a 'blessed plot', a 'blessed shore', or a 'blessed land' (as in R2 2.1.50; 2H6 3.2.90; 3H6 4.6.21) could refer to a kingdom marked by God's protection or benefits, or be merely an enthusiastic expression of patriotism or an observation about a frequently happy and victorious kingdom.

Shylock betrays his 'works ethic' when he says of the industrious Jacob and the pied sheep he earned, 'This was a way to thrive, and he was blest'. Antonio's disagreement with Shylock's usage of 'blest' seems based as much on a '**grace** ethic' as it is on his sense that breeding and interest are not the same thing: 'This was a venture, sir, that Jacob serv'd for, / A thing not in his power to bring to pass, / But sway'd and fashioned by the hand of **heaven**' (MV 1.3.89–93). Portia may use the word with both senses when she says of **mercy**, 'It is twice blest: / It blesseth him that gives and him that takes' (MV 4.1.186–7). The act of mercy, so conceived, both bestows and manifests spiritual blessings on the giver's part and undeserved grace on that of the receiver.

BLESSED (BLEST)³ *adj.*

(A) Saved, made eternal, often spoken of martyrs, saints and angels, in heaven and on earth.

(B) A 'blessed soul' is thus said to 'rest' 'in Elysium' (TGV 2.7.38). 'His blessed part' in H8 refers to Cardinal Wolsey's soul after he 'died fearing God' (H8 4.2.30, 66). Wolsey earlier tells his rival Cromwell that if he falls after serving 'thy country's [ends], / Thy God's, and truth's', he will die a 'blessed martyr' (H8 3.2.447–9). Alencon's comments to Joan of Arc reveal that a 'blessed saint', like this 'blessed martyr', is one who is 'reverenc'd' here as well as blessed by God (1H6 3.3.14–15). Henry VI cites the Beatitudes when he says, 'blessed are the peacemakers on earth' (2H6 2.1.33). 'Blessed ministers above' probably refer either to the angels or the saints who can be invoked by someone like the novice Isabella (MM 5.1.115). Antipholus asks another 'blessed power' to 'deliver us from hence' just before he is confronted by the Courtesan, whom they call the devil, a fiend, a sorceress and a witch (ERR 4.3.44–79).

For the Beatitudes, see Matt. 5.1–11.

BLESSED (BLEST)⁴ *adj.*

Consecrated.

Cymbeline refers to consecrated or 'blest altars' (CYM 5.5.478). The 'holy privilege of blessed sanctuary', that is the protection churches traditionally offered fugitives (but not apparently innocent children), is also frequently invoked and abused in Shakespeare (R3 3.1.42). Here 'blessed' can refer therefore to the protection of the Church as well as the consecrated **sanctuary**.

BLESSED (BLEST)⁵ *v.* and *adj.*

Said of the divine object of human praise or thanksgiving. Of '*Benedicamus Deum, Let us blesse God*', Donne says, 'The duty required of a Christian, is *Blessing*, Praise, Thanksgiving; To whom? To *God*, to God onely, to the onely God' (3: 258). 'Bless him therefore in speaking with him, in assenting, in answering that which he sayes to you in his word: And blesse him in speaking of him, in telling one another the good things that he hath done abundantly for you' (3: 260).

Fluellen says that God should be 'praised and plessed' in victory (H5 3.6.9–10). The words are almost synonymous here. 'God be blest' can also be used for casual emphasis, as when Kate, exasperated but getting wiser, says to Petruchio's silly comment about the sun being the moon, and then again the sun, 'Then, God be blest, it is the blessed sun' (SHR 4.5.18).

BLESSING *sb.*

(A) A parent's expression of approval and hope for a child's good fortune.

(B) Polonius's advice to Laertes, which ends, 'Farewell, my blessing season this in thee' (HAM 1.3.81) might be the most familiar father's blessing in Shakespeare. His blessing (and his advice) begins with his '*laying his hand on Laertes' head*', and his saying of this gesture, 'my blessing with thee' (HAM 1.3.57 *s.d.*). At such moments the familial and the liturgical gestures are closely associated. Lear would gladly enact with Cordelia for the rest of their lives such a ritual of his blessing and her forgiveness as they have just played out in the previous scene: 'when thou dost ask me blessing I'll kneel down, / And ask of thee forgiveness' (LR 5.3.10–11). There are mothers' blessing[s] too in Shakespeare, as when the Countess 'pray[s] God's blessing into [Helena's] attempt' to win her son (AWW 1.3.254). Paulina first thwarts Perdita's wish to 'kneel and then implore [Hermione's] blessing', but then, once the statue moves, invites her to 'Kneel, / And pray your mother's blessing' (WT 5.3.44, 119–20). Cf. MV 2.2.78, 84.

(C) On the utility of parental blessings in Shakespeare's time, see Young (1992a and 1992b). McAlindon (2001), 337–50, looks at blessing in TMP.

BLOOD[1]

(A) 'Flesh and blood' can occur together to suggest the family of Adam, mortal, imperfect humanity. Becon asks, 'What is flesh and blood? The circumlocution and very description of man. For man of himself is nothing but fleshly and carnal' (3: 611); Hooper also uses the phrase to speak of human limitations: 'The prophet by no means would have men put their trust in flesh and blood. . . . The best of flesh and blood is but vanity: the consolation and help of vanity is misery and wretchedness' (1852), 2: 278.

(B) Lavatch in AWW makes the same connection when he calls himself 'a wicked creature, as you and all flesh and blood are' (AWW 1.3.35–6). Berowne's witty evasion of moral responsibility evokes the same image to similar effect: 'We are as true as flesh and blood can be . . . Young blood doth not obey an old decree' (LLL 4.3.211–13).

(C) Quarlous reminds Adam Overdo of this connection in Ben Jonson's *Bartholomew Fair*, when he says, 'You are but Adam, **flesh** and blood. You have your frailty' (5.4.95).

BLOOD[2]

(A) 'Sacred blood' refers to the blood of kings because of the idea of their divine authority and the rituals that embody and perpetuate it.

(B) Gaunt twice calls his murdered brother Woodstock's blood 'sacred', a 'precious liquor' (R2 1.2.12, 17, 19), because he is, like Gaunt, a son of the anointed King Edward III. Duncan's 'silver skin' and 'golden blood' (MAC 2.3.112) suggests that Macduff considers him iconic, 'the Lord's anointed temple' (MAC 2.3.68).

(C) Murray (1966), combines Paracelsian medical theory and alchemical discourse to explain Duncan's 'golden blood'.

BLOOD[3]

(A) 'Blood' also flows with several biblical and liturgical associations in Shakespeare, on the one hand of the sacrifice of **Abel** and of **Christ** and on the other of the Catholic sacrament of marriage.

(B) The slain Woodstock's blood is compared by his wife with 'sacrificing Abel's', the first murder victim (R2 1.1.104–6). When Bolingbroke, holding a perfunctory trial of three of Richard's confederates before he kills them, says he does it 'to wash your blood / From off my hands' (R2 3.1.5–6), then promises 'To wash [Richard's] blood off from my guilty hand' by taking a journey to the holy lands (R2 5.6.49–50), he awkwardly evokes **Pilate**'s similar words about the trial of Christ. In ERR, when Adriana says 'My blood is mingled with the crime of lust', she must subscribe to the Catholic idea that marriage makes of two persons one flesh and one blood, since she reasons that her husband's adultery has become hers: 'For if we two be one, and thou play false, / I do digest the poison of thy flesh', and am 'strumpeted by thy contagion' (ERR 2.2.141–4).

(C) On Cain and Abel, see Gen. 4; on the shedding of blood, see Gen. 9.6. See also Donne, 1: 172; 8: 189; and Andrewes, 3: 321. Brockbank (1983) analyses LR and ANT in terms of ritual **sacrifice**.

BODKIN

Little body.

When he swears on 'God's bodkin', God's little body, in response to Polonius's promise to use the players 'according to their desert' (HAM 2.2.527–30), Hamlet is playfully referring either to the birth or the sacrifice of Christ, who won for fallen humans satisfaction by grace rather than merit or desert.

BODY

(A) The human body is often contrasted with the **soul** or in competition with its demands, especially when used by morally and theologically self-conscious characters. Donne says characteristically, 'My body is my prison . . . wee abhorre the graves of our bodies; and the body, which, in the best vigour thereof, was but the grave of the soule, we over-love' (7: 298).

(B) Isabella responds to Angelo's unlawful proposition that she have the 'sweet uncleanness' of sex with him, 'I had rather give my body than my soul' (MM 2.4.55). Buckinghan cynically distinguishes what he claims is Richard's 'watchful soul' from his brother's 'lewd' and 'idle body' (R3 3.7.72, 76–7). SON 146 is based upon this competition of body and soul.

(C) See also Andrewes, 1: 387; 2: 92–3; 2: 347; Bullinger, 1: 175; 3: 379; Donne, 6: 75; and *ST* I.75–6. Marshall (1991), 17–19, looks at the death of the body in CYM; on 38–48, she discusses bodily resurrection in WT. Hillman (2000) analyses the inner/outer body opposition and its relation to scepticism and belief in HAM. Waddington (1990) discusses the 'soul-in-body' motif in two of the Sonnets.

BOND

(A) Something that binds together, like the bond of matrimony; a contract or covenant. The 'bond' between children and their parents is more likely to be a personal than a religious one, though of course the fifth commandment is 'Honour thy father and thy mother' (*BCP*, 249).

(B) 'The bond of marriage' (JC 2.1.280), like 'my bond to wedlock' (H8 2.4.40), said once in a classical, once in a Christian context, may refer either to the marriage contract, to a personal relationship, or to both. In the case of Queen Katherine's husband Henry VIII, it has become a weak bond, except as it is still reinforced by the power of the Church. In the case of Portia, Brutus' wife, it is strong enough to support her request that he share his anxiety with her.

When Macbeth prays to 'seeling night' to 'Cancel and tear to pieces that great bond / Which keeps me pale!' (MAC 3.2. 46, 49–50), he is referring metaphorically to a contract which can be torn, something like conscience, natural law, brotherhood, even the fear of human or **divine** retribution. There is thus still left in Macbeth some of the moral and religious sensibility that once knew that 'deep damnation' would be the result of 'sacrilegious murther' (MAC 1.7.20; 2.3.67). On the other hand, Cordelia's 'I love your Majesty / According to my bond, no more, no less' (LR 1.2.92–3), though heartfelt, seems more about a natural than a religious connection.

(C) Canfield (1989) argues that 'word as bond' is a master trope of medieval and Renaissance English literature. Wasserman (1976) and Kronenfeld (1998), 95–100, discuss 'bond' in LR.

BOOK[1]

(A) The *Prayer Book*, a book of prayers, or the priest's service book. Donne speaks of such '*books* of pious and devout meditation' (10: 144). Red letters or rubrics sometimes marked liturgical gestures in the service books.

(B) The Priest, astonished at Petruchio's swearing during the service of matrimony, first 'let fall the book'; after he picked it up again, Petruchio 'took him such a cuff / That down fell priest and book, and book and priest' (SHR 3.2.161–4). In 2H6 the clerk is caught with 'a book in his pocket with **red letters** in't' (2H6 4.2.90–1). In both cases this is probably a service book. Buckingham observes of Richard's staged piety, 'And see, A book of prayer in his hand' (R3 3.7.98). In the same play, because 'A book of prayers on their pillow lay', one of the murderers almost changed his mind about killing the two young princes (R3 4.3.14–15). 'Bell, book, and candle' (JN 3.3.12) are three liturgical instruments used in the ritual of excommunication.

(C) See PEL, 617n; Arden JN, 75n; and Harper-Hill (1999), 296–9 on 'John and the Church of Rome'.

BOOK[2]

(A) The whole Bible or its distinct parts. Of 'that Booke, which they call the Scriptures, and the Gospell, and the Word of God' (3: 360), Donne says, 'There are not so eloquent books in the world, as the Scriptures' (2: 170). Donne also refers to David's 'book of Psalmes', 'the booke of Revelation', and 'the booke of the Acts of the Apostles' (1: 285; 3: 78).

(B) When Henry VI calls witchcraft and conjuring 'sins / Such as by God's book are adjudg'd to death' (2H6 2.3.3–4), he probably cites Ex. 22.18, 'Thou shalt not suffer a witch to live'. Canterbury cites 'the Book of Numbers' (H5 1.2.98) against the Salic Law.

(C) See Numbers 27.8; see also Shaheen (1999), 310.

BOOK[3]

(A) The book, wherein all virtuous and sinful acts were recorded for the last judgement. This was called for the saved 'the book of life' or 'the book of virtue' (from Rev. 3.5), and for the damned 'the book of trespasses' (from Ex. 32.32–3 – 'my booke that hath sinned against me'). The Reformer Sandys avoids the sticky problems of election and reprobation when he says of the books of Scripture and of our conscience (1841), 367, 'The books shall be laid wide open (Rev. 20.12) in the sight of all flesh; the book of God, and the book of man's conscience; the book of his law, and the book of our life. It shall be examined in the one, what God hath commanded; in the other it shall be testified how man hath obeyed' ... and 'according to the evidence (Matt. 25.34–46) both of the one and of the other, the eternal and irrevocable sentence shall pass from the mouth of God'.

(B) The proud thief and con man Autolycus assumes that he is enrolled among the damned and not the saved when he says, 'If I make not this cheat bring out another, and the shearers prove sheep, let me be unroll'd and my name put in the book of virtue' (WT 4.3.120–2). Mobray's 'If ever I were traitor, / My name be blotted from the book of life' (R2 1.3.202) refers more positively to the book of life. 'The book of **trespasses**' is also referred to in TNK (1.1.33). Richard threatens his deposers with a 'blot, damn'd in the book of heaven' (R2 4.1.236), and Hal teases Poins about thinking him 'in the devil's book' (2H4 2.2.45–6).

(C) With Aquinas and Augustine, Donne is much more comfortable with the 'The *Book of Life*... where all their names are written that are elect to Glory', than he is with the book of death and its implication of reprobation: 'I find no such *Book of Death*' (7: 353–4). See also Donne, 4: 187; 1: 236; 3: 252; Perkins (1597a), 34 (ch. 15 – 'Of Election'); Augustine (1950), XX.14; *ST* I.24.1.

BREAD

(A) One of the elements of communion. The bread represented or actually became the **body** of **Christ** during the service, depending upon one's sense of the **sacrament** as a memorial meal or a mysterious re-enactment of Christ's **sacrifice** on the **cross**.

(B) In AYL Rosalind says that Orlando's 'kissing is as full of sanctity as the touch of holy bread' (AYL 3.4.13–14). In TNK a Countryman says similarly of a love-promise, 'She swore by wine and bread she would not break' (TNK 3.5.47). Capulet unthinkingly swears in response to Juliet's refusing to marry Paris, 'God's bread, it makes me mad' (ROM 3.5.177).

(C) For several positions on the controversies about the elements of communion, see Andrewes, 5: 67; Donne, 2: 258; 7: 296; Perkins (1597a), 134–6 (ch. 34 – 'Of the Lords Supper'); Ridley (1841), 106; Becon, 3: 270; and Shacklock (1565), *sig.* C6ᵛ. The last, a recusant, exults of this intra-Reformation controversy: 'I have already opened, what heavyng & shoveing was betwene Luther, who affirmed the breade to be the body of Christ substantially and really, and Oecolampadius and Zuinglius, which sayde, that it was but a signe & bare figure only.'

BREASTPLATE

Part of the armour associated through a popular Pauline metaphor with moral protection: 'Put on the whole armour of God, . . . the breastplate of righteousness' (Eph. 6.11 and 14).

The pious King Henry VI uses the word similarly when he speaks to Warwick about just cause and moral rectitude: 'What stronger breastplate than a heart untainted!' (2H6 3.2.232–5).

BROTHER

Member of a religious **order**.

The Duke in MM poses as a **friar**, 'a brother of your order' (1.3.44), through much of the play, describing himself as 'Bound by my charity and my blest order' and 'a brother / Of gracious order' (MM 2.3.3; 3.2.219). The same duke answers Elbow's redundant 'Bless you, good father friar' with 'And you, good brother father' (MM 3.2.11–13). Friar John greets Friar Lawrence, 'Holy Franciscan friar! brother, ho!', then begins his story about missing Romeo in Mantua, 'going to find a barefoot brother out / One of our order' (ROM 5.2.1, 5).

BROWNIST

(A) Robert Browne was an important early Separatist leader, one who advocated the authority of Synods over individual congregations, and both over a more universal Church. The Puritans believed that they could reform the Anglican Church from within; the Brownists believed that they had to separate and start anew.

(B) Sir Andrew's comment 'I had as lief be a Brownist as a politician' (TN 3.2.31) shows that it was fashionable to speak poorly of both politicians and religious sects during the Reformation, and that it was hard to choose which group to dislike more.

(C) In 'Congregationalism', *OxfordEncyRef*, 1: 410–11, Browne is called 'the earliest major Separatist leader'; see also *NewCathEncy*, 4: 173–6. Though Congregationalism was not officially named until the 1640s, Browne is associated with that movement. On some of the Brownists' more extreme positions, see Donne, 8: 163; and the Parker Society Index, 'Brownist'. See also Milward (1977), 35–8, 172–4; Milward (1978), 48–53.

CACODEMON

An evil **spirit**, **devil**, or **demon**, the first part of the name coming directly from κακος, meaning bad, **evil** (*OED Caco, Cacodemon*).

Queen Margaret tells Richard of Gloucester early in the play, 'Hie thee to hell for shame, and leave this world, / Thou cacodemon, there thy kingdom is' (R3 1.3.142–3).

CAIN

(A) The brother of **Abel**; in slaying him because God favoured his offering to Cain's, Cain became the first murderer, and was therefore **cursed** to wander the earth. He was marked by God as a warning to others not to kill him. The story occurs in Genesis 4.3–15. In medieval legends the murder occurred in **Damascus** and the weapon became the jawbone of an ass. Cain was a popular figure in the mystery plays; even Simple knows that he wore 'a little yellow beard, a Cain-color'd beard' (WIV 1.4.23). The Gravedigger in HAM refers with strange syntax to 'Cain's jawbone, that did the first murder!' (HAM 5.1.77). Jawbones don't kill people; people kill people.

(B) To Constance, Cain is merely 'the first male', and an unusually 'gracious creature' at that (JN 3.4.79–81). One wonders why this mother, so worried about the life of her own son Arthur, would allude to Cain rather than Abel, who was killed. Northumberland more appropriately associates 'The spirit of the first-born Cain' with 'bloody courses' and secret burials (2H4 1.1.157–60). King Henry IV curses the murderers of Richard II, 'With Cain go wander through shades of night / And never show thy head by day nor light' (R2 5.6.43–4). Though he is only Gloucester's half-uncle, Winchester says of a threatening Gloucester, 'This be Damascus, be thou cursed Cain, / To slay thy brother Abel, if thou wilt' (1H6 1.3.39–40). Claudius laments more precisely an offence that 'hath the primal eldest curse upon't, / A brother's murther' (HAM 3.3.37–8).

(C) See Donne, 7: 241; 6: 220. Berninghausen (1987) looks at Cain as the pattern of kingship gone awry in R2. For the Cain-and-Abel story as an archetype for HAM, see Stump (1985). See also Shaheen (1999), 559.

CALLING

(A) Though this can refer to the summons to or propensity for any profession, it is commonly associated with a religious one, with the impulse often attributed to God (*OED vbl. n.* 9). As Donne says of 2 Cor. 4.6, 'the calling that is the root and foundation of all, [is] that we have this light shining in our hearts, the testimony of God's Spirit to our spirit, that we have this calling from above' (4: 109).

(B) The Friar in ADO emphasises his conviction that Hero is innocent by saying 'trust not my age, / My reverence, calling, nor divinity, / If this sweet lady lie not guiltless here / Under some biting error' (ADO 4.1.167–70). He invokes his appearance, his reputation in the world, and the calling bestowed upon him by God in asserting his authority in such a matter. A more complex prelate, the Bishop of Winchester, also tries to assert his honesty by invoking his true calling, against Gloucester's charge of his 'swelling heart': 'how am I so poor? / Or how haps it I seek not to advance / Or raise myself, but keep my wonted calling?' (1H6 3.1.30–2). Queen Katherine charges Cardinal Wolsey with the hypocritical abuse of his religious calling, 'You sign your place and calling, in full seeming, / With meekness and **humility**; but your heart, / Is cramm'd with arrogancy, spleen, and **pride**' (H8 2.4.108–10). Lest he misunderstand her, she adds, 'You tender more your person's honor than / Your high **profession spiritual**' (H8 2.4.116–17).

(C) See Tilley, C23. Daley (1994) argues that the disruption in AYL results from characters being denied their proper callings or vocations.

CAMEL
See **needle, word**.

CANDLE

(A) Taper. Besides being a traditional **symbol** of the shortness of human life, the candle is also with **bell** and **book** part of the ceremony of **excommunication**.

(B) 'Bell, book, and candle shall not drive me back' (JN 3.3.12) is the Bastard's way of telling King John that he will obey his command without fear of excommunication. Speaking of ephemerality, the Lord Chief Justice calls Falstaff 'a candle, the better part burnt out', to which Falstaff responds, 'a wassail candle, my lord, all tallow' (2H4 1.2.156–8). The wounded Clifford laments his death, 'Here burns my candle out' (3H6 2.6.1), and Macbeth mourns Lady Macbeth's death, and possibly his own, 'Out, out, brief candle!' (MAC 5.5.23).

(C) The Reformer Bradford says of excommunication, 'At the Pope's curse with book, bell, and candle, O how trembled we which heard it but only, though the same was not directed unto us but unto others!' (1848), 1: 58.

CANONISED
Made a **saint**.

The papal legate Pandulph makes this usage explicit, if also morally confusing, when he threatens King John with the promise that anyone who kills him will be called 'meritorious' and be 'Canonised and worshipp'd as a saint'. Constance bribes this same churchman that if he takes up her cause against Henry VI, 'thou shalt be canoniz'd, Cardinal' (JN 3.1.176–7; 3.4.52). King Henry VI's Queen Margaret complains of his piety and lack of sexual interest, 'his loves / Are brazen images of canonised saints' (2H6 1.3.59–60). Her 'brazen', usually applied to hussies, becomes the brass of which the **religious images** are made. Finally, Hamlet asks the ghost of his father to 'tell / Why thy canoniz'd bones, hearsed in death, / have burst their cerements' (HAM 1.4.46–8).

CANON
An ecclesiastical rule or law. Andrewes defines it: 'Then for the Church's laws, which we call canons and rules, made to restrain or redress abuses, they have always likewise been made at her assemblies in councils, and not elsewhere' (5: 146).

Timon complains about both ecclesiastical and secular laws when he says 'Religious canons, civil laws are cruel' (TIM 4.3.61–2). When Hamlet wishes that 'the Everlasting had not fix'd / His canon 'gainst self-slaughter' (HAM 1.2.131–2), he must instead be referring not to ecclesiastical laws but to the sixth commandment, 'Thou shalt not kill' (from Ex. 20.13).

CANTERBURY
The name of one of the great cathedrals and pilgrimage destinations in England, and the see of the Archbishop of all of England. Canterbury contains the shrine of Thomas à Becket, murdered in the cathedral 29 December 1170.

The cathedral itself is not referred to in Shakespeare, but we hear of several 'Archbishop[s] of Canterbury', as in JN 3.1.143–4 and R2 2.1.282. 'My Lord of Canterbury' is another way of referring to or addressing this prelate (H5 1.2.1; H8 2.4.219). 'Canterbury' is Henry VIII's more informal name for his trusted ally, Thomas Cranmer: 'Stand up, good Canterbury! / Thy **truth** and thy integrity is rooted / In us, thy friend' (H8 5.1.81, 113–14).

CARDINAL[1] *sb.*
(A) A high-ranking ecclesiast of the Roman Catholic Church, ranking just below the Pope.
(B) As a name, 'cardinal' refers to characters in JN (3.1.181; 3.4.76); 2H6 (1.1.174, 185; 1.2.94); H8 (1.1.51, 222), 1H6 (1.3.80), and R3 (3.1.32). 'The college of the cardinals' (the Pope's council) is mentioned as part of Margaret of Anjou's sarcasm about her husband's piety in 2H6 (1.3.61), and Gloucester refers angrily to the 'broad cardinal's hat' of the 'manifest conspirator' Beauford in 1H6 (1.3.36, 49). Norfolk, no friend of Cardinal Wolsey, once criticises both his inordinate ambitions and his great influence over King Henry VIII by calling him 'king-cardinal' (H8 2.2.19).

(C) Battenhouse (1991), 143–6, and Burgoyne (1977) discuss the figure of Cardinal Pandulph in JN. Saccio (1977), 214, speaks of Wolsey's great power by 1515: 'Subject only to the occasional intervening voice of the king, Wolsey governed England for nearly fifteen years.'

CARDINAL² adj.

(A) Chief, fundamental. The four cardinal or 'natural' virtues discussed by classical authors as well as Augustine and Aquinas are justice, prudence (or wisdom), fortitude (or courage) and temperance. When combined with the three 'theological virtues', faith, hope and charity, these seven could also be called 'cardinal virtues', and were as such incorporated into the Christian tradition. The distinction for many theologians was that the first four 'natural virtues' could be achieved by human effort, whereas the last three required an infusion of divine grace. Their counterpart could be called the 'cardinal sins' (*OED adj.* 2).

(B) Katherine puns on the 'cardinal' or chief virtues (and vices) when she says of Cardinal Wolsey and Cardinal Campeius, 'Holy men I thought ye, / Upon my soul, two reverend cardinal virtues; / But cardinal sins and hollow hearts I fear ye' (H8 3.1.102–4). However, it is unclear whether her 'cardinal sins' is meant to evoke the seven deadly sins or merely their own ecclesiastical sinfulness.

(C) See Augustine *Of Free Will*, I.13.27–8; ST II.2.47–170; ST II.1.61. Henry (1973), 'Virtue, Virtues', 697; Atkinson (1995), 881–2; and Roberti (1962), 'Virtues, Interrelation'.

CARDINALLY

Pompey's joke about 'a woman cardinally given' refers to the irony that some of the cardinals were accused of 'fornication, adultery, and all uncleanness' (MM 2.1.80–2), and of course puns on 'carnally'.

CARLISLE

The smallest of the cathedrals in England, founded in 1122; like Canterbury, this cathedral is not named in Shakespeare, but its bishop is.

The 'Bishop of Carlisle', once called 'a clergyman / Of holy reverence' (R2 3.3.28–30), is an important ally of King Richard II, one who eloquently warns Bolingbroke and his people about the dangers of deposing an anointed monarch (R2 4.1.114–49). As the play ends he is pardoned by King Henry IV, and twice called in the process merely 'Carlisle', once by Hotspur and once by the king. Certainly the king's usage implies no disrespect, since he concludes, 'High sparks of honor in thee have I seen'; Hotspur's 'Carlisle' might be more condescending, since he brings Carlisle before the king to receive 'the sentence of his pride' (R2 5.6.22–4, 29).

CAROL

A song of joy, usually celebrating the Christmas season.

Titania refers to such seasonal songs as she says of the repercussions on earth of her discord with Oberon, 'The human mortals want their winter here; / No night is now with hymn or carol blest' (MND 2.1.101–2). Her ambiguous historicity as an English fairy living in ancient Greece makes this in some ways an anachronism.

CASTIGATION
Systematic suppression of undesired impulses, sometimes considered a religious discipline.

When Othello offers to cure Desdemona's 'hot and moist hand' with 'fasting and prayer, / Much castigation, **exercise** devout' (OTH 3.4.39–41), the surrounding words establish a firm if also an ironic religious usage. Apemantus's question if the disillusioned Timon 'didst put this sour cold habit on / To castigate thy pride' (TIM 4.3.239–40) is a psychological comment possibly punctuated through '**habit**' by a pun on penitential garb.

CATECHISM (*v.* CATECHISE)
(A) An elementary book of formal religious instruction, using a question–answer format; also spoken of less formulaic religious instruction. In OTH 3.4.16–17, the Clown defines 'catechise', 'that is, make questions, and by them answer'. Hooker defines 'Catechising' as 'publique teaching or preaching' of 'a right opinion touchinge thinges divine', that is 'the sacred and saving truth of God' (V.18.1).
(B) Falstaff ironically refers to his long Nominalist question–answer soliloquy where he asks, 'What is honor? A word', as 'my catechism'. One reason is its catechistic 'yes' and 'no' answers to set questions like 'Can honor set to a leg? No. Or an arm? No' (1H4 5.1.129–41). Celia also compares Rosalind's barrage of questions about Orlando, which ends with 'answer me in one word', to the written catechism: 'To say aye and no to these particulars is more than to answer in a catechism' (AYL 3.2.224–8). Metaphoric uses include Feste's 'I must catechise you for it, madonna' (TN 1.5.62) as he is about to prove Olivia a fool by asking her a series of brief questions which demand brief answers. Hero calls Claudio's interrogation a 'kind of catechising' (ADO 4.1.78).
(C) The 'two *Catechismes*' Donne refers to (4: 202–3) might be those of Nowell (probably the longer 1570 version for the Anglican establishment), and Perkins (*The Foundation of Christian Religion Gathered Into Six Principles*; 1591). Perkins's catechism, with its Puritan slant, was reprinted seven times during Shakespeare's life. Vaux's is a very popular Catholic Catechism, offered in English in 1590. See '*Catechisms*', *OxfordEncyRef*, 1: 275–80; *NewCathEncy*, 3: 225–31.

CATHEDRAL
(A) The principal **church** of a diocese, which contains the **bishop**'s throne or seat.
(B) Eleanor the Duchess of Gloucester tells her husband Duke Humphrey that she dreamed she 'sate in seat of majesty / In the cathedral church of Westminster, / And in that chair where kings and queens were crown'd' (2H6 1.2.36–8).

(C) Cairncross (cited in Arden 2H6, 18n) reminds us that **Westminster** is technically an **abbey** and not a cathedral church.

CAUSE

(A) Machiavelli advised his Prince that the convincing assertion of just cause, that is moral rectitude and divine support, was crucial to military or political leadership. There must always be an axis of goodness and an axis of evil to justify war. This strategy is either explicit or implicit in most of Shakespeare's political plays. With stunning political realism, however, the claims behind the assertions of just cause in the histories and the tragedies often stand on slippery moral and religious ground.

(B) King Richard II instructs his herald to swear both Mowbray and Bolingbroke 'in the justice of his cause' (R2 1.3.10, 30), and Bolingbroke's father Gaunt also blesses his son just before the combat, 'God in thy good cause make thee prosperous!' (R2 1.3.78). Whose cause is just is, however, much more ambiguous than such formulae suggest. Even Richard claims that 'heaven still guards the right' (R2 3.2.62), but also fearfully interrupts the joust. King Henry IV, who is besieged for two whole plays (in Shakespeare at least) by the unjust murder of his predecessor Richard, still protests to his troops before the Battle of Shrewsbury, with an impressive blend of cheek, hypocrisy, and possible self-deception, both that 'our cause is just' and that our opponents' cause is not: 'And never yet did insurrection want / Such water-colors to impaint his cause' (1H4 5.1.120,79–80). Henry's supporter Westmoreland echoes the King's cheek when he says in the sequel, 'Our armor all as strong, our cause the best' (2H4 4.1.154), but his ally Worcester knows that there is 'a kind of question in our cause' (1H4 4.1.68). Since his opponent is the usurping and murderous Richard III, a better case could be made for Richmond's assertion to his troops before the Battle of Bosworth Field: 'God and our good cause fight upon our side' (R3 5.3.240). One suspects that Elizabeth I would have said 'Amen' to this assertion of her Tudor ancestor Henry VII (cf. R3 5.5.41), though theirs is not an entirely disinterested assessment of the eventual course of English history.

In between these events, of course, come the claims and counter-claims of the Lancastrians and the Yorkists during the reigns of Kings Henry V and Henry VI. In the case of the former king, the 'cause', later the 'well-hallow'd cause' (H5 1.2.125, 292–3), is his questionable right to invade France. Indeed, before the battle at Agincourt, a persistent Williams responds to the disguised Henry's claim 'his cause being just and his quarrel honorable', 'That's more than we know' (H5 4.1.126–7). Even the common soldiers are not sure 'If his cause be wrong', though they seem to agree that 'if the cause be not good, the King himself hath a heavy reckoning to make, when all those legs, and arms, and heads, chopp'd off in a battle, shall join together at the **latter** day and cry all, "We died at such a place" '(H5 4.1.129–38). Phrases like 'well-hallow'd cause', 'weighty cause', 'greatest cause', 'especial cause', 'so slight and frivolous a cause', 'rightful cause', and many more mere 'cause(s)' reveal how important the issue remains throughout Shakespeare's English histories, but also how intricately religious, legalistic and Machiavellian threads are interwoven in such assertions.

Though 'just cause' is neither as explicitly nor as frequently asserted in the tragedies, it is sometimes implicit in the use of the word 'cause'. Such is probably the case when Hamlet upbraids himself as having 'cause, and will, and strength, and means' to kill his uncle Claudius (HAM 4.4.45), and when Othello says before killing Desdemona, 'It is the cause, it is the cause, my soul' (OTH 5.2.1). In both cases, however, these assertions would be unnecessary if the speakers were really certain of their cause. Indeed, this sense of uncertainty is reinforced by its uniquely private assertion in soliloquy.

(C) On the assertion of just cause in medieval and early modern warfare, see Tuchman (1978), 73; Machiavelli (1560), *sig.* R1^v; and Sutcliffe (1593), 157. Starr (1966) explains the reference to Caesar's 'just cause' in JC. For a more general discussion of causation in Shakespeare, see Dean (1989).

CELEBRATE

Perform in a ritual observance.

Marcellus probably speaks of more than parties when he refers to 'that season . . . / Wherein our Saviour's birth is celebrated' (HAM 1.1.158–9); Perdita refers to the marriage ceremony when she laments that 'the heavens . . . will not have / Our contract celebrated' (WT 5.1.203–4). Of a darker ritual, we hear from Macbeth just before he will go on to kill Duncan, that this is a night during which 'witchcraft celebrates / Pale Hecate's off'rings' (MAC 2.1.51–2).

CELESTIAL

Pertaining to heaven and the heavenly, often merely as romantic or comic hyperbole.

Dion speaks of 'the celestial habits' and 'reverence / Of the grave wearers', that is, the heavenly clothing and manner of the priests at the temple of the oracle (WT 3.1.4–6). Canterbury contrasts 'th' offending Adam' of Prince Hal's sinfulness to the 'celestial spirits' which 'his body as a **paradise**' seems exclusively to contain since he was '**mortified**' (H5 1.1.26–31), thus opposing **Adam** and **Angel**, 'willfulness' and 'goodness.' Joan of Arc speaks literally of the activity of heaven when she refers to the 'celestial **grace**' that chose and inspired her (1H6 5.4.39–41), and Katherine of Aragon likewise uses 'celestial **harmony**' to describe (H8 4.2.80) the actual sounds she expects to hear after she is dead. Caliban's 'celestial liquor' (TMP 2.2.117) and Proteus' 'celestial Sylvia' (TGV 2.6.34) are characteristic metaphors.

CELL

The room of a person who holds religious office.

'Friar Patrick's cell' is associated with 'holy confession' and 'confession' (TGV 4.3.43–4; 5.2.41–2); Juliet will 'Be shrived and married' at 'Friar Lawrence's cell' (ROM 2.4.181–2).

CEREMONIAL
Liturgical, as of religious ritual or rites.

When Petruchio is late for the wedding service, Kate's father Baptista worries, 'What mockery will it be, / To want the bridegroom when the priest attends / To speak the ceremonial **rites** of marriage?' (SHR 3.2.4–6).

CEREMONY
(A) Can describe both **sanctimonious** and secular **rites** in Shakespeare. Though Cranmer (1846), 2: 158, speaks of the Roman Catholic Church having 'abused the ceremonies, as in . . . ringing of holy bells', Andrewes richly laments in a sermon 'Of Repentance and Fasting' to King James at Whitehall on Ash Wednesday, 1619, the discontinued ceremony of putting **ashes** on the forehead: 'There was wont to be a ceremony of giving ashes this day, to put us in mind of this *converteris* (this need to turn again to God before death). I fear with the ceremony the substance is gone too. If that conversion into ashes be well thought on, it will help forward our turning' (Andrewes, 1: 362).
(B) 'General ceremony' is secular ceremony to Henry V, the political 'place, degree, and form, / Creating fear and awe in other men' (H5 4.1.239–44). Laertes is distraught that Ophelia receives no more religious '**ceremony**' at her 'Christian burial, but the priest is just as obdurate, and just as sincere, about refusing 'To sing a requiem and such rest to her / As to peace-parted souls' (HAM 5.1.223, 225, 237–8). 'Twenty popish tricks and ceremonies'(TIT 5.1.76) is a characteristic Reformation association of ceremony with Catholism and deception. Even when Henry V speaks of the 'idol ceremony' in a secular context, he is using in 'idol' a word similarly charged with the Reformation controversy over **idolatry** (H5 4.1.240). Portia also uses 'ceremony' to refer to empty **ritual** (MV 5.1.206).
(C) On the continuation of disputes about ceremony within the Church of England near the end of the sixteenth century and the beginning of the seventeenth, see Hooker's '**Fourth Booke**, Concerning their third assertion, that our forme of Church-politie is corrupted with popish orders **rites** and ceremonies banished out of certaine reformed Churches whose example therein we ought to have followed' (from title page, 1593). See also Hooker V.5.1 (1597). Rose (1989), argues that JC stages the conflict between High Church ceremony and Puritanical anti-ritualism. Parker (1987) looks at Henry V's sceptical view of ceremony, notwithstanding his ability to use it for his own purposes. For the ceremony of 'touching for the king's evil', see Willis (1992). Levin (2002) argues that Shakespeare avoids staging religious ceremonies at all in the plays. Frye (1984), 144–51, relates some of the issues concerning ceremony to Ophelia's maimed funeral rites. Milward (1978), 24–33, catalogues some of the participants in controversies over church ceremony.

CHAFF
(A) The stalks and leaves of the wheat, corn or bran, and therefore the useless part of something. This is a fairly prominent biblical metaphor, as in Jer. 23.28,

Luke 22.31, Matt. 3.12, and Amos 9.9. Luke 3.17 says that Christ will 'gather the wheat into his garner; but the chaff he will burn with fire unquenchable'.
(B) When the churchman Cranmer kneels before King Henry VIII and welcomes an interrogation of his behaviour with this metaphor, his usage almost surely evokes a biblical resonance: '[I] am right glad to catch this good occasion / Most throughly to be winnowed, where my chaff / And corn shall fly asunder' (H8 5.1.109–11).
(C) See Shaheen (1999), 489.

CHALICE
(A) An ornamental cup, associated with both secular and religious celebrations as the cup of fellowship (*OED* 1) and the cup of the Eucharist (*OED* 2).
(B) When Macbeth reasons that Duncan's murder will be revenged both 'here' and in 'the life to come', he images this inevitable retribution as an 'even-handed justice' which 'Commends th' ingredience of our poison'd chalice / To our own lips' (MAC 1.7.7–12). The chalice readily represents both of his fears – divorce from good fellowship and divorce from God's **grace**.
(C) See Bradshaw (2002), 102–3.

CHANTRY (also chauntry)
A privately endowed chapel, sometimes dedicated to the saying of **mass** for the souls of designated persons.

Olivia probably directs Sebastian into such a private **chapel** for their marriage: 'Now go with me, and with this holy man, / Into the chantry by; there, before him, / And underneath that consecrated roof, / Plight me the full assurance of your **faith**' (TN 4.3.23–6). On the other hand, when Henry V describes 'Two chauntries' 'I have built', 'where the sad and solemn priests / Still sing for Richard's soul' (H5 4.1.300–2), he speaks of buildings specifically erected for prayers for the soul of the man whose murder was authorised by his father.

CHAPEL[1] *sb.*
A private place of prayer or worship; it can be part of a larger church, or housed in a private house; it can also be an independent structure, a place of worship (in England) for such dissenting groups as Baptists or Methodists.

Since Polonius is slain in the royal palace, Claudius must refer to the palace chapel when he says, 'bring the body / Into the chapel' (HAM 4.1.37–8; cf. 4.2.7–9). A royal residence is probably also the situation of the chapel mentioned in connection to Anne Boleyn's 'Going to chapel' (H8 3.2.405). In many cases, the chapel is referred to as a little place of worship or observance, with no further information about the venue. Touchstone's 'Will you dispatch us here under this tree, or shall we go with you to your chapel' (AYL 3.3.65–6) refers to such a building, and may suggest as well that Martext is not only a poor minister, but a dissenting one. 'Saint Mary's Chapel', apparently near Angiers, is named as the place where the 'rites of marriage shall be solemniz'd' between Louis and Blanch (JN 2.1.538–9). The Friar similarly directs Hero and Claudio 'to the chapel' to be married (ADO 5.4.71). Portia plays on the smallness of chapels (and their endowments) when she says, 'If to do were as easy as to know what were good to do, chapels had been churches and poor men's cottages princes' palaces' (MV 1.2.12–14).

CHAPEL[2] *v.*
To bury in a chapel.

In TNK the Queen asks Theseus, 'Give us the bones / Of our dead kings, that we may chapel them' (TNK 1.1.49–50).

CHAPLAIN
(A) An ecclesiastic attached to the chapel of a royal court, a college, a military establishment, or the like.
(B) Tyrrel says of the two murdered nephews of Richard III, 'The chaplain of the Tower hath buried them' (R3 4.3.29). Under examination, the Surveyor says in H8 1.2.162 that 'John de la Car', Buckingham's 'chaplain', has unethically revealed to the Surveyor an implied infidelity to Henry and his heirs which he heard during Buckingham's confession.
(C) See *NDS*, 4: 459–60, for Holinshed's somewhat garbled version of the story.

CHARBON
A corruption of *chairbonne*, good meat. See **Poysam**.

CHARITABLE
Generous; of good **works** stemming from a religious impulse.

The Abbess refers formally to her desire to minister to Adriana's apparently deranged husband as 'a branch and parcel of mine oath, / A charitable duty of my **order**' (ERR 5.1.106–7), and Lady Anne describes their participation in the funeral procession for King Henry VI as 'devoted charitable deeds' (R3 1.2.35).

CHARITY
(A) Sometimes Christian love, sometimes the good works or acts of charity that stem from that love. The conflict between *agape* and *caritas*, love and charity, becomes a flashpoint of Reformation theological and lexicographical controversy. This is manifest in such variant translations of Romans 13.10 as either 'Love worketh no ill to his neighbour: therefore love is the fulfilling of the law' or 'Charity worketh no ill to his neighbour, therefore the fulfilling of the law is charity'. *The Bishops' Bible* is unique among Protestant English translations when it prefers 'charity' to 'love'. Many religious issues hinge on this word, including distinctions between sacred and profane love, the question of celibacy versus marriage, and the efficacy of **rituals**, **sacraments** and the priesthood as mediators of **grace**. But the overriding issue, as More pointed out when he challenged Tyndale's 'Lutheran' translation of 'agape' as 'love' rather than 'charity', is also the core Reformation question of justification by **faith** versus **works**.

(B) Since the Protestant and Catholic controversialists were so notoriously uncharitable in discussing such issues, even the question of charity itself, Berowne's famous equivocation in LLL, 'For charity itself fulfills the law, / And who can sever love from charity?' (LLL 4.3.361–2) could make fun of their crude personal assaults as well as these conflicting meanings of love and charity. Longaville's 'thy love is far from charity' (LLL 4.3.125) is also informed by the controversy, as is the title of the play itself and its central action. For if their labours or works of love remain merely outward acts and do not manifest an indwelling spirit, 'generous', 'gentle', 'humble' (LLL 5.2.629), the Protestant lords of Navarre not only lack love, they will never win the Catholic ladies of France. More superficial references to Christian charity include Launce's 'thou hast not so much charity in thee as to go to the ale with a Christian' (TGV 2.5.56–7), and Feste's implication that 'the bells of Saint **Bennet**' [Benedict] 'may put [Orsino] in mind' of more charity, to which Orsino replies, 'You can fool no more money out of me at this throw' (TN 5.1.39–42). Angelo calls Isabella's forced **fornication** with him 'a charity in sin / To save this brother's life' (MM 2.4.63–4). In the same play, the Duke, disguised as a friar, also describes himself as 'Bound by my charity and my blest order' to 'visit the afflicted spirits / Here in the prison' (MM 2.3.3–5).

(C) More and Tyndale engage many of these issues with great vigour early in the century; Fulke and Martin clash later. See More (1927), 2: 208–12; Tyndale, 3: 21, 172–3; Fulke (1843), 1: 428; Fulke (1589), *fol.* 290ᵛ; Martin (quoted in Fulke, 1589), *fol.* 290ᵛ; Campbell (n.d.), 110; Pineas (1968), 40; Weigel (1949), 73–9; and George and George (1961), 174–256, 375–418. Responding to the usual verbal violence of such Protestant–Catholic exchanges, both the Catholic Persons and the Protestant Donne urge their respective parishioners to show charity towards the other party. Persons urges, 'Wherefore (gentle reader) if thow be of an other religion than I am, I beseche the most hartelye, that layenge a side all hatred, malice and wrathfull contention, let us joyne together in **amendment** of our lyves, and prayeng one for an other: and God (no doubt) will not suffer us to perishe finallye for want of right faithe' ([1582], 4). Donne warns specifically, 'entangle not your selves so with controversies about his body, as to lose reall charity, for imaginary zeale' (9: 78). On charity, see *ST* II.2.23–7, 44, and on the theological virtues, ST II.2.1–27. See also 'Justification', *Oxford-EncyRef.* Cunningham (1955), Noble (1935), 142–7, and Hassel (1977) connect 'charity' in LLL with the word's involvement in contemporary religious controversy. Streete (2002) suggests that a reference to charity in LLL derives from Calvin. For early modern charitable practices and LR, see Kronenfeld (1992). Koch (1990) argues that charitable gift-exchange is opposed to a destructive system of mercantile values in LR.

CHARITY, SAINT

St Charity was part of an Eastern allegory about the three daughters of St Wisdom (St Sophia or *Sapientia*); her sisters being St Faith and St Hope. All were said to have been martyred at the hands of the Emperor Hadrian; their mother died while praying at their grave.

The oath in Ophelia's mad song, 'By **Gis** and by Saint Charity', could possibly suggest her sense of shared martyrdom.

Delaney (1980) 144; *Book of Saints* (1966), 261; Voraigne (1941) describes the martyrdom in vivid detail (2: 592).

CHASTITY
(A) Abstinence from unlawful sexual intercourse, and sometimes from all sexual intercourse; purity even from sexual thoughts. Chastity among the religious was another flashpoint of Reformation controversy. As Erasmus once jokes, 'The Reformation, which began as a tragedy, ends as a comedy, with Luther marrying a **nun**.'
(B) Isabella's references to 'our chastity' and her 'sacred chastity' (MM 2.4.185; 5.1.405) are sympathetic responses to Angelo's attempted 'violation' of her novitiate's vow of chastity. However, the way she puts her decision not to yield to Angelo's lust, 'More than our brother is our chastity', is so unattractive in its severe and selfish righteousness that it might evoke overtones of Reformation controversy. In other references chastity is called both 'peevish' and 'spotless' (PER 4.6.122; TIT 5.2.176), 'ice' (AYL 3.4.17; HAM 3.1.135) and 'jewel' (AWW 4.2.46).
(C) Walker (1959), 317, translates the Erasmus quip from a letter dated 21 March 1528; cf. the Latin *Letters*, 7:369. See *ST* II.2.151–2 (under temperance) for a rich exploration of the virtues and vices attendant upon a religious commitment to chastity and virginity. See also Augustine on 'the violence which may be done to the body by another's lust, while the mind remains inviolate' (1950: I: 18). For chastity in MM, see Baines (1990) and Scolnicov (1998). Plant (1996) looks at the image of the 'chaste bee' in LUC. See Hull (1982) on conduct manuals for women. Williams (1984) argues that ADO displays an ambivalence about chastity. Shannon (1997) discusses chastity as a justification of same-sex friendships in TNK. See **compelled**.

CHAUNTS (CHAUNTED, CHAUNTING)
Sings songs, sometimes religious.

Religious associations are close to the surface of Prince Henry's comparison of his grief for his dying father to the swan, 'Who chaunts a doleful hymn to his own death, / And from the organ-pipe of frailty sings / His soul and body to their lasting rest' (JN 5.7.22–4). The mad Ophelia is described as chanting her own religious swan song: 'Which time she chaunted snatches of old lauds, / As one incapable of her own distress' (HAM 4.7.177–8). **Lauds**, of course, are **hymns**. Duke Theseus threatens Hermia with the barrenness of the sisterhood when he describes the sisters as 'Chaunting faint hymns to the cold fruitless moon' (MND 1.1.73). On an even lighter note, the Servant compares Autolycus's brilliance as a peddler of millinery to the chanting reverence of religious devotion: 'he sings 'em over as they were **gods** or **goddesses**: you would think a smock were a she-angel, he so chaunts to the sleeve-hand and the work about the square on't' (WT 4.4.207–10). See also **chantry**.

CHERTSEY

A monastery near London on the south side of the Thames.

Richard of Gloucester promises the lady Anne that he will take the corpse of King Henry VI to 'Chertsey monast'ry', 'And wet his grave with my repentant tears' (R3 1.2.214–15). Instead, he orders it 'to **White-Friars**' (R3 1.2.29, 214–15, 225–6).

CHERUBIN

(A) Mentioned in Gen. 3.24 and Ezek.10.1, as well as in the *Te Deum* ('To thee Cherubin and Seraphin, continually do cry'), these are one of the highest of the nine orders of **angels**, ranking only beneath the seraphin in their praise and contemplation of God (*OED* 2.b). They are often represented today as winged children, but in Shakespeare's time they could also evoke awe and fear, and Shakespeare's usage illustrates both understandings. Of the nine orders of angels in the Dionysian scheme, only the lowest two, Archangels and Angels, were thought to have an immediate mission to humans.

(B) The tonal range of Shakespeare's references to these beings is illustrated in Macbeth's imagining them as warlike figures of heavenly disapproval and pity, 'heaven's cherubin, hors'd / Upon the sightless couriers of the air' (MAC 1.7.19–23), and in Othello's reference to Desdemona, albeit ironically, as a blushing figure of childlike patience and innocence, a 'young and rose-lipp'd cherubin' (OTH 4.2.63). Timon refers similarly to the misleading look of innocence on the face of one of Alcibiades's mistresses as 'her cherubin look' (TIM 4.3.64). Imogen's chamber is described by the villainous Jachimo as 'fretted' 'With golden cherubins' (CYM 2.4.88), an image doubly ironic since they actually emblematise her great innocence but are used by Jachimo to prove his intimate knowledge of both the chamber and the woman. Miranda when she was just a baby is described by Prospero as 'a cherubin' 'that did preserve me' because she 'didst smile, / Infused with a fortitude from heaven' (TMP 1.2.152–8). A beautiful starry night inspires Lorenzo to describe the music of the spheres as an antiphonal exchange between the planets and the angels: 'There's not the smallest orb which thou behold'st / But in his motion like an angel sings, / Still quiring to the young-ey'd cherubins' (MV 5.1.60–2). Cf. H8 1.1.22–3. Of course, beloved women could also be compared to cherubins, as in SON 114.6: 'Such cherubins as your sweet self resemble'.

(C) For the *Te Deum*, see *BCP*, 53; see 'Angel', Cross and Livingstone (1997), 61–3.

CHESHU

Jesu with a Welch accent.

'By Cheshu' is uniquely Fluellen's form of this Welch oath on Christ's name (H5 3.2.63, 70, 79). With '**Chrish**' for **Christ** the Irishman MacMorris engages

Fluellen in a kind of antiphonal oathing here. See also H5 3.2.88, 92, 105, 109; **Jesu**, and **Jeshu**.

CHOIR¹ *sb.* (also QUIRE)
The place near the altar of a church, the choir-stall, where the choir might sit.

With rich but careful irony, the Gentleman describes part of the coronation of Anne Boleyn as her being brought 'To a prepar'd place in the choir' at the front of Westminster Abbey, there sitting 'In a rich chair of state' (H8 4.1.64–7). In SON 73.4, empty winter trees are compared to 'Bare ruin'd choirs, where late the sweet birds sang', evoking the empty but also disintegrating choir stalls of the abbeys or priories that were abandoned and partially dismantled as well as a result of Henry VIII's dissolution of such religious establishments beginning in 1535.

CHOIR² *sb.*
A group of religious singers.

At the end of Anne's coronation service in Westminster, 'the choir', 'With all the choicest music of the kingdom, / Together sung *Te Deum*' (H8 4.1.90–2).

While the other references to 'choir' are metaphoric, they still evoke the religious setting and its singers, as in 'choir of such enticing birds' (2H6 1.3.89) and 'still the choir of echoes answer so' (VEN 840). This last example vividly evokes the image of two antiphonally arranged choirs during a church service.

CHOIR³ (QUIRE) *v.*
Sing.

Lorenzo romantically describes **heavenly** music: 'There's not the smallest orb which thou behold'st / But in his motion like an **angel** sings, / Still quiring to the young-ey'd **cherubins**' (MV 5.1.60–2).

CHOLER
(A) Ire or wrath, one of the seven deadly **sins**. By Shakespeare's time choler is more commonly psychological than religious, describing an uncontrolled humour rather than a dangerous sin.
(B) The older religious paradigm might be especially present through the formula 'drunk with choler' (1H4 1.3.129; HAM 3.2.302–3), which combines two of the seven deadly sins, **wrath** and **gluttony**.
(C) Donne interestingly combines the moral and psychological meanings: 'The Devill had no hand in composing me in my constitution. But the Devill knows, which of these [four humours] govern, and prevail in me, and ministers such tentations, as are most acceptable to me' (3: 173).

CHRISH
The Irish dialectical version of this oath on Christ's name. In his scene with Fluellen MacMorris twice swears 'By Chrish' (H5 3.2.88, 109) and thrice 'so Chrish save me' (H5 3.2.92, 105, 133). Both oaths are casual, apparently habitual, and provoked by frustration.

CHRIST

(A) Shakespeare's characters make seven direct references to this name of Jesus, the prophesied Messiah, Son of God.

(B) During the scene of King Richard's deposition, Mowbray's reputation is redeemed when the Bishop of Carlisle says that he has gone to fight 'For **Jesu** Christ in glorious **Christian** field' and that he died peacefully and faithfully in the **holy land**, giving 'his pure **soul** unto his **captain**, Christ' (R2 4.1.93, 99). In such company King Richard comes off badly when he histrionically compares his own deposition to Judas's betrayal of Christ after he has said 'All **Hail**' to him: 'So **Judas** did to Christ; but he, in twelve, / Found truth in all but one; I in twelve thousand none' (R2 4.1.169–71). The newly crowned King Henry IV describes himself as 'engaged to fight' 'As far as to the **sepulchre** of Christ' (1H4 1.1.19–21), but he is only cynically waving that banner of his religious legitimacy before his subjects' eyes. Richard III threatens to kill his young opponent, Clifford, with 'you shall sup with Jesu Christ to-night'. Clifford's defiant response, 'Foul stigmatic, that's more than thou can'st tell', prompts Richard's witty response, 'If not in heaven, you'll surely sup in hell' (2H6 5.1.214–16). Either way, Clifford is a dead man.

(C) The Reformer Bullinger says that Christians 'by receiving the sacraments do profess and witness ourselves to be under Christ our captain's banner' (4.236), and the Jesuit Loarte (trans. Brinkley, 1596–97), 13, speaks of 'Jesus Christ our Lorde and **Captaine**'.

CHRISTEN[1] *v.*

(A) Baptise. This sacrament involved the naming and the sanctifying of children with 'water and the Holy Ghost', 'that they may be received into Christ's holy Church, and be made lively members of the same' (*BCP*, 270).

(B) Orlando responds to Jaques's dislike of Rosalind's name, 'There was no thought of pleasing you when she was christened' (AYL 3.2.266–7). A sardonic spin of the term occurs when Aaron the Moor in TIT is instructed by Tamora's nurse to kill their 'dismal, black, and sorrowful issue' with the words, 'christen it with thy dagger's point' (TIT 4.2.66, 70).

(C) Tyndale, 1: 272, criticises the Catholics, 'They pray in Latin, they christen in **Latin**, they **bless** in Latin, they give **absolution** in Latin; only **curse** they in the English tongue.'

CHRISTEN[2] *adj.*

(A) A variant of **Christian**[2].

(B) The Carrier says of his flea bites, 'there is never a king christen could be better bit' (1H4 2.1.16–18), and Prince Hal says of his tavern friends that he 'can call them all by their christen names' (1H4 2.4.8). In both of these cases, 'christen' could mean either Christian or christened.

(C) Cf. Tyndale, 2: 104, and Allen (1565), *sig.* G4ᵛ.

CHRISTENDOM[1]
(A) An area inhabited predominantly by Christians.
(B) Kate is called 'the prettiest Kate in Christendom' (SHR 2.1.187).
(C) For similar usage, see Donne, 4: 244; Tyndale, 2: 254; and Granada (trans. Hopkins, 1586), 115.

CHRISTENDOM[2]
One's Christian belief or baptism.
When the lad Arthur swears 'by my christendom' (JN 4.1.16), he has to mean either his Christianity or his baptism.

CHRISTENING
The service of baptism or the performance of its rites.
In H8 (5.4.37, 74, 83) the Porter and the Chamberlain mention the offstage christening of Princess Elizabeth in 1533 three times. The stage directions for 5.4 include 'two noblemen bearing great standing bowls for the christening gifts'.

CHRISTIAN[1] *sb.*
A member of the group which professes Christ and worships in his name.
There are 67 references to 'Christian' in Shakespeare. When Shylock says of Antonio, 'I hate him for he is a Christian' (MV 1.3.42), he uses this most common meaning. Shylock's final punishment, that 'He presently become a Christian' (MV 4.1.387), like his daughter's more voluntary 'Become a Christian and thy loving wife' (MV 2.3.21), are similar examples of the noun.
Launce associates 'the name of a Christian' with charity (or at least good fellowship in 'the alehouse') (TGV 2.5.53–7); to Antonio it means kindness (MV 1.3.178). Both oppose 'Christian' to 'Hebrew'. Shylock's 'the prodigal Christian' betrays his idea that most Christians waste money (MV 2.5.14–15). He also speaks sarcastically of the Christians' claims of 'humility' and 'sufferance' (forgiveness) (MV 3.1.69–70).

CHRISTIAN[2] *adj.*
Pertaining to members of the Christian community, or to places within **Christendom**.
Examples include the phrase 'Christian creatures' in WIV (4.1.71), 'Christian armies' (JN 5.2.37), 'Christian service' (R2 2.1.54), 'Christian climate' (R2 4.1.130), 'Christian blood' (1H6 5.1.9), and of course the many 'Christian king[s]' (H5 1.2.242), 'Christian prince[s]' (R3 3.7.96), and 'Christian soul[s]' (R3 4.4.408). The Chorus of H5 sincerely calls Henry V 'the mirror of all Christian kings' (2 pr.6); and the King of France prays for 'Christian-like accord' between his daughter and Henry V (H5 5.2.353). Richard III and Buckingham are more hypocritical as they repeatedly play this Christian card (as in R3 3.5.26; 3.7.96, 103, 116). Shylock's 'Christian fools with varnish'd faces' in MV (2.5.33) may refer to the masks that adorned **Shrovetide** revellers just before the Venetian

Lent; he also speaks sarcastically of 'Christian cur'sy' (MV 3.1.68–70, 48–9). In Christian mouths too a phrase like 'Christian care' can be sarcastic (H8 2.2.128–9; 2H4 4.2.115–23). 'The ensign of the Christian cross' (R2 4.1.94) is the banner which would have led Crusaders across 'glorious Christian field' (R2 4.1.93) into war. 'Christian' can also describe a rite of the Church, as with the three references to 'Christian burial' in the final act of HAM (5.1.1, 4–5, 23–5).

CHRISTOM
Either christened or Christian. Falstaff is described as making 'a finer end', dying as well 'as any christom child' (H5 2.3.10–12).

CHURCH¹
(A) The building; the 'holy edifice' as it is called in MV (1.1.29–30), and/or the Christian rites that might be performed therein.
(B) Beatrice speaks of the building: 'I can see a church by daylight' (ADO 2.1.71–2). However, when Don Pedro asks Claudio, 'When mean you to go to church?' (ADO 2.1.356), he is referring to the rites of his marriage to Hero as well as the building in which they will occur. Churches named in the plays include Saint Luke's (SHR 4.4.88), 'the cathedral church at Westminster' (2H6 1.2.37), Saint Peter's (ROM 3.5.154), and Saint Katherine's (1H6 1.2.100). Portia distinguishes between chapels and churches in MV (1.2.12–14). There are also references in Shakespeare to a 'church-bench' (ADO 3.3.89), a 'church-door' (ROM 3.1.97), and 'church-way paths' (MND 5.1.382).
(C) See Andrewes, 2: 409.

CHURCH²
(A) The organisation, the Christian Church.
(B) Parson Evans says 'I am of the church' (WIV 1.1.30–34), and Cardinal Pandolph refers to 'the Church, our holy mother' (JN 3.1.141). The possibility of confusing the building with the organisation lies behind Feste's pun, 'I do live by the church'. When Viola responds 'Art thou a churchman?' he responds, 'No such matter, sir. . . . I do live at my house, and my house doth stand by the church' (TN 3.1.4–7).
(C) See Andrewes, 3: 242; 3: 81; 5: 146; Donne, 7: 306; 4: 203.

CHURCHMAN
Man who does priestly work for the Church, ranging apparently from the most modest to the most exalted.
The 'two churchmen' in R3 are Friars Penker and Shaw (3.7.48). Cardinal Beauford is 'The imperious churchman' of (2H6 1.3.68–9).

CHURCHYARD
(A) The grounds of a church, including the graveyard.
(B) Mamillius begins his unfinished winter's tale 'There was a man . . . Dwelt by a churchyard' (WT 2.1.29–30). Menenius speaks metaphorically (and

anachronistically) of Coriolanus' Roman wounds as 'graves i' th' holy church-yard' (COR 3.3.51). 'Temple', not 'church', is the usual designation of Greek and Roman holy places; temples were also not usually burial sites or locations for congregational gatherings, but rather houses for the gods and sites for ritual sacrifices. Hamlet's 'when churchyards yawn' (HAM 3.2.389–90) speaks of graves releasing their horrible inhabitants. Romeo's macabre threat to the lad to 'strew this hungry churchyard with thy limbs' (ROM 5.3.36) also refers to the churchyard as a place for the dead and dismembered.

(C) See Pilkington (1842), 316; and Cranmer (1846), 2: 502. See also Eliade (1987), 'Temple'. On this reference as an anachronism, see NV COR, 378–9n, and Parker (1995).

CIRCUMCISED

(A) Purified spiritually, but more commonly, having the foreskin removed from the penis. This religious rite is prescribed in Gen. 17.14: 'Circumcise the flesh of your foreskin'. Donne associates it with the Jews (8: 208; 2: 257), but it is also a rite of passage for Muslim men. 'Circumcised' can therefore be 'allusively used for "Jewish" or "Mohammedan" ' (*OED adj.* 1.a). Donne says of 'unlawfull lust' and the penis: 'In this rebellious part, is the root of all sinne, and therefore did that part need this stigmaticall marke of Circumcision, to be imprinted upon it' (6: 192).

(B) Just before Othello kills himself, he calls the 'malignant and a turban'd Turk' he once slew a 'circumcised dog' (OTH 5.2.353–6).

(C) Circumcision was a highly controversial issue from the earliest history of the Christian Church, one which separated Paul and Barnabas and led the Council of Jerusalem (AD 51) to decree that it was not necessary for Christians. The Jew Barabas in Marlowe's *The Jew of Malta* complains of 'these swine-eating Christians, / Unchosen nation, never circumcised' (2.3.7–8). See Smith (1995), 273; and *ModCathEncy*, 178. See also John 7.21–3, and Acts 15. For an argument that OTH articulates anxieties about Jews and Muslims through the discourse of circumcision, see Lupton (1997); Lupton also (2000, 128–36), discusses circumcision as a mark of Jewish identity in reference to MV.

CLARE, SAINT

(A) A virgin of Assisi, born *c.* 1194, who with the assistance of St Francis and under his influence founded the Order of Minoresses of Poor Clares. Their poverty and austerity were so extreme that it exceeded even the severe Franciscan rule. Pope Gregory and St Francis were said to have asked St Clare to moderate 'her passion for self-torture'. There were four English convents. Feast Day: 12 August.

(B) When we meet Isabella, she is quickly identified as a novice among the 'votarists of Saint Clare'. The renowned severity of their rule could make Isabella's immediate 'wishing' for 'a more strict restraint' upon the order (MM 1.4.4–5) seem fanatical rather than just deeply committed.

(C) See BEV, 411n; Farmer (1978), 81–2; Attwater (1965), 87; Baring-Gould (1914), 9: 120–6.

CLAY

(A) Like 'dust,' another noun for human **mortality**, the **body** without the **soul** (*OED sb.* 4.a). This stems from both Gen. 3.19, 'for **dust** thou art, and unto dust shalt thou return', and Gen. 2.7, 'And the Lord God formed man of the dust of the ground, and breathed into his nostrils the breath of life'. Job 10.9 reads, 'Thou hast made me as the clay', and Isa. 64.8, 'we are the clay, and thou our potter'.

(B) Prince Henry in JN says at his father's death, 'When this was now a king, and now is clay' (JN 5.7.69). Prince Hamlet similarly reflects in the graveyard on 'Imperious Caesar dead and turned to clay' (HAM 5.1.213). 'A pit of clay' in the Gravedigger's song (HAM 5.1.96, 120) refers to the grave rather than the body.

(C) Donne says, '*God* could have made men of clay, as fast as they made Brickes of Clay in *Egypt*; but he began upon two, and when they had beene multiplying and replenishing the Earth One thousand six hundred yeares, the *Flood* washed all that away, and GOD was almost to begin againe upon eight persons' (4: 271).

CLERESTORIES

Windows in an upper wall, most commonly used in descriptions of the upper windows in sanctuaries.

We know that Feste is speaking nonsense to Malvolio when he says that the 'clerestories' in the 'house' in which he has been imprisoned are 'toward the south north' and 'as lustrous as ebony' (TN 4.2.37–8). On the other hand, Feste is appearing to Malvolio dressed as a curate, and he lives 'by the church' (TN 3.1.4–7), so the reference could be to a church building rather than merely a 'house'.

CLERGY

(A) Priests and others ordained to serve in the Church, as opposed to the laity or worshippers. Sometimes used for 'the Church'.

(B) The Archbishop of Canterbury speaks both of the Church and of the clergy-men who run it when he twice offers King Henry V substantial financial aid towards the costs of invading France: 'we of the spirituality / Will raise your Highness such a mighty sum / As never did the clergy at one time / Bring in to any of your ancestors' (H5 1.2.132–5; cf. H5 1.1.79–81). 'Clergy' may also mean both individuals and the Church they serve when Cardinal Beauford complains to the Lord Protector Gloucester that to pay for 'Thy sumptuous buildings and thy wife's attire', 'The commons thou hast rack'd, the clergy's bags / Are lank and lean with thy extortions' (2H6 1.3.128–30). The divorced Katherine of Aragon speaks of the negative influence Cardinal Wolsey's sexual depravity has had on individual churchmen: 'Of his own body he was ill, and gave / The clergy ill example' (H8 4.2.43–4).

(C) Saccio (1977), 215, tells us that Wolsey 'dressed, built, and entertained on a lavish scale', and that 'he kept mistresses'.

CLERGYMAN

A male member of the clergy, of various ranks.

The Bishop of Carlisle is called 'a clergyman / Of holy reverence' (R2 3.3.28–9) by Harry Percy, the Hotspur-to-be, and named among the few remaining supporters of King Richard II. At the end of what the Abbot calls the 'woeful pageant' of Richard's subsequent deposition, Richard's friend and ally Aumerle addresses both Carlisle and the Abbot, 'You holy clergymen, is there no plot / To rid the realm of this pernicious blot?' (R2 4.1.321, 324–5). Eighty years later, Buckingham and Richard of Gloucester use 'two clergymen' to clothe Richard's villainy as well as his desire for the crown in apparently pious indifference. Buckingham calls them 'Two props of virtue for a Christian prince, / To stay him from the fall of vanity' (R3 3.7.95–7; see also JN 4.2.141–2).

CLERK[1]

The minor church officer who sometimes leads or solely performs the congregational response to the priest. Whitaker complains of the Catholics' use of **Latin**: 'they say it is sufficient if one only, whom they commonly cal the *clerk*, understand them; who is to answer *Amen* in behalf of the whole congregation' (1849), 259–60.

There are two references to such a priest's assistant in Shakespeare. As he is being deposed, Richard II cries out 'God save the King', and, when no one answers responsively, he adds, 'Will no man say **Amen**? / Am I both **priest** and **clerk**? Well, then, amen. / God save the King, although I be not he!' (R2 4.1.172–4). This helps explain a similar usage of the word in ADO during the witty interlude at the masked dance:

> MARG. God match me with a good dancer!
> BOR. Amen.
> MARG. And God keep him out of my sight when the dance is done! Answer, clerk!
> BOR. No more words; the clerk is answered.
>
> (ADO 2.1.107–10)

This figure is twice associated with illiteracy. SON 85 speaks of the 'tongue-tied' lover who can only 'like unlettered clerk still cry "Amen" ' (1.6), and Smith the Weaver's comment that the 'clerk of Chartam' 'can write and read and cast accompt', provokes Cade's reply, 'O monstrous!' (2H6 4.2.85–7).

CLERK[2]

One trained in Christian theology.

When Cardinal Wolsey refers to consulting 'All the clerks / (I mean the learned ones in Christian kingdoms)' who 'have free voices' (H8 2.2.91–3), he speaks of the fact that Henry VIII has 'sent to all the universities in Italie and

France, and to the great clearks of all christendome, to know their opinions' concerning his proposed divorce from Katherine of Aragon (*NDS*, 4.466, quoting Holinshed's *Chronicles*).

CLOISTER
(A) Place of religious seclusion, like a convent or a monastery (*sb.*); entering or residing there (*v.*). This could be a residence for religious persons as well as a sanctuary for others.

(B) Claudio says of Isabella's imminent induction into the Sisterhood of St Clare, 'This day my sister should the cloister enter' (MM 1.2.177). Duke Theseus describes as severely as he can to Hermia the forbidding life of 'a nun, / For aye to be in shady cloister mew'd' (MND 1.1.70–1). The Lover likewise puts down this secluded life with the metaphor of the 'caged cloister' (LC 249). Because of the sacred associations, it would be particularly heinous to 'steal, sir, an egg out of a cloister' (AWW 4.3.250). Using the verb, Richard II advises his wife to 'cloister thee in some religious house' (R2 5.1.23).

(C) McFeely (1995) discusses monastic shelter in general and the convent in MM in particular as a 'green world'.

CLOISTER'D
Inhabiting a cloister or associated with such inhabitants (*OED* 2 *fig.*).

Macbeth uses this word metaphorically when he promises his Lady to do a 'deed of dreadful note' 'ere the bat hath flown / His cloister'd flight' (MAC 3.2.40–4). He could be imagining in the blackness of the bat (or of the night) the black clothing often associated with the cloistered religious, or associating the confines of the cave and those of the cloister.

CLOISTRESS
Female inhabitant of a cloister.

Because she has vowed to spend seven years in seclusion from men to honour her dead brother, Orsino says of Olivia, 'like a cloistress she will veiled walk' (TN 1.1.27).

COLLEGE
The assembly of all the **cardinals** of the Roman Catholic Church and its chief ecclesiastical body, which elects and advises the **Pope**.

Queen Margaret, never devoted to her husband's piety, once says of him, 'I would the college of the Cardinals / Would choose him Pope and carry him to **Rome**, / And set the **triple crown** upon his head – / That were a state fit for his holiness' (2H6 1.3.61–4). Her sarcasm, against Henry VI, the Pope, and the Roman Catholic Church, may reach here even to calling her husband by the Pope's name, 'his **holiness**'.

COLMEKILL
(A) Icolmkill. The cell of St Columba, located on the holy island of Iona, a sacred

and remote spot where Scottish and Pictish kings through the eleventh century were said to be buried.

(B) Ross tells Macduff in a scene shortly after the murder of King Duncan that his body has been 'Carried to Colmekill, / The sacred store-house of his predecessors / And guardian of their bones' (MAC 2.4.32–4).

(C) See Jackson (1910), 26–7.

COLME, SAINT

(A) The Isle of St Columba in the Firth of Forth was usually called 'Inchcolm' or 'Colmekill' (Colum-cille) in honour of St Columba of Iona, a well-known Irish missionary to Scotland, who died on the 'holy island' of Iona in 597. Feast Day: 9 June.

(B) Rosse names 'Saint Colme's inch' (MAC 1.2.61) as the place where Sweno, Norway's king, pays a tribute in order to be allowed to bury his dead.

(C) Farmer (1978), 87–8; Attwater (1965), 91–2; BEV 1224n.

COMMANDMENTS

(A) Sometimes used to refer to the ten laws given to Moses on the stone tablets on Mt Sinai, in Ex. 20; see also Ex. 34.28–9.

(B) Lucio, twitting the Gentleman for wanting peace, but only on his own terms, compares him to 'the sanctimonious pirate, that went to sea with the Ten Commandements, but scrap'd one out of the table', presumably 'Thou shalt not steal' (MM 1.2.7–10). When the Duchess of Gloucester wishes that she could fight back by scratching the 'proud Frenchwoman' Margaret of Anjou, she says, 'I could set my ten commandements in your face' (2H6 1.3.142).

(C) Parker (1853), 133, urges 'that the tables of the commandments may be comely set or hung up in the east end of the chancel, to be not only read for edification, but also to give some comely ornament and demonstration that the same is a place of religion and prayer', but Bradford (1848), 1: 9 laments, 'The commandments of God are continually, in the ears of all people, read openly in the churches, yea, written upon the walls, so that all men know them; yet is there none amendment.'

COMPELLED

(A) Committed under duress, thereby minimizing personal responsibility. Richard Hooker says, 'What we doe against our wills, or constrainedly, we are not properly said to do it' (I.9.1).

(B) Angelo, trying to convince Isabella that having sex with him to save her brother's life will not count against her at the Last Judgement, says with what seems like absolute theological certainty, 'our compell'd sins / Stand more for number than for accompt'. Isabella's disbelief provokes his retraction: 'Nay, I'll not warrant that; for I can speak / Against the thing I say' (MM 2.4.57–60).

(C) See Aquinas, *ST* II.1.6.4–5. Apparently the argument hinges on two biblical passages, Matt. 5.39, 'Do not resist an evil person', and Rom. 13.1, 4, 'if you do wrong, be afraid'. Cf. Tilley, S475, 'Compelled sins are no sins.' See also

'Force', Atkinson (1995); 'Coercion', Meagher (1979); and 'Force and Moral Responsibility', *NewCathEncy*, 5: 1004–5.

COMPT
Judgement Day.

Othello dreads either Desdemona's accusing look or the condemning remembrance of her murder at his own **judgement**: 'when we shall meet at compt, / This look of thine will hurl my soul from heaven, / And fiends will snatch at it' (OTH 5.2.273–5). The King in AWW threatens Bertram with a similar judgement when he says, with conscious irony, 'Well excus'd; / That thou didst love her strikes some scores away / From the great compt' (AWW 5.3.55–7).

CONCUPISCIBLE
(A) Concupiscence is ardent, usually sensuous longing, and therefore synonymous with lust.
(B) When Isabella describes Angelo's desire for her as 'his concupiscible, intemperate lust' (MM 5.1.98), she is being understandably redundant in her anger towards 'this pernicious caitiff' (MM 5.1.88).
(C) See *ST* II.1.30.

CONFESS[1]
Admit a **sin**.

Juliet in MM, being shriven by the Duke disguised as a friar, says of her fornication with Claudio, 'I do confess it, and repent it, father.' The religious focus of her language is obvious (MM 2.3.29). Most of the other references to 'confess' in Shakespeare seem more psychological than religious, though those categories were not as separable in the Renaissance as they are today. The religious environment is obvious when Mowbray says of his attempt on Gaunt's life, 'But ere I last received the sacrament, / I did confess it and exactly begg'd / Your Grace's pardon' (R2 1.1.140–1). Similarly, just after Melun in JN describes what 'Awakes my conscience to confess all this', he asks to be alone, 'Where I may think the remnant of my thoughts / In peace, and part this body and my soul / With contemplation and devout desires' (JN 5.4.43–8). Even when Cambridge, caught in his conspiracy against the life of his friend King Henry V, says 'I do confess my fault, / And do submit me to your Highness' mercy' (H5 2.2.76–7), the theological, the political and the personal are richly intertwined. Henry V exploits this complexity when he responds negatively to Cambridge's plea, 'God quit you in his mercy' (H5 2.2.166). Hamlet, trying to wring his mother Gertrude's heart with contrition, urges her to '**Confess** yourself to heaven, / **Repent** what's past, avoid what is to come' (HAM 3.4.149–50). Iago puts a sardonic theological spin on the word when he urges Cassio to 'confess yourself freely to' (OTH 2.3.318) Desdemona, thus casting her as one of those **intercessory** figures, a **priest** or a **saint**, so controversial during the Reformation. 'Confess' is also used commonly in Shakespeare as a metaphor connecting romantic and religious experience. In the speech in which he says that Love 'hath so humbled me as I confess', Valentine also uses the theologically loaded words **'penance'**, **'fasts'**, and **'penitential'** (TGV 2.4.128–37). For a fuller discussion, see **repentance**, penance and **confession**.

CONFESS²
Hear or direct confession, spoken of a **priest**.

When the Duke says of Mariana, 'I have confess'd her, and I know her virtue' (MM 5.1.527), he means that he has heard and directed her **confession**, in the prescribed (and controversial) manner of a Catholic priest

CONFESSION
(A) The formal admission of sins to a **priest**.
(B) When the Friar complains to Romeo, 'Riddling confession finds but riddling **shrift**' (ROM 2.3.56), he thinks he is hearing a confession of sin too vague to warrant absolution. Juliet also instructs the Nurse to tell her mother that she is 'gone, / Having displeas'd my father, to Lawrence' cell, / To make confession and to be **absolv'd**' (ROM 3.5.231–3). Silvia says that she is going to 'Friar Patrick's cell, where I intend holy confession' (TGV 4.3.43–4; cf. TGV 5.2.41–2).
(C) Vaux defends the role of the priest in **confession** (1590a), *sig.* G6. Among the many Reformers who permitted confession to a priest are Bradford (1848), 1: 51; Latimer (1844–45), 2: 13; and Coverdale (1846), 2: 481; opposed are Becon, 3: 3.4; Tyndale, 3: 22; Grindal (1843), 140; and Tyndale, 1: 263. Hooker also speaks against confession as a **sacrament** later in the century (VI.4). See also *ST* Suppl. 6–11. Hassel (1980), 80–90, examines confession in ADO. Morris (1985), 53–8, discusses confession in HAM. Lindley (1996), 342–6, looks at scaffold confessions as threats to the security of the state. Diehl (1998), 409–10, argues that the last act of MM is a scene of multiple public confessions.

CONFESSOR
The religious person who hears confession.

Angelo says of Claudio, who must 'Be executed by nine to-morrow morning' for his fornication with Juliet, 'Bring him his confessor, let him be prepar'd' (MM 2.1.34–5). Buckingham has two named confessors in H8, 'the duke's confessor, John de la Car' and 'Nicholas Henton', 'a Chartreux friar'. The second was said to have 'fed him every minute / With words of sovereignty' (H8 1.1.218; 1.2.146–9) rather than words of humility and contrition. Both Romeo and Juliet call Friar Lawrence a 'ghostly confessor' (ROM 2.6.21; 3.3.49). See also **penance**.

CONGREGATION
(A) Today 'congregation' more often means a 'gathering of worshippers'. In the Renaissance the more common usage is a secular gathering. Bullinger shows the connection when he says that 'Churches, which because of the companies gathered together in them are also called congregations, are the houses of the Lord our God' (1: 198–9).

(B) Claudio promises Don John that if he sees Hero's outrageous infidelity on the eve of their marriage, he will 'shame her' 'to-morrow in the congregation, where I should wed'. In the next scene, Borachio confirms that Claudio 'swore that he would meet her as he was appointed next morning at the temple, and there, before the whole congregation, shame her with what he saw o'er-night' (ADO 3.2.124–5; 3.3.160–3).

(C) Nicolson (2003), 25–6, discusses the controversial profile of 'congregation' in both translations and ecclesiastical affairs; Fulke (1843), 1: 231, and Bullinger, 4: 4, both prefer to translate the word '*Ecclesia*, the congregation'.

CONJOIN

Though it can refer to several forms of human (and material) connection, in almost half of Shakespeare's uses of the word, 'conjoin'd' means 'married'.

The Priest asks Hero and Claudio before the assembled congregation, 'If either of you know any inward impediment why you should not be conjoin'd, I charge you on your souls to utter it' (ADO 4.1.11–14). The *Prayer Book* reads, '. . . if either of you do know any impediment why ye may not be lawfully joined together in matrimony, that ye confess it' (*BCP*, 291). The word is used again at the end of the play (ADO 5.4.29). It also appears at the end of R3, where 'Richmond and Elizabeth', will 'By God's fair ordinance conjoin together!' (R3 5.5.31).

CONJURE

(A) To call upon or command devils or spirits to come or depart.

(B) Antipholus S., thinking the Courtesan a 'fiend', a 'sorceress' and a 'devil', tells her, 'Avoid', 'Avaunt' and 'I conjure thee to leave me and be gone' (ERR 4.3.48–67). 'Good Doctor Pinch, . . . a conjurer' in the same play, if also a 'doting wizard' (ERR 4.4.58), gives us a good example of the style of conjuring and its connection to religion when he says,

> I charge thee, Sathan, hous'd within this man,
> To yield possession to my holy prayers,
> And to thy state of darkness hie thee straight:
> I conjure thee by all the saints in heaven.
> (ERR 4.4.47–57; cf. H5 2.1.54)

'Margery Jordan, the cunning witch' and 'Roger Bolingbrook the conjurer' are the agents of Hume's promises to the superstitious Eleanor of 'A spirit rais'd from depth of under ground, / That shall make answers to' her concerning her ambitious dreams (2H6 1.2.75–6, 79–80). Shylock probably tries to offend the Christian Bassanio when he refers to eating pork, 'which your prophet the Nazarite conjur'd the devil into' (MV 1.3.34–5). Benedick and Mercutio both use 'conjure' metaphorically (ADO 2.1.257; ROM 2.1.23–9).

(C) See Luke 8.26–39. Rogers (1854), 258, speaks sarcastically of this 'order' of Catholic 'exorcists, or conjurers, which have power to expel the devils'.

CONSCIENCE

(A) Bullinger calls conscience 'a certain direction placed by God himself in the minds and hearts of men, to teach them what they have to do and what to eschew. And the conscience, verily, is the knowledge, judgement, and reason of a man, whereby every man in himself, and in his own mind, being made privy to every thing that he either hath committed, or not committed, doth either condemn or else acquit himself' (1: 194).

(B) Though the sense of what is right and wrong is not exclusively religious in Shakespeare, 'conscience' is often imbued with religious overtones. When Troilus says of Achilles in a classical play, 'I'll haunt thee like a wicked conscience still' (TRO 5.10.28), he is using conscience psychologically. However, when the Porter swears, 'on my Christian conscience this one christening will beget a thousand' (H8 5.3.36), his words demand to be set within a Christian context. As usual, the most interesting examples lie between such extremes. Claudius' 'How smart a lash that speech doth give my conscience' (HAM 3.1.49) seems neutral, but it comes in response to Polonius' more obviously Christian comments about their deceptive use of Ophelia, 'that with devotion's visage / And pious action we do sugar o'er / The devil himself' (HAM 3.1.46–7). 'Lash' also arguably suggests the monastic tradition of penitential flagellation. When Laertes says of his extreme revenge, 'To hell, allegiance, vows, to the blackest devil, / Conscience and grace, to the profoundest pit! / I dare damnation' (HAM 4.5.132–4), who could mistake the Christian text and sub-text? Hamlet's unanswered question to Horatio, 'is't not perfect conscience' to kill Claudius (HAM 5.2.67), loses complexity without some sense of the period's obsession with merit and grace, the Pauline and Lutheran sense of the impossibility of knowing or doing anything perfectly which is set so jarringly against the moral imperative, expressed by Christ himself, to 'be perfect' (Matt. 5.48). So does his glib dismissal of a Rosencrantz and Guildenstern executed by his order: 'They are not near my conscience' (HAM 5.2.58). Richard III dismisses the power of conscience more as a nominalist than as a casuist when he says, 'Conscience is but a word that cowards use, / Devis'd at first to keep the strong in awe: / Our strong arms be our conscience, swords our law!' (R3 5.3.309–10).

Some of Shakespeare's metaphors for conscience deserve special mention. Long after Margaret has cursed him, 'The worm of conscience still begnaw thy soul', Richard of Gloucester personifies his conscience as a many-tongued monster: 'My conscience hath a thousand several tongues, / And every tongue brings in a several tale, / And every tale proclaims me for a villain' (R3 1.3.221; 5.3.193–5). Conscience is also imaged as wringing or wounded (H8 2.2.27, 74), soft cheveril and bosomed (H8 2.3.32; 2.4.183), something that can be crept near to or that itself creeps up (H8 2.2.16–17). Conscience can witness and seal (CYM 3.4.46; 3.6.84), be fettered and heavy (CYM 5.4.8; 5.5.413) or be cold and frozen (against the hot will) (PER 4.1.4–5; LUC 247).

(C) Bullinger is quoting Augustine. See also Donne, 9: 408. Kaufman (1996) often discusses the importance of conscience in the Puritan inner life. Lukacher (1994) places Shakespeare philosophically and psychologically in the 'history of conscience'. McGrath (2001), 70–2, 74–6, briefly discusses relationships between nominalism and Reformation thought. Frye (1984), 135–43, 177–83, Waddington (1989) and Matheson (1995), 392–3, discuss conscience in HAM, the last two from a Protestant perspective. For conscience in H8, see Wegemer (2000) and Monta (2000). For an account of the 'erroneous' or 'doubting' conscience in HAM, see Wilks (1986). Slights (2001) discusses conscience as the basis for a sense of individual identity in Shakespeare's history plays. Kiefer (1996) argues that Lady Macbeth has a conscience, and Kinney (2001) looks at Macbeth's conscience. See **worm**.

CONSECRATE

To make or declare sacred. Bullinger defines the word when he criticises Catholic rites, 'By crossings and certain secret words, gestures, and breathings, they consecrate the water of baptism; all which things they beautify with the name of blessing' (4: 306).

In MND, when Oberon directs the blessing of 'each several chamber' of the palace, and its 'owner', 'with peace', he uses the religious word 'consecrate' to describe this equally traditional fairy activity (MND 5.1.415–20).

CONSISTORY

(A) The place where counsellors meet, the meeting itself; sometimes the ecclesiastical senate in which the Pope, presiding over the Cardinals, deliberates over the affairs of the Roman Catholic Church. The word can also be used for meetings of various bodies of Reformed clerics (*OED* 6, 8, and 9). There can also be a heavenly consistory, as of saints and martyrs (*OED* 4). The usage is similar in several Reformed churches, though the titles of the participants vary.

(B) The Catholic council is specifically referred to twice in H8, where Cardinal Wolsey assures Queen Katherine that he has not 'blown this coal' of Henry VIII's desire for the Church's permission that he divorce Katherine. In fact, he has sought the advice of Rome, and received 'a commission from the consistory, / Yea, the whole consistory of Rome' in this matter (H8 2.4.92–4). Richard III cynically if also enthusiastically calls Buckingham 'my counsel's consistory' (R3 2.2.151) for his willingness to advise him in evil.

(C) McGrath (2001), 212–15, discusses the consistory as an aspect of church life in Geneva.

CONSTANTINE

The Roman Emperor (AD 324–37) who made Christianity the religion of Rome. His mother Helen was the supposed discoverer of the holy **cross** and **sepulchre** of the **Lord**.

Praising Joan of Arc to the skies, the Dauphin Charles of France says of her 'Helen, the mother of great Constantine, / Nor yet Saint Philip's daughters, were like thee' (1H6 1.2.142–3).

(C) See BEV, 504n; RIV, 600n.

CONTRITE

(A) Characterised by contrition, feeling sorry; one of the parts of **repentance**.

(B) King Henry V uses this word with explicit theological meaning when he protests to God in the prayer before the Battle of Agincourt about his own efforts to amend his father's faults, 'I Richard's body have interred new, / And on it have bestowed more contrite tears, / Than from it issued forced drops of blood' (H5 4.1.295–7).

(C) See Donne, 8: 295; Becon, 3: 618; Vaux (1590a), *sig.* G6ʳ; *ST* Suppl. 1–5. See also **amendment**, **confession**, **forgiveness**.

CONTEMPLATION

(A) Religious reflection or consideration, often associated with the monastic life.

(B) Portia breathes a gentle lie when she tells Lorenzo, 'I have toward heaven breathed a sacred vow / To live in prayer and contemplation' (MV 3.4.27–8) until Bassanio's return. Berowne also likens their broken vow 'not to see ladies, study, fast, not sleep' to the 'leaden contemplation' (LLL 4.3.318) of a monastic vow. Buckingham depends upon the word's religious meaning to deceive the Mayor about Richard's piety: 'When holy and devout religious men / Are at their beads, 'tis much to draw them thence, / So sweet is zealous contemplation' (R3 3.7.92–4). King Henry VIII fears that Cardinal Wolsey's 'contemplation' is not 'above the earth / And fixed on spiritual objects' but 'below the moon' (H8 3.2.131–3).

(C) Donne speaks fairly often of 'The sight, and the Contemplation of God' (as in 6: 215; 10: 45; 2: 210; 3: 258).

CONTROVERSY

(A) Theological dispute.

(B) Lucio connects blessings before meals with the grace–works controversy when he says 'Grace is **grace**, despite of all controversy' (MM 1.2.24).

(C) Donne, moderating, advises 'Be this the issue in all Controversies, . . . That that most exalts the Grace and Glory of God, be that the Truth' (9.311). Milward (1978) catalogues some of the controversies between Anglicans and Puritans in ch. 1, some of the disagreements among the separatists in ch. 2, and some of the controversies between Catholics and Anglicans in ch. 4.

CONVERT *v.*

Change from one religion or belief into another. Shakespeare's usage is usually metaphoric.

In ADO, Benedick, called 'an **obstinate heretic** in the despite of beauty', proudly proclaims his desire to be martyred for this 'opinion', 'this **faith**', with 'I will die in it at the stake' (ADO 1.1.232–5, 255–6). This metaphoric connection of faith in love and faith in religion leads him to wonder later about himself falling in love, 'May I be so converted and see with these [a lover's] eyes?' (ADO 2.3.22). Margaret says of Beatrice's parallel experience, 'and how you may be converted I know not, but methinks you look with your eyes as other women do' (ADO 3.4.90–2). In MV Jessica is amused at the Christian Lancelot's caring supply-side wisecrack that 'in converting Jews to Christians, you raise the price of pork' (MV 3.5.35–6). An even stranger use of 'convert', but one with some theological nuance, is Timon's cynical comment to the two mistresses of Alcibiades that they should not be converted from whoredom: 'be whores still. / And he whose pious breath seeks to convert you, / Be strong in whore, allure him, burn him up' (TIM 4.3.140–2). What chance would the **'pious'** have against such conviction, such a sense of vocation as this?

CONVOCATION

A formal assembly of the clergy, technically referring exclusively to post-Reformation groups of Anglican and Episcopal clergy. Shakespeare's usage pertains, however, to a gathering of Catholic clergy.

The Archbishop of Canterbury mentions having discussed with King Henry V 'an offer' 'Upon our spiritual convocation' 'As touching [the invasion of] France, to give a greater sum / Than ever at one time the clergy yet / Did to his predecessors part withal' (H5 1.1.75–81). See also **worm**.

CORRECTION

Spiritual **amendment**, sometimes through physical punishment. Becon's definition combines both meanings: 'What is correction? An **amendment** of our former evil life, taming of our carnal will, **mortifying** our flesh, applying of ourselves to the commandment, will, and example of Christ, to take away and banish the evil, to bring in and establish the good' (3: 618).

Religious metaphor informs the words **'penance'**, 'correct' and 'correction' in the witty twelfth line of Sonnet 111, 'Nor double penance to correct correction'.

COVET (*v.*), COVETOUS (*adj.*), COVETOUSNESS (*sb.*)

(A) Inordinately wanting what others have. This is prohibited in the tenth commandment, and included among the seven deadly sins.

(B) Several characters explicitly connect 'covet' with 'sin'. Henry V protests as he rallies his troops on St Crispin's day, 'But if it be a sin to covet honor, I am the most offending soul alive' (H5 4.3.28–9), and Feste hopes that Orsino will not take 'my desire of having [as] the sin of covetousness' (TN 5.1.47). Malcolm, formally protesting his purity to Macduff, says that he 'Scarcely have coveted what was mine own' (MAC 4.3.127). The jealous Posthumus includes 'covetings' among 'All faults that name, nay, that hell knows' (CYM 2.5.25, 27). Falstaff invokes the traditional connection between 'age and covetousness' (2H4 1.2.229) to rationalise his own greed to the Lord Chief Justice: 'a man can no more separate age and covetousness than 'a can part young limbs and lechery' (2H4 1.2.228–30).

(C) Vaux (1590a), *sigs*. F1^{r-v}, on the authority of Matt. 3, focuses his commentary on coveting the neighbour's wife; however, when he says that 'Pride is an inordinate desire of honour and excellencie' (*sig*. e8^v), he also connects covetousness and **pride**. See also Loarte (trans. Brinkley, 1596–97), 205–14.

CRIMES

Sins rather than merely broken laws.

The Ghost of Hamlet's father speaks of inevitable but also unforgiven **sins** of nature which have condemned him to **purgatory**, where 'the foul crimes done in my days of nature / Are burnt and purg'd away' (HAM 1.5.12–13). Hamlet echoes him when he recalls his murder 'with all his crimes broad blown, as flush as May' (HAM 3.3.81). The Second Lord in AWW also probably uses 'crimes' to refer to the general sinfulness of human nature as well as specific sins when he says 'The web of our life is a mingled yarn, good and ill together: our virtues would be proud, if our vices whipt them not, and our crimes would despair, if they were not cherish'd by our virtues' (AWW 4.3.71–4).

CRISPIN, SAINT

(A) Crispin and Crispianus were early Christian martyrs (*c.* 285), Roman brothers who ... preached in Gaul. They became the patron saints of shoemakers. Feast Day: 25 October.

(B) If there is any connection beyond the common date of the Battle of Agincourt and Crispin's Day, it would seem to lie either in King Henry's disguise as a common man on the night before the battle, or in his promise to elevate all of his fellows-at-arms, 'howsoever vile', to gentlemen after the battle concluded. See H5 4.3.40–67 and 4.7.91.

(C) See BEV, 880n; Farmer (1978), 93; Baring-Gould (1914), 12: 628–30.

CROSS[1] *sb.*

(A) The structure which Christ bore on his back to **Golgotha** and on which he was crucified.

(B) Henry IV refers literally in his opening speech to 'those blessed feet / Which fourteen hundred years ago were nailed / For our advantage on the bitter cross' (1H4 1.1.25–7).

(C) See Andrewes, 5: 259.

CROSS[2] *v.*

(A) To make the **sign** of the cross for **blessing** or protection; this is associated during the Reformation with Catholic (and Anglican) **superstition**.

(B) Feeling threatened by 'goblins, owls, and spights', Dromio says of the protective signing, 'I cross me for a sinner' (ERR 2.2.188). When Horatio says to the Ghost, 'I'll cross it though it blast me' (HAM 1.1.127), he may refer both to an obstructive move and the protective sign.

(C) Donne says of baptism, '*We signe him with the signe of the Crosse, in token, that hereafter he shall not be ashamed, to confess the faith of Christ Crucified*' (10: 64). Hooker also defends 'the **Crosse** in **Baptisme**': 'Touchinge therefore the signe and ceremonie of the crosse, wee no waye finde our selves bounde to relinquish it, neither because the inventors thereof were but mortall men, ... nor finallie for any such offence or scandall as hertofore it hath bene subject unto by error now reformed in the mindes of men' (V.65.1; V.65.19, 21). The Recusant Rastell complains of the earlier Reformers like Jewel, 'That they shal have no more **Signe of Crosse**, or **Christ**, or our **Lady**, or any **Sainct** in their eye, nor any **memorie** of them in their hart' (1566), *sig.* A6ʳ. See **cross**[3].

CROSS[3] *sb.*

(A) Representations of the cross for religious devotion and ceremonial display.

(B) The Bishop uses 'cross' as a Christian symbol when he describes the crusader Mowbray 'streaming the ensign of the Christian cross' as he fights 'Against black pagans, Turks, and Saracens' (R2 4.1.94–5).

(C) Such representations were also controversial in Reformation England. The Reformer Grindal's Injunctions at York (140, item 16) say: 'nor shall worship any **cross** or any **image** or picture upon the same, nor give any reverence thereunto, nor superstitiously shall make upon themselves the **sign of the cross** when they first enter into any church to pray, . . . nor rest at any cross in carrying any corpse to burying, nor shall leave any little **crosses** of wood there'. Tyndale defends the 'right use, office, and honour' of the cross (3: 59). Nicolson (2003), 35–6, mentions the Puritan opposition to the **surplice** and the cross.

CROSS[4]

(A) A metaphor for human misfortunes.

(B) Richard II says metaphorically of his own deposition by Bolingbroke, 'you Pilates / Have here delivered me to my sour cross' (R2 4.1.240–1), but Richard compares himself too often to Christ for this to be merely a metaphor. Lady Grey speaks with less undercutting irony of 'my misfortune's cross' in 3H6 (4.4.20).

(C) Donne speaks of 'a feare of God too narrow, when we thinke every naturall crosse, every worldly accident to be a judgment of God, and a testimony of his indignation', and (3: 279) of 'a purgatory too in this life, Crosses, Afflictions, and Tribulations' (7: 183); Tyndale urges 'remembrance that whosoever will be Christ's disciple must suffer a cross of adversity, tribulations, and persecution, so doth the cross serve me, and I not it' (3: 59).

CROWN[1]

(A) The 'triple crown' refers to the ceremonial papal diadem, a beehive-shaped headpiece marked with three gold crowns possibly signifying the 'three churches', militant, suffering, and triumphant. Its use was ceremonial but not liturgical.

(B) Margaret sarcastically says of her too-pious husband King Henry VI, 'I would the college of the Cardinals / Would choose him Pope and carry him to Rome, / And set the triple crown upon his head – / That were a state fit for his holiness' (2H6 1.3.61–4).

(C) See *NewCathEncy*, 'Tiara', 14: 148; and BEV, 546n.

CROWN[2]

The shaved head of a priest, also called a tonsure. When the powerful Humphrey, Duke of Gloucester threatens his rival Cardinal Beauford, Bishop of Winchester, 'Now, by God's Mother, priest, / I'll shave your crown for this' (2H6 2.1.50), he probably refers to more than a shave and a haircut.

CUPID, SAINT
Saint Cupid never appears in the hagiographies.

The King of Navarre's romantic cry, 'Saint Cupid, then! and soldiers, to the field!' (LLL 4.3.360–3) probably makes fun of the usual invocation of the patron saints of either England or France, **George** or **Denis**, to rally the respective troops before battle. In a parallel reference, 'Saint Denis to Saint Cupid' (LLL 5.2.82–7), the Princess of France invokes her country's patron saint against the lords' St Cupid.

CURATE
Though a curate may be any **clergyman** charged with the care of souls, the office usually involves assisting a **rector** or **vicar**, or serving a small **parish**.

Alexander is thus a mighty large role for 'the parish curate' (LLL 5.2.535) in the Pageant of the Nine Worthies. Feste plays 'Sir Topas the curate' when he comes 'to visit Malvolio the lunatic', and Sir Toby also calls him 'Master **Parson**' in that same role (TN 4.2.2, 20–1, 27). With his usual blend of good sense and nonsense, Feste describes the curate's role in proclaiming his own inadequacy for it: 'Well I'll put it on, and I will dissemble myself in it, and I would I were the first that ever dissembled in such a gown. I am not tall enough to become the function well, nor lean enough to be thought a good student, but to be said an honest man and a good house-keeper goes as fairly as to say a careful man and a great scholar' (TN 4.2.4–10).

CURSE[1] *v.*
(A) To censure ecclesiastically, or to be under that censure; excommunicate.

(B) The formal, ecclesiastical curse occurs when Cardinal Pandulph, 'holy legate of the Pope', threatens King John, 'by the lawful power that I have, / Thou shalt stand cursed and excommunicate' (JN 3.1.173, 223). His excommunication is also called this 'heavy curse from Rome' (JN 3.1.205).

(C) Donne justifies excommunication as biblical, as in Isa. 65.20: 'These curses are deposited by God, in the Scriptures, and then inflicted by the *Church*, in her ordinary jurisdiction, by *excommunications*, and other censures' (7: 365). Tyndale, 1: 272, is less enthusiastic.

CURSE[2] *v. & sb.*
(A) To invoke (or the invocation of) supernatural retribution.

(B) In R3, we are repeatedly reminded of the pervasiveness and efficacy of Margaret's curses, as in Rivers' recollection as he is about to be executed, 'Then curs'd she Richard, then curs'd she Buckingham, / Then curs'd she Hastings' (R3 3.3.18–19). Some *v.* or *sb.* form of 'curse' occurs with this meaning thirty-seven times in this one play, with modifiers that range from 'frantic' to dismiss its power to 'dread' and 'quick' to credit it (R3 1.3.246, 190, 196); another twenty examples occur in the rest of the English histories, making the formal curse and varied responses to it a vital religious motif of the genre.

(C) Hassel (1987), 117–21, Frey (1976), 96–7, and French (1974), 321–4, discuss the efficacy of curses in R3.

CURSE³ *sb.*

(A) God's enacted vengeance or punishment.

(B) When Shylock says, 'The curse never fell upon our nation till now' (MV 3.1.85–6), he refers to the biblical idea that God might have cursed Israel either for disobedience (as in Deut. 28.15 – 'that all these curses shall come upon thee') or for putting Christ to death (see Matt. 27.25 – 'His blood be on us, and on our children'). When Claudius describes in his contrition 'a brother's murder' as carrying 'the primal eldest curse' (HAM 3.3.37), he speaks similarly of the curse God laid upon **Cain** for killing **Abel** (Gen. 4.10–11). Some have thought that when the Gentleman describes Cordelia, in a pre-Christian play, as one 'Who redeems nature from the general curse / Which twain have brought her to' (LR 4.6.206–7), he could refer not only to Goneril and Regan but also, anachronistically, to Adam and Eve and the first fall, which 'Brought' such curses as 'Death into the World, and all our woe' (see *PL* 1.3). Emilia's angry 'Let heaven requite it with the serpent's curse' (OTH 4.2.16) refers to the idea (from Gen. 3.14) that the serpent is cursed 'above all cattle, and above every beast of the field', 'because thou hast done this' to Adam and Eve, i.e., caused the Fall.

(C) Shaheen (1999), 174, discusses these biblical references. Elton (1966); Battenhouse (1969), 269–301; Hunter (1976), 183–96; and Jorgensen (1967), 9–11, 17, 26–31, all discuss the issue of Christian anachronism in LR.

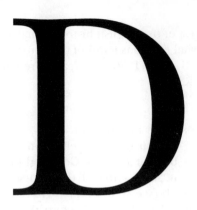

DAMASCUS

(A) In medieval legend, Damascus was founded on the site of Cain's murder of **Abel**. See Gen. 4.1–16 for the biblical story.

(B) The Bishop of Winchester, confronted by the threatening figure of Gloucester the Lord Protector of King Henry VI, refuses to be intimidated with the defiant words, 'Nay, stand thou back, I will not budge a foot: / This be Damascus, be thou cursed Cain, / To slay thy brother Abel, if thou wilt' (1H6 1.3.38–40). Actually Winchester was Gloucester's uncle, but the point is clear.

(C) Shaheen (1999), 288, attributes the tradition to the fictitious Travels of John Mandeville (1496), which was 'reprinted five times before the first performance of 1H6'.

DAMN

(A) To condemn to **eternal** punishment in **hell**, or to **tempt** towards such punishment. The first function was God's and the second Satan's. As Perkins' *Catechism* puts it, 'All men are wholly corrupted with sinne through Adam's fal: & so are become slaves of Sathan, and guilty of eternall damnation' (1591), *sig.* A4.

(B) Hamlet fears that the Ghost 'abuses me [with the request for revenge] to damn me' (HAM 2.2.603). Othello's 'Damn her, lewd minx, O damn her, damn her' (OTH 3.3.476) probably combines a serious desire for Desdemona's eternal punishment with the merely personal anger such an expression can also convey. Only when he persists with 'Come, swear it, damn thyself', to Emilia and to Desdemona, 'therefore be double damn'd: / Swear thou art honest' (OTH 4.2.35–8), do we know how seriously he is using this word. As a casual profanity, see 'God damn me' in ERR 4.3.53; in contrast, Macbeth's frightened curse of the Messenger, 'The devil damn thee black, thou cream-fac'd loon' (MAC 5.3.11), is meant casually, but it ironically reverberates with Macbeth's own looming **damnation**.

(C) On damnation, see *ST* II.1.87–9; Augustine (1950), 21.11. See also Andrewes, 1: 426; Donne, 2: 360. See also **sin**, **darkness**.

DAMNABLE[1] *adj.*

When used seriously, which is about half the time in Shakespeare, this means likely to deserve damnation. Donne calls 'why' (6: 188) 'a Damnable Monosillable, ... because it questions God's goodness, wisdom, and power. Becon, 2: 203 speaks of 'the dreadful dart of damnable desperation'.

Clarence warns the Murderers, 'The deed you undertake is damnable' (R3 1.4.192); Claudio asks Isabella of Angelo's proposed intercourse, 'If it were damnable, he being so wise, / Why would he for the momentary trick / Be perdurably fin'd?' (MM 3.1.111–12).

DAMNABLE[2] *adj. & adv.*

A handy profanity, condemnatory, but usually not to be taken with more than a grain of religious seriousness.

When Lucio expresses his annoyance at the disguised Duke with 'O thou damnable fellow' (MM 5.1.339), and Paulina calls Leontes 'damnable ingrateful' for all of her good advice (WT 3.2.187), they both mean merely annoying. Falstaff means the same thing when he says of Prince Hal's repeated moral admonitions, 'O thou hast damnable **iteration**, and art indeed able to corrupt a **saint**' (1H4 1.2.90–1). Ironically, his own danger of damnation is part of his annoyance; there is a moral edge to Hal's persistent wit-play, and Falstaff is getting nicked.

DAMNATION[1]

(A) The state of being damned, more often used seriously than casually.
(B) Speaking of the murder of Duncan, Macbeth acknowledges 'The deep damnation of his taking off' (MAC 1.7.20). Laertes says of his desire to avenge his father's death: 'To hell, allegiance, vows to the blackest devil!, / Conscience and grace, to the profoundest pit! / I dare damnation' (HAM 4.5.132–4). On the eve of Agincourt, Henry V and his men consider whether 'the master [can be] the author of the servant's damnation' or 'the king guilty of [the] damnation' of his subjects if either 'die unprovided' or unprepared by their own spiritual carelessness (H5 4.1.153–4, 173–5; cf. MV 2.7.49–50). Touchstone evidences some logical slippage when he reasons of Corin's deprived upbringing, 'thy manners must be wicked; and wickedness is sin, and sin is damnation' (AYL 3.2.42–3).
(C) For damnation in OTH, see Battenhouse (1969), 101–2; Ramsey (1978); Hassel (2001a); Vitkus (1997); West (1968), ch. 8; and Morris (1985), 76–114. Waswo (1974), 63–78, 97–9, studies damnation in MAC.

DAMNATION[2]

A name for the Tempter, or at least temptation.

Juliet, piqued at her fate as well as her Nurse's amoral advice that she marry Paris, calls the old woman 'Ancient damnation' (ROM 3.5.285).

DAMNED[1] *sb.*

Those who will go to hell.

Prospero compares Ariel's suffering in the cloven oak to 'a torment / to lay upon the damn'd' (TMP 1.2.289–90).

DAMNED[2]

The *adj.* and *v.* usages are often hard to distinguish. Both pertain to having been sent to hell, or destined to go there; as with the other 'damn' words, the usage ranges from casual to serious.

Ford calls Falstaff a 'damn'd Epicurean rascal' (WIV 2.2.287), and Hal refers comically, even lovingly, to Falstaff as 'that damn'd brawn' (1H4 2.4.110). Touchstone calls Corin 'damn'd, like an ill-roasted egg, all on one side' (AYL 3.2.37–8). A more serious fool, Lavatch, knows from the Bible story of **Dives** and **Lazarus** that 'many of the rich are damn'd' (AWW 1.3.17). Finally, Richard II presumptuously calls his friends 'damn'd without redemption' when he mistakenly thinks they have betrayed him (R2 3.2.129).

DAMNED[3]

Things that might result in or manifest damnation.

The usage in Lady Macbeth's 'Out, damn'd spot' (MAC 5.1.35) expresses both her surface annoyance at an imagined material stain on her hands and her deeper awareness, even in madness, that the spot manifests her damnation. The phrase 'damn'd despair' from VEN (743) suggests that despair causes and/or manifests damnation. Bassanio refers similarly to a 'damned error' 'in religion' (MV 3.2.77–8); this can be a heretical reading which could produce damnation by confusing believers or a reading produced by someone who would be damned for the interpretive heresy. We also read of 'damned incest' (HAM 1.5.83), a 'damned enterprise' (H5 2.2.164), and the like.

DANIEL

(A) In the apocryphal story, Susanna is the young and virtuous wife accused as an adulteress by two elders who first ask her to have sex with them, then slander her because she refuses. Daniel is the young man who turns the trial in Susanna's favour by asking her slanderers to name the tree under which they found her committing adultery. They name different trees, thus failing the test.

(B) Shylock, who obviously knows his Bible, exclaims 'A Daniel come to judgment! yea a Daniel! / O wise young judge, how I do honor thee!' when Portia begins to decide in his favour. When the legal tables are turned against Shylock, the Christian Gratiano says of this young judge, 'A second Daniel! a Daniel, Jew! / Now, infidel, I have thee upon the hip.' To her taking even the principal away from Shylock, Gratiano brays for a final time, 'A Daniel, still say I, a second Daniel! / I thank thee, Jew, for teaching me that word' (MV 4.1.223, 333, 340–1).

(C) 'The History of Susanna', *Geneva Bible, fols* 448–9. See Morris (1986), 303–6 for a discussion of the Book of Daniel's use in MV for Portia's judgement of Shylock. Luxon (1999) also looks at Daniel in MV.

DARKNESS

(A) The absence of **light**. This can be associated with prodigious **evil, devils, hell** and spiritual confusion. Andrewes says of human darkness, '*tenebrae* [darkness] is a plural word, . . . for they are many'. 'There is the senses' outward darkness, there is the darkness of the inward man; both the darkness of the understanding by ignorance and error, and the "darkness" of the will and heart by hatred and malice. There is the darkness of adversity in this world' (3: 371). Andrewes also traditionally calls 'the devil, the prince of darkness, who blindeth men's eyes' (5: 317), and says, 'they two, dark and evil, are as near of kin as light and good' (3: 373). Donne speaks of the darkness of the desperate and the damned, and says of the darkness of hell: 'They shall passe out of this world, in this inward darknesse of melancholy, and dejection of spirit, into the outward darknesse, which is an everlasting exclusion from the Father of lights, and from the Kingdome of joy' (2: 360); 'Darknesse is that, by which the holy Ghost himselfe hath chosen to expresse *hell*; hell is *darknesse*; and the way to it, to hell, is . . . blindnesse in our spirituall eyes' (4: 173).

(B) Feste also knows that the darkness in which Malvolio finds himself is not literal but figurative: 'There is no darkness but ignorance, in which thou art more puzzled than the Egyptians in their fog.' The room, then, is only incidentally dark; the true darkness is Malvolio's blindness to his share of the folly and madness that permeate Illyria. Cf. TN 4.2.28–39, 42–4, 87–93, 113–15, 131. Darkness is also despair when King Henry VI says of the apparent (but illusory) miracle of the blind man, 'Now God be prais'd, that to believing souls / Gives light in darkness, comfort in despair' (2H6 2.1.64–5).

The Clown in AWW says that the prince he serves is 'The black prince, sir, alias the prince of darkness, alias the devil' (AWW 4.5.42–3). To Banquo, the three Witches are clearly 'the instruments of darkness', despite the attractiveness of the 'honest trifles' they have promised him and Macbeth (MAC 1.3.124–5). The devil and hell are both associated with darkness in Poor Tom's mad words, 'The Prince of Darkness is a gentleman' (LR 3.4.87, 143). Lear, even more obviously mad and disillusioned, says of the world's body and the human body, hell and intestines, 'there's hell, there's darkness, / There is the sulphurous pit' (LR 4.6.127–8). Lear also naturally (and **supernaturally**) shouts 'darkness and devils' (LR 1.4.252) in his anger over Goneril's mistreatment of him. Caliban, the progeny of the witch Sycorax, is called 'this thing of darkness' by Prospero (TMP 5.1.275). To Falstaff, 'the sons of darkness' (1H4 2.4.172; 3.3.37) are apparently reprobates.

(C) Cf. Andrewes, 3: 371–4; Donne, 10: 56; and 2: 359. See also 1 John 1.5 and John 1.9 on God as 'the light that lighteneth every one', and 'cannot be comprehended of darkness'. Armstrong (1981) argues that the light/dark imagery in MAC suggests more than a simple distinction between good and evil. Maguin (1995) also looks at the association of darkness and evil in MAC.

DAVY, SAINT

(A) St David, late sixth-century monk and bishop, patron saint of Wales, indeed the only Welsh saint, is honoured on Saint David's day, March 1, by the wearing of a leek. This memorialises a Welch victory over the Saxons in 540, during which 'Saint David, the Welch leader, commanded his followers to wear leeks in their caps' (BEV, 876n).

(B) Pistol, blustering before Agincourt, says of the Welchman Fluellen, 'Tell him I'll knock his leek about his pate / Upon Saint Davy's day' (H5 4.1.54–5). After the battle, his friend Jamy asks Fluellen 'why wear you your leek to-day? Saint Davy's day is past' (H5 5.1.1–2). The answer is that he is about to beat Pistol with it.

(C) Farmer (1978), 102–3.

DEADLY

The **seven** deadly sins, one of the most familiar formulas of medieval Christianity, are sins so serious, so **mortal**, that they can result in the **eternal** punishment of the soul at **Judgement**.

That Shakespeare continues to trust its currency is clear when Claudio tries to persuade his sister the novice Isabella that 'of the deadly seven it [lust] is the least' (MM 3.1.110). He knows that she, and the audience, will finish the phrase correctly.

DEANERY

The residence of a Dean, who is the head of a cathedral chapter or a collegiate church.

Fenton is advised to marry his beloved 'at the dean'ry, where a priest attends', then urged again, 'away with her to the deanery, and dispatch it quickly'; her other suitor, Slender, learns to his dismay that 'she is now with the doctor at the dean'ry, and there married' (WIV 4.6.31; 5.3.3; 5.5.202).

DEATH[1]

(A) Since the end of life is crucial in most theologies, some of Shakespeare's references to death inevitably contain theological overtones. The idea that we owe God a death takes on both natural and supernatural dimensions in the theologians. Coverdale, for example, speaks to both associations when he says, 'Like as one should not withdraw himself from paying what he oweth, but gently to restore the money: so hath God lent us this life, and not promised that we may always enjoy it. Therefore death is described to be the payment of natural debt' (1846), 2: 49–50. Theologically, Coverdale traditionally calls death 'the just judgment of God; for out of the third chapter of the first book of Moses it is evidently perceived, that death is a penalty deserved, laid upon us all for the punishment of sin' (1846), 2: 49–50.

(B) When Prince Hal reminds Falstaff, 'Thou owest God a death' (1H4 5.1.126), and the recruit Feeble says, 'We owe God a death' (2H4 3.2.235), both of them refer to one of the costs of 'Man's First Disobedience', which, as Milton also says, 'Brought Death into the World, and all our woe' (PL 1.1–3). On the other hand, Justice Shallow's 'Death, as the Psalmist says, is certain to all, all shall die' (2H4 3.2.37), is as Shaheen says (1999), 441, as much proverbial as biblical.

(C) See *Certaine Sermons*, pp. 7–12, for the sermons of 'the miserie of all mankinde, and of his condemnation to death everlasting, by his owne sinne', and *Certaine Sermons*, pp. 59–68, for the sermons 'against the feare of Death'. For 'Death is common to all' see Tilley, D 142. See also Andrewes, 2:360–1; Latimer (1844–45), 1: 220; and Donne, 4: 52–75; 2: 197–212; 10: 229–48. Van Tassel (1983) examines the theme of preparation for death in MM and HAM. Flachmann (1992) also looks at the '*contemplatio mortis*' tradition as it relates to Claudio in MM. Farrell (1983), 75–93 gives a religious context to the strategy of feigned death; Farrell (1989), 135–7 considers 'faithful death' as a chance to share in God's patriarchal identity. See also Marshall (1991), 12–37, on death in CYM; Butler (1992) on the Erasmian idea of death as a passage to better things in LR; and Calderwood (1987) on *Shakespeare and the Denial of Death*.

DEATH[2]

(A) The imaging of death, as in the *memento mori* tradition of remembering death.

(B) The Lord says of the dead (or dead drunk) Christophero Sly, 'Grim death, how foul and loathsome is thine image' (SHR In. 35). Doll Tearsheet refers to the 'starved' Beadle as 'Goodman death, goodman bones' (2H4 5.4.28). Calling Holofernes 'a death's face in a ring' (LLL 5.2.612) points to the related tradition of wearing the **death's-head** ring as a *memento mori*. Morocco finds within the golden casket not Portia's picture but 'A carrion death' or **death's-head**, a skull 'within whose empty eye / There is a written scroll' which warns of the vanity of the world, 'All that glisters is not gold' (MV 2.7.63–5). Death imaged as the 'antic' or jester, 'Scoffing his state and grinning at his pomp' (R2 3.2.162–3) and laughing 'us here to scorn' (1H6 4.7.18) are also part of this general tradition. Equally traditional is the General's reference to John Talbot as the 'fearful owl of death' (1H6 4.2.15).

(C) For death as jester, see Illustration 1 in Wither's 1635 *Collection of Emblemes* (1635). The owl perched on the death's head in the same collection along with the accompanying commentary (168), shows its secure place in Christian tradition. Spinrad (1984) explores Claudio's resistance to death in MM and Cubeta (1987) explores the death of Falstaff in terms of the *ars moriendi* tradition. For medieval sources of the death imagery in PER, see Tristram (1983). MacKenzie (1998) discusses Shakespeare's use of death emblems in JN to emphasise a cycle of sin and death rather than death and rebirth.

DEATH'S-HEAD

(A) Either an actual skull or a replica could be prominently placed in a room or even worn as a constant reminder of death, of human mortality and human frailty.

(B) Falstaff, who often speaks in religious ways, says of Bardolph's red and pock-marked face, 'I make as good use of it as many a man doth of a death's-head

By Knowledge *onely*, Life *wee gaine*,
All other things to Death *pertaine*.

MORTIS ERVT VIVITVR INGENIO CÆTERA

ILLVSTRATIO I.   Book. I.

Fig. 1 Death holding a sceptre and mocking a man. Emblem #1 from *A Collection of Emblemes*, George Wither, 1635; STC 25900d. Courtesy The Newberry Library, Chicago.

or a *memento mori*. I never see thy face but I think upon hell-fire and **Dives** that liv'd in purple; for there he is in his robes, burning, burning' (1H4 3.3.29–33). In the next play, Falstaff, closer to death, evidences a similar awareness of this tradition when he responds to Doll's 'when wilt thou leave fighting a' days and foining a' nights, and begin to patch up thine old body for heaven?' with 'Peace, good Doll, do not speak like a death's-head, do not bid me remember my end' (2H4 2.4.231–5). This helps gloss Portia's even more flippant comment to Nerissa about one of her least attractive early suitors, the County Palatine, 'He doth nothing but frown . . . I had rather be married to a death's-head with a bone in his mouth' (MV 1.2.45–6, 50–2).

(C) The frontispiece to each book of Wither's 1635 *Collection of Emblemes* is a death's-head with a bone and a scythe in its mouth. Garber (1981) discusses the relevance of the genre of *memento mori* to Shakespeare's plays. Ogawa (1997), 200–4, discusses Hamlet's contemplation of the skull of Yorick.

Fig. 2 A death's-head with a bone in its mouth, from the title page of each of the four books of *A Collection of Emblemes*, George Wither, 1635; STC 25900d. Courtesy The Newberry Library, Chicago.

DEBORAH

Hebrew prophetess (from Judges 4. 5) who successfully led her Israelite people against their Canaanite oppressors. Donne says of Deborah in the 'great victory upon *Sisera*', '*Deborah* had a zeale to the cause' (4: 179–81).

When the Dauphin of France, overcome by Joan of Arc in single combat, says of her prowess, 'Thou art an Amazon, / And fightest with the sword of Deborah' (1H6 1.2.104–5), he refers to this story.

DEIFIES (DEIFYING)
Makes (making) a god of.

Shakespeare uses the word only metaphorically, once about the beloved in a romantic relationship, and once, oddly, about chance. Orlando is described as a worshipper, 'deifying the name of Rosalind' by hanging 'odes upon hawthorns, and elegies on brambles' (AYL 3.2.361–2). The 'unbounded tyrant' Creon is described by Palamon as one who 'deifies alone / Voluble chance'. The literal point is that by escaping unpunished he 'Makes heaven unfear'd' (TNK 1.2.63–7); the metaphoric point is that this makes Chance appear godlike.

DEITIES
Gods, usually at least quasi-literal in usage

In each of Shakespeare's five uses of this word, the classical setting requires a plural reference to the gods. Troilus attributes the loss of Cressida to the jealousy of the gods, who envy his idolatrous devotion: 'the blest gods, as angry with my fancy, / More bright in zeal than the devotion which / Cold lips blow to their deities, take thee from me' (TRO 4.4.24–7). Enobarbus uses 'their deities' to Antony to refer to the gods who have just delivered him of an unwanted wife, a wisecrack he prefaces with another religious reference, 'Why, sir, give the gods a thankful sacrifice' (ANT 1.2.161). Cf. TNK 5.4.108–9. Timon uses 'deities' in his sarcastic description of wealthy and powerful men (TIM 3.6.70–3).

DEITY[1]
'Her deity', like 'thy deity', can be a title of address, meaning 'her godship'.

Richard of Gloucester says sarcastically of Lord Hastings' pleadings to Queen Elizabeth, 'Humbly complaining to her deity / Got my Lord Chamberlain his liberty' (R3 1.1.76–7); Iris says of an actual goddess, Venus, 'I met her deity / Cutting the clouds towards Paphos' (TMP 4.1.92–3). Sicilius also prays to Jupiter to relent of his anger towards Posthumus, 'Or we poor ghosts will cry / To th' shining synod of the rest [of the gods, presumably] / Against thy deity' (CYM 5.4.88–90).

DEITY[2] *n.*
Godlikeness.

A Queen speaks of Theseus's earning 'a deity / Equal with Mars' (TNK 1.1.227); Sebastian, dumbfounded that he sees himself reflected in his sister, says 'Nor can there be that deity in my nature / Of here and every where' (TN 5.1.227–8).

DEITY[3] *n.*
God, literal and figurative.

Berowne speaks of 'the liver-vein, which makes flesh a deity' (LLL 4.3.72); Cominius says of Martius' warlike prowess, 'He is their god; he leads them like a thing / Made by some other deity than Nature' (COR 4.6.90–1); the cynical

Antonio says of the promptings of conscience, 'I feel not / This deity in my bosom' (TMP 2.1.277–8).

DELIVER, DELIVERANCE

(A) Set free, redeem, protect, or rescue, from sin, from death, or from both. The Recusant Persons says of Christ's deliverance of fallen mortals, 'whye came Christ into this worlde? whye laboured hee and tooke he so much paines heere? whie shed he his bloode? whie praied he to his father so often for thee? whie appointed he the **sacramentes** as conduites of grace? . . . is not all this to **delyver** us from sinne?' (1582), 190. The Protestant Marbeck agrees: 'The Lawe sayth, thou art bound and obliged to me, to the divell, and to hell: the Gospell saith, Christ hath delivered me from them all' (1581), 617. 'Deliver us from evil', the familiar phrase from the Lord's Prayer, can be taken to refer not only to the eternal effects of Christ's redemptive sacrifice, but also to his daily protection of both soul and body.

(B) 'From all such devils, good lord deliver us' (SHR 1.1.66), though spoken of the curst Kate, echoes the refrain of the Great Litany, which invokes the sins from which we need to be protected: 'From all evil and mischief, from sin, from crafts and assaults of the devil . . . Good Lord deliver us' (*BCP*, 68–9). 'The Welch Parson Evans' 'Got deliver to a joyful resurrections!' (WIV 1.1.52–3) speaks instead of the deliverance from death wrought by Christ's death and resurrection. 'Some blessed power deliver us from hence' (ERR 4.3.40–1, 44) invokes a vaguer supernatural protection, as does Marina in PER when she asks 'That the gods / Would safely deliver me from this place' (PER 4.6.179–80). When Norfolk in H8 says, 'We had need pray, / And heartily, for our deliverance' from Cardinal Wolsey (H8 2.2.44–5), his sarcasm probably overweighs his piety.

(C) Cf. Andrewes, 4: 207; 5: 424, 454–7; Donne, 2: 120; 1: 151.

DEMI-DEVIL

'Demi' being a prefix from French meaning half or little, a demi-devil is a person completely given over to evil deeds, but not literally a devil.

Speaking of Iago's treachery against him and Desdemona, Othello asks the assembled worthies at the end of the play, 'I pray, demand that demi-devil / Why he hath thus ensnar'd my soul and body?' (OTH 5.2.301–2). Prospero refers to Caliban, the son of a witch, as the 'demi-devil' who 'has plotted with' Stephano and Trinculo 'To take my life' (TMP 5.1.272–4).

DEMIGOD

From the French prefix 'demi-', 'demigod' can mean half or almost god.

Bassanio uses it positively when he asks of the maker of Portia's splendid portrait, 'What demigod / Hath come so near creation?' (MV 3.2.115). Claudio uses the word more critically when he complains to the Provost who arrests him of the Angelo who ordered the arrest: 'Thus can the demigod, Authority, / Make us pay down for our offense by weight' (MM 1.2.120–1). Berowne says of his own overhearing of confessions which are supposed to be soliloquies, 'Like a demigod here sit I in the sky, / And wretched fools' secrets heedfully o'er-eye' (LLL 4.3.77–8).

DEMI-PARADISE

Like 'demi-devil' and 'demigod', but not pejorative; a little paradise.

John of Gaunt eulogises England as 'This other Eden, demi-paradise' (R2 2.1.42).

DEMON (DAEMON)

(A) **Spirit** or **angel**, either good or evil, protective or destructive; this is something like the good and evil angel of the morality plays, and can refer as well to **Satan** himself. As Bullinger says, 'The devil is called *dæmon*, to wit, knowing, crafty, and cunning in many things. . . . Plato . . . doth think that devils, whom we commonly call by this word dæmons, are called and as it were named . . . wise, prudent, and knowing. . . . [T]he devil . . . is called the deceiver, the beguiler, and seducer of the world, the old serpent and dragon' (3: 356, 348).

(B) The Soothsayer advises Marc Antony to avoid Octavius Caesar because 'Thy daemon, that thy spirit which keeps thee, is / Noble, courageous, high unmatchable, / Where Caesar's is not; but near him, thy angel / Becomes a fear, as being o'erpow'r'd' (ANT 2.3.20–3). Henry V, arresting his friend Scroop for high treason against himself, uses 'demon' to mean tempter when he describes 'that same demon that hath gull'd thee thus' as returning 'to vasty Tartar back' and telling 'the legions', 'I can never win / A soul so easy as that Englishman's' (H5 2.2.121–5).

(C) See *NDS* (quoting Plutarch), 5: 280; see also ST I.64.

DENIS, SAINT

(A) St Denys, the patron saint of France, was an early **bishop** of Paris associated with the establishment of Christianity in France. He was martyred and buried near Paris *c.* 250. Feast Day: 9 October. The Abbey of St Denis, erected over his tomb, holds the remains of many French kings. Because Dionysius the god of wine was also worshipped around Paris at about the same time, harvest time, there has been speculation, mostly English, about the identity of these two figures.

(B) Besides the usual rallying cries before battle, the two invocations that stand out in Shakespeare are paradoxically those of an Englishman, King Henry V. About to launch into French as part of his romantic but also soldierly assault upon Katherine of France, Henry says, 'Saint Denis be my speed' (H5 5.2.183). He then asks her about their first child, 'Shall not thou and I, between Saint Denis and Saint George, compound a boy, half French, half English, that shall go to Constantinople and take the Turk by the beard?' (H5 5.2.206–9). The Princess of France calls upon her 'Saint Denis' to help her resist the advancing Lords' 'Saint Cupid' (LLL 5.2.87). More traditional rallying cries occur in 1H6 (1.6.28 and 3.2.18).

(C) Farmer (1978), 105–6; *Book of Saints* (1966), 205; Baring-Gould (1914), 11:190–4; Delaney (1980), 176.

DEPARTED

When used about souls having left their earthly for their heavenly or hellish abodes, 'departed' has religious implications, implying as it does an eternal spiritual life. Vaux speaks of 'praying for the lyving, & for the faithfull soules departed' (1590a), *sig.* K5ʳ, and Tyndale of 'the souls departed in the faith of Christ, and love of the law of God' (1: lxiii).

The Lord Say tries to convince Cade's rebels not to put him to death by reminding them, through reference to the 'forgive us our trespasses as we forgive those who trespass against us' part of the Lord's Prayer, of the spiritual dangers of their obduracy in revenge: 'Ah, countrymen! if when you make your pray'rs, / God should be so obdurate as yourselves, / How would it fare with your departed souls?' (2H6 4.7.114–16). Katherine of Aragon, divorced and dying, asks the sympathetic Captain to beg Henry VIII's kindness on their daughter Mary and her 'wretched women' with the invocation 'As you wish Christian peace to souls departed, / Stand these poor peoples' friend, and urge the King / To do me this last right' (H8 4.2.156–8).

DEPUTY

One given authority. Because God could be thought during the Renaissance to have chosen kings and other rulers and even, according to John of Gaunt in R2, to have witnessed their coronations, the word 'deputy' resonated with the idea of divinely deputed authority. The idea of a great chain of being, linking political, ecclesiastical and familial structures with parallel hierarchies among the elements, plants, animals, humans and angels in God's creation, reinforced this idea of deputed authority.

The King of Navarre makes fun of this idea, but also acknowledges its pervasiveness, when he reads from Armado's overblown letter which addresses him, 'Great deputy, the welkin's vicegerent, and sole dominator of Navarre, my soul's earth's god, and body's fostering patron' (LLL 1.1.219–21). John of Gaunt calls King Richard II 'God's **substitute**, / His deputy anointed in His sight', and 'His **minister**' (R2 1.2.37–41). Richard calls himself 'The deputy elected by the Lord (R2 3.2.57), and Richard's ally Carlisle tries during the deposition scene to reassert Richard's authority by calling him 'the figure of God's majesty, / His captain, steward, deputy, elect, / **Anointed**, crowned, planted many years' (R2 4.1.125–9).

DESCANT[1] *v.*

Sing (or compose variations on) a musical arrangement. Usually the descant is pitched above the melody, designed to provide harmony to a well-known tune, often a hymn. Shakespeare can use the word more generally than this as a song or as variations on a theme.

Richard of Gloucester promises now that the Yorkists are in power to 'descant on mine own deformity' (R3 1.1.27). Ironies abound here. 'Deformity' opposes the **harmony** that is usually associated with the descant; further, this compulsively individualistic character uses a word which usually refers to group singing to describe a solo; finally, the unholy Richard is using a religious metaphor. A more conventional lover describes himself banished to a 'cabin hang'd with care / To descant on the doubts of my decay' (PP 14.3–4).

DESCANT[2] *sb.*

(A) The song itself.

(B) When his henchman Buckingham later advises Richard III to stand between two churchmen for the appearance of piety, he directly associates the blend of his own imposture and Richard's with the tune and harmony of religious descant: 'For on that ground I'll make a holy descant' (R3 3.7.49).

(C) Bradford complains of the Romans, 'for singing of psalms and godly songs to our edification, all is done in Latin, with such notes, tunes, ditties, and descants, that utterly the mind is pulled from the consideration of the thing (if men did understand it) unto the melody' (1848), 1: 160. However, later Anglican voices like Hooker (V.38.1) and Donne (7: 407; 7: 165) approve of such holy embellishment. See **music**.

DESERT, DESERVE, DESERVING

(A) Something earned or merited, pertaining either to reward or punishment. Because of the high profile of the merit–grace controversy during the Reformation, various forms of this word can provoke religious associations.

(B) Morocco and Aragon in MV are marked deficient by their exaggerated sense of personal merit. Though Morocco knows that the inscription 'Who chooseth me shall get as much as he deserves' may be a trick, he lacks the humility to include himself among the undeserving, thereby losing fair Portia: 'I do in birth deserve her, and in fortunes, / In graces, and in quality of breeding; / But more than these, in love I do deserve' (MV 2.7.23, 32–4). Aragon, equally full of himself, concludes, 'I will assume desert', only to find 'a fool's head', to which he responds, 'Is that my prize? Are my deserts no better?' (MV 2.9.51, 59–60). When Polonius says of the players that he 'will use them according to their desert' (HAM 2.2.527–8), Hamlet retorts with a sophistication that derives in part from this same theological issue: 'God's bodkin, man, much better: use every man after his desert, and who shall scape whipping? . . . [T]he less they deserve, the more merit is in your bounty' (HAM 2.2.529–32). With ' 'Tis my deserving, and I do entreat it' (MM 5.1.477), Angelo asks to be condemned to death for having wrongly ordered Claudio's execution, invoking the Old Testament Law of 'measure for measure'. He is instead forgiven.

(C) Matt. 7.2 reads, 'with what **measure** ye mete, it shall be measured to you again'. See also **rights**.

DESPAIR

(A) Theological despair is the loss of hope or faith in God rather than what we might today call depression. It is considered a particularly dangerous spiritual state not only because such disbelief and loss of hope could lead to suicide, but also because the resultant death would preempt all chances of future repentance. Hooper describes 'desperation, when as men think they cannot be saved, but are excluded from all mercy. . . . [C]ontrary unto presumption, [such despair] taketh from God his mercy: for when they offend and continue in sin, they think there is no mercy left for them' (1843), 1: 422. Like Hooper, Andrewes connects the opposite sins of presumption and desperation: 'Between two such rocks lieth our way, that is, presumption and desperation: therefore blessed is he that so loveth God, that he can be content to creep on hands and feet to Him' (5: 535).

(B) Thus when the ghosts of the souls whom he has slain chant to Richard III a ninefold 'despair and die' (R3 5.3.120, 126, 127, 135, 140, 143, 149, 156, 163), they are urging upon him the worst possible theological outcome. The same context informs Lady Anne's 'hang thyself' and Richard's response, 'By such despair I should accuse myself' (R3 1.2.85–7). Edgar calls his father Gloucester's decision to kill himself in response to the apparent sadism of the gods 'despair': 'Why I do trifle thus with his despair, / Is done to cure it'; Edgar later claims that he 'saved him from despair' (LR 4.6 33–4; 5.3.192). When Richard speaks of 'that sweet way I was in to despair' (R2 3.2.205), his paradox suggests both that despair is comfortable because it is hopeless, without any possibility of disappointment, and that he has taken some delight as a poet and actor in feeling and speaking of his desperation.

Romeo plays on this religious word when he asks Juliet for a kiss, 'O, then, dear saint, let lips do what hands do, / They pray – grant thou, lest faith turn to despair' (ROM 1.5.103–4); he said earlier of Rosaline's disdain, 'She is too fair, too wise, wisely too fair, / To merit bliss by making me despair' (ROM 1.1.217, 221–2). Sonnets 99, 140 and 144 also play on this religious-romantic metaphor.

(C) See *Certaine Sermons*, pp. 52–8, for the sermons of 'falling from God'. See also *ST* II.2.20–1. Latimer (1844–45), 2: 182; Hooper (1843), 1: 415–22; and Andrewes, 5: 513–15, 535, all discuss the spiritual extremes of presumption and despair. Donne once cleverly rationalises desperation as a mark of faith and moral honesty: 'desperation may proceed from an excess of that which is good in it selfe, from an excessive over fearing of Gods Justice, from an excessive over hating thine own sinnes' (2: 332). George and George (1961), 95ff., as well as Devereux (1979) give a brief history of Renaissance ideas of despair; Devereux also explores the use of the word in the sonnets (33–7). Pinciss (2000), 48–57, outlines the theory of despair in the Renaissance, and argues that the Duke in MM uses his subjects' despair to test their faith. For Othello's spiritual despair as the result of racism, see Hogan (1998).

DESPERATE *adj.*
Prompted by theological **despair** to the point of suicide.

Leonato reports that Hero fears Beatrice 'will do a desperate outrage to her-self' (ADO 2.3.152) for Benedick's love, and the Friar says 'Hold thy desperate hand' as Romeo threatens to kill himself. Later he also explains that Juliet, 'too desperate, would not go with me' but remained behind in the crypt, to 'do violence to herself' (ROM 3.3.108; 5.3.263–4). Cf. similar references to Goneril (LR 5.3.162) and Brabantio (OTH 5.2.208).

DESPERATION

(A) A common name among theologians for the state of **despair**.

(B) This is used of suicidal impulses when Horatio warns Hamlet of the 'summit of the cliff', that it 'puts toys of desperation' in the brain (HAM 1.4.70, 75).

(C) See Hooper (1843), 1: 422; Andrewes, 5: 535; Donne, 2: 332.

DESTINY

Since 'destiny' means the predetermined course of events, it can be associated with the theological idea of **predestination**. For example, when Andrewes says, 'It seems chance, that is indeed destiny', he speaks explicitly of 'a high and wonderful disposition of God's heavenly **Providence**', but still calls it destiny, adding, 'For God will have it out certainly; rather than not, by some mere **accident**' (4: 139). Philpot (1842), 403, illustrates the same connection: 'Providence signifieth . . . a certain purveyance and administration of those things which be included in destiny.'

To Richard's evasion of moral responsibility, 'All unavoided is the doom of destiny', Elizabeth keenly retorts, 'True, when avoided grace makes destiny' (R3 4.4.218–19). Theologically, **grace** is abounding to sinners; its avoidance is a characteristic mark of **reprobation**. Donne, discussing Eccles. 8.11, on the 'setting of the heart upon evil', says of this theology of avoided grace, 'This is the evil of the heart, by the mis-use of Gods grace, to devest and lose all tenderness and remorse in sin' (1: 179). Richard has in a sense thus doomed himself to mere destiny, life without grace, and so he will eventually and inevitably 'Despair and die' forever (R3 5.3.120, 126, 135, 140, etc.).

DETERMIN'D

(A) Like 'destiny', 'determin'd' can mean prearranged or predetermined, and therefore have theological nuance. The Cambridge Puritan Perkins, for example, attempts to explain one of the severest parts of Calvinist orthodoxy to his contemporaries: 'The decree of Reprobation, is that part of predestination, whereby God, according to the most free and just purpose of his **will** hath determined to reject certaine men unto eternall destruction, and miserie, and that to the praise of his **justice**.'

(B) When Buckingham smiles to himself at the ironic calendar date of his reversal, he also with 'determin'd respite' acknowledges God's hand in his punishment:

> This, this All-Soul's Day to my fearful soul,
> Is the determin'd respite of my wrongs.
> That high All-Seer, which I dallied with,
> Hath turn'd my feigned prayer on my head,
> And given in earnest what I begg'd in jest.
> (R3 5.1.18–22)

In contrast, Caesar's resignation to whatever is fated, 'let determin'd things to destiny / Hold unbewail'd their way' (ANT 3.6.84–5), is more a philosophical than a religious resignation. See **predestinate**.

(C) See Perkins (1597a), 193–4, ch. 52 – 'Concerning the decree of Reprobation'.

TE DEUM

(A) The *Te Deum* is a hymn of thanksgiving to God, appropriated from the Catholic Mass, to be sung or said 'in English, daily through the whole year' (*BCP*, 53). It occurs during Morning Prayer, after the reading of the first lesson, and begins *Te Deum laudamus*: 'We praise thee, O God, we knowledge thee to be the Lord.'

(B) Just after his victory at the Battle of Agincourt, an exultant Henry V says 'Let there be sung **Non nobis** and *Te Deum*' as part of his determination to give all credit to God, 'For it is none but thine!' (H5 4.8.123, 112). The Gentleman reports, again on Holinshed's authority, that a *Te Deum* was also sung at Anne Boleyn's coronation: 'the choir, / With all the choicest music of the kingdom, / Together sung *Te Deum*' (H8 4.1.90–2).

(C) See *NDS*, 4: 398, 483; and Shaheen (1999), 470.

DEVIL[1]

(A) **SATAN**. The gist of the role is encompassed in Nowell's comment that 'The woman, deceived by the devil, persuaded the man to taste the forbidden fruit, which thing made them both forthwith subject to death' (1853), 148–9; Bullinger's that 'The devil . . . is called the deceiver, the beguiler, and seducer of the world, the old serpent and dragon' (3: 356); and Donne's epithet 'the father of lies, the devill' (9: 162).

(B) Over 300 references to 'devil' or a derivative word occur in Shakespeare. Antipholus of Syracuse identifies the Courtezan with Satan the tempter: 'Sathan avoid, I charge thee tempt me not'; his Dromio, stuck on the gender problem, asks in puzzled response: 'Master, is this Mistress Sathan?' to which his master replies without humour, 'It is the devil' (ERR 4.3.48–50). About half of the most colourful references to the devil in Shakespeare are proverbial: 'give the devil his due' (1H4 1.2.119; H5 3.7.112–13; Tilley, D273); 'the devil rides upon a fiddlestick' (1H4 2.4.487–8; Tilley, D263) and 'the devil fiddle 'em' (H8 1.3.42); 'a pox of the devil' (H5 3.7.116–17); 'the devil take order now' (H5 4.5.22; cf. Tilley, D235, D240 – 'The devil is a busy Bishop'); 'as good a gentleman as the devil is' (H5 4.5.137–8); 'a born devil' (TMP 4.1.188); 'he must have a long spoon that must eat with the devil' (ERR 4.3.63–4; Tilley, S771); 'the devil can cite Scripture for his purpose' (MV 1.3.98; Tilley, D230); 'lest the devil cross my prayer' (MV 3.1.19–20); 'the devil himself will have no shepherds' (AYL 3.2.84); seeking 'redemption of the devil' (MM 5.1.29; Tilley, R60); 'the devil shall have his bargain' (1H4 1.2.110–11); 'tell truth and shame the devil' (1H4 3.1.57–8, 61; Tilley, T588, T566); 'the devil understands Welch' (1H4 3.1.229); 'the devil is a niggard' (H8 1.1.70). The 'devil's dam' is his proverbial mother, but as often used to signify a particularly threatening woman (as in ERR 4.3.51; SHR 1.1.105; 1H6 1.5.5; and OTH 4.1.148; Tilley, D223, D225).

(C) *OED sb.* 1. See *ST* II.1.80 on the devil as the cause of sin, and *ST* I.64 on the punishment of devils. Paxson (2001) discusses the devils conjured by Joan in 1H6 in terms of the 'nether face' and devilish femininity (see especially 143–50); Cox (1993), 57–64, argues that the devils in 1H6 and 2H6 are used primarily to highlight human depravity.

DEVIL²

(A) The representation of this figure in art.

(B) 'A painted devil' (MAC 2.2.52) may refer to this or a subordinate devil in art, and 'this roaring devil i' th' old play' (H5 4.4.71) alludes to the devil as represented in the mystery or morality plays. When Jessica calls Lancelot 'a merry devil' as he is about to depart (MV 2.3.2), or Toby calls Maria 'a most excellent devil of wit' (TN 2.5.205–6), we are also reminded of the popularity of this theatrical figure.

(C) For the persistence of medieval stage devils in MAC, see Cox (1998), 941–7. For the source of the devils' names cited by Edgar in LR, see Lascelles (1973); more generally, of 'Daemonic Names, Places, and Ranks', see West (1939), ch. 5.

DEVIL³

(A) A subordinate evil spirit; often plural. Rogers sarcastically speaks of an 'order' of 'exorcists, or conjurers, which have power to expel the devils' (1854), 258; Bullinger of 'holy or good angels of God' and 'wicked angels', which are 'evil spirits, or devils' (3: 348).

(B) Ferdinand is described as saying in the midst of the storm, 'Hell is empty, / And all the devils are here' (TMP 1.2.214–15), and Margaret predicts that 'a hell of ugly devils' will populate Richard's 'tormenting dream' (R3 1.3.225–6). Duke Theseus speaks condescendingly of 'one' who 'sees more devils than vast hell can hold' (MND 5.1.9), and Othello imagines himself driven to hell by devils at the Last Judgement for his misjudgement of Desdemona: 'Whip me, ye devils, / From the possession of [her] heavenly sight' (OTH 5.2.277–8). Thersites says both sarcastically and blasphemously, ''Sfoot, I'll learn to conjure and raise devils' (TRO 2.3.5–6).

(C) See Bullinger, 3: 354. Brownlow (1993) discusses and reproduces the examinations of several who claimed in 1598 to be possessed and dispossessed.

DEVIL⁴

(A) A person of extraordinary evil or some other affinity with Satan.

(B) 'That devil Glendower' (1H4 1.3.117) probably refers to his fierceness; 'that devil monk / Hopkins' (H8 2.1. 21–2) is both a general anti-Catholic slur and an indictment for advising 'mischief' upon Buckingham. 'O devil', 'devil!' is spoken many times by Othello in ironic misjudgement of Desdemona (as in OTH 4.1.240, 244). '[T]hat irregulous devil Cloten' (CYM 4.2.315) is lawless; Shylock is often called 'devil' because he attempts murder and is not a Christian (MV 3.1.19, 32; 4.1.217, 281). The malevolent and almost demonically destructive Richard III is often called 'devil', sometimes even by himself (3H6 5.6.4; R3 1.2.45, 50; 1.3.337, etc.); so are Petruchio and Kate in their amusing but chaotic fierceness (as in SHR 3.2.155–6). 'The complexion of a devil' (MV 1.2.130) is proverbially black (Tilley, D217; cf. OTH 1.1.88–91), and so Othello is called both 'old black ram' and 'the devil' as Iago imagines his having sex with Desdemona (OTH 1.1.88–9).

(C) Morris (1985), 85–114, argues that Iago should be understood as a literal devil. Hassel (1999) and Doebler (1972) have argued that the Augustine commonplace of 'the mousetrap of the devil' may lie behind Hamlet's title 'The Mouse-trap' for a play which is designed to 'catch the conscience' (HAM 3.2.237; 2.2.605) of a Claudius often closely associated with 'devil' (as in HAM 3.1.48; 3.4.76, 162, 169).

DEVIL[5]

(A) Used metaphorically, sometimes almost allegorically, for anything capable of causing harm or facilitating sinfulness.

(B) Cassio says of wine that 'the cup is unblessed and the ingredient is a devil' (OTH 2.3.307–8); and Armado says 'love is a devil' (LLL 1.2.172–3). See also 'the devil of jealousy' (WIV 5.1.18); 'the devil luxury' (TRO 5.2.55); 'the devil drunkenness' and 'the devil wrath' (OTH 2.3.296–7).

(C) See *Certaine Sermons*, 2nd tome, pp. 94–101, for the sermons 'against Gluttonie and Drunkennesse'. See **exorcisms** for Donne's metaphoric take on such devils of temptation.

DEVIL[6]

Part of a more or less careless curse, like 'what the devil' (AWW 4.1.34) or 'the devil take thee, coward' (TRO 5.7.23, etc.).

DEVOTION[1]

(A) An act or image of worship or divine meditation.

(B) After asking Ophelia to pose reading a book in order to deceive Hamlet, Polonius laments 'that with devotion's visage / And pious action we do sugar o'er / The devil himself' (HAM 3.1.43–8). When Hamlet sees this pose and responds, 'Nymph, in thy orisons / Be all my sins rememb'red' (HAM 3.1.88–9), we see that '**devotions**' refers to the posture of **prayer**, and that the **book** too must be a religious one. Buckingham apologises for interrupting another hypocritical religious observance, Richard's 'devotion, and right Christian zeal' (R3 3.7.103) as he stands ''tween two **clergymen**'. Paris' 'God shield I should disturb devotion!' (ROM 4.1.41) refers to what he thinks to be Juliet's spiritual preparation to marry him.

The religious-romantic metaphor of 'devotion' is also common in Shakespeare. The most famous example is Romeo's elaborate comparison of himself to a pilgrim and Juliet to the shrine of his 'mannerly devotion' (ROM 1.5.98).

Richard III promises Queen Elizabeth less convincingly to love her 'beauteous princely daughter' with 'Immaculate devotion, holy thoughts' (R3 4.4.404–5). To emphasise his devotion to Cressida, Troilus promises that it will be 'More bright in zeal than the devotion which / Cold lips blow to their deities' (TRO 4.4.26–7). (C) See *ST* II.2.82; Donne, 7: 264; 10: 900.

DEVOTION[2]

A readiness to serve God. Donne illustrates both uses of **devotion** when he distinguishes between 'mine inward devotion' and 'such postures, and actions of reverence, as are required to testifie [it] outwardly', adding that 'these may well consist together' (7: 289).

Queen Margaret asks Simpcox, the man who has falsely claimed to have experienced a miracle of restored sight, 'Tell me, good fellow, cam'st thou here by chance / Or of devotion, to this holy shrine?' He answers, lying, 'God knows, of pure devotion' (2H6 2.1.85–90). Malcolm is probably also describing a religious attitude rather than a religious act when he includes 'devotion' among his list of personal virtues (MAC 4.3.94).

DEW

(A) A symbol of grace and benediction. Donne describes 'the dew of Gods grace sprinkled upon your souls' (2: 312). He expands the metaphor, 'he loves us most for our improvement, when by his ploughing up of our hearts, and the dew of his grace, and the seed of his word, we come to give a greater rent, in the fruites of sanctification than before' (1: 241).

(B) Katherine of Aragon says of her daughter Mary, 'The dews of heaven fall in blessing on her' (H8 4.2.133). Katherine similarly asks that 'God's dew quench' the coal of enmity between herself and Henry VIII (H8 2.4.79–80). Belarius blesses Cymbeline's sons: 'The benediction of these covering heavens / Fall on their heads like dew' (CYM 5.5.350–1). Lennox hopes that the forces of Malcolm, son of a 'sainted king' and supported by the army of 'the most pious' Edward the Confessor, said to be 'full of grace', will 'dew the sovereign flower and drown the weeds' by replacing Macbeth with Malcolm (MAC 4.3.109, 159; 3.6.27; 5.2.30). 'His dews fall every where' (H8 1.3.57) is Lovell's sarcastic metaphor about the bounty of Cardinal Wolsey.

(C) For biblical equivalents, see Gen. 27.28, 39; Dan. 4.15, 23, 25, 33. For a rich conceit on dew, pearls and grace, see Donne, 7: 306.

DIABLE (DIABLO)

Devil, usually in an exclamation uttered by a foreigner.

Dr Caius, the French physician, uses the proper French noun, 'O diable, diable!', when he finds John Simple in his closet (WIV 1.4.67), and says 'Diable!' again when Jack Rugby fails to appear for a duel (WIV 3.1.91). The Constable of France also says 'O diable' (H5 4.5.1) over their shameful loss at Agincourt. Iago shouts 'Diablo' (OTH 2.3.161), the correct Spanish form of the word, as a way of stirring up further chaos in the scene in which Cassio is dishonoured.

DIET

A legislative body, as in pre-Reformation Germany; also the assembled estates of the Holy Roman Empire. The Diet of Worms was the assembly before which Martin Luther defended his 95 theses.

It may therefore be a pun when Hamlet, a student from Luther's Wittenberg, says of the whereabouts of Polonius's hidden corpse, 'Not where he eats, but where 'a is eaten; a certain convocation of politic worms are e'en at him. Your worm is your only emperor for diet' (HAM 4.3.19–21).

DIRGE

(A) A funeral song or a funereal tone.

(B) King Claudius refers to the topsy-turvydom of the closely juxtaposed funeral of King Hamlet and his marriage with Hamlet's wife Gertrude as 'mirth in funeral, and dirge in marriage' (HAM 1.2.12). Capulet says that 'Solemn hymns' will be replaced by 'sullen dirges' in his lament for Juliet's apparent death (ROM 4.5.88).

(C) The word comes from the L. *dirige*, the first word in the antiphon sung in the Latin Office of the Dead (from Psalm 5.8). See Bradford (1848), 1: 589.

DISAPPOINTED

Spiritually unfurnished, unprepared (*OED ppl. a.* 2).

The Ghost of Hamlet's father describes his sudden murder as a spiritual catastrophe in which he was 'Cut off even in the blossoms of my sin, / Unhous'led, disappointed, unanel'd, / No reck'ning made, but sent to my account / With all my imperfections on my head' (HAM 1.5.76–9).

DIVES

(A) The rich man who went to hell in Jesus' parable about Lazarus (Luke 16.19–31), which begins, 'There was a certain rich man, which was clothed in purple and fine linen, . . . and in hell he lift up his eyes, being in torments.' Preaching to the privileged Court at Richmond, Andrewes says, 'Our comfort or torment eternal – comfort in Abraham's bosom, torment in the fire of hell – depend upon' our remembering this story of Lazarus and Dives (2: 78). *Dives* in Latin means rich man.

(B) Falstaff, characteristically both flippant and informed about such biblical matters, says that Bardolph's red nose reminds him of 'hell-fire and Dives that liv'd in purple; for there he is in his robes, burning, burning' (1H4 3.3.31–3).

(C) Donne refers to the story of Dives often and casually, in a manner that suggests that his audience knows it very well (as in 4: 237–8; 5: 82, 251, 386; 7: 54, etc.).

DIVINE[1] *adj.*

Pertaining to or proceeding from God. Becon calls 'a very sinner, a transgressor of God's precept, a breaker of the divine law' (1: 145), and Nowell says of God's providence, 'We also assuredly believe, that the whole order of nature and changes of things, which are falsely reputed the alterations of **fortune**, do hang all upon God: that God guideth the course of the heaven, upholdeth the earth, tempereth the seas, and ruleth this whole world, and that all things obey his divine power, and by his divine power all things are governed' (1853), 147.

Prospero tells Miranda that they 'came on shore' 'By providence divine' (TMP 1.2.158–9). Hermione hopes that 'powers divine / Behold our human actions' (WT 3.2.28–9). 'The divine Apollo' is also mentioned in WT (5.1.37), and 'you gods divine' in TRO (4.2.98). Imogen mentions the 'prohibition so divine' 'Against self-slaughter' (CYM 3.4.76–7). Caught in his sinfulness, Angelo compares Duke Vincentio to an omniscient and judgemental God: 'your grace, like pow'r divine, / Hath looked upon my passes' (MM 5.1.369–70).

DIVINE[2] *adj.*
(A) Godlike. When the Citizen says that 'men's minds mistrust / Ensuing danger' 'By a divine instinct' and then says 'leave it all to God' (R3 2.3.42–5), he suggests not only divining as foreseeing, but also that this instinct is godlike.
(B) As a metaphor for the extraordinary, 'divine' most often refers to things romantic. Speaking of Sylvia, Valentine asks 'is she not a heavenly saint?' and then says 'Call her divine', or 'if not divine, / Yet let her be a principality', one of the angelic orders (TGV 2.4.145–52). Kate in LLL (4.3.81), Helena in MND (3.2.137, 226), Anne in R3 (1.2.75), Desdemona in OTH (2.1.73) and Imogen in CYM (2.1.57) are also called divine. Berowne immediately calls the first metaphor 'profane'; the second is a drug-induced enthusiasm; the third blatant flattery; and the last two disinterested sincerity. When the Duke (in his disguise as Friar Lodowick) is called 'a man divine and holy' in testimony during the trial scene (MM 5.1.144), Friar Peter presumably connects and distinguishes his godliness from his sanctity.
(C) The angels were traditionally arranged into nine orders, Seraphin, Cherubin, Milton's 'Thrones, Dominations, Princedoms, Vertues, Powers' (PL 5.601), Archangels and Angels. 'Principality' was another name for 'Princedoms'. Only the lowest two were thought to interact with human beings. See **angel**[1].

DIVINE[3] *adj.*
Pertaining to theological study, occupation or consolation.
Richard II's 'Thoughts of things divine' (R2 5.5.12–17) refer not so much to God as to his own thinking theologically. He subsequently quotes two apparently conflicting biblical passages, one about the availability of Christ to the little children, the other about the difficulty for a rich man to come to heaven (Mark 10.14, 24–5). His enemy Westmoreland would prefer that the Archbishop of York would not turn his 'tongue divine / To a loud trumpet and a point of war' (2H4 4.1.51–2).

DIVINE[4] *v.*
To foresee or foretell.

The Queen wonders if a mere gardener can 'divine [the] downfall' of her husband King Richard II (R2 3.4.79). Stanley warns Hastings 'To shun the danger that his soul divines' (R3 3.2.18). Cassio 'divine[s]' that the business for the senate is 'something from Cyprus' (OTH 1.2.39), and Enobarbus wisely says of the marriage to Fulvia designed to unite Antony and Octavius, 'If I were bound to divine of this unity, I would not prophesy so' (ANT 2.6.116–17). Obviously some of these are mysterious divinings, others more like a hunch. Likewise, Henry VI's 'divining thoughts' that Richmond will someday become king are prophetic (3H6 4.6.68–70). While 'divining eyes' may play with the prophecies 'prefiguring' Christ, they are finally just love-struck (SON 106, 10–11).

DIVINE⁵ *sb.*
(A) Name for a minister or other church figure. Andrewes once warns his courtly congregation not 'to prescribe Bishops how to govern and Divines how to preach' (5: 15).
(B) Portia responds to Nerissa's appropriate criticism of her self-pity, 'It is a good divine that follows his own instructions' (MV 1.2.14), and Romeo calls the Friar in ROM 'a divine, a ghostly confessor' (ROM 3.3.49). The doctor says of the guilt-stricken Lady Macbeth, 'More needs she the divine than the physician' (MAC 5.1.74). Richard III is cynically described as 'meditating with two deep divines' (R3 3.7.75), and the Duke in MM asks that the condemned Claudio be 'furnish'd with divines, and have all charitable preparation' for death (MM 3.2.209–10).
(C) See also Andrewes, 3: 347: 'all Divines agree'.

DIVINITY¹
(A) Formal theology; religious instruction. Donne once asserts 'whatever is true in Philosophy, is true in Divinity too' (1: 225); Andrewes says that 'It hath ever been holden good divinity that the Church from Christ received power to censure and separate wilful offenders' (5: 63). Donne once calls 'Catechisticall divinity, and instructions in fundamentall things, . . . our Manna' (5: 276).
(B) In H5 the Archbishop is impressed to 'Hear [Henry] reason in divinity' (H5 1.1.38); and in PER the gentlemen, fresh from the brothel, are astonished to have heard 'divinity' 'preached there' by the virtuous Marina (PER 4.5.4–5). A religious metaphor informs Viola's comment to Olivia that her identity, 'What I am, and what I would, are as secret as maidenhead: to your ears, divinity; to any other's, profanation' (TN 1.5.215–17). When the Friar says that they should not trust 'my age, / My reverence, calling, nor divinity' (ADO 4.1.167–8) if Hero is guilty, he probably refers to his theological learning; godlike excellence would seem too egotistical for such a modest character, and religious calling is already covered by the previous word in his list.
   Lear probably uses 'divinity' as religious instruction when he analyses his daughters' flattery, 'To say "ay" and "no" to every thing that I said! "Ay" and "no" too, was no good divinity' (LR 4.6.98–100). Their false doctrine led him to misconceptions about himself and the universe that only the wind, the rain and the

thunder could silence: 'When the rain came to wet me once, and the wind to make me chatter, when the thunder would not peace at my bidding, there I found 'em, there I smelt 'em out. Go to, they are not men o' their words: they told me I was every thing. 'Tis a lie, I am not ague-proof' (LR 4.6.100–5).

(C) Donne wittily warns his feuding contemporaries of 'unlawfull and dangerous dallyings with **mysteries** of Divinity. Money that is changed into small pieces is easily lost; gold that is beat out into leaf-gold, cannot by coyned, nor made currant money: . . . so doth true, and sound, and nourishing Divinity vanish away, in those impertinent Questions. All that the wit of Man adds to the Word of God, is all *quicksilver*, and it evaporates easily' (5: 124).

DIVINITY[2]

God himself or providence.

'There's a divinity that shapes our ends / Rough-hew them how we will' is one of Hamlet's assertions of divine providence after his deliverance from the pirates and from death in England (HAM 5.2.10–11). Claudius asserts his own heavenly protection with 'There's such divinity doth hedge a king' (HAM 4.5.124).

DIVINITY[3]

The quality of being divine, **holy**, worthy of **reverence**.

Iago's oxymoron, 'Divinity of hell', helps him celebrate the scheme of blackening Desdemona's reputation by casting her in the Mary-like role of Cassio's **intercessor**, which he calls 'heavenly shows' (OTH 2.3.350–2).

DIVINITY[4]

Magic or good luck.

Falstaff says of his third try to seduce the women, 'They say there is divinity in odd numbers' (WIV 5.1.3–4). 'Third time's a charm', we might say today.

DOCTOR(S)

(A) Usually used of medical men, 'doctors' can also refer to those trained in theology.

(B) Thus, in WIV, 'justices and doctors and churchmen' (2.3.47) are distinguished, but when Henry VIII means to 'rectify [his] conscience' through the consultation with 'all the reverend fathers of the land / And doctors learn'd', he is obviously speaking of contemporaries of theological rather than medical education (H8 2.4.204–7). Similarly, the Doctor Shaw (R3 3.5.103) who helps deceive the Mayor and the Citizens into believing Richard's piety is a divine.

(C) Holinshed (cited in *NDS*, 3: 270) calls both Shaa (Shaw) and Penkie (Penker) 'doctours in divinitie, bothe great preachers, both of more learnyng then vertue'. The Recusant Rastell laments of the more extreme Protestants' throwing out so many of the old traditions of the Church: 'When it pleaseth them: all the bells shall goe, *With customes of primative churche, examples of good men, testimonies of blessed Doctors*' (1564), *sig.* C8ʳ. Earlier Reformers speak less nostalgically of the doctors' authority; see Fulke (1843), 1: 352; Whitaker (1849), 413; Cranmer (1844), 1: 325; and most outrageously Bale (1849), 321–2. For an account of Marina as a sacred physician in PER, see Willis (1992), 161–6; for a similar description of Cornelius in CYM as a 'heavenly physician,' see Kolin (1975). Bevington (1996) argues that medical doctors in Shakespeare are ineffectual, and that only religion offers cures to illness in the plays, and Richards (1978) that Hamlet is a divine physician, appointed by God to heal Denmark but failing to do so.

DOCTRINE

(A) An official religious position, principle or policy. Donne once proclaims 'That all that Doctrine, which wrought this great cure upon us, in the Reformation, is contained in the two *Catechismes*, in the 39. *Articles*, and in the 2. *Bookes of Homilies*' (4: 202–3).

(B) 'Doctrine' is often used metaphorically in Shakespeare, as when Berowne speaks twice of 'this doctrine I derive' 'from women's eyes' (LLL 4.3.298, 347), or Olivia says that Orsino's flattering if also conventional 'Most sweet lady' is 'A comfortable doctrine' (TN 1.5.221–4). Similar is Benvolio's conceited designation of Romeo's confidence that he will always love Rosaline as 'that doctrine' (ROM 1.1.238). On the other hand, when Polixenes says that as children he and Leontes 'knew not / The doctrine of ill-doing' (WT 1.2.69–70), he is referring to the familiar doctrine of original sin. Pretending to defend Cardinal Wolsey's extravagance, Lord Sands says, not altogether kindly, that 'Sparing would show a worse sin than ill doctrine' (H8 1.3.60); his ironic point is that not spending lavishly would be a greater sin in such a prominent churchman than religious heresy.

(C) Since Donne's sermon was 'by commandement of his Majestie Published' by Thomas Jones in 1622 (4: 178), his formal statement on approved doctrine seems to have been requested, and noticed.

DOOM

(A) The Last **Judgement** (*OED sb.* 6), from the OE *dóm* or law; the end of time, at which the good and the evil, the sheep and the goats, will be assigned their final places in heaven or hell.

(B) Macduff's response to all the corpses in Duncan's bedroom is to tell the thanes, 'Up, up, and see / The great doom's image' (MAC 2.3.77–8). Juliet makes a similar reference when she says, 'Is Romeo slaught'red, and is Tybalt dead? . . . Then, dreadful trumpet, sound the general doom' (3.2.65–7). In the masque in WIV, the elves are told to 'Strew good luck . . . that it may stand till the perpetual doom' (WIV 5.5.57–8).

(C) For the discovery of Duncan's death in MAC as a representation of doomsday and of MAC in general as a 'doomsday play,' see Kinney (2001).

DOOMSDAY

(A) The day of **judgement**; the day of one's death.

(B) In ROM, Romeo's 'What less than dooms-day is the Prince's doom?' (ROM 3.3.9) suggests that the Prince's worldly sentence of death or banishment is almost as severe as the Day of Judgement. However, 'Tybalt's dooms-day' (ROM 5.3.234), and Buckingham's as well (R3 5.1.12), are merely the days of their deaths (but see **All-Souls' Day**). Often the two meanings are conflated, as when Hotspur rationalises his divining of the rebels' upcoming deaths in battle with the idea that all are going to die anyway: 'Doomsday is near. Die all, die merrily' (1H4 4.1.134). When Hamlet responds to Rosencrantz's quip 'that the world's grown honest' with 'Then is doomsday near', he means either that the promised end would frighten everyone to be good or that the consignment of the dishonest ones to hell would leave the earth to the good (HAM 2.2.237–8). All of the deaths at the end of LR lead Kent and Edgar to ask, 'Is this the promis'd end, / Or image of that horror?' (LR 5.3.264–5). Cf. 'till doomsday', as in ERR (3.2.99), LLL (4.3.270), HAM (1.1.120), and anachronistically, ANT (5.2.232).

(C) Kaula (1984) traces references to doomsday and the Book of Revelation as part of Reformation ideology in HAM; see also Watson (1990). Marshall (1991) studies doomsday and eschatology in Shakespeare, especially CYM. For the rhetorical use of the word in LR, see Lascelles (1973), 69–70; cf. her 76–9 for Lear's envisioning of final judgement. See also Morris (1985).

DOVE

(A) A bird associated both with love, peace and innocence, as well as the Holy Spirit. Rogers complains that 'The Romish church' urges the worship of images 'Of God himself, even of God the Father, and that in the likeness of an old man with a long white beard; of the Son, in the similitude of a man hanging on the cross; of the Holy Ghost, in the shape of a dove' (1854), 222.

(B) The only obviously religious reference in Shakespeare is Charles' rhetorical question, 'Was Mahomet inspiréd with a dove?' (1H6 1.2.140). It is apparently a commonplace among Shakespeare's contemporaries to mention disparagingly that Mahomet claimed that he received divine inspiration from a dove whispering in his ear.

(C) Nashe is cited twice in regard to this tradition, as are Scot and Raleigh (see Arden 1H6, 20n). The story in a nutshell was that Mohammed trained a dove to peck corn out of his ear to make it appear that he was visited by the Holy Spirit. This claim was not mentioned in any of the consulted dictionaries of Islam.

DREADFUL

Inspiring awe or fear, sometimes spoken either directly or indirectly of God or the gods.

'Dreadful thunder' (HAM 2.2.486; LLL 4.2.115), 'dreadful thunder-claps' (TMP 1.2.202), and 'dreadful pudder' (LR 3.2.50) all refer to the fear-inspiring thunder of the gods. Lear hopes that such thunder will alert hypocrites, perjurers and 'covert' murderers to their hidden guilts; even more desperately, he hopes that such responses are part of a divine plan of the 'dreadful **summoners**' of heaven (LR 3.2.49–60). The Bishop of Winchester compares Henry V's victory at Agincourt with the final day of reckoning:

> He was a king blest of the King of kings.
> Unto the French the dreadful Judgment Day
> So dreadful will not be as was his sight.
> The battles of the Lord of Hosts he fought.
> (1H6 1.1.28–31)

'God's dreadful law' (R3 1.4.209–10) against murder is evoked by Clarence in a futile attempt to persuade Richard's murderers not to kill him.

DUST

(A) A metonym referring to creation from earth, and to the inevitable return to earth in death. Gen. 3.19 reads 'dust thou art, and unto dust shalt thou return', and Gen. 2.7, 'The Lord God formed man of the dust of the ground.'

(B) Beatrice thus opposes Benedick's preposterous self-image with his common mortality when she calls him 'a piece of valiant dust' (ADO 2.1.60–1). Hotspur says as he dies, 'No, Percy, thou art dust' (1H4 5.4.85); Hamlet asks similarly of this 'piece of work' which is man, 'What is this **quintessence** of dust?' (HAM 2.2.303–8).

(C) See Becon, 1: 110; Donne, 7: 322; and Shaheen (1999), 204. See also **clay**.

E

EARTH[1]

(A) Genesis describes human creation from earth, **clay** as well as **dust**. For this reason, earth can be associated with the vanity of human wishes and the modesty of human origins. Donne humbly exults: 'That this clod of earth, this body of ours should be carried up to the highest heaven, placed in the eye of God, set down at the right hand of God, *Miramini hoc*, wonder at this; That God, all Spirit, served with Spirits, associated to Spirits, should have such an affection, such a love to this body, this earthly body, this deserves this wonder' (6: 265–6).

(B) Beatrice wishes that 'god make men of some other mettle than earth, a clod of wayward marl' (ADO 2.1.59–60).

(C) Bullinger says that 'Paul calleth that natural body an earthly body, which we have of our first father Adam, . . . and he calleth the spiritual body an heavenly body, which we have of Christ' (1: 175).

EARTH[2]

(A) 'Earth' can also stand for this fallen world and the human waywardness in which it is played out.

(B) The Bishop of Carlisle refers to 'this cursed earth' and connects it 'to the field of Golgotha' where Christ was crucified (R2 4.1.144–7). Richard's Queen complains of 'this rebellious earth' that has deposed her husband (R2 5.1.5). Henry VIII reminds Archbishop Cranmer that Christ 'your Master, / Whose minister you are, whiles he here liv'd / Upon this naughty earth' also suffered 'perjured witness', false testimony (H8 5.1.136–8). Shakespeare's most religious sonnet begins 'Poor soul, the centre of my sinful earth', combining the idea of earth as the place of sinful rebellion with the metonym of earth as mere mortality (SON 146.1).

(C) See Donne, 7: 243–4.

EARTH[3]

Often opposed rhetorically and conceptually to the word '**heaven**', as when Andrewes says of **Dives**' 'forgetting God in heaven, no marvel if he remembered not **Lazarus** on earth' (2: 92); Donne says, 'the voice of *Abel's* bloud cryed from earth to heaven' (1: 172).

Juliet says 'My husband is on earth, my faith in heaven' (ROM 3.5.205) about her parents' insistence that she marry Paris while Romeo still lives. Hamlet describes his fallenness to Ophelia as a 'crawling between earth and heaven' (HAM 3.1.127). Unlike the frustrated moral idealism they both express with this opposition of heaven and earth, Richard III cynically says of Anne's comment about the murdered King Henry VI, 'He is in heaven, where thou shalt never come', 'For he was fitter for that place than earth' (R3 1.2.106–8). King Edward IV goes to his death hoping (with political and theological naiveté) that 'more in peace my soul shall part in heaven, / Since I have made my friends at peace on earth' (R3 2.1.5–6). 'Earth' is also commonly opposed rhetorically to 'hell', as when Richard's mother says 'Thou cam'st on earth to make the earth my hell' (R3 4.4.167).

EDEN

(A) The Garden of Eden was the site in Genesis of the story of the creation and the Fall. It is therefore associated with innocence, a timeless unawareness of good and evil, and with the primal perfection of creation as well as 'man's first disobedience and the fruit / Of that forbidden tree' (PL 1.1).

(B) During John of Gaunt's description of 'This blessed plot, this earth, this realm, this England' that was created perfect but has been damaged by King Richard's misgovernment, he calls it 'This other Eden, demi-paradise' (R2 2.1.50, 42). The Queen's later question to the Gardener, 'What Eve, what serpent, hath suggested thee / To make a second **fall** of **cursed** man' (R2 3.4.75–6), also connects Richard's misgovernment and his impending deposition with Eden and the Fall.

(C) On 'the Corruption of the Good of Nature', see *ST* II.1.85.

EDMUNDSBURY, SAINT

(A) A 'bury' (OE burg, byrig) is a place by the fort or stronghold. Bury St Edmunds is a Benedictine abbey and an ancient town in Suffolk, named for St Edmund, an East Anglian king and Saxon martyr who was brutally killed and buried here by the Vikings *c.* 870 for refusing to renounce his Christianity. St Edmunds soon became a shrine, and more than sixty churches were finally dedicated to Edmund; his legend also inspired a good deal of religious art. Feast Day: 20 November.

(B) Salisbury promises to meet Cardinal Pandulph 'at Saint Edmundsbury' (JN 4.3.11) to discuss an English revolt from King John; later King Philip of France is said to have sworn 'to recompense the pains' of these 'revolts of England', 'By cutting off your heads' (JN 5.4.7, 15–18). Some could have seen the irony of condemning English traitors in a place associated with an Englishman martyred for his loyalty.

(C) See *NDS*, 4: 42–6; BEV, 711n; Farmer (1978), 120–2; *Book of Saints* (1966), 223; Mills (1991), 61. For some early representations of St Edmund in religious art, see Davidson and Alexander (1985), 46.

EGYPT

The House of Egypt is 'the land of bondage' for the Israelites, from which they journeyed to the promised land in the Book of Exodus.

Egypt is once referred to as a biblical place in Shakespeare, where Jaques promises to 'rail against all the first-born in Egypt' (AYL 2.5.61). Though this is contrived nonsense, possibly having to do with the fact that he is suffering in the forest because he continues to follow in exile the rightful, first-born Duke Senior, it could refer as well to Ex. 11–12, in which all of the first-born of Egypt are slain as a mark of God's wrath against the Egyptians for enslaving the Israelites.

ELYSIUM

A classical name for **heaven** in plays of both Christian and classical setting, like '**Jove**' for 'God.'

In TN, a play in which the fool impersonates a curate and the title itself refers to a day in the Christian calendar, Viola says of her supposedly dead brother, 'My brother he is in Elysium' (TN 1.2.4). In TGV, similarly a play of Christian setting in which there is a single reference to 'Hallowmas' (TGV 2.1.26), 'Elysium' is named as a place, again heaven-like, in which 'a blessed soul doth' 'rest, as after much turmoil' (TGV 2.7.37–8). King Henry V, envying the heavenly sleep of the labourer, also says that he 'sleeps in Elysium' (H5 4.1.274). Two other English history plays have references to heaven as Elysium (2H6 3.2.399; 3H6 1.2.30). The reference also occurs in three works classically set, CYM (5.4.97), TNK (5.4.95) and VEN (600).

ENEMY[1]

(A) A common name for Satan; sometimes an epithet. Andrewes describes human sinfulness as being 'overwrought by the sleights of the enemy' (3: 208), and promises that 'Satan the arch-enemy (so signifies his name) will be sure to find Kings enemies' (4: 87).

(B) Macbeth literally acknowledges his remorse that in murdering Duncan he has given 'mine eternal jewel', his immortal soul, 'to the common enemy of man / To make them kings – the seeds of Banquo kings' (MAC 3.1.67–9). Angelo similarly says of his own temptation of lust for the novice Isabel, 'O cunning enemy, that, to catch a saint, / With saints do bait thy hook' (MM 2.2.179–80). 'Tempt', 'tempter', 'tempted' and 'temptation' in the same speech make his reference to Satan unmistakable. Toby Belch taunts the gulled Malvolio, 'What man, defy the devil? Consider he's an enemy to mankind' (TN 3.4.97–8).

(C) Donne, speaking of spiritual complacency, warns that 'All this while that thou enjoyest this imaginary security, the Enemy digges insensibly under ground, all this while he undermines thee, and will blow thee up at last more irrecoverably, then if he had battered thee with outward calamities all that time' (4: 293).

ENEMY[2]

A human reprobate.

Richard III is twice called 'God's enemy' by Richmond, who styles himself one of God's 'ministers of chastisement' (R3 5.3.252–3, 113).

ENSKIED

Placed in the heavens, either metaphorically or literally, as a saint.

Though Isabella takes it as sarcasm, Lucio's usage defines the word for us: 'I hold you as a thing enskied, and sainted, / By your renouncement an immortal spirit.' She is probably justified in saying of this, 'You do blaspheme the good in mocking me' (MM 1.4.34–8), since his praise is a bit over the top.

ENVY

(A) Jealousy; one of the seven deadly sins in the popular Christian formulation. Only a few of Shakespeare's 120 uses are explicitly theological rather than merely psychological, to the degree that such distinctions make sense in the Renaissance.

(B) Henry IV hopes he will not 'sin / In envy' by thinking that he is not Prince Hal's father but Hotspur's (1H4 1.1.78–9). Suffolk's description of 'full as many signs of deadly hate, / As lean-fac'd Envy in her loathsome cave' (2H6 3.2.314–15) draws explicitly upon the tradition of Envy's allegorical depiction in emblem books as well as literature.

(C) See Whitney (1586), Emblem 94: 'This, Envie is: leane, pale, and full of yeares.' Cf. Alciatus (1985r), Emblem 71; Spenser (1926), *Muiopotmos*, l.301; and Milton (1965), Sonnet 13.6. See also *ST* II.2.36.

EPHESUS; EPHESIANS

(A) City in Asia minor which St Paul visited and to which he sent an Epistle; its inhabitants. It is, however, from Acts 19.13 and from Menander, Shakespeare's Greek source for the play, that Shakespeare would have learned to associate Ephesus, the site of ERR, with exorcists or 'conjurers' (ERR 1.2.97–102).

(B) The Page's description of Falstaff and his tavern friends as 'Ephesians, my lord, of the **old church**' (2H4 2.2.150) may occur because of the biblical association of Ephesus with 'cozenage' and 'many such-like liberties of sin', vices Falstaff shares in abundance with them.

(C) Acts 19.13 is glossed in the *Geneva Bible, fol.* 64ᵛ. Shaheen (1999), 104–5, offers several versions of the key passage from Menander. Austen (1987), 57–8, argues that Shakespeare set *ERR* in Ephesus to capitalise on its biblical reputation as a place of disorder. Martin (2002) discusses the implications of the Page's reference to Falstaff's dining with the Ephesians in 2H4. For a discussion of Ephesus as a site for Anglican concerns over Catholic backsliding and superstitious ritual, in relation to PER, see Bicks (2000), 206–9. See also Kinney (1988) on the way the Christian Abbess supplants the witches and conjurers of old Ephesus.

EQUIVOCATE (EQUIVOCATOR, EQUIVOCATION)

(A) Answer ambiguously with the purpose of deceiving. During their trials for complicity in the Gunpowder Plot to blow up the English Houses of Parliament (1604–05), the Jesuits formulated a strategy of equivocation, the telling of only partial truths under oath to avoid the full discovery of their complicity in the treason. Donne says of them 'And though many have put names of disguise, as Equivocations, and Reservations, yet they are all children of the same father, the father of lies, the devill, and of the same brood of vipers, they are lyes' (9: 162).

(B) Near his own execution for a treasonous and 'most sacrilegious murder' (MAC 2.3.67), Macbeth describes 'the equivocation of the fiend, / That lies like truth' (MAC 5.5.42–3). However, most of Shakespeare's uses occur in the Porter's brief scene just after Macbeth's murder of Duncan, where he says, 'Faith, here's an equivocator, that could swear in both the scales against either scale, who committed treason enough for God's sake, yet could not equivocate to heaven. O come in, equivocator' (2.3.8–11). The Porter also says that 'drink may be said to be an equivocator with lechery', because it 'equivocates him in a sleep', 'makes him stand to, and not stand to' (MAC 2.3.30–6). All of these references may connect Macbeth's self-deceptive desire for power with the equivocation of the Jesuits.

(C) MAC was written around 1605. For a brief outline of the history of equivocation, see the exchange between Malloch and Huntley (1966); Milward (1978), 82–9, catalogues some of the controversialists. For the self-equivocation of both Macbeth and audiences, see Scott (1986). Hotine (1991), 482–6, looks at the wider historical context of the Porter's speech in MAC. For equivocation as a theme which underlies most of MAC, see Kinney (2001), 236–42.

ERMITES

Religious hermits or eremites.

When Lady Macbeth tells the gracious Duncan 'We rest your ermites' as she greets him before their castle, she means that though he has just thanked her profusely for her hospitality, like a eremite before God it is she who owes him prayers of thanks (MAC 1.6.20).

ETERNAL[1] *adj.*

(A) Lasting forever, used of God and the devil as well as the duration of the rewards and punishments of humans after death and judgement.

(B) Referring to God, Margery Jordan threatens the spirit she has conjured, whom she calls 'Asmath', 'By the eternal God, Whose name and power / Thou tremblest at'; later in the same play King Henry VI prays, 'O thou eternal Mover of the heavens, / Look with a gentle eye upon this wretch!' (2H6 1.4.24–6; 3.3.19–20). When Emilia unknowingly associates Iago with 'some eternal villain' (OTH 4.2.130), it is hard for us to ignore his own gleeful identifications of himself with the 'Divinity of hell' (OTH 2.3.350). The Roman Cassius gives the Christian devil his due when he says 'There was a Brutus once that would have brook'd / Th' eternal devil to keep his state in Rome' (JC 1.2.159–60). Of the Christian afterlife, the Friar equivocates faithfully with Capulet, 'Your part in her you could not keep from death, / But heaven keeps his part in eternal life' (ROM 4.5.69–70); Macbeth calls his immortal soul 'mine eternal jewel' as he thinks about what he has forfeited to make 'the seeds of Banquo kings' (MAC 3.1.67–9), and Othello swears ironically 'by the worth of mine eternal soul' as he tries to intimidate Iago into giving him 'ocular proof' of Desdemona's guilt (OTH 3.3.360–1).

(C) Andrewes preaches to the court at Richmond of 'Our comfort or torment eternal' (2: 78), and speaks of Christ's sacrifice, 'that purchased eternal redemption' (5: 260). Donne speaks similarly of the 'eternal Decree of thy Salvation' and of 'Gods eternall decree for my election' (3: 252). Bullinger (3: 381) and Perkins (1591), *sig.* A4, warn of 'eternall damnation'.

ETERNAL² *sb.*
A name for God.

When Valentine forgives Proteus with the words 'By penitence th' Eternal's wrath's appeas'd' (TGV 5.4.81) he evokes several aspects of the theology of **repentance**, including the fearsome aspect of Calvin's severely judgemental God. See **everlasting**.

ETERNAL³ *adj.*
(A) When combined with sleep, night and darkness, 'eternal' can refer more sceptically to nothingness or a state of unknowing after death.

(B) Pre-Christian references to death as a condition of 'silence and eternal sleep' (TIT 1.1.155; 2.4.15); or 'eternal sleeping' (VEN 951) manifest with some verisimilitude no belief in an afterlife. But when Richard III threatens to send Stanley's 'son George' 'Into the blind cave of eternal night' (R3 5.3.61–2), he may try to frighten this somewhat gullible Christian by implying that death is the end of everything. 'Eternal darkness', Fortinbras' brooding reference to death's 'eternal cell' may share this sense of theological emptiness (HAM 5.2.365); however, darkness is also one of the conditions of the damned.

(C) Donne says of the damned, 'They shall passe out of this world, in this inward darknesse of melancholy, and dejection of spirit, into the outward darknesse, which is an everlasting exclusion from the Father of lights, and from the Kingdome of joy' (2: 360).

ETERNITY¹
(A) Life after death as distinguished from life on earth; sometimes the rewards associated with that life.

(B) Gertrude speaks of 'passing through nature to eternity' as she tries to quiet Hamlet's grief (HAM 1.2.73). Thinking of the reward after death for a good life on earth, Tarquin worries about the imagined rape of Lucrece, who 'sells eternity to get a toy?' (LUC 214).

(C) Donne describes the eternity for which 'Christ took on himself all our sins' (2: 139): 'the sins of all places, and times, and persons, was upon him in an instant, in a minute. . . . And from this point, this *timelesse time*, time that is all *time*, time that is no *time*, from all eternity, all the sins of the world were gone over him.'

ETERNITY²

The end of time.

In the Sonnets, 'beyond all date, even to eternity' (SON 122.4) images eternity as the point when time ends. More ingeniously, 'time's thievish progress to eternity' (SON 77.8) casts time as a monarch in 'progress' around the realm, stealing hours rather than provisions from the inevitably finite stock.

EVE

The first woman, therefore the mother of all; she is sometimes associated with both sensuality and pride, and blamed with the serpent for Adam's fall.

The Queen challenges the Gardener, who has just prophesied Richard's deposition, 'What Eve, what serpent, hath suggested thee / To make a second fall of cursed man?' (R2 3.4.75–6). Berowne flatters Boyet, the self-possessed and apparently influential lord attending the Princess of France, 'Had he been Adam, he had tempted Eve' (LLL 5.2.322). In the same play Armado styles a tempting wench 'a child of our grandmother Eve, a female' (LLL 1.1.264, 251). In TGV, 'Eve's legacy' is pride rather than sensuality (TGV 3.1.72); more positive is Feste's reference to Maria as a clever woman, 'as witty a piece of Eve's flesh as any in Illyria' (TN 1.5.28). Cf. 'all Eve's daughters' (WIV 4.2.24).

EVEN-CHRISTEN

(A) Fellow Christians.

(B) Of Ophelia's suspected suicide, the Gravedigger laments that Christians of privilege are better treated in such matters than ordinary folk: 'the more pity that great folk should have count'nance in this world to drown or hang themselves, more than their even-Christen' (HAM 5.1.26–9). It is an odd privilege, to be sure, but one that he apparently resents.

(C) Hassel (2003), 115–17, connects the Gravedigger's class-consciousness as well as his literal reading of Scripture with the Puritans.

EVERLASTING¹ *adj.*

(A) Eternal, sometimes spoken of the duration of life after death and sometimes of the rewards or punishments that might accompany it.

(B) With war almost inevitable, King John says of all the combatants, 'Then God forgive the sin of all those souls / That to their everlasting residence / Before the dew of evening fall, shall fleet / In dreadful trial of our kingdom's king!' (JN 2.1.283–6). King Henry VI speaks similarly of 'The treasury of everlasting joy' in '**heaven**' (2H6 2.1.16–18). On the other side of the coin, Aaron the Moor says to the Lucius who has just condemned him to death and called him 'the devil', 'If there be devils, would I were a devil, / To live and burn in everlasting fire, / So I might have your company in hell, / But to torment you with my bitter tongue!' (TIT 5.1.145–50). Just after Macbeth has killed Duncan, the Porter speaks similarly of an offender going 'the primrose way to th' everlasting bonfire' (MAC 2.3.19). In a lighter moment, Dogberry tells Borachio that he will 'be condemn'd into everlasting **redemption**' (ADO 4.2.56–7) for slandering Hero. He means, of course, something like '**damnation**'.

(C) Of God's 'everlasting presence' see Donne, 6: 265; of hell as 'an everlasting exclusion from the Father of lights, and from the Kingdome of joy', see Donne, 2: 360; of 'the Gospell, everlasting', see Donne, 4: 172; of Christ as 'an everlasting mediator', see Bullinger, 3: 218; of 'everlasting joy', see Tyndale, 2: 101; and of the 'everlasting fire' of hell, see Hooper (1852), 2: 63; Latimer (1844–45), 2: 191. See *Certaine Sermons*, pp. 7–12, for the sermons of 'the miserie of all mankinde, and of his condemnation to death everlasting, by his owne sinne'.

EVERLASTING² *sb.*

'The Everlasting' can also be an epithet for God.

Hamlet wishes in his first soliloquy 'that the Everlasting had not fix'd / His canon 'gainst self-slaughter' (HAM 1.2.131–2). See **Eternal²**.

EVIL¹ *sb.*

A particular sinfulness or sin. Though 'evil' can mean merely 'bad' or 'wrong', it often carries theological weight in Shakespeare, suggesting actions which stem from some unholy alliance with 'the evil one', Satan, as well as a specific sense of sinfulness.

The pregnant Juliet in MM says of her fornication 'I do repent me as it is an evil' (MM 2.3.35). Barely twenty lines later, Angelo, who has condemned Juliet to prison, speaks remorsefully of 'the strong and swelling evil / Of my conception' (MM 2.4.6–7), by which he means his sinful obsession with possessing Isabella sexually, against both her religious vows and his own clear sense of right and wrong. Claudio, Juliet's mate, also speaks of their 'immoderate use' of sex as 'A thirsty evil' (MM 1.2.127, 130), implying that it is almost irresistible. Hamlet claims that he has not committed a 'purpos'd evil' when he asks Laertes to forgive him for killing his father accidentally (HAM 5.2.241).

EVIL² *sb.*

(A) Sin itself, the abstraction opposed to 'good'.

(B) One of the 'odd old ends stol'n forth of holy writ' with which Richard 'clothes' his 'naked villainy' is 'Tell them that God bids us do good for evil' (R3 1.3.333–6). This comes from Matt. 5. 44: 'Do good to them that hate you, and pray for them which despitefully use you, and persecute you'. Lafew also says scornfully of the Bertram who has disobeyed his king and abandoned his wife, 'I have spoken better of you than you have or will to deserve at my hand, but we must do good for evil' (AWW 2.5.46–8). The self-deceived Leontes calls Camillo, who has dared to defend Hermione's honour, 'a gross lout, a mindless slave, / . . . that / Canst with thine eyes at once see good and evil, / Inclining to them both' (WT 1.2.301–4). Finally, Iago, just having slain Roderigo but pretending to be an innocent, ironically asks the men who have almost discovered him in his treachery, 'Are you of good or evil?' (OTH 5.1.65).

(C) Cf. 1 Thess. 5.15 and Rom. 12.21, and see Shaheen (1999), 343. Sears (1974) examines how Shakespeare deals with the philosophical question of evil. Maguin (1995) examines the connection between darkness and evil in MAC. Tufts (1998) looks at Aquinas' account of evil as a failure to achieve good in relation to MAC.

EVIL[3] *adj.*

(A) Inevitably bad, spoken of persons born sinful, sinful deeds, or fallen angels.

(B) Edmund criticises the theory that we might be 'evil . . . by a divine thrusting on' (LR 1.2.120–6), reminding us that astrology and divinity are not readily separable in Shakespeare's time, and that predestination and what he has just called 'spherical predominance' may not be either. When the Duke says that 'evil deeds have their permissive pass' (MM 1.3.38), he asserts free moral choice rather than the compulsion of appetite. The 'evil angel' of the morality plays is referred to in ERR 4.3.20 and LLL 1.2.173.

(C) Becon asks 'What is Satan, or an evil angel? An adversary and enemy of God, a worker of all mischief and death unto us' (3: 605). However, Donne does not agree 'that there is a particular evill Angel over every sin' (10: 57).

EVILS

The plural 'evils' can mean just terrible events, but they often carry the theological weight of sinful thoughts, words and deeds.

Angelo, angry with himself for desiring the **novice** Isabella, compares his threat to her as a desire to 'raze the **sanctuary** / And pitch our evils there' (MM 2.2.171). His metaphor suggests his sense both of the uneven field of battle and of the **sacrilege** he is considering. When Helena calls Parolles's cowardice and his lying 'fix'd evils' (AWW 1.1.101–3), she implies that they are inseparable from him, thus marks of his **reprobation**. Macduff is convinced even before he learns of the slaughter of his family that 'Not in the **legions** / Of horrid **hell** can come a devil more damn'd / In evils to top Macbeth' (MAC 4.3.55–7).

EXCOMMUNICATE *adj.*

(A) In the condition of being excommunicated, expelled from the sacraments and fellowship of the Church by ecclesiastical sentence. Jewel makes it clear that excommunication is not limited to Catholics when he calls 'excommunication, a principal part of the discipline of the Church. . . . It cutteth us off from the body of Christ, and removeth us from the fellowship of the gospel. Let no man despise it: it is the sword of God, the power of the Holy Ghost, the discipline of Christ: it is an ordinance which the Church hath received from above. By it the goats are divided from the lambs, the weed from the good corn, and the sons of God from the sons of Belial. It hath continued from the beginning, and hath been used in the Church of Christ, in the synagogue of the Jews, in the law of Moses, and before Moses received the law' (Jewel [1845–50], 2: 942–3).

(B) The papal legate Pandulph twice uses this threat, first against King John of England, then against King Philip of France. John has not only refused to do the Pope's bidding but then set himself overtly and proudly 'against the Pope', whom he calls a 'meddling priest' (JN 3.1.163, 170–1). Once, in direct response to John's overt defiance, Pandulph says 'by the lawful power that I have, / Thou shalt stand curs'd and excommunicate' (JN 3.1.172–3). King Philip, momentarily aligned with John and therefore against the papacy, is similarly threatened that he is about to 'stand excommunicate and curs'd' (JN 3.1.223). Pandulph's frequent reiteration of this threatened 'curse' (JN 3.1.256–7, 318) finally succeeds in breaking the alliance.

(C) Jewel cites Matt. 18 and 2 Thess. 3.13–14 for biblical authority. See *ST* Suppl. 21–4; Tyndale, 1: 273; and Donne, 7: 148–19; 3: 87–8. See also **blasphemy**.

EXCOMMUNICATION

(A) The process or state of being divorced from the sacraments and fellowship of the Church.

(B) When Dogberry asks some 'learned writer to set down their excommunication' (ADO 3.5.63), he means he wants a written record of their legal hearing, their communication; his malapropism comically exaggerates the severity of Borachio's twinned crimes of slandering a virgin and insulting an officer of the law.

(C) See 'Excommunication', *OxfordEncyRef*, 2: 83–6; *NewCathEncy*, 5: 704–5.

EXERCISE

(A) A religious observance (*OED sb.* 10.a); an act of public worship (*OED sb.* 10.b); an act of preaching (*OED sb.* 10.c). Loarte's famous work on spiritual formation is called *The Exercise of a Christian Life* (trans. Brinkley, 1596–97). The Recusant Hopkins translates F. Lewis de Granada's complaint that the Reformers 'are directlie contrarie to doinge of penaunce, and unto all kindes of spirituall exercises of an austere vertuous life' (1586), 11.

(B) When Hastings tells 'good Sir John' the priest 'I am in debt for your last exercise' (R3 3.2.110), he refers to such a religious discourse.

(C) Though *OED* cites this line as its illustration of *sb.* 10.c, it could as well illustrate *sb.* 10.a, or *sb.* 10.b. See also NV R3 (225n) and Arden R3 (227n). See also **devotions**.

EXETER

(A) Like **Canterbury**, Exeter is the seat of a **bishop** and thus a **cathedral** city.

(B) A messenger warns King Richard that 'Sir Edward Courtney and the haughty prelate, / Bishop of Exeter, his older brother, / With many moe confederates, are in arms' against him (R3 4.4.500–2).

(C) This refers to Peter Courtenay, a zealous Lancastrian, who became bishop in 1478. See *NDS* (quoting the chronicler Edward Hall), 3: 283.

EXORCISMS

(A) The procedures of expelling and calling forth **spirits**.

(B) The conjurer Bolingbrook uses the second of these definitions when he asks if Eleanor the Duchess of Gloucester will 'behold and hear our exorcisms' (2H6 1.4.4). They 'make the circle' and 'then the Spirit riseth' (2H6 1.4.22 *s.d.*).

(C) Donne criticises exorcism through a metaphor, saying that when he feels himself becoming the slave of such distracting, worldly 'powers and principalities' as 'cheerful conversation, . . . musique, . . . feasting, . . . Comedies, . . . wantonnesse, . . . [and when] my Conscience spies no such enemy in all this, . . . I try then to dispossesse my selfe of them, and I make my recourse to the powerfullest exorcisme that is, I turne to hearty and earnest prayer to God' (10: 56). The Reformers Bullinger, 4: 115; Jewel (1845–50), 3: 273; and Rogers (1854), 258, all speak more literally against exorcism, but the Parker Society Index ('demons') indicates that there is a form of exorcism in the first Prayer Book of Edward VI (1549); Vaux's *Catechism* includes exorcists among the 'orders' of the Catholic Church (1590a), *sig.* H8^v. See **devil**[3]. See Hamilton (1992), ch. 4, 'Twelfth Night: The Errors of Exorcism'. Greenblatt (1985), 173–84, also argues that Shakespeare views and portrays exorcism as a dangerous fraud.

EXORCISER

The person who performs **exorcisms**; the **exorcist**.

As part of their pagan **'obsequies'** for Cloten, Guiderius says 'No exorciser harm thee' (CYM 4.2.276).

EXORCIST

Exorciser; conjurer of spirits.

Ligarius, pretending to be cured, says, 'Thou, like an exorcist, hast conjur'd up / My mortified spirit' (JC 2.1.323–4). The King in AWW uses the same metaphor when he says of the miraculously returned Helena, who was thought to be dead: 'Is there no exorcist / Beguiles the truer office of mine eyes? / Is't real I see?' (AWW 5.3.304–6).

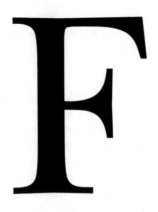

FAITH[1]

A religious system, like the Christian faith, the Jewish faith. The Recusant (Southern [1950], 168) speaks approvingly of 'the Catholicke faith' (168), and Vaux (1590a), *sig.* K8[r], of 'the Christian faith'.

When Henry VI laments 'That such inhumanity and bloody strife / Should reign among professors of one faith' (1H6 5.1.13–14), 'faith' refers clearly to the Christian system of belief, or at least professed belief. See **faith**[4].

FAITH[2]

(A) Trust in God and his promises; belief in religious **mysteries**; also the formal expression of such trust or belief in **prayer**. Since **justification** by faith alone was one of the lynchpins of the Reformation, it becomes a controversial word. Fr Granada complains of 'the late Apostatas, *Luther, Zuinglius, Calvin, Beza,* & other newe pretended Reformers of Christes Catholicke Churche' of 'all their doctrines beinge wholie grounded upon their newe Hereticall licentious doctrine of justification by onelie faith' (trans. Hopkins [1586], 115–16). Donne in contrast speaks of Paul's Epistle to the Romans as 'this precious ring, being made of that golden Doctrine, That Justification is by faith' (3: 377).

(B) When a gulled Parolles is advised to 'pray, pray, pray' at the apparent moment of his death, 'Sir, betake thee to thy faith' (AWW 4.1.75–6), the advice can concern religious practice as well as religious belief.

(C) See *Certaine Sermons*, pp. 21–9, for the sermons of 'the true, lively, and Christian Faith'. See also Donne, 10: 64; 4: 278; 7: 317; Becon, 3: 618; Latimer (1844–45), 1: 61; Vaux (1590a), *sig.* A3[r]. *ST* II.2.1–16. *ST* II.2.1–27 concerns 'the Theological Virtues', faith, hope and charity. Robert Watson (1997), 242–6, discusses the crisis of faith in OTH. McEachern (2000) explores how loss of faith in religion and order is expressed through loss of faith in female constancy in LR (see especially 215–30). See also McGrath (2001), 101–31; 'Faith', *OxfordEncyRef*,

2: 89–93; 'Faith', *NewCathEncy*, 5: 792–804; and 'Justification', *NewCathEncy*, 8: 77–92.

FAITH[3]

(A) 'Faith' is also a promise or a responsibility with religious dimensions.

(B) When Richard II says of the rebels, 'They break their faith to God as well as us' (R2 3.2.101), he illustrates the more common blending of religious and political fealty in the usage of 'faith'. A conflict between fealty to the authority of the Pope and Rome versus fealty to King John and England makes 'faith' an unusually prominent word in 3.1 of JN. Blanch says, for example, that 'The Lady Constance speaks not from her faith, / But from her need' in urging Louis, Dauphin of France, to 'stand fast' with the Pope and with Catholicism (see JN 3.1.207–16). The Pope's legate Pandulph similarly challenges Philip the King of France, 'So mak'st thou faith an enemy to faith, / And like a civil war set'st oath to oath' (JN 3.1.263–4), about his competing commitments to the Pope and to King John. Philip finally relents, but it is the threat of excommunication rather than the persuasion that one of these faiths or oaths is superior to another that carries the day.

The phrase 'plighted faith' (LLL 5.2.283), meaning promised fidelity, sometimes echoes the moment in the Service for Matrimony when the man says 'thereto I plight thee my **troth**' (*BCP*, 292). The same phrase occurs in 1H6 (5.3.162) to announce Margaret's engagement to Henry VI, and Olivia also asks Sebastian (thinking him to be Cesario) to 'Plight me the full assurance of thy faith' (TN 4.3.26). This use of 'faith' as 'vow' is probably one of Juliet's meanings when she refuses to be unfaithful to the banished Romeo by marrying the proffered Paris: 'My husband is on earth, my faith in heaven' (ROM 3.5.205).

(C) Kehler (1989) argues that the rhetoric of faith in JN is used mainly to attain secular goals.

FAITH[4] *fig.*

(A) Erasmus once calls romantic and religious faith and love 'nere sybbe', almost siblings (*Praise of Folly* [1965r], 122). Shakespeare often uses this delightful metaphor.

(B) Most familiar is Romeo's request of a kiss from the Juliet whom he newly worships, 'Lest faith turn to **despair**' (ROM 1.5.104). Silvia complains to the fickle Proteus, 'Thou hast no faith left now, unless thou'dst two, / And that's far worse than none: better have none / Than plural faith, which is too much by one' (TGV 5.4.50–2). This resonates especially well in a time of Reformation turmoil, both between Catholics and Protestants and also within Protestantism. Benedick twice swears 'in faith', ironically or sarcastically, in the scene in which he proudly announces his 'suspicion' of all women. Referring to 'this faith', Don Pedro calls him 'ever an obstinate **heretic** in the despite of beauty' (ADO 1.1.172, 197, 226, 234–5). Good examples of the romantic-religious metaphor also occur in MND 4.1.169; AYL 5.2.89; and WIV 4.3.8–10. When Henry V tells Katherine of France, 'I have a saving faith within me tells me thou shalt' be mine (H5 5.2.204–5), he may extend the romantic metaphor to a core issue of the Reformation, **salvation** by an indwelling **grace** or saving faith rather than outward **works**. A non-romantic example of the metaphor is Maria's comment about Malvolio's demonic self-love, 'It is his grounds of faith that all that look on him love him' (TN 2.3.151–2).

(C) Hassel (1980) discusses the Pauline and Erasmian dimensions of the close kinship of romantic and religious faith and folly in Shakespeare's romantic comedies.

FAITH[5]

Of the many oaths using 'faith', a few convey more theological import than the speaker might have intended. The best example is the Murderer's 'faith, some certain dregs of conscience are yet within me' as he ponders killing Clarence (R3 1.4.121–2).

FAITHFUL; FAITHFULLY

Believing (*adj.*); in a way that manifests belief (*adv.*).

Clarence swears 'as I am a Christian faithful man' about his horrible dream of **death**, **judgement** and **damnation** (R3 1.4.4). The Bastard in JN, illegitimate son of Richard the Lion-Hearted, denies himself the son of Faulconbridge 'As faithfully as I deny the devil' (JN 1.1.252). Orsino's complaint to Olivia in the final scene of TN is metaphoric: 'My soul the faithfull'st off'rings have breathed out / That e'er devotion tender'd' (TN 5.1.114–15).

FAITHLESS

(A) Not faithful; not a Christian.

(B) When Claudio asks her to 'sin ... to save a brother's life' and Isabella responds 'O faithless coward', she impugns both his lack of personal loyalty and his lack of religious faith. He would not only consign a novice to fornication and a sister to dishonour, but is afraid 'to die, and go we know not where' (MM 3.1.136, 133, 117). 'Faithless Jew' refers to the Jew Shylock's lack of Christian belief (MV 2.4.33–7).

(C) Dachslager (1986) argues that Jews, pagans and Turks are counted among the unfaithful by Shakespeare, but see **Jew**, **synagogue**.

FALL[1] *sb.*

'The Fall' refers to 'man's first disobedience' against God (PL 1.1). The Cambridge Puritan Perkins says that 'Adam's fall, was his willing revolting to disobedience by eating the forbidden fruite' (1597a), 25 (ch. 11 – 'Of mans fall, and disobedience').

Richard's Queen challenges the Gardener, who has just prophesied her husband's deposition, how dare you 'make a second fall of cursed man?' (R2 3.4.76). Henry V calls the 'revolt' that attempts his assassination 'like / Another fall of man' (H5 2.2.141–2).

FALL² *v.*

Submit to temptation.

Angelo is obviously speaking theologically when he says ''Tis one thing to be tempted, Escalus, / Another thing to fall' (MM 2.1.17–18). Gratiano suggests that had Desdemona's father seen her murdered body, 'This sight would make him do a desperate turn; / Yea, curse his better angel from his side, / And fall to reprobance' (OTH 5.2.206–9).

FALL³ *v.*

To descend (from heaven), said of blessings or curses.

Katherine asks that 'the dews of heaven fall thick in blessings' upon her daughter Mary (H8 4.2.133), and Belarius wishes for Cymbeline's recovered sons that 'The benediction of these covering heavens / Fall on their heads like **dew**' (CYM 5.5.350–1; cf. TMP 4.1.18). The counterpart is Timon's curse, 'the gods fall upon you' (TIM 3.4.99), or Lear's that 'All the stored vengeances of heaven fall' on Goneril (LR 2.4.157). Macbeth also threatens the Witches, 'an eternal **curse** fall on you' (MAC 4.1.105).

FARTUOUS

Virtuous.

When Mistress Quickly says of Mistress Page, 'she's as fartuous a civil modest wife, and one (I tell you) that will not miss you morning nor evening prayer' (WIV 2.2.97–9), she associates virtue with civil behaviour and frequent church attendance. At the same time, neither she or Shakespeare cannot resist the dialectical pun on flatulence.

FAST

(A) An **abstinence** from some or all foods for religious purposes. Donne says of this abstinence, 'Fast with a holy purpose; and it is a holy action' (5: 221–2). Hooker calls 'daies appointed as well for ordinary as for extraordinary **fasts** in the Church of God', 'daies of pensive humiliation and sorrow' (V.72.1). Cranmer's 'proclamation for the abstaining from flesh in Lent time', issued on 'the 16th day of January', [1548] is more pragmatic: 'whereof many [of his majesty's realm] be fishers . . . and also, divers of his loving subjects have good livings, and get great riches thereby in uttering and selling such meats as the sea and fresh water doth minister unto us . . . all manner of person and persons, of what estate, degree, or condition he or they be . . . [should] observe and keep from henceforth such fasting days, and the time commonly called Lent, in abstaining from all manner of flesh' (2: 508).

(B) The Ghost in HAM says of purgatory that he is each day 'confined to fast in fires' (HAM 1.5.11). The Bastard in JN disclaims any kinship to his mother's husband Fauconbridge with the metaphor, 'Sir Robert might have eat his part in me / Upon Good Friday and ne'er broke his fast' (JN 1.1.234–5). The Steward speaks cryptically about the praise Timon has purchased with his extravagant entertaining, 'Feast-won, fast-lost' (TIM 2.2.171). Common combinations include 'study and fast' (MM 1.4.61), 'fast and pray' (ERR 1.2.51), and 'priest-like fasts' (COR 5.1.56). 'I will fast, being loose' (LLL 1.2.155) is one of Shakespeare's best puns on the proverbial phrase and the game of the same name, 'fast and loose' (PEL, ANT 4.12.28n).

(C) For other uses of 'fast and pray', or 'prayer and fasting', see Donne, 9: 166; Andrewes, 1: 381; Tyndale, 1: 82. For proverbs involving 'fast and loose', see Tilley, F77 and 78. See also *ST* II.2.147.8.

FASTING

(A) The act of abstinence, sometimes as a penitential exercise. Fasting-days were the days like Fridays and the forty days during Lent which were marked by religious dietary restrictions. Flesh (red meat) is usually prohibited, fish allowed. See **fast**.

(B) The Fisherman says in PER, 'we'll have flesh for holidays, fish for fasting-days' (2.1.81–2). Paulina tells Leontes after his great transgressions, 'A thousand knees, / Ten thousand years together, naked, fasting, / Upon a barren mountain, and still winter / In storm perpetual, could not move the gods' to accept his **repentance** (WT 3.2.210–13). More lightly, Rosalind advises the scornful Phebe, who is, we recall, beloved of Silvius even though she is 'not for all markets', 'Down on your knees, / And thank heaven, fasting, for a good man's love' (AYL 3.5.57–8).

(C) See *Certaine Sermons*, 2nd tome, pp. 81–94, for the sermons of 'Fasting'. Donne says 'For certainly, he that uses no *fasting*, no *discipline*, no *mortification*, exposes himselfe to many dangers in himselfe. [We] nourish our soules, with that wholesome bread of taming our bodies' (4: 152). Gutierrez (1992), 80–3, looks at male fasting in LLL, HAM and MM.

FATHER[1]

Though never used in Shakespeare as a name for God, 'father' can name a member of the clergy from priest through Pope. Both Vaux (1590a), *sig.* G6ᵛ, and Bale (1849), 498, speak of a '**ghostly** Father', and Tyndale, 2: 113, sarcastically, of 'our holy father the **Pope**'.

Friar Lawrence is once called 'holy father' by Juliet (ROM 4.1.37), and both 'good father' and 'holy father' name the priest who marries Olivia and Sebastian (TN 4.3.34; 5.1.151). In JN 'our holy father' is 'Pope Innocent', his legate Cardinal Pandulph 'My reverend father' (JN 3.1.145–6). **Friar** Thomas in MM is also called 'holy father' (MM 1.3.1). The Duke disguised as a friar and his associate are called 'father' many times (MM 2.3.29; 4.3.48–9; 5.1.126). There is also a 'father **Abbott**' (H8 4.2.20).

FATHER[2]

(A) The founder of a religion. Sandys says 'God made a covenant with our father Abraham, . . . this covenant of grace and mercy' (1841), 180; Bullinger, 1: 39 speaks of 'the history of Adam, Noe, and Abraham, the first and great grandfathers'.

(B) Shylock refers to 'Father Abram' as a Jewish ally who would share his opinion of 'what these Christians are' when they suspect him of 'hard dealings' about the bond (MV 1.3.160–1).

(C) For 'Father Abraham' see Luke 16.24, 30, and Shaheen (1999), 168.

FAULT

Sin or its enactment. Tyndale says of Matt. 6.14–15, 'If ye shall forgive men their faults, your heavenly Father shall forgive you; but and if ye shall not forgive men their faults, no more shall your Father forgive you your faults' (1: 470). Andrewes says of Christ before Pilate, 'His judge . . . examined Him, and "found no fault in Him" '(2: 126).

The distinction between the sin and the sinner informs the discussion between Isabella and Angelo about her brother's crime, fornication, and its punishment, death. Isabella says, 'I have a brother is condemned to die; / I do beseech you, let it be his fault, / And not my brother' (MM 2.2.34–6). Angelo responds, 'Condemn the fault, and not the actor of it? / Why, every fault's condemn'd ere it be done' (MM 2.2.37–8). On the eve of the Battle of Agincourt, King Henry V asks God not to factor in his father's past sin, the deposition and murder of King Richard II, in processing his son's present prayer for victory: 'think not upon the fault / My father made in compassing the crown!' (H5 4.1.293–4). King Claudius also refers to one sin, a brother's murder, when he prays, 'My fault is past, but O, what form of prayer / Can serve my turn? "Forgive me my foul murther"?' (HAM 3.3.51–2). Prince Hal uses 'fault' more generally to characterise his prodigal past: 'My Reformation, glitt'ring o'er my fault, / Shall show more goodly and attract more eyes / Than that which hath no foil to set it off' (1H4 1.2.213–15). 'Fault' means both moral responsibility and enacted sin when Angelo asks of his 'seduction' by Isabella, 'Is this her fault, or mine? / The tempter, or the tempted, who sins most?' and then honestly concedes, 'Not she, nor doth she tempt; but it is I' (MM 2.2.162–4).

FEAST[1]

A banquet, sometimes in honour of a marriage or a baptism.

Amelia invites everyone to 'a **gossips**' feast' (ERR 5.1.406), a feast of the godparents after the baptismal rites. Of course she speaks figuratively, since she and her children have only experienced a kind of 'nativity', a reunion after her 'Thirty-three years' of 'travail' (ERR 5.1.405–6, 401). Duke Theseus, the King of France and Petruchio all refer to a marriage feast (MND 4.1.185; AWW 2.3.180; SHR 2.1.316). Capulet speaks in conscious contrast of Juliet's 'sad burial feast' when they expected a wedding celebration (ROM 4.5.84–90).

FEAST[2]

(A) A day of great religious celebration, like Easter, can be called a feast day.

(B) Two traditional English festival days named in Shakespeare are 'The Feast of **Crispin**' (H5 4.3.40), 25 October, and '**Saint George**'s feast' (1H6 1.1.154), 23 April. The classical plays include references to a 'feast of Lupercal' (JC 1.1.67), the Roman festival celebrated on 15 February, and 'the god Neptune's annual feast' (PER 5 ch. 17), 23 July. See **fast**.

(C) The Reformer Bale (1849), 262, complains of the Catholics' 'diversity of feasts, constrained vows, fastings, processions, and prattlings', and the Reformer Ridley asks, even closer to home, 'If saints be not to be worshipped, why keep we Saint George's feast?' (1841), 502. Defending liturgical feasts nearer the end of the sixteenth century, Hooker says, 'The sanctification of dayes and times is a token of that thankfullnes and a part of that publique honor which wee owe to God for admirable benefites, . . . daies which are chosen out to serve as publique memorials' (V.70.1). For the Feasts of 'Neptune' and 'Lupercal', see Grimal (1986).

FEET

Associated with both the devil and Christ.

King Henry IV speaks with apparent piety of 'those holy fields, / Over whose acres walk'd those blessed feet / Which fourteen hundred years ago were nail'd / For our advantage on the bitter cross' (1H4 1.1.224–7). Cf. the anachronistic ' 'Sfoot, I'll learn to conjure and raise devils' from the profane Thersites in the pre-Christian TRO (2.3.5–6). Othello refers to the traditionally cloven feet of the devil when he says about the exposed Iago, 'I look down towards his feet; but that's a fable' (OTH 5.2.286–7).

FIEND[1]

The devil.

Launcelot Gobbo tells us in MV that 'the fiend [who] is at my elbow and tempts me' to leave Shylock 'is the devil himself' (MV 2.2.2–3, 26–7).

FIEND[2]

A diabolically wicked person, or one possessed by devils.

Lady Macbeth is called Macbeth's 'fiend-like queen' (MAC 5.9.35), and Joan of Arc a 'vile fiend' by Burgundy and a 'foul fiend' by Talbot (1H6 3.2.45–53). Talbot is called a 'fiend of hell' in the same play (1H6 2.1.46). Though both are called 'a devil, a devil, a very fiend', the shrew Katherine and her counterpart Petruchio, on the other hand, are only metaphorically possessed (SHR 1.1.88; 3.2.155).

FIENDS

(A) Devils; fallen angels.

(B) Satan is once called 'the prince of fiends' (H5 3.3.16). In hell, fiends can be 'arrayed in **flames**', and they can suffer hell's **torments** (as in R3 1.4.58, or 4.4.75, where 'hell burns, fiends roar'); they are also associated with temptation or deception on earth, as in Macbeth's famous lament, 'be these juggling fiends no more believ'd' (MAC 5.8.19). Othello imagines that 'fiends will snatch' his soul 'from heaven' (OTH 5.2.274–5). In JN the Bastard warns Hubert, 'There is not yet so ugly a fiend of hell / As thou shalt be, if thou didst kill this child' (JN

4.3.123–4). Fiends are more than once called 'legion' in Shakespeare (as in R3 1.4.58; TN 3.4.85; MAC 4.3.55); they are once 'a thousand' (TIT 2.3.100).

(C) Mark 5.9 describes fiends as '**legion**', many; see also Shaheen (1999), 344. Brownlow (1993), 9–10, mentions several readers who have attributed the fiend-lore in LR to Shakespeare's awareness of Harsnett's Declaration (1603); they include Muir (1951), Elton (1966) and Milward (1973).

FIERY

(A) In flames. One of the traditional descriptions of **hell** and **purgatory**, in painting and in literature, is of a fiery gulf or a furnace.

(B) Othello expects as his eternal punishment for killing Desdemona that 'devils' will wash him 'in steep-down gulfs of liquid fire' (OTH 5.2.277, 280). Claudio also fears that in death 'the delighted spirit / Will bathe in fiery floods, or . . . reside / In thrilling region of thick-ribbed ice' (MM 3.1.120–2).

(C) When Becon speaks sarcastically of 'the papists, which say that the souls of the faithful go not straight unto heaven, but unto purgatory, there to be boiled in the fiery furnace of the bishop of Rome, till they have made satisfaction for their sins' (3: 182), his indirect point is that purgatory is non-biblical. On the imagining of purgatory, see Greenblatt (2001), ch. 2; Frye (1984), 16–19; and Harbison (1976), figs 79, 102.

FISH

(A) Fish was the white meat permitted during Catholic **fast** days; **flesh**, red meat, was prohibited.

(B) The simple (but well-fed) fisherman promises his invited guest Pericles, 'we'll have flesh for holidays, fish for fasting-days' (PER 2.1.81–2). A joke also informs Falstaff's wisecrack about Hostess Quickly, 'She's neither fish nor flesh, a man knows not where to have her.' Though he may mean in which country, or under which religious regime, she takes him more literally: 'Thou art an unjust man in saying so. Thou or any man knows where to have me' (1H4 3.3.127–30).

(C) Andrewes jokes about the powerful fish lobby when he says that fasting is controversial within 'reformed Churches', France having prohibited it as superstitious, but England having retained it because 'God will have fish to be used' (5: 492). For the Proclamation that led to this complaint, see **fast**. See also **Charbonne**, **Poyson**.

FLAMES

(A) **Hell** and **purgatory** were traditionally **fiery**.

(B) The Ghost of Hamlet's father speaks to his son about 'the hour' 'When I to sulph'rous and tormenting flames / Must render up myself' (HAM 1.5.2–4), apparently in reference to his current residence in purgatory. When King Henry V threatens Harfleur with a hellish conflagration, he describes an 'impious War, / Arrayed in flames like to the prince of fiends' (H5 3.3.15–16).

(C) *Mirrour* (1986), 202, reproduces an impressive medieval woodcut of the devil dressed in flames. On Shakespeare, ghosts, and the flames of hell or purgatory, see Frye (1984), 16–22, and Greenblatt (2001), ch. 2.

FLESH¹

(A) Red meat, as distinct from fish. 'Flesh' can refer to the diet prohibited to both Catholics and some Protestants during fasting-days. Pilkington says 'because generally every man loves flesh better than fish . . . generally it was well appointed in fasting to forbear flesh' (1842), 558–9.

(B) Falstaff not only uses the fish–flesh dichotomy in his wisecrack about Mistress Quickly, 'she's neither **fish** nor flesh, a man knows not where to have her' (1H4 3.3.127–8); he also charges her with disobeying the prohibitions against serving red meat during Lent: 'Marry, there is another indictment upon thee, for suffering flesh to be eaten in thy house, contrary to the law, for the which I think thou wilt howl.' Her retort is hardly penitential, but it does help us complete the gloss: 'All vict'lers do so. What's a joint of mutton or two in a whole Lent?' (2H4 2.4.343–7). Equally complex is Mercutio's taunt of Romeo (as a new lover) 'O flesh, flesh, how art thou fishified' (ROM 2.4.38). Romeo the lover, gaunt and emaciated, looks more like a fasting than a fleshed man, but puns on the sexual associations of both 'fish' and 'flesh' again complicate the reference.

(C) See Williams (1997): 'mutton', 212; 'fish', 126; and 'flesh', 127–8, for the sexual implications of Falstaff's charge.

FLESH²

Merely mortal as distinct from supernatural or immortal.

Richard II, just beginning to discover his own mortality, asks his respectful friends to 'Cover your heads, and mock not flesh and blood / With solemn reverence' (R2 3.2.171–2). As he dies, Richard says of the final divorce of the soul and the body, hopefully if also hyperbolically, 'Mount, mount, my soul! thy seat is up on high, / Whilst my gross flesh sinks downward, here to die' (R2 5.5.111–12). Pericles' question to his rediscovered child Marina, whom he thought dead, 'But are you flesh and blood? / Have you a working pulse, and are no fairy? / Motion?' (PER 5.1.152–3), again shows 'flesh and blood' being used to distinguish mortal from immortal beings.

FLESH³

(A) The sensual, bodily part of human being as opposed to the **spiritual** part. Donne says of 'This flesh, this sensuall part of ours', 'that flesh, that sensuality' (3: 77), 'in every man there are two sides, two armies: the flesh fights against the Spirit. This is but a *Civill warre*, nay it is but a *Rebellion* indeed' (4: 194).

(B) King John's 'Within this wall of flesh, there is a soul' (JN 3.3.20) is much like Hamlet's 'When we have shuffled off this mortal coil' (HAM 3.1.66), since both of them image the flesh or body as the mere covering for the spirit. More explicit than either is Bolingbroke's way of telling Mowbray that one of them would now be dead if King Richard II had allowed their joust to occur: 'One of our souls had wand'red in the air, / Banish'd this frail sepulchre of our flesh' (R2 1.3.195–6).

Falstaff's 'His grace says that which his flesh rebels against' (2H4 2.4.350) opposes '**flesh**' and '**grace**' theologically. A religious sensibility is also opposed to 'the flesh' of general worldliness when King Henry VI's protector Gloucester charges his rival and brother the Bishop of Winchester 'Name not religion, for thou lov'st the flesh, / And ne'er throughout the year to church thou go'st / Except it be to pray against thy foes' (1H6 1.1.41–3).

(C) See also Andrewes, 5: 427, 451; a recusant [Copley?] similarly translates Cardinal Pole on 'the battaile whiche remaineth with the flesh, with the worlde, and with the divel' (1569), *sig*. Z3ᵛ.

FLESH⁴

(A&B) In a Lutheran (and a Pauline) context, the 'works of the flesh' can refer to the fallenness of even the higher human faculties. One of Donne's discussions of this concept suggests its possible relevance to Hamlet's laments about both 'this too too sallied [i.e. sullied, or solid (F1)] flesh' and the 'shocks / That flesh is heir to' (*HAM* 1.2.129; 3.1.61–2): 'The flesh may signifie the *lower faculties* of the soule, or the weaker works of the higher faculties thereof; There may bee a Carnality in the understanding; a concupiscence of disputation, and controversie in unnecessary points. . . . The mind of a curious man delights to examine it selfe upon Interrogatories, which, upon the Racke, it cannot answer, and to vexe it selfe with such doubts as it cannot resolve' (Donne, 2: 84).

(C) Luther speaks often (in part from Gal. 5.19 – '*The works of the flesh are manifest*') of the prudence, the wisdom, the righteousness of the flesh. See LW 26: 216; 25: xi, 135, 350–1. Under Luther's influence, *Tyndale's New Testament*, in its preface to Romans, also speaks of the 'lusts of ignorance' (211–14). See also Donne, 6: 197; 3: 131; 2: 84; 6: 197; Tyndale, 1: 139; 1.494; and Bradford (1848), 1: 301. Hassel (1994a) connects Hamlet's obsession with 'perfect conscience' (HAM 5.2.67), i.e. perfect knowing and perfect doing, with Luther's concept of the prudence of the flesh.

FLOOD¹

The liquid fires of hell.

Claudio imagines himself after death as a 'delighted spirit' forced to 'bathe in fiery floods' (MM 3.1.120–1).

FLOOD²

(A) The deluge during the biblical story of Noah (Gen. 6–9).

(B) When his master tells him that 'a little water will mend' the sweat and darkness of the kitchen wench who has assaulted him, Dromio responds, 'Noah's flood could not do it' (ERR 3.2.106). 'The great flood' (JC 1.2.152) may be the classical equivalent to Noah's flood, appropriately referred to in a Roman play.

(C) However, Donne, 2: 351; 3: 108; 4: 98; 4: 271 speaks similarly of 'the generall flood'.

FOOL (and **FOLLY**)

(A) The praise of fools and folly has a rich Christian tradition, one associated biblically with some Pauline passages and in the Renaissance particularly with Erasmus. The Christian value of humility lies at its core. Paul speaks of the folly of trying to preach either the 'good news' of Christ crucified or the inexpressible and incomprehensible mysteries of faith and grace to sceptical rationalists like the Romans and the Corinthians. Good preachers, like good jesters, can also be fools for Christ in ministering humility to their prideful flocks. Erasmus's *The Praise of Folly* repeatedly stresses the close kinship between the follies of romantic and religious love. Humility lies at the heart and mind of each of these paradoxes. Andrewes once says even of **saints** and **angels** that 'In His Saints He found folly, and in His Angels *pravitatem*, somewhat awry; they both need a **Redeemer**, themselves. That they want themselves, they cannot perform to others; and if neither Saint nor Angel, then no Redeemer but God' (2: 259). Finally, Donne, preaching on the text *He came not to call the righteous, but sinners'*, says, 'for that was the end of **miracles**, and it is the end of preaching, to make men capable of **salvation** by acknowledging themselves to be sinners. And this hath brought us to the last part of this text, that which at first we called the fruit of the Gospel, Humility.'

(B) Thus, while 'fool' is often an insult in the Bible and in Shakespeare, it can also express profound admiration and, if the title is taken to heart, deep **humility**. The abundance of paradoxical phrases in Shakespeare in praise of folly are inevitably informed by these traditions. Characters like Touchstone, Feste, Lavatch, and of course Lear's Clown all try to teach the wisdom of folly and the folly of wisdom. As Lavatch says to Parolles, who has tried to put him down with 'Go to, thou art a witty fool; I have found thee': 'Did you find me in yourself, sir, or were you taught to find me? . . . The search, sir, was profitable, and much fool may you find in you' (AWW 2.4.32–6). In TN, Feste's 'Good Madonna, give me leave to prove you a fool', provokes her good-natured response to his proof, 'What think you of this fool, Malvolio? Doth he not mend?' Malvolio's negative response, 'Infirmity, that decays the wise, doth ever make the better fool', and Feste's effective rejoinder to this attempted putdown, 'God send you, sir, a speedy infirmity, for the better increasing your folly' (TN 1.5.58–76) all refer to the spiritual health of this paradoxical acknowledging of 'fool'. Jaques's 'noble fool', 'worthy fool' and 'material fool' (AYL 2.7.33–4; 3.3.32) are among the many oxymorons in Shakespeare that verbally celebrate this folly. So do such paradoxes as Feste's 'better a witty fool than a foolish wit' (TN 1.5.36), Touchstone's 'The fool doth think he is wise, but the wise man knows himself to be a fool' (AYL 5.1.31–2), and Viola's 'This fellow is wise enough to play the fool': 'This is a practice / As full of labor as a wise man's art; / For folly that he wisely shows, is fit, / And wise men, folly-fall'n, quite taint their wit' (TN 3.1.60–8). See also TN 4.2.88–90; TN 5.1.373.

As a corollary, calling others 'fool' is inadvisable in Shakespearean comedy. Portia calls all of the losing suitors, 'deliberate fools', but she also says, 'I know it is a sin to be a mocker' (MV 2.9.80; 1.2.57). Rosaline says of the foolish actors in the Pageant, 'I dare not call them fools', though she too immediately trans-gresses: 'but this I think, / When they are thirsty, fools would fain have drink' (LLL 5.2.371–2). Shakespeare suggests in both of these light but pointed cases the difficulty among even the best of his characters to obey Christ's injunction about charity and humility: 'Whosoever shall say, Thou fool, shall be in danger of hell fire' (Matt. 5.22).

This folly tradition also informs the histories and the tragedies. The arrogant Richard II calls Gaunt 'a lunatic lean-witted fool' R2 2.1.115) for trying like a professional fool to tell him the truth about both his personal folly and his political vulnerability. The suddenly repentant and conflicted Richard III finds himself unexpectedly playing his own truth-telling fool in soliloquy when he says 'Fool, of thyself speak well' and immediately contradicts, 'Fool, do not flatter' (R3 5.3.192). Hal, just after becoming Henry V, calls his presumptuous 'fool and jester' Falstaff both 'surfeit-swell'd' and 'profane', and orders him, 'Make less thy body hence, and more thy grace' (2H4 5.5.48–51). Against the Pauline and Erasmian traditions, Falstaff is neither wise nor humble enough to play the fool, for all his great width and wit.

Lear, the character who arguably needs more self-knowledge and more humil-ity than any other in Shakespeare, receives his own painful wisdom of folly in many cruel and loving ways, one of them through the ministry of his wise, Festean fool. Lear once says to him, 'Dost thou call me fool, boy?' The Fool's answer is also his persistent lesson for his master: 'All thy other titles thou has given away; that thou wast born with' (LR 1.4.148–50). Lear's refusal to acknowledge his own folly leads his fool to observe that he has thereby forfeited basic human identity: 'I am better than thou art now: I am a Fool, thou art nothing' (LR 1.4.126, 193–4). Slowly, Lear embraces the wisdom of folly. He tells Gloucester 'When we are born, we cry that we are come / To this great stage of fools'; then he confides in Cordelia, 'I am a very foolish, fond, old man. Pray you forget and forgive. I am old and foolish' (LR 4.6.183–4; 4.7.59). How much he has learned; how much learning remains.

(C) For some Pauline comments on blessed folly, see 1 Cor. 1.18–27, 2.9; for comments in Erasmus, see *The Praise of Folie* (1965r), 115–27; see also Kaiser (1963). John Evans (1990), 7–19, examines Christian folly in LR in this Erasmian context. Hassel (1980) discusses from Erasmian and Pauline perspectives the roles of acknowledged and celebrated folly in the comedies. Stockard (1997) suggests that MND stages a Christian folly which grows to resemble the folly of the cross. See also Battenhouse on Falstaff's 'perhaps holy' folly (1975). For the tension in TN between Malvolio and Feste as a reflection of the Puritan oppos-ition to laughter and foolery, see Ghose (2002); for the fool in LR as philosopher, see Bate (2000). Wenzel (1982), 225–6, 240, claims that the moral depth of Lear's fool comes from medieval traditions. See also **faith, reason**.

FOOL'S HEAD

(A) A representation of a fool that emblematises human folly.
(B) Aragon, still self-deceived, asks 'Did I deserve no more than a fool's head?'

His parting line more graciously acknowledges that folly: 'With one fool's head I came to woo, / But I go away with two' (MV 2.9.59, 75–6). The picture of 'we three' referred to in TN, which is a picture of two fools or two asses which can be called 'we three' only if we count the viewer, is also part of this tradition. So, probably, is Maria's related comment to the fools Toby Belch and Andrew Aguecheek, about Malvolio, 'Let the fool make a third' (TN 2.3.15–16, 174).

(C) See Wither's English Emblem Book of 1635 (1975r), 211, for a fool's head.

Fig. 3 Fool's head. Emblem # 211 from *A Collection of Emblemes*, George Wither, 1635; STCC 25900d. Courtesy The Newberry Library, Chicago.

FORFEIT *sb.* and *adj.*

(A) A debt whose due date has passed (as in MV 1.3.148), or an obligation, moral, financial, legal or theological, which must still be fulfilled; subjected to such a debt. Theologically, this can image the human debt to the God of justice, eternal damnation, which could only be paid, in the Christian scheme, by Christ's sacrifice on the cross.

(B) In their theological debate, Isabella and Angelo once mention this theological scheme directly, and link it to legal indebtedness on earth. To Angelo's 'Your brother is a forfeit of the law', Isabella responds, 'Why, all the souls that were were forfeit once, / And He that might the vantage best have took / Found out the remedy' (MM 2.2.71–5).

(C) Andrewes speaks of this financial metaphor when he says, 'Oft we have heard, in redemption there is emption, a buying, and re, that is back; a buying back of that, which formerly hath been lost or made away.' 'Redemption real [speaks] of our estates, lands, or goods; redemption personal, of our own selves, souls, and bodies' (3.208).

FORFEND

Forbid, prohibit, spoken in Shakespeare exclusively of or to God.

Thus the Bishop of Carlisle, arguing against the deposition of King Richard II, appeals, 'O, forfend it, God, / That in a Christian climate souls refin'd / Should show so heinous, black, obscene a deed!' (R2 4.1.129–31). Cf. 1H6 5.4.65; 2H6 3.2.30–1; TRO 1.3.302; TIT 1.1.434.

FORGIVE

(A) Excuse or pardon. Because Christ taught the prayer, 'Forgive us our trespasses, as we forgive those who trespass against us', and also enacted his own forgiving sacrifice to redeem erring humanity, forgiveness has become one of the central virtues of Christian precept, if not always Christian practice. Andrewes says, 'And when we pray, "Forgive us our debts," we learn that it is our duty to crave forgiveness for others as for ourselves' (5: 428); 'for by mercy shewed, sins are forgiven' (1: 442–3).

(B) 'Heaven forgive you' and 'Heaven forgive me' (as in WIV 2.1.28; 2.2.56) may be casual statements of regret; something like Parson Evans's 'heaven forgive my sins at the day of judgment' (WIV 3.3.212) is more explicitly theological. Mistress Ford's 'Heaven forgive our sins!' (WIV 5.5.31) falls somewhere between these extremes. The kind Judge Escalus warns his severe colleague Angelo after he has condemned Claudio to death for fornication, 'Well; heaven forgive him! and forgive us all! / Some rise by sin, and some by virtue fall' (MM 2.1.37–8).

There are many fascinating manipulations of the 'God forgive you' formula in the histories. Falstaff pretends to have an eroding religious sensibility, and great moral scrupulousness about it, when he says, topsy-turvy, 'Thou hast done much harm upon me, Hal, God forgive thee for it!' (1H4 1.2.90–7). Prince Hal's 'And God forgive them that so much have sway'd / Your Majesty's good thoughts away from me!' (1H4 3.2.130–1) blames his damaged reputation on a false report which he now pretends to pardon. Falstaff is no less nor more hypocritical than Hal when he says to Mistress Quickly 'Hostess, I forgive thee' (1H4 3.3.170), when in fact it is she who will have to forgive him tavern debts that he will never repay. Most outrageously, when Richard of Gloucester is about to kill King Henry VI, the King, pious to a fault even now, says to his murderer, 'O God, forgive my sins, and pardon thee!' Richard, unmoved but amused, responds, 'Down, down to hell, and say I sent thee hither' (3H6 5.6.60, 67). There are also of course many more honest and conventional uses of this 'God forgive' formula, but they are inevitably less interesting. Henry IV prays from his deathbed 'How I came by the crown, O God forgive' (2H4 4.5.218). Buckingham, escorting Lovell to the scaffold, says to him, 'I as free forgive you / As I would be forgiven' (H8 2.1.82–3).

The conflict of revenge motifs and Christian scruples in some of the tragedies, not to mention their greater psychological and epistemological depth, often complicates their usage of 'forgive'. The Doctor's 'God, God, forgive us all' (MAC 5.1.175) may sound formulaic, but it is prompted by the revealed guilt of Lady Macbeth's sleepwalking scene. Macduff is so desperate to repay Macbeth for the wholesale slaughter of his entire family that he says, 'If he scape, heaven forgive him too' (MAC 4.3.235), trying perhaps to rachet up his own intensity, but also revealing his dread of a nonsensical universe if Macbeth escape his vengeance. Several references to 'heaven forgive' 'and 'God forgive us our sins' in OTH (2.3.111; 3.3.373; 4.2.8) manifest naiveté as much as they do spiritual health, especially when the characters seem increasingly to lack the heavenly protection they so frequently assume, and invoke (see **God**, **heaven**). The newly blinded Gloucester's formulaic 'Kind gods, forgive me that, and prosper him' (LR 3.7.92) similarly prefaces his fall into spiritual despair. Claudius also sounds conventional enough when he asks God in prayer, 'Forgive me my foul murther'. However, 'That cannot be' immediately complicates his contrition with a disarming spiritual honesty and theological understanding. Unwilling to give up 'those effects' for which he killed Old Hamlet, 'My crown, mine own ambition, and my queen' (HAM 3.3.52–5), he knows that his prayer will not be granted.

(C) In a sermon which rhetorically echoes his 'Hymn to God the Father', Donne meditates brilliantly on sin and forgiveness (5: 81). The passion and the detail of his analysis reveal the vital importance of this subject to Donne and his contemporaries. See also Hutchinson (1842), 333; Sandys (1841), 229 (citing Luke 6.37); Tyndale, 1: 470 (citing Matt. 6): 'If ye shall forgive men their faults, your heavenly Father shall forgive you; but and if ye shall not forgive men their faults, no more shall your Father forgive you your faults.' For forgiveness in CYM, see Marshall (1991), 19–33; for the problematic nature of Hero's forgiveness of Claudio in ADO, see Hassel (1980), 80–90.

FORNICATION

(A) A formal word for having sex outside of wedlock.

(B) In MM, Claudio is as Isabella says 'Condemn'd upon the act of fornication / To lose his head' (MM 5.1.70–1). Angelo, his 'just but severe' judge, is himself accused of 'fornication' (MM 2.2.41; MM 5.1.195) by Mariana, who stood in, or laid in, for Isabella (cf. MM 2.1.79–81). When the Porter calls the throng of commoners who are trying to glimpse the infant Elizabeth's christening 'a fry of fornication' (H8 5.3.35–6), he means the offspring of unauthorised sex. The word's presence in an alliterative, genitive phrase, self-righteously disapproving, also feels like parody of Puritan-speak. Parson Evans similarly disapproves of Falstaff as 'given to fornications' (WIV 5.5.158).

(C) On Puritan representation and the alliterative language of disapproval, see Barish (1960), 197–203; Waith (1963) [see Jonson, Ben], 12–13; and Kernan (1974) [see Jonson, Ben], 6. See also Hassel (2003), 105–9.

FORTITUDE

(A) Courage. One of the four **cardinal** or 'natural' virtues which were appropriated into the Christian scheme. In a funeral sermon the Reformer Grindal praises the deceased's 'fortitude, travails, and continuance in wars against infidels and sworn enemies of the Christian name and religion, I mean the Turks' (1843), 13.

(B) Miranda is described by Prospero as 'a cherubin' 'that did preserve me' because she 'didst smile, / Infused with a fortitude from heaven' during their desolate abandonment to the sea (TMP 1.2.152–8). Malcolm includes 'fortitude' among his list of twelve 'king-becoming graces', a list that includes justice and temperance, but not prudence (MAC 4.3.91–4). Several of his 'graces', especially **'lowliness'**, **'mercy'**, **'devotion'** and 'bounty', are more clearly Christian than classical.

(C) See *ST* II.2.123–40; Roberti (1962), 515–17; Atkinson (1995), 265–6 ('Courage'); Becker and Becker (2001), 352–5; 'Fortitude', *NewCathEncy*, 5: 1034. See **unfortified**.

FRANCIS, SAINT

(A) St Francis of Assisi (1181–1226), called Francis because he spoke some French and had a French mother, is renowned as the founder of the Franciscan Order, one known for its brown habits and its commitment to the poor and the sick. Feast Day: 4 October.

(B) The Friar in ROM, himself a Franciscan (ROM 5.2.1), swears by 'Holy Saint Francis' (ROM 2.3.65) when he learns that Romeo no longer loves Rosaline; he also prays 'Saint Francis be my speed' (ROM 5.3.121) as he tries to get to Juliet's tomb in time to avert a tragedy. He arrives too late, and leaves too soon. In AWW (3.5.35–6) 'the Saint Francis here beside the port' is an inn.

(C) Farmer (1978), 157–9; Voraigne (1941), 2:600–1; Baring-Gould (1914), 11:80–3.

FRANCISCAN

(A) An order of begging friars founded by St Francis in the thirteenth century.

(B) Friar John calls the Friar Lawrence who has tried to help Romeo and Juliet a 'Holy Franciscan friar' (ROM 5.2.1), adding two precise details about the

Franciscans style, that they went 'barefoot' in sympathy for the poor, and that they went out as 'associate brothers', that is, in pairs (ROM 5.2.1, 5–6).
(C) See Lambert (1961), and RIV, 1135n.

FRIAR

(A) A member of a religious order; sometimes a mendicant. The Franciscans ('Grey Friars'), Dominicans ('Black Friars'), Carmelites ('White Friars') and Augustinians ('Austin Friars') were the most common orders.
(B) Among the actual friars named in Shakespeare are Friar Penker (R3 3.5.104) and Nicholas Henton (H8 1.2.148), the latter according to *NDS* a mistake in the F1 for the monk Nicholas Hopkins, who is later correctly named in H8, 2.1.22. Friar Peter and Friar Lodovick (the disguised Duke) appear in MM. The 'friar of orders grey' (SHR 4.1.145) is a Franciscan. 'Robin Hood's fat friar', Friar Tuck, is given the traditional 'bare scalp' (TGV 4.1.36). 'As the nun's lip to the Friar's mouth' (AWW 2.2.26–7) is one of the fool Lavatch's perfect fits, 'as the nail to his hole' (AWW 2.2.24–5). Shakespeare's imagined friars, in MM, ROM and ADO, are all well-meaning manipulators of events, some of them more successful than others.
(C) See *Mod.Cath.Ency* (1994), 330; BEV, 903n. *NDS* quotes Hall's chronicle on Friar Penker in R3 (3: 269–70) and Holinshed's on Friar Hopkins in H8 (4: 458). Voss (2000), 133–6, relates the history of the Reformation to the character of the Friar in ROM . Thatcher (1996) argues that the Duke in MM acts as an incompetent friar; Rosenheim (1982) argues that the Friar-Duke is Stoic rather than Christian, and must learn to be a more Christian ruler by the end of MM. Box (1988), Parker (1987), 150–3, Brenner (1980), Bryant (1974) and Battenhouse (1969), 120–7, all argue for a negative reading of Friar Lawrence in ROM.

FRIDAY

(A) Good Friday is the Friday before Easter Sunday, the most prominent of the Christian fasting days. Each Friday, however, is a traditional day of religious fasting. Donne urges moderation in this tradition: 'and if wee give our selves as much *mortification* as our body needs, we live a life of *Fridays*, and see no *Sabbath*, we make up our years of *Lents*, and see no other *Easters*, and whereas God meant us *Paradise*, we make all the world a *wildernesse*' (2: 63).
(B) The Bastard in JN disclaims any relationship to his mother's husband Faulconbridge by saying 'Sir Robert might have eat his part in me / Upon Good Friday and ne'er broke his fast' (JN 1.1.234–5). He could not keep his fast unless he ate no meat at all. Poins twits fat Jack Falstaff, 'how agrees the devil and thee about thy soul that thou soldest him [that soul] on Good Friday last, for a cup of Madiera and a cold capon's leg' (1H4 1.2.114–16). When Lucio slanders the disguised Duke to his face about his lack of moral discipline, 'The Duke ... would eat mutton on Fridays' (MM 3.2.181–2), the mutton he speaks of is probably whores.
(C) See also *Certaine Sermons*, 2nd tome, pp. 175–88, for the homilies 'for good Friday, concerning the death and passion of our Saviour Jesus Christ'. See Williams (1997) 'mutton' (212); see also **fast**, **flesh**.

FURIES
(A) Female classical divinities, thought to punish crimes at the urging of the victims.
(B) In R3, Clarence dreams of going to a Christian 'hell', replete with 'foul fiends', but his conveyors, prompted by the ghost of Prince Edward, are 'Furies', urged to 'take him into torment' (R3 1.4.56–8, 62). This interesting mixture of classical and Christian occurs again in AWW, where Parolles says that Bertram 'talk'd of Sathan and of Limbo and of Furies and I know not what' (5.3.260–1) before he bedded (as he thought) Diana.
(C) McGee (1966) relates the witches in MAC to the classical Furies. Battenhouse (1951), 190, discusses the common mixture of pagan and Christian words for hell and the underworld.

GARDEN, GARDENER

(A) Eden was the garden home of Adam and Eve, Adam the chief gardener. Donne, quoting Gen. 2.15, says, '*Adam* in the state of **Innocency** had abundant occasion of continuall rejoycing; but yet even in that joyfull state he was *to labour, to dresse and to keep the Garden*' (10: 219).

(B) Richard's Queen associates the royal garden with the Garden of Eden, the Gardener who works it with **Adam**, and her husband's pending deposition with the **Fall** when she calls the Gardener 'Old Adam's likeness, set to dress this garden', then asks him if he is come 'To make a second fall of **cursed** man' (R2 3.4.73, 76). Jack Cade says that 'Adam was a gardener' (2H6 4.2.134; see also HAM 5.1.29–37). Iago develops his notion of absolute freedom of the will with his metaphor of the will as gardener: 'Our bodies are our gardens, to the which / Our wills are gardeners' (OTH 1.3.320–1).

(C) Berninghausen (1987) relates the garden scene in R2 to the Genesis account of Eden and the Fall. McFeely (1995), 204–11, discusses the cloister as garden in MM. Battenhouse (1969), 380–4, and Hunter (1976), 129–33, both call Iago's garden metaphor and his position on free will Pelagian; Wiggers (1840), 107, illustrates this usage in Pelagius by citing Augustine's *Of the Grace of Christ*, ch. 4; Luther opposes grace to works (in LW 17: 335–6) by positing 'Christ [as] the gardener', citing Isa. 61.3: 'they may be called trees of righteousness, / The planting of the Lord'. See McGrath (2001), 72–4, on the relationship between the Pelagius–Augustine dispute and the issues of the freedom of the will. See also **will**[1].

GEORGE, SAINT

(A) The patron saint of England, St George was a Christian martyr who died *c.* 303 under the persecution of Diocletian. By killing the famous dragon, often associated with evil itself, he was reputed to have saved a maiden and converted a large pagan community to Christianity. In Shakespeare 'George' is invoked most frequently for inspiration and courage, but the name can also serve for casual emphasis; 'George' can also be used to designate membership in the Order of the Garter, the order itself, and/or various objects associated with the insignia of such membership. According to *OED sb.* 2, the garter is 'a ribbon of dark-blue velvet, edged and buckled with gold, and bearing [certain] words embroidered in gold, and is worn below the left knee; garters also form part of the ornament of the collar worn by the Knights'. The order was, according to Froissart, instituted by Edward III about 1344. Feast Day: 23 April.

(B) Petruchio's playful quip to Kate, 'Now, by Saint George, I am too young for you' (SHR 2.1.236), may identify the shrew with the dragon. Henry V, also being playful with his Katherine of France, wrongly assumes that 'between Saint Denis and Saint George' he and she will 'compound' a heroic boy (H5 5.2.206–9). Bedford, English Regent of France, promises 'Bonfires in France forthwith I am to make, / To keep our great Saint George's feast withal' (1H6 1.1.153–4), a tradition unlikely to have endeared him to the still-occupied country. Because Saint George was also the patron saint of the Order of the Garter, Lord Falconbridge can be called a 'Knight of the noble order of Saint George' instead of 'the Garter' (1H6 4.7.68), and Suffolk can say, 'Look on my George' (2H6 4.1.29) when he means some insignia of the order, like the pendant inscribed with the image of St George slaying the dragon (Arden 2H6, 291n; BEV, 561n) or the jewel associated with this insignia (*OED* 3). Richard III also swears 'by my George, my Garter, and my crown' (R3 4.4.366). When Elizabeth responds, 'Thy George profan'd' (R3 4.4.369), she imbues his charm with religious significance. One cannot profane things that are not holy. Berowne's silly reference to 'Saint George's half-cheek in a brooch' (LLL 5.2.616) attests to a tradition of wearing images of the saint as either an ornament or a fastening device. There are also, of course, many stirring invocations of Saint George for courage, among them JN 2.1.288; R2 1.3.84; H5 3.1.34; and 1H6 4.2.55.

(C) On the St George legends, see Farmer (1978), 166–7; Voraigne (1941), 1: 233–5; Baring-Gould (1914), 4:301–10. Baring-Gould (1914), 4:306, in what is apparently a competition among different nationalities to discredit their rival patron saints, says that Calvin declared George a myth (see **Denis, Saint** and **Jaques, Saint**). The English Reformer Becon calls the idea that 'St George will defend us in battle against our enemies' 'superstition and idolatry' (2: 536); Donne agrees (4: 311). Ridley similarly complains that 'if a man place an image in the Church, or hang it about his neck (as all use to do to the image of the cross, and the knights of the order of St George), this is some piece of worship' (1841), 498. See also Florio (1611), 193; NV R3, 350 n. For some early representations of St George in the art of Warwickshire, see Davidson and Alexander (1985), 46–7, 73–4, 157–8.

GHOST[1]

(A) The soul or spirit of a dead person.

(B) The objective reality of ghosts is questioned more than once in Shakespeare, most notably by Lady Macbeth (MAC 3.4.59–60) and Hamlet's mother Gertrude (HAM 3.4.116–18,131–3), both on essentially the same grounds, not Scotland or Denmark but the sanity of the perceiver. However, their common motive may be moral self-deception rather than scepticism about the supernatural. The ghost is most common in revenge plays like HAM and MAC or their counterparts in the histories like JC, R3 and R2. Richard II speaks in this tradition of kings 'haunted by the ghosts they have deposed' (R2 3.2.158). Richard III is visited by the ghosts of eleven of his victims, and each of them bids that he 'despair and die' (R3 5.3.120–200) and his opponent Richmond 'live and flourish' (R3 5.130, 138). 'Ghosts wand'ring here and there' are also mentioned in MND (3.2.381). Bedford prays to the 'ghost' or spirit of the dead King Henry V to protect England: 'Prosper this realm, keep it from civil broils' and 'Combat with adverse planets in the heavens' (1H6 1.1.52–4). That such spirits may be good or evil is clear when Hamlet first calls his father's 'an honest ghost', then wonders if it is not 'a damned ghost that we have seen' (HAM 1.5.138; 3.2.82).

(C) Cranmer helps us understand Hamlet's distrust of the Ghost: 'If dead men should come again from thence unto us, the devil might have brought to us false doctrine; and that very easily. For he might have shewed oftentimes ghosts, and have suborned men that should counterfeit death and burial, and within a while after shew themselves as though they were raised again from death, and through them to persuade the people so beguiled whatsoever him list.' Even if it is not the Devil's guile, 'yet dreams seen of many men in their sleep, as though it were of them that are **departed** hence, have deceived, destroyed, and overthrown many men'. Even 'if many of the dead had returned again to life, that wicked devil would have wrought innumerable deceits, and brought much fraud into the life of men. And for that cause God hath shut up that way, neither doth he suffer any of the dead to come again hither, to tell what is done there' (1846), 2: 43. Cf. Bullinger, 3: 400–1. For more recent discussions of the ambiguity of the ghost in HAM, see Prosser (1971), 97–143; Morris (1985), 17–34; Greenblatt (2001), chs. 4 and 5; Frye (1984), 14–23; Low (1999); and Dean (2002). Thatcher (1993) discusses ghosts who appear in dreams, specifically Antigonus' deceptive dream in WT. Stott (1992) argues that Banquo's ghost in MAC is a true ghost and signifies the eventual return of providential justice to Scotland. See Greenblatt (2001), ch. 4, and Smidt (1996) for more general discussions of ghosts in Shakespeare. Diehl (1997), 145–6, speaks of Shakespeare's subtlety in handling the objective and subjective reality of ghosts. See also West (1939), ch. 9.

GHOST²

The immortal soul; the 'ghost' (*OED sb.* 8.a) or '**spirit**' (*OED sb.* Spirit 2.a) that outlives the body.

'Gave up the ghost' or 'yield the ghost' (3H6 2.3.22; R3 1.4.37) often refers to the moment of death. When Kent says of Edgar's attempt to revive Lear as he is about to die, 'Vex not his ghost. O, let him pass' (LR 5.3.314), he speaks about Lear's just-departing spirit.

GHOSTLY
(A) Spiritual, that is ministering to the **spirit**, spoken often of a **priest** or other **confessor**.
(B) The Friar in ROM is referred to twice as a 'ghostly father' and twice as a 'ghostly confessor' (ROM 2.2.188; 2.3.45; 2.6.21; 3.3.49). There are similar references in MM (4.3.48; 5.1.126) and 3H6 (3.2.107).
(C) See Becon (1848), 1: 102, 46; and Vaux (1590a), *sig.* G6.

GIS
The *OED* calls this 'a mincing pron. of Jesus', used as 'an oath or exclamation'.
'By Gis and by Saint Charity' (HAM 4.5.58) occurs in Ophelia's song about the maid who was tricked by her lover into having intercourse before marriage.

GLASS
(A) The mirror or glass can serve as a spiritual emblem for looking inward.
(B) Hamlet tells his mother as she tries to escape his shriving during the bedroom scene, 'You go not till I set you up a glass / Where you may see the [inmost] part of you' (HAM 3.4.19–20). Richard II, challenged by Northumberland during the deposition scene to admit his 'crimes', or in Richard's words his 'weav'd-up follies', asks for 'a looking-glass', calling it 'the very book indeed / Where all my sins are writ' (R2 4.1.223, 229, 268, 274–5).
(C) Frye (1984), 153–66, discusses this emblem in HAM and in Shakespeare's time. Becon urges that as one sees his own physical deformity 'in some mirror or glass', so 'Semblably', 'the soul of a Christian man' profitably 'looketh in the glass of truth, which is the law of God, and by that means perceiveth his own deformity, misery, and wretchedness' (1: 97). See also **mirror**.

GLUTTONY (GLUTTON)
(A) Excessive desire for or consumption of food or drink (one who indulges that desire); one of the seven deadly sins.
(B) Falstaff's 'Let him be damned, like the glutton' (2H4 1.2.34) refers to Dives, the rich man who in his own excessive plenty refused to aid the beggar Lazarus (Luke 16.19–31).
(C) See (under **temperance**) *ST* II.2.148, where Augustine is quoted as calling gluttony 'one of the lesser sins'. See also *Certaine Sermons*, 2nd tome, pp. 94–101, for the sermons 'against Gluttonie and Drunkennesse'.

GOD
(A) The supreme being.
(B) Shakespeare's works contains 796 refs to the word 'God', 362 more to 'Gods', another 127 to 'God's', and one to 'Gods''. Another 82 contain 'God' as part of a compound word. Some form, then, of the word 'God' appears 1367 times in Shakespeare. For all the insights these references provide, God is one thing in Shakespeare, the supreme being and ruler of the universe.
'God' is often addressed in Shakespeare in habitual but not necessarily

unthinking prayers of petition, like Antipholus's 'Pray God, our cheer / May answer my good will and your good welcome here' (ERR 3.1.19–20); or Margaret's 'God match me with a good dancer' (ADO 2.1.94–5, 107). Quirkier examples of this usage are Falstaff's 'God help the wicked' (1H4 2.4.470) or Edmund's 'Now, gods, stand up for bastards' (LR 1.2.22). The more serious of these expressions may also invoke blessings for others or for oneself, as when Beatrice says, 'Cousins, God give you joy!' (ADO 2.1.301) and 'God give me patience' (ADO 2.3.148). Similar usage, which is abundant in Shakespeare, includes: 'God amend' (LLL 4.3.71), 'God rest his soul' (MV 2.2.71–2), 'God shield us' (MND 3.1.30), 'God bless' (LLL 2.1.77) and 'God have mercy' (TN 3.4.166). Benedick's 'God forbid it should be so' (ADO 1.1.217) belongs to another large set of 'please don't' prayers. Hero's 'God defend the lute should be like the case' (ADO 2.1.95) is another good example.

Other brief prayers express praise rather than petition, again both casually and seriously. Verges says, 'I thank God I am as honest as any man living', and Beatrice tells Benedick, 'I thank God and my cold blood I am of your humor' for loving none (ADO 3.5.13–14; 1.1.130). Kate, with a mixture of irony and joy, responds to Petruchio, 'Then God be blessed, it is the blessed sun' (SHR 4.5.18).

Many of these casual prayers and comments reveal commonly understood and frequently invoked characteristics of God, especially in an age so indoctrinated with the theology of **grace** (and depravity). God has been asked (or thanked) in these expressions already cited for **mercy**, honesty, protection, **rest, amendment** of life, joy, **patience**, help and defence, as well as finding a good dance partner. Prayers for 'the grace of God' (R2 1.3.22), 'the love o' God' (TN 2.3.85), God's blessing (ROM 3.5.169) and God's 'tuition' [protection] (ADO 1.1.281) are also common, as is 'God save the king' (as in MAC 1.2.47).

Because 'God' is also associated in the plays and in Christian theology with words like 'displeas'd', '**revenge**' (as in R3 2.1.139; 2.2.89), and '**angry**' (MAC 4.3.17), we find, repeatedly, phrases and prayers like 'God shall **pardon**' (R2 5.3.131), 'God **forgive**' (JN 2.1.283), 'O God defend my soul from such deep sin' (R2 1.1.87), and 'God forgive the sins of all those souls' (JN 2.1.283). As a result of this divine anger a phrase like 'God buy you' (OTH 3.3.375) is both a general blessing, a 'God b' wi' you' (as emended in PEL) and also a reference, however casual, to Christ's redemptive death.

Frequently repeated phrases like 'God he knows' (as in ERR 5.1.229) or 'God knows' (as in LLL 5.2.290) refer more or less casually to matters of human perplexity and godly knowledge. The casual curse 'God damn me' (ERR 4.3.53) occurs only once. More common are the completely neutral if technically blasphemous verbal tics like Hamlet's 'O God, I could be bounded in a nutshell' (HAM 2.2.254), or Cassio's drunken ' 'fore God' (OTH 2.3.75). Validating phrases like 'in God's name' or 'for God's sake' are especially common in the English histories (as in R2 1.3.11; 2.2.76; 4.1.113; 5.3.74; 1H4 2.4.393; 4.3.29), and they cross class lines.

Other references form part of a formal oath like 'so help you truth and God' (R2 1.3.183); a series of corresponding figures of authority like 'a traitor to his

God, his king and him' (R2.1.3.108); or a formal pledge like 'by the grace of God and this mine arm' (R2.1.3.22). Both this last and Henry V's 'Praised be God, and not our strength, for it' (H5 4.7.87) also refer to the **grace–merit** issue.

There is considerable disagreement, even within single plays and single characters, about God's providential control. Dogberry's 'Well, God's a good man' (ADO 3.5.36) is a wonderful comic reference to this ingrained impulse towards anthropomorphism and clarity. In the same play in which Richmond assumes that 'God and our good cause fight upon our side', Queen Elizabeth wonders about the murder of her two boys, 'Wilt thou, O God, fly from such gentle lambs / And throw them in the entrails of the wolf?' (R3 5.3.240; 4.4.22–3). Indeed, Dorset warns the Duchess of York earlier in the play that she complains too much about God's sendings: 'God is much displeas'd / That you take with unthankfulness his doing' (R3 2.2.89–90). After his eyes have been plucked out, Gloucester sees in his cruel fate at the hands of Cornwall and Regan the cruelty of the gods: 'As flies to wanton boys are we to th' gods, / They kill us for their sport' (LR 4.1.36–7). Such 'sad times' in both the Christian and the pre-Christian plays require characters to 'Speak what we feel, not what we ought to say' (LR 4.2.78–82; 5.3.324–5).

References to God the creator include the thoughtful but also sarcastic 'He's a god or a painter, for he makes faces' (LLL 5.2.643); Portia's caustic 'God made him, and therefore let him pass for a man' (MV 1.2.56–7); and Beatrice's vow that she will not love 'till God make men of some other mettle than earth' (ADO 2.1.59–60).

Even more selectively, references to classical gods include: Mars 'the god of war' (JN 5.1.54), 'the fire-rob'd god, / Golden Apollo' (WT 4.4.29), Cupid, 'imperial Love, that god most high' (AWW 2.3.75), Hymen, 'god of every town' (AYL 5.4.146), and 'the god Priapus', whom the virtuous Marina is 'able to freeze' (PER 4.6.3–4). Vaguer references include Ferdinand's 'some god o' th' island' (TMP 1.2.390), which probably implies in its neutrality nothing negative about the young speaker, and Morocco's 'Some god direct my judgment!' (MV 2.7.13), which might mark him as even more of an alien in the very Christian worlds of Venice and Belmont.

(C) Jorgensen (1975) shows how the perceived role of God in military victory shifts from the first tetralogy to the second. Keefer (1987) argues that Calvin's God is present throughout LR. Elton (1966), 171–263, argues instead a consistent pre-Christian awareness of the **Gods** in LR. Reed (1984) looks at God's retribution for crimes in the plays. See also Morris (1972).

GOD-A-MERCY

A colloquial variant of 'God have mercy'.

Usually this is just a casual expression, or sometimes a friendly greeting, though the Bastard in JN refers to it sarcastically as a way 'new-made honor' tries to speak 'respective and sociable' and thereby fit in (JN 1.1.185–8). Hamlet uses the phrase as a mocking greeting for Polonius, but also perhaps as an indication that he is not quite himself (HAM 2.2.171–2).

GODDAUGHTER
(A) A girl whom a godfather or a godmother has sponsored in baptism by taking liturgical vows.
(B) When Justice Shallow asks Justice Silence, 'How doth . . . your fairest daughter and mine, my goddaughter Ellen?' (2H4 3.2.5–7), the personal nature of his words implies a close relationship to Silence, and a serious sense of commitment to the child.
(C) For these vows, see **godfather** and *BCP*, 273.

GODDED
Cared for like a god.
Coriolanus speaks of an 'old man' who 'loved me above the measure of a father, / Nay, godded me' (COR 5.3.11).

GODDESS
Female god or deity; usually a romantic compliment in Shakespeare, 'goddess' can also refer literally to classical goddesses.
Miranda (TMP 1.2.422; 5.1.187), Maria (LLL 4.3.63), Rosaline (LLL 5.2.36), Helen (MND 3.2.137, 226), Emilia (TNK 2.2.134), the beloved in SON 111 (2), and, chillingly, the evil Tamora (TIT 2.1.22) are all called 'goddess' in Shakespeare, often with some delightful self-consciousness of the hyperbole. Fortune (AWW 1.3.111; H5 3.6.28; COR 1.5.20), Nature (MM 1.1.36–8; WT 2.3.104; LR 1.2.1), Isis (ANT 3.6.17), Venus (TNK 5.1.74) and Diana (AWW 4.2.2) are also called 'goddess', though in the last case Diana is also the name of the maid whom Berowne is complimenting. Diana is also called 'Celestial Dian, goddess argentine' (PER 5.1.250) in Pericles' reference to her silvery glow.

GODFATHER
(A) The man who sponsors a child in **baptism**. Traditionally he names the child and answers for it during the baptismal ritual such questions as 'Dost thou forsake the devil and all his works?', 'Dost thou believe in the Holy Ghost, the holy catholic Church, the communion of saints, the remission of sins, the resurrection of the flesh, and everlasting life after death?', and 'Wilt thou be baptised in this faith?'
(B) Shakespeare refers more than once to the fact that such a person is asked to name the child during the service. When Clarence complains that he has been imprisoned merely 'Because my name is George', Richard comes back with 'Alack, my lord, that fault is none of yours; / He should for that commit your godfathers' (R3 1.1.46–8). Similarly Berowne, arguing against too much study, complains about 'These earthly godfathers of heaven's lights', the astronomers, 'That give a name to every fixed star', adding of them, 'Too much to know is to know nought but fame; / And every godfather can give a name' (LLL 1.1.88–9, 92–3). Of the vows, we hear Henry VIII ask Cranmer to be Elizabeth's godfather by saying, somewhat tongue-in-cheek, 'You must be godfather, and answer for her' (H8 5.2.197, 212–13).
(C) See *BCP*, 273–4; Vaux (1590a), *sig.* G2.

GODHEAD
(A) The essential being, nature or condition of God.
(B) Jupiter speaks of his own 'godhead' uplifting the fortunes of Cymbeline's son (CYM 5.4.103); Rosaline in LLL refers playfully to Cupid's godhead waxing in the long love letter from the King (LLL 5.2.10–11). In AYL a metaphoric use of the word expresses Phebe's romantic worship of the disguised Rosalind (AYL 4.3.44–5).
(C) See also Donne, 4: 100–1; Bullinger, 3: 11.

GOD-I-GOD-EN
PEL glosses this as the Nurse's colloquial version of 'for God's sake' (ROM 3.5.172). BEV (1009n) emends to the phrase 'God-i'good-e'en', i.e. 'God give you good evening'.

GODLY[1], GODLIKE, GODDESS-LIKE
Like a god. Andrewes calls 'Solomon, not only wise, but godly wise, with the "wisdom that is from above" ' (4: 299).
Included in the list of the divine traits attributed in Shakespeare to humans are 'Godlike amity' (MV 3.4.3), 'godlike reason' (HAM 4.4.38), 'godly shame' (TRO 2.2.32), 'godly jealousy' (TRO 4.4.80), 'godlike honors' (TNK 1.1.230), and 'godlike power' (TNK 5.1.89). In addition, Marina is called 'godlike perfit' (PER 5.1.206), and 'Things hid and barr'd from common sense' are called 'study's godlike recompense' (LLL 1.1.57–8). 'Goddess-like' (WT 4.4.10; CYM 3.2.8; PER 5. Cho. 4) is usually a romantic compliment.

GODLY[2]
Religious, righteous. Donne distinguishes between 'the afflictions of the godly', and 'the afflictions of the wicked' (2: 300); elsewhere he uses 'the righteous Man, the godly man' (6: 243) as synonyms.
Justice Slender once promises to amend his drunken life, 'I'll ne'er be drunk whilst I live again, but in honest, civil, godly company. . . . If I be drunk, I'll be drunk with those that have the fear of God, and not with drunken knaves' (WIV 1.1.181–4).

GODLINESS[1]
The quality of being godlike.
Iago protests to Othello that he lacked godlike forbearance and therefore almost throttled Roderigo for slandering his master: 'That with the little godliness I have / I did full hard forbear him' (OTH 1.2.9–10).

GODLINESS[2]
Piety.
When Maria says of Malvolio 'He will not hear of godliness' and 'Get him to say his prayers, good Sir Toby, get him to pray' (TN 3.4.118–21), she refers to his lack of piety.

GODS

(A) Not surprisingly, plural references to the gods occur almost exclusively in classical plays like WT, TRO, COR, TIT, TIM, JC, LR, ANT, CYM, PER and TNK.
(B) Predominant again are the thoughtful as well as the barely considered prayers of petition and praise and the even more casual and sometimes profane words of divine address. LR is probably richest in the range of such references. Kent challenges Lear early in the play, 'Thou swear'st thy gods in vain', then blesses the banished Cordelia, 'The gods to their dear shelter take thee, maid'; Edmund prays more profanely, 'Now, gods, stand up for bastards!' (LR 1.1.161, 182; 1.2.22). We hear as well of 'the revengive gods', 'the kind gods', 'the mighty gods' and 'the clearest gods' (LR 2.1.45; 3.7.35; 4.6.34, 73), all this in a play in which the nature and even the existence of the gods are anything but clear.
(C) Williams (1986) discusses the gods as Roman deities. For Lear's attitudes towards the gods, see Elton (1966), 171–263; Whitehead (1992) argues that LR moves towards a realization that there are no benevolent gods who guide humanity. McCoy (2003), 53, briefly discusses the cruelty of the gods in LR.

GOD'S BODY

Swearing by 'God's body' (1H4 2.1.26) is swearing by the body of Christ, either on the cross or in the **mass**. In fact, the profane Carrier who says this has just earlier sworn 'By the mass' (1H4 2.1.16).

GOD'S MOTHER

Mary, mother of Christ.

Three of the four references are merely oaths, but Joan of Arc's testimony that 'God's Mother deigned to appear to me / ... And in a vision full of majesty' (1H6 1.2.78–9) is part of a sincere attempt to authenticate her calling. Gloucester, on the other hand, profanes Mary's name to belittle Cardinal Beauford: 'Now, by God's Mother, priest, I'll shave your crown for this' (2H6 2.1.50). The notoriously lustful King Edward's swearing 'by God's Mother' is even more grotesque, punctuating as it does his lack of respect for the Lady Grey he is courting as well as all of the women he has already enjoyed (3H6 3.2.102–5). Finally Richard III swears with false **piety** and false **repentance**, 'By God's holy Mother' for the wrongs that he has done to Queen Margaret (R3 1.3.305–7).

GODSON

The male child sponsored in baptism.

In asking Gloucester of Edgar, 'What, did my father's godson seek thy life?' Regan seeks to reinforce her case, and Goneril's, that all of Lear's 'consort' of associates were 'riotous' (LR 2.1.91–5). On the question of such Christian anachronisms in LR, see also **curse**[3] and **redeem**.

GOGS-WOUNS

A dialectical variant of the profane oath, 'God's wounds', or **''zounds'**.

Petruchio's outrageous blasphemy during the wedding includes his shouting 'Ay, by gogs-wouns' so loudly that the 'priest let fall his **book**' in amazement and fear (SHR 3.2.160–1).

GOLGOTHA

Calvary, the hill outside **Jerusalem**, called the 'place of a skull', where Jesus was crucified (see Mark 15.22; John 19.17).

The Bishop of Carlisle, threatening disasters for England if King Richard II is deposed, prophesies such 'Disorder, horror, fear, and mutiny' that England will be 'call'd / The field of Golgotha and dead men's skulls' (R2 4.1.142–4). Similarly, the Captain who says that the battle that preserved Duncan's kingship 'Would memorise another Golgotha' speaks of its bloodiness rather than its sacrilege (MAC 1.2.40).

GOLIAH

Goliath, the giant whom David slew. In 1 Samuel 17.7, we read in the *Geneva Bible* that 'the shaft of [Goliath's] spear was like a weavers beam' (*fol.* 128ᵛ).

Falstaff boasts to Ford of a courage he obviously lacks when he says, 'I fear not Goliah with a weaver's beam' (WIV 5.1.20–2). When Alanson wants to heroicize the English combatants, he calls them 'none but **Samsons** and Goliases' (1H6 1.2.33).

GOOD FRIDAY

See **Friday**.

GOSPELL'D

Instructed according to Gospel teachings, New Testament principles.

Macbeth challenges the murderers 'Are you so gospell'd / To pray for this good man and for his issue / Whose heavy hand hath bow'd you to the grave, / And beggar'd yours for ever?' (MAC 3.1.87–90). The Gospel precept to which he attributes their mildness is probably Christ's injunction, 'Love your enemies, . . . and pray for them which despitefully use you, and persecute you' (Matt. 5.44).

GOSPELS

The first four books of the New Testament are called Gospels because they contain the 'gospel truth', the good news of Christ the Redeemer. The rest of the New Testament is largely composed of epistles, letters to the Christian community, though Acts is history and Revelation vision.

When Feste explains why he took so long to deliver Malvolio's letters of complaint – 'as a madman's epistles are no gospels, it skills not much when they are deliver'd' (TN 5.1.287–8) – he refers to their unimportance and their untruthfulness.

GOSSIP *sb.* & *v.*

As a noun, this refers to a godparent, often a female godparent. Becon speaks of 'Christian gossips, that is to say, those men and women that have been godfathers and godmothers together of one child at baptism' (3: 532). As a verb, it can refer to being a godparent, but more often describes the idle chattering that accompanies christenings. 'Gossips' can therefore also be busybodies, and is usually a misogynistic usage. It can also be a title, like 'Master'.

Richard of Gloucester calls Lady Grey and Mistress Shore 'mighty gossips in our monarchy' (R3 1.1.83) for what he considers their undeserved influence on his brother King Edward IV. The fact that he just 'dubb'd them gentlewomen' (R3 1.1.82), makes him ironically their godfather too. Of literal godparents, Paulina tries unsuccessfully to have 'needful conference' with Leontes 'About some gossips' for the newborn Perdita (WT 2.3.40). Helena, so in love with Bertram that she comes up with many names for him, concludes that she could add 'a world / Of pretty, fond, adoptious christendoms / That blinking Cupid gossips' (AWW 1.1.173–5). In other words, Cupid inspires her nicknames.

There are several references in Shakespeare to the gossips' feast that follows the christening, many of them misogynistic. Puck says 'sometimes lurk I in a gossip's bowl' and he delights in spilling the drink down her chin (MND 2.1.47). Capulet, with similar condescension towards what he considers unwarranted self-importance, says to the Nurse who is defending Juliet, 'Peace, you mumbling fool! / Utter your gravity o'er a gossip's bowl, / For here we need it not' (ROM 3.5.173–5). Because the Abbess compares their concluding festivity to 'a gossips' feast' (ERR 5.1.406), two puns follow, the Duke's 'With all my heart I'll gossip at this feast' (ERR 5.1.408) and Dromio's 'Will you walk in to see their gossiping?' (ERR 5.1.420). In both the verb and the gerund 'prattle' and 'sponsor' are punningly mixed. Benedick insults Claudio's inappropriate wit-play and frivolity after the slander of Hero by referring to 'your gossip-like humor' (ADO 5.1.186).

As a title, Mrs Ford calls out, 'What ho, gossip Ford!' to her female friend (WIV 4.2.9), and Mistress Quickly says to Falstaff about her unaccustomed respectability, and her consequent desire that Falstaff marry her, 'Did not goodwife Keech, the butcher's wife, come in then and call me gossip Quickly?' (2H4 2.1.93–5).

GOWN

(A) The alb or black liturgical vestment worn by ministers of many different denominations. This dress evolved from Greek and Roman garments, and has changed shape several times in the twenty Christian centuries. In northern Europe these were often fur-lined against the chill, requiring a very loose-fitting **surplice**, the white over-garment. Some Reformed preachers, starting with Andreas Karlstadt in Wittenberg in 1521, wore their academic gown rather than clerical garb in celebrating the Eucharist, and the academic gown remained standard Eucharistic dress in some Reformed congregations until the last quarter of the twentieth century. This is sometimes called the 'preaching' or 'Geneva' gown. The alb has now become once again more common.

(B) When the Clown Lavatch says of spiritual pride, 'Though honesty be no puritan, yet it will do no hurt; it will wear the surplice of **humility** over the black gown of a big heart' (AWW 1.3.94–5), he conceivably refers to the new academic dress code of some Reformed ministers. He more clearly criticises spiritual pride and spiritual hypocrisy among the clergy. Feste also associates hypocrisy and religious gowns when he poses as Sir Topas the Curate to gull and edify Malvolio. Maria instructs him to 'put on this gown and this beard, make him believe thou art Sir Topas the curate'. He responds, 'I will dissemble myself in't, and I would I were the first that ever dissembled in such a gown' (TN 4.2.1–6).

(C) See 'Vestments' in Bradshaw (2002); Nicolson (2003), 43. See also **apparel**, **almsman**.

GRACE[1]

(A) The indwelling presence and influence of God on a person's spiritual and moral life. Andrewes gives the range of such influence in one of a series of Whitsunday sermons 'Of the Sending of the Holy Ghost'. It includes: '1. The grace reproving and checking them within, when they are ready to go astray.' 2. The grace ' "guiding them", and giving them a good pass "into all truth". 3. The grace, teaching them what they knew not, and calling to their minds that they did know and have forgot.' 4. 'The grace, quickening them and stirring them up, when they grow dull, and even becalmed. 5. The grace, inspiring and inditing their requests, when they know not what or how to pray. 6. The Spirit breathing, and "shedding abroad His love in their hearts" '. 7. 'The spirit "sealing" them an assurance of their estates to come' (3: 207).

(B) Richard III is branded a reprobate when Queen Elizabeth responds to his moral and theological rationalization, 'All unavoided is the doom of destiny', with 'True, when avoided grace makes destiny'. She more clearly adds God's decree of reprobation to Richard's free choice of evil, however, with 'My babes were destined to fairer death, / If grace had blessed thee with a fairer life' (R3 4.4.219–21). The Friar in ROM similarly tells Romeo 'Two such opposed kings encamp them still / In man as well as herbs, grace and rude will' (ROM 2.3.27–8). The former is the divinely implanted capacity for virtue, the latter the tendency to want and to choose the wrong thing despite a knowledge of what is right. When York criticises Bolingbroke for returning to England against his holy allegiance to King Richard II: 'Grace me no grace, nor uncle me no uncle. / I am no traitor's uncle, and that word "grace" / In an ungracious mouth is but profane' (R2 2.3.85–7), it is clear that the holiness is religious as well as political.

In his troubling moral idealism, Hamlet refers to 'virtues' 'as pure as grace', and he calls for both material and spiritual protection when he says upon seeing his father's Ghost, 'Angels and ministers of grace defend us' (HAM 1.4.33, 39). Hamlet speaks to Horatio of 'grace and mercy' helping him keep up his confidence (HAM 1.5.180), and says when he urges his mother to be repentant, 'For love of grace / Lay not that flattering unction to your soul, / That not your trespass but my madness speaks' (HAM 3.4.144–6). 'Grace' here refers both to her respect for the moral capacities she has been supernaturally given, **grace**[1], and '**unction**' stresses the need for the recipient of extreme unction, or any of the sacraments of contrition, to be 'truly sorry and to earnestly repent' their own sins if she is to receive their liturgical benefits, **grace**[2]. Finally, to stress his resolution to achieve absolute revenge without regard for his own immortal soul, Laertes says, 'Conscience and grace, to the profoundest pit! / I dare damnation' (HAM 4.5.133–4).

(C) The Andrewes sermon was 'preached before the King's Majesty at Whitehall' Whitsunday, 23 May 1613. The Catholic Persons (1582), 4, and the Protestant Tyndale (1: 273) share Andrewes's sense of grace. Andrewes, 3: 207; and Fulke (1843), 1: 376–7, comment on the complex interrelationship of grace and good works in the individual's life. Baker (1985) stresses the central position of grace in English Protestant discourse; Davies (1970), 23, calls the related faith–works issue 'the central theological tenet of the Reformation'. See also 'Predestination' (3: 332–8), and 'Grace' (2: 184–9), *OxfordEncyRef*. Rom. 7.19 is a classic Pauline statement on human sinfulness and the need for grace: 'For the good that I would I do not: but the evil that I would not, that I do.' On Richard III's 'avoided grace' and St Paul, see Shaheen (1999), 513–14. McAlindon (1995) sets 1 and 2 H4 in the context of the Pilgrimage of Grace and argues that the idea of grace – secular and religious – is deeply imbedded in the plays. Hamlin (1995), 117 and 184–5, discusses the use of the word in TMP. Beauregard (1999) argues that AWW advocates the Roman Catholic theology that places merit over grace as a means of salvation. Tiffany (2000) suggests that the late romances would be tragedies were it not that the intercession of divine grace inspires repentance in the plays' flawed heroes.

GRACE[2]

(A) The unmerited favour and love of God, as it is spiritually transmitted through the sacraments. The Recusant Persons says 'a **Sacrament**, according to the common definition asscribed to S. *Augustine, is a visible signe of an invisible grace*, as in baptisme, the externall washinge by water, is the signe of the internall washing of the soule by grace: So heere also in this Sacrament of the Eucharist, the externall & visible signe are the consecrated formes of bread and wyne, as they conteyne the body of Christ; the internall or invisible grace signified, is the inward nourishinge and feedinge of our soule' (1604b), 186–7. The Protestant Andrewes similarly calls sacraments 'the conduit-pipes of His grace, and seals of His truth unto us' (1: 100).

(B) Shakespeare almost insists that his audience engage the essentially Pauline conflict of grace and rude will in MAC by letting several of these meanings of grace, including several references to **grace**[2], interact and overlap in the play. The protagonist, whose will overwhelms the considerable **grace**[1] which he manifested in the initial moral clarity of his early soliloquies (see, for example, 1.7.1–31 or 1.3.120–47), presumably laments of both himself and the 'gracious' king he has murdered that 'Renown and grace is dead' (MAC 3.1.65; 2.3.94). The king he has killed manifested God's indwelling grace to such an extent that Macduff can call his murder 'most sacrilegious' (MAC 2.3.67). But Macbeth also refers here to other, more personal losses of grace. In deciding to murder Duncan, he has turned his back on **grace**[1], his own God-given sense of right and wrong ('False face must hide what the false heart doth know' – MAC 1.7.82). In the immediate aftermath of the murder he is surprised by his divorce from **grace**[2], liturgically given grace. This is implicit in associated laments like 'I could not say "Amen," / When they did say "God bless us!" ', 'our poison'd chalice', and 'The wine of life is drawn, and the mere lees / Is left this vault to brag of' (MAC 2.2.26–7; 1.7.11; 2.3.95–6). More explicitly, Macbeth later says, 'For them the gracious Duncan have I murther'd, / Put rancors in the vessel of my peace / Only for them, and mine eternal jewel / Given to the common enemy of man, / To make them king – the seeds of Banquo kings' (MAC 3.1.65–9). For other interesting examples of this intertwined usage of several meanings of grace, see the paragraph on HAM at the end of **grace**[1], and subsequent paragraphs on MAC under **grace**[3] and on MM at **grace**[5].

(C) On 'What Is a Sacrament', see Augustine, *City of God*, X:5. See also *ST* II.1.109–13; Vaux (1590a), *sig.* F7[v]; Bullinger, 3: 11; Donne, 5: 350. Young (1992b) in 'Ritual as an Instrument of Grace', examines parental blessings as ritual communications of grace. Sexton (1994) discusses grace in AWW in relation to the sacrament of baptism.

GRACE[3]

The manifestations of God's favour in the more material blessings of this life. Once again, this usage sometimes overlaps with the first two.

Of one of Macbeth's opponents, the pious Edward the Confessor, it is said 'He hath a heavenly gift of prophecy, / And sundry blessings hang about his throne / That speak him full of grace' (MAC 4.3.157–9). He and his kingdom are marked by the blessings **grace**[1] and **grace**[3]. Macbeth is also to be succeeded by Duncan's son Malcolm, who promises in his last speech fairly to reward and punish 'and what needful else / That calls upon us, by the grace of grace' (MAC 5.9.37–8). The gift and the giver are both named 'grace' in these pious and hopeful last words. The phrase 'by God's grace' or 'by the grace of God' is occasionally used in Shakespeare's histories to legitimise political and personal causes, as when Mowbray and Bolingbroke, sworn enemies, both invoke God's favour in their upcoming duel (R2 1.3.22, 37), or when both the English Harry and the French Katherine invoke 'God's grace' and 'la grace de Dieu' (H5 1.2.262; 3.4.40–1) before two very different encounters. Hastings' lament after Richard turns on him in R3 interestingly contrasts the material and the spiritual meanings of 'grace', **grace**[3] versus **grace**[1&2]: 'O momentary grace of mortal men, / Which we more hunt for than the grace of God' (R3 3.4.96–7).

GRACE[4]

(A) The blessing of meals. The Recusant Brinkley translates Loarte, 'Thus having spent the day til *Dinner* time, see when thou goest thereto, that being nowe at *Table*, either thou, or some other say **Grace** before thou eate, or at least-wise say a

Pater noster and Ave Mary' (1596–97), 17. The Reformer Cranmer prescribes 'That all graces to be said at dinner and supper shall be always said in the English tongue' (1846), 2: 504.

(B) For an example of this usage, see **grace**[5].

(C) Nuttall (1989), 115–24, discusses grace before meals in TIM.

GRACE[5]

Part of a verbal blessing, often in farewell.

MM is a play like HAM and MAC fraught with the complexity of 'grace' as a word and an issue. 'Grace go with you, benedicite' (MM 2.3.39), is merely the disguised Duke's uttered blessing (**grace**[5]) of the pregnant Juliet. However, when the Duke, already taken with Isabella, calls 'grace' just two scenes later 'the soul of your complexion' (MM 3.1.183), he refers both to the gift of her physical beauty (**grace**[3]) and her divinely inspired virtue (**grace**[1]). The profane Lucio challenges a Gentleman's piety by saying 'I think thou never wast where grace was said.' Then he moves quickly from this 'grace' as prayers before meals (**grace**[4]) to 'grace' as a prominent theological issue when he adds 'Grace is grace, despite of all controversy' (**grace**[1&2]). Finally he condemns the gentlemen as a reprobate who not only shows no marks of God's unmerited favour and love but seems to have resisted their spiritual influence in his own life: 'thou thyself art a wicked villain, despite of all grace' (**grace**[1]) (MM 1.2.18–26). Isabella's stridently self-righteous response to her brother's weakness in 3.1 is hardly **gracious** in either the secular or the religious sense of the word. And when the Duke later promises Isabella 'Grace of the Duke, revenges to your heart, / And 'general honor' if she will let him, godlike, direct her 'wisdom / In that good path that I would wish it go' (MM 4.3.132–6), the 'Grace' and the 'general honor' which the Duke promises may be both **grace**[3] and **grace**[1], worldly prominence if she marries him and a heightened capacity to forgive both Angelo and her brother if she follows his gracious lead during the trial. Of course, the Duke's proposal is also full of dangers and ambiguities, not the least his wish that she leave her vocation and grace him with marriage. Is the Duke godlike here in wisdom and direction, or merely in desire? His grace, and hers, have justifiably been the subject of considerable disagreement.

Angelo's lament just after this veiled promise of a marriage proposal is almost as complex: 'Alack, when once our grace we have forgot, / Nothing goes right – we would, and we would not' (MM 4.4.33–4). He once assumed his divinely inspired virtue (**grace**[1]), even his election, thus the still-pregnant name 'Angelo'. His contrite words to the godlike Duke once his sinfulness has been discovered, 'When I perceive your grace, like pow'r divine, / Hath look'd upon my passes' (MM 5.1.369–70), is accompanied only by his request for the grace of death, the *coup-de-gras* which would also be the measure-for-measure dispensation of the Old Testament. Angelo will receive from this gracious Duke and this gracious Isabella much more than that, however: a New Testament forgiveness for his trespasses, and from the Mariana whom he has wronged, love. Their image of grace, an undeserved, almost inconceivable love and forgiveness, caps off the play's rich interest in what 'measure for measure' can mean in a world so fully informed by this rich religious word.

GRACIOUS[1]

When spoken of God in Shakespeare's usage, the word can imply either God's protection or his capacity of dispensing both rewards and punishments appropriately.

Richmond asks God both to 'Look on my forces with a gracious eye' and to 'Abate the edge of traitors, gracious lord.' He glosses both requests when he asserts that 'God and our good cause fight upon our side' (R3 5.3.109; 5.5.35; 5.3.240).

GRACIOUS[2]

When spoken of a person, full of piety, supernaturally endowed powers, and blessings.

Most of the uses of 'gracious' in the histories are merely polite forms of human address, but when Duncan is called 'gracious' three times in MAC (3.1.65; 3.6.3, 10) and Edward twice (MAC 4.3.49, 189), personal piety as well as good kingship are the point. Of Edward the Confessor it is explicitly said that he 'solicits heaven' with 'holy prayers' and has 'a heavenly gift of prophecy' (MAC 4.3.141–56). Indeed, 'sundry blessings hang about his throne / That speak him full of grace' (MAC 4.3.157–9). See **grace**[1&3].

HABIT

Garb characteristic of a particular rank, profession, religious order. Donne puns on this meaning when he says, 'When a man curses out of *Levity*, and makes a loose habit of that sinne, God shall so gird it to him, as he shall never devest it' (7: 367).

When Duke Vincentio asks Friar Thomas to 'supply me with the habit', what he needs is the clothing appropriate to 'a brother of your order' (MM 1.3.44–6; cf. MM 3.1.177–8). Since the novice Isabella is wearing her own religious habit when the Duke proposes marriage to her at the play's end, his references to his unfrocking and hers is potentially unsettling:

> Come hither, Isabel,
> Your friar is now your prince. As I was then
> Advertising and holy to your business,
> Not changing heart with habit, I am still
> Attorneyed at your service.
>
> (MM 5.1.381–5)

She never responds, verbally at least, to his proposal.

HAG

(A) Not merely an ugly old woman, but sometimes a **witch**, a **fiend**, an enchantress or a **demon**; once in the plural a reference to the **Furies**.

(B) Joan of Arc is called by the Englishman York, for her excellence at cursing, 'hag of all despite' and 'Fell banning hag, enchantress' (1H6 3.2.52; 5.3.42). Richard of Gloucester also calls Margaret a 'hateful with'red hag' for her 'charm' or curses against all of her assembled enemies (R3 1.3.214). Macbeth calls the witches 'secret, black and midnight hags' and 'filthy hags' (MAC 4.1.48,

115), and Prospero calls 'This damned witch Sycorax' 'This blue-ey'd hag' (TMP 1.2.263, 269; cf. 1.2.258). 'You witch, you hag' also seem synonymous in WIV (4.2.179). When the Lieutenant curses Suffolk, 'And wedded be thou to the hags of hell' (2H6 4.1.79), he combines Christian and classical reference.

(C) Kiessling (1977) argues that the references in WT to 'hag' evoke the image of the 'hag-incubus'.

HAGAR

(A) Sarah's Egyptian maid, who bore Ishmael by Sarah's 87-year-old husband, Abraham. Ishmael is therefore a non-Jew, and by God's will also an outsider. However, in Gen. 21.13 and 18, God promises Abraham that he will 'make a nation of the son of the bondwoman, because he is your seed'. Though this 'great nation' is not Christian but 'Ishmaelite' or Northern Arabian, Moham-medan Arabs, popular tradition came to associate Ishmael with all the Gentiles, including the Christians.

(B) Shylock thus means 'outsider' when he calls the Christian Lancelot Gobbo 'that fool of Hagar's offspring' (MV 2.5.44).

(C) See Noble (1935), 267; see also Gen. 6.1–16 and 21.9. See 'Ishmael' in Jackson (1910) and Jeffrey (1992). See also Vaughan's 'Providence', 'Begging' (2), and 'The Timber' (1965).

HAIL
See **All-hail**.

HALIDOM (HOLIDAM, HOLIDAME)

Holiness. All five references constitute a casual swearing.

Thus Falstaff's companion the Hostess says 'By my halidom, I was fast asleep' (TGV 4.2.135; cf. SHR 5.2.99); the Nurse says of the child Juliet, 'by my holidam / The pretty wretch left crying and said "ay" ' (ROM 1.3.43–4). Henry VIII, only a little more seriously, asks the accused Cranmer whom he will protect and trust, 'Now, by my holidame / What manner of man are you?' (H8 5.1.116–17).

HALLOWED

(A) Formally blessed. Andrewes in a sermon on 'Hallowed be Thy Name', says that those persons, places and things which are to be hallowed are 'holy' and 'consecrated' things, 'priests, . . . the sanctuary . . . the Sabbath . . . the word of God, . . . the element consecrated in the Sacrament' (5: 384). The Catholic prac-tice of blessing and selling religious **relics** for the remission of sin had become controversial certainly by Chaucer's time and was still controversial enough dur-ing the Reformation for Luther to make it a prominent part of his 95 theses about indulgences. Indeed, the Castle Church in Wittenberg where he posted his document was one of the great repositories of relics in Germany.

(B) Mrs Page says of the object with which Falstaff was beaten, 'I'll have the cudgel hallow'd and hung o'er the altar; it hath done meritorious service' (WIV 4.2.204–5), and Autolycus says of his wares, 'They throng who should buy first, as if my trinkets had been hallow'd and brought a benediction to the buyer' (WT 4.4.600–2). Obviously both cases are tongue-in-cheek, but they also suggest religious tensions. Pericles uses the word to lament that his dead queen must receive only a sea burial: 'nor have I time / To give thee hallow'd to thy grave, but straight / Must cast thee . . . in the ooze' (PER 3.1.58–60). Marcellus refers to the Christmas season as the 'hallowed' time 'Wherein our Saviour's birth is celebrated' (HAM 1.1.159, 164).

(C) See also Hooker on the permissible 'hallowing' of new churches (V.12.1).

HALLOWMAS

(A) The feast of All Hallows or All Saints', 1 November.

(B) Pompey's two references to Hallowmas are corrected by Froth to 'All-hallond eve' (MM 2.1.125–6) as if such calendrical precision proves the truthfulness of their testimony. Simple recalls that a Book of Riddles was lent 'to Alice Shortcake upon All-hallowmass last, a fortnight afore Michaelmas' (WIV 1.1.203–5); since Michaelmas is 29 September, he is a month and a half off. When Richard II laments that his queen, who 'came adorned hither like sweet May', was 'sent back like Hollowmas or short'st of day' (R2 5.1.79–80), his metaphor is also essentially seasonal. Hal refers with equal appropriateness to Falstaff as 'All-hallown summer' (1H4 1.2.158–9); his life and his happy summer days with the Prince are both almost over. 'Like a beggar at Hallowmas' (TGV 2.1.24) reminds us that it was a day of special alms for beggars (BEV, 84n).

(C) Barber (1967), 58–67, relates the pageant *Summer's Last Will and Testament* to Falstaff's seasonal end.

HARMONY

(A) Musical concord. The planets in the Ptolemaic system were thought to make a celestial music inaudible to humans since the Fall; the angelic intelligences, thought to cause the spheres to revolve, were also members of the choirs of angels, and therefore constantly praising God in both their motions and their songs.

(B) Lorenzo evokes many of these connections when he speaks to Jessica about the 'sweet harmony' Stephano begins to play:

> There's not the smallest orb which thou behold'st
> But in his motion like an angel sings,
> Still quiring to the young-ey'd cherubins;
> Such harmony is in immortal souls,
> But whil'st this muddy vesture of decay
> Doth grossly close it in, we cannot hear it.
> (MV 5.1.60–5)

Katherine of Aragon, Henry VIII's divorced, sick and dying queen, also connects musical and heavenly harmony when she asks her gentleman usher Griffith to 'Cause the musicians play me that sad note / I nam'd my knell, whilst I sit meditating / On that celestial harmony I go to' (H8 4.2.78–80).

(C) Hooker's eloquent defence 'Of **Musique** with Psalmes' in church services claims of the 'pleasinge effectes' of 'musicall harmonie . . . that the soule it selfe by nature is, or hath in it harmonie'. He especially praises 'The prophet David' as 'the author of addinge unto poetrie melodie in publique prayer, melodie both vocall and instrumentall for the raysinge up of mens hartes and the sweetninge of theire affections towardes God', adding, 'They must have hartes verie drie and tough, from whome the melodie of psalmes doth not sometimes draw that wherein a minde religiously affected delighteth' (V.38.1–3). See **tuned**.

HAUNT

To visit supernaturally, referring to ghosts, devils and fiends, as well as conscience.

MacDuff's 'My wife and children's ghosts will haunt me still' (MAC 5.7.16), and Richard II's 'Some haunted by the ghosts they have deposed' (R2 3.2.158) both illustrate the usage with ghosts. Bianca's angry outburst to Cassio, 'Let the devil and his dam haunt you!' (OTH 4.1.148) connects the word with the Devil and his kith and kin, as does Prince Hal's metaphoric reference, 'a devil haunts thee in the likeness of an old fat man' (1H4 2.4.447–8). Troilus's simile, 'I'll haunt thee like a wicked conscience still' (TRO 5.10.28) illustrates the usage of 'haunt' for the activity of the conscience, as does Richard of Gloucester's 'Suspicion always haunts the guilty mind' (3H6 5.6.11). When Richard later puts a romantic spin on the word: 'Your beauty, that did haunt me in my sleep / To undertake the death of all the world, / So I might live one hour in your sweet bosom' (R3 1.2.122–4), her image as a revengeful ghost and a tempting fiend both figure into his metaphor.

HEATHEN

(A) Either non-Christian or believing or behaving in a manner inappropriate for Christians.

(B) Iago describes his service to the Moor in many lands, '**Christen'd** and heathen' (OTH 1.1.30). Norfolk's description of the French as 'All clinquant, all in gold, like heathen gods' (H8 1.1.19) associates their golden armour with the gilded idols of heathen worship. The Gravedigger asks his associate, 'What, art a heathen?' for daring to question his assertion that Adam was the first gentleman that 'ever bore arms'; he follows with a biblical proof (from Gen. 3.23) that in its interpretive contortions entertains more than it edifies: 'The Scripture says Adam digg'd; could he dig without arms?' (HAM 5.1.32–7).

(C) Donne associates 'the stone Idols of the Papists' with 'the stone Gods of the heathen' (2: 190). Of 'heathen' as the opposite of 'christened', the *Father* in Becon's *Catechism* asks, 'Of what favour from God is baptism a sign and testimony unto thee?' and the *Son* replies, 'Baptism declareth evidently unto me, that God doth so dearly love and favour me, that whereas before I was an heathen, I am now become a Christian' (2: 203–4).

HEAVEN

Shakespeare's works contain over 900 references to some form of the word 'heaven', including the compound words. Often as with **grace**, the meanings overlap.

HEAVEN¹

(A) Another name for God and God's omnipotence, his providential agency, or his dispensing of eternal justice and mercy.

(B) The first confrontation between Shylock and Antonio involves a dispute about whether Jacob's 'venture' with Laban's sheep (Gen. 30.25–43) was 'swayed and fashioned by the hand of heaven', a gift of grace, or rather something 'Jacob did' (MV 1.3.77, 91–3). Isabella contrasts Angelo's legalistic severity against her condemned brother to the more measured judgements of 'merciful heaven' (MM 2.2.114). The Duke probably uses 'heaven' for 'God' as he distinguishes between a contrition which stems from our fear of worldly shame and one which results from a sincere desire not to offend that God who hears our contrition when he says that the wrong 'sorrow is always towards ourselves, not heaven, / Showing we would not spare heaven as we love it, / But as we stand in fear' (MM 2.3.32–3). When Isabella frightens her brother with her vivid wish that he become in death a heroic ambassador conveying 'affairs to heaven' (MM 3.1.56), **heaven**¹ and **heaven**² are almost indistinguishable.

In the histories and the tragedies, 'heaven' sometimes problematically invokes or asserts the role of God or Divine Providence in the affairs of state. To Desdemona's plaintive but ultimately ineffective protestation of innocence and invocation of divine protection, 'Heaven doth truly know it', Othello counters, 'Heaven doth truly know that thou art false as hell' (OTH 4.2.38–9). Macduff, learning that 'all my pretty chickens, and their dam' have been killed 'at one fell swoop', wonders briefly, 'Did heaven look on, / And would not take their part?' Four lines later, however, his reflexive 'Heaven rest them now' (MAC 4.3 223, 227) seems to revert to a more simplistic theodicy. Richard II asserts, desperately, that 'heaven still guards the right' as his kingdom totters on the edge of ruin (R2 3.2.62). York justifies his broken alliance with Richard with the rationalization: 'But heaven hath a hand in these events' (R2 5.2.37), just as Gaunt has rationalised his declining to kill Richard II by saying 'Let heaven revenge, for I may never lift / An angry arm against His minister' (R2 1.2.40–1. 'His' makes it clear that 'heaven' is Gaunt's way of saying 'God'. 'Heaven' can also mean heaven's agency in human affairs and / or God's will in R3 (1.3.190, 194; 2.1.83; 2.2.94; 4.4.353; 5.5.8, 19–20).

On a lighter note, characters often emphasise their veracity by invoking divine sanction in phrases like 'by heaven', 'witness heaven', 'heaven knows', 'heaven be judge', or 'so help me heaven' (like R2 3.2.207; TGV 2.6.25; H8 3.1.145; TGV 5.4.36; ERR 5.1.268). Others say 'thank heaven' or 'praise heaven' to express gratitude (WIV 3.4.58; MM 2.1.72; WIV 1.4.141). There are also many casual requests, hardly justifying the name 'prayer', where heaven is asked to 'forgive', 'prosper', 'pardon', 'keep', 'speed', 'guide', 'give', 'restore' or 'send' (as in WIV

3.3.212; WIV 3.1.20; OTH 4.2.135; OTH 3.4.163; JC 2.4.41; TIT 4.1.75; MM 4.2.70; TN 3.4.46; WIV 3.4.101). Occasionally these oaths and prayers seem more theologically aware, as when the formula 'so defend me heaven' continually marks the confrontation of Mowbray and Bolingbroke (R2 1.3.15, 25, 34). Left unsettled is the possibility that both of their causes, or neither of them, might be just.

(C) Hunter (1976), 70–9, discusses what he calls the God-devising (or perceiving) characters in R3. See also Hassel (1987), ch. 5, on 'Perceptions of Providence in R3'. Stritmatter (1999) discusses the concept of 'all-seeing Heaven' in several plays. Kehler (1989) discusses references to heaven in JN.

HEAVEN[2]

The abode of the departed dead. Donne once offers a map to heaven when he imagines 'my soule, as soone as it is out of my body, . . . ascended through ayre, and fire, and Moone, and Sun, and Planets, and Firmament, to that place which we conceive to be Heaven' (7: 71).

Lady Anne, with pious defiance, tells Richard III that Henry VI 'is in heaven, where thou shalt never come' (R3 1.2.106). Lorenzo, betrothed to Jessica, once says of Shylock, 'If e'er the Jew her father come to heaven, / It will be for his gentle daughter's sake' (MV 2.4.33–4). Jessica, however, quotes the fool Lancelot as having told her 'flatly there's no mercy for me in heaven because I am a Jew's daughter' (MV 3.5.32–3). The sinister anti-Semitism of such a theology, however inadequately it represents mainstream Christianity, intersects uncomfortably with Portia's assurances about the quality of mercy during the trial scene. Hamlet worries that if Claudius' soul 'goes to heaven' after he kills him at prayer, the revenge would be imperfect; he had rather kill him in the midst of 'an act, / That has no relish of salvation in't', 'that his heels may kick at heaven, / And that his soul may be as damn'd and black / As hell, whereto it goes' (3.3.73–4, 91–5). When Richard III decides to have his brother Clarence killed, he refers with characteristic sarcasm first to 'heaven' as this place of eternal rest, then to 'heaven' as its ruler: 'I do love thee so, / That I will shortly send thy soul to heaven, / If heaven will take the present at our hands' (R3 1.1.118–19). Isabella uses 'heaven' as both a place where the prayers of 'fasting maids' will be heard, and as the divine ear which might hear them: 'true prayers / That shall be up at heaven and enter there' (MM 2.2.151–2).

HEAVEN[3]

Christ's body as one of the elements of Communion.

Angelo, dissatisfied with his own **contrition**, reflects, 'Heaven hath my empty words, / Whilst my invention, hearing not my tongue, / Anchors on Isabel: Heaven in my mouth, / As if I did but only chew his name, / And in my heart the strong and swelling evil / Of my conception' (MM 2.4.2–7). His first 'heaven' refers to God as the auditor of prayers (**heaven**[1]); his second refers to the word 'heaven' he has just spoken, merely chewed, in the ineffectual prayer. But 'only chew his name' suggests as well a merely ritualistic participation in the Eucharist, eating Christ's body but not intending to digest his grace or amend his life.

HEAVEN[4]

'Heaven' is also used commonly as a romantic metaphor, as in 'the heaven of her brow' (LLL 4.3.223), 'my sole earth's heaven' (ERR 3.2.64), and 'now heaven walks on earth' (TN 5.1.97).

HEAVENLY[1]

Spoken of beings like God, the gods, or the angels, as in 'Some heavenly power' (TMP 5.1.105), 'you heavenly guards' (HAM 3.4.104), or Edmund's cynical reference to divine (or astrological) predestination as 'heavenly compulsion' (LR 1.2.122). Also used of things located in heaven, as when the sun is called a 'heavenly car' (TGV 3.1.154), eternal blessedness 'heavenly bliss' (3H6 33.182), and the Pythagorean music of the spheres, 'heavenly harmony' (H5 3.1.5).

HEAVENLY[2]

Heaven-like or godlike.

This can be spoken of extraordinary earthly things like 'heavenly music' (TMP 5.1.52), the 'heavenly Rosaline' (LLL 4.3.217), or 'heavenly eyes' (LLL 5.2.767); also something bestowed by or analogous to the divine, like 'a heavenly gift of prophecy' (MAC 4.3.157). Othello refers with a misguided piety to the suffering of Christ, or perhaps better to God's suffering the necessity of Christ's suffering on the cross, when he says of his own inner turmoil about killing Desdemona, 'This sorrow's heavenly, it strikes where it doth love' (OTH 5.2.21–2).

HEAVENLY[3]

Things pious, holy, or of theological origin, as in 'make her heavenly comforts of despair' (MM 4.3.110), 'heavenly oaths' (LLL 5.2.356), or 'holy and heavenly thoughts' (H8 5.4.29).

HEAVENS

Most often refers to, invokes, or complains about the influence of god or the gods.

As an oath we hear 'O heavens it cannot be' (MM 3.1.98). Leontes' 'Apollo's angry, and the heavens themselves / Do strike at my injustice' (WT 3.2.146) speaks of the retributive justice of the gods.

HEBREW (also EBREW)

(A) Jew.

(B) In three of the four uses by Shakespeare's characters, the reference is condescending. When Falstaff challenges Peto's testimony about a detail of the Gadshill robbery, 'You rogue, they were bound, every man of them, or I am a Jew else, an Ebrew Jew' (1H4 2.4.178–9), he is probably relying on the age's stereotype that Jews are liars. Launce tells Speed that if he will not 'go with me to the alehouse', 'thou art an Hebrew, a Jew, and not worth the name of a Christian' (TGV 2.5.53–5). This 'Christian', like Falstaff's **Corinthian**, refers to 'a good ole boy' rather than a certain kind of believer, but good fellowship is part of the package, and obviously not associated with Jews. Antonio's response to Shylock's decision to lend him the money gratis is similar: 'The Hebrew will turn Christian, he grows kind' (MV 1.3.178); in this case it is being kind rather than being fun that distinguishes 'Christian' from 'Hebrew'. Only when Shylock calls his friend Tubal in the same scene 'a wealthy Hebrew of my tribe' (MV 1.3.57), do we see in Shakespeare's usage that a Jew as well as a Christian could use 'Hebrew' for 'Jew,' and not use it condescendingly.

(C) See **Jew, Turk**. Hassel (1980), 181–9, and Dessen (1974), 233, 242–3, both urge a distinction between anti-Semitism in theatrical characters and anti-Semitism in the playwrights who draw those characters.

HECATE (also HECAT)

(A) Goddess of witchcraft and the moon. Also an eponym for furious and ominous speaking.

(B) Lear swears (in vain) to Kent by 'the mysteries of Hecat and the night' (LR 1.1.110). Macbeth imagines himself just before the murder of Duncan as living in a nighttime world in which 'witchcraft celebrates / Pale Hecat's off'rings' (MAC 2.1.51–2); later, while elusively mentioning the upcoming murder of Banquo, he again associates Hecate with the literal and figurative things of darkness: 'ere to black Hecat's summons / The shard-borne beetle with his drowsy hums / Hath rung night's yawning peal, there shall be done / A deed of dreadful note' (MAC 3.2.41–4). Hecate is, of course, also a character in the play.

When Talbot describes Joan of Arc as 'that railing Hecate' (1H6 3.2.64), he refers to her scoffing words as well as her dark alliance with the powers of hell. He has already called her 'witch', 'sorceress', 'vile fiend' and 'hag' earlier in the scene (1H6 3.2.38, 45, 52).

(C) Roberts (1987–88) examines the concept of the 'Triple Hecate' in the plays.

HEDGE-PRIEST

(A) A priest of modest talent, little learning and low status.

(B) Sir Nathaniel is such a figure in LLL, 'the hedge-priest' who forms part of the ill-qualified cast of the Pageant of the Nine Worthies (LLL 5.2.542). Oliver Martext is another such priest, of whom Jaques asks Touchstone 'will you (being a man of your breeding) be married under a bush like a beggar? Get you to church, and have a good priest that can tell you what marriage is' (AYL 3.3.83–6).

(C) Whitgift (1851–53), 3: 382, admires the simple lifestyles of hedge-priests.

HELEN

See **Constantine**.

HELL

(A) The place for damned humans and fallen angels or devils. Donne says of its material and spiritual realities: 'But when we shall have given to those words, by which hell is expressed in the Scriptures, the heaviest significations, that either the nature of those words can admit, or as they are types and representations of hell, as *fire*, and *brimstone*, and *weeping*, and *gnashing*, and *darknesse*, and *the worme*, . . . *deepe and large*, . . . *a pile of fire and much wood*, . . . *and the breath of the Lord to kindle it, like a streame of Brimstone*, . . . when all is done, the hell of hels, the torment of torments is the everlasting absence of God, and the everlasting impossibility of returning to his presence' (5: 265–6).

(B) Othello speaks of 'burning hell' (OTH 5.2.129), Lear of 'the sulph'rous fires' (LR 3.2.4), Lady Macbeth of 'the dunnest smoke of hell' (MAC 1.5.51). Queen Margaret says that 'Earth gapes, hell burns, fiends roar, saints pray, / To have him suddenly convey'd from hence' (R3 4.4.75–6), and Antony dreads 'th' abysm of hell' (ANT 3.13.145–7). Hamlet fears that the Ghost brings 'blasts from hell' and hopes that Claudius's 'soul may be as damn'd and black / As hell, whereto it goes' (HAM 1.4.41; 3.3.94–5); Othello says that Desdemona's 'like a liar gone to burning hell' (OTH 5.2.129), and Feste teases Olivia about her dead brother, 'I think his soul is in hell, madonna' (TN 1.5.68). Ariel speaks of 'all the devils' of hell (TMP 1.2.214), Iago of 'all the tribe of hell' (OTH 1.3.357), Posthumus of 'the fiends of hell' (CYM 2.4.129), Cade of 'the devils and hell' (2H6 4.8.60–1), and Margaret of 'a hell of ugly devils' (R3 1.3.226). Philip the Bastard says 'the devil is come from hell' (JN 4.3 100).

Metaphorically, hell can refer to some earthly torment, like 'the hell of having a false woman' (WIV 2.2.291–2). The shrew Kate is 'this **fiend** of hell' (SHR 1.1.88), and Jessica says 'Our house is hell' (MV 2.3.2). But when Anne calls Richard 'thou dreadful **minister** of hell' (R3 1.2.46), she probably means that he is hell's literal **agent**. The idea of hell within us is also common (H8 1.1.72; JN 5.7.46).

Casual curses include 'O hell' (MND 1.1.140; 3.2.145; MV 2.7.62) and 'go to hell' (MV 3.2.21), the latter spoken not to a person but of fortune.

Common phrases which suggest attributes of hell include 'deep as hell' (WIV 3.5.13; cf. Job 11.8), 'dark as hell' (TN 4.2.46; cf. Tilley, H397); 'false as hell' (OTH 4.2.39; cf. Tilley, H398); 'grim as hell' (OTH 4.2.64); 'the pains of hell' (R2 3.1.34; cf. Ps. 116.3); and 'wide as hell' (H5 3.3.13). Usually self-explanatory compounds include 'hell-black' (LR 3.7.60); 'hell-born' (LUC 1519); 'hell-broth' (MAC 4.1.19); 'hell-fire' (1H4 3.3.31–3); 'hell-govern'd' (R3 1.2.67); 'hell-hated' (LR 5.3.147–8); 'hell-pains' (OTH 1.1.154); 'hell-hound', and 'hell-kite' (MAC 5.8.3; 4.3.211, 217; R3 4.4.48, 51; cf. TIT 5.2.144). 'Hell-hound', like 'hell-governed' and 'hell-kite', often designates a **scourge** and **reprobate**, someone completely abandoned to **evil** and self-destruction; usually in Shakespeare it refers either to Macbeth or Richard III.

(C) On hell within, Mephastophilis famously says in *Dr Faustus* (1990), 3.75, 'Why this is hel, nor am I out of it'; Mephastophilis describes hell more fully, but still subjectively, later (5.122–9). 'The Hell within him' similarly describes Satan's condition in *Paradise Lost* (1965): IV.20. Wickham (1966) and Lancashire (1984) both examine the medieval stage convention of the 'hell-castle' emblem and its relevance to MAC. Nosworthy (1984), 215–17, argues for the 'intrusion of hell' upon the action of MAC. Morris (1985) deals generally with the fears of hell and damnation exhibited in the plays.

HELLISH
Extraordinarily evil; perhaps also inspired by hell.

'[H]ellish cruelty' (MV 3.4.21) and 'hellish obstinacy' (AWW 1.3.180) are good examples. Richard III claims that Queen Elizabeth and 'that harlot, strumpet Shore' have 'prevail'd / Upon my body with their hellish charms' (R3 3.4.61–2, 70–1).

HERESY
(A) A religious doctrine or opinion contrary to established belief. In Shakespeare 'heresy' pertains, through metaphor, more often to romantic than to religious experience.

(B) An extended reference which combines the religious meaning and the romantic metaphor occurs when Lysander says to the sleeping Hermia he is about to leave for Helena, 'as the heresies that men do leave / Are hated most of those they did deceive, / So thou, my surfeit and my heresy, / Of all be hated, but the most of me!' (MND 2.2.139–42).

(C) Persons, paraphrasing Aquinas in the second part of his *Three Conversions*, says: 'The nature of heresie conteineth two points, first Election, or choice of a private discipline or sect, & then Pertinacity & obstinacy in defence of the same: And no marvaille truly, that these two kinswomen do ever go so conjoined togeather, for that heresie being the daughter of pride, . . . and pertinacity the child of vayne glory, . . . which vayne glory also is the daughter of pride: yt cometh to passe that heresie is the aunt of pertinacity, and she her neece' (1604a), 158–9. See also *ST* II.2.11. For the 'heresy of merit' in OTH, see Hunt (1996). Klause (1999) deals with heresy as it relates to the deaths of martyrs, which he argues is a theme in TIT and SON 124.

HERETIC
A person who believes in or professes heresies. That this term can be applied with equal fervour to both Protestants and Catholics is clear when we hear the Reformer Ridley call Catholics 'whoso stubbornly and stiffly maintaineth an untruth . . . in matters of religion and concerning our faith' 'an heretic' (1841), 155, and the Recusant Hopkins translate F. Lewis de Granada on the 'newe Heretical licentious doctrines' of 'the late Apostatas, *Luther, Zuinglius, Calvin, Beza,* & other newe pretended Reformers of Christes Catholicke Churche' (1586), 5. Many of Shakespeare's references to 'heretics' concern their traditional disposal, burning at the stake. In classic catch–22 fashion, if accused heretics and witches could be drowned, then they were dead but proven not to be heretics or witches; if they survived the drowning, they were obviously witches or heretics, and would have to be burned.

Pandulph, the papal legate in JN, proclaims King John 'an heretic' and his followers 'curs'd and excommunicate' (JN 3.1.172–5) for John's famous defiance of Rome in the matter of who should be appointed Archbishop of Canterbury. Cranmer, an actual sixteenth-century Reformer, is also proclaimed 'An heretic, an arch-one' by the Catholic Cardinal Wolsey (H8 3.2.102). The Fool in LR also refers anachronistically to 'heretics burn'd' (LR 3.2.84).

Death by fire is prominent in several romantic metaphors. Romeo says of the idea that he could love anyone more than Rosaline,

> When the devout religion of mine eye
> Maintains such falsehood, then turn tears to fires,
> And these, who often drown'd, could never die,
> Transparent heretics, be burnt for liars!
>
> (ROM 1.2.988–91)

Benedick, the mocker of love and lovers, is once called 'an obstinate heretic in the despite of beauty' in response to his wisecrack that his scepticism about all women 'is the opinion that fire cannot melt out of me; I will die in it at the stake' (ADO 1.1.232–5). Paulina calls Leontes for his disbelief in Hermione, 'an heretic that makes the fire, / Not she which burns in't' (WT 2.3.115–16), and Ford similarly calls himself 'heretic' for disbelieving in his wife's fidelity (WIV 4.4.9). The speaker in SON calls policy 'that heretic' for its tendency to proceed on the basis of the trendy, 'leases of short-numb'red hours', rather than that timeless and unshakable love he professes, which 'nor grows with heat, nor drowns with show'rs' (SON 124.9–12).

HEROD

(A) King of Judea at the time of the birth of Christ. Herod achieved his greatest notoriety by ordering the slaughter of all of the first-born children of Israel in a vain and futile attempt to frustrate the prophecy that a new 'King of the Jews' had been born.

(B) Shakespeare reveals a considerable knowledge of the Herod figure from popular art as well as the mysteries. Hamlet uses the name as the theatrical eponym for overacted villainy: 'It out-Herods Herod' (HAM 3.2.14). Henry V overcomes Harfleur by threatening to match Herod's cruel slaughter of the innocents even as he imitates the ranting tyrant with his own purposeful overacting:

> Your naked infants spitted upon pikes,
> Whiles the mad mothers with their howls confus'd
> Do break the clouds, as did the wives of Jewry
> At Herod's bloody-hunting slaughter-men.
>
> (H5 3.3.38–41)

Mrs Ford's 'What a Herod of Jewry is this' (WIV 2.1.20) probably associates Falstaff's preposterous love letters and the equally preposterous self-image which wrote them with Herod's over-inflated ego and his usual obliviousness to the possibility of failure. This same Herod is often named as a contemporary in ANT (1.2.28–9; 3.3.3; 3.6.73; 4.6.13).

(C) The main biblical account of the Herod story comes from Matt. 2. 2–4, 16, 19–20. See Grant (1971) on the historical Herod. Colley (1986) discusses parallels between the various biblical Herods and Richard III. Harris (2000–01) argues that SHR is informed by the character of Herod from the Coventry play cycle, and also notes references to Herod in HAM and WIV. Hassel (2001b) reveals detailed echoes in MAC of the characters, actions, themes, props, stage business and language of the Herod plays.

HIGH, HIGHEST

(A) Because of the common sense of analogous vertical hierarchies, 'high' and 'highest' can refer to a superiority of authority or location, and sometimes to both at once. As the recusant Sander says, 'as the angels occupie the highest place, so doe the heavens with the lights and starres in them occupie the second place, & the foure elements are beneath them' (1565), *sigs.* F1–2. 'Glory be to God on high' (from the *Gloria* – *BCP*, 265) is the most familiar liturgical formulation.

(B) 'Heaven so high above our heads' and 'as high as heaven itself' (ROM 3.5.22; 4.5.74) both illustrate a sense of literal vertical relationship. York speaks more of superior authority than location when he says of the turmoil surrounding King Richard's deposition, 'But heaven hath a hand in these events, / To whose high will we bound our calm contents' (R2 5.2.37–8). Buckingham, near his death and contrite at the last, concedes ruefully of this same combination of location and authority, 'That high All-Seer, which I dallied with, / Hath turn'd my feigned prayer on my head, / And given in earnest what I begg'd in jest' (R3 5.1.20–2). Brutus's 'the providence of some high powers / That govern us below' (JC 5.1.106–7) also speaks of both authority and location. 'High' is also used once, in the phrase 'your high profession spiritual' (H8 2.4.117), to describe the elevated place of the spiritual life in the hierarchy of occupations. Shakespeare's one use of the phrase 'high-judging' probably means judging from heaven, but it also implies great authority and power. It occurs when King Lear, in high anger but still trying to control himself, says to Goneril 'I do not bid the thunder-bearer shoot, / Nor tell tales of thee to high-judging Jove' (LR 2.4.227–8).

(C) Vaux (1590a), *sig.* B4, speaks of 'the glory of the most high and mighty God the Father'; Bullinger, 3: 337, calls angels 'messengers and ambassadors of the most high God'.

HOLIDAM
See **halidom**.

HOLY[1]

(A) Consecrated, spoken of a person, place, object, institution or activity. Andrewes includes among the holy 'The priests . . ., because they are consecrated to the Lord'; 'Those places . . . which are consecrated to holy uses, as the sanctuary'; and 'Those times which are kept holy to the Lord, as the Sabbath.' Donne calls '*holy ground*' 'a place *accustomed to Gods presence*' (6: 284).

(B) 'Holy **father**' (TN 5.1.142), 'holy **friar**', and 'holy **nuns**' (ROM 3.3.81; 5.3.157) are common references to persons holding religious office. 'Holy

saint(s)' (as in R3 5.3.241; ERR 3.2.14) refers to unnamed departed spirits, while 'holy **Abram**' (MV 1.3.72), 'holy **Paul**' (R3 1.3.45) or 'God's holy **Mother**' (R3 1.3.305) all refer to particular biblical persons of unusual importance or **sanctity**. 'Holy **confession**' (TGV 4.3.44), 'holy **rites**' (ADO 5.4.68), 'holy edifice' (MV 1.1.30), 'holy **bell**' (AYL 2.7.121), 'holy **bread**' (AYL 3.4.14), 'holy **cross**es' (MV 5.1.31), 'holy **Sabaoth**' (MV 4.1.36), 'holy **abstinence**' (MM 4.2.81), 'holy **prayers**' (ERR 4.4.55), and 'holy **rood**' (R3 3.2.75) are some of the references to sanctified places, times, objects and activities. Most of these phrases occur several times in Shakespeare. 'Holy **text**' (2H4 4.2.7) and 'holy **writ**' (R3 1.3.336) refer to a passage from the Bible or the entire book. The English histories contain one reference to 'the holy wars in Palestine' (JN 2.1.4) and several to the '**Holy Land**' (as in 1H4 1.1.48). The 'holy **Church**' (JN 5.2.71) refers to the 'universal Church'. The references to 'holy **vestments**' (TIM 4.3.126), a 'holy **altar**' (TNK 5.1.164), a 'holy hat' or 'holy **oil**' (H8 3.2.325; 4.1.88), like those to holy bread, holy crosses and holy water above, might have evoked controversies about the accoutrements of formal worship during the Reformation. At particular issue was the question of whether such objects should or could be sanctified and then venerated, and then if such sanctification and veneration might not lead to **idolatry**.

(C) Donne calls 'the holy ones [those] whom God will heare, who are of the houshold of the faithfull, of the Communion of Saints, matriculated, engraffed, enrolled in the Church, by that initiatory Sacrament of Baptisme' (9: 319); and 'his Saints, his holy ones in this world' (2: 103). Marx (1995) discusses 'holy war' in H5. Barnes (1984) argues that in LR 'holy cords' refer to the 'three-fold cords of Solomon'. See **hallowed**.

HOLY[2]

fig. 'Holy' as a metaphor also marks romantic description.

Examples include the frequent phrase 'holy kiss' (TGV 2.2.7). Oxymorons like 'holy-cruel' (AWW 4.2.32), 'th' offence is holy' (WIV 5.5. 225), 'holy traitors' (AYL 2.3.13), 'holy witch' (CYM 1.6.166), 'holy fox, or wolf' (H8 1.1.158–9) are also common.

HOLINESS

The quality of being holy; also one title of the Pope.

Suffolk refers to the Pope as 'his Holiness' in H8 (3.2.32); so does the Duke in MM (3.2.220).

HOLY-ROOD DAY

14 September. The holy rood is the holy cross.

In 1H4 (1.1.52) 'Holy-rood day' seems merely to mark the date in 1402 of Hotspur's encounter with Archibald.

HOLY WATER

(A) Water that has been sanctified for use in rituals that effect or signify religious purification and devotion. Of the 'holy water' available to Catholic parishioners in basins or 'stoups' near the entries of churches, the Recusant Vaux says, 'It is used, to put men in minde of the water of Baptisme, wherein their sinnes were cleansed' (1590a), *sig.* K6.

(B) 'Holy water' occurs four times, always in plays not set in the Christian era. In TIT, a Roman play, Saturnius swears that he will marry Tamora immediately by 'all the Roman gods, / Sith priest and holy water are so near, / And tapers burn so bright' (TIT 1.1.322–4). In LR, the tears of Cordelia's compassion for her father are described by the Gentleman as the 'holy water from her heavenly eyes' (LR 4.3.30). The fool in LR earlier refers to flattery as 'court holy-water' (LR 3.2.10). In CYM, also set in pre-Christian Britain, a father prays to his daughter that 'My tears that fall [may] / Prove holy water on thee!' (CYM 5.5.269). Since blessed water was presumably universal to religious practice, such pre-Christian usage is not necessarily anachronistic; it could, however, reverberate with the energy of religious controversy.

(C) Reformers critical of 'superstitious' trust in 'holy water and holy bread' include Latimer (1844–45), 1: 497; Cranmer (1846), 2: 158; Pilkington (1842), 527; Grindal (1843), 159; and Becon, 2: 65. See *Prayer Book Dictionary* (1912), 819; and Meagher (1979), 1699. Eliade (1987), 15: 357, mentions many other-than-Christian understandings and uses of water, including the 'purifying' and the 'sacralizing'.

HOMILY

Sermon. Though we think of a homily today as a brief, informal sermon, in the Renaissance the word could refer to sermons of much greater length and formality. The title of the famous Elizabethan book of homilies is *Certain sermons or homilies appointed to be read in Churches in the time of Queen Elizabeth I.*

Shakespeare's only usage is metaphoric. Rosalind asks Celia, who has just read one of Orlando's poems to her, 'what tedious homily of love have you wearied your parishioners withal, and never cried, "Have patience, good people!" ' (AYL 3.2.155–7). We can read between the lines some impatience with the sermons of the time, but whether it is Rosalind's or Shakespeare's, only the forest can tell. See **sermon**.

HOOD

Katherine of Aragon's proverbial expression, 'But all hoods make not monks' (H8 3.1.23) reminds us that the hooded robe was associated with religious dress. When Lucio insults the Duke, still disguised as a friar, as a 'bald-pated, lying rascal', he adds, 'you must be hooded, must you' (MM 5.1.352–3).

HOPE

(A) Theological hope is more than the feeling that things will turn out for the best; as part of the Pauline triad of faith, hope and love (from 1 Cor. 13.13), it is one of the theological virtues and suggests a belief in God's providential control, here and hereafter. Vaux (1590a), *sig.* B2^v, defines 'Hope [as] a vertue geven from God above, wherby we looke for the goodnes of our salvatio[n] & everlasting life with a sure trust'.

(B) The words 'hope' and 'grace' are connected syntactically in both MM (1.4.68–9) and in WIV (2.2.111–12), suggesting even in the silliness of these examples that hope, like faith and love, can be considered a gift of **grace**. Portia's question of Shylock, 'How shalt thou hope for mercy, rend'ring none?' and Shylock's quick retort, 'What **judgement** shall I dread, doing no wrong' (MV 4.1.88–9), raises a similar issue more seriously; since Portia is leading up to the point 'That in the course of justice none of us / Should see **salvation**' (MV 4.1.199–200), it is certainly theological hope she refers to.

As he is about to die, Cardinal Wolsey speaks twice explicitly of his theological 'hopes for [or in] heaven' (H8 3.2.385, 459); Warwick swears his innocence 'by the hope I have of heavenly bliss' (3H6 3.3.182). Clarence also speaks of theological hope when he advises the Murderers not to kill him, 'as you hope to have **redemption**, / By Christ's dear blood shed for our grievous sins' (R3 1.4.189–90). Bolingbroke echoes both the Psalms and Proverbs when he says of his cause against Mowbray, 'strong as a tower in hope, I cry amen' (R2 1.3.102). Several times Shakespeare has characters juxtapose the general words 'hope' and '**despair**' (as in 3H6 2.3.9), but nowhere with clearer theological point than when Cymbeline tells Imogen that in marrying Posthumus against his will she is 'Past grace? obedience?' She responds with a spirited theological analogy, 'Past hope, and in despair, that way, past grace' (CYM 1.1.136–7). Here 'hope', 'despair' and 'grace' combine formulaically if also anachronistically to bring wisps of Christian theology into Roman Britain, but Imogen's main point is that grace is more a matter of hope than obedience.

(C) See *ST* II.2.17–18; and on the three 'theological virtues', *ST* II.1.62; *ST* II.2.1–27. Vaux quotes the Lord's Prayer and the Ave Maria as the basic documents about hope (1590a), *sig.* B3ʳ. Of the close connection between faith and hope, see Coverdale (1846), 2: 86; Norden (1847), 18; Bullinger, 2: 90 (on Heb. 40.1); and Donne, 3: 197; 5: 149. Shaheen (1999), 366, comments on Mowbray's allusion to Ps. 61.3: 'thou hast been my hope, and a strong tower for me against the enemy'. Marshall (1986) writes about the hope of reunion after death as it relates to the resurrection of the body. Cox (1992) argues that Shakespeare uses comedy to inspire spiritual hope in the tragedies.

HOWL

Sometimes this long, mournful sound is associated with fiends or the **damned**, as when Donne asks 'what extraction of **Wormwood** can be so bitter, what exaltation of fire can be so raging, ... what confection of gnawing **worms**, of gnashing teeth, of howling cries, of scalding brimstone, of palpable darknesse, can be so, so insupportable, so inexpressible, so in-imaginable, as the curse and malediction of God?' (7: 367).

Clarence describes 'a legion of foul fiends' that 'howled in mine ears / Such hideous cries' that he 'Could not believe but that I was in hell' (R3 1.4.58–62). The howl is also the sound of the damned. Laertes threatens the 'churlish priest' who will not give full burial rites to Ophelia that she will become 'a minist'ring angel' when he 'liest howling' (HAM 5.1.241–2). Pistol says that 'fiends for food howl on' (H5 2.1.93), and Falstaff tells Hostess Quickly that one woman 'is in hell already', and that he thinks she too 'wilt howl' 'for suffering flesh to be eaten in thy house, contrary to the law' against serving meat during **Lent**. She responds, 'What's a joint of mutton or two in a whole Lent?' (2H4 2.4.345–7).

HUMBLE

Not characterised by **pride**, the deadliest of the seven deadly **sins**; as a consequence, a chief symptom of **spiritual** health, one that could be cultivated by spiritual **discipline**. Andrewes, for example, calls **abstinence** 'an act or fruit of **repentance**' and 'an act of humiliation, to **humble** the **soul**' (1: 380; cf. 5: 341).

Holofernes correctly diagnoses a spiritual fault in the lords that only their enactment of the ladies' penance can relieve when he says of their mocking response to the poor actors in the Pageant of the Nine Worthies, 'This is not generous, not gentle, not humble' (LLL 5.2.629). Suffolk's description of Margaret of Anjou's 'humble lowliness of mind' (1H6 5.5.18) is an ironic example of this usage. See **lowliness, meek, fool, humility**.

HUMILITY

(A) The absence of pride, the admission of fallenness, and the acknowledged need for forgiveness and grace. The anonymous Recusant work *A Breefe Collection* (1603), 9, calls humility 'the ground & foundation of all Vertue'. Preaching on the text '*He came not to call the righteous, but sinners*', Donne says of what he calls 'the fruit of the Gospel, Humility': 'for that was the end of **miracles**, and it is the end of preaching, to make men capable of salvation by acknowledging themselves to be sinners . . . To know that we have no strength in our selves, and to know that we can lack none if we ask it of God, these are St. *Augustines* two Arts and Sciences, and this is the **humility** of the **Gospel** in general' (1: 314–15).

(B) Shylock says about the discrepancy between Christian precept and practice: 'If a Jew wrong a Christian, what is his humility? **Revenge**' (MV 3.1.68–9). Another ironic reference occurs in AWW, where the Clown Lavatch says of spiritual pride, 'Though honesty be no puritan, yet it will do no hurt; it will wear the surplice of humility over the black gown of a big heart' (AWW 1.3.94–5). Here he connects the often-represented **Puritan** pride and the false surface of humility with the liturgical garb of black **gown** and **surplice** (cf. TN 4.2.5–6). Richard, enjoying his hypocrisy, says of his pretended attempt to unite the warring political factions, forgive them, and seek their forgiveness, 'I thank my God for my humility' (R3 2.1.73).

(C) According to Andrewes, 'Man was to be recovered by the contrary of that by which he perished. By pride he perished, that is confessed. Then, by humility to be recovered, according to the rule, *Contraria curantur contrariis*' (1: 206; cf. Donne, 1: 315; and *ST* II.2.161.). Norden (1847), 22, warns, 'In a counterfeit humility many come near unto their duty in the eye of man, as when they can bow down their heads like bulrushes, as the prophet saith, and yet are puffed up in mind'. Sandys (1841), 407, speaks similarly of Absalon the 'holy hypocrite' who 'would hide his treason under the cloak of religion'. Butler (1982) looks at humility as a requirement for public office in COR, and examines rituals of humility and penance for both ordinary sinners and monarchs in early modern England. See **folly** and **revenge**.

HYMN

(A) Though usually these are religious songs of praise and joy (*OED sb.* 1), a 'hymn' may also be secular (*OED sb.* 2). The religious hymn is usually distinguished from the **anthem** as designed for congregational rather than choral singing, and from psalms in not setting a biblical passage to verse. Shakespeare's usage, however, is only once simply religious.

(B) Shakespeare names several metaphoric hymns of love, which are all, interestingly, solos rather than congregational pieces (as in SON 85.7; 29.12; 102.10; MV 5.1.66). The classical Hymen prescribes 'a wedlock-hymn' (AYL 5.4.137). In another play which mixes Christian and classical settings, English fairies and labourers with Athenian lords and ladies, Titania's 'No night is now with hymn or carol blessed' (MND 2.1.102) refers to the traditional singing of joyful religious and secular pieces during the 'winter' season. Duke Theseus also threatens Hermia with a cloistered life which will consist of 'chaunting faint hymns to the cold fruitless moon' (MND 1.1.73) if she refuses to marry Demetrius. Capulet's lament that Juliet's untimely death will 'Our solemn hymns to sullen dirges change' (ROM 4.5.88) is probably the most unequivocally religious usage.

(C) See J. R. Watson (1997) on *The English Hymn*. See also 'Hymns', *Oxford-EncyRef*, 2: 290–9; *NewCathEncy*, 7: 295–304.

IDOLATRY (IDOLATROUS)

(A) To the Master's question in Nowell's *Catechism* of 1570, 'What is idolatry, or to have strange gods?', his Student answers, 'It is in the place of the one only true God . . . to set other persons or things, and of them to frame and make to ourselves as it were certain gods, to worship them as gods, and to set and repose our trust in them' (1853), 122. This is the traditional Reformation interpretation of the second commandment. The Reformer Grindal (1843), 159, requires that 'all vestments, albs, tunicles, stoles, phanons, pixes, handbells, sacringbells, censers, chrismatories, **cross**es, **candlesticks**, holy-water-stocks, **image**s, and such other relics and monuments of superstition and idolatry be utterly defaced, broken, and destroyed'. Hooper says, 'To pray or trust in any dead saint departed out of this world is idolatry against this commandment' (1843), 1: 307. Donne, speaking of 'a Rome of superstition and idolatry' (1: 245), says 'We charge them with *Idolatry*, in the *peoples practise* . . . in the greatest mystery of all their Religion, in the *Adoration* of the Sacrament' (3: 132). This variety of usage reveals that idolatry can pertain to setting up false objects of worship, saints, say, or the Virgin Mary, to worshipping the religious image instead of God, to venerating icons in a church, the Cross, the elements of communion, even candles. In a sense, this prior act of capitalization is a form of idolatry. In Shakespeare's usage 'idolatry' is always metaphoric.

(B) Juliet once calls Romeo 'the god of my idolatry', and Romeo styles Juliet at their first meeting a 'holy shrine', himself as a pilgrim or palmer. 'Prayer', 'sin', 'faith', 'despair', 'saints', all form a part of this hyperbolic dialogue (ROM 2.2.114; 1.5.93–110). The question, about which there has been little agreement, is whether this sort of exuberance is theologically problematic or merely very romantic. SON 105 begins 'Let not my love be call'd idolatry', and defends the denial with the Donne-like assertion, verging on blasphemy, of a trinitarian constancy of 'Fair, kind, and true' in himself, 'Which three till now never kept seat in one' (SON 105.1, 9–10, 14). Lysander says of Helena that 'she, sweet lady, dotes, / Devoutly dotes, dotes in idolatry, / Upon this spotted and inconstant' Demetrius (MND 1.1.108–10); Julia laments Proteus's senseless 'idolatry' for Silvia (TGV 4.4.200). As serious a character as Helena says similarly of her extreme and equally hopeless love for the departed (and faithless) Bertram, 'But now he's gone, and my idolatrous fancy / Must sanctify his reliques' (AWW 1.1.97–8). Berowne also places the romantic idolatry of the lords in the realm of religious sin when he says of the lovelorn Longaville's poem, 'This is the liver-vein, which makes flesh a deity, / A green goose a goddess; pure, pure idolatry. / God amend us, God amend!' (LLL 4.3.72–4). Finally, Hector calls Paris's love of Helen of Troy, and the war which it has caused, a 'mad idolatry', that makes 'the service greater than the god' (TRO 2.2.56–7). When Henry V contemplates 'idol ceremony' before the Battle of Agincourt with questions like 'What kind of God art thou?' and 'What is thy soul of adoration?' (H5 4.1.240–1, 245), he refers in religious terms to an excessive worship of political symbols and rituals.

(C) See also *ST* II.2.94; Foxe (1641), 182–3; and Donne, 4: 92. Augustine's position is similar to the Reformers: 'Anything invented by man for making and worshiping idols, or for giving Divine worship to a creature or any part of a creature, is superstitious' (*On Christian Doctrine*, II.20). See 'Iconoclasm', *OxfordEncyRef*, 2: 302–6; *NewCathEncy*, 7: 327–9. Roche (1989), ch. 8, argues that a problematic idolatry of the beloved was an element of much Petrarchan poetry, including Shakespeare's. Battenhouse (1969), 102–30, 231–3, considers the same problem in ROM and HAM. Diehl (1997), 164–70, also comments on idolatry and romantic love. Kaula (1973) looks at various kinds of idolatry in TRO. Bicks (2000) notes that Ephesus as portrayed in PER draws upon English Protestant associations of the city with both pagan and Roman Catholic idolatry. Kamps (2000), 43, briefly discusses Romeo and Juliet's love as idolatrous. Diehl (1998), 400–1, discusses Angelo's lust in MM as idolatry. See also **image** and **holy water**.

ILL[1] *sb.*

Sin or sinfulness (*n.*).

Williams agrees with Hal that 'every man that dies ill, the ill upon his own head, the King is not to answer it' (H5 4.1.186–7). Miranda also says of Caliban's resistance to positive nurturing that he 'any print of goodness wilt not take, / Being capable of all ill' (TMP 1.2.352–3).

ILL[2] *adj.*

Evil, as when the Lord Chief Justice calls Falstaff Hal's 'ill angel' (2H4 1.2.164).

ILL-DOING, DOCTRINE OF

When Polixenes says 'we knew not / The doctrine of ill-doing', he seems to refer to the idea of original sin at the very moment when Leontes is about to be struck by an obsessive, murderous jealousy. 'Temptations' are opposed in surrounding speeches to the 'innocence for innocence' that they 'exchanged' when as youths they 'were as twinn'd lambs that did frisk i'th'sun'. Polixenes adds that had they lived on in such innocence they 'should have answer'd heaven / Boldly "Not guilty"; the imposition clear'd / Hereditary ours' (WT 1.2.66–4). Though this is a difficult sentence, not to mention a strange subject in a play whose God is Apollo rather than Jehovah, Polixenes claims that they were so innocent that the divine imposition of hereditary fallenness would have been waived in their case.

IMAGE

(A) Representation in religious art. Since Shakespeare's father was apparently forced by the Anglican authorities to whitewash over the wall painting of the Last Judgement in the Guild Chapel in Stratford, his son must have been aware from an early age of the importance of religious images during the Reformation. The recusant Sander, complaining of the Reformers, asks of their iconoclasm, 'Did they not by that colour ['the sincere word of God'] overthrow monasteries, Churches, **altar**s, **image**s of **Saint**es, and mine owne image and **cross**e?' (1565), *sigs*. PPpp2[r]. Donne is characteristically circumspect: '*Væ Idololatris*, woe to such advancers of Images, as would throw down Christ, rather then his Image: But *Væ Iconoclastis* too, woe to such peremptory abhorrers of Pictures, and to such uncharitable condemners of all those who admit any use of them, as had rather throw down a Church, then let a Picture stand' (7: 433).

(B) When York refers to 'all the walls with painted imagery' welcoming Boling-broke home with their 'Jesu preserve thee' and mentions too the people's 'desiring eyes' (R2 5.2.14–17), Shakespeare may paint some of this Reformation turmoil into his picture of an earlier revolution. Vernon's description of Hal 'Glittering in golden coats like images' (1H4 4.1.100) may also evoke the parallel tradition of gilded and otherwise painted religious statuary. Queen Margaret's sarcastic image of her husband's worshipping before '**brazen** images of **canonised** saints' is directly associated by her with the 'beads' and the Pope of Rome (2H6 1.3.55–62). When King Edward IV laments that some drunken subjects have 'defac'd the precious image of our dear **Redeemer**', we might think the iconoclasts are at work, but actually he refers to a 'drunken slaughter' (R3 2.1.123–4) of persons made in the image and likeness of God, the defacing of 'God's handiwork' (R3 4.4.51) and not man's.

(C) See *Certaine Sermons*, 2nd tome, pp. 11–76, for the sermons 'against perill of **Idolatry**'. Tyndale, 3: 125, cites More as saying 'He trusteth that men know the image from the saint' (More's *Dialogue*, II.11). The Catholics Vaux (1590a), *sig*. C2v, and Sander (1567), *sig*. H5[v]-J1[r], also defend the use of images. Among the defenders of the iconoclasts are Grindal (1843), 140; Bale (1849), 262; and Tyndale, 1: 33. Diehl (1983) argues that MAC is about the failure properly to interpret visual images. Carson (1984), 34–6, discusses the Puritan distrust of spectacle as it relates to the plays. Davidson (1989), 35–7, reminds us, citing Frere's edition of *Visitation Articles*, 90, that Shakespeare's father was forced to whitewash the Last Judgement in the Guild Chapel at Stratford.

IMMORTAL[1] *adj.*
(A) Living forever, referring to the human soul. As Bullinger says 'All the ancient writers . . . and all that followed them, have said that souls are everlasting or immortal' (3: 385).
(B) Hamlet calls his 'soul', 'a thing immortal as' the Ghost (HAM 1.4.66–7). The Man tells Romeo of the apparently dead Juliet's soul, 'her immortal part with angels lives' (ROM 5.1.19). Poins speaks profoundly of Falstaff: 'Marry, the immortal part needs a physician, but that moves not him; though that be sick, it dies not' (2H4 2.2.104–5).
(C) See Bullinger, 3: 385; Nowell (1853), 178; Andrewes, 1: 4. See also **soul**[1&2], **spirit**[1].

IMMORTAL[2] *adj.*
Living forever but also omniscient, omnipotent, spoken of divinities.
    When Ferdinand describes Miranda to his father Alonso, who has asked if she is a goddess, he says, 'Sir, she is mortal; / But by immortal providence she's mine' (TMP 5.1.188–9). Vincentio's 'O immortal gods' (SHR 5.1.66) refers simply to their being eternal.

IMPEDIMENT
(A) In ecclesiastical law, a bar to marriage, usually in matters of morality or affinity. In the Service for Matrimony the priest asks the couple 'if either of you do know any impediment why ye may not be lawfully joined together in matrimony, that ye confess it' (*BCP*, 291).
(B) The Friar in ADO follows this closely in his own service for Hero and Claudio when he says, 'If either of you know any inward impediment why you should not be conjoined, I charge you on your souls to utter it' (ADO 4.1.12–14). This liturgical context may also inform the famous line from Sonnet 116.2: 'Let me not to the marriage of true minds / Admit impediments'.
(C) See *ST* Suppl. 50–63; see also 'Marriage, Impediments', in *NewCathEncy*, 9: 274–6, and Sokol and Sokol (2000), 139–46.

IMPERFECTIONS
(A) Sins, taken theologically. In the **Last Judgement**, sins are weighed in the balance against good deeds and the result of that **account**ing is condemnation to **hell** or blessedness in **heaven**. In the Catholic scheme, **purgatory** could be an intermediate resting place, where, as the Ghost of Hamlet's father tells him, 'foul crimes . . . Are burnt and purg'd away' (HAM 1.5.12–13).
(B) The Ghost of Hamlet's father says that because he was killed sleeping, he was deprived of the last **rites** of the **church** and therefore sent to purgatory 'With all my imperfections on my head' (HAM 1.5.76–9).
(C) Andrewes says traditionally, 'To supply the defect that is in nature grace is added, that grace might make that perfect which is imperfect' (5.315).

IMPIOUS[1]; IMPIETY
Unfaithful, impure, profane, without piety; blasphemous.

Claudius advises Hamlet that his extended grief is 'a course of impious stubbornness', adding the gloss, this 'shows a will most incorrect to heaven' (HAM 1.2.93–4, 101). In contrast, when Eleanor calls the Cardinal 'impious' and 'false priest' (2H6 2.4.53) because he has betrayed her husband Humphrey Duke of Gloucester, she is using religious words to express a sense of personal betrayal. Shakespeare reveals the flexibility of the word by applying it as well to the claim of an 'impious War' (H5 3.3.15) and an 'impious priest' (2H6 2.4.53). 'Impious acts' describe rape, and 'impious breach' broken wedlock vows (LUC 199, 809). 'Impiety' is similarly used both for religious and romantic faults (as in 3H6 5.1.90 and MM 1.2.57), as when Claudio describes the Hero he imagines to be false but wants to be true as 'pure impiety and impious purity' (ADO 4.1.104).

IMPIOUS[2]
Non-Christian.

Though 'impious turbands' in CYM may refer, through synecdoche, to impious pagans (3.3.6, 9), it more literally calls the turbans themselves impious, that is, non-Christian.

IMPORTUNE
Pray.

The Boy says of his father Clarence's murder at Richard's command, 'God will revenge it, whom I will importune / With earnest prayers all to that effect' (R3 2.2.14–15).

INCARNATE *adj.*
Said of spirits who have assumed bodies.

This is used in Shakespeare only metaphorically, only in reference to devils, and in half of the cases, only with some funny malapropism. The fool Lancelot says in the midst of his struggle with his hard conscience, 'Certainly the Jew is the very devil incarnation' (MV 2.2.24). The fool Andrew similarly calls Sebastian 'the devil incardinate' (TN 5.1.182) for fighting so fiercely that he draws blood. The Boy in the tavern says that Falstaff called women 'dev'ls incarnate' as he lay dying (H5 2.3.32), and Lucius calls Aaron 'the incarnate devil' for his villainy (TIT 5.1.40).

INCENSE
This sweet but controversial smoke of liturgy is mentioned twice metaphorically.

As Tarquin tries to convince himself not to rape Lucrece, he says he should rather 'offer pure incense to so pure a shrine' (LUC 194). Salisbury emphasises the seriousness of his promise to avenge young Arthur's death by describing himself 'Kneeling before this ruin of sweet life, / And breathing to his breathless excellence / The incense of a vow, a holy vow' never to experience pleasure or delight until the murderer is dead (JN 4.3.65–72).

INDIAN

(A) Probably Judaean, referring either to Judas, who betrayed Christ, or Herod, 'who slew Miriamne in a fit of jealousy' (BEV, 1166n).

(B) One of the most famous textual cruxes in Shakespeare concerns the right reading of Othello's late lament. Was he in killing Desdemona 'like the base Indian' or the 'base Judaean' who 'threw a pearl away, / Richer than all his tribe' (OTH 5.2.347–8)? The Folio reads 'Iudean', the Quarto 'Indian'. Since 'J' was in those days printed as 'I', the question is whether the second letter, the *u* or the *n*, is upside down.

(C) Fleissner (1981) and (1995), Poisson, (1975), Gutierrez (1985) and Levin (1982) prefer the reading 'Indian'; Holmer (1980) argues that 'Judaean' fits the Mediterranean context better. Battenhouse (1969), 93–4, avoids a firm judgement but clearly prefers the 'Judaean' reading, as do Milward (1989) and Shaheen (1980).

INDULGENCE

In the Catholic Church a partial remission of the temporal punishment that is still due for sin after absolution. The selling of indulgences, often abused, became a flash-point of the Reformation and was in fact criticised and parodied much earlier, as in the character of Chaucer's **Summoner**.

Prospero refers metaphorically to this practice when with 'Let your indulgence set me free' he begs the audience for their 'good hands' and their 'gentle breath', their applause and their forgiveness (TMP ep. 10–11, 20).

INFERNAL

(A) Spoken of **hell**, or the regions **below** (*OED adj.* 1).

(B) Pistol mixes Christian and classical references when he says of Doll Tearsheet, 'I'll see her damn'd first, to Pluto's damned lake, by this hand, to th' infernal deep, with Erebus and tortures vile also' (2H4 2.4.156–8).

(C) On the common interweaving of classical and Christian hells, see Battenhouse (1951).

INFIDELS

(A) Non-Christians in both belief and behaviour.

(B) Jessica and Shylock are both called 'infidel' by the anti-semite Gratiano in MV (3.2.218; 4.1.332), once fondly, once fiercely. The paired 'Turks and infidels' (R2 4.1.139; R3 3.5.41) shows that 'infidels' can apply to Turks as well as Jews, and suggest barbarity as well as non-Christianity.

(C) Among the theologians, Donne laments the opposition 'Not onely of the *Christian* against *Jewes, Turkes,* and *Infidels,* but of the *Protestant* against the *Romane Church*' (4: 206); Hooper twice professes belief in 'hell for the infidels and reprobate' (1852), 2: 31, 63; Grindal, in a funeral sermon for the Emperor Ferdinand praises among his virtues 'his fortitude, travails, and continuance in wars against infidels and sworn enemies of the christian name and religion, I mean the Turks'

(1843), 13. Dachslager (1986) argues that infidels in Shakespeare include atheists, Jews, Turks and pagans. See **impious**[2].

INIQUITY

(A) A name of the allegorical vice figure from the morality play (*OED* 4.a).

(B) Richard III praises his own deceptive twisting of words, 'Thus, like the formal Vice, Iniquity, / I moralise two meanings in one word' (R3 3.1.82–3); Hal calls Falstaff 'that reverend Vice, that grey Iniquity' (1H4 2.4.454).

(C) In Jonson's *Devil An Ass* (1970: 265–6), 1.1, Pug. says 'Lend me but a Vice, to carry with me . . . Fraud, Or Covetousness, or Lady Vanity, Or old Iniquity'; moments later the *s.d.* read, '*Enter* Iniquity'. Iniquity is also a name for the devil (*OED* 4.b).

INNOCENCE, INNOCENCY

(A) Freedom from sin or an awareness of it is sometimes associated with Eden and the story of the Fall. Donne once refers to '*Adam* in the state of Innocency' (10: 219), and elsewhere advises praying, 'Begin with me againe, as thou begunst with *Adam*, in innocency; and see, if I shall husband and governe that innocency better then *Adam* did' (5: 357).

(B) Falstaff rationalises his 'frailty' by telling Hal 'Thou knowest in the state of innocency Adam fell, and what should poor Jack Falstaff do in the days of villainy' (1H4 3.3.164–5). Polixenes says that he and Leontes not only 'chang'd . . . innocence for innocence' but 'knew not / The doctrine of ill-doing' (WT 1.2.67–70). His phrase 'the imposition cleared / Hereditary ours' intensifies his reference to the pre-lapsarian world of Adam and Eve before the Fall.

(C) See BEV, 1488n and RIV, 1571n on Leontes's allusion. Guilfoyle (1985–86) reads the theme of the murder of innocence allegorically in OTH; Adamson (1980) argues that Desdemona must be seen as a total innocent. Taylor (1982a and 1982b) analyses malignant and pure innocence in WT and PER.

INNOCENT

'Pope Innocent' III is referred to in JN (3.1.146).

INTERCESSOR

(A) Advocate, defence attorney. Andrewes speaks of Christ's 'intercession to make atonement for them as sinners, whose innocency as an Advocate He cannot defend' (3: 158).

(B) When Shylock complains about 'these Christian intercessors' (MV 3.3.16), he is only annoyed that Bassanio and Gratiano are trying to save Antonio from his judgemental knife. Shakespeare's audience, on the other hand, could have heard in the word the Reformation controversy about the saints, angels and priests who might (or might not) intervene with a judgemental God. See **advocate**.

(C) Donne is sceptical of saintly intercessors, even of St George: 'Why should I pray to *S. George* for victory, when I may goe to the Lord of Hosts, Almighty

God himselfe; or consult with a Seargeant, or Corporall, when I may goe to the Generall? Or to another Saint for peace, when I may goe to the Prince of peace Christ Jesus?' For the full and lively passage, see Donne, 4: 311. Hassel (2001a), 44–8, has argued that the 'heavenly shows' Iago creates for Desdemona includes an intercessory role that will 'turn her virtue into pitch' by making it appear that she loves Cassio more than the Moor (OTH 2.3.352, 360).

INVESTMENTS
Sometimes religious **habits** or **vestments**.

The warlike Archbishop of York is described by his enemy Westmoreland as someone 'Whose white investments [should] figure innocence'; instead, he has turned his 'tongue divine / To a loud trumpet and a point of war' (2H4 4.1.45, 48–9).

IRRELIGIOUS[1]
Pagan, as when Aaron's bastard child in TIT is called 'the issue of an irreligious Moor' (TIT 5.3.121).

IRRELIGIOUS[2]
Actions which would deviate from Christian idealism.

Master Fenton speaks of 'A thousand irreligious cursed hours, / Which forced marriage would have brought upon' (WIV 5.5.229–30).

ISCARIOT
(A) Judas Iscariot is the disciple who betrayed Christ; Judas Maccabaeus is the Hebrew warrior.

(B) Dumaine pretends to confuse them when he responds to the lines 'Judas I am', 'A Judas?', to which the actor Holofernes says, 'Not Iscariot, sir. / Judas I am, ycliped Maccabaeus' (LLL 5.2.595–8).

(C) Most of those who discuss the '**Indian/Judean**' crux mention **Judas** Iscariot. Dawson (1987) connects the name of the character Enobarbus in ANT with him.

ISRAEL
(A) 'The people descended from Israel or Jacob' (*OED sb.* 1); the **Jews**.

(B) Hamlet once calls Polonius '**Jepthah**, judge of Israel' (HAM 2.2.403).

(C) See Judges 11.30–40.

ITALIAN PRIEST
King John belittles the authority of Pope **Innocent** III to his **legate** Pandulph: 'no Italian priest / Shall tithe or toll in our dominions' (JN 3.1.153–4), thus demoting Innocent from Pope to priest.

ITERATION
(A) Verbal repetition or amplification. Waith and Barish describe this as one of the characteristic speech patterns of Puritan satire, especially in their represented moral diatribes.

(B) Thus when Falstaff says to a Prince Hal who has been repeatedly upbraiding him for his own moral faults, 'O, thou hast damnable iteration, and art indeed able to corrupt a saint' (1H4 1.2.90–1), he is accusing Hal of speaking annoyingly like a **Puritan**; at the same time he implies that Hal is so persuasively immoral that he could undermine a **saint**, a name the Puritans called themselves.

(C) On Puritan iteration, see Mallette (1997), chs 1 and 2; Waith (1963), 12–13; Barish (1960), 198–204; and Hassel (2003), 105–9. Bloom (1989), 84; and Poole (1995) notice that Falstaff parodies Puritan preachers.

JACK-A-LENT

(A) A puppet in human form pelted by boys during **Lent**.

(B) 'Jack-a-Lent' is referred to twice in WIV (3.3.27; 5.5.127), once describing Falstaff's battered wit.

(C) See BEV, 272 n; Jonassen (1991) relates the symbolism of the Jack-a-Lent puppet figure to the figure of Falstaff.

JACOB

(A) The son of Isaac, who once tricked his uncle Laban into giving him all of the sheep which were born pied (Gen. 30.32–43).

(B) As Shylock and Antonio dispute the proper interpretation of the scriptural passages concerning Jacob's service as Laban's shepherd, the issue gradually shifts from Shylock's using Jacob 'to make interest good' (MV 1.3.94) to Antonio's very Protestant insistence that **grace** rather than **merit** informs these strange events (MV 1.3.71–91). To Antonio, Jacob's reward was 'sway'd and fashion'd by the hand of **heaven**' (1.3.93); to Shylock, it was Jacob's hard work and good wit, his works, which made him 'thrive' (MV 1.3.89). Shylock also later swears 'By Jacob's staff' (MV 2.5.36), the one that helped produce the 'parti-colored lambs' (MV 1.3.88).

(C) Among Reformation theologians, Andrewes concedes Jacob's humility but stresses his physical and mental 'strength' (5: 461; from Gen. 32.28 and in Gen. 27.36); Donne concedes his strength but stresses his humility (1: 268–9; from Gen. 32.9). See Shaheen (1999), 162–4, on the reference to Laban's shepherd. Holmer (1985) argues that a source for MV may have been a contemporary treatise which uses the Jacob-Laban story to argue against usury. Nathan (1987) looks at names of characters in the plays which are derived from the name Jacob.

Josipovici (1999), 25–7, examines Jacob as a positive example of Jewish identity and resourcefulness for Shylock, as does Lupton (2000), 127.

JAPHET
(A) Noah's son Japheth; the traditional progenitor of all the peoples of Europe.
(B) Prince Hal sarcastically puts down Falstaff's spurious claim to be related by blood: 'Nay, they will be kin to us, or they will fetch it from Japhet' (2H4 2.2.117–18).
(C) See Gen. 10.2–5, and *Britannica* 12: 967.

JAQUES, SAINT
(A) 'Saint Jaques le grand' is Saint James the Greater, one of the apostles of Christ. His shrine, in Santiago de Compostela, St James's purported burial place in Galicia in northwestern Spain, was 'one of the great pilgrimage centres of the Middle Ages', and his emblem was the scallop shell. The emblem and the place were known well enough in Renaissance England for Sir Walter Raleigh to have begun his poem 'Pilgrimage', 'Give me my Scallop shell of quiet', and for Queen Elizabeth's dashing pirate, Sir Francis Drake, to have tried in 1589, the year after the defeat of the Spanish Armada, to plunder this site's unusual material and symbolic wealth. Shrines, bridges, roads and churches to St Jaques and Santiago dot the four ways across France to Santiago.
(B) AWW contains several references to this saint and this site. Helena calls herself 'Saint Jaques' pilgrim, thither gone' (AWW 3.4.4), characteristically using the name in reference to the place and the saint at once. Shakespeare also has the Widow identify Helena as 'a pilgrim', presumably because she is dressed like one, with the broad-brimmed hat, the staff, the cloak and the cockle shell. To the welcome, 'God save you, pilgrim, wither are you bound?' Helena responds 'To Saint Jaques le Grand', adding 'Where do the palmers lodge?' She is repeatedly called 'pilgrim' and 'holy pilgrim' as the scene goes on, and finally united by the widow with other 'enjoin'd penitents, / There's four or five, to great Saint Jaques bound' (AWW 3.5.30–4, 39, 44, 93–5). See also AWW 4.3.48–53.
(C) Bond, the ecclesiastical authority, counts 414 churches in England dedicated to Saint James the Greater, and in his famous fifteenth-century book about pilgrimages, Samuel Purchas mentions 'the Way . . . from the land of England unto Saint Jamez in Gales', equating its importance, as his contemporaries would, with Rome and Jerusalem. Boorde, a sixteenth-century English pilgrim, calls Santiago 'the greatest journey that any Englishman mae goe' (Bond, Purchas and Boorde are cited in Neillands [1985], 8–12, 30). For Raleigh and Drake, see Bentley (1992), 134, and Mullins (1974), 14. In chapter XI of the *Vita nuova* (1294), Dante, a rather more famous Italian traveller, 'reserves the name of "pilgrims" [*peregrini*] for those who go to the house of Galicia; seeing that no other apostle was buried so far from his birthplace as was the blessed St James' (cited in Davies and Davies [1982], 52). Apparently millions of pilgrims 'took the cockle' and made the trek in the seven centuries before 1600, including the famous Valencian El Cid. People are still doing so today (Hitt [1994], 248).

JAW-BONE
Hamlet refers to 'Cain's jaw-bone, that did the first murder' (HAM 5.1.77).
See Genesis 4.8, and **Cain**.

JEPHTHAH
(A) Jephthah was one of the judges of Israel who promised to God that if he defeated the Ammonites he would sacrifice whatever first appeared to him from his house (Judges 11.30–39). His daughter appeared, and he 'most cruelly' performed the foolish promise.
(B) Clarence excuses his own oath-breaking to Warwick by referring to the impious oath 'of Jephthah when he sacrific'd his daughter' (3H6 5.1.91). Hamlet's three references to Polonius and Ophelia as Jephthah and his daughter (HAM 2.2.403–12) seem to imply that Polonius is also foolishly sacrificing his daughter for his own ends.
(C) Johnston (1962), 21–2, discusses the use of the Jephthah story in HAM, as does Spencer (2001), 616–21.

JERUSALEM[1]
(A) The city in Israel where Christ was crucified and buried, and therefore a major destination of the crusades.
(B) Henry IV makes much of 'our holy purpose to Jerusalem', where he locates 'the **sepulchre** of Christ' (1H4 1.1.102, 19); however, he only manages to die in the Jerusalem chamber, thrice named, of his own castle (2H4 4.5.234–40).
(C) Oz (1998) discusses Jerusalem as a symbol serving various early modern 'imagined communities' and as a presence behind H4.

JERUSALEM[2]
(A) Heaven.
(B) When a defeated Queen Margaret is parted from her allies Oxford and Somerset, she refers to heaven as the new Jerusalem (from Rev. 21): 'So part we sadly in this troublous world, / To meet with joy in sweet Jerusalem' (3H6 5.5.7–8).
(C) Of this 'New Jerusalem' as heaven, see Bradford (1848), 1: 272; and Pilkington (1842), 260–1.

JESU MARIA
Though **Jesu** is a fairly common oath in Shakespeare, this version, 'Jesu Maria' (ROM 2.3.69), swearing in Latin by the child and the mother, occurs only once. Friar Lawrence utters it to emphasise his astonishment that Romeo now loves Juliet. Friar Lawrence also greets Romeo in Latin, '*Benedicite*' (ROM 2.3.31).

JESU
Latin form of Jesus.
Mowbray is described by the Bishop of Carlisle as fighting 'for Jesu Christ in glorious Christian field' (R2 4.1.93); Richard III once cries out 'Have mercy,

Jesu' (R3 5.3.178) in frightened prayer, and more cynically he prays 'which Jesu pardon' about his brother Clarence's oath-breaking (R3 1.3.135). Hostess says, 'O Jesu, this is excellent sport, i'faith' (1H4 2.4.390), and Shallow recollects, 'Jesu, Jesu, the mad days that I have spent' (2H4 3.2.33). Since the Hostess swears by 'Jesu' four times in this scene and Shallow twice pairs 'Jesu, Jesu' (2H4 3.2.33, 43), Shakespeare is obviously using the mild blasphemy as a characterizing verbal tic for both figures. Mercutio is instead mocking the fashionable language of upstarts when he says 'O Jesu, a very good blade' (ROM 2.4.29–30). Friar Lawrence swears by 'Jesu **Maria**' and 'Holy Saint Francis' as he speaks about Romeo's fickleness in love (ROM 2.3.65, 69), and the Nurse says 'Jesu what haste' when Juliet demands news of her meeting with Romeo (ROM 2.5.29). The other 'Jesu's' are the same invocations of blessing and protection that we found with **Jesus**.

JESUS

The Son of God. Though the name of Christ can serve as a casual blasphemy, as in Shallow's 'Jesus, the days that we have seen' (2H4 3.2.219), it is also invoked for blessing and protection. The priest John Hume says, 'Jesus preserve your royal majesty' to the Duchess of Gloucester, and follows it with a reference to 'the grace of God' (2H6 1.2.70–2). The 'women cried, / "O Jesus bless us, he is born with teeth" ' at Richard III's prodigious birth (3H6 5.6.75). A Traveller, about to be robbed, also says 'Jesus bless us!' (1H4 2.2.82).

JESHU

Welch form of Jesus.

Fluellen once says 'By Jeshu' for emphasis (H5 4.7.111), and Evans (WIV [Q2] 3.1.11), says '[Jeshu] pless my soul'.

JEW

(A) A person whose religion is Judaism.

(B) The word takes on many connotations in Shakespeare, most of them negative. This says little, however, about Shakespeare's own attitudes towards Jews, since many of the speakers who use the word are drawn as anti-Semites. In MV, which contains 90 per cent of the references, 'the Jew' and 'Jew' often merely replace Shylock's name, frequently with disapprobation or disgust. This happens most often during the trial scene, where Portia and Gratiano use 'Jew' nineteen times for Shylock's name (MV 4.1.313–46). The anti-Semitism of some of the Christian characters in MV also reveals that for them words like 'kindness' and 'gentle' can only modify 'Jew' with irony or surprise. Antonio will 'say there is much kindness in the Jew' if he does not demand collateral, and his 'Hie thee, gentle Jew' follows Shylock's decision to ask in 'a merry sport' only for the pound of his flesh (MV 1.3.145, 153, 177). Gobbo once says of Shylock and his daughter Jessica, 'If e'er the Jew her father come to heaven, / It will be for his gentle daughter's sake' (MV 2.4.33–4). Gratiano, the most outspoken anti-Semite in the play, once says of Jessica's liberality with gold coins, 'Now, by my hood, a gentle and no Jew', and the Duke expects a 'gentle answer' of Shylock during the trial scene, long before Portia asks Shylock to display 'the quality of **mercy**' enjoined by the Lord's Prayer (MV 2.6.51; 4.1.34, 184, 200–2). The word 'Jew' in the play is also associated with and defined by such words as 'faithless', 'devil', 'villain', 'dog', 'currish', 'wealthy', and 'rich' (MV 2.4.37; 2.2.24; 2.8.4, 14; 4.1.292; 5.1.15, 292).

In the other plays, the fool Launce's 'a Jew would have wept to have seen our parting' (TGV 2.3.10–11) implies that Jews usually lack empathy (cf. TGV 2.5.57). Benedick's comment about Beatrice, 'If I do not love her, I am a Jew' could also refer to the Jew's presumed lack of love, but the phrase is probably an unexamined bit of verbal shorthand, the counterpart of Marvell's 'Till the Conversion of the Jews' ('To His Coy Mistress' [1966], 251). Benedick has just been 'converted' from romantic disbelief (ADO 2.3.240, 22). Lancelot Gobbo's pun 'I am a Jew if I serve the Jew any longer' (MV 2.2.112–13) works because of such negative associations. The Witches in MAC complete this sorry array of prejudice when they throw 'Liver of blaspheming Jew' into the charmed pot (MAC 4.1.26). (C) For similar anti-Semitism among the theologians, see Andrewes (2: 25) and Becon (1: 359). Donne is usually more respectful (as in 2: 251; 6: 161–2; 10: 164), but he once says of God's partial blessings, 'if he would have given thee a religion, He might have left thee a Jew; or if he would have given thee Christianity, He might have left thee a Papist' (8: 177). Hassel (1980), 181–9, Dessen (1974), 233, 242–3, and Yaffe (1997) warn against calling a play anti-Semitic merely because it has anti-Semitic characters. On anti-Semitism in MV see Cohen (1980), (1990), Dachslager (1986), and Shapiro (1996). Luxon (1999) claims that Shylock would have been regarded as a 'false Jew,' one who refused to admit Christ, as opposed to the 'Christian Jew' model presented by the biblical Daniel. Edelman (1999) challenges the notion that MV would have been first seen by an entirely anti-Semitic audience. Marx (2000), 103–24, reviews discussions of the Christian/Jew issue in MV. See Adelman (2003) and Metzger (1998) on the converted Jew as a disturbing presence in MV. See **Hebrew**.

JEWESS
Female Jew; used only once in Shakespeare.

Lancelot uses the word in advising Shylock's daughter Jessica that her lover Lorenzo is about to come for their elopement: 'There will come a Christian by, / Will be worth a Jewess' eye.' Though the word can be used condescendingly, like 'negress', there is little reason to assume that Lancelot is doing so here, since he so obviously loves his mistress Jessica, and she him (MV 2.5.43; 2.3.1–3, 10–11).

JEWISH
Of or pertaining to Jews.

Shylock speaks early in the play of Antonio's having 'spet upon my Jewish gaberdine', and Antonio allows during the trial scene that there would be nothing more difficult than trying to 'soften . . . His Jewish heart' (MV 1.3.112; 4.1.79–80). Since both Shylock the **Jew** and the obviously anti-Semitic Antonio use the word 'Jewish' to categorise Shylock ethnically, it is clear that the word could be used both neutrally and pejoratively in Shakespeare.

JEWRY
The Jewish people.

The phrase 'Herod of Jewry' refers more than once to the bloody tyrant who slaughtered the innocent children of Israel (WIV 2.1.20; ANT 1.2.28–9; 3.3.3). 'The wives of Jewry' also refers, sympathetically, to the Jewish mothers of the innocents whom Herod slaughtered (H5 3.3.40). Gaunt refers with prejudice to Christ's 'sepulchre in stubborn Jewry' (R2 2.1.55).

JEZEBEL
The proud queen of Ahab, from 1 Kings 18.4,13; 21.23–6.

Andrew Aguecheek probably criticises his pride when he says of Malvolio, 'Fie on him, Jezebel' (TN 2.5.41).

JOB
(A) Biblical character renowned for his suffering and his patience.

(B) Shakespeare's references to Job are brief and to the point. 'As poor as Job' 'And as wicked as his wife' (WIV 5.5.155–6) refer to his losses and his wife's advice that he 'curse God, and die' (Job 1.21, 2.9). Falstaff tells the Lord Chief Justice, 'I am as poor as Job, my lord, but not so patient' (2H4 1.2.126–7).

(C) Job 1.21 refers to Job's poverty, and James 5.11 to his proverbial (but not perfect) patience. Donne says of Job's tempters, 'The Devill could oppresse him with *deceit*, corrupt the wife of his bosome, to tempt him to desperation' (8: 276–7). Blakemore Evans (1990) compares Dogberry and Job.

JOSHUA
Joshua was Moses's successor as leader of the Israelites and the namesake of one of the books of the Old Testament.

Joshua is a named character in the Pageant of the Nine Worthies (LLL 5.1.126).

JOVE
(A) Jove is often referred to as the chief member of the classical Pantheon, 'the king of gods' (as in TRO 2.3.11). He is the bull for Europa (WIV 5.5.3ff.; ADO 5.4.46–51); the thunderer (MM 2.2.111; H5 2.4.100); the heavenly visitor to a 'thatch'd house' (AYL 3.3.10–11). Like the Christian 'God', he is sworn to in Shakespeare, prayed to, thanked, and subjected to casual and serious curses.

(B) 'Jove' is named repeatedly by Christian as well as non-Christian characters. Malvolio sounds like a Puritan in thanking and praising God, but he often says 'Jove' instead, as in 'Jove and my stars be prais'd!', 'Jove I thank thee', 'It is Jove's doing, and Jove make me thankful!', and 'Well, Jove, not I, is the doer of this, and he is to be thank'd' (TN 2.5.172–3, 178; 3.4.74–5, 82–3). Only once, exasperated at the revellers, does Malvolio say 'For the love o' God, peace' (TN 2.3.85).

Perhaps this usage is related to the Parliamentary prohibition of oaths in plays in 1606, but this is far from certain since sixteen times in TN, characters use 'God' rather than 'Jove'. Shakespeare may rather be making a little fun of the Puritan scrupulousness about oaths and the Puritan tendencies to attribute all things to God in Malvolio's frequent invocations of Jove.

Jove is also a metaphor and a simile, as in Falstaff's flattery of Hal, just kinged, as 'my king, my Jove' (2H4 5.5.46), or Exeter's more serious threat to the French in H5 that Henry V is 'coming / In thunder and in earthquake, like a Jove' (H5 2.4.100).

(C) On this usage see NV TN, 176–7n; Arden TN, 96–7n; Halliwell first speculated that 'Jove' was substituted for 'God' in TN to comply with the statute of 1606 forbidding profanity in plays. Velie (1972), 86–8, argues that Jupiter/Jove in CYM is intended to represent God.

JOY

(A) Eternal blessedness in heaven.

(B) Jessica says metaphorically that Bassanio, who has chosen correctly, 'finds the joys of heaven here on earth' (MV 3.5.76). The Murderer also taunts Clarence with Richard's desire to have him murdered by pretending to believe that death is a benefit: 'he delivers you / From this earth's thralldom to the joys of heaven' (R3 1.4.247–8). We also find everlasting life called 'everlasting joy' (2H6 2.1.18) and 'joy in sweet Jerusalem' (3H6 5.5.8). Varieties of 'God give you joy' also serve as a casual blessing (as in ADO 2.1.336; LLL 5.2.448; SHR 4.2.52).

(C) See Donne, 3: 339; 3: 212; and 7: 70, for parallel usage.

JUDAS[1]

(A) Judas **Iscariot** betrayed Christ with a kiss, for which betrayal the Roman authorities paid him thirty pieces of silver (Matt. 27.3).

(B) Richard II associates the many subjects he blames for his deposition with Judas **Iscariot**: 'So Judas did to Christ; but He, in twelve, / Found truth in all but one; I, in twelve thousand, none' (R2 4.1.169–71). Richard also mistakenly calls his executed friends 'Three Judases, each one thrice worse than Judas' for betraying him to Bolingbroke (R2 3.2.132). The lords say of the actor's 'shame' in the Pageant of the Nine Worthies that this 'Judas [should] hang himself' like the biblical one (LLL 5.2.600–4; see Matt. 27.5). Rosalind and Celia also mention Judas in teasing one another about the colour of Orlando's hair and the honesty of his heart:

> ROSALIND. His very hair is of the dissembling color.
> CELIA. Something browner than Judas's. Marry, his kisses are Judas's own children.
> (AYL 3.4.9–10)

(C) On Judas's traditional red hair and beard, see Shaheen (1999), 225–6. See also *OED* Judas 4.b. For the common association of Judas with betrayal, see Donne, 7: 241; 1: 240; 2: 224; 3: 313; Tyndale, 2: 288; Sandys (1841), 230–1. See also **Indian**.

JUDAS[2]
Eponym for betrayer.

In LLL when the character playing Machabeus says 'Judas I am' the audience responds 'A Judas', provoking the clarification, 'Judas I am, ycliped Machabeus' (LLL 5.2.595–8). Perversely, the witty and theologically educated audience of Navarre continues to pretend to confuse 'Judas' with 'betrayer'.

JUDAEAN
See **Indian** and **Iscariot**.

JUDGE[1] *sb.*
(A) Sometimes spoken of the God who renders judgement.
(B) Though phrases like 'heaven be judge' (as in TGV 5.4.36) or 'God's my judge' (MV 5.1.157) are usually just a manner of speaking in Shakespeare, they can reveal theological context. Katherine of Aragon challenges the unfriendly 'Christian counsel' of Cardinal Wolsey with a possible biblical allusion and a certain theological assertion, 'Heaven is above all yet; there sits a judge / That no king can corrupt' (H8 3.1.100–1). Iago's 'Heaven is my judge' (OTH 1.1.59) is particularly redolent with irony since he is in the midst of proclaiming his diabolical anger. When King Philip of France uses a phrase like 'that supernal judge' in JN, he invokes heavenly authority so strongly that King John has to respond, 'Thou dost usurp authority' (JN 2.1.112, 118).
(C) Andrewes reminds us that Abraham calls God 'Judge of the world' (1: 123–4; of Gen. 18.25); Donne speaks of 'that eternall Judge' (9: 320).

JUDGE[2] *v.*
(A) Render legal or moral judgement.
(B) When King Henry VI says of Warwick's judgement of Cardinal Beauford's 'monstrous life' and current madness, 'Forbear to judge, for we are sinners all' (2H6 3.3.30), he echoes Christ's 'Judge not, that ye be not judged' (Matt. 7.1).
(C) See Shaheen, (1999), 481–2; cf. Rom. 2.11; Ps. 7.8, Ps. 50.6; and Isa. 11.3–4. Diehl (1998), 403–7, argues that MM invokes the Calvinist theory that one must reject the temptation to judge others. See **judgement**[2].

JUDGEMENT[1]
(A) The 'day of judgement' is that time at the end of time when Christ would according to the Apostles' Creed 'come to judge the quick and the dead' (*BCP*, 58). 'God's judgement' can also refer to his apparent retribution against living sinners.
(B) Parson Evans says 'heaven forgive my sins at the day of judgement' (WIV 3.3.212). Dromio refers more cryptically to the cheating devil who 'before the judgement carries poor souls to hell' (ERR 4.2.40). The two Murderers discuss the 'remorse' that can be 'bred' by 'the great Judgement Day' (R3 1.4.104–7), and Macbeth implies a distinction between 'judgement here' and judgement hereafter, in 'the life to come' (MAC 1.7.7–8). Cardinal Beauford spitefully

invokes one aspect of the Calvinist idea of predestination when he refers to 'God's secret judgement' (2H6 3.2.31) in Gloucester's death.

(C) Rogers (1854), 217, speaks of sinners 'continually in torment till the day of judgement'. See also the 17th Article of Religion, 'Of Predestination and Election'. On secret judgement, see Hunter (1976), 41. Weedin (1975), 301–8, discusses judgement and reason in OTH. Morris (1986) argues that 'eschatological judgement' is the theme of MV. Kaula (1984) discusses apocalyptic references in HAM and the characters' readiness for judgement.

JUDGEMENT[2]

(A) The theology of justice, 'the old dispensation', as distinguished from the theology of **mercy**, 'the new dispensation'.

(B) Though Shylock's 'I stand for judgement' stands for many things, including his vengefulness and his legalistic, literal interpretation of the law, it also suggests his alignment with the Old Law instead of the New Law, Judaism rather than Christianity. When the Christian Duke asks him, 'How shalt thou hope for mercy, rend'ring none?' Shylock responds in this same vein, 'What judgement shall I dread, doing no wrong?' (MV 4.1.88–9, 103).

(C) Donne says that 'No attribute of God is so often iterated in the Scriptures, no state of God so often inculcated, as this of **Judge**, and Judgement, no word concerning God so often repeated' (2: 313).

JUST

(A) Fair in **judgement** and protection. Donne says of God, 'therefore he will be feared, not as a wilfull Tyrant, but as a just Judge' (1: 262).

(B) Queen Elizabeth makes a similar claim against Queen Margaret, albeit with a desperate vindictiveness: 'So just is God, to right the innocent' (R3 1.3.181). On the other extreme, Lear resolves during the storm to do extraordinary acts of charity to the 'poor naked wretches' of the world, 'shake the superflux' of abundance to them, 'To show the heavens more just' (LR 3.4.36). He may mean in this difficult passage that his kingly acts of charity might teach the gods to be more just. He may mean that those acts would make the gods appear more just than they are in the eyes of the wretched. In either case, only a deep religious scepticism could provoke such a desperate plan.

(C) Coverdale (1846), 2: 49, calls death 'the just judgement of God: . . . a penalty deserved'. For 'just cause', see '**cause**'.

JUSTICE

(A) One of the four **cardinal** or 'natural' virtues, meaning something like behaving justly and judging others fairly if also sternly. With temperance, fortitude and patience, justice is appropriated into the Christian scheme of virtues. However, because of the prominence of God's **grace** (and consequent calls for human **mercy**) in Reformation theology, justice assumed an increasingly uncomfortable seat amongst the human virtues during that time.

(B) Such tension is revealed in Portia's argument that Shylock show mercy to

Antonio and forgive him the pound of flesh he is justly owed. This centres on her distinction between **salvation** by grace and salvation by **works**, God's mercy versus God's justice:

> Therefore Jew,
> Though justice be thy plea, consider this,
> That in the course of justice, none of us
> Should see salvation.
>
> (MV 4.1.197–200)

The Duke also tries unsuccessfully to persuade Shylock to give a 'gentle answer' of 'commiseration' and not justice for Antonio (MV 4.1.30–4). Isabella refers to the same idea when she advises Angelo to use 'the deputed sword' with 'grace' and 'mercy' rather than mere justice (MM 2.2.60, 62–3). Her own later call for 'justice, justice, justice, justice' against this same Angelo is therefore not unequivocally virtuous (MM 5.1.25, 89). On the other hand, the newly crowned (and apparently irresponsible) King Henry V praises the Lord Chief Justice for his stern administration of the law: 'You are right justice, and you weigh this well, / Therefore still bear the balance and the sword' (2H4 5.2.102–3). Othello, casting himself ironically in the godlike role of just judge, also recalls the familiar iconography of Justice when he observes of the still-sleeping Desdemona that her 'balmy breath . . . dost almost persuade / Justice to break her sword!' (OTH 5.2.16–17). His grotesque misjudgement of her caps off the moment.

(C) See Roberti (1962), 673–6; 'Justice', *NewCathEncy*, 8: 68–72, 75–7; *ST* II.2.58; *ST* I.21. Wilks (1986), 123–4, discusses how 'providential justice' is executed in HAM. Lindley (1996) argues that MM tries to reconcile justice and mercy. Lemercier (2001) argues that justice moves from a religious, supernatural concern in R3 to an absolutist model in MM. For discussions of this Last Judgement imagery in Tudor literature and art, see Sheingorn (1985), 22; Emmerson (1985), 89; and Harbison (1976), 127–8.

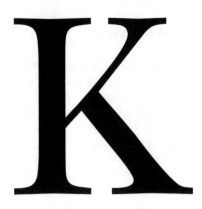

KATHERINE, SAINT

(A) The mythical Saint Katherine (Catherine) of Alexandria (4th c.) was martyred for her faith; though she successfully disputed with fifty philosophers, she was tortured on the 'Catherine wheel'; when it broke in the process (such things often happened as the saints were being persecuted), she was beheaded.

(B) Joan of Arc (1412–31), who names 'Saint Katherine's churchyard' in Touraine (1H6 1.2.100) as the place where she got her sword, was also a virgin martyr who, something like Katherine, successfully passed three weeks of theological examination at Poitiers. Joan, who was burned rather than beheaded for refusing to recant her radically personal faith, also claimed to have heard Katherine urge her to defend France. Feast Day: 25 November.

(C) See Farmer (1978), 69–70, 212; Baring-Gould (1914), 14: 540–2. Katherine had a widespread cult in England, with 62 churches; 162 medieval bells still bear her name. She is also commonly represented in English miracle plays as well as a variety of art forms, including wall murals and stained glass. For a variety of extant artistic representations of St Katherine in Warwickshire, see Davidson and Alexander (1985), 44–5, 96, 152–4; for such art in York, see Palmer (1990), 194–6.

KINE

'Kine' is an archaic plural of cow. In Gen. 41.1–4, 19–21, the Pharaoh of Egypt dreamed of seven 'fatfleshed' kine and seven 'leanfleshed' ones, which ate up the first seven; Joseph correctly interpreted this as seven years of plenty followed by seven years of famine.

When Falstaff tries to persuade Prince Hal not to banish him with the analogy: 'If to be fat be to be hated, then Pharaoh's lean kine are to be lov'd', he asks, 'who would prefer famine over plenty?' (1H4 2.4.472–4).

KING OF KINGS, KING OF HEAVEN
God.

Winchester says that Henry V 'was a king, blest of the King of kings' (1H6 1.1.28). Clarence warns the Murderers, to no avail, that 'the great King of kings / Hath in the table of his law commanded / That thou shalt do no murther' (R3 1.4.195–7). King Edward also prophetically warns Hastings and Rivers to tell the truth lest 'the supreme King of kings / Confound your hidden falsehood and award / Either of you to be the other's end' (R3 2.1.13–15). See also R2 3.3.101–3, and R3 1.2.105.

KISS
(A&B) Several religious rituals and stories are associated with the kiss in Shakespeare. When Stephano tells Caliban to 'kiss the book' (TMP 2.2.142), he alludes to the tradition of swearing an oath by kissing the Bible, though literally he offers a bottle rather than a Bible. Julia's 'seal the bargain with a holy kiss' (TGV 2.2.7) may refer to the 'holy kiss' of Christian greeting in 1 Thess. 5.26. In MV Morocco's description of Portia's suitors ('From the four corners of the earth they come / To kiss this shrine, this mortal breathing saint' – MV 2.7.39–40) derives like Romeo's 'holy palmers' kiss' (ROM 1.5.100) from the pilgrim's veneration of holy persons, places and things. Richard of Gloucester, proud of his hypocrisy when he kisses the young prince he will soon kill, recalls, 'so Judas kiss'd his master, / And cried "All hail!" when as he meant all harm' (3H6 5.7.33–4). Cf. Berowne's 'A kissing traitor' (LLL 5.2.600–4).
(C) The Gospel for the Sunday next before **Easter** reads, 'And forthwith he came to Jesus, and said, Hail Master, and kissed him' (*BCP*, 121; cf. Matt. 26.49). See also Donne, 1: 240; 3: 313). Of the holy kiss in church, Tyndale complains, 'We have turned kissing in the Church into the **pax**' (3: 126); Jewel, similarly complaining of the Roman rite, says, 'The peace given to the bishop was not a little table of silver or somewhat else, as hath been used in the Church of Rome, but a very kiss indeed, in token of perfect peace and unity in faith and religion' (1845–50), 1: 265. See **all-hail**; see also BEV, 1544n; Noble, (1935), 272–3, and Shaheen (1999), 82, 335.

KNEE, KNEEL
(A) Whether cynically or devoutly, kneeling can signify political or religious obedience and humility. Like the holy kiss, this gesture was controversial among the more extreme Reformers. In response, Hooker calls kneeling and standing acceptable '*Gesture*[*s*] *in prayinge*': 'When we make profession of oure faith wee stand; when we acknowledge our synnes or seeke unto God for favour, we fall downe, because the gesture of constancie becometh us best in the one, and in the other the behavior of humilitie' (V.30.2).
(B) With a word and a gesture, 'Here on my knee' or its close equivalent 'here I kneel' can assert a speaker's merely secular honesty (AWW 1.3.192–4) or sincerity (JN 3.1.309–10; see also 3H6 2.3.29–35; 3H6 1.1.74–5; 3H6 2.2.81). The Bastard in JN says more cynically of his brother's genetic inheritance, 'on my knee / I

give heaven thanks I was not like to thee' (JN 1.1.82–3). Iago's 'Here I kneel' (OTH 4.2.151) appropriates this potentially holy word and gesture to convince Othello of his total commitment to the Moor's cause against Desdemona.

(C) Nowell (1853), 123; Hutchinson (1842), 253; Cranmer (1846), 2: 502; Becon, 3: 270; and Grindal (1843), 340, are among the early Reformers opposed to kneeling in church; Donne, 8: 331; 8: 174; 7: 275, has mixed feelings. Andrewes says of 'Come, let us worship and fall down, and kneel before the Lord our Maker', with which 'We begin our Liturgy every day', 'He will not have us worship Him like elephants, as if we had no joints in our knees; He will have more honour of men than of the pillars in the Church. He will have us "bow the knees" ' (2: 334; citing Ps. 95.6). See also *BCP*, vii.

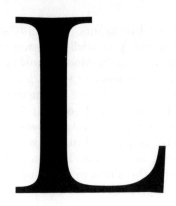

LABAN

Jacob's uncle from Gen. 28.2 and 29.13. See **Jacob**.

LADY

(A) 'Our Lady' is Mary, Mother of **Christ**.

(B) To establish her own authority, Joan of Arc proclaims to King Charles, 'Heaven and our Lady **gracious** hath it pleas'd / To shine on my contemptible estate'; she quickly adds, glossing and underlining this claim, 'God's **Mother** deigned to appear to me' (1H6 1.2.74–5, 78). The Catholic Princess of France says a little more sarcastically about the king's broken vow, 'Our Lady help my lord! He'll be forsworn' (LLL 2.1.97).

(C) Reformers like Jewel (1845–50), 86, Pilkington (1842), 535, and Bradford (1848), 1: 45–6, disapprove of Mary's invocation and worship in speaking of the 'feast of Lady-day' and 'Lady Psalters'.

LADY, BY'R

'By our Lady' is a mild oath occurring fourteen times in Shakespeare, and fairly evenly spread among the genres.

The most interesting example is Desdemona's usage of the oath (in Q1) to express both frustration and determination as she tries to intercede on Cassio's behalf with the sternly judgemental Othello: 'By'r lady, I could do much' (OTH 3.3.74). One of the Virgin's most common roles is that of intercessor. Verges and Prince Hal both use the phrase twice (ADO 3.3.77, 83; 1H4 2.4.45, 298), Hal probably to achieve a more common touch in the tavern.

LAKIN, BY'R

(A) A variation of 'By'r Lady', shortening 'By our ladykin' (*OED* lakin[2]).

(B) Both the gentle Gonzalo, the reverend counsellor, and Snout the joiner use the phrase in Shakespeare (TMP 3.3.1; MND 3.1.13).

(C) BEV, 968n; RIV, 1090n.

LAMBERT'S DAY, SAINT

(A&B) Richard II announces 'Saint Lambert's Day' (R2 1.1.199), 17 September, as the time of the combat between Mowbray and Bolingbroke. Holinshed, Shakespeare's source, offers two possible dates, St Lambert's day or the more neutral 'mondaie in August'. The fact that St Lambert, like the two rivals in Shakespeare, was a political exile involved in both a blood-feud and struggles for familial property, may have influenced Shakespeare's choice of the religious day.

(C) See BEV, 728n; see also *NDS*, 3: 391; Farmer (1978), 236–7; Baring-Gould (1914), 10: 274–8.

LAMMAS

A harvest festival of the early English Church, celebrated on 1 August and associated with the ripening corn (*OED sb.* 1 & 4). The word might literally be 'loaf-mass' from the OE hláfmæsse.

When the Nurse says of Juliet, 'Come Lammas-eve at night shall she be fourteen' (ROM 1.3.21), the audience might therefore have associated the ripening young woman with the ripening grain. See also ROM 1.3.15, 17.

LASH

Literally an implement of the mortification of the flesh, applied as a spiritual discipline; both of Shakespeare's uses are figurative.

Claudius responds 'How smart a lash that speech doth give my conscience' when he hears Polonius ask Ophelia to hold a holy book when Hamlet approaches her. In Polonius' reluctant words, he is thereby staging a 'pious action' which will look like 'devotion's visage' even though it will actually be 'The devil himself' in its religious hypocrisy (HAM 3.1.45–7). Luciana also uses the word metaphorically when she warns her sister Adriana that 'headstrong liberty is lash'd with woe' (ERR 2.1.15).

LATIN

(A) In 1500, Latin was still the universal language in Europe of diplomats, scholars and universities, as well as the official language of the Roman Church. The liturgy, including the mass, the Bible (the 'Vulgate'), the provincial synods, the ecclesiastical courts and the papal letters were all in Latin. The introduction of vernacular liturgies and of course vernacular translations of the Bible were two hallmarks of the Reformation. Despite agitation within the Roman Catholic community during the sixteenth century for similar use of vernacular liturgies and Bible translations, and with the clear exception of the Rhemish New Testament in 1582, the Catholic equivalent for the next three hundred years of the English King James version, Latin remained the language of the Roman Church until the last four decades of the twentieth century.

(B) When Rosalind compares 'a priest that lacks Latin' to 'a rich man that hath not the gout' (AYL 3.2.318–19), she implies that neither group would have many members. When she adds of such a priest that 'he sleeps easily because he cannot study' (AYL 3.2.320–1), her point is based on the exclusivity of Latin texts for religious study before the Reformation. By 1600, of course, this is no longer the case in Western Europe. When Katherine of Aragon says to Cardinal Wolsey's Latin, 'O, good my lord, no Latin', she is speaking more generally of Latin as the universal language of the Catholic Church. She glosses her own comment, 'I am not such a truant since my coming, / As not to know the language I have liv'd in' and 'Lord Cardinal, / The willing'st sin I ever yet committed / May be absolv'd in English' (H8 3.1.42–9). Such Reformed sentiment from such obviously Catholic lips catches the ear.

(C) Grindal's Injunctions at York prescribe 'That no person or persons whatsoever shall wear beads, or pray, either in Latin or in English, upon beads, or knots, or any other like superstitious thing' (140, item 16). Whitaker (1849), 273, also complains of 'the use of the Latin tongue in the Catholic service': 'When we raise a Psalm, we should not only sing, but understand it' (273). So does Bradford: 'for singing of psalms and godly songs to our edification, all is done in Latin, with such notes, tunes, ditties, and descants, that utterly the mind is pulled from the consideration of the thing (if men did understand it) unto the melody' (1848), 1: 160. See also *Certaine Sermons*, 2nd tome, pp. 133–42, for the sermon 'wherein it is declared that Common Prayer and Sacraments ought to bee ministred in a tongue that is understood of the hearers'. See 'Latin Language', *OxfordEncyRef*, 2: 400–1; see also *NewCathEncy*, 8: 412–17; 2:436–57, 463–74. See Lang (1989), 'Latin' and 'Vatican II'. Moisan (1995), 106–16, examines the implications of a woman learning Latin in SHR. Binns (1982) argues that Shakespeare did know Latin well and surveys Latin citations in the plays. See Cross and Livingstone (1997), 1758. See also **curse**.

LATTER

Last, pertaining to the end of the world (*OED adj.* 3.a). The latter day can thus be the Day of **Judgement**.

Williams says of King Henry V before Agincourt, 'But if the **cause** be not good, the King himself hath a heavy reckoning to make, when all those legs, and arms, and heads, chopp'd off in a battle, shall join together at the latter day and cry all' against him (H5 4.1.134–7).

LAUD

Religious praise, as a noun or a verb.

Henry IV says, 'Laud be to God' when he learns in the hour of his death that he will indeed die in Jerusalem, even if it is just a chamber of his palace (2H4 4.5.235–40). As part of his complicated rhetorical parody of the Puritan figure, Falstaff says of competent thieves, 'I laud them, I praise them' (1H4 3.3.191–2).

LAUDS
(A) Religious songs of praise; hymns.
(B) Gertrude says that Ophelia, just before her death, 'chaunted snatches of old lauds' (HAM 4.7.177).
(C) See *OED sb.* 3.

LAW
(A) Often 'the law' of God. Christ preaches from the Mount, 'Thou shalt love the Lord thy God with all thy heart, and with all thy soul, and with all thy mind. This is the first and great commandment. And the second is like unto it, Thou shalt love thy neighbour as thyself. On these two commandments hang all the law and the prophets' (Matt. 22.37–40; cf. Mark 12.30–1, Luke 10.27). These two commandments contrast the old dispensation of law with the new dispensation of love. The Reformer Marbeck offers this clear and resonant distinction: 'The Law saith, pay thy debt: the Gospell saith, Christ hath payed it. The Lawe saith, thou art a sinner, dispaire and thou shalt be damned: the Gospell saith, thy sinnes are forgiven thee, be of good comfort thou shalt be saved. The Lawe saith, make amends for thy sinnes: the Gospell saith, Christ hath made it for thee. The Law saith, the father of heaven is angry with thee: the Gospell saith, Christ hath pacified him with his bloud' (1581), 616.
(B) Clarence refers to one cornerstone of this Judaic law, the ten commandments, when he reminds the Murderers that God 'Hath in the table of His law commanded / That thou shalt do no murther' (R3 1.4.196–7). Berowne speaks of Christ's two commandments (just quoted above), when he reminds his friends that '**charity** itself fulfills the law / And who can sever love from charity?' (LLL 4.3.361–2).
'The law' in MM and MV resonates with both judicial and theological nuance. Angelo's 'Your brother is a forfeit of the law' or 'Redeem your brother from the angry law' (MM 2.2.71; 3.1.201–2) combine theologically loaded words like '**forfeit**' and '**redeem**' with '**law**' in ways which encourage both understandings (cf. MM 1.4.63; 2.2.41, 80, 90; 2.4.61, 93–4, 114; 3.2.15). The play's title and one of its chief phrases too, 'measure for measure' (MM 5.1.411), also come from Christ's Sermon on the Mount: 'Judge not, that ye be not judged. For with what judgement ye judge, ye shall be judged: and with what measure ye mete, it shall be measured to you again' (Matt. 7.1–2). In MV, Shylock the Jew says to the assembled Christians about his rightful bond for a pound of Antonio's 'fair flesh' (MV 1.3.150), 'I stand here for law', and 'I crave the law'. He also asks 'Is that the law?' when the tables of literal interpretation are turned against him. Portia then exults, 'The law hath yet another hold on you' (MV 4.1,142, 206, 314, 347). Jew and Christian, the Old Dispensation and the New, the law of justice and the law of mercy, are resonant in the tensions of this exchange.
(C) On the new and the old law, see *OED sb.* 10.a & 10.b; *ST* II.1.98–107, *esp.* 106. See also Andrewes, 1: 367; 1: 96; Donne, 1: 56; 7: 226–9; 8: 208. Freinkel (1995) argues that Shakespeare's sonnets are filled with Lutheran anxiety over humanity's inability to fulfil the Law. Stritmatter (2000b) notes the use of 'old' and 'new'

religious law discourse in MV, while Isaac (1992), 352–72, looks at Portia's use of Talmudic law. Barnaby and Wry (1998), 1237–52, argue that MM unsettles the relationship between religious and civil law. Levin (1996) suggests that MM stages the replacement of mercy by tolerance. Lupton (1990) argues that in MM, mercy becomes the internalization of the law, not its opposite. Cox (1983) asserts that MM is linked to the medieval mystery plays in its theme of the conflict between the 'old' and the 'new' religious law. Young (1986), 102–4, notes that in early modern theology nature's fall was seen as a consequence of Adam's fall, and that therefore natural law participates in the fallen nature of man. See also 'Law, Theological understanding of', *OxfordEncyRef*, 2: 404–8; and 'Law, Mosaic', *NewCathEncy*, 8: 554–6.

LAY
Not clergy; the laity.

Lucio says of the Duke disguised as a Friar, 'had he been lay, my lord, / For certain words he spake against your Grace, / . . . I had swing'd him soundly' (MM 5.1.128–30). Sands in H8 bawdily contrasts his 'lay thoughts' to the apparently more divine preoccupations of Cardinal Wolsey (H8 1.4.11).

LAZARUS
(A) The beggar in Christ's parable (Luke 16.19–21), who, 'full of sores', 'desired to be refreshed with the crumbs that fell from the rich man's table; yea, and the dogs came and licked his sores'.
(B) Falstaff refers to 'slaves as ragged as Lazarus in the painted cloth, where the glutton's dogs lick'd his sores' 1H4 4.2.25–6).
(C) Andrewes pointedly reminds the privileged court at Richmond to heed the lesson of Lazarus (2: 78–9). See Shaheen (1999), 421 on Lazarus.

LECHERY
Excessive or irresponsible expression of sexual desire. The usage is arguably religious rather than merely moral when several of the seven deadly sins are mentioned together.

Falstaff, for example, full of disease and empty of purse, proclaims, 'A man can no more separate age and covetousness than 'a can part young limbs and lechery' (2H4 1.2.228–30). 'Lechery' is also a favourite malapropism in Shakespeare. The Watch in ADO calls the **slander** of Hero a 'dangerous piece of lechery' (ADO 3.3.167–8), and the drunken Toby Belch responds to Olivia's charge of '**lethargy**' or **sloth**, 'Lechery? I defy lechery' (TN 1.5.125).

LEGACY
Something bequeathed.

'Eve's legacy' in TGV (3.1.338) is **pride**, and more generally the consequences of the **Fall**.

LEGATE

(A) An official representative of the **Pope**.

(B) 'Here comes the holy legate of the Pope' is spoken of Cardinal Pandulph in JN (3.1.135). Besides the five references to Pandulph as legate, there is also a papal legate in 1H6 (5.1.51); Surrey also charges that Wolsey 'sought to be a legate' 'Without the King's assent or knowledge' (H8 3.2.310–12).

(C) Jewel mentions several criticisms of these papal representatives (1845–50), 4: 679.

LEGION

Any great host or multitude. Because Christ speaks in Matt. 5.8–9 to the 'unclean spirit' possessing the man, 'What *is* thy name?, And he answered, saying, My name *is* Legion: for we are many', this word and name can be associated with both devils and the devil.

When Sir Toby says of the apparently mad Malvolio, 'Legion himself possess'd him' (TN 3.4.85–6), he is talking about these biblical demons. Clarence also dreamed that 'a legion of foul fiends / Environ'd me' (R3 1.4.58–9), and Macduff allows that 'Not in the legions / Of horrid hell can come a devil more damn'd / In evils to top Macbeth' (MAC 4.3.55–7). Cf. TMP 3.3.102–3; and H5 2.2.124–5.

LENT (LENTEN)

(A) The period of **abstinence** and **penitence** from **Ash Wednesday** through **Easter Eve**.

(B) When Falstaff pretends to charge Mistress Quickly with 'suffering **flesh** to be eaten in thy house, contrary to the **law**, for the which I think thou wilt **howl**', she responds with a discretion that surely rivals Falstaff's, 'What's a joint of mutton or two in a whole Lent?' (2H4 2.4.346–7). Mercutio's 'a hare, sir, in a lenten pie, that is something stale and hoar ere it be spent', followed by the song about the 'old hare hoar' which 'is very good meat in Lent' (ROM 2.4.132–9) draws bawdy connotations out of the meat that is eaten so seldom during Lent that it spoils. The rebel Jack Cade promises to reward Dick the butcher for his valour in battle by doubling the length of Lent but providing him, against the Elizabethan law against slaughtering meat during Lent, with 'a license to kill for a hundred lacking one' (2H6 4.3.6–7).

(C) Tyndale speaks of corrupt Lenten practices (2: 113); Bullinger gives a taste of some Lenten controversies, 'touching the time and manner of fastings, and also the choice of meats' (1: 431). Cranmer reveals in 'A proclamation for the abstaining from flesh in Lent time' (dated 'the 16th day of January', [1548]) that fish might have been an especially popular fasting choice in a country like England whose 'subjects have good livings, and get great riches thereby in uttering and selling such meats as the sea and fresh water doth minister unto us' (1846), 2: 508. On the injunction, see BEV, 572n. Bristol (1987) examines COR, Laroque (1998) the Falstaff scenes in 1&2 H4, and Hassel (1979) several masques and plays, including TN and MV, all in relation to the traditional Battle of Carnival and Lent. See also **Jack-a-Lent**.

LENTEN *fig.*

Sparse, associated with **fasting**.

Rosencrantz teases Hamlet, 'if you delight not in man, what lenten entertainment the players shall receive from you' (HAM 2.2.315–17). When Maria says that Feste's witty response is 'A good lenten answer', she implies that it is too brief, therefore Lenten; he is abstaining from the use of many words (TN 1.5.9).

LETHARGY

(A) **sloth** or idleness.

(B) Olivia charges the drunken Toby Belch, 'how have you come so early by this lethargy?' (TN 1.5.123–4). The drunken Toby Belch responds to Olivia's charge of 'lethargy' or sloth, by pretending to misunderstand: 'Lechery? I defy lechery' (TN 1.5.125).

(C) See *Certaine Sermons*, 2nd tome, pp. 249–55, for the 'Homily against Idlenesse'. See also *ST* II.2.35.

LIGHT

(A) Tyndale reveals that light has a variety of symbolic uses in sixteenth-century religious discourse: 'As the devil is darkness and lies, so is God light and truth only. . . . And the brightness of his light is his word and doctrine, as the hundred and eighteenth Psalm saith, "Thy word is a lantern unto my feet, and a light to my paths." And Christ is "the light that lighteneth all men". And the apostles are called "the light of the world", because of the doctrine. And all that know truth are light: "Ye were once darkness", saith Paul, "but now light in the Lord; walk therefore as the children of light" [Eph. 5]. And good works are called the fruits of light. And all that live in ignorance are called darkness; as he saith afterwards, "He that hateth his brother walketh in darkness [citing 1 John 2.11]. For if the light of the glorious gospel of Christ did shine in his heart, he could not hate his brother." To walk in darkness [is to] consent and work wickedness' (2:149).

(B) Several phrases in Shakespeare imbue the word 'light' with such theological associations. When King Henry VI responds to news of the miracle of restored sight to 'a blind man at Saint Albon's shrine', 'Now God be prais'd, that to believing souls / Gives light in darkness, comfort in despair' (2H6 2.1.61, 64–5), he moves from the literal light of seeing to light as God's gift of enlightenment and comfort. Light is often associated with divine beings and holy promptings, as when Macbeth says 'Let not light see my black and deep desires' (MAC 1.4.51). Vows by 'this light of heaven' and 'this heavenly light' are common but also ironic in OTH (4.2.150; 4.3.65), given the darkness Iago is able to bring into its world. When Dromio says of devils, 'It is written, they appear to men like angels of light' (ERR 4.3.55–6), he apparently refers to 2 Cor. 11.14, where Paul writes that 'Satan is transformed into an angel of light'. Berowne may refer to the same passage when he says of the fair ladies who are tempting them to break their vows, 'Devils soonest tempt, resembling spirits of light' (LLL 4.3.253). Doll Tearsheet swears twice by 'God's light' in 2H4 (2.4.132, 147), and Hostess Quickly does the same in 1H4 (3.3.62). Andrew Aguecheek also uses the contraction

' 'slight' (for God's light) twice in TN (3.2.13; 2.5.33). Such mild blasphemies seem without theological point, just the personal verbal tics of one unenlightened fool and two light women of the tavern world.

(C) Cf. Jewel (1845–50), 2: 1036; Tyndale, 1: 256; Grindal (1843), 339; Hooper (1852), 1: 26; Vaux (1590a), *sig*. A3; K8ᵛ. For proverbial references to the devil as an angel of light, see Tilley, D231. See also BEV, 21n.

LIMBO

(A) A controversial site located somewhere between hell and heaven and inhabited (according to Roman Catholics) by unbaptised infants and good people who died before the coming of Christ. Like many Reformers, Hooper finds limbo unscriptural: 'I do clearly reject and esteem as fables all the limbos of the fathers, and of young children, purgatory, and such other like, to be follies, mockeries, and abuses, which are invented and found out by man, without the word of the Lord. For I neither believe nor receive more than two places in the world to come; that is to say, heaven for the faithful and elect, with the angels; and hell for the infidels and reprobate, with the devils' (1852), 2: 31. Fulke agrees (1843), 1: 84.

(B) Titus laments that Lavinia is in her sorrow 'As far from help as Limbo is from bliss!' (TIT 3.1.149). In H8 '*Limbo Patrum*' (5.3.64) is the Porter's slang name for a jail. When Dromio tells Adriana that her husband his master is 'in Tartar Limbo, worse than hell' (ERR 4.2.32), he also means that he is in jail, but refers to Tartarus, the pagan hell, rather than the limbo of Catholic tradition. Cf. Parolles's garbled description of Bertram's talk 'of Sathan and of Limbo and of Furies' (AWW 5.3.260–1).

(C) Like Shakespeare, Philpot uses limbo as a metaphor for prison, this one Newgate (1842), 160; see BEV, 20n. *Mirrour* (1986), 162, reproduces a medieval woodcut of the Patriarchs freed from limbo. See BEV, 535n.

LORD

In 99 per cent of its 800 occurrences, 'lord' refers to a nobleman, not to God. Even in the remaining 1 per cent of the cases, 'lord' is usually part of a casual, unconsidered emphasiser like 'By the Lord' (as in WIV 3.3.61); 'Lord, Lord' (as in TGV 1.2.15); 'Good Lord' (as in ADO 2.1.285). Old Gobbo's 'Lord worshipp'd might he be, what a beard hast thou got!' (MV 2.2.93–4) is a syntactically grotesque example. Salisbury and Gargrave, dying, say more religiously, 'O Lord have mercy on us, wretched sinners' and 'O Lord have mercy on me, woeful man' (1H6 1.4.70–1). Desdemona's prayer upon learning that Othello plans to kill her immediately, 'Then Lord have mercy on me' (OTH 5.2.57) is another more serious reference, while the usage of her dying 'Lord, Lord, Lord' (OTH 5.2.83) may refer to Othello, God, or both.

Among the more serious uses of 'Lord' as a name for God, Henry V is described heroically as fighting 'the battles of the Lord of Hosts' (1H6 1.1.31); Richmond prays to God after his victory over Richard III, 'Abate the edge of traitors, gracious Lord' (R3 5.5.35); and Macduff calls the murdered Duncan

'The Lord's anointed temple' (MAC 2.3.66–8). The Bishop of Winchester says of the deceased King Henry V, 'The battles of the Lord of Hosts he fought' (1H6 1.1.31). Surrey's clever wisecrack, 'The Lord forbid', about the question of whether Henry VIII will yield to Cardinal Campeius's authority and not marry Anne Boleyn, provokes his ally Norfolk to say with a wry liturgical overtone, 'marry amen' (H8 3.2.54–5).

Pompey uses the phrase 'for the Lord's sake' as a synonym for begging prisoners, apparently because that was their constant way of begging (MM 4.3.19 and PEL 423n). And when Berowne tells Rosaline to 'write "Lord have mercy on us" on those three' 'infected' lovers, he refers to the words inscribed on the houses of plague victims (PEL). He adds, 'They have the plague, and caught it of your eyes' (LLL 5.2.419–21).

LOVE[1]

(A) Theological love, the reciprocal love of God and man, is only occasionally referred to in Shakespeare, and then usually only occurs in casual expressions whose religious dimension is difficult to determine.

(B) Andrew Aguecheek's panicked cry for the wounded Sir Toby, 'For the love of God, a surgeon' (TN 5.1.172–3), is possibly more than an unconscious blasphemy, since acts of human charity were traditionally associated with God's love. Similar is Gertrude's protective 'For love of God, forbear him' (HAM 5.1.273) as Hamlet grapples with both Laertes and sacrilege over Ophelia's grave. Hamlet seems to manifest only excitement when he says 'For God's love, let me hear' Horatio's tale of the ghost (HAM 1.2.195), but when he commands his 'Mother, for love of grace' (HAM 3.4.144) to listen to his shriving words and thus preserve her immortal soul, his words, though formulaic, seem explicitly religious.

(C) See *Certaine Sermons*, pp. 40–5, for the sermons 'of Christian love and charity'; see also *ST* I.20. Sexton (1994), 263–8 and 279–83, argues that the Countess's maternal love in AWW is linked to divine grace through the metaphor of baptism. Simonds (1989b), 33–7, argues that AWW is concerned with both sacred and secular love. Lewalski (1962) asserts that MV is concerned with Christian love.

LOVE[2]

(A) The liturgically prescribed love of a man for a woman and a woman for a man. The service for matrimony still contains the question, 'Wilt thou obey him and serve him, love, honour, and keep him, in sickness and in health?' However, the ten commandments and the catechisms also contain the potentially conflicting direction, 'Honour thy father and thy mother' (*BCP*, 249). As Tyndale writes in *The Obedience of a Christian Man*, 'The honour of parents containeth love, fear, and reverence, and consisteth in the proper work and duty of it, in obeying them, in saving, helping, and defending them, and also finding and relieving them if ever they be in need' (1:175).

(B) Cordelia echoes both the wedding service and the Fifth Commandment, then, when she tells her father Lear 'I . . . obey you, love you, and most honor you' but I cannot 'love my father all' (LR 1.1.96–8, 104).

(C) See *BCP*, 292; Shaheen (1999), 607; and Nowell (1853), 130. Siegel (1961) notes the medieval belief in sexual love as an expression of God's love and argues this as a theme in ROM. Stockard (1997) argues that human love in MND grows to resemble divine love through Christian folly. See also **holy**, **heavenly**, **idolatry**, **charity**.

LOWER

Thinking of the universe as a vertical construct, morally and spatially, leads to phrases like 'this lower world', that is, this world below heaven. See **above**, **below**, **beneath**.

Richard II, desperate to believe that 'heaven still guards the right' (R2 3.2.62), nevertheless concedes 'That when the searching eye of heaven is hid / Behind the globe that lights the lower world, / Then thieves and robbers range abroad unseen, / In murthers and in outrage [boldly] here' (R2 3.2.37–40). Prospero asserts a 'Destiny, / That hath to instrument this lower world' (TMP 3.3.53–4).

LOWLINESS

Humility.

Malcolm includes 'lowliness' among his list of twelve 'king-becoming graces', a formula that includes the other arguably (though not exclusively) Christian virtues 'mercy', 'devotion' and 'bounty' (MAC 4.3.91–4). If subsequent history is to be believed, Suffolk's description of Margaret of Anjou's 'humble lowliness of mind' (1H6 5.5.18) is not entirely accurate, but it does illustrate this same usage.

LUCIFER

(A) The proud, rebellious archangel, expelled from heaven and subsequently called the devil, prince of hell.

(B) The Bastard refers to this narrative when he calls Hubert 'damn'd as black . . . more deep damn'd than Prince Lucifer. . . . if thou did'st kill this child' (JN 4.3.121–4); so does Cardinal Wolsey, lamenting all falls from power, including his own; 'And when he falls, he falls like Lucifer / Never to hope again' (H8 3.2.371–2). Unlike Lucifer, however, Wolsey seems to recover spiritually. Cf. WIV 1.3.76; 2.2.297–9; 1H4 2.4.336–7; H5 4.7.137–8.

(C) See Shaheen (1999), 403–4; Isa. 14.12.

LUKE'S, SAINT

(A) St Luke is the Greek physician who wrote one of the Gospels and the Acts of the Apostles. There were 28 ancient churches named St Luke's in England.

(B) An 'old priest of Saint Luke's Church' will secretly marry Lucentio and Baptista's daughter Bianca in SHR (4.4.88, 103).

(C) Baring-Gould (1914), 12: 467–70; Farmer (1978), 251–2. For some early representations of St Luke in the art of Warwickshire, see Davidson and Alexander (1985), 150.

LUST

(A) Uncontrolled or illicit sexual desire; another of the 'deadly seven' (MM 3.1.110) sins.

(B) Isabella speaks a theological mouthful when she rails against her pretended subjugation to Angelo's 'concupiscible intemperate lust' (MM 5.1.98); lust is also called 'ruffian' (ERR 2.2.133); 'wanton' (3H6 3.3.210); 'killing' (TIT 2.3.175); 'murd'rous' (SON 129.3); 'perjur'd' (SON 129.3); and styled an opponent to 'truth' (VEN 804); to 'light' (LUC 674); and to 'honor' (LUC 156). Iago's 'unbitted lusts' suggests its associations with bestiality (OTH 1.3.331), and its 'boundless' insatiability (LUC 653–4). Malcolm speaks similarly of the bottom-less 'cestern of my lust' (MAC 4.3.60, 63). Lust is often associated with heat and fire, as when Ferdinand promises Prospero that nothing will 'melt / Mine honour into lust' for Miranda (TMP 4.1.27–8). Mrs Ford advises teasing Falstaff 'till the wicked fire of lust have melted him in his own grease'; and their song later torments him, 'Lust is but a bloody fire, / Kindled with unchaste desire' (WIV 2.1.67–68; 5.5.95–6).

(C) See Pilkington (1842), 558; Tyndale, 1: 273; Hutchinson (1842), 142; Becon, 1: 159; Marbeck (1978), 150; and, typically, Nowell (1853), 201: 'we be most sharply and continually assaulted both by crafty and violent men, and by con-cupiscence and our own lusts, by the enticements of the flesh'. Loarte offers detailed advice for avoiding the 'dartes of lust' (trans. Brinkley, 1596–97), 177–88. See also (under temperance) *ST* II.2.153–4. Waters (1973) argues an association of lust with the Roman Catholic mass in H8.

LUTHERAN

(A) Follower of Martin Luther's Reformation movement. Gregory Martin, the Catholic translator of the Rheims New Testament into English (1582), is repre-sented by the Reformer Fulke as complaining about the general animosity of such competing Protestant groups as 'the Calvinists and Puritans at home; the Lutherans, Zuinglians, and Calvinists abroad. Read their books written vehe-mently, one sect against another' (1: 204). Donne admires the liturgical moder-ation of 'That Church, which they call Lutheran', because it 'hath retained more of these Ceremonies, then ours hath done; And ours more then that which they call Calvinist' (8: 331).

(B) As his authority as advisor to Henry VIII and as a representative of Catholicism is threatened by Henry's attraction to Anne Boleyn, Cardinal Wolsey refers directly to this prominent Reformist group:

> What though I know her virtuous
> And well-deserving? Yet I know her for
> A spleeny Lutheran, and not wholesome to
> Our cause, that she should lie i' th' bosom of
> Our hard-rul'd king.
>
> (H8 3.2 97–101)

(C) PEL (803n) glosses 'spleeny' passionate; BEV (919n) 'hot-headed, contentious'. Waddington (1989) considers possible connections between Luther and Hamlet.

LUXURY

(A) Sensuality, **lechery** or **lust**, one of the seven deadly sins.

(B) Mistress Quickly incongruously sings to Falstaff, 'Fie on lust and luxury' (WIV 5.5.93). Lear expresses his moral disillusionment as well as his sense of personal and political powerlessness when he says, 'The wren goes to't, and the small gilded fly / Does lecher in my sight. / Let copulation thrive. . . . / To't luxury, pell-mell, for I lack soldiers' (LR 4.6.112–17).

(C) De Grazia (1998), 273, discusses the use of the word as a metaphor for lechery and argues (267–71) that Gloucester is identified with this sexual luxury in LR.

M

MACHABEUS

(A) Judas Maccabaeus, the great Jewish military hero who helped resist the oppressive rule of Antiochus Epiphanes, 'who had defiled the temple and outlawed the Jewish religion'.

(B) Five times in LLL this Judas is confused with the man who betrayed Christ (5.1.127; 5.2 536, 598, 599, 631).

(C) See Shaheen (1999), 136; this story is recounted in 1 Maccabees 2.66; 3.1–2.

MADE¹

Created, said of God, heaven or the gods.

Hamlet speaks of God the Maker in the words 'He that made us with such large discourse' (HAM 4.4.36). Othello describes Desdemona's wishing 'That heaven had made her such a man' (OTH 1.3.163) as Othello spoke to her father of his exploits. Emilia later complains of Othello's calling Desdemona 'whore' by asking of her 'Was this fair paper, this most goodly book, / Made to write "whore" upon?' (OTH 4.2.71–2). Portia, anatomizing her first wave of suitors, says of 'the French lord, Monsieur Le Bon', 'God made him, and therefore let him pass for a man' (MV 1.2.54–7), and Orlando says of his brother's refusal to give him an education, 'I am helping you to mar that which God made' (AYL 1.1.32–3). Trying to calm Isabella's moral outrage, the Duke says to her, 'The hand that hath made you fair hath made you good' (MM 3.1.181).

MADE²

Ordained by God.

The Bishop of Carlisle advises King Richard II to take arms against his sea of troubles by saying 'Fear not, my lord, that Power that made you king / Hath power to keep you king in spite of all' (R2 3.2.27–8). Here the reference is arguably more to 'made' as ordained than to 'made' as created, since Carlisle asserts God's predetermination of Richard's kingship. Statements like 'This hand was made to handle nought but gold' or 'Thy hand is made to grasp a palmer's staff' (2H6 5.1.7, 97) could refer to psychological or divine predispositions.

MADE[3]

Executed by God, as of Last Judgement.

The last judgement is considered an event that will be executed by God when King John wrongly accuses Duke Humphrey of their mutual hand in Arthur's death, 'O, when the last accompt 'twixt heaven and earth / Is to be made, then shall this hand and seal / Witness against us to damnation!' (JN 4.2.216–18).

MADE[4]

Converted or baptised into the Christian religion.

Henry VIII says of his infant daughter Elizabeth, 'I long to have this young one made a Christian' (H8 5.2.212–13). Jessica is 'made' 'a Christian' through her marriage to Lorenzo (MV 3.5.19–20).

MADONNA

The Virgin Mary; in ancient Italian, 'my lady', a form of address.

Feste is the only character in Shakespeare who uses this word. The almost exclusive associations between the name 'madonna' and the Virgin Mary is instrumental in Feste's attempt to help Olivia to a little humility. She has vowed to be celibate, a veiled cloistress, for seven years 'in sad remembrance' of her brother's death (TN 1.1.25–33). He begins his fool's work with 'Good madonna, give me leave to prove you a **fool**.' The sarcastic title 'madonna' and 'good madonna' that mark each of his next five lines inevitably underline Olivia's preposterous vow of virginity, not to mention the inflated self-image that led her to such an expression of perfect love (TN 1.5.58–72). Even after she has accepted his proof of her **folly**, Feste continues to call her 'madonna' (TN 1.5.112–13; 1.5.137–8; 5.1.295–300). In Illyria, 'Foolery . . . does walk about the orb like the sun' (TN 3.1.38–9); Feste often uses 'madonna' to mark Olivia's most prideful path.

MAGNUS, SAINT

(A) St Magnus Martyr, the Earl of Orkney (1075–116), died praying for his political murderers. A church near London Bridge was dedicated to him, and rebuilt by Wren. Feast Day: 16 April.

(B) There must therefore be some irony when Jack Cade unforgivingly mentions 'Saint Magnus' Corner' as he commands his mob to 'kill and knock down' the establishment (2H6 4.8.1–2).

(C) Farmer (1978), 257; Baring-Gould (1914), 4:211–17.

MAHOMET

(A) Muhammed, the founder of Islam.

(B) When Charles of France asks in 1H6, 'Was Mahomet inspired with a dove?'

(1H6 1.2.140), he refers to the claim, often disputed in Shakespeare's time, that a dove whispered divine inspiration into Muhammed's ear. See **dove**.

MAKE

Render, cause to occur, spoken of God. Andrewes recites the benediction, '*The God of peace . . . make you perfect . . . through Jesus Christ*' (3: 80).

Hamlet responds to Laertes's offer to 'exchange forgiveness' for their mutual death-dealing with 'Heaven make thee free of it!' (HAM 5.2.332). Gaunt similarly blesses his son, 'God in thy good cause make thee prosperous!' (R2 1.3.78).

MAKER, MAKING

(A) God the creator is frequently called 'maker', as in the Apostles' Creed, and his work, including his providential control, 'making'. Donne says of God's making and women's make-up, citing Jerome, '*manus Deo inferunt*, they take the pencill out of Gods hand, who goe about to mend any thing of his making' (2: 343).
(B) When the Queen of France calls 'God, the best maker of all marriages' (H5 5.2.359) in her blessing of Katherine and Henry, 'maker' implies both the religious dimension of the service and God's hand in the union. As the wedding service states, 'Those whom God hath joined together, let no man put asunder.' Cardinal Wolsey says to his ecclesiastical rival Cromwell that since the angels fell by ambition, 'how can man, then / (The image of his Maker) hope to win by it?' (H8 3.2.441–2). Rosalind also asks of Orlando, who is making a fool of himself by praising her so lavishly in the forest, 'Is he of God's making?' (AYL 3.2.205).
(C) See Andrewes, 2: 334 (from Ps. 95.6); Norden (1847), 172; Vaux (1590a), *sig*. A4; and the Apostles' Creed (*BCP*, 293).

MANNA

(A) The substance that miraculously appeared in the desert each morning during the exodus of the Jews from Egypt: 'It is manna . . . the bread which the Lord hath given you to eat.'
(B) Lorenzo says upon learning from Portia that he and Jessica will finally inherit all of Shylock's wealth, 'Fair ladies, you drop manna in the way / Of starved people' (MV 5.1.294). The contrast between the free gift from God and the forced gift from Shylock reverberates with ironies.
(C) See Sandys (1841), 371–2, and Ex. 16.15.

MARIA

Mary's Latin name.

The Friar mocks Romeo's apparent fickleness with the mild blasphemy, '**Jesu** Maria, what a deal of brine / Hath wash'd thy sallow cheeks for Rosaline' (ROM 2.3.69–70).

MARRIAGE

(A) The ceremony of matrimony, or the liturgical vows it contains.
(B) Kate's father Baptista speaks of 'the ceremonial rites of marriage' (SHR

3.2.6). There is also a reference to the 'rites of marriage' in JN (2.1.539), a 'marriage to be solemniz'd' in 1H6 (5.3.168), 'holy marriage' in ROM (2.3.61), 'the vow / I made to her in marriage' in HAM (1.5.49–50), and 'marriage rite' in PER (4. ch. 17). Hamlet later complains that Gertrude 'makes marriage vows / As false as dicers' oaths' (HAM 3.4.44–5). Since the vows clearly state 'as long as you both shall live' (*BCP*, 291), Hamlet is either excessively scrupulous here or charging his mother with committing adultery before King Hamlet's death.

(C) See *Certaine Sermons*, 2nd tome, pp. 239–48, for 'An Homilie of the state of Matrimony'. Ranald (1979) examines the context of canon and civil laws on marriage with regards to ADO, MM, MV and SHR; Chamberlain (2000) discusses the same topic in MM. Simonds (1989b), 48–59, considers AWW's parody of the sacred language of marriage, and Simonds (1992), 248–68, studies the vine/tree emblem of marriage in CYM. Wayne (1991), 166–7, places differing Protestant and Roman Catholic views on sexual pleasure within marriage in relation to OTH. Belsey (1996) argues that CYM and WT exhibit anxieties about women in marriage which stem from the story of the Fall. See also Hopkins (1998). Bevington and Riggio (2002), 128–32, explore royal marriage rituals in connection with the staging of such rituals in MND and TMP.

MARRIED

'Married' refers to the religious service rather than the matrimonial condition which follows it in WIV (5.5.203), MM (2.1.171, 175), ADO (3.2.89, 4.1.9, 5.4.118), AYL (5.2.42, 73, 114, 116) and OTH (1.3.79).

MARRY

A common pun on the name of Mary, used as a substitute oath. 'Marry' as 'matrimony' is also sometimes part of this pun; this is more common in the comedies than it is in the other plays.

The convergence of 'Mary' and 'marry' is especially obvious when the two uses occur side by side, as when 'Marry [by Mary], after they closed in earnest' is followed two lines later by 'But shall she marry him', and 'Shall he marry her' is followed by 'Marry, thus' (TGV 2.5.12–22). 'The question is concerning your marriage' is likewise quickly followed by 'Marry, is it' in WIV (1.1.220–3). Cf. ROM 3.5.112, 234. Sometimes the pairing calls attention to itself, as when the reiterated question (with the oath), 'What, marry, may she?' is followed by 'Marry with a king' (R3 1.3.99). But 'Marry' as merely an oath for 'Mary', without the other pun, is much more common in Shakespeare. An example is Dogberry's answer to 'Which be the malefactors?' 'Marry, that am I and my partner'; another is Conrade's response to the charge of 'villain': 'Marry, sir, we say we are none' (ADO 4.2.3–4, 24).

MARTEXT

The incompetent clergyman whom Touchstone picks so that he can be badly married to Audrey is named Oliver Martext. Because Sir Oliver is a '**hedge-priest**', i.e. uneducated (LLL 5.2.542), he is likely to mar any religious text he reads, and therefore unlikely, at least in Touchstone's mind, 'to marry me well' (AYL 3.3.64, 92–4).

MARTIN, SAINT

(A) Martin of Tours (*c.* 316–97) was a monk and bishop, popular enough in the Middle Ages in France for over 4000 French churches to be dedicated to him, as well as 500 villages. There were also 173 St Martin's churches in England by 1800.
(B) When Joan of Arc advises Prince Charles to 'Expect Saint Martin's summer, halcyon days' (1H6 1.2.131), she is promising an 'Indian summer', an unseasonably warm, calm, political climate. St Martin's Feast Day is 11 October.
(C) Farmer (1978), 265–6; Baring-Gould (1914), 13: 241–61.

MARTLEMAS

(A) Actually Martinmas (11 November), the day sacred to St Martin of Tours; a traditional time for slaughtering previously fattened beef. Ironically, St Martin was associated with the very non-Falstaffian qualities of humility, kindness to the poor, prayerfulness, and above all, abstinence.
(B) Falstaff is called by Poins 'the martlemas your master' (2H4 2.2.102), and even more explicitly 'that roasted Manningtree ox with the pudding in his belly' (1H4 2.4.452–3), not only because he resembles such fattened meat, but also because he is about to be sacrificed as a scapegoat and a liability.
(C) See Voraigne (1941), 2: 663–74; Attwater (1965), 233–4. For a seminal discussion of Falstaff as 'the scapegoat of saturnalian ritual', see Barber (1967), 205–13.

MARTYR

(A) Someone who dies for a cause, like a religious faith.
(B) Shakespeare refers to both Catholic and Protestant martyrdom. The Epilogue proclaims Falstaff's connection to the Lollard Reformer by disclaiming it: 'Oldcastle died a martyr, and this is not the man' (2H4 Epi. 31–2). In contrast, Cardinal Wolsey advises his servant Cromwell about himself, 'thou fall'st a blessed martyr' if you 'Let all the ends thou aim'st at be thy country's, / Thy God's, and truth's' (H8 3.2.447–9). Wolsey, however, is glossing over the truth, since he apparently served himself better than these other three. Mowbray's 'royal faiths martyrs in love' (2H4 4.1.191) is a political metaphor, and 'here they stand martyrs, slain in Cupid's wars' (PER 1.1.38) is a romantic one. Standing slain is indeed miraculous.
(C) Foxe's *Acts and Monuments* (1563; 1641r) is the famous Protestant martyrology of Shakespeare's time. McCoy (1997) examines martyrdom for love and religion in SON and PHT. Monta (2000) looks at the 'rhetoric of conscience' used by both Protestant and Roman Catholic martyrs in relation to H8. Moschovakis (2002), 470–2, discusses the use of 'martyr' in TIT.

MARY

(A) The mother of Christ. This is once used in a mild oath, once as the name of a chapel (JN 2.1.538–9), and once with reference to the crucifixion of Christ.

(B) Henry VIII, planning to listen unobserved to the proceeding against his ally Archbishop Cranmer, tells his physician of the conspiracy: 'By holy Mary, Butts, there's knavery' (H8 5.2.33). There is delightful irony in this very Catholic oath coming out of the mouth of this very independent king, and uttered in connection to the arch-Reformer Cranmer. John of Gaunt refers to Christ's tomb as 'the sepulchre in stubborn Jewry / Of the world's ransom, blessed Mary's Son' (R2 2.1.55–6). See **marry**.

(C) Farmer (1978), 268–9.

MASS

(A) The preferred Catholic word for Communion or the Eucharist.

(B) 'By the mass' is a common mild blasphemy in Shakespeare, characterizing at least half of his 32 uses of 'mass'. Polonius's 'By the mass, I was about to say something' (HAM 2.1.50) shows that the gentle as well as the vile could use the phrase, though he is speaking to his servant Reynaldo here. Sometimes this is shortened, as when the Gravedigger's helper says 'Mass, I cannot tell' (HAM 5.1.55), or Verges responds to what Dogberry calls the 'burglary' of Hero's slander, 'by mass, that it is' (ADO 4.2.51). Henry V also tells the French messenger Montjoy of the English resolve, 'By the mass, our hearts are in the trim' (H5 4.3.115). The only reference to the mass that is not an oath occurs when Juliet asks the Friar, 'Or shall I come to you at evening mass?' (ROM 4.1.38).

(C) See *ST* III.73–83, and **sacrament**. Milward (1978), 171–6, catalogues some of the participants in controversies concerning the mass. See also 'Eucharist', *OxfordEncyRef*, 2: 71–81; and 'Mass', *NewCathEncy*, 9: 414–26.

MASTER

(A) Used as a name for Christ or God.

(B) Richard of Gloucester says of his plan to betray the princes his nephews, 'so Judas kiss'd his master, / And cried "All hail!" when as he meant all harm' (3H6 5.7.33–4); also speaking of Christ, Henry VIII reminds Archbishop Cranmer that your Master, / Whose minister you are, whiles here he liv'd / Upon this naughty earth' also suffered 'perjur'd witness' (H8 5.1.136–8). Richard II threatens the rebels with 'Armies of pestilence' sent by 'my master, God omnipotent' (R2 3.3.85–7).

(C) Donne warns of 'an *ungratefulnesse*, that we will not apply his example, and do to his servants, as he, our Master, hath done to us' (3: 158). See also Donne, 7: 241; Pilkington (1842), 316.

MEASURE

(A) A coded, biblically resonant word for severe justice. Speaking against the eye-for-an-eye legalism of Ex. 21.23–5: 'And if *any* mischief follow, then thou shalt give life for life, eye for eye, tooth for tooth', Christ not only says to turn the other cheek, but also, 'Judge not, that ye be not judged. For with what judgement ye judge, ye shall be judged; and with what measure ye mete, it shall be measured to you again' (Matt. 7.1–2).

(B) The Duke seems to espouse the severity of Exodus when he condemns Angelo to a deserved judicial death for his own unjust judicial killing of Claudio: 'An Angelo for Claudio, death for death! / Haste still pays haste, and leisure answers leisure; / Like doth quit like, and *Measure* still *for Measure*' (MM 5.1.409–11). The case can be made, however, that the Duke feigns such severity to manipulate the wronged but also legalistic Isabella into the position of asking that Angelo be forgiven. Warwick says of the eye-for-an-eye trade of the severed head of his murdered father York for that of the Clifford who killed him: 'Measure for measure must be answered' (3H6 2.6.55).

(C) See Andrewes, 5: 434–8.

MEDITATION, MEDITATING

(A) This can refer to religious contemplation, or to the manuals that direct it. Donne speaks of '*books* of pious and devout meditation' (10: 144), and the Recusant Gibbons translates F. Lewis de Granada's description of two kinds of meditation, 'Intellectual' and 'Imaginarie', the former about doctrinal matters and the latter about those biblical narratives and places that illustrate them (1599), 116.

(B) 'Meditation' is used deceptively when Richard III is described three times by Buckingham as 'Divinely bent to meditation', 'on his knees at meditation', and 'meditating with two deep divines' (R3 3.7.62, 73–5). Katherine of Aragon more honestly describes herself 'meditating / On that celestial harmony I go to' (H8 4.2.79–80). Also in H8, Norfolk sarcastically tells the ruined Cardinal Wolsey, 'And so we'll leave you to your meditations / How to live better' (H8 3.2.345–6), but Griffith, Katherine's gentleman usher, finally praises Wolsey's good death as 'full of repentance, / Continual meditations, tears and sorrows, / He gave his honours to the world again, / His blessed part to heaven, and slept in peace' (H8 4.2.27–30).

(C) On Protestant and Catholic traditions of religious meditation during the sixteenth and seventeenth centuries in England, see Lewalski (1979) and Martz (1962).

MEEK

(A) Not proud; humble and mild-mannered. The meek are listed among the blessed in Christ's Sermon on the Mount (Matt. 5.5).

(B) Only a few of Shakespeare's thirteen references are definitely religious. When Richard's mother says 'God bless thee, and put meekness in thy breast, / Love, charity, obedience, and true duty' (R3 2.2.107–8), she clearly places the virtue in a theological setting, however despairing she may be of her son's potential to attain salvation. Longaville's 'To hear meekly, sir' after Berowne's 'hope in God for high words' (LLL 1.1.192–8) may echo the Litany, 'To hear meekly thy Word' (*BCP*, 70). Henry VIII calls his wife Katherine's 'meekness saint-like' (H8 2.4.139), and the threatened Cranmer ruefully tells his inquisitor Gardiner,

'Love and meekness, lord, / Become a churchman better than ambition' (H8 5.2.97–8). Macbeth's lament that Duncan 'Hath borne his faculties so meek . . . in his great office' that his 'virtues / Will plead like angels, trumpet-tongu'd, against / The deep damnation of his taking off' (MAC 1.7.17–20) probably also refers to the religious as well as the merely social virtue.
(C) See Latimer (1844–45), 1: 480; and Tyndale, 1:19. See also Shaheen (1999), 123.

MEMENTO MORI
(A) Literally from the Latin, the imperative, 'remember that thou must die' (*OED* memento 5); usually this refers to a reminder of death, often a skull or its replica, used for contemplating one's mortality.
(B) Falstaff speaks of using Bardolph's burning and whelked face as 'many a man doth of a death's-head or a *memento mori*' (1H4 3.3.30–1).
(C) Morris (1970), Frye (1984), 206–20, and Malsen (1983) all study *memento mori* references in HAM. Morris (1985), 208–16, 270–8, and Garber (1981) consider this theme more generally.

MEMORY
(A) One of the three moral faculties humans possessed as potential assistance against the snares of the devil. The others in this common trinity of powers were **understanding** and **will**, though **imagination** was sometimes added to the mix, and **reason** added as a sub-category of understanding. 'Reason' was also sometimes synonymous with 'understanding'. The Reformer Hutchinson thus says of the three moral faculties, 'There is in man's soul reason, discerning good from evil, truth from falsehood; there is memory, by the which he remembereth things past; there is will, by the which he chooseth what him liketh. . . . In these things man was formed after the likeness of God' (1842), 24–5.
(B) Lady Macbeth calls 'memory, the warder of the brain' and promises to diminish its function in Duncan's grooms 'with wine and wassail' (MAC 1.7.64–6). By promising the Ghost to erase from 'the table of my memory' 'all saws of books' (HAM 1.5.98–100) Hamlet is thus playing a dangerous spiritual game. On the other hand, the 'book of memory' Plantagenet refers to is a record of grudges, not moral or spiritual precepts (1H6 2.4.101).
(C) Augustine in *On the Trinity* (2002), X.11.18, refers to this trinity of our intellectual powers. See also ST I.79.6–7. Donne calls 'the Memory . . . oftner the Holy Ghosts Pulpit that he preaches in, then the Understanding' (8:261). The Jesuit Puente (1619), 1: 3, says of memory and meditation: 'with the memory to be mindefull of God our Lorde, with whom wee are able to speake, and to negociate; and to be mindefull also, of the mysterie that is to be meditated, passing through the memorie, with clearnesse, and distinction, that which is to be the matter of meditation'. Memory is allegorised in Book II of Spenser's *Fairie Queene*. See Hamilton (1990), 467–9, on Spenser and the art of memory. For a discussion of the place of memory, understanding and will in the Catholic meditative tradition, see Martz (1962), pt 1. On the prominence and persistence of

Fig. 4. Owl perched on a skull. Emblem #168 from *A Collection of Emblemes*, George Wither, 1635; STC 25900d. Courtesy The Newberry Library, Chicago.

memory in various meditative traditions, see also Engel (1995, 2002). A useful general discussion of the word in the plays may be found in Salingar (1994). Alexander (1968) and Richards (1988) discuss memory systems in HAM. Mazzaro (1985) argues that madness disrupts memory in HAM and LR; Mazzaro (2001–02) examines Shakespeare's phrase 'books of memory' in the H6 plays. Baldo (1996), 152–7, looks at memory in H5 in regard to the liturgical calendar.

MERCIFUL

(A) The quality, human or divine, of showing **mercy** when justice or revenge might be legally allowed. Donne says of human mercy, 'The root of all Christian duties is *Humility*, meeknesse, that's . . . violated in an *unmercifulnesse*' (3: 158), and Sandys says of Luke 6.37, 'Forgive, and ye shall be forgiven'; 'follow the example of our Saviour: "Be merciful and forgive" '. (1841), 229.

(B) Isabella refers to 'Merciful heaven' (MM 2.2.114) as she tries to persuade Angelo to be more lenient to her brother Claudio. Banquo, either worried that Macbeth might harm Duncan in response to the Witches' prophecy or himself be tempted to kill his gracious king, prays, 'Merciful powers, / Restrain in me the cursed thoughts that nature / Gives way to in repose' (MAC 2.1.7–9). Finally Malcolm, having just learned that Macbeth has slaughtered Macduff's whole family, utters the perplexed and perplexing phrase 'Merciful heaven' (MAC 4.3.208).

(C) On human mercy, see *ST* II.2.30; see also Augustine, *The City of God* (1950), IX.5. Of the mercifulness of God, see *ST* I.21; Becon, 3: 618; and Tyndale, 3: 59.

MERCY

(A) Spoken theologically both of God's compassionate forbearance towards human sinfulness and of the recommended human imitation of this quality. If the word 'justice' is associated with the Old Testament God, divine 'mercy' describes its mitigation through the new dispensation of Christ's sacrifice. As Sandys says, 'God made a covenant with our father Abraham, . . . that he would shew mercy, and in mercy work our **deliverance**. To perform this covenant of grace and mercy made unto our fathers, and comprehending also us, he gave up his only-begotten Son in the fulness of time to death. There was no other motive why he should work our deliverance but only this, his mercy' (1841), 180. Donne reminds the worldly judge of the traditional association of mercy here and mercy hereafter: 'Waigh the mercy of thy Judge then, and think there is such mercy required in thy judgement now' (3: 291).

(B) Portia's 'mercy is above this sceptred sway, / . . . / It is an attribute to God himself, / And earthly power doth then show likest God's, / When mercy seasons justice' illustrates the theological intersection of these two meanings. So does her subsequent reference to the Lord's Prayer: 'We do pray for mercy, / and that same prayer doth teach us all to render / The deeds of mercy.' '[I]n the course of justice, none of us / Should see salvation' (MV 4.1.193–200. The Lord's Prayer, here referred to, reads, of course, 'Forgive us our trespasses, as we forgive them that trespass against us' (*BCP*, 51). Like Portia, Isabella associates human mercy with the grace of God, once saying that not even 'the judge's robe' becomes him 'with one half so good a grace / As mercy does' (MM 2.2.61–3). But both Isabella and Portia find it very difficult to forgive a 'precise' Angelo (MM 1.3.50) or a vengeful Shylock, both of whom would murder in the name of the law, and both of whom have refused to temper the 'just but severe law' with mercy (MM 2.2.41). Portia finally cries out 'The Jew shall have all justice' during the trial scene, and Isabella says at her parallel moment, 'The very mercy of the law cries out' for what she has earlier demanded – 'justice, justice, justice, justice' (MM 5.1.407, 25).

In Shakespeare the frequent phrases, 'God have mercy' (TN 3.4.167), 'Mercy, mercy' 'mercy on us' (TMP 2.2.97; 1.1.60), and the like are sometimes, as today, casual, almost unthinking, but they are seldom devoid of theological implications, especially when uttered as in these examples in times of trouble. We are sure that Desdemona invokes heaven's forgiveness at the hour of her death when she says both 'heaven have mercy on me' and 'Lord have mercy on me' just before Othello kills her (OTH 5.2.34, 57). As Salisbury and Gargrave fall in battle, they utter a refrain so reminiscent of the Litany's reiterated plea for mercy, and so relevant to the occasion of sudden death, that there is no question that it too is consciously liturgical:

> SALISBURY. O Lord, have mercy on us, wretched sinners!
> GARGRAVE. O Lord have mercy on me, woeful man!
> (1H6 1.4.70–1)

York's 'Open thy gate of mercy, gracious God' (1.4.177) hopefully associates the open gates of heaven with the theology of mercy and grace. York's son Richard Hunchback curses Clifford, 'ask mercy, and receive no grace' (3H6 2.6.69), and prays only ironically for his own brother, 'God take King Edward to his mercy', since this will merely 'leave the world for me to bustle in' (R3 1.1.151–2). Paradoxically, God's revenge, or perhaps merely Tudor revenge, comes when Richard's dream of the eleven ghosts leads him to the momentarily serious prayer, 'Have mercy, Jesu', and the sure 'despair' thereafter that for him heaven's gates are closed: 'All several sins . . . Throng to the bar, crying all, "Guilty! guilty!" '(R3 5.3.178, 198–200).

(C) See *Certaine Sermons*, 2nd tome, pp. 154–66, for the sermons of 'Almes deedes, and mercifulnesse toward the poore and needy'. As Shaheen says (1999), 289, the words 'Have mercy upon us miserable sinners' occurs repeatedly in the 'opening petitions and responses of the Litany' (see *BCP*, 68). Bevington and Sheingorn (1985) contains several essays on the just judgement plays. Of the traditional difficulty of blending justice and mercy, see Sandys (1841), 147. Lupton (1990) argues that mercy is the internalization of the law in MM, not its opposite. Thatcher (1995) suggests that mercy might be related to the guilt of the judge. Lindley (1996) considers ways in which MM tries to reconcile justice and mercy. See **justice**, **law**, **revenge**.

MERIT

(A) Theologically, the works that save; sometimes opposed therefore to grace in theological discourse. In Nowell's *Catechism*, the *Master* asks, 'Cannot we then, with godly, dutiful doings, and *works*, satisfy God, and by ourselves **merit** pardon of our sins?' and the Reformed *Student* dutifully replies, 'There is no mercy due to our merits, but God doth yield and remit to Christ his correction and punishment that he would have done upon us. For Christ alone, with sufferance of his pains, and with his death, wherewith he hath paid and performed the penalty of our sins, hath **satisfied** God. Therefore by Christ alone we have access to the grace of God' (1853), 176.

(B) Shakespeare's usage, especially in the comedies, suggests a playful awareness of this crucial Reformation word and its theological associations. The Princess in

LLL, having almost forced the Forester to praise her beauty, then upbraids him for changing his tune under the pressure of her wit, her position, and her generous gratuity: 'See, see, my beauty will be sav'd by merit. / O heresy in fair, fit for these days!' (LLL 4.1.21–2). See **heresy** for a fuller discussion of the religious nuance. In MV, another comedy full of religious tensions, these usually between Jew and Christian rather than Catholic and Protestant, the Catholic Prince of Aragon, one of 'fair Portia's' suitors, reveals as he assesses the inscriptions on the silver casket ('Who chooseth me shall get as much as he deserves') his own predisposition towards merit, and it finally dooms him to failure. His is 'the stamp of merit', not grace or 'undeserved dignity'. His success will manifest 'the merit of the wearer' (MV 2.9.36–43); he will 'assume desert'. His reward is 'the portrait of a blinking idiot' (MV 2.9.50–1, 54). See also **right**, **title** and **desert**. A nice pun on this religious usage comes when Duke Theseus says of all such inadequate human performances, that 'what poor duty cannot do, noble respect / Takes it in might, not merit' (MND 5.1.91–2). Cf. MND 1.1.97, 99–105; AWW 2.1.148–52.

For all the desperation of his own spiritual position, Falstaff also asserts a theology of grace when he says of Bardolph, 'O, if men were to be sav'd by merit, what hole in hell were hot enough for him?' (1H4 1.2.107–8). Hamlet, also only partly joking, sounds like a combination of Falstaff and Duke Theseus when he advises Polonius about the housing of the visiting players, 'use every man after his desert, and who shall scape whipping? Use them after your own honor and dignity – the less they deserve, the more merit is in your bounty' (HAM 2.2.529–32). Hamlet, however, may be on more dangerous grounds when, just later, he styles himself 'patient merit' and everyone who opposes him 'the unworthy' (HAM 3.1.73). Romeo refers to the same religious issues when he says of the disdainful Rosaline, 'She is too fair, too wise, wisely too fair, / To merit bliss by making me despair' (ROM 1.1.221–2). Playfully buying into the theology of works, Romeo hopes that she would not earn her own salvation by driving him to despair.

(C) For a measured assessment of the relationship of merit and grace, see *ST* II.1.114; see also Andrewes, 5: 282; and Donne, 1: 193–4. *Certaine Sermons*, pp. 30–9, has the 'Sermon of Good workes annexed unto Faith'. Hunt (1996), 354–8, Robert Watson (1997) and (2002), and Beauregard (1999) all associate the use of the word 'merit' or 'merits' in OTH with the Reformation issue of salvation by merit rather than by grace; the first two associate the preference for merit with Catholicism, Beauregard with Calvinism.

METAPHYSICAL

(A) When he says 'in a regenerate man, all is Metaphysicall, supernaturall' (9: 230), Donne identifies the two words.

(B) This usage characterises Lady Macbeth's comment after reading Macbeth's letter about the Witches' prophecies, that 'fate and metaphysical aid doth seem / To have thee crown'd' King of Scotland (MAC 1.5.29–30).

(C) Curry (1968r) discusses *Demonic Metaphysics of Macbeth*.

MICHAELMAS

This festival, celebrated on 29 September, honours 'Saint Michael and All Angels' (*BCP*, 239–40). One assigned reading for this day, Rev. 12, is about the war in heaven and Satan's defeat at the hands of 'Michael and his angels' and his subsequent residence among 'the inhabitants of the earth'. Another is from Matt. 18, where Jesus warns against misleading a child and instructs his followers to cut off all members that offend.

Both references in Shakespeare (WIV 1.1.205 and 1H4 2.4.54) are mostly calendrical. However, Hal also calls Falstaff 'old white-bearded Satan' during the scene in which Michaelmas is mentioned, and resolves as it concludes to 'banish plump Jack, and banish all the world' (1H4 2.4.62–3, 479–80) as he moves from what he calls 'the old days of goodman Adam' (1H4 2.4.92–3) into the days of 'my Reformation, glitt'ring o'er all my faults' (1H4 1.2.213). Hal is also said at the end of that scene to have been 'violently carried away from grace', and Falstaff is called the 'devil', 'vice' and 'iniquity' who did this violence (1H4 2.4.462–3, 446–54). The festival is also mentioned in close proximity to Falstaff (WIV 1.1.205), but not with the same thematic and verbal resonance.

(C) For some early representations of St Michael in the art of Warwickshire, see Davidson and Alexander (1985), 39–40, 141–2.

MIGHT

(A) Occasionally a synonym for theological **merit**, the might or strength of **works** that saves in contrast to what Luther might call the **grace** or **faith** which only justifies a sinner in the court of God's **judgement**. Tyndale explains the Lutheran concept of 'Thraldom of will' (from Rom. 7.24): 'Unto the devil's will consent we with all our hearts, with all our minds, with all our might. . . . This is the captivity and bondage, whence Christ delivered us, redeemed and loosed us' (1: 17–18).

(B) Berowne similarly rationalises the inevitable failure of the lords to live up to their vow:

> Necessity will make us all forsworn
> Three thousand times within this three years' space:
> For every man with his affects is born,
> Not by might mast'red, but by special grace.
>
> (LLL 1.1.149–52)

The arrival of four ladies from France is the immediate necessity, but the more general one is human nature, original sin, 'the devices and desires of our own hearts', as the *Prayer Book* puts it (*BCP*, 50), over which one does not have absolute or even moderate control.

More subtle is Theseus's charitable response to the menials' performance. If they 'offend', and they do, 'they come not to offend'; Theseus has such grace that he 'Takes it in might not merit' (MND 5.1.108–9, 92). Because his 'might' literally means what they intended in contrast to what they actually executed, it can suggest in Pauline terms the 'would' that they 'do not' (Romans 7.19). It is this inevitability that requires Luther's theology of grace.

(C) Donne has a particularly vivid passage relating the poison of original sin to limited human might (1: 293).

MINISTER[1]

(A) A preacher or a priest.

(B) 'The minister is here' (TN 4.2.94) announces Feste's change back from the role of Malvolio's fool to the role of his curate; Mistress Quickly refers similarly to 'Master Dumbe, our minister' (2H4 2.4. 88).

(C) Grindal (1843), 159, Item 7, uses the *v.* and the *sb.* when he asks about possible remnants of Catholicism 'Whether your parson, vicar, curate, or minister, do . . . minister the holy Communion in any chalice heretofore used at mass.'

MINISTER[2]

(A) A mortal or immortal hand that does heaven's or hell's will on earth. Tyndale says of 'Kings, Princes, and Rulers', 'If thou do evil, then fear: for he beareth not a sword for nought; for he is the minister of God, to take vengeance on them that do evil' (1: 174).

(B) Of the representatives of heaven or hell, Joan of Arc is called 'foul accursed minister of hell' by Richard Plantagenet (1H6 5.4.93); Anne calls Richard of Gloucester a 'dreadful minister of hell', and his opposite Richmond asks God, 'whose captain I account myself', 'Make us thy ministers of chastisement' (R3 1.2.46; 5.3.108, 113). Gaunt declines to kill Richard II, whom he calls God's 'deputy' (R2 2.1.38), by saying, 'Let heaven revenge, for I may never lift / An angry arm against His minister' (R2 1.2.40–1). Hamlet laments after killing Polonius 'but heaven hath pleas'd it so / . . . / That I must be their **scourge** and minister' (HAM 3.4.173–5). To Young Clifford it is 'War', not a person, 'Whom angry heavens do make their minister' (2H6 5.2.34). Of supernatural ministers, Hamlet asks that 'Angels and ministers of grace defend us' upon seeing his father's ghost (HAM 1.4.39.); Isabella similarly prays during the trial scene, 'you blessed ministers above, / Keep me in patience' (MM 5.1.115–16). On the darker side, Lady Macbeth invokes 'murth'ring ministers' to transform her into something more wicked but less human than is her 'nature' (MAC 1.5.48).

(C) Dent (1978), argues that 'scourge' and 'minister' in HAM may be synonyms; Desai (1993) asserts that Hamlet is a 'minister of God' to revenge his father.

MINISTER[3]

The verb can refer to an act of spiritual nurturing.

In describing his role as Friar, the Duke says: 'Bound by my charity and my blest order, / I come to visit the afflicted spirits / Here in the prison' to 'make me know / The nature of their crimes, that I may minister / To them accordingly' (MM 2.3.3–8). Macbeth asks Lady Macbeth's Doctor 'Canst thou not minister to a mind diseas'd' (MAC 5.3.40), but he has already diagnosed her malady as beyond his medical skills: 'More needs she the divine than the physician' (MAC 5.1.74).

MIRACLE

(A) Something occurring beyond human knowledge or power. Assorted comments by Donne reveal that the moderate Protestant belief that miracles ceased after New Testament times was more a pragmatic response to Roman Catholic claims of miraculous power than an absolute theoretical stance: 'Neither must the profusion of miracles, the prodigality and prostitution of miracles in the Romane Church, (where miracles for every naturall disease may be had, at some Shrine, or miracle-shop, better cheap, then a Medicine, a Drugge, a Simple at an Apothecaries) bring us to deny, or distrust all miracles, done by God upon extraordinary causes, and to important purposes' (8: 366). To him the greatest danger is that 'In the Roman Church, they multiply, and extend miracles, til the miracle it selfe crack, and become none, but vanish into nothing, as boyes bubbles, (which were but bubbles before, at best) by an overblowing become nothing' (7: 294).

(B) Lafew, pointedly an old French (and therefore Catholic?) Lord, thoughtfully disagrees: 'They say miracles are past, and we have our philosophical persons, to make modern and familiar, things supernatural and causeless. Hence it is that we make trifles of terrors, ensconcing ourselves into seeming knowledge when we should submit ourselves to an unknown fear' (AWW 2.3.1–6; see **minister**). The Archbishop of Canterbury would like to call Hal's transformation a miracle in H5, but because of this same disputed doctrine, he is obliged to agree with the Bishop of Ely that it is as natural as 'the strawberry [that] grows underneath the nettle': 'for miracles are ceas'd / And therefore we must needs admit the means / How things are perfected' (H5 1.1.60, 67–9). With the subtle anachronism so common to the histories, though this Catholic archbishop is speaking to a Catholic bishop in Catholic England around 1422, well before the Reformation, a Reformation issue informs their conversation. This rich context of religious scepticism and belief could also underlie Benedick's and Beatrice's calling their love 'A miracle' with a mixture of joy and sarcasm at the end of ADO (5.4.91); Perdita similarly calls Camillo's promise to reconcile father and son 'almost a miracle' near the end of WT (WT 4.4.534).

Joan of Arc proclaims herself 'Virtuous and holy, chosen from above / By inspiration of celestial grace / To work exceeding miracles on earth' (1H6 5.4.39–41); of course, none of the English agree with her, and Joan is about to be burned alive as a witch and a heretic. In 2H6 Simpcox, an imposter cripple, runs away as soon as he is beaten, prompting the scoffing response, 'A miracle'. The false 'miracle' of his restored sight has already been exposed earlier in the scene (2H6 2.1.157, 129).

Only in the romances are miracles relatively uncontested sites. Gonzalo calls their 'preservation' from the tempest 'a miracle' (TMP 2.1.6), and even the cynical Sebastian claims that Alonso's son Ferdinand's deliverance from death is 'A most high miracle' (TMP 5.1.177). Pericles proclaims it a 'great miracle' that his wife and daughter were both delivered from death and restored to him (PER 5.3.58).

(C) See *ST* II.2.178; Donne, 6: 91, 251–2. For some of the participants in controversies over miracles, see Milward (1978), 159–64. See also Shaheen (1999), 452.

MIRROR

(A) Like the **glass**, the mirror can serve as a spiritual emblem for looking inward.
(B) The just-deposed Richard II commands 'a mirror hither straight', expecting to find in it 'the very book indeed / Where all my sins are writ, and that's myself' (R2 4.1.265, 274–5).
(C) Frye (1984), 153–66, discusses this emblem in HAM and in Shakespeare's time.

MISBELIEVER, MISBELIEVING

Technically someone who does not believe in Christianity; also a demonizing epithet which seems to imply as much a destructive cruelty as a different belief.

Thus Shylock charges Antonio, 'You call me misbeliever, cut-throat dog, / And spet upon my Jewish gaberdine / And all for use of that which is mine own' (MV 1.3.111–12), and Marcus can order that someone 'hither hale that misbelieving Moor' forth to judgement 'for his most wicked life' (TIT 5.3.143–5).

MISCREANT

A **misbeliever**, one holding false or unorthodox religious **belief**; a **heretic** or an **infidel**. Becon says that 'A preacher of the Lord's word is bound to do good unto all men; not only to such as be of the household of faith, but also to Turks, Jews, Saracens, and such other miscreants' (1: 22).

However, Mowbray, whom Bolingbroke calls 'a traitor and a miscreant' (R2 1.1.39), eventually dies as a holy crusader; similarly, the 'miscreant' Basset is merely a Lancastrian (1H6 3.4.44), and the 'miscreant' (LR 1.1.161) Kent has simply disagreed with Lear's banishment of Cordelia. Of this group, only Joan of Arc, who is variously called a witch, a hag, an enchantress, and a devil by her English enemies, technically deserves the title 'miscreant' (1H6 5.3.44). The play shows her conjuring devils (1H6 5.3.1–29).

MONASTERY

A habitation for monks or other religious persons.

Richard of Gloucester falsely promises Anne to inter 'At Chertsey monast'ry this noble king' Henry VI (R3 1.2.214, 226). Portia remembers 'a monast'ry two miles off' from her house in Belmont (MV 3.4.31). The Goth in TIT says he 'stray'd / To gaze upon a ruinous [ruined] monastery' (TIT 5.1.21).

MONASTIC

Characteristic of the reclusive life of a monastary.

Rosalind-Ganymede tells Orlando that she-he once cured a lover by convincing him to 'forswear the full stream of the world, and to live in a nook merely monastic' (AYL 3.2. 419–21).

MONDAY, BLACK
See **Black Monday**

MORNING PRAYER
An order prescribed in the *Prayer Book* for daily morning worship.

Mistress Quickly describes Mistress Page as one 'that will not miss you morning nor evening prayer' (WIV 2.2.98–9). Isabella's phrase 'morn-prayer' (MM 2.4.71) refers instead to a daily prayer she will utter to have her brother's pardoning, 'if it be a sin', added to the 'faults of mine' rather than those Angelo would have to 'answer' (MM 2.4.69–73).

MORTAL¹
Human, that is, subject to both death and varieties of imperfection. Both of these human limitations are deeply interwoven into Christian theology. Touchstone's 'but as all is mortal in nature, so is all nature in love mortal in folly' (AYL 2.4.55–6) touches both definitions. 'Mortal' can also distinguish body from soul, as when Anne tells Richard over the corpse of Henry VI, 'Thou hadst but power over his mortal body, / His soul thou canst not have' (R3 1.2.47–8). The Witches in MAC have 'more than mortal knowledge' (MAC 1.5.3).

MORTAL²
(A) Mortal sins were thought to lead to spiritual death, separation from God, if not repented; venial sins were less serious. Vaux says of 'mortal and deadly sins': 'that dede or negligence is a deadly sinne, in which of purpose and advisedly with notable contempt of God, or manifest harme of our selfe or our neighbour, any of the ten commaundements are broken, or els when wee doe anie thing against that, whiche our owne conscience doth teache us, . . . as for example to despise God, and to despaire of his mercie, to forsweare, or sweare falsely, to steale any thing of valew, not to give almose [alms], if we be able, to such as we know to be in necessitie' (1590b, *sigs.* a6$^{\text{r–v}}$).
(B) Though he speaks about earthly rather than heavenly judgement, Cassio makes such a distinction when he asks Desdemona, 'If my offense be of such mortal kind' (OTH 3.4.115).
(C) See *ST* III.86, on 'the Pardon of Mortal Sin'; and *ST* II.1.88, 'Of Venial and Mortal Sin'. See also *Certaine Sermons*, pp. 52–8, for the sermons of 'falling from God'. Donne once says, 'when all is done, the hell of hels, the torment of torments is the everlasting absence of God, and the everlasting impossibility of returning to his presence' (5: 265–6).

MORTIFIED
(A) Said of the penitential discipline that can strengthen the will or subjugate the flesh.
(B) Canterbury's description of 'his wildness, mortified in him' refers both to Prince Hal's new sense of responsibility as King Henry V and to the spiritual discipline that produced that change. In a nice pun, the wildness has been both

controlled and killed. As the Archbishop says, 'Consideration like an angel came / And whipt th' offending Adam out of him' (H5 1.1.26–9). Edgar compares the beggars he will imitate to religious penitents who 'Strike in their numbed and mortified bare arms / Pins, wooden pricks, nails, sprigs of rosemary' (LR 2.3.15–16). 'Dumaine is mortified' refers to his formal commitment to 'pine and die' 'To love, to wealth, to pomp' (LLL 1.1.28–31).

(C) Donne warns against an overdependence on such spiritual disciplines: 'They ['*the Romane Church*'] magnifie *sanctification*, and *holinesse of life* well; . . . *fasting*, and *prayer*, and *almes*, and other Medicinall Disciplines, and *Mortifications*. But all this to a wrong end; Not to make them the more acceptable to God, but to make God the more beholden to them' (7: 264).

MOTE

(A) A common word meaning 'speck'.

(B) 'Mote' is often, as in JN 4.1.91–3 and HAM 1.1.112, associated literally with the eyes, but figuratively with sins: 'You found his mote, the King your mote did see; / But I a **beam** do find in each of three' (LLL 4.3.159–60). All have betrayed their vows, and are now being exposed.

(C) This clearly alludes to Matt. 7.3 and Luke 6.41, Jesus's words about seeing 'the mote, that is in thy brother's eye, but . . . not the beam that is in thine own eye'.

MOTION

(A) Puppet show which sometimes enacted biblical stories.

(B) Autolycus makes up a story of a man who after a chequered life 'compass'd a motion of the Prodigal Son, and married a tinker's wife' (WT 4.3.96–7).

(C) BEV, 816n; PEL; *OED sb*. 13.a.

MOUSETRAP

See **devil**⁴.

MURDER (also **MURTHER**)

(A) The unlawful killing of one human by another.

(B) Clarence reminds his murderers that 'the great King of kings / Hath in the table of his laws commanded / That thou shalt do no murther' (R3 1.4.195–7). Hamlet refers to 'Cain's jaw-bone, that did the first murder' (HAM 5.1.77), and Claudius refers to this same biblical event when he says that his 'offense' 'hath the primal eldest curse upon't, / A brother's murther' (HAM 3.3.37–8).

(C) The story of Cain's murder of Abel is told in Gen. 4.8–11.

MUSIC

(A) 'Music' in Shakespeare refers more than once to the Neoplatonic notion that the heavenly bodies, set in hollow concentric spheres in heaven, made music inaudible to fallen human ears but available to the angels (BEV, 346n).

(B) Prospero's 'heavenly music' (TMP 5.1.52) may be just extraordinarily beautiful, but Olivia's 'music from the spheres' (TN 3.1.110) definitely refers to this heavenly orchestra. Pericles also thinks he hears 'the music of the spheres' (PER 5.1. 229).

(C) As Tillyard says (1944), 96–101, John Davies' 'Orchestra' richly celebrates this cosmic concert. Donne's cynical speaker in 'Love's Alchemy' (1971) says that the gullible lover who believes 'tis not the bodies marry but the minds' would also swear 'that he hears / In that day's rude, hoarse minstralsy, the spheres' (19–22). In his sermons Donne's scepticism is more muted, but his 'belief' is often metaphoric: 'if you can heare a good Organ at Church, and have the musique of a domestique peace at home, peace in thy walls, peace in the bosome, never hearken after the musique of the sphears, never hunt after the knowledge of higher secrets, than appertaine to thee' (7: 407); cf. Donne's 'God multiplies his mercies to us, in his divers ways of speaking to us. . . . This is the true harmony of the Spheares, which every man may heare' (10: 109). Ingram (1972), 159–60, briefly discusses the Elizabethan connection between music and religious belief in the plays. Blick (1999) argues that the references to music in SONs 8 and 128 draw upon the theories of Pythagoras. See also 'Music', *OxfordEncyRef*, 3: 104–16.

MYSTERIES

(A) Both things impossible to understand and secret rites.

(B) In two pre-Christian plays, Volumnia speaks of 'those mysteries which heaven / Will not have earth to know' (COR 4.2.35–6), and Lear swears, more darkly, by 'the mysteries of Hecate and the night' (LR 1.1.110).

(C) Donne, who often tries to defuse Reformation tensions, warns against 'unlawfull and dangerous dallyings with mysteries of **Divinity**', calling them 'forc'd dishes of hot brains, and not sound meat, . . . perverse wranglings. . . . Money that is changed into small pieces is easily lost; gold that is beat out into leaf-gold, cannot by coyned, nor made currant money. . . . [T]rue, and sound, and nourishing Divinity [doth] vanish away, in those impertinent Questions. All that the wit of Man adds to the Word of God, is all *quicksilver*, and it evaporates easily' (5: 123–4).

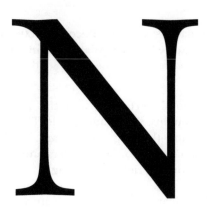

N

NAIL'D

Directly associated with the crucifixion of Christ when King Henry IV speaks of 'those blessed feet / Which fourteen hundred years ago were nail'd / For our **advantage** on the bitter cross' (1H4 1.1.26–7).

NAKED

(A) Going almost without clothing can be associated in both religious art and penitential acts with the extreme expression of religious devotion.

(B) Paulina tells Leontes after he has defied the oracle and apparently caused Hermione's death that 'A thousand knees / Ten thousand years together, naked, fasting, / Upon a barren mountain, and still winter / In storm perpetual, could not move the gods' to forgive him (WT 3.2.210–13).

(C) Becon, speaking vividly but disdainfully of the artistic representations of saints, includes 'some naked' (2: 65).

NATURE[1]

(A) The diminished human moral condition after the Fall. 'Nature' is equivalent to moral inadequacy when we read in Nowell's *Catechism* (1853), 137: 'we be by nature most inclined to the love of ourselves'.

(B) Touchstone may lightly touch on both the imperfection and the temporality of nature when he says 'as all is mortal in nature, so is all nature in love mortal in folly' (AYL 2.4.55–6). Of sinfulness, the Captain says of the rebel Macdonwald, 'The multiplying villainies of nature / Do swarm upon him' (MAC 1.2.11–12). Hamlet laments the 'vicious mole of nature' in the best of people, and his father's ghost admits 'the foul crimes done in my days of nature' (HAM 1.4.24; 1.5.12). 'The stamp of nature' in that same play is Hamlet's way of describing what he considers Gertrude's fallen sexuality (HAM 3.4.168).

(C) On fallen human nature, see also Becon, 3: 608. Young (1986), 102–4, discusses the belief that nature fell with Adam's fall in reference to LR.

NATURE[2]

Original, prelapsarian moral perfection and the grace which still prompts humans towards good thoughts, words and deeds. The 'law of nature' is in *The Catechism* authorised during the reign of Edward VI, 1553 (in *Two Liturgies* [1844], 499), prelapsarian perfection, the understanding of 'what difference is between honesty and dishonesty, right and wrong'.

(B) 'Nature' in Shakespeare is innate human goodness, or innate moral sensibility when Lady Macbeth fears that Macbeth's 'nature' 'is too full of the milk of human kindness / To catch the nearest way' and worries that 'compunctious visitings of nature' might 'shake my fell purpose' (MAC 1.5.16–18, 45–6).

(C) For Aquinas on original human perfection, see *ST* I.94–6.

NAVARRE

(A) A region in France associated with the Huguenots, proto-Reformers.

(B) The King and his friends in LLL live in Navarre, and the play occurs there. See *s.d.* 1.1: '*Enter* Ferdinand, *King of Navarre*'.

(C) Hassel (1977) and Cunningham (1955) both argue that Shakespeare plays on several Reformation tensions, including questions about merit, ministers, penance and innate fallenness, when he juxtaposes the Protestant lords of Navarre against the Catholic ladies of France in LLL. Richmond (1979) also suggests that the King in LLL is based on Henry IV and his court in Navarre.

NAZARITE

(A) Someone from Nazareth.

(B) In speaking to the Christian Bassanio, Shylock the Jew disparagingly calls Jesus 'your prophet the Nazarite' (MV 1.3.34).

(C) When Matt. 2.23 speaks of that 'which was spoken by the Prophetes, which was, That he should be called a Nazarite' (*Geneva Bible, fol.* 3), it refers to Judges 13.5–7.

NEBUCHADNEZZAR

(A) The biblical king who falls from blind pride to bestial nakedness, even to the eating of grass or hay (Dan. 4).

(B) Shakespeare refers directly to the biblical figure only when Lavatch says of Lafew's correction of his herbal metaphors for Helena, 'I am no great Nebuchadnezzar, sir; I have not much skill in grass' (AWW 4.5.20–1).

(C) Several have suggested parallels between Lear and Nebchadnezzar, including Mack (1965), 49–52; Battenhouse (1969), 297; and Hamilton (1974), 173–91. Doob (1974) discusses Nebuchadnezzar's influence on the representations of madness in middle English literature.

NEEDLE'S EYE

(A) This refers to a very small opening, and therefore a very slim possibility, in the passage in Mark 10.25–7 where Jesus says, 'It is easier for a camel to go through the eye of a needle, than for a rich man to enter into the kingdom of God.' However, Jesus immediately reassures his listeners of the possibility of divine grace by adding, 'With men it is impossible, but not with God: for with God all things are possible.'

(B) Richard II apparently recalls only the harshness of these verses when he despairs in prison of finding consolation in Scripture:

> As thoughts of things divine, are intermix'd
> With scruples and do set the word itself
> Against the word,
> As thus: 'Come, little ones', and then again,
> 'It is as hard to come as for a camel
> To thread the postern of a small needle's eye.'
> (R2 5.5.12–17)

The apparently contradictory verse he cites here is Mark 10.14: 'Suffer the little children to come unto me'.

(C) Metzger and Coogan (1993), 553, mention patristic traditions of softening the harshness of this passage by reading 'rope' (Gr. *kamilos*) rather than 'camel'. Latimer follows this tradition when he calls the 'camel' 'a great cable of a ship; which is more likelier than a beast that is called a camel' (1844–45), 2: 202. However, Richard's reading was (and is still) more common. Indeed, Talmudic traditions exaggerate the impossibility by speaking of an elephant rather than a camel. See **word**, **camel**. See also Edgerton (1951).

NEIGHBOURLY

(A) Like a good neighbour. Christ summarises the commandments, 'Thou shalt love the Lord thy God with all thy heart, and with all thy soul, and with all thy mind. This is the first and great commandment. And the second is like unto it, Thou shalt love thy neighbour as thyself. On these two commandments hang all the law and the prophets' (Matt. 22.37–40). St Paul subsequently tells the Romans (13.10), 'therefore love *is* the fulfiling of the law'.

(B) Portia ironically refers to revenge rather than love when she says that her Scottish suitor 'hath a neighborly charity in him, for he borrow'd a box of the ear of the Englishman, and swore he would pay him again when he was able' (MV 1.2.79–81). The disdainful Phebe also tells the lovelorn Silvius, not very charitably, 'Thou hast my love; is not that neighborly?' (AYL 3.5.89–90).

(C) Nowell's *Catechism* (orig. 1570) essentially paraphrases Christ's summary of the Law when he divides the Ten Commandments into 'our duties both of . . . the true worshipping of God, and of charity toward our neighbour' (118); cf. Latimer (1844–45), 1: 466. See **love**, **charity**.

NEVER-QUENCHING
(A) Inextinguishable.
(B) When Richard II curses Exton for killing him: 'That hand shall burn in never-quenching fire' (R2 5.5.108), he evokes one of the conditions of the damned in hell.
(C) Andrewes speaks traditionally of 'torment eternal – . . . torment in the fire of hell' (2: 78).

NICHOLAS, SAINT
(A) St Nicholas (d. *c.* 350), Bishop of Myra, was a very popular and often represented 'saintly bishop' and miracle worker who was considered the patron saint of scholars, children, sailors, unmarried girls, merchants, pawnbrokers, apothecaries and perfumiers. Voraigne tells of the legend of a statue of St Nicholas that was beaten black and blue by an angry Jew in place of the thieves who had stolen the Jew's property.
(B) Perhaps because of this last tradition, highwaymen are once called in Shakespeare 'Saint Nicholas' clerks' (see *OED* 2.b) and their devotion to their craft his 'worship' (1H4 2.1.61–5). Using the parallel connection to scholars (*OED* 2.b), Launce first challenges Speed as an 'illiterate loiterer', then gives him a 'paper' to read, saying, 'Saint Nicholas be thy speed' (TGV 3.1.296, 300). Perhaps coincidentally, Speed speeds well in the subsequent reading.
(C) Farmer (1978), 292–3; Voraigne (1941), 1: 22–3; Baring-Gould (1914), 15: 64–8.

NICK
(A) 'Old Nick' is a name for Satan (*OED sb.*^{2}).
(B) Shakespeare may therefore be punning on 'Satan' and 'sin' when Katherine of France, while learning 'the English' for body parts, calls the neck and the chin, 'le col, de nick; le menton, de sin', and then twice more, 'de nick, et de sin', 'de nick, de sin' (H5 3.4.33, 36, 49).
(C) For a proverbial reference, see Tilley, N161.

NOAH
(A) The famous biblical sailor and shipbuilder who survived the Great Flood in the Ark he built with his family.
(B) Toby uses the name to mean merely 'long ago' when he says that judgement and reason 'have been grand-jurymen since before Noah was a sailor' (TN 3.2.16–17). A more complicated reference occurs when Antipholus S. and Dromio S. discuss the 'fault' of Nell the kitchen wench's sweating. 'That's a fault that water will mend' is the master's merely physiological observation. Dromio's hyperbolic dissent has a theological edge: 'No, sir, 'tis in grain, Noah's flood could not do it' (ERR 3.2.103–7). To him, Nell's sweaty flesh is apparently more immune to the cleansing effects of the Flood than the universe of sinfulness it was designed to wash away.
(C) See Gen. 6–8.

NON NOBIS

(A) *Non Nobis* (BEV, 886n) refers to the first two words of the Latin Vulgate version of Ps. 115 (113 in the Vulgate), which begins 'Not unto us, O Lord, not unto us, but unto thy name give glory.' This refers to the successful exodus of the Jews from Egypt.

(B) Henry V calls for the singing of *Non Nobis* and *Te Deum* to acknowledge 'that God fought for' the English at Agincourt (H5 4.8.123). This order corresponds with his modest wish upon his return to London to give 'full trophy, signal, and ostent, / Quite from himself to God' (H5 5 Cho. 17–22).

(C) Shaheen (1992) discusses this psalm's use in H5, as does Candido (2003).

NOTHING

(A) The first gloss in the *Geneva Bible*, for Gen. 1.2, 'The earth was without form, and void', reads, 'First of all, & before that anie creature was, God made heaven and earth of nothing' (*fol.* 1).

(B) It is possible that Lear's 'nothing can be made out of nothing' (LR 1.4.132) encourages a glance at the theological controversy about God's creation of the universe out of nothing, *ex nihilo* from the Vulgate.

(C) On the controversy, see Donne, 3: 96; 3: 195; Nowell (1853), 146; and Tyndale, 3: 234. Elton (1966), 181–8, reconstructs the animated discussion of this issue among some of Shakespeare's contemporaries. Fleissner (1962) also analyses 'nothing' in LR.

NOVICE

Someone spending probationary time before being admitted into a religious order.

Isabella is identified as 'a novice of this place', the 'sisterhood . . . of Saint Clare' (MM 1.4.5, 19–20).

NUMBERS, BOOK OF

(A) One of the books of the Old Testament.

(B) The Archbishop of Canterbury justifies Henry V's claim to the throne of France by this biblical citation: 'in the book of Numbers it is writ, / When the man dies, let the inheritance / Descend unto the daughter' (H5 1.2.98–100).

(C) He refers to Num. 27.8; see Shaheen (1999), 453.

NUN

(A) A woman bound to a religious order and living under the vows of poverty, chastity and obedience. The unmarried and celibate priesthood was another locus of Reformation controversy. As Erasmus once jokes, 'The Reformation, which began as a tragedy, ends as a comedy, with Luther marrying a nun' (see *Letters* 7:369). Tyndale speaks more indelicately of the tradition of celibacy: 'With their chastity they have filled all the world full of whores and sodomites' (2: 123).

(B) Shakespeare's characters give mixed reviews to such a life. Duke Theseus wonders if Hermia 'can endure the livery of a nun, / For aye to be in shady cloister mew'd, / To live a barren sister all your life, / Chaunting faint hymns to the cold fruitless moon.' Though he calls 'they that master so their blood' 'Thrice blessed', he also compares such 'single blessedness' to 'withering on the virgin thorn' (MND 1.1.70–8). On the other hand, Queen Elizabeth knows that 'praying nuns' may be happier than 'weeping queens' (R3 4.4.202), at least if the husband is Richard III. Venus describes the 'fruitless chastity' and 'barren dearth' of 'love-lacking vestals and self-loving nuns' (VEN 751–4), but the Friar speaks more becomingly of placing the just-widowed Juliet with 'a sisterhood of holy nuns' (ROM 5.3.157). Lavatch the Clown speaks cynically of the 'fit' of 'the nun's lip to the Friar's mouth' (AWW 2.2.26–7), but when the Lover says to his reluctant mistress, 'My parts had pow'r to charm a sacred nun' (LC 260), he implies that such a woman is least likely to be seduced. Finally, when Rosalind says that Orlando's kissing is 'as full of sanctity as the touch of holy bread', Celia delightfully declines the simile by pretending to accept it: 'A nun of winter's sisterhood kisses not more religiously; the very ice of chastity is in them' (AYL 3.4.13–17).

(C) Holdsworth (1993) argues that since **nunnery** was slang for 'brothel', 'nun' could be slang for 'whore'. See also Williams (1997), 219–20, and *OED sb.*[1] 1.c. See also *NewCathEncy*, 'Nuns', 10: 575; 'Monasticism', 9: 1032–48; and *OxfordEn-cyRef*, 'Nuns', 3: 158–60; 'Monasticism', 3: 78–83; and 'Marriage', 3: 18–23.

NUNN'RY

(A) A place where **nuns** might live; also a slang word for a whorehouse (*OED* 1.b).
(B) Hamlet directs Ophelia five times 'to a nunn'ry' (HAM 3.1.120–49). But if his 'nunn'ry' is compassionate, a retreat from the world as well as the flesh, its association with bawdy houses also expresses his anger that she has betrayed him. Her father has commanded her to stop seeing Hamlet, lest she 'tender [Polonius] a fool' by becoming pregnant (HAM 1.3.108–10).
(C) Partridge (1968), 154, Bland (1965), Holdsworth (1993), and Williams (1997), 219–20, all argue in favour of reading nunnery as slang for 'brothel' in HAM. French (1967) and Levin (1994) argue against that reading. McFeely (1995), 201–4, examines the nunnery as a refuge in the plays, especially MM.

NUPTIAL

The marriage ceremony.

Shakespeare's funniest reference occurs in LLL, where Armado proclaims, 'the catastrophe is a nuptial' (LLL 4.1.77), intending to mean that a wedding ends their play, not that the wedding will be a disaster.

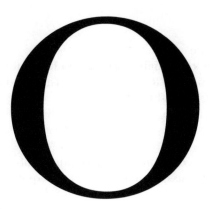

OBEY, OBEDIENT

(A) The woman vows in the marriage ceremony to 'obey him and serve him, love, honor, and keep him' (*BCP*, 292). But because Paul also commands 'Servants obey your masters' and 'Children obey your parents in all' (Col. 3.20, 22), the word can highlight what Desdemona once calls a 'divided duty' (OTH 1.3.81).

(B) A child's obedience, and a wife's, is a persistent issue in HAM. Witness Hamlet's reluctant 'I shall in all my best obey you, madam' to his mother, Ophelia's equally reluctant 'I shall obey, my lord' to Polonius, Gertrude's 'I shall obey you' to Claudius, and Hamlet's angry and perplexing, 'We shall obey, were she ten times our mother' when Rosencrantz and Guildenstern tell him of Gertrude's desire to see him after The Mousetrap play. Polonius also speaks twice to Claudius and Gertrude of Ophelia's 'duty and obedience' towards him (HAM 1.2.120; 1.3.136; 3.1.36; 3.2.333; 2.2.107, 125). Hamlet's own divided duty, to a father who commanded him to 'revenge' and to a God who commanded 'Thou shalt not kill', lurks behind these other examples (HAM 1.5.25). When Brabantio challenges Desdemona to look around the Senate chamber and determine 'where most you owe obedience', she chooses her husband Othello (OTH 1.3.180). Cordelia reveals the same 'divided duty' as Desdemona but also an ear for the words of the wedding rites when she lists 'Obey you, love you, and most honor you', among her daughterly 'duties' to Lear. 'I shall never marry like my sisters, / To love my father all' makes this tension even clearer (LR 1.1.98, 103–4). Kate reveals her apparent taming as well as her knowledge of the Pauline passage when she describes the wife as 'bound to serve, love and obey' (SHR 5.2.164).

(C) See *Certaine Sermons*, pp. 69–77, for the sermons 'of Obedience', and *Certaine Sermons*, 2nd tome, pp. 275–320, for the homilies 'against disobedience and wilfull rebellion'. See also Tyndale, 1: 175 (*The Obedience of a Christen Man*); and Nowell's *Catechism* (1853), 130. See also Hull, *Chaste, Silent, & Obedient* (1982).

OBLATIONS
Any religious observance.

Pericles promises to 'offer night-oblations' to Diana for her help in reuniting him with his wife Thaisa (PER 5.3.70, 57–8). The word occurs as a romantic metaphor in SON 125.10 and LC 223.

OBSEQUIOUS
Fawning, servile.

When King Claudius complains about Hamlet's 'obsequious sorrow' (HAM 1.2.92) for his father, his usage might pun on **obsequy**, the funeral rites due to the dead.

OBSEQUY
Funeral rite or ceremony.

Shakespeare's most famous reference occurs in the 'churlish' Priest's response to Laertes's complaint about the inadequate '**ceremony**' at Ophelia's funeral: 'Her obsequies have been as far enlarg'd / As we have warranty'. Because 'Her death was doubtful', she is deprived of 'charitable **prayers**', 'a **requiem**, and such **rest** to her, / As to peace-parted souls'. Under political pressure she is allowed burial in **sanctified** ground, 'virgin crants' and 'maiden strewments' or flowers, 'and the bringing home / Of **bell** and burial' (HAM 5.1.226–38). Richard Plantagenet mourns his son Rutland's murder and Margaret's mockery with 'tears [that] are my sweet Rutland's obsequies', knowing that he too is about to be murdered and that both of them will be given only a traitor's burial (3H6 1.4.147). Henry VI's 'mean obsequies' seem to suggest that no services could adequately express his personal sadness over Duke Humphrey's murder (2H6 3.2.141–6).

OBSERVANCE
(A) Ceremony, rite, or the proper keeping of it.

(B) In Shakespeare's figurative usage, lovers may 'do observance to a morn of May' (MND 1.1.167; see also 4.1.132), or promise in a litany of love 'all adoration, duty, and observance', 'all purity, all trial, all observance' (AYL 5.2.96, 98).

(C) Bale calls ceremonies, albeit pejoratively, 'holy observations' (1849), 262.

OBSTINATE
(A) Stubborn, unmovable. Two of Shakespeare's six uses are explicitly connected to religious matters.

(B) To Benedick's decision never to marry, not even to trust a woman, Don Pedro says 'Thou wast ever an obstinate **heretic** in the despite of beauty' (ADO 1.1.234–5). 'Heretic' is metaphoric here, but the pairing with 'obstinate' seems quite traditional, oddly suggesting today the deep convictions of these 'heretics', not to mention their courage. Possibly connected to this usage is Claudius's description of Hamlet's refusal to be consoled after the death of his father as 'obstinate condolement', or mourning, which he defines as 'a course / Of impious stubbornness' (HAM 1.2.93–4).

(C) The Catholic Persons says, 'The nature of heresie conteineth two points, first Election, or choice of a private discipline or sect, & then Pertinacity & obstinacy in defense of the same' (1604: II: 158); he also stresses that Protestant heretics 'were worthilie condemned and burned for this pride, selfe-will and obstinacy' (1603), 252. From the Protestant side, Hooper speaks similarly against the 'obstinacy and contempt of God's laws and the king's majesty's' in the maintaining of Roman rites and practices after the Reformation in England (1843), 1: 135–6.

OCCULTED

In astronomy (and astrology), a star is occulted when it disappears behind, say, the moon. Thus the occult deals with hidden but present things, mysteries.

Hamlet shows his propensity towards the stacking up of complex metaphors when he tells Horatio of Claudius's response to The Mousetrap, 'If his occulted guilt / Do not itself unkennel in one speech, / It is a damned ghost that we have seen' (HAM 3.2.80–2).

OFFENCE

Though usually used to denote an action which displeases or a misdemeanour, 'offence' can also refer to a transgression of religious or moral law.

Claudius repeatedly uses the word in his **contrition**. He compares his sin with **Cain**'s: 'O, my offense is rank, it smells to **heaven**, / It hath the primal eldest curse upon't, / A brother's murther.' He tries to salve his resultant theological **despair** with the assurance, 'Whereto serves **mercy**, / But to confront the visage of offense?' But when Claudius honestly answers 'no' to the question, 'May one be pardoned and retain th' offense?' (HAM 3.3.36–8, 46–7), we know that his **repentance** is unsuccessful. Cassio adds a theological dimension to his impropriety in Cyprus when he asks Desdemona 'If my offense be of such mortal kind' (OTH 3.4.115); '**mortal**' sins were thought to lead to spiritual death; '**venial**' were less serious. Even when the superficial Proteus asks Valentine's pardon, he connects the word 'offence' with the liturgically loaded phrase 'hearty **sorrow**' and the equally resonant word '**ransom**': 'Forgive me, Valentine. If hearty sorrow / Be a sufficient ransom for offense, / I tender't here' (TGV 5.4.74–6). Henry V also plays the spiritual priest as well as the worldly judge as he condemns the three traitors 'to your death' but also prays, 'God of his mercy give / You patience to endure and true repentance / Of all your dear offenses' (H5 2.2.178–81).

OFFERINGS

Gifts to the Church. Poins describes their potential victims as 'pilgrims going to Canterbury with rich offerings' (1H4 1.2.126).

OFFICE[1]

The liturgical service that a priest might conduct.

Of Angelo and Mariana the Duke commands the Friar, 'Go take her hence, and marry her instantly. / Do you the office' (MM 5.1.376–7). When Queen

Katherine criticises Cardinal Wolsey for serving himself rather than the Church, 'I must tell you, / You tender more your person's honour than / Your high profession spiritual', she puns on the close connection between **office**[1] and **office**[2]: 'Your words / (Domestics to you) serve your will as't please / Yourself pronounce their office' (H8 2.4.113–17).

OFFICE[2]

The religious position that a priest holds and its related duties. Andrewes says, 'For not only the power to pray, to preach, to make and give the Sacrament; but the power also to bless you that are God's people, is annexed and is a branch of ours, of the Priests' office' (3: 81).

Wolsey and Henry VIII speak of the conflicts of 'holy offices' and worldly offices just before Henry turns against Wolsey (H8 3.2.144).

OIL

(A) Consecrated oil, sometimes mixed with balsam, is used in such religious rites as extreme unction, baptism and confirmation. Grindal warns the young Church of England against any Romish 'parson, vicar, curate, or minister' who uses 'any gestures, rites, or ceremonies, not appointed by the book of Common Prayer, as **crossing** or breathing over the sacramental bread and wine, or shewing the same to the people to be worshipped and adored, or any such like, or use any oil and chrism, tapers, spattle, or any other popish **ceremony** in the ministration of the **sacrament** of **Baptism**' (1843), 159–60.

(B) The Gentleman says that Anne Boleyn, during her coronation ceremony, 'had all the royal makings of a queen', including 'holy oil' (H8 4.1.88).

(C) Bale is characteristically outrageous when he says of the Catholics, 'No end is there of their babbling prayers, their portasses, **beads**, **temples**, altar-songs, hours, **bells**, **images**, **organs**, ornaments, jewels, lights, oilings, shavings, . . ., **fastings**, **processions**, and prattlings, that a man would think that they were proctors of paradise' (1849), 262. There are many similar complaints, as in Pilkington (1842), 163, 527, 493.

OLDCASTLE

(A) Oldcastle was the Lollard knight and martyr, executed in 1417. He was still celebrated in the sixteenth century as a Puritan hero. Shakespeare originally named one of his most famous characters Oldcastle, but the family's intervention with the Stationer forced Shakespeare to change the name to Falstaff.

(B) Shakespeare did not erase all traces. The Epilogue of 2H4 says of Falstaff, 'for Oldcastle died a **martyr**, and this is not the man' (2H4 Ep. 31–2). Hal calls him 'my old lad of the castle' in their first scene together, and Falstaff preposterously claims to be a man of virtue, indeed 'a **saint**', corrupted by the Prince (1H4 1.2.91).

(C) See Bale's 'A brefe Chronycle concerning the examination and death of the Blessed martyr of Christ Sir John Oldcastle'. See Scoufos (1979) on the Oldcastle–Falstaff issue: 44–69 gives a biography of Oldcastle, 70–133 analyses H5, and 188–220 discusses WIV. Honigmann (1987) argues that Shakespeare was deliberately trying to insult the Cobham family in the portrayal of Falstaff as Oldcastle. Poole (1995), 62–75, considers Falstaff more generally as a figure of the 'grotesque Puritan,' even connecting him to the Marprelate Tracts, and Spencer (2001), 622–5, discusses the religious violence related to the Oldcastle story. See also Kastan (1998).

ORACLE

Formal pronouncement of the pagan **gods**, then delivered by priests to the waiting people.

An oracle of Apollo is consulted by Leontes to affirm his conviction of Hermione's infidelity, and then denied when the judgement comes back 'not guilty' (WT 3.2.115–18, 140; cf. 1.2.74).

ORDER¹

Monastic institution, as of friars or nuns. See **friar, nun, brother**.

The Duke in MM poses as a friar, 'a brother of your order' (1.3.44), through much of the play. He elsewhere describes himself as 'Bound by my charity and my blest order' and 'a brother / Of gracious order' (MM 2.3.3; 3.2.219); he also refers to 'a vow of mine order', and assures Isabella, 'Trust not my holy order / If I pervert your course' (MM 4.2.169; 4.3.147–8). The Gentleman refers to the 'Learned and **reverend** members of [Canterbury's] order' (H8 4.1.26), and Friar Lawrence swears 'By my holy order' (ROM 3.3.114). See also **vot'ress**.

ORDER²

Established sequence, ceremony or procedure, as the order of worship.

Antony asks to 'Speak in the order of [Caesar's] funeral' (JC 3.1.230).

ORDINANCE

Ordering or direction, sometimes of God.

Two assertions of **providence** in R3 use a form of this word. Richard's mother hopes before his final battle with Richmond that 'thou wilt die by God's just ordinance'. Richmond, after winning the battle, attributes his coming marriage with Elizabeth to 'God's fair ordinance' (R3 4.4.184; 5.5.31).

ORDINANT *adj.*

(A) Spoken of God, meaning capable of or exercising governance; provident.

(B) Hamlet, telling Horatio of a newfound sense of the 'divinity that shapes our ends, / Rough-hew them how we will' and of the 'special providence in the fall of a sparrow', says of his useful but unplanned mastery of clerical penmanship and his possession of the royal seal on his 'father's signet', 'Why, even in that was heaven ordinant' (HAM 5.2.10–11, 219–20, 34, 48–9).

(C) *OED adj.* reads: 'that orders, arranges, regulates, or directs'.

ORGAN

(A) This musical instrument was another controversial appurtenance of church worship during the Reformation.

(B) Though Shakespeare's usage does not evoke any explicit sense of the religious controversy, his characters refer to the organ five times with some sense of awe (HAM 2.2.593–4; 3.2.367–8; TMP 3.3.98–9; JN 5.7.22–4; AWW 2.1.175–6).

(C) See Donne in favour of organs in church (7: 407), and Philpot against (1842), 427–8. Reformers George Withers and John Barthelot complain of English church officials: 'They say that they disapprove the chanting of choristers, and the use of organs.' 'Nevertheless they all adopt them in their churches, and the archbishop of Canterbury especially has caused an organ to be erected in his metropolitan church at his own expense' (*Zurich Letters* [1845], 2: 150, letter LVIII). See also Holden (1954), 68.

ORISONS

Prayers, devotions.

Perhaps already mocking her false piety and posture as she holds the religious book, what her father has just called 'devotion's visage', Hamlet asks Ophelia, 'Nymph, in thy orisons / Be all my sins remember'd' (HAM 3.1.44–7, 88–9). Juliet tells her Nurse 'I have need of many orisons / To move the heavens to smile upon my state' (ROM 4.3.3–4). Cf. 3H6 1.4.110; CYM 1.3.31–2.

OSTENTATION

Formal show. Today we use the word pejoratively; in Shakespeare's time it could obviously describe appropriate formality in worship, or the observance itself.

Laertes is not only angry that the Priest will give Ophelia no more ceremony. He also complains that his father's 'obscure funeral' contained 'No noble rite nor formal ostentation' (HAM 4.5.214–16). The Friar in ADO advises Leonato to 'maintain a mourning ostentation' (ADO 4.1.205).

OUTWARD

(A) The deceptive surface of persons or things as against their inner substance.

(B) The word is used to distinguish between the flesh and the spirit in Shakespeare's most explicitly religious sonnet. 'Poor soul, the centre of my sinful earth' laments early that the soul would 'pine within and suffer dearth, / Painting thy outward walls so costly gay', then ends, 'Within be fed, without be rich no more' (SON 146.1–4, 12). The word also designates the deceptive surface of religious hypocrisy, most obviously when Angelo is called an 'outward-sainted deputy' and 'angel on the outward side' by the angry Isabella and the disappointed Duke (MM 3.1.88; 3.2.272). Bassanio speaks similarly of the vice that commonly 'assumes / Some mark of virtue on his outward parts'; he also says of 'all that glisters' in the material world, 'So may the outward shows be least themselves' (MV 3.2.81–2, 73; 2.7.65).

(C) Andrewes uses 'outward show' to describe a 'counterfeit show of holiness' (5: 492); Donne speaks non-pejoratively of 'the outward Ceremoniall, and Rituall worship of God in the *Church*' (4: 203). The Reformer Philpot complains about the 'outward ornaments', the 'sumptuous temples, with images, signs, tables, organs, vessels, vestiments, lights, gold, silver, precious stones, purple, and with such other like, with which we see churches and chapels trimmed withal' (1842), 427–8.

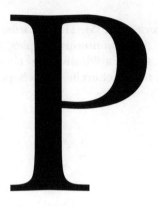

PABYLON
See **Babylon**.

PAGAN
(A) Non-Christian.
(B) Shylock's daughter Jessica is called 'most beautiful pagan, most sweet Jew' by their servant Gobbo (MV 2.3.10–11), and Mowbray is described as carrying 'the ensign of the **Christian cross** / Against black pagans, **Turks**, and **Saracens**' (R2 4.1.94–5). Henry IV also hopes 'to chase those pagans in those holy fields' of the crusades (1H4 1.1.24), but he specifies neither their colour, nationality nor religion. Hamlet distinguishes simply between Christian and pagan in his advice to the players (HAM 3.2.31–2), and Othello is implicitly called a 'pagan' by the angry Brabantio even though he has been converted to Christianity (OTH 1.2.99).
(C) Elton (1966) looks at the Elizabethan understanding of pagan belief in LR (see *esp.* 147–70). Simmons (1973) argues that the essential difference of the Roman plays from Shakespeare's other tragedies is their pagan setting. Moschovakis (2002), 470–2, examines the impact of martyrdom in the pagan world of TIT.

PAINTED
(A) Rendered visually on walls or cloth. When Donne refers to 'a *painted Church*, on one side, or . . . a *naked Church*, on another' he speaks of the controversies about the proper use of religious representation in sanctuaries (6: 284). At these extremes, the naked church would be the most undecorated Protestant sanctuary, entirely without religious imagery, the painted one the elaborately decorated Catholic one. Donne in his Holy Sonnet 18 speaks of the Catholic Church as 'richly painted', in contrast to the 'robbed and tore' (ll. 3–4) German Church

after the work of the iconoclasts. Herbert speaks of 'The British Church' as 'Neither too mean, nor yet too gay', in contrast to 'all they either painted are, / Or else undrest' (1974), ll. 8–12.

(B) Richard's queen may be referring to the many religious wall-paintings of medieval England when she describes Bolingbroke's enthusiastic welcome into England as though 'all the walls / With painted imagery had said at once, / Jesu preserve thee! Welcome Bolingbroke!' (R2 5.2.15–17). Falstaff probably refers in contrast to 'the cheap hangings of a room' when he calls his pathetic company of soldiers 'As ragged as **Lazarus** in the **painted** cloth' (1H4 4.2.25; see Luke 16.19–31). When Orlando promises Jaques to 'answer you right painted cloth' (AYL 3.2.273) he therefore means in clichés, since these cheap religious tapestries were usually hackneyed. Mistress Quickly also says that Falstaff's room 'is painted about', appropriately enough, 'with the story of the Prodigal' (WIV 4.5.6–7). Lady Macbeth refers to a more general tradition of religious iconography when she taunts Macbeth that it is only 'the eye of childhood, / That fears a painted devil' (MAC 2.2.51–2). When Borachio likens fads in fashion to '**Pharaoh**'s soldiers in the reechy painting' (ADO 3.3.133–4), he probably refers to some grimy representation of the Israelites crossing the Red Sea (Ex. 14).

(C) Of such painted cloth, see BEV, 309n, PEL, 260n. For those religious representations in England which survived the iconoclasts, see Davidson and Alexander (1985) and Alston (1989). Caiger-Smith (1963), 119–20, reminds us that the unique temperature and humidity of churches in northern Europe led artists to paint rather than fresco the walls of religious and secular buildings.

PALESTINE

The Holy Land and destination of most of the Crusades.

King Philip of France identifies Richard the Lion-Heart as one who 'fought the holy wars in Palestine' (JN 2.1.4); saltier is Emilia's comment to Desdemona about Cassio that she knows 'a lady in Venice would have walked barefoot to Palestine for a touch of his nether lip' (OTH 4.3.38–9).

PALMER

Religious **pilgrim**, so called because someone who had returned from a pilgrimage to the Holy Land might bear a palm leaf.

Richard II offers to exchange his 'sceptre for a palmer's walking staff' as he imagines his divestiture (R2 3.3.151); similarly, Richard Plantagenet calls Henry VI unfit for political affairs by saying, 'Thy hand is made to grasp a palmer's staff' (2H6 5.1.97). Juliet expresses her hope that they might just hold hands when Romeo requests a kiss: 'For palm to palm is holy palmers' kiss'. He persists, 'Have not saints lips, and holy palmers too?' (ROM 1.5.100–1).

PANCAKE

See **Shrove Tuesday**.

PAPIST
(A) Derogatory term for Catholic; a supporter of the Pope and the papistry.
(B) The cynical Lavatch says of 'young **Charbon** the puritan and old **Poysam** the Papist', 'howsome'er their hearts are severed in **religion**, their heads are both one' as cuckolds (AWW 1.3.51–4).
(C) BEV, 370n, glosses these names as French puns on 'the fast-day diets of Puritans and Catholics, respectively', 'chair bonne' for 'good meat' and 'poisson' for fish. For various pejorative uses of Papist, see Andrewes, 1: 403; Donne, 4: 202–4; 8: 177; Whitaker (1849), 259; and Fulke (1843), 1: 218.

PARADISE
(A) Eden before the Fall, thus metaphorically a perfect place (see TMP 4.1.124; MM 3.1.130; LLL 4.3.71).
(B) The King in LLL uses the romantic-religious metaphor paradoxically: 'You would for paradise break faith and troth' (4.3.141). Juliet, bewildered that Romeo has just killed Tybalt, asks, also metaphorically, how nature could 'bower the spirit of a fiend / In mortal paradise of such sweet flesh?' (ROM 3.2.81–2). Dromio wittily turns 'Paradise' into the name of the first pub: 'Not that Adam that kept the Paradise, but that Adam that keeps the prison' (ERR 4.3.17–18).
(C) Donne similarly translates Gen. 2.15, '*Adam* himself was commanded to *dresse* Paradise, and to *keep* Paradise' (7: 424). Scoufos (1981), 218–25, discusses the 'earthly paradise' in AYL.

PARDON[1] *v.*
Forgive; *sb.* forgiveness. Requests in Shakespeare for God to pardon sins are often complicated by rationalization, deception or negotiation. In a sense that is merely to say that most of them occur in political rather than purely spiritual environments, and are public rather than private expressions.
    Part of Richard II's formula of deposition is his explicit if also self-serving request, 'God pardon all oaths that are broke to me' (R2 4.1.214). Later in the play the usurper Bolingbroke, just crowned Henry IV, says of Richard's ally Aumerle, 'I pardon him as God shall pardon me' (R2 5.3.131). In 1H4 Northumberland, Bolingbroke's ally in Richard's deposition, if not his death, seems also to be negotiating with God when he calls Henry IV an 'unhappy king / (Whose wrongs in us God pardon!)' (1H4 1.3.148–9). Bolingbroke is essentially refusing to grant his own son Hal's request for 'pardon' when he responds to it, 'God pardon thee' (1H4 3.2.28–9). Henry V, as clever as his father, declines the traitors' request for 'pardon, sovereign' with 'God quit you in his mercy' (H5 2.2.160, 165–6).
    Henry V later describes the 'Five hundred poor I have in yearly pay, / Who twice a day their wither'd hands hold up / Toward heaven to pardon blood', mentions 'two chantries' 'I have built' 'Where the sad and solemn priests still sing / For Richard's soul', and finally acknowledges, 'More will I do, / Though all that I can do is nothing worth, / Since that my penitence comes after all, / Imploring pardon' (H5 4.1.298–305). An audience at the start of the twenty-first

century, like one in the middle of the Reformation, might be uncomfortable with this extraordinary bribery of God. On the other hand, doing such good works on such a large scale with such a clear spiritual agenda is arguably appropriate behaviour for a Catholic king in the Middle Ages.

The son who asks 'Pardon me God, I knew not what I did' for killing his father in 3H6 asks for God's pardon with a possible echo of Christ's last words on the cross, 'Father forgive them, for they know not what they do' (Luke 23.34). In another mouth, at another time, the prayer could be distrusted; here the echo probably adds to our sense of the speaker's sincerity and innocence. The ever-pious Henry VI also dies at Richard of Gloucester's hands knowing that Richard is 'ordained' for 'much more slaughter after this' and asking for God's forgive-ness of both of them: 'O God, forgive my sins, and pardon thee' (3H6 5.6.59–60). Richard's response is less charitable: 'Down, down to hell, and say I sent thee hither' (5.6.67). See **forgive**.

PARISH

An ecclesiastical district, with its own church and clergyman.

The role of Alexander the Great is given to 'the parish curate' (LLL 5.2.535), possibly because he could read. Jaques' 'The why is plain as way to parish church' (AYL 2.7.52) and the fisherman's reference to the imaginary whale that first swallows and then 'casts bells, steeple, church, and parish up again' (PER 2.1.42) also connect the district with the Church building. Cf. H8 1.2.152–3.

PARISHIONERS

Members of a parish church.

In LLL (4.2.74) Nathaniel the curate refers to 'my parishioners', and Rosalind compares Celia's reading of Orlando's bad verse to a curate's bad reading of a prescribed **homily**: 'what tedious homily of love have you wearied your parishioners withal, and never cried, "Have patience, good people"' (AYL 3.2.155–7).

PARSON

A clergyman, minister or preacher.

'Master Parson' Evans is described as 'a gentleman born'; since he always 'writes himself Armigero' or Esquire, he is probably a bit proud of his birth, certainly possessive of what privilege it affords him (WIV 1.1.7–9). Shallow calls him 'no jester' (WIV 2.1.1210); the implication may be that parsons could some-times become objects of ridicule. When Feste plays the Curate for Malvolio, he too is called 'Master Parson' several times. Interestingly, Feste enters his role with a thoughtful description of what a parson should and should not be: 'I would that I were the first that ever dissembled in such a gown. I am not tall enough to become the function well, nor lean enough to be thought a good student; but to be said an honest man and a good house-keeper goes as fairly as to say a careful man and a great scholar' (TN 4.2.4–10). The other two references, to 'coughing' which 'drowns the parson's saw' (LLL 5.2.922) and Queen Mab 'Tickling a parson's nose as 'a lies asleep' (ROM 1.4.80) are both humanizing details which gently undercut these figures of authority.

PASSES

By ellipsis, 'trespasses'.

Angelo expresses 'shame' when he learns that the Duke, 'like pow'r **divine**, / Hath look'd upon my passes' (MM 5.1.366–7).

PASTOR

Preacher (*OED sb.* 2) responsible for the care of his flock or **congregation**.

Ophelia warns Laertes, 'Do not, as some ungracious pastors do, / Show me the steep and thorny way to heaven, / Whiles like a puff'd and reckless libertine, / Himself the primrose path of dalliance treads / And reaks not his own rede' (HAM 1.3.47–51).

PATIENCE

(A) A willingness to abide the providence of God. In addition to being one of the four cardinal virtues, this is also one of the traditional marks of religious humility and faith. Aquinas quotes Augustine as saying (in *De Patiencia* i): 'The virtue of . . . patience is so great a gift of God, that we even preach the patience of Him who bestows it upon us.' Aquinas calls it 'a virtue to safeguard the good of reason against sorrow'.

(B) Several characters pray for this virtue. Henry V prays for the three traitors, 'God of his mercy give / You patience to endure and true repentance / Of all your dear offenses' (H5 2.2.178–81). Isabella asks during her trial with Angelo, 'O, you blessed ministers above, / Keep me in patience' (MM 5.1.115–16). Longaville also asks, 'God grant us patience' (LLL 1.1.192–8). The Duchess of York calls Queen Elizabeth's 'black despair' and her subsequent threat to kill herself 'rude impatience' (R3 2.2.36–8). Rosalind wonders sarcastically of a bad preacher, 'what tedious homily of love have you wearied your parishioners withal, and never cried, "Have patience, good people!" ' (AYL 3.2.155–7).

(C) For Augustine and Aquinas on patience, see *ST* II.2.136.1.

PATRICK, SAINT

(A) The English missionary and bishop (*c.* 390–461) who was traditionally credited with bringing Christianity to Ireland. He was said to be potent against serpents (Voraigne), and to have revealed one opening into purgatory, thence called St Patrick's purgatory. Also the patron saint of Ireland. Feast Day: 17 March.

(B) As in many of the references to saints in Shakespeare, the name becomes a mild oath when Hamlet says to Horatio's 'no offense my lord', 'Yes, by Saint Patrick, but there is' (HAM 1.5.135–6). He refers to the 'offense' that the ghost has uncovered. The Ghost describes himself as coming from a place much like purgatory, where 'the foul crimes done in my days of nature' will be 'burnt and purg'd away' (HAM 1.5.12–13); he also describes his murderer as a 'serpent' (HAM 1.5.39).

(C) See Voraigne (1941), 1:192–3 (on purgation and serpents); BEV (1076n); Farmer (1978), 312–13; Baring-Gould (1914), 3:285–306; for St Patrick and purgatory, see also Greenblatt (2001), 75–7, 233–4.

PAUL, SAINT

(A) The early persecutor of Christians who was suddenly converted on the road to Damascus. St Paul wrote many of the Epistles of the New Testament, advising the fledgling congregations and their leaders about affairs of the Church and the Spirit; the writings of this 'apostle of the gentiles' were also the basis of a good deal of the language of the Book of Common Prayer. St Paul according to some traditions was beheaded under Nero's persecution of the Christians *c.* 65. Before his conversion Paul (then Saul) was known for his 'wanton boldness and insolence', especially against the early Christian apostles. St Paul was also known for his 'triumph over magical arts' in **Ephesus**. Feast day: 29 June.

(B) Richard of Gloucester gleefully swears five times by Paul. The first two oaths (R3 1.2.36, 41) probably occur because the funeral procession he has interrupted started at St Paul's Cathedral, London. The third (R3 1.3.45) may ironically contrast Richard's self-imputed Pauline peace-making to the dissension around him. The fourth, against the witches he claims have deformed him, could connect Richard to the St Paul who spoke of the witches and conjurers in Ephesus (R3 3.4.76). Invoking the beheaded St Paul as he orders the beheading of Hastings is another likely connection here. The last 'by Saint Paul' is uncharacteristically reflective, admitting that the eleven ghosts of his victims have at least briefly 'struck . . . terror to my soul' (R3 5.3.217–18).

(C) On St Paul, see Farmer (1978), 313–14; Voraigne (1941), 1:126–7; Baring-Gould (1914), 6:432–54. Hassel (1971b) considers Pauline allusions concerning faith and folly in the romantic comedies. Whall (1996) suggests that references to magic in the comedies allude to Paul. Shaheen (1999), 352, suggests that Richard's use of St Paul's name before Hasting's execution may echo a passage in Acts 23.12–15, in which some Jews swear to kill St Paul before they eat or drink again. Carnall (1963) argues that Richard III is an impersonation of St Paul. On St Paul in R3, see also Hassel (1980), 9–17, 23–7, 53–76, 172–5, 208–22, and Colley (1986). Lupton (1997) looks at the relevance of Paul's categories of Jew, Christian and Gentile to OTH. Go (2002) notes a reference to Paul in Sonnet 121. See **folly** and **fool**.

PAUL'S (Powles)
St Paul's Cathedral, London.

Shakespeare's five references each reveal something different about the place. Hal's comment about Falstaff suggests its fame: 'This oily rascal is known as well as Paul's' (1H4 2.4.526); the Man's 'We may as well push against Powle's as stir 'em' (H8 5.3.16) suggests its great size. That it was both a labour exchange and a site for the public reading of official documents is revealed when Falstaff says of Bardolph, 'I bought him in Paul's' (2H4 1.2.50), and the Scrivener describes his phoney indictment of Hastings as designed to be 'read o'er in Paul's' (R3 3.6.3).

Finally, it was a site for state funerals. Henry VI's body was 'Taken from Paul's to be interred' at Chertsey monastery near London (R3 1.2.29–30).

PAX

(A) According to Bullough (*NDS*, 4: 361) the object that Bardolph stole from the French church was a *pyx*, the 'vessel in which the consecrated bread of Holy Communion is reserved', rather than Shakespeare's *pax*, 'a tablet bearing a picture of the crucifixion . . . kissed by worshipers at Mass'.

(B) Pistol laments of Bardolph, 'he hath stol'n a pax, and hanged must'a be – / A damned death!' and also 'Exeter hath given the doom of death / For pax of little price' (H5 3.6.40–5). Whereas 'damned death' seems to suggest that the theft is a sacrilege, 'little price' takes it more materially.

(C) Either *pax* or *pyx* would have resonated with Reformation dissonance. Jewel argues, for example, that 'The peace given to the bishop was not a little table of silver or somewhat else, as hath been used in the Church of Rome, but a very kiss indeed, in token of perfect peace and unity' (1845–50), 1: 265. Grindal more literally lists the *pax* among the 'relics and monuments of superstition and idolatry, [that must] be utterly defaced, broken, and destroyed' (1843), 135–6. See also Knapp (1993), 39–40.

PEACE[1]

Eternal rest in heaven after death; also by metonymy heaven itself.

When Macbeth, lamenting his fear and penitence as 'the torture of the mind', says of Duncan, 'Whom we, to gain our peace, have sent to peace' (MAC 3.2.20), the religious usage is fairly clear. The holy Katherine of Aragon once says, 'as you wish Christian peace to souls departed' (H8 4.2.156). This 'peace of heaven' is often personified in JN (as in 2.1.35; 3.1.246; 3.3.9; 4.3.150; 5.2.76), and frequently invoked, both hypocritically and sincerely, throughout the English histories. The richest cluster of references occurs in 4.1 and 4.2 of 2H4, the scenes at Gaultree Forest in which the rebels are first pardoned and then betrayed, arrested and condemned to death by the king's party (see *esp.* 2H4 4.1.29–48, 175–86; 4.2.29–31, 70–89).

PEACE[2]

(A) Spiritual composure. Part of a formulaic benediction, as in the famous Pauline blessing at the end of communion, 'The peace of God, which passeth all understanding, keep your hearts and minds in the knowledge and love of God, and of His Son Jesu Christ our Lord' (*BCP*, 265; cf. Phil. 4.7).

(B) The formulaic blessing 'Peace be with you' is especially common in the comedies (as in MM 3.2.260; WIV 3.5.56; MV 4.1.48). Ecumenically, one of these blessings is by the Duke disguised as a friar, one by Mistress Quickly in the tavern; the third is Portia's ironic farewell when she leaves the trial scene pretending anger because she has been denied Bassanio's ring.

(C) Donne plays on several meanings of 'peace': '*Peace* in this world, is a pretious *Earnest*, and a faire and lovely *Type* of the everlasting peace of the world to come:

And warre in this world, is a shrewd and fearefull *Embleme* of the everlasting discord and tumult, and torment of the world to come: And therefore, our *Blessed God*, blesse us with this externall, and this internall, and make that lead us to an eternall peace' (4: 182–3). See *ST* II.2.29.

PEACEMAKERS

Henry VI makes a futile attempt to cool hot tempers, including that of his queen Margaret of Anjou, when he says from the Beatitudes (Matt. 5.9), 'I prithee, peace, / Good queen, and whet not on these furious peers, / For blessed are the peacemakers on earth.' The Cardinal's immediate wish that he could make 'peace' 'against this proud protector with my sword', not to mention the fact that the warlike Margaret is still holding her hawk on her fist (2H6 2.1.32–4, *s.d.*), predict little success.

PEARL

(A) This precious object is often associated with great value and purity.
(B) If the 'base Iudean' Othello compares himself to (OTH 5.2.347) is Judas, the 'pearl' he 'threw . . . away', whom he compares to Desdemona, would be Christ himself.
(C) See, however, **Indian**.

PELICAN

(A) In the Christian iconographic tradition the pelican, who pierces her own breast to feed her young, can stand for Christ's sacrifice on the cross, and in fact sometimes accompanies representations of the Crucifixion. Andrewes blends the natural and supernatural in his description of 'the pelican's bill of mercy, striking itself to the heart, drawing blood thence, even the very heart-blood, to revive her young ones, when they were dead in sin, and to make them live anew the life of grace' (4: 331). This posture, called 'the pelican in her piety', is vividly illustrated in Wither's English Emblem Book of 1635 (1975r), fig. 154.
(B) Shakespeare gives both a picture of 'the kind, life-rend'ring pelican' (HAM 4.5.147) and of its ungrateful children who 'tapped out and drunkenly caroused' 'that blood' (R2 2.1.126–7). Lear's angry reference to his 'pelican daughters' and Edgar's to the 'side-piercing sight' of the mad and banished Lear (LR 3.4.75; 4.6.85) are other complex references to this tradition.
(C) For a small illustration and a brief discussion of the pelican in its piety, see Friedmann (1980), 267, 170. The website http://www.kwantlen.bc.ca/~donna/sca/pelican/ offers a rich online selection of medieval representations. See also Clark (1992), 169–71.

PENALTY

(A) According to Gen. 3.17–18, 'a curse on the earth' which included both death and the end of Eden's perpetual spring, resulted from the Fall. Coverdale calls death ' "the just judgment of God" . . . a penalty deserved, laid upon us all for the

Our Pelican, *by bleeding, thus,*
Fulfill'd the Law, *and cured* Vs.

ILLVSTR. XX.   *Book.*3

Fig. 5 The Pelican in her Piety. Emblem #154 from *A Collection of Emblemes,* George Wither, 1635; STC 25900d. Courtesy The Newberry Library, Chicago.

punishment of sin' (1846), 2: 49–50. Milton says of the second penalty 'Else had the Spring / Perpetual smil'd on earth' (PL 10.678–9.

(B) This curse is called 'The penalty of Adam' in AYL, and defined as 'the seasons' difference' (AYL 2.1.5–6).

(C) See also Sandys (1841), 168; Nowell (1853), 176; Shaheen (1999), 218. Hankins (1964) discusses the 'penalty of Adam' in AYL.

PENANCE

(A) A formal sacrament in the Roman Catholic Church, involving contrition, confession, absolution, and a penitential discipline imposed by a priest; more generally, any punishment undergone in token of repentance. Reformers were concerned about the reputed outwardness of penance versus the inwardness of repentance, the reputed redundancy of the priest's role in an essentially personal act of contrition, confession and amendment of life, and the question of whether any person could do an individual or a liturgical work that effected satisfaction for sins, since Christ only made his sacrifice once and for always for that purpose. See **repentance**.

(B) When Armado says 'The naked truth of it is, I have no shirt. I go woolward for penance' and Boyet responds sarcastically, 'True, and it was enjoined him in Rome for want of linen' (LLL 5.2.710–13), he speaks of the woollen sackcloth that was traditionally worn by penitents to remind them of their duty to feel uncomfortable in and to punish the flesh; 'Rome' further connects his formally prescribed penance with Catholicism. In ADO, Claudio, having learned how much he has wronged Hero, and still thinking her dead, asks her father Leonato to 'impose me to what penance your invention / Can lay upon my sin'. He is given the penance of proclaiming her innocence and his guilt throughout Messina, writing and singing an epitaph in her memory, and marrying Leonato's niece (ADO 5.1.273–4, 281–5). Dame Eleanor Cobham's 'three days' open penance' for her treason against 'God and us [King Henry VI]' is elaborately portrayed as a blending of religious and political rites. She enters '[barefoot] in a white sheet [with verses pinned upon her back] and a taper burning in her hand, . . . a crowd following', and it is clear in what she says that public humiliation is her chief penalty: 'Look how they gaze' (2H6 2.3.2, 11; 2.4.s.d., 20). There are also the usual metaphoric references (TGV 2.4.129; SON 111.12).

(C) For a taste of the controversy about penance versus **repentance**, see the Protestants Tyndale, 1: 260; Bradford (1848), 1: 45–6; Fulke (1843), 1: 429; and the Catholics Vaux (1590a), *sig.* G6^{r-v}, and Granada (trans. Hopkins, 1586), 11. See also *ST* III.84–90; *ST* III.90, treats 'the parts of penance'. Butler (1982), 88–90, connects an early modern ritual for public penance with the use of humiliation in COR. Morris (1985), 53–8, argues that Hamlet puts Ophelia and Gertrude through the sacrament of penance. Hassel (1977, 1980, ch. 4) discusses the 'penance' imposed on the lords in both LLL and ADO. See also 'Penance', *OxfordEncyRef*, 3: 242–4; *NewCathEncy*, 11: 72–83.

PENDANT

The earth was thought in the Ptolemaic picture to hang suspended from the vault of heaven on a golden chain, like a pendant on a necklace.

Though Claudio once speaks of 'this pendant world' (MM 3.1.125), his dread of death and whatever '**howling**' might follow leaves little space for the potential comfort of such an image of proximity to God.

PENITENCE

Feeling truly sorry for **sins**.

Valentine, believing the sincerity of Proteus's expression of 'hearty sorrow', forgives him, citing the divine analogy: 'By penitence th' Eternal's wrath's appeased' (TGV 5.4.74, 81). The Duke, speaking to pregnant Juliet in MM, says he will 'try your penitence, if it be sound', and through a systematic interrogation is satisfied both that she repents out of love of heaven, and not in fear of shame, and that she embraces 'the shame with joy' (MM 2.3.22–36). The same question, if 'Fear, and not love, begets his penitence' comes up as York tries to convince Henry IV to execute his son Aumerle as a traitor (R2 5.3.56).

PENITENT
One who is truly sorry for sins.

Angelo, caught red-handed but also 'sorry that such sorrow I procure', says of his sin, 'so deep sticks it in my penitent heart / That I crave death more willingly than **mercy**' (MM 5.1.474–6). By having Camillo call Leontes 'the penitent King' and 'that penitent' after the passage of sixteen years (WT 4.2.6, 22), Shakespeare can assure us that time, Paulina, and Leontes's own **contrition** have readied him for our **forgiveness**, Hermione's, and his own. 'Enjoin'd **penitents** . . . to great Saint **Jaques** bound' (AWW 3.5.94–5), describes people literally on a penitential **pilgrimage** to Santiago in Spain. Valentine's metaphoric 'penance for contemning love', 'bitter **fasts**, with penitential groans' (TGV 2.4.130–1), reveals two possible details of a formal act of religious **penance**.

PENTECOST
(A) The Christian festival commemorating the descent of the Holy Ghost upon the Apostles, celebrated on the seventh Sunday after Easter, called Whitsunday.
(B) Shakespeare's characters use it mainly as a reference to springtime (ERR 4.1.1; ROM 1.5.36).
(C) Andrewes, in a Whitsunday sermon before the king at Greenwich, 1606, not only calls '**Prayer**', 'the **Word**' and 'the **Sacraments**' 'every one of them . . . an artery to convey the **Spirit** into us', but also 'three means to procure the Spirit's coming' (3: 127–8).

PEOPLED
(A) Populated. The first 'cause for which matrimony was ordained', according to the *BCP* (290), was 'the procreation of children'. God's first commandment to Adam and Eve was also this blessing: 'Be fruitful, and multiply' (Gen. 1. 28).
(B) Benedick comically rationalises his unexpected love for Beatrice by citing this rule: 'the world must be peopled' (ADO 2.3.242).
(C) See Donne, 8: 101: 'Man is borne into the world, that others might be born from him.'

PERDITION
Usually merely loss; in religious usage it is a state of **spiritual** ruin, **damnation** and the experience of **hell**.

Othello says with prophetic irony after his first argument with Desdemona, 'perdition catch my soul / But I do love thee! and when I love thee not, / Chaos is come again' (OTH 3.3.90–2).

PERDURABLY

(A) Eternally, sometimes applied to the eternal damnation of the soul.

(B) Claudio, desperate for life, asks his sister Isabella of Angelo's proposition that she have sex with him, 'If it were damnable, he being so wise, / Why would he for the momentary trick / Be perdurably fin'd?' (MM 3.1.112–14).

(C) *OED adv.* defines it 'everlastingly, eternally'.

PERIL

Grave danger, occasionally applied to the soul, as in such constructions as 'a peril to my soul', 'at peril to your soul' (MM 2.4.65, 67) and 'On thy soul's peril' (WT 2.3.181).

PERJUR'D

(A) Of the person who has testified falsely and broken oaths.

(B) The Princess seems to echo the 'Sermon Against Swearing and Perjury', part 2 of which ends, 'Thus you see how much God doth hate perjurie', when she tells the King, who has lied about the Russian pageant and broken his oath not to see ladies, 'Nor God, nor I, delights in perjur'd men' (LLL 5.2.346).

(C) Sandys also consigns (from Rev. 21.8) 'the perjured, the usurer, the adulterer, the liar, the idolater . . . into the lake which burneth with fire and brimstone; into that utter **darkness**, where shall be wailing, weeping, gnashing of teeth, endless horror, and everlasting wo' (1841), 367. See Shaheen (1999), 139; *Certaine Sermons* 51.

PERJURY

(A) The act of lying; also, breaking an oath.

(B) Leonato's desperate hope about Hero, accused of **adultery**, is 'that she will not add to her damnation / A sin of perjury' (ADO 4.1.172–3). Shylock refers to breaking an 'oath in heaven' when he asks Portia, 'Shall I lay perjury upon my soul?' (MV 4.1.228–9).

(C) See *Certaine Sermons*, pp. 45–51, for the sermons 'Against Swearing and Perjury'.

PERNICIOUS

Destructive, ruinous. This word is cited twice in the *OED* as used in connection with the doctrines of the Reformation, as in Fisher's 'ye pernicyous doctryne of Martin luuther' (1521) and More's 'those perylouse and perniciouse opinions' (1529).

  In H8, a play set in the early sixteenth century, and culminating in the rise to power of the great English **Reformer Cranmer** and the birth of his protegé the Protestant Queen Elizabeth, the Catholic Lord Chancellor similarly calls these 'new opinions, / Divers and dangerous', '**heresies**', which if 'not **reform'd**, may prove pernicious' (H8 5.2.52–4). Otherwise, as in Othello's curse of Iago ('May his pernicious soul / Rot half a grain a day') or Isabella's 'somewhat madly spoken' description of Angelo as 'this pernicious caitiff deputy' (OTH 5.2.155;

MM 5.1.88–9), Shakespeare's usage is about wicked and destructive persons rather than religious movements.

PETER, SAINT

(A) The holder of the keys to the kingdom of heaven and the rock upon which Christ built his Church. Simon Peter, brother of Andrew, was the leader of the **Apostles**; he died *c.* 64.

(B) Beatrice tells a joking Don Leonato that after she delivers her old maid's 'apes into hell', she will 'away to Saint Peter. For the heavens, he shows me where the bachelors sit, and there live we as merry as the day is long' (ADO 2.1.41, 47–9). When Othello calls Emilia someone who has 'the office opposite to Saint Peter, / And keeps the gates of hell!', he accuses her of being an insufficient gatekeeper for Desdemona's purity. His allusion to St Peter's role (and emblem) continues with 'I pray you turn the key and keep our counsel' (OTH 4.2.91–4). 'Saint Peter's' is thrice mentioned as the name of the Church where Juliet is to wed Paris (ROM 3.5.114, 116, 154).

(C) Farmer (1978), 320–2; Voraigne (1941), 1: 331; Baring-Gould (1914), 6: 419–32.

PETITION *sb.*

(A) The prayer asking for something; *v.* the asking. As Bullinger says 'By petition we lay open unto God the requests and desires of our heart' (4: 163).

(B) The Gentleman is honest if cynical when he says, 'There's not a soldier of us all, that in the thanksgiving before meat, do relish the petition well that prays for peace' (MM 1.2.14–16). The victorious Coriolanus says to his mother, 'You have, I know, petition'd all the gods / For my prosperity' (COR 2.1.170).

(C) The NV MM (1980), 22, suggests several sources for the Gentleman's prayer, including *Preces Privatae* (1573), *sig.* Gg6: 'The Acts of Thanksgiving in Eating shall always be concluded by these short prayers', ending, '*pacem nobis donet perpetuam. Amen*'.

PEW-FELLOW

(A) Someone who shares a pew, which is either a bench or a family enclosure in a church.

(B) Margaret exults metaphorically that Richard, by killing his own brother, has made his mother 'pew-fellow with others' moan' (R3 4.4.58).

(C) For a similar metaphoric usage among the theologians, see Andrewes, 2: 91; 5: 33–4; Fulke quotes Martin as calling all 'Protestants, Calvinists, Bezites, and Puritans . . . brethren and pew-fellows' in their 'more or less corrupting the holy Scriptures' (1843), 1: 65.

PHARAOH

(A) An Egyptian king; *esp.* the rulers during the Egyptian bondage of Israel who were associated first with Joseph and later with Moses and the exodus of the people of Israel from Egypt (see *OED* 1).

(B) When Falstaff defends his own lovable fatness by saying in ironic disbelief that 'Pharaoh's lean kine are to be lov'd' (1H4 2.4.473), he speaks of the Pharaoh who consulted **Joseph** about his dreams of seven fat and seven lean **kine**. Borachio's reference to 'Pharaoh's soldiers in the reechy **painting**' (ADO 3.3.133–4) focuses on the moment near the end of the Egyptian bondage of Israel when the charioteers of Rameses II are drowned by the returning waters of the Red Sea after the Israelites have crossed over to the other side.

(C) See Gen. 41.3–21; Ex. 14.28. See *Mirrour* (1986), 204, for a vivid medieval woodcut of Pharoah's soldiers overwhelmed by the Red Sea.

PHILIP, SAINT

(A) Known as the evangelist, St Philip was popularly misunderstood to have been the father of the four daughters, 'virgins, which did prophesy' in Acts. This father was actually Philip the Deacon.

(B) The Dauphin Charles of France, newly infatuated with Joan of Arc's prophetic and military prowess, says of her confidence about raising the siege of Orleans, that none of the many famous prophets of the past, including 'Saint Philip's daughters, were like thee' (1H6 1.2.143).

(C) Baring-Gould (1914), 5: 1–5; Attwater (1965), 282; Farmer (1978), 328.

PHILIP AND JACOB

When Mistress Overdone testifies that Lucio's 'child is a year and a quarter old come Philip and Jacob' (MM 3.2.201–2), she refers to the feast of the Apostles Philip and **Jacob**, 1 May.

PHILOSOPHY

(A) That branch of knowledge often traditionally opposed to religion. Donne proudly follows 'the **Apostle**' in opposing the truth of religion and the truth of philosophy: 'Christ *Crucified*, that is, the Gospell of Christ, is said by the Apostle, to be ... *Græcis stultitia*, to the Grecians, to the Gentiles, *meer foolishnesse* .... [T]he wise men, the *learned*, the *Philosophers* of the world: they thoght that Christ induced a religion improbable to Reason, a silly and foolish religion' (9: 113–14, citing 1 Cor. 1.18–27).

(B) Though his words may also refer to Horatio's particular philosophy, Hamlet's 'There are more things in heaven and earth, Horatio, / Than are dreamt of in your philosophy' (HAM 1.5.166–7) similarly distinguishes 'philosophy' from a branch of learning like theology that might more comfortably embrace **mystery**. Hamlet refers to this distinction again an act later when he finds 'something in this more than natural, if philosophy could find it out' (HAM 2.2.367–8).

(C) Whitaker finds a similar 'difference between theology and philosophy', 'because the things of **faith** are not subject to the teaching of mere human **reason**' (1849), 364.

PIBLE

A Frenchman's pronunciation of Bible.

Caius, a doctor, says condescendingly of the Welch Parson Evans's failure to appear for the duel, 'he has pray his Pible well, dat he is no come. By gar, Jack Rugby, he is dead already, if he be come' (WIV 2.3.6–9).

PIETY

(A) Reverence for God or strict religious observance.

(B) A contrite Leontes contrasts his 'profaneness' in denying the **truth** of the **oracle** to Camillo's 'piety' in accepting it (WT 3.2.154, 171). Tamora calls it a 'cruel **irreligious** piety' that her son is chosen 'religiously' by Titus's Romans as 'a **sacrifice**' (TIT 1.1.130, 124). Henry V, perplexed that Cambridge has betrayed him, reflects that devils who would tempt traitors usually plate their sin with **religion**, 'glist'ring semblances of piety' (H5 2.2.117).

(C) See *ST* II.2.101.

PILATE

(A) Pontius Pilate was the governor who presided over the trial of Christ, found no cause to execute him, but capitulated anyway to 'the chief **priests** and **elders** of the people' by releasing him in exchange for **Barabbas**. Pilate is most famous for washing his hands of the matter to absolve himself of guilt (Matt. 27.1–24).

(B) The Second Murderer of Clarence repents of the crime but does nothing to stop it, lamenting instead 'How fain (like Pilate) would I wash my hands / Of this most grievous murther' (R3 1.4.272–3). In Shakespeare's other direct reference, Richard II complains of the citizens who have witnessed his deposition, 'Though some of you, with Pilate, wash your hands, / Showing an outward pity, yet you Pilates / Have here deliver'd me to my sour cross, / And water cannot wash away your sin' (R2 4.1.239–42).

(C) On this exculpatory hand-washing, see Andrewes, 2: 126; Donne, 9: 65.

PILGRIM

Person who undertakes a religious journey.

'Pilgrim' and '**palmer**' are interchangeable in the first exchange between Romeo and Juliet, in which his request for a kiss and her denial are couched in terms of a pilgrimage. He says that though touching her 'with my unworthiest hand' might '**profane**' 'This holy **shrine**' which is her body, 'My lips, two blushing pilgrims, ready stand / To smooth that rough touch with a tender kiss.' She first demurs: 'Good pilgrim, you do wrong your hand too much, / Which mannerly **devotion** shows in this: / For **saints** have hands that pilgrims' hands do touch, / And palm to palm is holy palmer's **kiss**.' Then she grants his **prayer** (ROM 1.5.93–105). The oft-mentioned pilgrim in AWW is Helena, disguised and bound for Saint **Jaques**' (Santiago's) famous shrine at Compostella (AWW 3.4.4; 3.5.30, 32; 4.3.48). Poins mentions as 'quarry' 'pilgrims going to **Canterbury** with rich offerings' (1H4 1.2.126).

PILGRIMAGE
(A) The pilgrim's journey.
(B) Usually this is used metaphorically, especially for life as a journey (as in MM 2.1.36; AYL 3.2.130; R2 2.1.154; LR 5.3.197), or for a romantic quest (SON 27.6). There are literal references too, two general (in LUC 791; and R2 1.3.49) and one specific (AWW 4.3.48: to 'Saint **Jaques** le Grand').
(C) Maxwell (1969) discusses Helena's pilgrimage in AWW. Black (1983) argues that King Henry is on pilgrimage throughout R2 and H4, only realizing it on his deathbed.

PIOUS[1]
Full of piety, devout in matters of religious belief or practice.
   In two relatively simple references, Hamlet speaks of a 'pious chanson' or song (HAM 2.2.419) that he almost sang for Polonius, and the Duke in MM calls the good **Friar** in whom he will confide 'pious sir' (MM 1.3.16). Much is said in MAC of 'the most pious Edward' the Confessor, king of England; indeed, they 'speak him full of grace' (MAC 3.6.27; 4.3.159).

PIOUS[2]
Sometimes used pejoratively, meaning excessively zealous.
   When Lennox describes Macbeth 'in pious rage' tearing 'the two delinquents' who were supposed to be guarding Duncan (MAC 3.6.12), he uses this meaning metaphorically as well as ironically.

PLESS
Welch pronunciation of 'bless', as in Fluellen's 'God pless you, Aunchient Pistol! you scurvy, lousy knave, God pless you' (H5 5.1.117–18).

PLUTO
(A) Keeper of the underworld in classical mythology.
(B) Sometimes this place is intertwined with the Christian myth of hell and damnation, as when Pistol says with typical hyperbole, 'I'll see her damn'd first, to Pluto's damned lake' (2H4 2.4.156).
(C) On the interweaving of classical and Christian hells, see Battenhouse (1951), 190.

PONTIFICAL
Of the Pope or Pontiff.
   Henry IV advises his son Hal to show himself less often to the people, so that his 'presence, like a robe pontifical', might be more valued, 'Ne'er seen but wonder'd at' (1H4 3.2.56–7).

POPE
(A) Head of the Roman Catholic Church, whose represented tensions with England extend in Shakespeare's plays from King John's reign in the early thirteenth

249

century through the first half of the sixteenth and the reign of Henry VIII, a contemporary (and sometime opponent) of Luther and the Protestant Reformation. Since Shakespeare wrote in a Protestant England still churning with Catholic–Protestant tensions, indeed, like most of his generation, had Catholic parents, it is not surprising that Reformation issues inform many references to the Pope.

(B) Pope Innocent, represented in JN by Cardinal Pandulph, his 'holy legate', is referred to as 'the Pope' or as 'Pope Innocent' ten times in the play. Pandulph in fact reiterates the holy name 'Pope Innocent' as a charm, and tries to use other charged words like 'religiously' and 'holy errand' to intimidate those who 'So wilfully dost spurn' 'against the Church, our holy mother'. King John immediately disarms him by calling all these words 'earthy name[s]' and then saying of the 'Pope', 'no Italian priest / Shall tithe or toll in our dominions' (JN 3.1.135–54). In a play set two centuries later, Gloucester says to the Pope's man Winchester, 'Under my feet I stamp thy Cardinal's hat; / In spite of Pope or dignities of church'. He also calls him 'Winchester goose', the name of a venereal disorder (see BEV 505n, and *OED* goose *sb.* 3), and asks for 'a rope' to 'beat them hence', calling him with commonplace epithets of anti-Catholic derision, 'wolf in sheep's array' and 'scarlet hypocrite' (1H6 1.3.49–56). In H8, a play set in the midst of the Reformation, Suffolk says of the threats of the Pope's man Cardinal Wolsey, 'I love him not, nor fear him; there's my creed'; 'his curses and his blessings / Touch me alike; th'are breath I not believe in. / I knew him, and I know him; so I leave him / To him that made him proud, the Pope' (H8 2.2.49–54).

(C) Bradford's 'filthy puddle of popery' (1: 390) is among the more colourful phrases of papal derision; Tyndale's 'as good is the prayer of a cobbler as of a cardinal, and of a butcher as of a bishop; and the blessing of a baker that knoweth the truth is as good as the blessing of our most holy father the Pope' (1: 258) is a fairly characteristic assertion of Reformation democratization. See Saccio (1977), 195.

POPISH *adj.*

(A) Pejorative for Catholic.

(B) Aaron the Moor calls Lucius 'religious', makes fun of the 'thing called conscience' within him, and says 'I have seen thee careful to observe' 'twenty popish tricks and ceremonies' (TIT 5.1.74–7). Though this statement is complicated by Aaron's Machiavellian atheism, it does parallel the Protestant distrust of Catholic rites.

(C) For similar usage, see Grindal (1843), 140; Hooper (1852), 2: 127; Fulke (1843), 1: 564; Becon, 3: 259.

PORK

All three of Shakespeare's references to pork occur in MV, and each pertains to Jewish dietary law.

When Shylock is invited by Bassanio to dinner, he responds 'Yes, to smell pork, to eat of the habitation which your prophet the Nazarite conjur'd the devil into . . . . I will not eat with you, drink with you, nor pray with you' (MV 1.3.30–7). Jesus did command a legion of spirits from a possessed man into a herd of swine in Matt. 8.28–32, but this is not the reason for the Jewish prohibition of pork. The Christians in the play are equally good at using this dietary difference condescendingly. When Shylock's daughter Jessica tells her servant Lancelot Gobbo that her husband Lorenzo 'hath made me a Christian', Lancelot teases her, 'This making of Christians will raise the price of hogs. If we grow all to be pork-eaters, we shall not shortly have a rasher on the coals for money.' In a good-natured if also ethnically challenged response, Jessica then teases her husband Lorenzo that 'in converting Jews to Christians, you raise the price of pork' (MV 3.5.19–36).

POSSESS'D

(A) Occupied or dominated by demons.

(B) Maria's 'He is sure possess'd' about Malvolio's acting like a lover might seem merely to mean mad or obsessed, but Toby's follow-up comment makes it clear that they are talking about demonic possession: 'If all the devils of hell be drawn in little, and Legion himself possess'd him, yet I'll speak to him' (TN 3.4.9, 85–6). Toby alludes here to the 'unclean spirit' Christ cast from the possessed man, who said, 'My name is **Legion**, for we are many' (Mark 5.8–9). Other clear references to **demonic** possession include the **exorcist** Pinch's 'Mistress, both man and master is possess'd: / I know it by their pale and deadly looks. / They must be bound and laid in some dark room' (ERR 4.4.92–4), and the scholar Say's hope that Jack Cade will not kill him, 'Unless you be possess'd with devilish spirits' (2H6 4.7.75). Cade disappoints him.

(C) On the religious authority to exorcise demons, see Vaux (1590a), *sig.* H8ᵛ. Milward (1977), 168–72, lists some of the participants in debates about possession and exorcism. Holden (1954), 79–83, 97–8, speaks of the 'idiom of madness and possession usually directed against the nonconformists'.

POWERS

(A) Deities; also an order of angels; in actual usage these are sometimes hard to distinguish.

(B) Ophelia says of the apparently mad Hamlet, 'O heavenly powers restore him' (HAM 3.1.141), and Othello responds to Desdemona's prayer that 'our loves and comforts should increase' 'Amen to that, sweet powers' (OTH 2.1.194–5). Pericles tries to accept Thaisa's death at sea, 'We cannot but obey / The powers above us' (PER 3.3.10), and during the scene of the oracle in WT, Hermione says 'if pow'rs divine / Behold our human actions (as they do)' (WT 3.2.28–9, 202). There are also of course 'wicked powers', though Paulina 'protest[s] against' their assistance in the 'lawful' magic of Hermione's restoration (WT 5.3.91, 111).

(C) Bullinger speaks of the 'three hierarchies or holy principalities, [each] of which . . . have three orders: the first, seraphim, cherubim, thrones; the second, lordships, virtues, powers; the third, principalities, archangels, and angels' (3: 336). Donne characteristically uses the angelic designation metaphorically when he speaks of becoming 'the subject, the slave' of such distracting, worldly 'powers and principalities' as 'cheerful conversation, . . . musique, . . . feasting, . . . Comedies, . . . wantonnesse' (10: 56).

POYSAM

(A) Corruption of the French poisson, fish. Catholics and some higher-church Anglicans too observed fasting-days by eating fish; dissenters opposed the tradition as superstitious.

(B) Speaking cynically of the universality of cuckoldry, and the need therefore for all husbands to resign themselves to having a cuckold's horns, Lavatch says to the Countess, 'for young Charbon the puritan and old Poysam the Papist, howsome'er their hearts are sever'd in religion, their heads are both one: they may jowl horns together like any deer i' th' herd' (AWW 1.3.51–5).

(C) For a glance at the controversy over eating fish on **fasting-days**, see Pilkington (1842), 558–9; Cranmer (1846), 2: 508. See also BEV, 370n, **fish**, and **flesh**.

PRAISED

Commended; credited. Petition and praise are two of the most common reasons for prayer.

Phrases like 'God be prais'd' (WIV 2.2.309) and 'prais'd be the gods' (AYL 3.3.40) are fairly common in Shakespeare, though the objects of praise in these two cases, 'my jealousy' and 'thy foulness', are more unusual. Richmond's 'God and your arms be praised, victorious friends' (R3 5.5.1), or Henry V's 'Praised be God, and not our strength, for it' at Agincourt (H5 4.7.87) are more traditional and more self-consciously religious.

PRAY

(A) Usually merely 'please', as in 'I pray thee', but of almost eight hundred uses of 'pray' in Shakespeare, about eighty, 10 per cent, include 'God', 'heaven', or the like, and can therefore properly be said to have something to do with the petition or praise of God usually associated with prayer.

(B) More than half of these say something like 'pray heaven' or 'I pray' so casually as to mean 'I hope', though of course religion always has something to do with such phrases. An example is the devout Provost's 'Pray heaven she win him' (MM 2.2.125) about Isabella's attempt to persuade Angelo not to execute her brother for fornication. Meditating on his desire for Isabella, Angelo uses 'pray' both literally and figuratively: 'When I would pray and think, I think and pray / To several subjects. Heaven hath my empty words, / Whilst my invention, hearing not my tongue, / Anchors on Isabel' (MM 2.4.1–4). Later an angry Isabel takes 'pray' quite literally when she says to the Claudio who has refused to die gladly for her chastity, 'I'll pray a thousand prayers for thy death, / No word to save thee' (MM 3.1.145–6).

Of the sixty uses of 'pray' in ERR, LLL and ADO, only four actually refer to the act of religious devotion; even the most obviously theological of these, Dromio's 'But we that know what 'tis to fast and pray, / Are penitent for your default to-day' (ERR 1.2.51–2), merely uses the devotional cliché 'fast and pray' to suggest Dromio's expectation of more beatings. In MV, Shylock associates the act of prayer with Christians dining together when he declines Bassanio's invitation to dinner with, 'I will not eat with you, drink with you, nor pray with you' (MV 1.3.36–7). Portia's 'We do pray for mercy / And that same prayer doth teach us all to render / The deeds of mercy' (MV 4.1.200–2) refers to the Lord's Prayer, in which the Lord, Christ, instructed his followers to say 'forgive us our trespasses, as we forgive them that trespass against us' (*BCP*, 51). This prayer is so familiar in Anglican England that several references to it in the *Book of Common Prayer* read 'Our Father, which art, etc.' (*BCP*, 59, 61).

A flurry of deadly serious 'prays' are directed at Richard and Richmond in R3. Margaret's 'Earth gapes, hell burns, fiends roar, saints pray, / To have him suddenly convey'd from hence. / Cancel his bond of life, dear God, I pray' or the Ghosts' 'The wronged heirs of York do pray for thee' and 'Thy adversary's wife doth pray for thee' are good examples (R3 4.4.75–7; 5.3.137, 166). To the queen's angry and impotent prayer in R2, 'Pray God the plants thou graft'st may never grow', the Gardener responds sceptically but compassionately, 'Poor queen, . . . I would my skill were subject to thy curse' (R2 3.4.101–3). In H8, the English history that most often engages theological issues, Buckingham's early valediction sounds formulaic but sincere: 'All good people, / Pray for me . . . . The last hour / Of my long weary life is come upon me . . . . And God forgive me!' (H8 2.1 131–6) Interestingly, each of these history plays raises the question of the efficacy of prayers and curses in human affairs; in a classical play like TRO or COR, which does not raise such issues, 'pray' is always merely 'please' or 'I hope', a completely secular utterance.

Though some of Hamlet's 'wild and whirling words' after he sees the Ghost are 'I'll go pray' (HAM 1.5.132), we are as perplexed as Horatio by what he means, since Hamlet is represented as a thoughtful but not a prayerful character. Much clearer is Claudius's 'Pray can I not, / Though inclination be as sharp as will.' This anticipates the eventual admission of the failure of his rather strenuous attempt at contrition, confession and repentance: 'Words without thoughts never to heaven go' (HAM 3.3.38–9, 98). Lear tells Kent and the Fool, 'I'll pray, and then I'll sleep'; then like Claudius, though more productively, he offers a substantial prayer for the 'Poor naked wretches . . . / That bide the pelting of this pitiless storm' (LR 3.4.25–9). We see Lear changing during his prayerful experience, and Claudius remaining the same.

(C) Donne says, 'Pray personally, and pray frequently; *David* had many stationary times of the day, and night too, to pray in. . . . It is not enough to have prayed once . . . . Christ does not onely excuse, but enjoine Importunity' (7: 269). He cites Luke 11.5, 18.5. See **prayer**[1].

PRAYER[1]

(A) A devout petition to God. Donne speaks of devout and superficial personal prayer, 'hearty and earnest prayer to God' (10: 56), and less optimistically, of 'that short Prayer, . . . that halfe-minute of our Devotion' (7: 264). Hooker says,

'Prayers . . . doe best testifie our dutifull affection, and are for the purchasinge of all favour at the handes of God' (V.23.1).

(B) Despite his resolution not to kill her soul, Othello kills Desdemona before she can 'say one prayer' (OTH 5.2.83). With his usual theological sophistication and pragmatism, Claudius speaks of prayer in terms of its traditional usefulness as either a deterrent to sin or a means for its forgiveness: 'And what's in prayer but this twofold force, / To be forestalled ere we come to fall, / Or pardon'd being down' (HAM 3.3.48–50). Leontes describes himself as having said 'many a prayer upon [Hermione's] grave' (WT 5.3.140–1).

(C) See *Certaine Sermons*, 2nd tome, pp. 110–32, for the homilies 'concerning Prayer'. See also *ST* II.2.83; and Hooker, 'Of publike Prayer' (V.23–4). Williams (1986) looks at prayers in LR. Nuttall, (1989), 115–24, discusses prayer in TIM, and McAlindon (2001) in TMP. Targoff (1997), 61–5, argues that HAM reflects contemporary anxieties over the efficacy of prayer.

PRAYER[2]

(A) A prescribed order of worship.

(B) Falstaff's old friend Mistress Quickly says of his new quarry Mistress Page, in a way that should be daunting to him but is not, 'she's as **fartuous** a civil modest wife, and one (I tell you) that will not miss you morning nor evening prayer' (WIV 2.2.96–9).

(C) See Hooker, 'Of the forme of common prayer' (V.25).

PRAYER[3]

A devotional exercise or lifestyle. Andrewes calls 'the vital parts of Religion, Preaching, Prayer, the Sacraments' (2: 407), and also speaks of the 'sanctity' in 'fasting and prayer' (1: 381).

Quickley's comment about the prayerful habits of the 'honest, willing, kind' servant Rugby is another example of the topsy-turvydom of Falstaff's world of misrule: 'His worst fault is, that he is given to prayer; he is something peevish that way; but nobody but has his fault' (WIV 1.4.12–15). Though she is fibbing a little, Portia tells Lorenzo 'I have toward heaven breath'd a sacred vow, / To live in prayer and contemplation', that is within a disciplined religious life, 'Until her husband's and my lord's return' (MV 3.4.27–30). Othello, misreading Desdemona's 'moist hand' as evidence of her loose morals, directs her towards a similar discipline: 'fasting and prayer, / Much castigation, exercise devout' (OTH 3.4.40–1). See **fast**.

PRAYER[4]

A devotional book.

'A book of prayer in his hand' is Buckingham's evidence that Richard is 'a holy man' (R3 3.7.98–9).

PRAYER[5] *fig.*

The word can also be used in romantic metaphor, as when Helena laments of

Demetrius's inattention, 'The more my prayer, the lesser is my grace' (MND 2.2.89).

PRAYERS

(A) The plural of prayer in Shakespeare tends to refer to habitual devotions rather than individual expressions of praise or petition.

(B) Though Titus is being sarcastic, his reference to 'begging hermits in their holy prayers' (TIT 3.2.41) is one good example of this common usage. 'Thy prayers', 'my prayers', and the like also suggest that these prayers are regular occurrences which allow for particular petitions. As examples, Ferdinand wants to learn Miranda's name so that he 'might set it in my prayers' (TMP 3.1.35); Margaret tells Balthasar in ADO that one of her faults is 'I say my prayers aloud' (ADO 2.1.104); the Countess refers to Helena's 'prayers, whom heaven delights to hear' (AWW 3.4.27); and the Widow in 3H6 naively thinks that King Edward wants 'My love till death, my humble thanks, my prayers' instead of her body (3H6 3.2.62, 69). Macbeth notices that Duncan's grooms woke up while he was in the chamber, 'and one cried "Murther"', 'But they did say their prayers and address'd them / Again to sleep' (MAC 2.2.20–3). These references describe men and women who habitually said their prayers, often before bedtime.

The Mariners' cry on the sinking ship, 'All lost! To prayers, to prayers! All lost!' (TMP 1.1.51), is a different matter, a call to prayer when all else has failed. 'Prayers' are also said just before death. Hal tells Falstaff before battle that he must 'Say thy prayers, and farewell', and when Falstaff pretends to misunderstand, 'I would 'twere bed-time, Hal, and all well', Hal persists, 'Why, thou owest God a death' (1H4 5.1.124–6). The overconfident Constable of France says of the English before Agincourt, 'They have said their prayers, and they stay for death' (H5 4.2.56). Richmond's 'God and our good cause fight upon our side; / The prayers of holy saints and wronged souls' (R3 5.3.240–1) reveals the (contested) belief that the dead could continue to pray for the living.

(C) Donne urges 'a thankfull acknowledgement of the ministery and protection of Angels, and of the prayers of the Saints in heaven for us' (5: 360), and says of prayers as personal devotional acts, 'Blesse him therefore in speaking to him, in your prayers' (3: 260).

PRAYING[1] v.

Uttering petitions to God, or meditating thoughtfully.

Portia and Nerissa say, 'We have been praying for our husbands' welfare' (MV 5.1.114), and Buckingham pretends that Richard is engaged in a spiritual discipline, 'praying, to enrich his watchful soul' (R3 3.7.77).

PRAYING[2]

A pious vocation or lifestyle.

Hal teases Falstaff that he has good 'amendment of life in thee, from praying to purse-taking' (1H4 1.2.102–3); Elizabeth asserts in the same play that if

Richard is their only choice she would prefer her daughters to enjoy the vocation of 'praying nuns' to that of 'weeping queens' (R3 4.4.202).

PREACH

(A) Offer a sermon, sometimes metaphorically.

(B) Henry VI criticises Cardinal Beauford when he refuses Gloucester's hand of reconciliation, 'Fie, uncle Beauford, I have heard you preach / That malice was a great and grievous sin; / And will you not maintain the thing you teach, / But prove a chief offender in the same?' (1H6 3.1.127–30). Lear pretends to be a minister to the blinded Gloucester, first saying 'I will preach to thee', then catching the high style: 'When we are born, we cry that we are come / To this great stage of fools' (LR 4.6.180–3). The virtuous Marina, kidnapped by pirates, is then sold to a brothel; it amazes (and emasculates) everyone 'to have divinity preach'd there'; indeed one lord says, 'I am for no more bawdy-houses', the other promises, 'I am out of the road of rutting for ever', and a bawd complains, 'she's able to freeze the god Priapus, and undo a whole generation' (PER 4.5.3–9; 4.6.3–4).

(C) Donne says that 'the first course' of the 'great Feast' of the Church 'is Manna, food of Angels, plentifull, frequent preaching' (6: 223); Andrewes calls 'the vital parts of Religion, Preaching, Prayer, the Sacraments' (2: 407).

PRECISE

(A) One who adheres tenaciously to rules or forms. The word was applied to English Puritans during the sixteenth and seventeenth centuries because of their behavioural, doctrinal and procedural scrupulousness.

(B) 'Lord Angelo is precise' thus probably connects Angelo's moral and legal absolutism with that of the Puritan movement. Hamlet's 'thinking too precisely on the event' (HAM 4.4.41) resonates similarly. See also **saint** and **angel** (MM 1.3.50; 2.2.180; 2.4.16).

(C) Holden (1954), 41, reminds us that 'precise' was associated with the Puritan 'willingness to debate infinitely any smallest detail of doctrine or rite'. Hamilton (1992), 11–12, calls 'precise' 'a word that was used to stigmatise a theological or ecclesiological position and one often applied to Puritans'. See also Milward (1973), 156; Holden (1954), 117; and Hamilton (1992), 11–12.

PREDESTINATE

(A) Predestined or pre-ordained by God. The Cambridge Puritan Perkins is defending this central and severe doctrine of Calvinism when he says that 'Predestination hath two parts; **Election** and Reprobation . . . . Election, is God's decree, whereby of his owne free will, he hath ordained certaine men to **salvation**, to the praise of the glorie of his **grace**.' 'The decree of Reprobation, is that part of predestination, whereby God, according to the most free and just purpose of his **will**, hath determined to reject certaine men unto **eternall** destruction, and miserie' (1597a), 34, 193.

(B) Shakespeare's only usage comes in a playful insult. Benedick says of Beatrice's comment that she never wants to hear 'a man say he loves me', 'God keep your ladyship still in that mind! so some gentleman or other shall scape a predestinate scratch'd face' (ADO 1.1.133–5). 'God' is in his sentence, and so are the theological connotations of 'predestination', but Benedick's 'predestinate' literally means only 'predictable' here.

(C) On the question of predestination, see *ST* I.23. The Recusant Hopkins illustrates Benedick's usage in a more traditionally religious realm when he translates F. Lewis de Granada's complaint that the Reformers act as though 'Almightie God had reveiled unto everie *Calvinist*, and *Puritan*, by such a speciall divine revelation that every one of them is of the number of the Elect, & **predestinate** unto salvation' (1586), 11. On the struggle between Lutheranism and Calvinism in England, see Hall (1979), 104–6; and Baker (1985), 115. McGrath (2001), 135–40, discusses Calvin's positions on predestination. See also Milward (1977), 157–63, on debates about predestination and free will. Matheson (1995), 394–7, argues that Hamlet finally comes to believe in predestination and to trust in the moral authority of conscience.

PRELATE

(A) A high-ranking churchman.

(B) In 1H4 the 'noble prelate', at least to the other rebels, is Lord Richard Scroop, the Archbishop of York (1H4 1.3. 266–7; 5.5.37). Humphrey Duke of Gloucester, Protector of the young Henry VI, calls Henry Beauford, Bishop of Winchester and afterwards Cardinal, 'arrogant Winchester, that haughty prelate' (1H6 1.3.18–32).

(C) For pejorative usage among the Reformers, see Bale (1849), 498; Calfhill (1846), 82, and Donne, who warns, 'to submit the kingdome to the government of a *forein Prelate*, was to destroy the Monarchy, to annihilate the Supremacy, to ruine the very forme of a kingdome' (4: 244).

PREPAR'D (PREPARE)

Made (make) spiritually ready for death.

The word is used three times in relation to Claudio's impending execution for fornication. Angelo orders, 'Bring him his confessor, let him be prepar'd; / For that's the utmost of his pilgrimage' (MM 2.1.34–6); Isabella pleads in his defence, 'He's not prepar'd for death'; finally Claudio calls himself 'prepar'd to die' after the Duke's spiritual advice (MM 2.2.84; 3.1.4), though in fact he is not (cf. 3.2.239; 4.2.69; 4.3.54). Antonio similarly calls himself 'armed, and wellprepar'd' for Shylock's knife (MV 4.1.264). The Murderer even gives Clarence a chance to 'prepare to die' (R3 1.4.180).

PRIDE

(A) The chief of the seven deadly sins. Donne calls it 'the principall spiritual sin', and Augustine says, 'you will find no sin that is not labelled pride'. Andrewes succinctly says of pride and its cure: 'Man was to be recovered by the contrary of that by which he perished. By pride he perished, that is confessed. Then, by humility to be recovered, according to the rule, *Contraria curantur contrariis.*'

(B) Though pride is often a fault of character in Shakespeare's works, only a few of his references feel obviously theological. The Chorus assures us that Henry V resists his advisors' tempting advice to bear 'His bruised helmet and his bended sword / Before him through the city' because, 'free from vainness and self-glorious pride', he wished to give 'full trophy, signal, and ostent, / Quite from himself to God' (H5 5 Cho. 17–22). In H8 Abergavenney says of Cardinal Wolsey: 'I cannot tell / What heaven hath given him – let some graver eye / Pierce into that – but I can see his pride / Peep through each part of him. Whence has he that? / If not from hell, the devil is a niggard' (H8 1.1 66–70). This may be jealousy, but it is theologically informed jealousy. The humbling of pride, accompanied by the often grudging acceptance of personal folly, is one of Shakespeare's most characteristic comic actions. Beatrice explicitly stands 'condemn'd for pride' and then, changed by the loving foolery of her friends, bids 'maiden pride, adieu' (ADO 3.1.108–9). Viola charges Olivia, 'I see you what you are, you are too proud' even as she plays Olivia's edifying fool by becoming the impossible object of her love (TN 1.5.250). The puritannical Angelo expresses embarrassment that 'I take pride' in 'my gravity' (MM 2.4. 9–10), and in the end he too is shriven of this pride, humiliated, humbled, and also forgiven, by those very people his pride has harmed.

(C) Donne, 9: 377; Augustine, *Of Nature and Grace*, xxix. cited in *ST* II.2.162.2; Andrewes, 1: 206. See also Vaux (1590b), *sigs*. e8ᵛ-f2ᵛ. In 'Against Pride, or Vain Glory', Becon (1: 448–9) cites at least twenty scriptural passages useful in defence against pride. Loarte (trans. Brinkley, 1596–97), 214, calls pride the temptation 'whereunto [the Divill] principally induceth us'. See **proud**, **humility**, **fool**.

PRIEST

(A) The name for the minister in both Catholic and Church of England traditions. More extreme Reformers, wanting to do away with all things Catholic, preferred 'minister' or 'preacher'. In some services and parishes then (as now) the priest would read the service and his assistant or **clerk** would lead the responsive 'Amens'.

(B) Richard II refers to this tradition when he asks of the silence which follows his ironic 'God save the king', 'Will no man say **amen**? Am I both priest and clerk?' (R2 4.1.172–3). Of the performance of marriages, the Host tells Fenton, 'Bring you the maid, you shall not lack a priest' (WIV 4.6.53). An oft-abused 'priest' tries to 'perform the **ceremonial rites** of marriage' between Kate and Petruchio (SHR 3.2.5–6, 154–79; 4.6. 86–104). Rosalind tells her friend Celia of her lover Orlando, 'You shall be the priest, and marry us', then 'goes before the priest' and speaks some of the service words herself (AYL 4.1.112–26). Shakespeare's characters also associate priests with having **Latin** (AYL 3.2.319); with religious instruction ('a good priest can tell you what marriage is' – AYL 3.3.85–6); with **prayer** ('priests pray for enemies, but princes kill' – 2H6 5.2.71); with singing penitential **psalms** (H5 4.1.301–2); and with presiding over funerals (HAM 5.1.240; WT 4.4.458). Of garments, we hear of a '**surplice** white' (PHT 13), a 'long coat' (H8 3.2.276), and a '**gown**' (TN 4.2.6). 'Priest and **holy water**' are associated in TIT (1.1.323). Pagan priests are associated with saying prayers (COR 1.10.21); **shriving** (WT 1.2.236–37); **fasting** (COR 5.1.56); **sacrifice** (JC 2.2.5); martyrdom ('priests in holy **vestments** bleeding' – TIM 4.3.126); and **blessings** (ANT 2.2.239); there are also 'maiden priests' (PER 5.1.242).

'Jack priest' and 'jack-a-nape priest' is a frequent insult uttered by the French physician Caius in WIV (as in 1.4.109, 117); it means basically worthless, an ape or a fop. He refers to the Welch priest Hugh Evans.

(C) Bullinger quotes Boniface, on 'Whether it were lawful to minister the sacrament in vessels of wood' as saying 'In old times . . . golden priests used wooden cups; but now contrariwise, wooden priests use golden cups' (4: 420). See **temple**.

PRIORESS

A woman holding superior office in a priory, a religious house or order.

A 'prioress' is Isabella's superior in the Order of St Clare (MM 1.4.10–11).

PRIORY

The establishment run by a prior or prioress. Abbeys and priories (technically offshoots of **abbeys**) were often prosperous little farming and processing communities scattered throughout rural England until the dissolution of the monastic houses by King Henry VIII in the 1530s.

An **Abbess** heads the priory in ERR (5.1.37), and carries herself with great authority. King John anticipates Henry VIII's looting and dissolution of these establishments when he says three hundred years earlier, 'Our abbeys and our priories shall pay / This expedition's charge' (JN 1.1.48–9).

PRISON-HOUSE

(A) *Fig.* for **purgatory**.

(B) The Ghost probably refers to purgatory when he speaks of 'my prison-house' in which 'the foul crimes done in my days of nature / Are burnt and purg'd away' (HAM 1.5.12–14).

(C) Shaheen (1999), 544, calls this passage a 'clear reference to the Roman Catholic doctrine of purgatory that rests largely on church tradition rather than on Scripture'. Hell is the prison in Rev. 20.7: 'Satan shall be loosed out of his prison'. Greenblatt (2001), 66–70, also discusses the common image of purgatory as a prison.

PRIVILEGE

(A) Right; protection.

One of the many kinds of 'privilege' in the Renaissance is 'the holy privilege / Of blessed **sanctuary**' (R3 3.1.40–2), the granting of protection in a church against arrest by civil authority. Because the Inns of Court were 'ancient religious houses and . . . courts of law' (PEL), one could claim their 'place's privilege' as well (1H6 2.4.86). The *v.* usage occurs when the Abbess tells Adriana of her husband, 'he took this place for sanctuary, / And it shall privilege him from your hands' (ERR 5.1.94–5).

PROBATION

A period of testing before full acceptance into a religious order.

Isabella speaks of being in 'probation of a sisterhood' when she was asked to intervene on Claudio's behalf (MM 5.1.72).

PROCESSION

(A) Liturgical marching.

(B) Charles of France says of Joan of Arc, 'And all the priests and friars in my realm / Shall in procession sing her endless praise' (1H6 1.6.19–20).

(C) Fulke complains about 'Popish' processions (1843), 1: 564; Vaux crisply defends them: 'Procession was ordeined, partly to protest and to shew everywhere by our deedes the Christian faith (as by carrying openly before us the baners and tokens of Christs death' (1590a), *sig.* K8ʳ. For other complaints, see Fulke (1848), 2: 182; and Cranmer (1846), 2: 502.

PRODIGAL

(A) Wastefully extravagant. The most famous prodigal is the biblical son who was forgiven by his father (Luke 15.11–32).

(B) 'The story of the Prodigal' is said to be 'painted about' Falstaff's chamber (WIV 4.5.7–8); Falstaff too mentions a 'story of the Prodigal' 'for thy walls' (2H4 2.1.144–5). Dromio mentions 'the calve's-skin that was kill'd for the Prodigal' (ERR 4.3.19); and a '**motion** of the Prodigal' refers to a puppet show of the story (WT 4.3.96–7). The clown Launce seems to think size matters when he says of himself, 'I have receiv'd my proportion, like the prodigious son' (TGV 2.3.3–4). Cf. LLL 5.2.64 and R2 3.4.31.

(C) See *Mirror* (2002), fig. 55, for a medieval woodcut of the welcomed prodigal. Snyder (1966) notes parallels between LR and the story of the Prodigal Son; Pastoor (2000) and McLean (1996) do the same for MV.

PROFANE

As a *v.* or an *adj.*, something that undermines or contrasts with the sacred; irreverent, unholy, sacrilegious.

The Priest says of his refusal to bury the suspected suicide Ophelia with full religious **rites**, 'We should profane the service of the dead / To sing a **requiem** and such **rest** to her / As to peace-parted **souls**' (HAM 5.1.236–8). Brabantio calls Iago a 'profane wretch', in part for insulting him and his daughter with coarse references, but also because of his irreligious language, words like ' '**Zounds**' and phrases like 'will not serve God if the devil bid you' (OTH 1.1.114, 108–9). Using a romantic metaphor, Romeo says of touching Juliet, 'If I profane with my unworthiest hand / This holy **shrine**' (ROM 1.5.93–4). Viola similarly calls her story 'to your ears, **divinity**; to any other's **profanation**' (TN 1.5. 216–17). See **blasphemy**.

PROFESS

Claim or express (a faith).

Vincentio mentions 'the saint whom I profess', which PEL glosses as 'the patron saint of my order' (MM 4.2.179).

PROFESSORS

Those who claim or speak out about a faith. The Recusant Hopkins translates Granada's wondering 'howe the devill coulde prevaile so farfoorthe, as to induce a whole newe late **secte** of **heretikes** that be called **Puritans** (professinge in gaie wordes to be more pure, more sincere, and better **professours** of Christes **gospell** than anie other **Christians** either be or have bene in anie age since the **Apostles** time . . .)', (1582), *sig.* aiiii.

Henry VI calls it 'most impious and unnatural' that 'bloody strife / Should reign among professors of one faith' (1H6 5.1.12–14), England and France. With a blend of romantic metaphor and religious hyperbole, the Servant describes Perdita as a 'creature [who], / Would she begin a sect, might quench the zeal / Of all professors else' (WT 5.1.106–8). See also **office**.

PROMIS'D END

See **doomsday**.

PROPHECY

(A) Though sometimes it can merely mean a threat or a prediction, 'prophecy' can also be used theologically.

(B) Malcolm, praising his sanctity, says that Edward the Confessor 'hath a heavenly gift of prophecy' (MAC 4.3.157). R3 dramatises the question of prophecy's supernatural agency by representing a full range of attitudes. Richard refuses to believe in them; the often-cursing Margaret desperately believes. Clarence, Hastings, Rivers, Grey and even Buckingham are all first sceptical of dreams, curses and prophecies, but later bludgeoned into reluctant belief. See R3 1.1.33, 54; 1.4.1–74; 3.2.10–11, 26–7; 3.3. 15–23; 3.4. 82–3; 4.4.79–80; 5.1.12–27.

(C) Garber (1986) examines prophecy in the history plays, and Jacobs (1986) argues that R3 is fundamentally a prophetic play. Farrell (1987) examines how the characters of Richard III and Prince Hal are shaped by prophecy. Hassel (1987), 92–107, Hunter (1976), 70–9, and Frey (1976), 120, discuss prophecy in R3. See also *ST* II.2.171–2.

PROPHESY

To utter prophecy.

Even the sceptical Richard III remembers at the height of his own power that 'Henry the Sixth / Did prophesy that Richmond should be king' though he only says about it, 'Perhaps, perhaps' (R3 4.2.95–6).

PROPHET[1]

One who prophesies or is claimed to do so.

Joan of Arc is often called a 'prophet' by the still-sceptical but also hopeful French in the first half of 1H6, and once described as having 'the deep gift of prophecy' (1H6 1.2. 55, 150); subsequently she is burned as a witch. The puritanical Angelo apparently believes in the 'prophet' who 'looks in a glass that shows ... future evils' (MM 2.2.94–5). The Welchman's 'lean-look'd prophets [who] whisper fearful change' (R2 2.4.11) expresses admiration for contemporary prophets.

PROPHET[2]

(A) A prominent religious teacher or writer, often from the Old Testament. Andrewes distinguishes among 'the **law**, the prophets, and the **gospel**' (1: 367).
(B) Queen Margaret sarcastically complains about her young husband's piety, 'His champions are the prophets and apostles' (2H6 1.3.57), meaning writers of selected books of the Old and New Testaments. Shylock would likely have been thought insulting when he marginalises Christ by calling him 'your prophet the Nazarite' (MV 1.3.34). Gaunt, who calls himself 'a prophet new inspir'd' (R2 2.1.31), utters dire warnings that sound like the Old Testament prophets.
(C) For similar usage, see Andrewes, 2: 134; 1: 378–9; Donne, 7: 365; 1: 285.

PROUD

Guilty of the greatest of the spiritual **sins**, **pride**, **self-love** and self-worship.

Suffolk says of the threats of the Pope's man Cardinal Wolsey, 'I love him not, nor fear him; there's my creed'; 'his curses and his blessings / Touch me alike; th'are breath I not believe in. / I knew him, and I know him; so I leave him / To him that made him proud, the Pope' (H8 2.2.49–54). Viola charges Olivia, 'I see you what you are, you are too proud' (TN 1.5.250). A young King Henry V, proclaiming his '**Reformation**' (1H4 1.2.213) to the Archbishop of Canterbury, calls his past excesses or **affections** 'the tide of blood in me [that] / Hath proudly flowed in **vanity** till now' (2H4 5.2.129–30). When Hotspur describes himself as 'whipt and **scourg'd** with rods' (1H4 1.3.239) at the very mention of Boling-broke's name, he unknowingly describes a spiritual scourging that he himself needs and will eventually receive as 'Ill-weav'd ambition', the proud holder of 'proud titles' (1H4 5.4.88, 79).

PROVIDENCE[1]

(A) God's or the gods' control over worldly affairs. Donne speaks of God's 'providence upon his people throughout the Old Testament' (7: 323), and prays as well about contemporary events, 'Preserve our soules *O Lord*, ... and enlarge thy providence towards us' (8: 62).
(B) Prospero tells Miranda that though old Gonzalo helped save them, they 'came ashore' 'By providence divine' (TMP 1.2.159). Brutus professes himself to be a Stoic who rather than commit suicide will arm himself 'with patience / To stay the providence of some high powers / That govern us below' (JC 5.1.105–7).

He is not as good as his word. Hamlet's assertion of 'special providence in the fall of a sparrow' probably refers to the biblical assurance (Matt. 10.29) that even though they cost only two for a farthing, 'one of them shall not fall on the ground without your Father' (HAM 5.2. 219–20). Hamlet also says, 'There's a **divinity** that shapes our ends / Rough-hew them how we will' (HAM 5.2.10–11).

(C) Of the fall of sparrows and men, Donne says, 'God exercises another manner of Providence upon man, then upon other creatures. *A sparrow falls not without God*, says Christ (Mat.10.29): yet no doubt God works otherwise in the fall of eminent persons, then in the fall of Sparrows. *For yee are of more value then many sparrows*, says Christ there of every man' (9: 74). See also *ST* I.22. Of Hamlet's assertion of 'special providence', see Frye (1984), 254–7; Mack (1952); Levin (1959); Hunter (1976), 117–26; and Sinfield (1980), 91–7. Hunt (1993) argues that in TN and TMP Shakespeare endorses a liberal rather than a literal view of providence. Stritmatter (2000a) suggests that Shakespeare's references to providence in HAM, R2 and AWW come from the textual notes to 1 Samuel in the *Geneva Bible*.

PROVIDENCE[2]
God Himself, who exercises such control.

Ferdinand says of Miranda, 'Sir, she is mortal; / But by immortal Providence she's mine' (TMP 5.1.188–9).

PROVIDENTLY
With providential control and care.

Old Adam's pious 'He that doth the ravens feed, / Yea, providently caters for the sparrow, / Be comfort to my age' (AYL 2.3.43–5) alludes to Matt. 10.29. See **providence**.

PRUDENCE *sb.* (**PRUDENT** *adj.*)
(A) Wisdom or discretion. One of the **cardinal** or 'natural' virtues, sometimes appropriated into the Christian scheme.

(B) Katherine of Aragon, trying to dissuade her husband Henry VIII from divorcing her and marrying Anne Boleyn, uses the word traditionally, and defines it to boot: 'The King your father was reputed for / A prince most prudent, of an excellent / And unmatch'd wit and judgment' (H8 2.4.45–7). Capulet condescendingly calls Juliet's nurse 'Good Prudence' for defending her mistress against his anger (ROM 3.5.171), and Antonio similarly calls Sebastian's conscience 'Sir Prudence' for urging him not to kill his own brother (TMP 1.2.286).

(C) See *ST* II.2.47–56; Roberti (1962), 981–3; Becker and Becker (2001), 1397–401; *NewCathEncy*, 11: 925–8.

PSALMIST
(A) Writer of the Psalms.

(B) Shallow says, 'Death, as the Psalmist saith, is certain to all, all shall die' (2H4 3.2.37).

(C) Ps. 89.48 reads, 'What man is *he that* liveth, and shall not see death?' Tilley, D142, M505, lists the proverbs 'Death is common to all' and 'All shall die', both of which are closer to Shallow's words.

PSALMS

(A) The works of the biblical Psalmist.

(B) When Falstaff says 'I would I were a weaver, I could sing psalms' (1H4 2.4.133), he refers to a very familiar habit of the weavers, who were often associated with the Puritans, of singing Psalms as they worked. The Clown refers similarly in WT (4.3.43–5) to 'but one Puritan amongst' the workers in pagan Bohemia, 'and he sings Psalms to hornpipes'. Mrs Ford says that Falstaff's words and truth 'no more adhere and keep place together than the hundred Psalms to the tune of "Green-sleeves" ' (WIV 2.1.62–3). Apparently she was unimpressed by the lack of variety and discretion in the use of familiar tunes for the psalms.

(C) The Recusant Hopkins translates F. Lewis de Granada's complaint that the Reformers 'are moved to singe **psalmes** in their Schismaticall Congregations, and at home' (1586), 11. Clark (1983), 34, mentions as one indication of 'the great popularity of sermons and moral philosophy' during Shakespeare's lifetime that the Sternhold-Hopkins Psalter, originally published in 1547, was in its forty-seventh edition by 1600. On the weavers, the Puritans, and psalm-singing, see also Collinson (1967), 372–82; Holden (1954), 102–3; and Poole (1995), 66.

PURE

Spiritually unsullied.

Shakespeare seems to enjoy occasional oxymoronic combinations between this word and an irreligious one, as with Claudio's perplexed 'pure impiety' (ADO 4.1.104) or Berowne's cynical 'pure idolatry' (LLL 4.3.73). In less paradoxical references, 'conscience' is once said to be 'wash'd / As pure as sin with baptism' (H5 1.2.32), 'pure as grace' implies that in Hamlet's mind grace is the ultimate purity (HAM 1.4.33), and Mowbray is described as having dedicated 'his pure soul unto his Captain Christ' (R2 4.1.99).

PURGATION

Religious cleansing.

Duke Frederick declines to accept Rosalind's protest that she is innocent of any thoughts or actions of treachery with 'Thus do all traitors: / If their purgation did consist in words, / They are as innocent as grace itself' (AYL 1.3.53–4).

PURGATORY

(A) The place or condition, associated with Roman Catholic belief, in which those who die penitent are cleansed, some say of their **venial** sins (Vaux [1590a], *sig.* G8ᵛ), some of 'venial and mortal sins too (for which in this life men have done no penance)' (Rogers, [1854], 216–17). This was an extremely controversial site during the Reformation, one not only underpinning and supporting many of the institutions and practices of the Roman Catholic Church, but also deeply imbedded in the popular imagination, and slow to be disinterred.

(B) When Emilia tells Desdemona of making 'her husband a cuckold to make him a monarch', 'I should venture purgatory for't' (OTH 4.3.77), she rightly assumes that adultery is a venial rather than a mortal sin, but may forget that the blasphemy of manipulating judgement or presumptuously taking it for granted is more dangerous. Her word 'venture' might also suggest some scepticism about the place and the doctrine. The Ghost of Hamlet's father probably speaks of purgatory when he describes 'my **prison-house**' in which he is 'for the day confin'd to fast in fires, / Till the foul crimes done in my days of nature / Are burnt and purg'd away' (HAM 1.5.11–14).

(C) Vaux (1590a), *sig.* G8^v, confirms purgatory theologically: 'a temporall paine is due for venial sinne, either in this life, or in Purgatorie'; Allen confirms it pragmatically: 'this faithe of purgatory and respecte of Goddes **judgements** to come, feared the holyest persons that ever were in goddes Churche. This drove many a blessed man to perpetuall **paenaunce** . . . filled the desertes with many a noble heremite, this raysed uppe the cloisters and all the holy houses of mowrning and praiers in the whole worlde, and hathe in all agyes appeared bothe in the wordes and woorkes of all **Christen** people' (1565), *sig.* G4^{r-v}. Donne uses this controversial word metaphorically (7: 183), but he is less sure of its literal reality, once speaking of the 'dream of purgatory' (4: 141) and 'their *Purgatorie* Fires' (6: 250); and elsewhere calling it 'controverted now' (3: 316). Also sceptical are Hooper (1843), 1: 197; Bullinger, 3: 400–1; Becon, 3: 181; Rogers (1854), 214–17; and Ridley (1841), 320. Greenblatt (2001), *esp.* ch. 5, Dean (2002), Shaheen (1999), 544; and Frye (1984), 14–24, all look at the relevance of controversies about purgatory in readings of HAM.

PURGED

(A) Cleansed of sins. Vaux says of '*the Sacrament of extreme Unction*', 'The effect of the Sacrament of annoyling is, to put away and purge veniall sinne commited by mispeding of our senses, & to purge and put away sinnes forgotten' (1590a), *sigs.* H5v–6v.

(B) Old Hamlet's Ghost tells his son that he is 'Doom'd for a certain time to walk the night, / And for the day confin'd to fast in fires, / Till the foul crimes done in my days of nature / Are burnt and purg'd away' (HAM 1.5.10–13). Suffolk may draw through metaphor upon the tradition that venial but not mortal sins could be worked off in purgatory or by extreme **unction** when he says of Gloucester's treason, 'mightier crimes are laid unto your charge, / Whereof you cannot easily purge yourself' (2H6 3.1.134–5). Romeo also playfully tells Juliet that by her kiss 'my sin is purg'd' (ROM 1.5.107).

(C) See Rogers (1854), 216–17; Vaux (1590a), *sigs.* H5^v–6^v. See also **purgatory**, **anoyl'd**.

PURGING

Process of theological cleansing.

Hamlet speaks of Claudius's attempted prayer of contrition when he says it would be 'hire and salary, not revenge' to 'take him in the purging of his soul' (HAM 3.3.79, 85), i.e. kill him while he prays.

PURITAN

(A) A member of the Anglican communion who preferred reforming or purifying it of what he or she considered its Catholic errors and excesses of theology, church polity, and **worship** to forming a separatist denomination or **sect**, like the **Anabaptists** or the **Brownists**; also someone of extreme, some would say excessive, moral and religious purity.

(B) 'Charbon the puritan' is distinguished from 'Poysam the Papist' in AWW (1.3.52–4) as 'sever'd in religion' but united in cuckoldry. Malvolio, on the other hand, is called 'a kind of puritan' (TN 2.3.140) for being so opposed to revelry, personal rather than ecclesiastical misrule. The Clown refers to the shearers at the feast as having as their best voice 'a Puritan amongst them', who 'sings psalms to hornpipes' (WT 4.3. 44–5), drawing upon the traditional association of Puritans and the singing of psalms. The Bawd complains that Marina's words and deeds have so reformed the patrons of the brothel where she was taken 'that she would make a puritan of the devil' (PER 4.6.9).

(C) The moderate Protestant Donne disapproves of '*purifying Puritans*, quarrelling with men, with States, with Churches, and attempting a purifying of Sacraments, and Ceremonies, Doctrine and Discipline, according to our own fancy' (1: 189); so does the Catholic Persons (1604a), 144–53. For discussions of English Puritanism, see Collinson (1987), Hill (1964), Lake (1982), Durston and Eales (1996), Bremer (1993) and Todd (1995). Hassel (2003) discusses Puritan motifs in HAM, and Hunt (1993), 278–84, analyses Malvolio's puritanical traits in TN. Poole (1995) discusses Falstaff as a kind of 'grotesque Puritan'. Milward (1977) catalogues controversies between Protestants and Puritans in ch. 7. See **professors**.

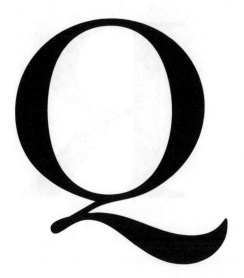

QUINTESSENCE

In ancient, medieval, and Neoplatonic philosophy, the fifth essence, or ether, supposed to constitute the heavenly bodies.

It may be because human beings were thought uniquely constituted of body and soul, 'crawling between earth and heaven' that Hamlet can ask in his odd blend of idealism and scepticism 'to me, what is this quintessence of dust' (HAM 3.1.128; 2.2.308).

(C) On this fifth essence or *quinta essentia*, see Cassirer (1963), 24–5.

QUIRE

See **choir**[1–3].

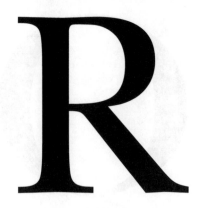

RAIN *sb.* & *v.*

When Portia compares mercy to 'the gentle rain from heaven' (MV 4.1.185), she draws upon a biblical simile in Ecclus. 35.19, 'Oh, how faire a thing is mercie in the time of anguish and trouble! It is like a cloude of raine, that cometh in the time of a drought' (*Geneva Bible, fol.* 438). Prospero similarly prays for Miranda and Ferdinand, 'Heavens rain grace / On that which breeds between 'em' (TMP 3.1.75–6).

See Shaheen (1999), 180, for other suggested biblical parallels. See also **dew**.

RANSOM

(A) Buy back, **redeem**, or rescue from punishment for a sin, as Christ did on the cross. Becon's *A New Year's Gift* defines it, 'To redeem us is to buy us again, when we are lost, to pay our **ransom**, to **satisfy** for our sin, to **deliver** us out of captivity, to bring us home again to our true owner, to restore us to our old liberty, to set us again in that **favour**, wherein we were with God the Father, before we offended. All this hath Christ, and none other, done for us, by his most precious blood' (1: 329).

(B) The sure reference to this theological usage occurs in R2, where Gaunt speaks of 'the sepulchre in stubborn Jewry / Of the world's ransom, blessed Mary's son' (R2 2.1.55–6). Christ is described as giving 'his life a ransom for many' in Matt. 20.28. Shakespeare may tease our ears with echoes of the same meaning near the end of WT, when the Gentleman describes the indescribable joy of the reunited Leontes and Camillo with 'they look'd as they had heard of a world ransom'd, or one destroy'd' (WT 5.2.14–15).

(C) Key biblical passages include Rom. 3; Gal. 2; 1 John 1; Heb. 9; Col. 1. Cranmer says of this 'ransom for us', 'so the **justice** of God and his **mercy** did embrace together, and fulfilled the mystery of our **redemption**' (1846), 2: 128. See also Donne, 7: 437; and Andrewes, 3: 208.

RAVENS

(A) Like sparrows, associated with God's providential care.

(B) The famished Old Adam in AYL refers appropriately to this passage when he says 'He that doth the ravens feed, / Yea providently caters for the sparrow, / Be comfort to my age' (AYL 2.3.43–5).

(C) Luke 12.24 reads, 'Consider the ravens: for they neither sow nor reap, . . . and God feedeth them: how much more are ye better than the fowls?'

REASON

(A) Sometimes used interchangeably with 'understanding' as that human moral faculty capable of grasping the difference between right and wrong and the consequences of misdoing, and therefore of directing the will towards right desiring and right action. A beast 'wants discourse of reason' (HAM 1.2.150); a person has it, or should. As the Reformer Marbeck says, 'The **law of nature** is, that light and judgement of reason, whereby we do discerne betwixt good and evill. Thomas Aquinas saith, that the law of nature is nothing els, but the perticipation of the eternal law in a reasonable creature' (1581), 608. Bullinger says similarly, 'And the conscience, verily, is the knowledge, judgment, and reason of a man, whereby every man in himself, and in his own mind, being made privy to every thing that he either hath committed, or not committed, doth either condemn or else acquit himself. And this reason proceedeth from God, who both prompteth and writeth his judgments in the hearts and minds of men' (1: 194).

The theologians also understood that reason, even if it functions well, can be an impediment to knowing or belief. Donne, for example, twice praises 'the light of reason' (4: 104; 3: 277), but he also concedes that 'Christ *Crucified*, that is, the Gospell of Christ, is said by the Apostle, to be . . . to the Grecians, to the Gentiles, *meer foolishnesse*. . . . [T]he *wise men*, the *learned*, the *Philosophers* of the world: they thoght that Christ induced a religion improbable to Reason, a silly and foolish religion' (9: 113–14). The doctrine of the Resurrection is for Donne particularly 'out of the compasse of reason' (7: 99–100). Whitaker also warns (from Paul in Col. 2) 'Assuredly, this is the difference between theology and philosophy: since it is only the external light of nature that is required to learn thoroughly the arts of philosophy; but to understand theology aright, there is need of the internal light of the Holy Spirit, because the things of faith are not subject to the teaching of mere human reason' (1849), 364.

(B) In two interesting paradoxes from the tragedies, Macbeth speaks explicitly of reason as a moral guide when he tries to explain his rash murder of the sleeping grooms: 'Th' expedition of my violent love / Outrun the pauser, reason' (MAC 2.3.110–11); and Hamlet calls us 'noble in reason' and praises 'that capability and Godlike reason', while also trying to persuade himself to stop 'thinking so precisely on th' event'. Hamlet thinks he wants to act impulsively, amorally, like Fortinbras or Laertes, or like Macbeth (HAM 2.2.304; 4.4.38–41). There are, of course, less problematic uses of reason as a moral guide in the tragedies, including Claudius's advice to Hamlet that his long, intense mourning for his father is 'To reason most absurd, whose common theme / Is death of fathers' (HAM 1.2.103–5).

The ironies behind Lysander's certainty that 'The will of man is by his reason sway'd', that 'Reason becomes the marshal to my will', and the like (MND 2.2.115, 120), are informed by the tradition of the distrust of reason. His words sound both traditional and assured, but we know that he is dead wrong. Under the influence of the love-potion, Lysander is not acting reasonably at all. None of the lovers in the forest are acting reasonably. The fool Bottom underlines this when he says, 'reason and love keep little company together now-a-days' (MND 3.1.143–4). 'Lord, what fools these mortals be' is Puck's similar assessment (MND 3.2.115). The narrowly reasonable Theseus is also almost entirely wrong when he calls 'The lunatic, the lover, and the poet' 'of imagination all compact' (MND 5.1.6–7). Otherwise, Shakespeare the poet, not to mention Shakespeare in love, is as mad as a hatter. Under the influence of love, the forest world, and the love-potion, the lovers come to accept the blessed madness of love, its transcendence of reason. No less a fool than Bottom and no less a wise man than Erasmus both gloss this paradox by alluding to the famous passage from St Paul: 'eye hath not seen, nor ear heard, neither have entered into the heart of man, the things which God hath prepared for them that love him' (1 Cor. 2.9; Bottom's version occurs in MND 4.1.211–14).

(C) Aquinas quotes Augustine as saying that 'virtue is the rectitude and perfection of reason' (*ST* II.58.2). Augustine, however, also says that 'the gift of understanding is incompatible with faith', for 'the thing which is believed is bounded by the comprehension of him who understands it' (QQ. lxxxiii. qu.15, cited in *ST* II.2.8.2). Even Aquinas, the great champion of reason, reluctantly concedes that 'certain things, of themselves, come directly under faith, because they surpass natural reason, such as the mystery of three Persons in one God, and the incarnation of God the Son' (*ST* II.2.8.2); see also *ST* II.58.1–2. On 'faith and reason', see *NewCathEncy*, 5: 807–11. On the distrust of reason, see 1 Cor. 1.17–27, Erasmus (1509; 1965r), 115–16, 118, 126–7. See also Martz (1962), 34–9; Manley (1963), 48; Stein (1962), ch. 3; Bryant (1961); Greenfield (1968), 236–44; Hassel (1971a & b); Hassel (1980), ch. 3, 163–9; and Kaiser (1963), pt. 3. Parker (1987) argues against Bottom that love often goes hand-in-hand with 'right reason' in Shakespeare; Morse (1990) that overly rationalist theories of behaviour are critiqued in HAM; and Levy (2002) that reason is questioned and reconstituted in HAM. Platt (1997) discusses 'Reason Diminished' in the romances. See also Hawkes (1965); Frye (1984), ch. 4, and Battenhouse (1969), 156–61, 183–203.

RECKONING

Paying up an account; used theologically to refer to the religious rituals that might weigh against sins in determining both the pains and the duration of purgatory torments and to the weighing of virtues and vices at the Last Judgement.

The Ghost in HAM says that because he was killed while sleeping, there was 'No reck'ning made'; instead he was 'sent to my account / With all my imperfections on my head', '**Unhous'led**, disappointed, **unanel'd**' (HAM 1.5.77–9). Williams also clearly refers to the accounting at the Last Judgement when he says before Agincourt, 'But if the **cause** be not good, the King himself hath a heavy reckoning to make, when all those legs, and arms, and heads, chopp'd off in a battle, shall join together at the **latter day** and cry all' against him (H5 4.1.134–7).

RECTOR
Clergyman in charge of a parish.

Helena's death was 'faithfully confirm'd by the rector of the place' (AWW 4.3.58–9) in order to deceive Bertram.

RED LETTERS
(A) Rubrics; liturgical instructions for the enactment of rituals were written in red ink in Western liturgical books, like the Elizabethan *Book of Common Prayer*, to distinguish them from the actual words of the liturgy.

(B) When the clerk is caught with 'a book in his pocket with red letters in't' (2H6 4.2.90–1), the revolutionary Jack Cade apparently associates these descriptions of a priest's liturgical gestures with the darker performative arts of conjuring. Red letters also marked the name of a saint in a church calendar, thus 'red-letter days' (*OED* rubric *sb.* 3.a and 4).

(C) See Bradshaw (2002), 413.

REDEEM, REDEEMED, REDEEMING
(A) Buy, bought, buying back; spoken theologically of the way Christ's **sacrifice** and death expiated, paid off, the sins of Adam and Eve and had similar religious consequences for all subsequent humans. Andrewes says of Gal. 4.4–5, Christ came 'that He might redeem them that were under the Law' (1: 57): 'The first and main benefit his Redeemer will raise him to, is to see God. That he lost when he became aliened; that he recovers, being redeemed. Here begins all misery, to be cast out of His presence; here all happiness, to be restored to the light of His countenance' (2: 261).

(B) Iago hopes that Othello's love for Desdemona is so strong that it will persuade him to 'renounce' 'All **seals** and **symbols** of redeemed **sin**', including his recent 'baptism' (OTH 2.3.342–4). Though the Duke's promise to help Isabella 'Redeem your brother from the angry law' (MM 3.1.201–2) speaks about the severity of human rather than divine law, it resonates too well with the 'measure-for-measure' theological context of the play to be without religious associations. The Gentleman also suggestively describes Cordelia, albeit in a pre-Christian play, as one 'Who redeems nature from the general curse / Which twain have brought her to' (LR 4.6.206–7).

(C) Elton (1966); Battenhouse (1969), 269–301; Hunter (1976), 183–96; and Jorgensen (1967), 9–11, 17, 26–31, all discuss the issue of Christian anachronism in LR. See also **redeemer**, **ransom**, **reckoning**, **godson** and **curse**[3].

REDEEMER

He who redeems; Christ. Donne says of Isa. 52.3, 'ye shall be redeemed without money': 'it is a deliverance from the sting and bondage of death by sin; and so it appertains to the whole world, and the Redeemer of the whole world is Christ Jesus' (1: 151).

The deeply flawed and only briefly penitent King Edward IV says at the hour of his death, 'I every day expect an embassage / From my Redeemer, to redeem me hence' (R3 2.1.3–4). However, once he learns that his brother Clarence has been put to death before he could stay the execution he has himself ordered, and recalls other murders that have 'defac'd / The precious image of our dear Redeemer', he is less sure of that deliverance: 'O God! I fear thy justice' (R3 2.1.3–4, 123–5, 132). See also **redeem**.

REDEMPTION

(A) The state of being redeemed by Christ's sacrifice.

(B) Wrongly thinking them traitors, and probably exaggerating his own worth as well, Richard II calls his murdered friends 'villains, vipers, **damned** without redemption' (R2 3.2.129); one of Dogberry's finest malapropisms is that the slanderers of Hero should be 'condemn'd into everlasting redemption' (ADO 4.2.56–7).

(C) Becon (1: 329–30) names Heb. 9, Col. 1 and 1 John 1 as key biblical texts about redemption. The last reads, 'By Christ we have redemption, and by his blood remission and **forgiveness** for our sins'. See also **Judas**.

REFORM, REFORMED, REFORMATION

(A) These words refer to the movement in northwestern Europe, spearheaded by Martin Luther in Germany and John Calvin in Switzerland, to 'reform' the Roman Catholic Church. Prominent among the many liturgical, doctrinal and ecclesiastical issues: the question of salvation by faith or grace rather than merit or works; the question of whether there were two sacraments, baptism and communion, or seven, including in addition marriage, ordination, confirmation, extreme unction and penance; the question of the central authority of each church, or the Church, including the head; questions concerning intermediaries such as priests, saints and angels in the individual's process of faith and forgiveness; questions concerning the sacraments themselves, especially what happened to the elements and the worshippers during communion; and questions about providing to all readers access to the Bible in their own vernacular languages, rather than in the Latin Vulgate version authorised by the Roman Catholic Church. Scriptural authority was paramount among the more extreme Reformers in matters of belief and practice, as against the traditions that had accumulated within Roman Catholicism. Though such issues had been discussed for most of Christian history, the sixteenth century marked their culmination, as well as the actual separation of the one Western Church into many.

(B) Shakespeare never refers directly to this important religious movement by this name, though such a meaning of the word is in use by 1563 (*OED* 3.b). H8, however, a play which depicts some of the events leading up to the Reformation in England, contains an extensive discussion of these 'new opinions, / Divers and dangerous', these 'heresies', which if 'not reform'd, may prove pernicious'. Bishop Gardiner immediately responds, 'Which Reformation must be sudden too' (H8 5.2.52–5). The curiosity here lies in the Catholic Lord Chancellor's and Gardiner's reverse spin on the word. That it is the Reformation which must be reformed is clear when their conversation specifies the 'commotions' and 'uproars' in 'upper Germany' (H8 5.2.63–6), referring to the Peasants' Wars in 1524, and the Anabaptists' uprising (and subsequent massacre) in Münster in 1535. Earlier, the powerful Catholic Cardinal Wolsey also calls Anne Boleyn a 'spleeny Lutheran' (H8 3.2.99). A pun on the theological meaning of 'reform' could also be present when Hamlet, preaching to the players about the abuses of the stage, says 'O reform it altogether' after the players said 'we have reform'd that indifferently' (HAM 3.2.36–8). The Puritans, of course, wanted absolute and not indifferent reform of the stage as well as the Church.

(C) Andrewes speaks of the 'Reformed' (1: 403); Donne of 'the Reformation in this *Kingdom*' (4: 202–4) as well as 'persons born since the Reformation of Religion' (4: 92). He also frets about the Reformers who 'make too much haste to mend all at once' (3: 182–3). Pilkington speaks of 'Poor cities in Germany, compassed about with their enemies, [who] dare reform religion throughly, without any fear' (1842), 38. Rowley (1632, *sig*. H3ᵛ) similarly refers to 'Much blood-shed there is now in Germanie, / About this difference in religion, / With *Lutherans, Arians* and *Anabaptists*, / As halfe the Province of *Helvetia*, / Is with their tumults almost quite destroy'd'. Foxe (cited in Arden H8, 159n), similarly refers to the Peasants' Revolts of 1521–22 in Saxony when he speaks of the 'horrible uproars, like as in some partes of Germanie'. On the Gardiner–Cranmer episode, see Hamilton (1992), 180–2. On this turmoil in upper Germany, see BEV, 932n; Berdan H8 (1925), 144; Maxwell (1962), 218; and Hamilton (1992), 180–1. Frye (1984) and Diehl (1997), 81–91, both discuss Reformation patterns and pressures in HAM. Healy (1999) argues that H8 is anti-Roman Catholic but not unambiguously pro-Reformation. McMullan (1998) discusses 'the dialogics of Reformation' in H8. Shuger (2001) looks at the Reformation background of MM. See also 'Reformation' (3: 396–8); 'Reformation Studies' (3: 398–410), and 'Riots, Religious' (3: 437–9) in *OxfordEncyRef*.

RELIGION[1]

A group (or sub-group) of organised beliefs and practices. 'The Articles of Christian Religion' (as in Becon, 3: 396) is a familiar example of this usage.

The Gentleman's quip that grace could be said 'in any religion' (MM 1.2.23) uses the word generally. When the Pope's legate Pandulph charges that Philip of France is 'sworn against religion' (JN 3.1.280), he means against the Catholic Church, not the more general Christianity. Implicit in the charge, of course, is Pandulph's assumption that Christianity is Catholicism.

RELIGION²

The study of theology.

Bassanio reflects over the caskets, 'In religion / What damned error but some sober brow / Will bless it, and approve it with a text?' (MV 3.2.77–9).

RELIGION³

(A) The beliefs and practices of these groups. Nowell says 'Of religion . . . there are principally two parts; obedience, which the law, the perfect rule of righteousness commandeth, and faith, which the gospel, that embraceth the promises concerning the mercy of God, requireth' (1853), 118. Hooper says 'The first point therefore of religion is the *fear* of God' (1843), 1: 298.

(B) Jachimo's 'I see you have some religion in you, that you fear' (CYM 1.4.136–7) is informed by this last assumption, as is the joke in LLL that the Schoolmaster Holofernes does 'this in the fear of God, very religiously' (LLL 4.2.147–8). On the other hand, when Gloucester tells Bishop Beauford, 'Name not religion, for thou lov'st the flesh, / And ne'er throughout the year to church thou go'st' (1H6 1.1.41–2), the word refers to obeying (or not obeying) some combination of the rules of abstinence and regular church attendance.

(C) Hooper (1843), 1: 298, cites Ps. 111.10, 'The fear of the Lord is the beginning of wisdom' (cf. Job 28.28).

RELIGION⁴

Liturgical vows.

When Hamlet tells Gertrude that in breaking her marriage vows she makes of 'sweet religion' 'a rhapsody of words' (HAM 3.4.47–8), he connects the commitment of the marriage vows with the religious ceremony which contains them.

RELIGION⁵

Metaphorically, commitment or devotion.

Orlando promises to keep his promise to Rosalind 'With no less religion than if thou wert indeed my Rosalind' (AYL 4.1.197–8); Romeo speaks of his love for Rosaline as 'the devout religion of mine eye' (ROM 1.2.88).

RELIGIOUS¹ *adj.*

Said of a place, a person or a lifestyle devoted to holiness.

The Friar plans to hide and protect Hero in 'some reclusive and religious life' (ADO 4.1.42). Richard similarly advises his queen, 'cloister thee in some religious house' (R2 5.1.23). Rosalind's 'old religious uncle', though imaginary, apparently refers to someone who belongs to a religious order and practices celibacy, though technically it could merely refer to someone to whom religion is important (AYL 3.2.343–4). There are enough references to 'religious churchmen' (1H6 1.1.40) and 'holy and devout religious men' (R3 3.7.92) in Shakespeare to suggest that then as now some churchmen were known to be neither devout nor religious.

RELIGIOUS² *adj.*
Ecclesiastical. Timon of Athens, in saying that 'Religious canons, civil laws are cruel' (TIM 4.3.61), distinguishes between ecclesiastical and civil courts of law only to link them in cruelty.

RELIGIOUS³ *adj. Fig.*
Deeply committed.
    When Fabian calls Viola 'a most devout coward, religious in it' (TN 3.4.388), he means deeply committed, though in this case to cowardice.

RELIGIOUSLY
Both rigorously and with the support of religious texts.
    Henry V, demanding that the Archbishop 'justly and religiously unfold / Why the law Salique' supports his claim to the throne of France (H5 1.2.10–11), probably uses both meanings.

RELIQUES
(A) Items venerated for their association with religious persons or events, like pieces of the cross, vials of Mary's milk, or bits of the bones of saints. Donne takes the classic Reformer's stance: 'What their counterfait Reliques may doe, against their counterfait hell, against their purgatory, I know not: That powerfull, and precious, and onely Relique, which is given to us, against hell it selfe, is onely the Communion of the body, and blood of Christ Jesus, left to us by him, and preserved for us, in his Church, though his body be removed out of our sight' (6: 271).
(B) Helena plays metaphorically on this tension when she laments Bertram's departure with 'But now he's gone, and my **idolatrous** fancy / Must sanctify his reliques' (AWW 1.1.97–8). Sebastian's request of Antonio upon their arrival in Illyria, 'Shall we go see the reliques of this town' (TN 3.3.19), could refer to any antiquities of interest to a traveller, but these things were often religious relics in the sixteenth and seventeenth centuries, about which there was a fascinating blend of scepticism and credulity.
(C) For a good example of such complex responses to religious relics, see the anonymous English gentleman's *Travels Through France and Italy* (1647–49), 23–4, 54–9, 67–70. On relics, see also Tyndale, 2: 216. The Schlosskirche of Wittenberg, on which Luther posted his 95 theses on the eve of All Saints Day, 1517, was one of the great repositories of relics in Europe.

REMORSE
A religiously based regret for or fear of wrongdoing. Donne credits 'St *Bernard*' as saying, 'as long as we are ashamed of sin, we are not growne up, and hardned in it; we are under correction; the correction of a remorse' (6: 57).
    The Second Murderer in R3 says 'the urging of that word "judgment" hath bred a kind of remorse in me', connecting his fear of God's judgement with his misgivings about murdering Clarence. He is not 'afraid to kill him, having a

warrant, but to be damn'd for killing him, from the which no warrant can protect me' (R3 1.4.107–12).

RENOUNCE

To give away something for religious reasons; to take back a religious vow. Andrewes says, 'The will of the flesh wills one thing, and the will of God another: therefore that God's will may take place, we must renounce our own will and, as Christ saith, willingly "deny ourselves" ' (5: 400).

The blinded Gloucester says to the Gods, 'This world I do renounce, and in your sights / Shake patiently my great affliction off', though in fact he has committed himself to suicide because he cannot 'bear it longer, and not fall / To quarrel with your great opposeless wills' (LR 4.6.35–8). Iago hopes that Othello worships Desdemona so much that he would 'renounce his baptism' if she asked (OTH 2.3.343). This religious meaning is evoked more playfully when Lovell describes the French as 'renouncing clean / The faith they have in tennis and tall stockings' (H8 1.3.29–30).

REPENT, REPENTANCE

(A) Shakespeare uses variants of this word eighty times, always with the general meaning of feeling sorry. *Certaine Sermons* (264–8) and the 'General Confession' (*BCP*, 259–60) both assert 'four parts' of repentance: contrition, confession, faith in forgiveness, and amendment of life.

(B) The fourfold contrition, confession, faith in forgiveness, and amendment of life often inform Macbeth's potential moments of repentance. His contrition dominates the scene with his wife just after the murder of Duncan, as when he laments, 'I could not say "Amen" and 'I had most need of blessing, and "Amen" / Stuck in my throat' (MAC 2.2. 26–30). Macbeth even shouts at the end of the scene, 'Wake Duncan with thy knocking! I would thou could'st.' But lacking faith in forgiveness, he also concludes that 'all great Neptune's ocean [will not] wash this blood / Clean from my hand' (MAC 2.2. 71, 57–8). Soon Macbeth will confess to murdering Duncan's grooms, 'O, yet I do repent me of my fury, / That I did kill them' (MAC 2.3.106–7), but only a keen ear would hear in 'Th' expedition of my violent love outrun the pauser, reason' a confession of his reason for murdering Duncan and not the grooms (MAC 2.3.110–11). Finally, Macbeth resists the impulse to amend his life, most obviously when he says after seeing Banquo's ghost: 'Returning were as tedious as go o'er' (3.4.137). Richard III tries to convince a stubbornly undeceived Queen Elizabeth that he is worthy of her daughter by promising, 'As I intend to prosper and repent, / So thrive I in my dangerous affairs' (R3 4.4.397–8). Earlier he has dismissed repentance with a glib 'Which after hours give leisure to repent' (R3 4.4.293). That he does not thrive in his enterprise, or have time to repent at the end, may or may not suggest that some supreme being is hearing these false promises and responding to them with an ironic sense of humour in a universe of judgement that Richard III is loath to acknowledge.

The depictions of Claudius and Gertrude involve two of the most dynamic uses of 'repentance' in Shakespeare. Attempting to pray after his sense of guilt is aroused by 'The Mousetrap' play, Claudius confesses his sin and expresses his contrition: 'O my offense is rank, it smells to heaven'. Unlike Macbeth, Claudius does not assume that his sin is too great for God's blessing, God's grace: 'What if this cursed hand were thicker than itself with brother's blood, / Is there not rain enough in the sweet heavens / To wash it white as snow?' The very purpose of mercy is to 'confront the visage of offense'. The problem for Claudius concerns the fourth ingredient in the formula of repentance, amendment of life. 'Pray can I not' he says, not because of God's incapacity to forgive but because 'I am still possess'd / Of those effects for which I did the murther: / My crown, mine own ambition, and my queen.' 'May one be pardon'd and retain th' offense?' The conclusion is inevitable, the fault fully his own: 'Try what repentance can. What can it not? / Yet what can it, when one cannot repent?' (HAM 3.3.36–66). It is this brutal honesty with himself, combined as it is with his theological sophistication about the doctrine of repentance, that wins a grudging admiration for Claudius, for all his evil thoughts, words and deeds. Hamlet seems less honest with himself when he says of the murdered Polonius, 'For this same lord, / I do repent', then connects this contrition with the rationalization that 'heaven hath pleased it so, / That I must be their scourge and minister' (HAM 3.4.172–5).

Gertrude's is a rue with a difference. For one thing, she needs Hamlet to 'wring [her] heart'; for another, she would all-too-readily 'lay that flattering unction to [her] soul / That not [her] trespass but [his] madness speaks' (HAM 3.4.145–6). Finally, at Hamlet's sometimes overzealous prompting, Gertrude feels contrition and confesses, however vaguely, her sense of sinfulness: 'Thou turn'st mine eyes into my very soul, / And there I see such black and grained spots / As will not leave their tinct.' This contrition, not unlike Claudio's in ADO, is imposed from without, though it is perhaps still deeply felt: 'These words like daggers enter in mine ears, / No more, sweet Hamlet' (3.4.35, 145–6, 90–2, 95–6). Hamlet must therefore, priest-like, lay out for Gertrude a precise route to repentance involving confession, contrition, and amendment of life. 'Mother for love of grace', he says, 'Confess yourself to heaven, / Repent what's past, avoid what is to come, / And do not spread the compost on the weeds / To make them ranker' (HAM 3.4.144, 149–52). She must nurture the amended garden of restraint if her repentance is to work any better than that of Claudius. What we cannot know is how deeply she takes this to heart, and for how long.

Shakespeare may introduce into LLL the controversy in which the Reformers would have distinguished a personal spiritual repentance from a liturgically pre-scribed penance. The Ladies of Catholic France, also like **priests** at **confession**, lay formal penance upon the lords of Protestant Navarre. Their lords need their spiritual guidance for many reasons, among them their lack of contrition for their broken vows, their lack of compassion for the poor players in the Pageant of the Nine Worthies, and their insensitivity to the Princess of France, who has just lost her father. Even when the Princess says of this last insensitivity, 'My griefs are double', they do not comprehend (LLL 5.2.752). All four are 'Full of dear **guiltiness**' that only a 'twelvemonth' of 'frosts and **fasts**, hard lodging and thin weeds', a 'forlorn and **naked hermitage**' (LLL 5.2.752, 791, 833, 801) will purge. As usual, Berowne is the focal point of this prescribed amendment of life: 'You must be purged too, your sins are rack'd' (LLL 5.2.818). His priest Rosaline tells him that if he spends his penitential year well, vainly trying 'To enforce the pained impotent to smile', 'To move wild laughter in the throat of death', and therefore learning a little compassion and a little humility, 'I shall find you empty of that fault, / Right joyful of your Reformation' (LLL 5.2.854–5, 868–9). 'A twelvemonth and a day' may be 'too long for a play', but it is just about the right amount of time for the successful enactment of such penance. The word 'penance' occurs three times in the play (LLL 1.1.115; 1.2.129; 5.2.711). The last, Armado's 'I go woolward for penance', comments on the even coarser cloth the four lords must wear if their ladies are to accept their amendment of life, and marry them.

(C) Hooker speaks 'Of . . . Twoe kinds of **pœnitency**: the one a private dutie towards God: the other a dutie of externall discipline, and also 'Of the vertue of **repentance** from which the former dutie procedeth. And of **contrition** the first part of that dutie' (VI.3). See also Becon (3: 618) and the sermon by Andrewes 'On Repentance and Fasting', preached to King James at Whitehall on Ash Wednesday, 1619 (1: 356). Hassel (1977, 1980) and Cunningham (1955) discuss penance in LLL. Velie (1972) speaks of Shakespeare's 'repentance plays', TGV, ADO, AWW, MM, CYM, WT and TMP; and Hunter (1965) discusses *Shakespeare and the Comedy of Forgiveness*. Matthews (1975) and Battenhouse (1969), 293–302, look respectively at Edmund's and Edgar's repentance in LR. Cubeta (1987) examines whether Falstaff's reported last words might constitute a moment of deathbed repentance.

REPRIEVE

The commutation of a capital sentence or postponement or remission of an execution. The word can refer theologically to the results of Christ's sacrifice on the cross or of Mary's intervention on our behalf for 'the remission of our sins'.

The Countess probably speaks of Mary's intercession, though she may speak of Helena's, when she says of her son Bertram's mistreatment of Helena, 'He cannot thrive, / Unless her prayers, whom heaven delights to hear / And loves to grant, reprieve him from the wrath / Of greatest justice' (AWW 3.4.25–9). MM's repeated opposition of the ethos of equitable punishment for wrongdoing, measure for measure, against that of loving and forgiving even one's enemies (Matt. 5.38–44), probably gives even its two essentially secular uses of 'reprieve' some religious resonance. When Isabella argues with Angelo for her brother's 'reprieve' from 'the most just law', his response is to offer her the chance to 'redeem him' with the 'sweet uncleanness' of having sex with Angelo (MM 2.4.39, 53–5). Her angry reference to a 'bending down' which might 'reprieve thee from thy fate' could describe both a sexual submission to Angelo and what she now decides not to offer for Claudio, the posture of intercessory prayer: 'I'll pray a thousand prayers for thy death, / No word to save thee' (MM 3.1.143–6).

REPROBANCE
(A) The state of being a reprobate, that is someone hardened in sin, and even cast off by God. The second-generation English Calvinist Perkins says that, 'The decree of Reprobation, is that part of predestination, whereby God, according to the most free and just purpose of his will, hath determined to reject certain men unto eternall destruction, and miserie, and that to the praise of his justice' (1597), 193–4 (ch. 52).
(B) Gratiano says of Brabantio, Desdemona's father, a reasonably good man, that the sight of her murdered body, were he not already dead, 'would make him do a desperate turn, / Yea, curse his better angel from his side, / And fall to reprobance' (OTH 5.2.206–9). Here despair rather than habitual sinfulness would mark his reprobation.
(C) On Perkins's position in the English Reformation, see Perkins (1970), 171–2.

REPROBATE *sb.* & *adj.*
Someone hardened in sin, and even cast off by God; also descriptive of desires and actions characterised by such a spiritual state. Hooper distinguishes 'the evil, wicked, and reprobate' from 'the good, the faithful, and the **elect**' (1852), 2: 38.

Barnadine is such a character in MM, a 'rude wretch' who 'apprehends death no more dreadfully but as a drunken sleep, careless, reakless, and fearless of what's past, present, or to come' (MM 4.2.142–4). The Duke decides therefore to delay his execution, 'omit / This reprobate till he were well inclin'd' (MM 4.3.74). More sinister, if also a bit melodramatic, is the narrator's reference to Tarquin's 'reprobate desire' for Lucrece (LUC 300).

REQUIEM
A mass said or sung for the peace of the departed soul.

When Laertes complains to the 'churlish priest' about Ophelia's perfunctory or 'maimed' burial rites, he attributes their paucity to the suspicion of suicide: 'We should profane the service of the dead / To sing a requiem and such rest to her / As to peace-parted souls' (HAM 5.1.236–8). A metaphor makes 'the death-divining swan' the 'priest in surplice white' who sings 'the requiem' for the departed Phoenix and Turtle, Love and Constancy (PHT 13–16).

REQUITE
(A) Pay back a debt or a wrong, sometimes used of heaven's reward or punishment for human deeds.
(B) Emilia unknowingly curses her husband Iago when she says of Othello's jealousy, 'If any wretch have put this in your head, / Let heaven requite it with a serpent's curse!' (OTH 4.2.15–16). Volumnia says similarly about the banishment of her son, 'The hoarded plague a'th'gods / Requite your love!' (COR 4.2.11–12). When Palamon and his Knights in TNK offer their purses to the daughter of the man who is about to execute them, the Jailer responds with a blessing, 'The gods requite you all, and make her thankful!' (TNK 5.4.36). The note from Pericles which accompanies his wife's (still living) body also uses

'requite' as 'reward': 'Who finds her, give her burying . . . The gods requite his charity!' (PER 3.2.72, 75).
(C) In Gen. 3.14, God cursed the Serpent for deceiving Eve.

REST[1] *sb.*

(A) The soul's peace. Donne says that 'our rest . . . is Christ himselfe. Not onely that rest that is *in Christ,* (peace of conscience in him) but that Rest, that *Christ is in*; eternall rest in his kingdome' (5: 213). Heb. 4.11 reads, '*Let us study to enter into that Rest*'.
(B) Isabella, unwilling to give up her virginity to save her brother Claudio's life, purposes to 'fit his mind to death, for his soul's rest' (MM 2.4.187). 'Rest' is more specifically associated with the formal rite of requiem when the priest declines to 'sing a requiem and such rest' to Ophelia, 'As to peace-parted souls' (HAM 5.1.237–8). Romeo's 'O, here / Will I set up my everlasting rest' (ROM 5.3.109–10), spoken of his proposed suicide, is more ambiguous theologically than it is romantically. Suicides were denied the rites of the Church because they did not part in peace and would not rest in peace; but in romance, even Bottom knows that 'A lover, that kills himself most gallant for love' (MND 1.2.24) earns eternal fame. Hamlet's last words, 'the rest is silence' (HAM 5.2.358), are less theologically turbulent. Granted, 'silence' can mean absence from God as well as presence with him; and 'rest' can mean merely 'remainder'. But when Horatio follows just a few lines later with his benediction of Hamlet, 'And flights of angels sing thee to thy rest' (HAM 5.2.360), Horatio at least seems to understand that this 'rest' he speaks of is 'that peace of God, which passeth all understanding'.
(C) *BCP*, 265; cf. Phil. 4.7.

REST[2] *v.*

Abide in peace; give peace to, as requested in the *Requiem.*

The Gravedigger says to Hamlet with compassion and wit that Ophelia 'was a woman, sir, but rest her soul she's dead' (HAM 5.1.135). The common phrase, 'rest in peace' also occurs in HAM 5.1.135; and MAC 4.3.227. When Hamlet tells his father's ghost 'Rest, rest, perturbed spirit', he is trying vainly to impart some peace to this departed soul (HAM 1.5.182).

RESURRECTIONS

(A) Resurrection, the rising of the dead at the Last Judgement, as promised in the Apostles' and the Nicene Creeds.
(B) The Welch parson Evans mispronounces the word when be blesses the memory of Mistress Ann Page's grandsire in the line 'Got deliver to a joyful resurrections!' (WIV 1.1.52).
(C) For both creeds, see *BCP*, 58 and 250–1. The Nicene Creed ends, 'I look for the resurrection of the dead, and the life of the world to come. Amen'. See *Certaine Sermons*, 2nd tome, pp. 189–96, for the 'Homily of the Resurrection of our Saviour Jesus Christ. *For Easter Day*'.

REVEALED

Made known by supernatural means.

When Peter kills his master Horner and thus demonstrates his own just cause, King Henry VI says, 'God in justice hath revealed to us / The truth and innocence of this poor fellow'; the more worldly York, however, advises the servant that he won because his master was drunk: 'Fellow, thank God, and the good wine in thy master's way' (2H6 2.3.95–6, 102–3).

REVENGE *sb. & v.*

(A) Retribution; extract retribution for. Because the *sb.* and the *v.* are so often used in tandem, their usage will not be separated here. 'Revenge is mine, saith the Lord', Donne's version of the more common 'Vengeance is mine . . .', is a two-edged theological sword. On the one hand, God asserts his just wrath, and promises a vengeful response; on the other, he forbids a similar human response to a sense of wrong. Thus Donne can say of Deut. 32.35, '*Revenge is mine, saith the Lord*', 'since Revenge is in Gods hands, it will certainly fall upon the Malefactor, God does not mistake his marke; And then, since Revenge is in his hands, no man must take revenge out of his hands, or make himselfe his owne Magistrate, or revenge his owne quarrel' (8: 315). Revenge is also a crucial issue because of the close relationship in Christian thought between forgiveness and humility. Donne says again, this time from Matt. 18.21, '*How oft shall my brother sinne against me, and I forgive him?*', 'The root of all Christian duties is *Humility*, meeknesse, that's . . . violated in an *unmercifulnesse*, and *inexorablenesse*, for that implies an *indocilenesse*, that we will not learn by Christs doctrine; and an *ungratefulnesse*, that we will not apply his example, and do to his servants, as he, our Master, hath done to us' (3: 158)

(B) Old Queen Margaret is the most outspoken of the many voices in the histories asking that 'God revenge' (R3 1.3.136). Her 'I am hungry for revenge' (R3 4.4.61) reveals how subjective, even guttural, these calls can be, but she seems convinced that her hunger and God's will have coincided in the deaths of 'thy Edward', 'my Edward', 'Thy other Edward', 'Young York', 'Thy Clarence', 'Th' adulterate Hastings, Rivers, Vaughan, Grey' (R3 4.4.63–70). The Lady Anne, lamenting the death of her husband Edward over the corpse of her dead father-in-law Henry the Sixth, also prays to both God and earth, supernature and nature, for revenge upon the chief perpetrator of these murders, Richard of Gloucester: 'O God! which this blood mad'st, revenge his death! / O earth! which this blood drink'st, revenge his death! / Either heav'n with lightning strike the murth'rer dead; / Or earth gape open wide and eat him quick' (R3 1.2.62–5). Even the blasphemous Richard once says with the unconscious irony of self-condemnation, 'God will revenge it' (R3 2.1.139) of Clarence's untimely but well-timed death (cf. R2 1.2.40; R3 2.2.14–15). 3H6 is equally rich in these interwoven and often theologically and psychologically complicated references to God's revenge and man's (see, for example, 3H6 1.1.100, 190; 1.3.31–3, 40–2, 35–7; 1.4.175–8; 2.1.86; 5.6.83).

The treatment of revenge in HAM acknowledges more explicitly the moral and psychological complexity of a Christian ethic of forgiveness that flies in the face of the Senecan ethic of revenge. 'Thou shalt not kill', God's commandment, directly contradicts Hamlet's father's commandment to 'Revenge his foul and most unnatural murther' (HAM 1.5.25). When Hamlet says to the Ghost, 'Speak, I am bound to hear', the Ghost immediately replies, 'So art thou to revenge, when thou shalt hear' (HAM 1.5.6–7). But Hamlet cannot 'sweep to my revenge' (HAM 1.5.31) until he is convinced not only that the murder occurred as the ghost described it, but also that it is meet and right to seek revenge in a Christian universe. For one thing, 'The spirit that I have seen / May be a dev'l', and it may be that this devil 'Abuses me to damn me' (HAM 2.2.598–603). Even when Hamlet tries to make himself think and act impulsively (complaining, for example, of 'Thinking too precisely on th' event' – HAM 4.4.41–3), even when he tries to distance himself from the act with a theatrical analogy ('Prompted to my revenge by heaven and hell' – HAM 2.2.584), he cannot be sure who wrote the script, or what his role should be in it. And once Claudius's guilt is revealed, Hamlet still cannot 'do it pat' (HAM 3.3.73). His Senecan conscience says kill him immediately; paradoxically, his Christian worldview resists this impulse to kill Claudius not so much because killing is prohibited in the Ten Commandments but because by killing him while he is praying he might send his soul 'to heaven' and not to hell. In truth 'That would be scann'd' (HAM 3.3.73–9). Perfect revenge would not be served by such impulsiveness. When Claudius tells the gullible Laertes 'Revenge should have no bounds' (HAM 4.7.125–8), he valorises instead a thoughtless revenge, and therefore reminds us of the proper bounds Hamlet's wisdom places upon his anger. Laertes is the better revenger not because he has more courage but because he lacks Hamlet's moral and intellectual complexity.

Shylock plays most directly on the ironic breach between Christian precept and Christian practice when he declares a Jew to be as human as a Christian not only in 'hands, organs, dimensions, senses, affections, passions' (MV 3.1.59–60). but also in 'revenge':

> And if you wrong us, shall we not revenge? If we are like you in the rest, we will resemble you in that. If a Jew wrong a Christian, what is his humility? Revenge. If a Christian wrong a Jew, what should his sufferance be by Christian example? Why, revenge. The villainy you teach me I will execute, and it shall go hard but I will better the instruction.
> (MV 3.1.66–73)

Donne (8: 315; quoted above) helps us see just how theologically germane it is that Shylock would oppose Christian revenge with Christian 'humility'.

(C) On the biblical 'Vengeance is mine' and close variants, see also Rom. 12.19; Ps. 94.1; Jer. 50.28 and Heb. 10.30. Becon warns like Donne of persistence in revenge (2: 183). For a range of critical positions on the moral rightness, wrongness or ambiguity of revenge in HAM, see Prosser (1971), Hallett and Hallett (1980), 181–222, Rappaport (1987), Watson (1990), Girard (1986), Desai (1993) and Whitaker (1969, Ch. 11). Anderson (1987) studies revenge in the comedies.

Keyishian (1995) looks at revenge and victimization in all the plays. Hassel (1987), 92–107, Hunter (1976), 70–9, and Frey (1976), 120, discuss distinctions between personal revenge and divine vengeance in R3. Frye (1984), 29–37, discusses 'Retribution in Doctrine and Fact'.

REVENGIVE

(A) Revenging.

(B) When Edmund says, 'I told him, the [revengive] gods / 'Gainst parricides did all the thunder bend' (LR 2.1.45–6), he is trying to deceive his father by catering to his simplistic sense of divine justice (cf. LR 1.2.126–7).

(C) See RIV, 1266n, and **revenge**.

REVENGEFUL

Highly motivated to seek **revenge**.

Hamlet includes 'revengeful' among the imperfections he lists to Ophelia: 'I am very proud, revengeful, ambitious, with more offenses at my beck than I have thoughts to put them in, imagination to give them shape, or time to act them in' (HAM 3.1.123–6).

REVERENCE

Sometimes this means merely dignity or respect, as when Benedick says of the dignified Leonato, 'Knavery cannot sure hide himself in such reverence' (ADO 2.3.119–20).

'Reverence' can, however, signify the respect or trust due to religious persons, offices or vows. The Friar in ADO, for example, cites his religious occupation in asserting his authority to judge Hero guiltless: 'trust not my age, / My reverence, calling, nor divinity, / If this sweet lady lie not guiltless here / Under some biting error' (ADO 4.1.167–70). Likewise, when Olivia wants airtight testimony that she has married Cesario, she says to the Priest, 'Father, I charge thee by thy reverence / Here to unfold ... what thou dost know / Hath newly pass'd between this youth and me' (TN 5.1.151–5). Hotspur also refers to 'a clergyman / Of holy reverence' (R2 3.3.28–9). One can hear a churchman's 'exposition of the holy text' 'with reverence' (2H4 4.2.4–7), and describe, albeit naively, 'the due reverence of a sacred vow' (OTH 3.3.461).

REVEREND, REVERENT

Holy, spoken of a person or a place. Though the word is more likely to describe secular respect in Shakespeare, it sometimes carries religious nuance. At least once it carries both meanings simultaneously.

King Henry IV refers to the 'reverend bishops' he led (1H4 3.2.104); West-moreland refers to the Archbishop of York as 'reverend father' in his speech accusing him of rebellion (2H4 4.1.38); Suffolk includes 'twenty reverend bishops' of France among the witnesses of the espousal of Henry VI and Marga-ret (2H6 1.1.8); Richard III and Buckingham twice play the 'reverend fathers' card to deceive the citizens about Richard's piety. Since he is 'within, with two right reverend fathers, / Divinely bent to meditation', how can he be anything but pious? (R3 3.5.100; 3.7.61–2). A heated exchange between the Bishop of Winchester and Gloucester relies upon both the secular and the religious meanings:

> WIN. Unreverent Gloucester!
> GLOU.   Thou art reverent
> Touching thy spiritual function, not thy life.
>   (1H6 3.1.49–50)

Henry IV pronounces as the Bishop of Carlisle's 'doom' this pardon: 'Choose out some secret place, some reverent room, / More than thou hast, and with it joy thy life. / So as thou liv'st in peace, die free from strife.' He speaks here of a holy cell, a hermitage, generous 'doom' for an enemy he nevertheless respects (R2 5.6.24–9).

REVERENTLY
With religious devotion.

When Charles, still Dauphin of France, asks Joan of Arc, 'How may I reverently worship thee enough?' (1H6 1.2.145), his praise is part Petrarchan and part religious.

REVOLT
Rising against or falling away from an established power or belief. Two major biblical revolts, the uprising of the angels in heaven (from Rev. 12.7) and the subsequent fall of man (Gen. 3) allow Shakespeare to use this word with religious nuance. Bullinger says of this narrative, 'Evil angels are corrupt and wicked spirits, and, for their revolting or falling away, everlastingly condemned' (3: 349). Milton asks rhetorically near the beginning of PL, 'Who first seduc'd them to that foul revolt' (PL 1.33); later he calls Satan 'Author of evil, unknown till thy revolt' (PL 6.261).

Henry V's anger and surprise over the attempted betrayal of his friend Scroop explicitly evokes one of these biblical moments: 'I will weep for thee; / For this revolt of thine, methinks, is like / Another fall of man' (H5 2.2.140–2; cf. R2 3.4.73–6; 3.2.100–1). When Ford, suspecting his wife's (and Page's wife's) infidelities with Falstaff, says 'Our revolted wives share damnation together' (WIV 3.2.39–40), he associates marital revolt with revolt against God. Cf. TRO 5.3.144–5.

RIGHT[1] *sb.*
(A) What is just, a fair claim; also, the person or cause entitled to such a claim.
(B) 'The right' is often associated with God, though there can be a personal agenda in the assertion. The Marshall of the joust assumes a neutral stance when he hands Bolingbroke his lance with the formulaic words 'and God defend the right' (R2 1.3.101). Vindictiveness, however, marks Margaret's claim about the

death of Queen Elizabeth's two young sons, 'say that right for right, / Hath dimm'd your infant morn to aged night' (R3 4.4.15–16). When Richard II later proclaims 'for heaven still guards the right' (R2 3.2.62), **desperation** and self-deception colour his claim. The young King Henry V seems to know in his first conference with the Archbishop, who is about to advise him about his 'right and title' to France, that asserted 'right' does not always '[Suit] well in native colors with the truth' (H5 1.2.89, 16–17). The young Edward Prince of Wales shows a similar sophistication when he says 'If that be right which Warwick says is right, / There is no wrong, but every thing is right' (3H6 2.2.131–2). Peter's victory and Horner's death prove at least to Henry that Peter's cause was right: 'O Peter, thou hast prevail'd in right!' A cynic, however, attributes the win to Horner's drunkenness (2H6 2.3.98–101). In JN, the assembled leaders of Spain, France, Austria, Rome and England so relentlessly press their competing, ambiguous, shamelessly self-serving claims of 'God and our right' (JN 2.1.237, 299, 112–17; 176–7; 236–8; 2.1.267–8; 2.1.299; 112–17; 176–7) that even the cynical Bastard is disillusioned, or at least pretends to be: '[If] kings break faith upon commodity / Gain, be my lord, for I will worship thee' (JN 2.1.597–8). An even darker movement occurs in LR. Edgar's 'pray that the right may thrive' is followed only four lines later by 'King Lear hath lost, he and his daughter ta'en'; this reversal in hope returns his father to 'ill thoughts again', a theological despair that had already led Gloucester to the edge of the cliffs of Dover, and over the edge, earlier in the play (LR 5.2.2–9). (C) See (under prudence) ST II.2.57. See also **revenge**.

RIGHT² v.
Make reparation for, avenge, vindicate.
  Queen Elizabeth says of the death of the innocent Rutland, 'So just is God, to right the innocent' (R3 1.3.181).

RIGHT³ adj., adv.
Rightful, rightfully; possessing the authority of God or the Church.
  Bolingbroke concludes his initial challenge to Mowbray, 'What my tongue speaks, my right drawn sword may prove' (R2 1.1.46).

RIGHTEOUS adj.
Just, virtuous and law-abiding, said of persons, actions or God. Donne describes human righteousness in clearly religious terms as 'the exaltation and perfection of all true holinesse' (1.406). Donne also uses 'the righteous Man, the godly man' (6: 243) as synonyms.
  'So help you righteous God' formulaically ends the oath the Governor of Paris takes to support the new king Henry VI (1H6 4.1.8). Katherine of Aragon uses the word to punctuate her hopes that the visiting cardinals will be as good as their costumes: 'I do not like their coming. Now I think on't, / They should be good men, their affairs as righteous. / But all hoods make not monks' (H8 3.1.21–3). In two classical plays, Titus says 'Rome and the righteous heavens be my judge' (TIT 1.1.426), and Flavius speaks of 'the righteous gods' (TIM 4.2.4).

RIGHTFUL

Usually meaning someone who has the rights to, like a proper heir to a throne; sometimes referring to the idea of the divine right of kings, or some prerogative or authority deriving from it.

In his final scene with his wife, Richard II laments 'the deposing of a rightful king' (R2 5.1.50); York has earlier said that Bolingbroke 'deposed the rightful king' (2H6 2.2.24). When Henry V assures the French Ambassador that his invasion of France will be a 'rightful hand in a well-hallow'd cause' (H5 1.2.293) his 'hallow'd' makes it clear that he has a religious sense of the rightness of his cause.

RING[1]

(A) Wedding band. Though there are many symbolic rings mentioned in Shakespeare (as in AWW 3.2.57–8; ROM 3.3.163) and some that come extensively into play in the plots, there is only one sure reference to a wedding band.

(B) When the Priest in TN testifies to the wedding of Olivia and Sebastian (whom she still thinks to be Cesario), he says that their marriage was 'Strength'ned by interchangement of your rings' (TN 5.1.159). Engagement rings include Portia's to Bassanio (MV 3.2.311), Leah's to Shylock (MV 3.1.121–2) and Richard's to Lady Anne (R3 1.2.201).

(C) In the marriage service in the Elizabethan *Book of Common Prayer*, the rubrics dictate that 'the man shall give unto the woman a ring', and 'put it upon the fourth finger of the woman's left hand', saying, 'With this ring I thee wed' (292). Hooker explicitly defends the 'ringe', not only because it 'hath bene alwaies used as an especiall pledg of faith and fidelitie', but also because there is 'Nothing more fit to serve as a token of our purposed endlesse continuance in that which wee never ought to revoke' (V.73.6). On the Puritan opposition to the ring in the marriage ceremony, see Nicolson (2003), 53, 85

RING[2]

(A) 'Ring' also refers to the sounding of church bells on special civic and religious occasions, both joyful and mournful.

(B) At the recovery of the town of Orleans, Reignier says, 'Why ring not out the bells aloud throughout the town? / Dolphin, command the citizens make bonfires, / And feast and banquet in the open streets, / To celebrate the joy that God hath given us' (1H6 1.6.11–14). Henry IV tells his son Hal near the end of his life, 'And bid the merry bells ring to thine ear / That thou art crowned, not that I am dead' (2H4 4.5.111–12). When Lucius says of 'that ravenous tiger Tamora', 'No mournful bell shall ring her burial' (TIT 5.3.195–7), we hear of the customary ringing of funeral bells by its prescribed absence. 'The doleful knell' that 'rings out' in LUC (1495) sounds a metaphoric mourning of her loss of virginity. Benedick speaks more literally in ADO of the short time that 'the bell rings and the widow weeps' (ADO 5.2.79–80).

(C) See Cressy (1989), 67–92, on the inclusion of bells in 'the vocabulary of celebration' in Protestant England.

RITE

A ritual or formal religious observance.

Shakespeare uses this term literally of marriages and funerals, and metaphorically of sexual celebrations. Prospero warns the eager Ferdinand and Miranda not to 'break' Miranda's 'virgin-knot before / All **sanctimonious ceremonies** may / With full and **holy** rite be minist'red' (TMP 4.1.15–17). Romeo and Juliet are also in sexual haste, and so the Friar decides to 'perform the rite' quickly, make 'short work' of it, 'For by your leaves, you shall not stay alone / Till Holy **Church** incorporate two in one' (ROM 2.2.146; 2.6.35–7). 'The rites of marriage', 'the ceremonial rites of marriage', 'the holy rites', and 'our nuptial rites' all refer to the performance of the ceremony of holy matrimony' (JN 2.1.539; SHR 3.2.6; ADO 5.4.68; MV 2.9.6). The word 'rite' is sometimes associated figuratively with the sexual rather than the religious observance of love, as in Claudio's 'Time goes on crutches till love have all his rites' (ADO 2.1.357–8), and Bertram's 'great prerogative and rite of love' (AWW 2.4.41).

The 'funeral rite' is denied to Tamora in TIT (5.3.196), and Laertes complains of the politics that allowed 'no noble rite nor solemn **ostentation**' for his father, and only 'maim'd rites' for Ophelia (HAM 4.5.216; 5.1.219). She is 'allow'd her virgin crants, / Her maiden strewments, and the bringing home / Of bell and burial', but neither 'charitable prayers' nor a 'requiem' (HAM 5.1.230–7).

Henry V ordains celebratory religious rites after the great victory at Agincourt: 'Do we all holy rites: / Let there be sung *Non nobis* and *Te Deum*, / The dead with charity enclos'd in clay' (H5 4.8.122–4). In the classical worlds of JC and TIT, we also hear of having 'perform'd / Our Roman rites', of 'all true rites and lawful ceremonies', and 'all respects and rites of burial' (TIT 1.1.142–3; JC 3.1.241; 5.5.77). See **Roman**.

ROBE

(A) Sometimes an ecclesiastical garment. The Pope's robe was obviously a symbol of extravagance and superstitious show in Reformation England.

(B) When King Henry IV describes to his son Hal his effective manipulation of public opinion before his usurpation of Richard II's kingship, he compares his public 'presence' to a 'robe **pontifical**, / Ne'er seen but wond'red at' (1H4 3.2.56–9). Political and religious iconoclasm possibly merge in Henry V's later inclusion of 'The intertissued robe of gold and pearl' among the items of 'idol **Ceremony**' that he says dresses the kingship and often weighs it down. Both 'idol' and 'ceremony' here could suggest papal as well as royal dress (H5 4.1.240, 262). When Cardinal Wolsey says to his close associate (and successor) Cromwell near his death 'My robe, / And my integrity to heaven, is all / I dare now call my own' (H8 3.2.452–4), he speaks of his ecclesiastical garb.

(C) Nicolson (2003), 43, elaborately describes what he calls 'the uniform the Church required and which the Puritans loathed', which included the tippet, the elaborate episcopal surplice or rochet, the chimere, and the three- or four-cornered caps worn by divines and scholars.

ROD
(A) Straight, round stick used sometimes for flogging, and standing therefore as a symbol of authority and discipline. There are several biblical uses of the rod as a symbol of God's corrective and punitive power, as in Ps. 89.31–2: 'If they break my statutes, and keep not my commandments; Then will I visit their transgression with the rod, and their iniquity with stripes.'
(B) Shakespeare's usage usually pertains only to parental, schoolmasterly or political authority and discipline (as in MND 3.2.410; R2 5.1.32; LR 1.4.172–4; and MM 1.3.23–7). However, King Henry IV's usage is religious when he predicts a heavenly chiding of both himself and his prodigal son, who seems to him 'mark'd / For the hot vengeance, and the rod of heaven, / To punish my mistreadings' (1H4 3.2.9–11).
(C) Lam. 3.1 speaks of 'the rod of his wrath'. See Shaheen (1999), 417, and **chastise**.

ROMAN
(A) Of or associated with Rome, and sometimes Roman Catholicism.
(B) In phrases like 'Roman coin' (LLL 5.2.613), 'ancient Roman honor' (MV 3.2.395), 'Roman conqueror' (AYL 4.2.3), 'Roman disciplines' (H5 3.2.73), 'Roman state and territories' (COR 1.1.69; 4.6.40), etc., Roman refers to a heroic classical place and time. On the other hand, as Donne illustrates when he speaks of 'the *Protestant* against the *Romane Church*' (as in 4: 206), or of 'they of the Romane perswasion' and 'their Saints' (8: 329–31), phrases in Shakespeare like 'Roman rites', 'Roman gods' (TIT 1.1.143, 322; 4.2.6;), and 'all the gods that Romans bow before' (JC 2.1.320), could refer to Reformation claims about the Roman Catholics' praying to saints as though they were gods, their superstitious reverencing of religious iconography and statuary. Similarly, 'secret Romans' (JC 2.1.125) could suggest the secretive Jesuit plots against the Protestant establishment of England.
(C) Parker (1995) has suggested in relationship to JC that some apparently neutral references to Roman, like 'Roman Emperor' (TIT 5.1.157) or the 'Roman empire' (CYM 5.5.461), might also have reverberated with Reformation tensions.

ROME
(A) The **Roman** Catholic Church, and its authority as embodied in the Pope. Donne speaks of 'the Religion of Rome . . . in their superstitious errors' (8: 330), calls the Pope 'the Bishop of Rome' (5: 258; 3: 211), and actually uses 'Rome' as an eponym in 'a *Rome* of Superstition and Idolatry' (1: 245).
(B) 'Rome' is a controversial religious place-name in Shakespeare's history plays, especially in JN and H8, which both dramatise issues of papal versus kingly authority. In JN, Pandulph, 'the holy legate of the Pope' (JN 3.1.135), challenges 'Philip of France, on peril of a curse' to 'Let go the hand of that arch-heretic [King John], / And raise the power of France upon his head, / Unless he do submit himself to Rome' (JN 3.1.191–4). Here Rome is the centre of papal

authority, and Pandulph its representative on stage. Because King John was considered a proto-Reformer by some English Protestants, the English Reformation audience might have been disappointed after seeing him defy Rome for three acts to learn that King John 'hath reconcil'd / Himself to Rome, his spirit is come in' or that 'King John hath made / His peace with Rome' (JN 5.2 70, 92). In H8, 'Rome' is from Henry's point of view a place of 'dilatory sloth and tricks' (H8 2.4.237–8) designed to frustrate the king's desire to marry Anne Boleyn. Phrases like 'The court of Rome commanding' and 'whilst our commission from Rome is read' (H8 2.2.104; 2.4.1; 3.2.212–13) also cast Rome as heavily bureaucratic and authoritarian.

(C) *NDS* calls one precursor of Shakespeare's JN, Bale's *King Johan*, 'violently anti-Catholic' (3: 3). Burgoyne (1977) briefly analyses Rome (via Cardinal Pandulph) as the source of England's problems in JN.

ROOD

The cross of Christ or its representation, as in a crucifix.

All five of the references to the rood in Shakespeare occur in oaths; some are more seriously religious than others. Surely superficial is Justice Shallow's calling Justice Silence, 'An early stirrer, by the rood' (2H4 3.2.2–3), or the Nurse's 'by th' rood' (ROM 1.3.36). '[R]ood' might be taken with slightly more than a grain of religious salt in Hamlet's warning to his mother, 'No, by the rood, not so: / You are the Queen, your husband's brother's wife' (HAM 3.4.14–15) and in the Duchess of York's curse of her demonic son Richard III, 'No, by the holy rood, thou know'st it well, / Thou cam'st on earth to make the earth my hell' (R3 4.4.165–7). Stanley's use of the oath punctuates his dreadful sense that Hastings is not taking Richard seriously enough: 'You may jest on, but by the holy rood, / I do not like these several Councils, I' (R3 3.2.75–6). In two scenes, Hastings will die acknowledging his own foolish 'scorn' (R3 3.4.83) of supernatural things.

ROSEMARY

(A) This fragrant evergreen shrub is an emblem of immortality, traditionally strewn over corpses.

(B) Perdita knows of the natural side of this tradition that 'rosemary and rue . . . keep / Seeming and savor all the winter long' (WT 4.4.74–5). Friar Lawrence, a herbalist as well as a priest, mentions the funeral tradition when he says of first rites for the apparently dead Juliet, 'Dry up your tears, and stick your rosemary / On this fair corse' (ROM 4.5.79–80). Finally, when Edgar as Poor Tom speaks of seeing beggars' arms 'mortified' with 'sprigs of rosemary' (LR 2.3.15–16), we see this symbol of immortality used upon and against mortal flesh. Ophelia's 'rosemary . . . for remembrance' might also refer to this tradition (HAM 4.5.175).

(C) See *OED sb.* 1&2, which cites Bourne in Brand, *Pop. Antiq.* 1777, iii.29: 'The carrying of Ivy, or Laurel, or Rosemary, or some of those Ever-Greens [at funerals], is an Emblem of the Soul's Immortality'. See also BEV, 1014n.

RUE

(A) This bitter herb is probably associated with repentance both because of its inevitable association with the 'rue' that means regret (unrelated etymologically) and because repentance also has a bitter taste. 'Herb of grace' was possibly once a popular name for rue because of the idea that true repentance, however painful, was a gift of grace.

(B) The Gardener in R2 plants 'a bank of rue, sour herb of grace' (R2 3.4.105–6) where Richard II's Queen 'did fall a tear' for his 'news of woe'. Ophelia also calls the rue she gives to Gertrude and keeps for herself 'herb of grace a' Sundays' (HAM 4.5.180–3).

(C) See BEV, 1103n, RIV, 569n, and *OED* rue *sb.* 1&2; see also *OED* herb-grace.

SABA

Sheba. The Queen of Sheba journeyed a great distance to see Solomon because of her desire for wisdom (1 Kings 10).

Knowing this story, Archbishop Cranmer prophesies of the infant Elizabeth at her baptism that 'Saba was never / More covetous of wisdom and fair virtue / Than this poor soul shall be' (H8 5.4.23–5).

SABBATH (SABAOTH)

Seventh day of the week, the day appointed for rest for the Israelites and the day of Jewish worship. It can also refer to Sunday, the traditional Christian day of worship. As Whitgift says, 'The sabbath-day mentioned by Ambrose and Augustine is not the "Lord's day," which we call the Sunday, and whereof both Ignatius and Tertullian speak; but it is the Saturday, which is called *Sabbatum*' (1851–53), 1: 228; Bullinger explains, 'They of the primitive church, therefore, did change the sabbath-day, lest, peradventure, they should have seemed to have imitated the Jews, and still to have retained their order and ceremonies; and made their assemblies and holy restings to be on the first day of the sabbaths, which John calleth Sunday, or the Lord's day, because of the Lord's glorious resurrection upon that day' (1: 259–60).

Linking the Jewish Sabbath and his own revenge, Shylock tells the Duke of Venice, 'by our holy Sabaoth have I sworn / To have the due and forfeit of my bond' (MV 4.1.36–7). Hastings uses the word of the Christian day of worship: 'I thank you, good Sir John, with all my heart. / I am in debt for your last exercise; / Come the next Sabbath, and I will content you' (R3 3.2.109–11). Hastings will not live long enough to deliver the promised offering.

See Milward (1978), 44–7, on sabbatarian disputes between Anglicans and Puritans.

SACRAMENT

(A) Hooker is right when he says that 'Sacramentes, by reason of theire mixt nature, are more diverslie interpreted and disputed of then anie other parte of religion.' Even the most basic and oft-repeated Augustinian definition, 'a visible **sign** of an invisible **grace**', is not completely without controversy. Fortunately, Shakespeare's characters only use the word 'sacrament' to refer to one of them, holy communion; also, only once does 'sacrament' refer to the controversies themselves, and that only generally. Basically, the controversies concerned the number and the nature of the sacraments. The **Roman** Catholic Church held that there were seven sacraments – **baptism**, the **mass**, **confirmation**, **penance**, extreme **unction**, ordination and **marriage**; the Protestants held that there were only two, baptism and communion. 'Communion' itself is of course a controversial word, its various names, among them the Sacrament, the Eucharist, the Mass, the Holy Communion, and the Lord's Supper, reflecting major differences of opinion within Christianity and within Protestantism about its form and substance. Among the issues were the appropriate language, Latin or a vernacular; the role of the **priest** in the re-enactment of Christ's **sacrifice** upon the **Altar**; the question of whether and how such a re-enactment occurred; who ate the bread; who drank the wine; whether, and how, these 'elements' of communion changed during the ceremony; whether, and how, these elements should be honoured during and after the service; what sorts of gestures should be made by the priest and the parishioners during the ceremony and what they signified. By the middle of the sixteenth century there were four main positions on the most essential of these matters. The Council of Trent reaffirmed 'transubstantiation', the idea that the bread became Christ's body and the wine his blood once the priest blessed it, as the official Roman Catholic position. Luther's position, which came to be called 'consubstantiation', was that the bread and the wine coexisted with the body and the blood after the consecration. The German Swiss Reformer Zwingli preferred to think of communion as a memorial rite, with no change in the elements. Calvin proposed a compromise called virtualism, also popular with many Anglican Reformers, in which the faithful received the power or virtue of the body and blood of Christ.

By Shakespeare's time, however, thoughtful middle-of-the road-Anglicans like Hooker, Andrewes and Donne had tired of these controversies. As Hooker once said, 'I wishe that men would more give them selves to meditate with silence what wee have by the sacrament, and lesse to dispute of the manner how', since 'this heavenlie foode is given for the satisfyinge of our emptie soules, and not for the exercisinge of our curious and subtle wittes' (V.67.3; V.67.4). The ingenious language of the Book of Common Prayer also embraces many of the possible 'readings' of Holy Communion in its juxtaposition of phrases like 'full, perfect, and sufficient sacrifice, oblation, and satisfaction for the sins of the whole world' and 'Do this in remembrance of me' (*BCP*, 263).

(B) Taking the sacrament is often associated in Shakespeare with taking a vow seriously or adding religious dimensions to a solemn promise. In AWW 'I'll take the sacrament on't' is Parolles' way of emphasizing his truthfulness, but his immediate addition of 'how and which way you will' refers to the controversial state of this memorial or mystery during the Reformation. Bertram, hardly a moral exemplum in the play, complains of this sane if also non-sectarian approach 'All's one to him. What a past-saving slave is this!' (AWW 4.3.136–9). The General of Bordeaux tells John Talbot, who is threatening the city, 'Ten thousand French have ta'en the sacrament / To rive their dangerous artillery / Upon no Christian soul but English Talbot' (1H6 4.2.28–30), and Louis the Dauphin of France says that he and many other disaffected nobles 'took the sacrament' to 'keep our faiths' 'firm and inviolable' against King John's abuses of their customary rights (JN 5.2.6–7). The same assumption applies to York's comment to his wife that 'A dozen of them have ta'en the sacrament, / And interchangeably set down their hands / To kill the King at Oxford' (R2 5.2.97–99). Cf. R2 4.1.328–9. When Richmond says at the end of R3, 'And then, as we have ta'en the sacrament, / We will unite the White Rose and the Red' (R3 5.5.18–19), he also promises to seal his sincerity with the Eucharistic act. Mowbray, who will later die on a crusade but whose hands are no cleaner than anyone else's in R2, says of his prior attempt on Gaunt's life, 'But ere I last receiv'd the sacrament, / I did confess it, and exactly begg'd / Your Grace's pardon' (R2 1.1.139–41). Confession to a priest was a common precursor to communion in the Catholic tradition of Mowbray's time.

(C) On 'What Is a Sacrament', see Augustine's *City of God*, X: 5; and *ST* III.60; on their 'Principal Effect, Which Is Grace', see *ST* III.62; 'Of the Number of the Sacraments', see *ST* III.65. See *Certaine Sermons*, 2nd tome, pp. 197–205, for the sermons of 'the worthy receiving and reverend esteeming of the Sacrament of the body and blood of Christ'. See also Hooker, V.57.5. On seven versus two sacraments, see Andrewes, 3: 81, 219, 348; and Donne, 8: 77; 9: 319. Donne like York above uses 'the sacrament' for 'communion' (as in 8: 331; 2: 258; 7: 332; 3: 132). See also **sacrifice**[1&3], **sanctify**. Bradshaw (2002), 172–204, discusses these issues during the Reformation. Cross and Livingstone (1997), 566–9, distinguish clearly among the most prominent positions during the sixteenth century. Diehl (1997), ch. 4, discusses Eucharistic controversies and revenge tragedies.

SACRED

(A) Hallowed, made holy by religious association, consecrated to a deity, safeguarded by religion. Andrewes in a sermon on the Gowrie Conspiracy calls kings, '*christus Domini*', saying of 'God's own express words, "Touch not Mine anointed" ', that the monarch is sacred because of the religious service that consecrated him: 'To the Sanctuary he goeth, . . . and from thence fetcheth this term of "the Lord's anointed," and . . . from that place it cometh, that maketh both their callings and persons sacred and holy: therefore not without sacrilege to be violated, nay not to be touched' (4: 32). However, Andrewes knows that this anointing is not a guarantee of grace or goodness in a king (4: 56–7, citing Isa. 45.1).

(B) It is therefore no surprise that when Richard II's sense of his divine right to rule England is persistently threatened by effective political rivals, the word 'sacred' is often used to evoke the supernatural foundations of his authority, as in phrases like 'our sacred blood', 'his sacred head', 'such a sacred king', 'the sacred handle of our sceptre' (R2 1.2.12; 3.3.9, 80; 5.2.30). However, because Richard has not lived up to his sacred heritage, what York calls the 'customary rights' that time has bestowed on him, the 'sacred blood' of his grandfather Edward can also be invoked against Richard. Richard may even have ordered the sacrilegious murder of his uncle Woodstock, who is called 'One vial full of Edward's sacred blood' (R2 1.2.12, 17). Richard finally deposes himself with the words 'With mine own tongue deny my sacred state' (R2 4.1.209; cf. R2 5.6.6). The Archbishop of Canterbury greets Henry V, 'God and his angels guard your sacred throne', though from his memory of Hal's unsteady past he quickly adds the warning note of scepticism: 'And make you long become it!' (H5 1.2.7–8). Joan of Arc asserts her own divine mission, 'For my profession's sacred from above' (1H6 1.2.114), and Henry VIII's Queen Katherine of Aragon tries to strengthen her position with her sensually distracted husband by reminding him that he is a 'sacred person' (H8 2.4.39–42). Wolsey also tries ineffectively to appeal to Henry's 'most sacred person' (H8 3.2.171–7), with the result that Archbishop Cranmer, who will become England's great Protestant leader, says at the infant Elizabeth's christening that she will 'from the sacred ashes of her honor / . . . star-like rise as great in fame as she was, / And so stand fix'd' (H8 5.4.39–46).

In the comedies and the romances 'sacred' is used with greater variety. It metaphorically marks something that is precious in a romantic rather than a religious sense, like 'Sacred Silvia' (TGV 3.1.212; see also WT 1.2.76; SHR 1.1.176; TNK 5.1.165; LUC 1172). Duke Senior's 'Drops that sacred pity has engend'red' (AYL 2.7.121–3) seems to refer to tears evoked by funeral rites, but it could just mean deeply felt. When another Duke, disguised still as a friar, tells Isabella he will not be present at her accusation of Angelo because he is bound 'by a sacred vow' (MM 4.3.144), 'sacred' can mean solemn, sworn in God's name, or sworn by his holy order and profession. The 'sacred chastity' Angelo is accused of violating (MM 5.1.405), is similarly Isabella's religious vow of celibacy. Shylock's 'our sacred nation' (MV 1.3.48) can just mean revered and ancient, but it is also a nation of Jews, the chosen people of God. In WT, 'Sacred Delphos' refers to the site of the oracle they consult to test Hermione's chastity (WT 2.1.183), and 'Their sacred wills be done' (WT 3.3.7) refers to the apparently 'angry' 'heavens' (WT 3.3.4–7). Hermione blesses Perdita by asking 'You gods, look down / And from your sacred vials pour your graces / Upon my daughter's head!' (WT 5.3.121–3).

The usage of 'sacred' is less rich and frequent in the tragedies. In HAM 'sacred bands' (HAM 3.2.159–60) refers to holy marriage rites. When Macduff says that Duncan's remains will be 'Carried to Colmekill, / The sacred store-house of his predecessors / And guardian of their bones' (MAC 2.4.32–4), he speaks of an island holy for its reputation as the place where Christianity entered Scotland and as the resting-place for the bones of most of the Scottish kings.

(C) See **anointed** and **sacrilegious**. See also Andrewes, 4: 55–6; Donne, 8: 116. Willis (1992), 157–66, looks at the relationship between royalty and the sacred in MAC and PER.

SACRIFICE[1]

(A) A pre-Christian offering to a deity in the form of a slaughtered animal, person or possession. Andrewes says of this sort of sacrifice, 'Therefore had the heathens . . . their expiations for the guilt, by shedding of blood ever, . . . without which they held no remission of sins. The Jews, they likewise had their . . . slain sacrifice, the "blood" whereof done on their "posts", the destroyer passed by them, the guilt by it being first taken away'. 'But . . . the Apostle, he tells us, "it was impossible the blood of bulls or goats should satisfy for the sins of men" ' (3: 347). Donne says of the Mosaic Law and Christ, 'Before, under the Law, it was . . . In the bloud of Goats, and Bullocks; here it is *in sanguine ejus*, in his bloud' (4: 294). The Reformers mention this fairly often as a way of challenging the Roman Catholic assertion that the priest reenacts the sacrifice of Christ each time he makes Eucharist at the altar. That issue lies behind the reiterations in the Anglican liturgy that Christ's 'death upon the cross for our redemption' was 'a full, perfect, and sufficient sacrifice, oblation, and satisfaction for the sins of the whole world', 'once offered' for the remission of sins (*BCP*, 263).

(B) There are several explicit references in Shakespeare to pagan sacrifice, but none which necessarily evoke this controversial religious context. Caesar commands his servant, 'Go bid the priests do present sacrifice, / And bring me their opinions of success' (JC 2.2.5–6) as he is trying to decide whether to go forth to the senate chamber. When Aufidius lists former situations that would have prohibited him from an act of violence, two of them are 'The prayers of priests [and] times of sacrifice' (COR 1.10.21). Aeneas refers to a similar Grecian or Trojan custom when he says the exchange of prisoners must occur 'Ere the first sacrifice, within this hour' (TRO 4.2.64). Later in the same play, Cassandra says of Hector's heated vows, 'The gods are deaf to hot and peevish vows; / They are polluted off'rings, more abhorr'd / Than spotted livers in the sacrifice' (TRO 5.3.16–18). 'Why, sir, give the gods a thankful sacrifice' (ANT 1.2.161) is Enobarbus's 'light' but honest 'answer' to Antony's discovery that Fulvia, whom he no longer loves, is dead. Lucius mentions the 'entrails [which] feed the sacrificing fires' (TIT 1.1.144), and Cymbeline 'smok[ing] the temple with our sacrifices' (CYM 5.5.398; cf. 1.2.2). Lear reassures Cordelia after she loses the crucial battle against her sisters, 'Upon such sacrifices, my Cordelia, / The gods themselves throw incense' (LR 5.3.20–1). Othello, about to kill Desdemona and frustrated by her refusal to confess, accuses her of making him do 'A murther, which I thought a sacrifice' (OTH 5.2.65). This reference to 'a sacrifice' images Othello's regression to his pagan past even as he expresses his present Christian concern for Desdemona's immortal soul: 'I would not kill thy soul' (OTH 5.2.32).

Twice characters refer to Old Testament acts of sacrifice. The Bible makes it clear that Abel offered an animal sacrifice, 'the firstlings of his flock', which God accepted, and that Cain, a farmer, offered 'the fruit of the ground', which God, no vegetarian apparently, refused to accept (Gen. 4.4, 10). But though 'sacrificing Abel' (R2 1.1.104) must therefore refer to this successful ritual act, the blood that cries out for vengeance is also that of the sacrificed Abel, after Cain killed him in response to the divine disfavour. To rationalise his own oath-breaking to Warwick, Clarence refers less ambiguously to 'Jephthah when he sacrific'd his daughter' (3H6 5.1.91) as an example of a religious oath that should not have been kept.

(C) On the Eucharist as a memorial of this sacrifice once offered, see also Nowell (1853), 216, and *Certaine Sermons*, 198–203. Hager (1988) looks at human sacrifice in JC. O'Meara (1990) compares Othello's intended sacrifice of Desdemona to the Abraham-Isaac story in the Bible. Little (2000), 112–18 and 163–70, discusses sacrificial death in ANT. Girard (2002), 120–4, argues that Caesar's death is the ritual sacrifice around which JC revolves. McCoy (1997) suggests that sacrifice in the SON and in PHT only leads to martyrdom. Moschovakis (2002), 468–70, discusses sacrifice in TIT. See also **sacrifice**[3].

SACRIFICE[2]

(A) An act of prayer, thanksgiving or penitence offered as propitiation. Andrewes says of the Christians' threefold sacrifice, 'alms, prayer, and fasting', 'with such sacrifices God is pleased' (1: 381); elsewhere he also quotes 'the Church of England in her Reformed Liturgy' of the worshippers offering 'ourselves, our souls, and bodies to be a living sacrifice, holy and acceptable to God, which is our reasonable service of Him' (5: 266–7). Donne also speaks of 'the Sacrifice of Prayer' (3: 213).

(B) Nearing his execution in H8, Buckingham says to his remaining friends,

> Go with me like good angels to my end,
> And as the long divorce of steel falls on me,
> Make of your prayers one sweet sacrifice,
> And lift my soul to heaven.
>
> (H8 2.1.75–8)

(C) Aquinas characteristically understands 'sacrifice' as both 'outward' and 'inward' (*ST* II.2.85). So does Augustine (*City of God* X.6).

SACRIFICE[3]

(A) The thing or person sacrificed, sometimes suggesting Christ's offering of himself in the crucifixion. Andrewes says of Christ's 'sacrifice of Himself upon the cross', ' "the cross of Christ was the altar" of our Head, where he offered . . . "the only, true, proper sacrifice, propitiatory" for the sins of mankind, in which all other sacrifices are accepted, and applicatory of this propitiation' (5: 259). We notice again the Protestant emphasis that Christ's sacrifice is offered only once, on the cross, not each time the Eucharist is made.

(B) The usage of 'sacrifice' in Shakespeare is especially complex in MV. When Portia says 'I stand for sacrifice' (MV 3.2.57) as Bassanio peruses the three caskets, she may be advising Bassanio that the right choice is the sacrificial choice, the 'give and hazard' of the leaden casket rather than the 'get' of the silver and gold (MV 2.7.9, 16). She may also be comparing her role in the casket scheme to that of the sacrificial victim. Bassanio offers Antonio to 'sacrifice them all', 'life itself, my wife, and all the world', 'Here to this devil to deliver thee' (MV 4.1.284–7). Since Christ was sacrificed to deliver humankind from the clutches of the devil, both 'deliver' and 'sacrifice' can resonate here with religious overtones. Shylock's inexplicable longing for a pound of Antonio's flesh, like his finally being denied even 'one drop of Christian blood' (MV 4.1.310) as he compulsively tries to perform his own mysterious blood sacrifice on the Christ-like Antonio, adds more complexity to the mix of Christian, Jew, and 'sacrifice'.

(C) Guilfoyle (1985–86), discusses Desdemona as a sacrifice in OTH; Hassel (1980, 1987) discusses Shylock's frustrated communion in MV. See also **sacrifice**[1].

SACRIFICE[4] *fig.*
From defns. 1–3 above; sometimes a *v.*

Hotspur desperately asserts that the finely dressed forces of Prince Hal 'come like sacrifices in their trim' (1H4 4.1.113) to put a hopeful spin on the momentum of Hal's apparent Reformation. Beasts were apparently well dressed for blood sacrifice. The Chorus of H5 similarly compares his threatened troops the night before Agincourt to 'sacrifices [who] by their watchful fires / Sit patiently, and inly ruminate / The morning's danger' (H5 2 pr. 6; 4 pr. 23–5). Cf. Proteus's 'Say that upon the altar of her beauty / You sacrifice your tears, your sighs, your heart' (TGV 3.2.72–3). Orsino uses 'sacrifice' as a *v.* when, angry that his favourite Cesario has apparently married Olivia and therefore undermined his own marriage suit, he threatens to kill him/her: 'I'll sacrifice the lamb that I do love, / To spite a raven's heart within a dove' (TN 5.1.130–1).

SACRILEGIOUS
Describing the robbery or profanation of a sacred building, an outrage on a consecrated or **anointed** person, or more generally any violation of something **sacred**. Andrewes invokes 'God's own express words, "Touch not Mine anointed"' against killing kings, saying that their consecration in a 'Sanctuary', 'maketh both their callings and persons sacred and holy: therefore not without sacrilege to be violated, nay not to be touched' (4: 32). Donne says that 'in the Schooles we call Sedition and Rebellion, Sacriledge; for, though the trespasse seeme to be directed but upon a man, yet in that man, whose office (and consequently his person) is sacred, God is opposed, and violated' (8: 116).

Macduff describes his outrage upon discovering his murdered King Duncan's body to witnessing the forced entry into a consecrated sanctuary:

> Most sacrilegious murther hath broke ope
> The Lord's anointed temple, and stole thence
> The life o' th' building!
>
> (MAC 2.3.66–9)

Duncan's murder is here both the desecration of a holy building and the theft of whatever is most sacred in it; in a church it would be the consecrated Host. Posthumus similarly expresses his fury at Jachimo's slander of his wife Imogen and his own painful complicity in her death by comparing himself to 'A sacrilegious thief' 'That kill'd thy daughter' and Imogen to 'The temple / Of virtue' (CYM 5.5.217–21).

SACRING

(A) The sacring bell is the bell rung during the most sacred portion of the Catholic mass, the consecration of the Host.

(B) In an imagined vignette as vivid as any moment in Robert Browning's monologues about Renaissance Church figures, Surrey compares catching Cardinal Wolsey in an act of political treachery to catching him in the arms of a wench in the middle of a mass in which he should be participating, even officiating: 'I'll startle you / Worse than the sacring bell, when the brown wench / Lay kissing in your arms, Lord Cardinal' (H8 3.2.294–6).

(C) Hooper (1852), 2: 127–8 and Ridley (1841), 319, both warn against the 'ringing of the sacring-bell' as 'Popish'. See also Grindal (1843), 159, and Becon, 3: 270.

SAINT[1] *sb.*

(A) The title of a person canonised by the Catholic Church as exceptionally holy, as in 'Saint Clare'.

(B) Almost half of the 117 references to 'Saint' in Shakespeare serve as the prefix to a specific saint's name. St George, the patron saint of England, is predictably the most popular of these, with close to twenty references. These saint's names often merely designate a church, a tavern, a town, a field, or a date in the Church year. Several are also sworn by, as in 'by Saint Paul' or 'By Saint Jamy' (R3 3.4.76; SHR 3.2.82). The 33 saints Shakespeare names individually include, alphabetically, **Albon** Anne, **Bennet**, **Charity**, **Clare**, **Colme**, **Crispian**, **Cupid**, **Davy**, **Denis**, **Edmundsbury**, **Francis**, **George**, Gregory, Jamy, **Jaques**, Jeronimy, John, **Katherine**, **Lambert**, Lawrence Poultney, **Luke**, **Magnus**, **Martin**, **Mary**, **Michael**, **Nicholas**, **Patrick**, **Paul**, **Peter**, **Philip**, **Steven**, and **Valentine**.

The individual saints are most often invoked for protection or assistance (for the appropriateness of the saint to the request, see each individual item), as in TGV 3.1.300; R3 5.3.270; H5 3.1.34. They can also be the destination or focal point of a pilgrimage, like Helena's pretended one 'to Saint Jaques le grand', Santiago de Compostela in Spain (AWW 3.5.34); however, 'at the Saint Francis here beside the port' (AWW 3.5.36) refers to an inn rather than a shrine. Saints can be referred to as objects of worship, as in 'thou worshippest Saint Nicholas as truly as a man of falsehood may' (1H4 2.1.64–5), though here the veneration comes from St Nicholas's popular association with thieves.

(C) Hooker says against Puritan objections, 'Of the names whereby wee distinguish our Churches', 'Touchinge the names of Angels and Sainctes whereby the most of our Churches are called; as the custome of so naminge them is verie ancient [it is not] . . . at this present hurtefull, [since] as oft as those buildinges came to be mentioned, the name should put men in minde of some memorable thinge or person. [This does not mean] 'that those places which were denominated of Angels and sainctes should serve for the worship of so glorious creatures . . . for defense protection and patronage of such places. A thinge which the ancient do utterly disclaime' (V.13.1–2). Vanita (2000) argues that the memory of female saints is a powerful force in WT and H8.

SAINT² *sb.*

(A) The generic noun for a canonised person.

The worship of the saints was a particularly controversial (and confusing) subject during the Reformation, when both their naming and their invocation were officially discouraged but often personally practised. Donne, e.g., says critically of prayers to saints, '[W]hy should I pray to *S. George* for victory, when I may goe to the Lord of Hosts, Almighty God himselfe'? (4: 311), yet he speaks easily of 'Saint *Paul*' and others as authorities on theological matters (6: 197; 1: 285), and in fact once speaks 'of the prayers of the Saints in heaven for us' (5: 360). Andrewes is even more enthusiastic, calling heaven 'even the "inheritance of the Saints in light" ' (3:372), and speaking of 'God's saints that pray for us with all instancy' (5: 339). Luther repeatedly teases his parishioners who would idolatrously 'hie yourself to St. Iago', 'run to St. Iago', 'go to St. Iago or to Rome': 'it is in vain. . . . It is the greatest tragedy that we will go in quest of all this after we have thrust Christ aside.'

(B) Thus, when the Pope's representative Pandulph promises canonization to anyone who 'takes away by any secret course' King John's life, says indeed that he shall be 'Canonised and worshipp'd as a saint' (JN 3.1.177–8), he is treading on both English and Protestant toes. Similarly controversial would have been the Bastard's promise to Joan of Arc, 'We'll set thy statue in some holy place, / And have thee reverenc'd like a holy saint' (1H6 3.3.14–15). On the other hand, it is probably less troublesome when a heroic Englishman like Richmond assures his troops before the Battle of Bosworth Field that 'prayers of holy saints and wronged souls' protect them 'Like high-rear'd bulwarks' (R3 5.3.241–2), or when Margaret asserts against Richard III that 'saints pray / To have him suddenly convey'd from hence' (R3 4.4.75–6).

(C) For other examples of Luther's criticism of praying (and going) to Santiago, see LW 23: 24, 43, 121, 178, 179, 263; on what Luther considers the analogous Marian 'idolatry', see LW 22: 37, 165; 23: 57, 59, 104, 123, 137. See also 'Mariology', *OxfordEncyRef*, 3: 10–14.

SAINT³ *sb.*

A good person, often a member of the Christian Church; sometimes one of the Puritan elect. Andrewes calls the Church 'the public place whither the saints of God from time to time assemble themselves to call upon God together' (5: 357).

The 'precise' and Puritan-like Angelo refers to the devil, his own weakness, and Isabella's tempting attractiveness with 'O cunning enemy, that to catch a saint, / With saints dost bait thy hook!' (MM 2.2.179–81). For his conceit to work, Isabella must be both the figurative saint (**saint⁶**) of romantic metaphor and the 'saint' (**saint**[3]) as a chosen one of God, the saint Angelo thought himself to be until this moment of temptation and fall.

SAINT[4] *sb.*

A representation of a saint in art, like sculpture or painting. Becon says of such representations of saints, 'What a garnishing of the Church is this, to see a sort of puppets standing in every corner of the Church, some holding in their hands a **sword**, some a sceptre, some a spit, some a butcher's knife, some a gridiron, some a pair of pinsons, some a spear, some an anchor of a ship, some a shoemaker's cutting-knife, some a shepherd's hook, some a **cross**, . . . some weeping, some laughing, some gilded, some **painted**, some housed, some unhoused, some rotten, some worm-eaten, . . . some **naked**, . . . some with **holy water** sprinkled, some with flowers and garlands garnished, &c.' (2: 65).

Richard II refers to the sculptural tradition when he promises to trade 'My subjects for a pair of carved saints' as he imagines himself deposed and in a hermitage (R2 3.3.152).

SAINT[5] *v.*

To act virtuously.

In PP we find this odd usage: 'Think women still to strive with men, / To sin and never for to saint' (PP 18.44).

SAINT[6] *fig.*

A romantic metaphor.

When Valentine asks Proteus about his Sylvia 'Is she not a heavenly saint?' Proteus twice corrects him for the excess of both this love and this comparison. Just before this reference, he asks Valentine, 'Was this the idol that you worship so?' Just after, he answers Valentine's question, 'No; but she is an earthly paragon' (TGV 2.4.144–6). Portia is similarly referred to by the Catholic Prince of Aragon as 'this shrine, this mortal breathing saint' (MV 2.7.40). Contrasting the forgiving, charitable religious saints to the more disdainful ones of Petrarchan tradition, Richard of Gloucester tells a reluctant but also praying Lady Anne, 'Sweet saint, for charity, be not so curst' (R3 1.2.49). Romeo tries to get a first kiss by styling Juliet as the saint and himself as her prayerful pilgrim: 'O then, dear saint, let lips do what hands do'; later, when she seems to have cursed his name of Montague, he agrees: 'My name, dear saint, is hateful to myself' (ROM 1.5.103; 2.2.55). Speakers in Shakespeare are also fond of the combination of saint and devil or the like, as when SON 144.7 finds within a romantic metaphor the paradox 'would corrupt my saint to be a devil'. Lucrece is 'This earthly saint, adored by this devil' Tarquin (LUC 84). Juliet, perplexed by the news that Romeo has murdered Tybalt, names him 'a damned saint, an honorable villain!' (ROM 3.2.79).

SAINTED

Holy or pious; sacred; saint-like.

Macduff, distressed at Malcolm's (false) admission of sinfulness, recalls 'Thy royal father' as 'a most sainted king', and 'the queen that bore thee, / Oft'ner upon her knees than on her feet' (MAC 4.3.108–10). The second detail, of the queen's obvious **piety**, suggests the gloss for the first. When Leontes calls his wife Hermione, still assumed dead, a 'sainted spirit', he may mean both just dead and extremely virtuous (WT 5.1.57). Helena's letter to her mother-in-law describes her imaginary pilgrimage to Santiago as one taken 'With sainted vow my faults to have amended' (AWW 3.4.7). She could mean here that her vow is directed to a saint, Jaques, or that the promise itself is sacred. Lucio teases the novice Isabel when he says 'I hold you as a thing enskied and sainted, / By your renouncement an immortal spirit, / And to be talk'd with in sincerity, / As with a saint' (MM 1.4.34–8).

SAINT-LIKE
Like a saint.

Characters in Shakespeare associate 'saint-like' with 'meekness', 'sorrow', 'pensiveness', 'patience' in 'suffering', and 'an humble gait' (H8 2.4.139; WT 5.1.2; LUC 1497, 1505, 1508). Henry VIII's virtuous Queen, Katherine of Aragon, reminds the 3rd Gentleman of the traditional iconography of saints:

> At length her Grace rose, and with modest paces
> Came to the altar, where she kneel'd, and saint-like
> Cast her fair eyes to heaven, and pray'd devoutly.
> (H8 4.1.82–4)

SALVATION
(A) Saving of the soul, deliverance from the consequences of sin, and admission into the joys of heaven.

(B) Hamlet decides not to kill Claudius whilst he is at prayer, but rather 'When he is drunk asleep, or in his rage / Or in th' incestuous pleasure of his bed, / At game a-swearing, or about some act / That has no relish of salvation in't' (HAM 3.3.86–92). Portia's argument that Shylock show mercy to Antonio and forgive him the pound of flesh he is justly owed centres on her distinction between salvation by grace and salvation by **works**, God's **mercy** versus God's **justice**:

> Therefore Jew,
> Though justice be thy plea, consider this,
> That in the course of justice, none of us
> Should see salvation.
> (MV 4.1.197–200)

When the Gravedigger in *Hamlet* says that Ophelia 'willfully seeks her own salvation' (HAM 5.1.2), he probably means damnation (HAM 5.1.227), because if she willed her own suicide she may wilfully have damned herself. The cynic Parolles may be flippant about the word 'salvation' (AWW 4.3.278–9), but he understands its theological implications: 'Sir, for a cardecue he will sell the fee-simple of his salvation, the inheritance of it'. 'Fee-simple' and 'entail' both refer to provisions in English property law for 'absolute and perpetual possession'. Parolles is saying, therefore, that for two shillings, the approximate value of this French coin, he will sell not only his own salvation but also that of all of his heirs. The priest and the people use a similar metaphor during Communion when they give thanks that their receiving of 'the most precious body and blood of thy Son our Saviour Jesus Christ' will make them 'heirs through hope of thy everlasting kingdom' (*BCP*, 265). When Prince Hal says of his tavern friends in 1H4 that 'they take it upon their salvation' that he will always be their friend (1H4 2.4.9–15), he is metaphorically referring to the doctrine of **grace** over that of **merit**, and implying their presumption of his grace in the process.

(C) See *Certaine Sermons*, pp. 13–21, for the sermons of 'the salvation of man-kinde, by only Christ our Saviour'. See Sokol and Sokol (2000): 'fee-simple'; 'entail'.

SALVE (SALVING)

Apply (applying) a healing ointment. *OED v.* 2.a & 2.b illustrate the two *fig.* usages in Shakespeare, to heal some sin or spiritual malady and to heal a person so afflicted.

The mortified Dumain asks for 'Some salve for perjury' (LLL 4.3.285); the speaker of SON 35 complains that excusing his beloved's sins against him is 'Myself corrupting, salving thy amiss' (7).

SAMSON

Samson is described in Judges 16 as the physically strong man who was tempted by Delilah to reveal the secret of his strength, his long hair, and thus betray himself.

LLL speaks the most of Samson's strength and weakness. Moth says of him (from Judges 16.3) that 'he carried the town gates on his back like a porter; and he was in love'. Armado the schoolteacher replies, 'O well-knit Sampson, strong-jointed Sampson' (LLL 1.2.71–3). The French Duke of Alanson uses 'Samsons and Goliases' to stress the strength and greatness of the English soldiers (1H6 1.2.30, 33).

(C) See Judges 14–16; 1 Sam. 17.4, 10; and Shaheen (1999), 286.

SANCTIFY[1] (*adj.* sanctified)

To bless or make sacred in a ceremony like baptism, communion, consecration, ordination, or by holy use; this can be said of a person, a place, or an object. Vaux says that the Holy Ghost 'sanctifieth us by the holy **Sacramentes**' (1590a, *sig.* A6^v), and Donne calls 'holy ones' those 'enrolled in the Church, by that initiatory Sacrament of Baptisme', but asserts 'a sanctification in a worthy receiving of the other Sacrament too' (9: 319). Donne says of a church building, 'His house is *Sanctum Sanctorum*, The holiest of holies, and you make it onely *Sanctuarium*; It should be a place sanctified by your devotions' (7: 318).

Parolles's cynical comment that virgins, like suicides, should be 'buried in highways out of all sanctified limit' (AWW 1.1.139–40) distinguishes consecrated or blessed places from unholy, totally secular ones. Henry IV refers figuratively to the ceremonial act when he complains to his apparently wayward son Prince Hal, 'Let all the tears that should bedew my hearse / Be drops of balm to sanctify thy head' (2H4 4.5.113–14). With 'crown up the verse, / And sanctify the numbers' (TRO 3.2.183), Troilus speaks metaphorically of making the metre right.

SANCTIFY[2] (*adj.* sanctified)
Make holy or pious.

When a nun is referred to as a 'sister sanctified, of holiest note' (LC 233), 'sanctified' refers to both her piety and the religious ceremony (**sanctified**[1]) which made her a consecrated person. Polonius negatively compares Hamlet's love-vows to Ophelia to 'mere implorators of unholy suits, / Breathing like sanctified and pious bonds [bawds BEV] / The better to beguile' (HAM 1.3.129–31); their hypocrisy impersonates holiness. Adam similarly calls Orlando's 'virtues' 'sanctified and holy traitors' in a world that despises 'what is comely' (AYL 2.3.12–15).

SANCTIFY[3] (*adj.* sanctified)
Make legitimate by religious sanction.

When King Henry IV promises God that if they win at Gaultree Forest then their next action will be in the crusades, where they shall 'draw no swords but what are sanctified' (2H4 4.4.4), he refers to swords or actions which have received the formal blessing of the Church (**sanctify**[1]) and to a cause that has religious sanction.

SANCTIFY[4] (*adj.* sanctified)
(A) Named as or included among the saints.
(B) Desdemona's 'So help me every spirit sanctified' (OTH 3.4.126) says something like 'so help me [God]' to the blessed spirits of heaven, the angels and the saints.
(C) See *ST* III.27 on 'the Sanctification of the Blessed Virgin'.

SANCTITY
(A) Holiness of life, piety, purity, saintliness; also the mysterious powers deriving from these qualities.
(B) The Doctor illustrates both sides of this definition when he describes Edward the Confessor's power to cure scrofula, 'the king's evil', with his touch: 'but at his touch, / Such sanctity hath heaven given his hand, / They presently amend' (MAC 4.3.143–5). When Toby Belch asks after the gulled and apparently mad Malvolio, 'Which way is he, in the name of sanctity?' he adds, 'If all the devils of hell be drawn in little, and Legion himself possess'd him, yet I'll speak to him' (TN 3.4.84–6). Without the second sentence, his usage of 'sanctity' is no more than a casual oath; with it, Toby is invoking, however hypocritically, both his own saintliness and the saints themselves in holy opposition to demonic possession.

Antigonus describes Hermione's ghost, who appeared to him in a dream in 'pure white robes', as 'Like very sanctity' (WT 3.3.22–3). Here simile and the literal almost merge; he thinks he has seen sanctity itself, a very saint; even if he has not (she is not actually dead, though only Shakespeare, Paulina and Hermione know it at this moment), what he sees is almost the same thing, the image of holiness. The nun Thaisa, just recovered from apparent death, and miraculously reunited with her husband Pericles, says upon seeing him, 'O let me look! / If he be none of mine, my sanctity / Will to my sense bend no licentious ear, / But curb it, spite of seeing' (PER 5.3.28–31). As a nun, a wife, and a holy woman besides, she is vowing not to be seduced from either marriage or religious vows by what she so desperately wants to see, her husband alive. But this is a world of romance and miracles, and so at the end she can be true to all of these holy things. Finally, Rosalind speaks figuratively of the purity and holiness of Orlando's interest in her by saying 'his kissing is as full of sanctity as the touch of holy bread' (AYL 3.4.13–14).

(C) Greenblatt (2001), 200–4, comments on the complex reality of Hermione's 'ghost'.

SANCTIMONIOUS

Making a show of sanctity or piety. Today this is usually pejorative, suggesting hypocritical or at least excessive show, but in Shakespeare's usage it can be either positive or negative.

Thus, when Prospero refers to the 'sanctimonious ceremonies' which must precede any sex between Miranda and Ferdinand, he speaks of the 'full and holy rite' of marriage that 'must be minister'd' before Ferdinand 'dost break her virgin knot' (TMP 4.1.15–17), not something false or ostentatious. On the other hand, when the cynical Lucio speaks of the 'the sanctimonious pirate, that went to sea with the Ten Commandements, but scrap'd one out of the table', 'Thou shalt not steal' (MM 1.2.7–10), he is obviously referring to some sort of religious hypocrisy.

SANCTIMONY[1]

Personal holiness; religious sincerity.

When the Lord describes the 'most austere sanctimony' with which Helena accomplished her pilgrimage to Santiago (AWW 4.3.48–50), he probably means either that she performed it well or that she undertook it with religious devotion. A pathetic Troilus, trying to deny what he has just seen, Cressida promising to meet Diomedes that night in his tent, says 'If souls guide vows, if vows be sanctimonies, / If sanctimony be the gods' delight, / . . . This was not she' (TRO 5.2.139–42).

SANCTIMONY[2]

The blessings of a religious service, like that of matrimony.

Both meanings of **sanctimony** pertain when Iago vows to Roderigo, 'If sanctimony and a frail vow betwixt an erring barbarian and a super-subtle Venetian be not too hard for my wits and all the tribe of hell, thou shalt enjoy her' (OTH 1.3.355–8).

SANCTUARY[1] *sb.*
A church within which someone can seek protection from civil authorities. Donne says of the Church building – 'It should be a place sanctified by your devotions, and you make it onely a Sanctuary to priviledge Malefactors' (7: 318).

Arcite refers literally to the Church when he tells Palamon that he would speak out anywhere in his friend's defence: 'your silence / Should break out, though i' th' sanctuary' (TNK 3.1.61–2). When Queen Elizabeth says in 3H6, 'I'll hence forthwith unto the sanctuary, / To save, at least, the heir of Edward's right; / There shall I rest secure from force and fraud' (3H6 4.4.31–3), she also refers literally to the safety of a church building, though implicitly she invokes the right to protection that is associated with the word (**sanctuary**[2]).

SANCTUARY[2]
(A) The protection the Church affords (*sb.*); also said of those seeking protection (*adj.*). Philpot, defending himself against judgement in the wrong diocese, says that it is wrong to think that 'a sanctuary man, being by force brought forth of his place of privilege, doth thereby lose his privilege, but always may challenge the same wheresoever he be brought' (1842), 71–2.
(B) Queen Elizabeth, fearing the dangers from Richard of Gloucester to her two sons and heirs to the crown of Edward IV, tells her younger son 'Come, come, my boy, we will to sanctuary' (R3 2.4.49, 51, 66). According to Holinshed (quoted in *NDS*, 3: 257) as soon as Elizabeth heard the 'heavy tidynges' that Rivers, Grey and Vaughan had been imprisoned: 'she and all her chyldren and compaignie were registered for sanctuarye persons'. Buckingham soon informs Richard and Prince Edward: 'The Queen your mother and your brother York / Have taken sanctuary' (R3 3.1.27–8). During a debate on the appropriateness of sanctuary for two innocent children, the Cardinal first briefly demurs, 'God in heaven forbid / We should infringe the holy privilege / Of blessed sanctuary! Not for all this land / Would I be guilty of so deep a sin' (R3 3.1.27–8). Buckingham's 'You break not sanctuary in seizing him': 'Oft have I heard of sanctuary men, / But sanctuary children, never till now' (R3 3.1.47, 55–6) persuades him otherwise, and within an act the children have been smothered in the Tower, and Richard has become king (cf. R3 4.1.93). Cf. ERR 5.1.94–5; COR 1.10.19–24.
(C) See Sokol and Sokol (2000), 333–39. See also Baker (1990), 8–13.

SANCTUARY[3] *fig.*
Angelo, overwhelmed with lust for the novice Isabella, imagines a field of battle in which the Church building as well as Isabella's chastity which should be protected by it have both been razed to the ground, and replaced by the pitched or erected tents of a desire which destroys both camps at once: 'Shall we desire to raze the sanctuary / And pitch our evils there?' (MM 2.2.170–1).

SANCTUARIZE
Afford protection.

Claudius, agreeing with Laertes's resolution 'To cut [Hamlet's] throat i' th' church', responds 'No place indeed should murther sanctuarize, / Revenge should have no bounds' (HAM 4.7.126–8). He means that to a revenger, not even a church should afford protection for a murderer. The syntax is morally ambiguous because a revenger is a murderer in a Christian context, but not in a Senecan one.

SANCTUS
See **sacring**.

SARACENS
Arabs or Muslims during the time of the Crusades. More generally, any 'others', especially unbelievers and evildoers. Becon says with some charity, 'A preacher of the Lord's word is bound to do good unto all men; not only to such as be of the household of faith, but also to Turks, Jews, Saracens, and such other miscreants' (1: 22).

Mowbray is said, with his own age's sense of political correctness, to have gone to fight 'For Jesu Christ in glorious Christian field, / Streaming the ensign of the Christian cross / Against black pagans, Turks, and Saracens' (R2 4.1.93–5).

SATHAN
(A) Satan. One of the legion of names for Lucifer, the arch-enemy of God and all goodness, and the chief tempter of humankind. Also his representation in the mystery plays. Satan's chief sin was pride.

(B) Prince Hal calls Falstaff 'That villainous, abominable misleader of youth, Falstaff, thou old white-bearded Sathan' (1H4 2.4.462–3), suggesting both the **Tempter** and the bearded **Vice** character in the miracle and morality plays. He has just called Falstaff 'That reverent Vice, that grey **Iniquity**' (1H4 2.4.453–4). Ford also refers to Falstaff as 'one that is as slanderous as Sathan' (WIV 5.5.155). Pinch the conjurer tries to conjure Satan out of Antipholus of Ephesus: 'I charge thee, Sathan, hous'd within this man, / To yield possession to my holy prayers, / And to thy state of darkness hie thee straight' (ERR 4.4.54–6; see also ERR 4.3.48–50, and **devil**). With similar zeal but more artifice, Feste, disguised as Sir Topas the Curate, pretends to conjure the devil (and his preoccupation with Olivia) out of the possibly mad and certainly prideful Malvolio: 'Fie, thou dishonest Sathan!' (TN 4.2.31). Sir Toby has also charged Malvolio with a dangerous dalliance with the devil, 'to play at cherry-pit [a child's game] with Sathan', and Olivia has called him 'sick of self-love' (TN 3.4.116; 1.5.90). Cf. AWW 53.260–1.

(C) See Andrewes, 2: 409; Donne, 9: 400.

SATISFIED

(A) Satisfaction, in theology, refers to Christ's atonement for the sins of humankind, from the term for the payment of debt or the fulfilment of obligation; being satisfied, therefore, is having forgiven a debt, theological or monetary. Nowell, stressing the Protestant position that humans could not 'merit **pardon** for our sins', says, 'There is no mercy due to our merits, but God doth yield and remit to Christ his correction and punishment that he would have done upon us. For Christ alone, with sufferance of his pains, and with his death, wherewith he hath paid and performed the penalty of our sins, hath satisfied God. Therefore by Christ alone we have access to the grace of God' (1853), 176.

(B) When Proteus asks Valentine to '**forgive**' him, contiguous words like '**ransom**', and '**paid**' emphasise the analogy between wrongs committed and forgiven in religion, friendship and romance. He adds: 'Who by **repentance** is not **satisfied** / Is nor of heaven nor earth, for these are pleas'd; / By **penitence** th' **Eternal**'s **wrath**'s appeas'd' (TGV 5.4.74–81).

(C) See also Tyndale, 1: 260; Andrewes, 3: 347; Hooker, 'Of Satisfaction' (VI.5.2); and Donne, 9: 120. Vaux (1590a), *sig.* G6ᵛ, illustrates the Catholic usage of 'satisfaction' as a word for the penitential act.

SAVE¹ (often **SAV'D**)

'Save' can refer to the result of Christ's redemptive death on the cross, where as Saviour he delivered sinful humankind from the wrath of God. The word receives additional emphasis during the Reformation because of the question of salvation by faith or grace versus salvation by merit or works. Andrewes says of 'this freedom of Christ' (from John 8.36), 'He only is able perfectly to save us out of the thraldom of Satan' (5: 454).

The drunken Cassio uses this 'sav'd' four times in succession in a conversation with Iago: 'Well, God's above all; and there be souls must be sav'd, and there be souls must not be sav'd'. 'I hope to be sav'd'. 'The lieutenant is to be sav'd before the ancient' (OTH 2.3.102–10). Desdemona responds similarly to Othello's 'What, not a whore?', 'No, as I shall be sav'd' (OTH 4.2.86). When the Princess complains to the Forester that he has overpraised her beauty, she cleverly refers to this theological issue: 'See, see, my beauty will be sav'd by merit. / O heresy in fair, fit for these days!' (LLL 4.1.21). Why should someone who is merely born beautiful, or someone who has been saved by grace, receive credit for it? Falstaff also concedes the theological possibility that men are not saved by merit when he flippantly condemns Poins for his misdeeds: 'O, if men were to be sav'd by merit, / What hole in hell were hot enough for him?' (1H4 1.2.107–8). Clarence, pleading for his life to the two murderers sent by his brother Richard III, futilely asserts a more works-based argument when he tells them to 'Relent, and save your souls' (R3 1.4.256), because 'the great King of kings / Hath in the table of his law commanded / That thou shalt do no murther' (R3 1.4.195–7). 'Save' can also occur as part of a mild emphasising oath (*OED v.* 2.b). The Hostess says 'so God save me law!' (2H4 2.1.155); Macmorris's repeated 'so **Chrish** [or Christ] save me, law' (as in H5 3.2.92, 105, 113) is a more casual expression of the same usage.

SAVE[2]

Protect, as asked of God, the angels or human intercessors. Andrewes praises God, 'How often hast Thou rid us from plague, freed us from famine, saved us from the sword, from our enemies compassing us around, from the fleet that came to make us no more a people!' (4: 339–40).

Hamlet, frightened by the second appearance of the ghost of his father, invokes angelic protection with 'Save me, and hover o'er me with your wings, / You heavenly guards!' (HAM 3.4.103–4). Since he has already expressed fear that the ghost 'Abuses me to damn me' (HAM 2.2.603), he must be speaking of spiritual as well as physical protection. When Isabella, having turned down her brother's understandable but also repulsive request that she save his life by laying down her own precious virginity, promises 'prayers for thy death, / No word to save thee' (MM 3.1.145–6), she is declining to intervene for him spiritually. She has just earlier virtually proclaimed his reprobation: 'Thy sin's not accidental but a trade. / Mercy to thee would prove itself a bawd' (MM 3.1.148–9).

SAVE[3]

Part of a frequent, often merely formulaic phrase of greeting, farewell, or emphasis like 'God save you, sir (or madam)' (as in WIV 2.2.154; LLL 5.2.716; HAM 2.2.221), 'Save you, sir' or 'Save your honor' (as in COR 4.4.6; MM 2.2.161). A similar formula, as in 'God save the King (or Queen)', blesses nobility (as in R2 4.1.172, 174, 220; R3 4.4.94; MAC 1.2.47). See *OED v.* 3.a & 3.b. In a few instances the response to the usage indicates an awareness of its religious component. Richard II, during his deposition scene, laments the lack of a traditional response: 'God save the King! Will no man say amen? / Am I both priest and clerk? Well then, amen. / God save the King! although I be not he, / And yet amen, if heaven do think him me' (R2 4.1.172–5). He later blesses the new king, however ironically: 'God save King Henry, unking'd Richard says, / And send him many years of sunshine days!' (R2 4.1.220–1). More flippantly, Falstaff first carelessly greets Prince Hal with 'God save thy grace', then hears the religious dimensions of the phrase and amends it to 'Majesty, I should say, for grace thou wilt have none'. To Prince Hal's 'What, none?' Falstaff's relentless wit connects this 'grace' to the blessing of meals: 'No, by my troth, not so much as will serve as to be prologue to an egg and butter' (1H4 1.2.17–21). First seeming to declare that Hal is devoid of all grace, that is, a reprobate, Falstaff backs off to the milder insult that he has never heard a blessing even long enough for such a small meal. In many other occasions like 'God save you, brother', followed by 'And you, fair sister', or 'God save thee!' then 'And you sir' (AYL 5.2.17–18; TN 3.4.218–19), only the actor can reveal whether or not the response sounded like a liturgical exchange.

SAVIOUR

'Our Saviour' is Christ the redeemer.

Marcellus the watch, speaking to the scholar Horatio about the 'crowing of the cock' that seems to have frightened away the Ghost, says, 'Some say that ever 'gainst that season comes / Wherein our Saviour's birth is celebrated, / This bird of dawning singeth all night long, / And then they say no spirit dare stir abroad' (HAM 1.1.157–61).

'SBLOOD

(A) A popular contraction of the usually casual blasphemy on Christ's blood which was shed on the cross. ' 'Swounds', or more commonly ' '**Zounds**' is a similar blasphemy.

(B) In Shakespeare this blasphemy occurs disproportionately in 1H4, and is almost the exclusive property of Falstaff, though Bardolph and Hotspur each use it once. Interestingly, several of his apparently casual references to Christ's blood occur in contexts associated with Falstaff's own great body and his even greater fear of losing blood. To Hal's taunts about putting his ear to the ground to listen for 'the tread of travellers', Falstaff replies, 'Have you any levers to lift me up again, being down? 'Sblood, I'll not bear my own flesh so far afoot again for all the coin in thy father's exchequer' (1H4 2.2.33–7). When Hal calls him 'this sanguine coward, . . . this huge hill of flesh', Falstaff replies with ' 'Sblood, you starveling, you eel-skin' (1H4 2.4.244) and other epithets of thinness. The word 'sanguine', meaning of the humour of blood and implying spiritual sloth, also provokes Falstaff's ' 'Sblood'. Poins' ' 'Sblood, I would my face were in your belly!' provokes Falstaff's response, 'God-a-mercy' (1H4 3.3.49–51), combining, however inadvertantly, Christ's blood and God's mercy. Falstaff even rationalises his cowardly feigning of death with: ' 'Sblood, 'twas time to counterfeit, or that hot termagant Scot had paid me scot and lot too. Counterfeit? I lie, I am no counterfeit' (1H4 5.4.113–16). One wonders if any of Shakespeare's contemporaries would have sensed the irony of Falstaff's apparent death and resurrection in the midst of all of these references to Christ's blood.

(C) On the precious blood of Christ, see also Nowell (1853), 212; Donne, 7: 321; Andrewes, 5: 94. During the communion service, the priest says, 'The blood of our Lord Jesus Christ which was shed for thee, preserve thy body and soul into everlasting life: and drink this in remembrance that Christ's blood was shed for thee, and be thankful' (*BCP*, 264).

SCHOLAR

Someone who has studied for one of the professions at university, including that of divinity (*OED* 2.a).

When the Archbishop of Canterbury says of the apparently reformed Prince Hal, now King Henry V, 'Never was such a sudden scholar made; / Never came Reformation in a flood' (H5 1.1.32–3), he compares Hal's miraculous trans-formation to the knowledge and wisdom that might come from years of uni-versity study in divinity. He also marvels, 'Consideration, like an angel, came / And whipt th' offending Adam out of him'; 'Hear him but reason in divinity, / And, all-admiring, with an inward wish / You would desire the King were made a prelate' (H5 1.1.28–29, 38–40). When Cardinal Wolsey asks Henry VIII to determine the legality of his marriage to Katherine of Aragon by allowing

'Scholars . . . freely to argue for her' (H8 4.2.50–1; 2.2.112), he also speaks of university-educated divines.

SCOURG'D *v.*

Literally beaten for spiritual chastising; penitents habitually inflicted such punishments upon themselves, in acts of flagellation.

When Hotspur describes himself as 'whipt and scourg'd with rods' (1H4 1.3.239) at the very mention of Bolingbroke's name, he metaphorically compares his discomfort with the self-inflicted pain of religious penitents. Since such mortification supposedly purged pride, Hotspur unknowingly describes a scourging that he himself needs and will eventually receive as 'Ill-weav'd ambition', the proud holder of 'proud titles' (1H4 5.4.88, 79).

SCOURGE *sb.*

(A) Literally, a 'scourge' might be an object like a whip with which a penitent lashes himself. Figuratively it is a person or an event (like Richard III or the plague) sent by divine agency for vengeance or punishment against another person or a country.

(B) The scourge can be in Shakespeare persons like Joan of Arc, who calls herself 'Assign'd . . . to be the English scourge' (1H6 1.2.129), Talbot, the 'scourge of France' (1H6 2.3.15), or Richmond, God's 'minister of chastisement' (R3 5.3.113), all of whom consider themselves good, persons like Richard III who delight in evil, and persons like Hamlet who dwell ambiguously between these extremes. Hamlet clearly considers himself the good minister of God as he urges his mother to repent what he considers her sinful behavior with Claudius. He also considers himself 'born to set it right' (HAM 1.5.189). But when Hamlet accidentally kills Polonius, he is perplexed that 'heaven hath pleas'd it so / To punish me with this, and this with me, / That I must be their scourge and minister' (HAM 3.4.172–5). In contrast, when Clarence, about to be killed at his brother Richard's direction, recounts a dream in which his victim asks, 'What scourge for purjury / Can this dark monarchy afford false Clarence?' (R3 1.4.50–1), everyone except Clarence knows the answer. His brother Richard is both scourge and reprobate.

(C) Both Pilkington (1842), 24 and Jewel (1845–50), 4: 679 use 'scourge' to speak of God's just punishments of England. See also **minister**.

SCRIPTURE

(A) The Bible. When Donne, calls 'the onely tryall of Doctrines, the Scriptures' (7: 174) and says elsewhere that the 'Authority of the Church is founded in the Scriptures' (1: 169), we are reminded that Scripture is almost reflexively cited in Reformation doctrinal disputes. The first-generation Reformers repeatedly cited the absence of scriptural authority against the contested practices and beliefs of the Roman Catholic Church. Interestingly, by the time Shakespeare is writing his plays, both Church of England apologists like Hooker, Andrewes, and Donne and Catholic apologists like Vaux are responding to the more radical Puritan and Separatist complaints about the sole authority of Scripture with appeals to the traditions of the old church and the authority of the old fathers.

(B) After Shylock has used the story of Joseph and Laban's sheep to justify charging interest for loans, Antonio warns Bassanio, 'The devil can cite Scripture for his purpose', then calls Shylock in his self-justification 'An evil soul producing holy witness' (MV 1.3.98–9). Richard III boasts about his manipulative veneer of piety: 'But then I sigh, and, with a piece of Scripture, / Tell them that God bids us do good for evil: / And thus I clothe my naked villainy / With odd old ends stol'n forth of holy writ, / And seem a saint, when most I play the devil' (R3 1.3.333–7). In both of these cases, the user of Scripture is described as a devil and a dissembler in the use of holy writ, one by an opponent critical of the man and his Scripture-based argument, the other in an ironic piece of self-congratulation. The Gravedigger in HAM, in one of the finest bits of false reasoning in Shakespeare, uses Scripture to prove to his sceptical friend that Adam was a gentleman: 'What, art a heathen? How dost thou understand the Scripture? The Scripture says Adam digg'd; could he dig without arms?' (HAM 5.1.32–7; Gen. 2.15). His assertion that only a heathen would not understand the Scripture is ironic since he, though obviously a Christian, can hardly be said to do so. A coat of arms has little to do with the biceps required of a gravedigger. Shakespeare is poking fun at literal biblical interpretation here as well as the unreliability of argument by formal logic. In an interesting figurative usage, Imogen, reading her husband's contract on her life, asks if the letter itself and the lost faith in her that caused it to be written are 'The Scriptures of the loyal Leonatus, / All turn'd to heresy?' (CYM 3.4.80–2).

(C) See *Certaine Sermons*, pp. 1–7, for the sermons of 'the reading and knowledge of holy Scripture'. On the use of Scripture to test doctrine, see, for example, Jewel (1845–50), 3: 351 (about authorised kinds of confession); Cooper (1850), 146–7 (about men becoming angels); Tyndale, 1: 260 (on penance versus repentance); Cranmer (1846), 2: 43 (about ghosts returning from purgatory); and Pilkington (1842), 527 (on the efficacy of holy water). Of course, Vaux and his Catholic fellows could also cite Scripture for their purpose, as on the controversial seven sacraments: '*How many Sacramentes did Christ institute?*' 'Seven, which be expressed in the Scripture, and they have continually bene kept in the Catholike Church, & used by tradition from the Apostles, from man to man, until these our dayes' (1590), *sig.* F8[r]; see also *sigs.* K4[v]–5[r]. Throughout Book II, Hooker agrees with Vaux and argues extensively against the Puritan and Separatist view 'That Scripture is the onely rule of all things' (Book II. title page). His position (as in III.9.1), similar to the one that emerged from the Hampton Court Conference of 1603, is that the Puritans must show by Scripture that the polity and ceremonies of the established church are wrong, not prove them wrong by their absence from Scripture. See also Hooker IV.4.2 on their similar opposition to ceremonies: 'The burthen of proving doth rest on them'; the whole of Hooker's Books II and III concern this vital topic of the rule of Scripture. Nicolson (2003), 53 says of this reversal:

James . . . put the burden of proof on the Puritans. Unless they could show that there was something in Scripture explicitly condemning the bishops' administration of confirmation, or the use of the **cross** in **baptism**, or of the **ring** in a wedding service, or kneeling to receive communion, or the wearing of the surplice, of about the institution of episcopacy itself, he would not interfere with the accustomed **ceremony** or government of the Church.

See also 'Bible', *NewCathEncy*, 2: 381–6; and on the Latin and English versions, *NewCathEncy*, 2: 436–57, 463–74; 'Scripture', *OxfordEncyRef*, 4: 36–9.

SCRUPLE

(A) Technically 20 grams of weight, 'scruple' comes to refer to a small but vital moral objection. The comical Puritan figure Ananias in Ben Jonson's *The Alchemist* assures the conning alchemists 'I make no scruple', indicating the willingness of his sect to take and use counterfeit coins; Ananias adds with similar rhetorical parody, 'the holy synod / Have been in prayer, and meditation, for it' (1974), 4.7.75–8.

(B) Hamlet uses two words sometimes associated with Puritan style, '**precise**' and 'scruple', when he upbraids himself for taking too long and thinking too carefully about his right to murder Claudius as having 'some craven scruple / Of thinking too precisely on th' event' (HAM 4.4.40–1). Malvolio's anal-obsessive 'No dram of a scruple, no scruple of a scruple' (TN 3.4.79) also sounds a lot like this represented Puritan rhetorical tic.

(C) Cf. Jonson, *The Alchemist* 4.7.45–58, for similar satire of the way Puritans spoke morally.

SEAL(S)

(A) Something signifying agreement or commitment; its impression in stamp or wax. Andrewes calls sacraments 'the conduit-pipes of His grace, and seals of His truth unto us' (1: 100); Donne also uses the word of both **sacraments**: 'God hath afforded me the seale of that *Sacrament*' of baptism; then he asks, 'how many that are *baptiz'd*, and so eas'd in *originall sinne*, doe yet proceed to *actuall sins*, and are surpriz'd by death, before they receive the *Seale* of their *Reconciliation* to *Christ*, in the *Sacrament* of his body and his bloud' (8: 77).

(B) 'Seals' suggests both baptism and communion when Iago imagines Othello's love for Desdemona to be so strong that she could if she wished 'win the Moor' to anything, even 'were't to renounce his baptism, / All seals and symbols of redeemed sin' (OTH 2.3.343–4). The seal that marked official legal and political documents becomes in all these references the new covenant, the sealed, agreed-on promise of God's forgiveness and grace. 'The holy seal' (WT 3.2.129) that the Officer refers to in WT is a literal seal of the document recording the oracle from Apollo testifying to Hermione's innocence. Cf. WT 3.1.18–19; 3.2.127). Westmoreland's complaint to his opponent the Archbishop of York, 'What peer hath been suborn'd to grate on you? / That you should seal this lawless bloody book / Of forg'd rebellion with a seal divine' (2H4 4.1.90–2), metaphorically equates the seal divine with the Archbishop's authority, the book with the rebellion against King Henry IV that he has authorised.

(C) See also Eph. 4.30: 'The holy Spirit of God, by whom ye are sealed unto the day of redemption', and Eph. 1.13–14: 'Ye were sealed with the holy Spirit of promise . . . until the redemption'. On sacraments as 'seals and confirmations', see also Bullinger, 4: 318. Shaheen (1999), 588, cites Tomson's note to 1 Cor. 7.14: 'Baptisme is added as the seal of that holiness'.

SECT[1] (sectary)

(A) A group of persons who share a preference for certain religious doctrines, ecclesiastical structures, or practices; usually this group has broken from the larger body, therefore the term can be used pejoratively. Separatists like Anabaptists would be an obvious example within Protestantism during the Reformation, but to the Catholic establishment so would Lutherans and Calvinists. A **sectary** is a member of this group.

(B) In a confrontation between the Catholic Gardiner, Bishop of Westminster and his two Protestant opponents Cromwell and Cranmer, Gardiner calls Cranmer 'a sectary' and Cromwell, who rises to Cranmer's defence, also 'a favorer / Of this new sect' (H8 5.2.105, 115–16). Cranmer and his people will in time raise both Elizabeth and Edward as Protestants, and finally suffer the consequences of their sectarian efforts at the hands of Henry's Catholic daughter, Mary. Once Elizabeth becomes queen six years later, Protestantism is a sect no more, at least in England.

(C) Donne is characteristically nervous about such name-calling: 'Where two contrary opinions are both probable, they may be embraced, and beleeved by two men, and those two be both learned, and discreet, and pious, and zealous men. And this consideration should keep men from that precipitation, of imprinting the odious and scandalous names of Sects, or Sectaries upon other men who may differ from them, and from others with them, in some opinions', so long as they are 'things that are not fundamentall' (7: 97). The Recusant Hopkins speaks pejoratively of the 'whole newe late **secte** of **heretikes** that be called **Puritans**' (1582), *sig*. aiiii; his fellow Catholic Persons says of 'sectaries condemned by K. Henry' . . . that they were worthilie condemned and burned for this pride, selfe-will and obstinacy' (1603), 251–2. The Reformer Becon plays payback by using the word ironically to describe Catholics: 'I here recite how great and how wide a chapel, how ample and how large a synagogue, the devil hath built him in the satanical sect of the pernicious papists' (3: 401); and the Reformer Foxe speaks sympathetically of 'the co-sectaries Anthony Peerson and Henry Filmer' (1397–98), two of his Protestant martyrs.

SECT[2]

(A) *Fig*.

(B) The Servant in WT calls Perdita 'a creature, / Would she begin a sect, might quench the zeal / Of all professors else, make proselytes / Of who she bid but follow' (WT 5.1.106–9). Based on the idea of the religious zeal inspired by charismatic preachers, this metaphor is enriched by the assertion that both the preacher and his followers or 'proselytes' would abandon their faiths and follow her. Falstaff calls prostitutes a sect (2H4 2.4.37), and Iago calls love 'a sect, or scion' of 'our raging motions, our carnal stings, our unbitted lusts' (OTH 1.3.330–2). The image of something wild, lust, being grafted on to a more civilised tree is a nice counterpart here of the religious offshoot.

(C) Donne uses a similar gardening metaphor when he calls 'Sects . . . rotten boughes, gangrened limmes, fragmentary chips, blowne off by their owne spirit of turbulency, fallen off by the waight of their owne pride, . . . hewen off by the Excommunications and censures of the Church' (3: 87–8).

SEE

The seat of an archbishop or the Pope.

Pandulph, the papal legate, confronts King John about defying the Pope's orders and thus keeping 'Stephen Langton, chosen Archbishop / Of Canterbury, from that holy see' (JN 3.1.143–4). Later Pandulph rejoices that John has changed his mind 'That so stood out against the holy Church, / The great metropolis and see of Rome' (JN 5.2.71–2).

SEIGNEUR

Also signieur. 'O Seigneur Dieu;' is French for 'O Lord God'.

Katherine the Princess of France uses 'O Seigneur Dieu' twice in exasperation over the difficulty of learning the English (H5 3.4.31, 52). A French soldier says it later in fearful response to Fluellen's challenge, to which Fluellen replies three times in a row, 'O Signieur Dew', thinking it to be his name (H5 4.4.6–9).

SELF-LOVE

(A) The love of oneself, when considered sinful rather than merely psychologically aberrant (or natural), has religious meaning. Donne explains Aquinas's saying, 'selfe-love cannot be called a distinct sin, but the roote of all sins': 'To love our selves, to be satisfied in our selves, to finde an omni-sufficiency in our selves, is an intrusion, an usurpation upon God' (4: 330). Aquinas in turn has cited Augustine, who says: '[T]wo cities have been formed by two loves: the earthly by the love of self, even to the contempt of God; the heavenly by the love of God, even to the contempt of self'. 'Self-love is the origin of sin' (*City of God* XIV.28, cited in *ST* II.2.21.1). **Pride**, the more common name of self-love, is sometimes called 'the devil', as in 'the world, the flesh, the devil', so closely is it associated with Satan's rebellion, fall, and continuing revolt, and humanity's, against God.

(B) Sometimes in Shakespeare self-love is explicitly a sin. His theology if not his patriotism stands on slippery ground when the French Dauphin says to his fearful father 'Self-love, my liege, is not so vile a sin / As self-neglecting' (H5 2.4.74–5). Venus is also less than disinterested when she refers to celibates as 'self-loving nuns' (VEN 752). Sonnet 62 refers more traditionally to the 'sin of self-love', ending with the acknowledgement that 'Self so self-loving were iniquity' (SON 62.1,12).

(C) See also **pride, humility**; Nowell (1853), 137, 216–27; Latimer (1844–45), 1: 434.

SELF-SLAUGHTER

(A) Such a phrase links suicide to the commandment against murder. The *Geneva Bible* glosses the biblical text about Razi's suicide, 2 Maccabees 14.41, 'contrary to the worde of God' (*fol.* 473). Bullinger prohibits suicide even if it were used to obtain immortality or 'to avoid imminent evil. . . . For it must be understood that we are forbidden so to do by the law which saith, "Thou shalt not kill." ' However, of 'uncertain' deaths like Ophelia's (HAM 5.1.cite), Bullinger adds, 'So also must wee think the best of the unwilful death of men beside their wits, that in their madness kill themselves' (2: 414).

(B) Hamlet, lamenting both his father's untimely death and his mother's 'o'er-hasty marriage' to Claudius (HAM 2.2.59), connects suicide to the sixth commandment when he wishes 'that th' Everlasting had not fix'd / His canon 'gainst self-slaughter!' (HAM 1.2.131–2). The same prohibition constrains Imogen from taking her life after she has been abandoned by her husband: 'Against self-slaughter / There is a prohibition so divine / That cravens my weak hand' (CYM 3.4.76–8). In both cases the dramatic figure is in a sense experiencing psychologically the tension between a classical tradition that sometimes valorises suicide and a Christian tradition that categorically forbids it. Horatio highlights this tension when he calls himself 'more an antique Roman than a Dane' (HAM 5.2.341) as he considers taking his own life. Both Hamlet and Imogen are conflicted enough to associate the word 'coward' or 'craven' with failing to kill oneself (HAM 3.1.82; CYM 3.4.78). There is a similar moral ambiguity when Lucrece is described as 'self-slaught'red' (LUC 1733), since the act is simultaneously valorous from a classical perspective and desperate from a Christian one. Othello's suicide is likewise described both as something which 'mars all' and as a mark that 'he was great of heart' (OTH 5.2. 361).

(C) Donne's *Biathanatos* (1984) discusses possible religious justifications of suicide; see also Bullinger, 2: 414–15. Whitaker (1969), ch. 11, discusses the conflict between Senecan and Christian morality in HAM. For the legal implications of this term, including its association with homicide, see Sokol and Sokol (2000), 339–45. See also Shaheen (1999), 539.

SEPULCHRE[1]
Tomb.

Twice in Shakespeare this refers to the place where Christ was interred after the Crucifixion. This was one of the great destinations of religious pilgrims and of the crusaders.

Henry IV begins his kingship by promising to take his friends on a crusade 'As far as to the sepulchre of Christ' (1H4 1.1.19). His father John of Gaunt also refers to 'the sepulchre in stubborn Jewry / Of the world's ransom, blessed Mary's Son' (R2 2.1.55–6). Both men seem to understand the value of such spiritual window-dressing, but Gaunt's reference may be more sincere than his son's.

SEPULCHRE[2]
Metaphorically this suggests the **body's** imprisonment of the **soul**.

Bolingbroke tells Mowbray that if they had been permitted to fight, by now 'One of our souls had wand'red in the air, / Banish'd this frail sepulchre of our flesh' (R2 1.3.195–6).

SERMON[1] *sb.*
(A) **Homily**. Almost from the beginning of the Church of England (1547), the first year of King Edward the Sixth, authorised sermons were 'appointed to be read' from the official collection, *Certain Sermons or Homilies*. As their twentieth-century editors have said (1968), viii, 'Read in every church and heard of all congregations, designed for the maintenance of the Establishment, as well as the "maintenance of true religion and vertue" – for the suppression of Catholicism and the discouragement of Puritanism, as well as for the teaching of "what duty they owe both to God and man" – these homilies were probably, next to the Book of Common Prayer, as well known and influential as any writings produced between 1547 and 1640.'
(B) Though Shakespeare elsewhere shows his knowledge of this work (see **perjur'd** and **repent**), all of his uses of 'sermon' are figurative. Petruchio is said to be 'In her chamber, making a sermon of continency' to his new wife Kate just after their marriage (SHR 4.1.182); Duke Senior says that he finds 'Sermons in stones, and good in every thing' (AYL 2.1.17) in the forest. By metonymy he refers to the lessons sermons contain.
(C) See also Hooker V.21–2, '*Of* **preaching** *by Sermons, and whether Sermons be the onely ordinarie way of teachinge whereby men are brought to the savinge knowledg of Gods truth.*'

SERMON[2] *v.*
To preach.

Timon says to his steward's protestations of loyalty, 'Come, sermon me no further' (TIM 2.2.172).

SERPENT
(A) The serpent is associated with **Satan**, who assumes this form to tempt Eve in the **Garden**. The serpent is also one of the most common manifestations of evil in religious art. The sting, the hiss, the egg, the tooth, and the poison all find their way into Shakespeare, as well as the serpent's tendency to lurk, deceive, and tempt.
(B) The Queen in R2 refers directly to the tempting serpent and to Eve as well when she asks the Gardener who has just been describing Richard's impending deposition, 'What Eve, what serpent, hath suggested thee / To make a second fall of cursed man?' (R2 3.4.75–6). The image of the serpent hidden in the garden lurks behind Juliet's perplexed 'O serpent heart, hid with a flow'ring face' (ROM 3.2.73). Emilia's angry curse of Iago, 'If any wretch have put this in your head, / Let heaven requite it with the serpent's curse!' (OTH 4.2.15–16) refers to God's

punishment of the serpent in the story of the Fall (Gen. 3.14–15), that he should hiss and speak no more and that he should forever crawl on his belly in the dust; it also predicted his eventual defeat at the heels of a woman.

(C) Andrewes says of the serpent's temptation, ''The devil indeed is subtle and playeth the serpent' (5: 454), and Coverdale of his punishment, 'Therefore doth the Lord righteously curse the serpent, . . . and saith, "Upon thy body shalt thou go, and earth shalt thou eat all the days of thy life" '(1844), 1: 19.

SERVICE
A liturgical rite. Andrewes gives insight into the connection between service as an act of worship and service as an act of duty when he says 'for though there be other parts of God's service, yet prayer hath borne away the name of service from them all'. Hebrews, Greeks, Anglicans all serve God best in their 'Common Prayer, and that is service' (4: 76).

The clearly liturgical usage comes in HAM, where the Priest says of Ophelia's limited funeral rites, 'We should profane the service of the dead / To sing a requiem and such rest to her / As to peace-parted souls' (HAM 5.1.236–8). See also **anthem**.

SEVEN – see **deadly**.

SEXTON
(A) The custodian of a church, often charged with bell-ringing and grave-digging.

(B) The Gravedigger says out of his grave, 'I have been sexton here, man and boy, thirty years' (HAM 5.1.161–2); Hamlet also refers to 'a sexton's spade' (HAM 5.1.90). When the Bastard calls Time 'the clock-setter, that bald sexton' (JN 3.1.324), we hear of another of his jobs. We also learn that he is in charge of the 'jangling of the bells' when the Third Fisherman says of the tale of whales that 'swallow'd the whole parish, church, steeple, bells, and all', 'If I had been the sexton, I would have been that day in the belfry' (PER 2.1.33–41). See also ADO 4.2.70, 2; 5.1.254.

(C) On the duties of sextons, see Cross and Livingstone (1997), 'Sexton'.

'SFOOT
By God's or Christ's foot. Another little blasphemy on the body of the crucified Christ in which the process of definition probably overstates the seriousness of the reference.

Anachronism marks the cynical Thersites' promises of revenge: ''Sfoot, I'll learn to conjure and raise devils' (TRO 2.3.5–7). A pre-Christian Greek can no more swear on Christ's foot than he can later let the 'devil Envy say amen' (TRO 2.3.21). Shakespeare's references in the same speech to Mercury, Jove and Olympus exaggerate the discrepancy.

SHADOW

(A) Literally a ghost or an apparition; figuratively, its ambiguous reality.

(B) 'Shadows' in Shakespeare often refer to a contested site of experience where a character cannot tell whether what he has seen is a **ghost**, a dream or something otherwise imagined. After Richard III cries out 'O Ratcliffe, I fear, I fear!' in response to his 'fearful dream' of the ghosts of his eleven victims, Ratcliff responds, 'Nay, good my lord, be not afraid of shadows.' This provokes one of Richard's most honest moments: 'By the **apostle Paul**, shadows tonight / Have strook more terror to the soul of Richard / Than can the substance of ten thousand soldiers / Armed in proof and led by shallow Richmond' (R3 5.3.212–19). These shadows may be things dreamed as distinguished from things seen, but they are more frightening, and spiritually more substantial too, than literal soldiers. Richard's brother Clarence reveals a similar complexity of usage and insight when he describes a dream in which 'A shadow like an **angel**, with bright hair / Dabbled in blood, ... shriek'd out aloud, / "Clarence is come false, fleeting, perjur'd Clarence, / That stabb'd me in the field by Tewksbury: / Seize on him, **Furies**, take him unto **torment**!"' (R3 1.4.52–7). Was this an avenging ghost, a ministering angel, or just a dream? Again neither we nor Clarence can know. Shadow and substance are sometimes indistinguishable.

The ghosts and apparitions in MAC are similarly hard to pin down. The word 'apparition' illustrates that ambiguity, since it means both 'that which is only imagined' and 'that which appears supernaturally'. Even the word 'appears' means both 'seems' and 'becomes visible'. Shakespeare further complicates matters with a character's rationalization. Macbeth, who has every reason not to want to believe in the objective reality of Banquo's ghost, says to it understandably but not definitively, 'Hence, horrible shadow!' and 'Unreal mock'ry hence!' (MAC 3.4.105–6). However, the three Witches also say to the apparitions 'Come like shadows, so depart' (MAC 4.1.111). Are they conceding mere trickery, bits of deceptive magic? Or are they able, as Glendower says of himself, to 'call **spirits** from the vasty deep' (1H4 3.1.52)?

(C) Are their 'shadows' real if intangible, or are they merely illusory? We just don't know, and neither do Shakespeare's contemporaries. That is why there is still such energy in such shadowy glances in Shakespeare at what Robert West aptly called 'the outer mystery' (1968), and sometimes the inner mystery as well.

SHAVE

(A) The priest's head is tonsured or shaved. The penitent might also shave his head in an act of mortification or as a sign of contrition.

(B) Thus when Humphrey of Gloucester taunts the Lord Cardinal about their upcoming swordplay, 'Now, by God's Mother, priest, / I'll shave your crown for this' (2H6 2.1.49–50), he is both reducing his title and threatening to make a thrust very close to his head. The Duke, possibly tonsured in his disguise as a friar, tells the Provost to disguise the dead Barnadine as a penitent: 'Shave the head, and tie the beard, and say it was the desire of the penitent to be so bar'd before his death' (MM 4.2.175–7).

(C) Hooper asks disparagingly if 'a good priest, must have necessarily that shaven crown and long gown? . . . Restore it to Rome again, from whence it came' (1843), 1: 245. Pilkington also disapproves of 'their shavelings, priests, and bishops' (1842), 163.

SHREWSBURY
(A) Shrewsbury Cathedral.
(B) When Falstaff refers to fighting with the Douglas 'a long hour by Shrewsbury clock' (1H4 5.4.148), he refers to the clock on the tower of Shrewsbury Cathedral. '[T]he clock-setter, that bald sexton' (JN 3.1.324) suggests the common association of clocks and church towers.
(C) See NV 1H4, 332n, and **sexton**.

SHRIEK
Like owls, ghosts can make shrieking sounds.

Calphurnia warns Caesar that 'ghosts did shriek and squeal about the streets' (JC 2.2.24). Paulina describes herself as the ghost who would haunt Leontes if he ever remarried, indeed 'shriek, that even your ears / Should rift to hear me' (WT 5.1.65–6). Antigonus, thinking that he has seen Hermione's ghost, says 'And so, with shrieks, / She melted into air' (WT 3.3.36–7); the Ghost of Prince Edward, 'dabbled in blood', 'shriek'd out aloud' against the Clarence who had a hand in his death (R3 1.4.54). When Lady Macbeth says just as Macbeth 'is about' Duncan's murder, 'Hark! Peace! / It was the owl that shriek'd' (MAC 2.2.2–3), she thinks for a moment that she has heard a ghost, then reassures herself that it was only an owl. Ross later describes how accustomed Scotland has become to murders during Macbeth's reign of terror by describing 'shrieks that rent the air / Are made, not mark'd' (MAC 4.3.168–9). He could refer to the cries of murder victims, their ghosts, or both.

SHRIFT
(A) Shriving; the giving or hearing of confession, the assignment of penance and absolution; also the submission of oneself to a priest for such discipline (see *OED sb.* 1–2, 4–6).
(B) Romeo 'confesses' his new love to the Friar in such elaborately Petrarchan terms that the Friar, failing to understand, reprimands him: 'Riddling confession finds but riddling shrift' (ROM 2.3.56). Here 'shrift' refers to that absolution which follows satisfactory confession. The Nurse asks Juliet, 'Have you got leave to go to shrift to-day?' ROM 2.5.66), then says naively, 'See where she comes from shrift with merry look' (ROM 4.2.15) when Juliet returns with the Friar's potion rather than his absolution. Richard's henchman says just before Hastings' execution, 'Make a short shrift, he longs to see your head' (R3 3.4.95); the Duke resolves about the condemned reprobate Barnadine, 'I will give him a present shrift, and advise him for a better place' (MM 4.2.207–8). He means heaven, of course.

A metaphoric usage of 'shrift' occurs when Desdemona promises to be relentless in her priest-like attempt to convince Othello to forgive Cassio: 'His bed shall seem a school, his board a shrift' (OTH 3.3.24). Gloucester and Clarence have some cynical fun about their brother King Edward's lust for Lady Grey by saying of his advice to her that she marry him, 'The ghostly father now hath done his shrift', and 'When he was made a shriver, 'twas for shift' (3H6 3.2.107–8). His shifty, as against his 'ghostly' or spiritual purpose, conflates nicely with the other meaning of 'shift' here, the woman's smock or chemise he will soon be removing if she follows his advice.

(C) See Grindal (1843), 140, for an injunction against 'shrift or auricular confession in Lent, or at any other time'. On Puritan methods of self-examination, see Kaufman (1996), ch. 2; on the Catholic tradition of 'spiritual exercises' and 'spiritual combat', see Martz (1962), ch. 3.

SHRINE

A place often holding objects of religious veneration like the remains of a **saint**; the shrine is therefore often the destination of religious **pilgrims**. Cranmer's is a typical Reformer's complaint and requirement: 'That they shall take away, utterly extinct, and destroy all shrines, covering of shrines, all tables, candlesticks, trindles or rolls of wax, pictures, paintings, and all other monuments of feigned **miracles**, pilgrimages, **idolatry**, and **superstition**; so that there remains no memory of the same in walls, glass windows, or elsewhere within their churches or houses.' Interestingly, the order had to be reiterated because it was originally ignored (2: 503, 2: 155).

Queen Margaret refers literally to the shrine of **Saint Alban**, the first British martyr, when she asks Simpcox, who has falsely claimed the miracle of restored sight, 'Tell me, good fellow, cam'st thou here by chance / Or of devotion, to this holy shrine?' He responds that Saint Alban has often called him, 'Simon, come; / Come offer at my shrine, and I will help thee' (2H6 2.1.61, 85–90). Jachimo also refers literally to a classical religious site, 'The shrine of Venus or straight-pight Minerva' (CYM 5.5.164), though here 'shrine' probably refers to religious statuary rather than the chapel which might contain it.

The other uses are metaphorical. The famous sonnet which marks the first verbal exchange between Romeo and Juliet is driven by Romeo's conceit that Juliet is a 'holy shrine' and he a **pilgrim** or **palmer** eager to touch and kiss her **relics**, but afraid lest 'I **profane** [them] with my unworthiest hand' (ROM 1.5.93). Morocco uses the same metaphor when he says of fair Portia, 'From the four corners of the earth they come / To kiss this shrine, this mortal breathing saint' (MV 2.7.39–40). Tarquin also calls Lucrece 'so pure a shrine' as he considers the sacrilege of ravishing her (LUC 194).

SHRIVE

Give **shrift; confess**, give **penance**, and **absolve** of **sins**.

With his 'Bid her devise / Some means to come to shrift this afternoon, / And there she shall at Friar Lawrence' cell / Be shriv'd and married' (ROM 2.4.179–82), Romeo refers to the confession and absolution that traditionally preceded marriages. Portia says of Morocco, the next unwanted suitor who will arrive, 'If he have the condition of a saint, and the complexion of a devil, I had rather he should shrive me than wive me' (MV 1.2.129–31). To her a black skin is apparently better for frightening away sins than for attracting hearts. 'Shrive' like 'shrift' can also be used metaphorically (ERR 2.2.208).

SHRIVING
Hearing confession and giving absolution. See **shrift**.

Hamlet tells Horatio that he has rewritten the letter from Denmark to England in a way that will send Rosencrantz and Guildenstern 'to sudden death, / Not shriving time allow'd' (HAM 5.2.46–7). This is arguably the cruellest of Hamlet's actions, since it seems designed to punish the old schoolfellows eternally by depriving them of time for spiritual preparation. Buckingham, knowing that Hastings is in grave danger, sadistically pretends otherwise when he says, 'Your friends at Pomfret, they do need the priest, / Your honor hath no shriving work in hand' (R3 3.2.114–15).

SHROVETIDE
(A) The Sunday, Monday and Tuesday before Lent. Shrovetide was therefore simultaneously a time when the pious were preparing themselves spiritually for the Lenten disciplines of abstinence and the worldly fortifying themselves gastronomically against its enforced fastings.
(B) Though it literally means 'shriving-time,' Shakespeare's one verbal reference occurs in a song Silence sings for Falstaff. Predictably, his 'welcome merry Shrove-tide' (2H4 5.3.35) leans more towards self-indulgence than self-abnegation.
(C) See Hassel (1979), 112–39, for a fuller discussion of possible Shrovetide references in Shakespeare.

SHROVE TUESDAY
The Tuesday just at the end of Shrovetide and just before Ash Wednesday, which marks the beginning of Lent. This is also called Mardi Gras or Fat Tuesday because it marked the rioters' last hurrah before the severities of Lent. Pancakes were traditionally served on Shrove Tuesday as families tried to use up all the remaining meat, fat, eggs, and dairy products before their consumption was prohibited.

This explains the Clown's famous comment that 'a pancake' is as 'fit' 'for Shrove Tuesday' 'as the nail to his hole, the cuckold to his horn, as a scolding quean to a wrangling knave, as the nun's lip to the friar's mouth' (AWW 2.2.23–7).

SHUTTLE
(A) The implement used for tossing the yarn across the loom between each weaving action. Because Job 7.6 reads, 'My days are swifter than a weaver's shuttle', the shuttle is associated biblically with the shortness of human life.
(B) Thus, when Falstaff, who knows his Bible unusually well for such an old

reprobate, says 'I fear not Goliah with a weaver's beam, because I know also life is a shuttle' (WIV 5.1.22–3), he is seasoning his cowardice with a little biblical wisdom.

(C) For **Goliath** and the weaver's beam, see also 1 Samuel 17.7.

SIGN¹ *sb.*
Something supernatural which foretells or reveals. Pilkington says of what he perceives to be Catholic excesses in worship, 'As in St Paul's church in London, ... "it is no marvel, if God have sent down fire to burn part of the Church as a sign of his **wrath**"' (1842), 483.

Often in Shakespeare this usage is merely superstitious (as in 3H6 5.6.44–5; R2 2.4.15; 1H4 3.1.13–19, 40). Superstition and religion mix when the cynical papal legate Cardinal Pandulph advises the 'green' and 'fresh' Louis, Dauphin of France, that he is safe from King John's jealous rage because his prior crimes have so lost the heart of his people that they will seek in all natural events supernatural omens of divine vengeance against him:

> No natural exhalation of the sky,
> No scope of nature, no distemper'd day,
> No common wind, no customed event,
> But they will pluck away his natural cause
> And call them meteors, prodigies, and signs,
> Abortives, presages, and tongues of heaven,
> Plainly denouncing vengeance upon John.
> (JN 3.4.153–9)

SIGN² *v.*
(A) Make the sign of the cross.
(B) King Henry VI may refer to the sign of the cross or merely a raised hand when he advises his uncle Cardinal Beauford as he is dying, 'Lord Cardinal, if thou think'st on heaven's bliss, / Hold up thy hand, make signal of thy hope.' After 'He dies, and makes no sign', Henry adds, 'O God forgive him!' The less forgiving Warwick concludes of this signless moment, 'So bad a death argues a monstrous life', to which Henry replies, 'Forbear to judge, for we are sinners all. / Close up his eyes, and draw the curtains close, / And let us all to meditation' (2H6 3.3.27–33).
(C) Grindal's Injunctions at York includes: 'nor shall worship any **cross** or any **image** or picture upon the same, nor give any reverence thereunto, nor superstitiously shall make upon themselves the **sign of the cross** when they first enter into any church to pray' (140); cf. Calfhill (1846), 288.

SIN¹ *sb.*
(A) Theologically designated wrongdoing or offence. Since the central reason for Christ's sacrifice on the cross was humanity's sinfulness, 'sin' is a crucial word in Christian theology and a central concept in sacraments like baptism and communion. Iago refers to such religious rituals as 'All **seals** and **symbols** of

redeemed sin' (OTH 2.3.344), and Malcolm accuses Macbeth of 'every sin / That has a name' (MAC 4.3.61). The Ten Commandments and the seven deadly sins are the two formulations of the named sins most familiar to Shakespeare and his contemporaries, and they often come into play in Shakespeare's usage of 'sin' and 'sins'.

(B) Five sins from the Ten Commandments are actually labelled with the word 'sin' in Shakespeare. 1. Coveting. An apologetic (but still-begging) Feste speaks amusingly of 'The sin of **covetousness**' (TN 5.1.47), and Henry V says, 'If it be a sin to covet honour, / I am the most offending soul alive' (H5 4.3.28–9). Having just denied 'covetous[ness] for gold' and 'garments', he wonders if 'coveting' applies to abstract as well as tangible things. 2. **Adultery**. The Abbess calls adultery 'unlawful love' and describes it as 'A sin prevailing much in youthful men' (ERR 5.1.52). 3. Lying. The distraught and deceived father Leonato hopes that his daughter Hero will 'not add to her damnation / A sin of **perjury**' (ADO 4.1.172–3); Berowne calls 'falsehood', 'in itself a sin' (LLL 5.2.775). 4. 'Honour thy father and thy mother'. Jessica calls it a 'heinous sin ... in me / To be ashamed to be my father's child' (MV 2.3.16). 5. Murder. Humphrey refers to '**murther**, ... that bloody sin' as the fault he punished most severely as Lord Protector (2H6 3.1.131). When Malcolm says that Macbeth has committed 'every sin / That has a name', 'bloody' is in his long list (MAC 4.3.59–60). Tybalt opposes the revenge ethic against this commandment when he threatens to kill Romeo by swearing 'Now, by the stock and honour of my kin, / To strike him dead I hold it not a sin'; Romeo also refers to murder as a sin ((ROM 1.5.58–9; 5.3.61–2).

The word 'sin' also directly designates four of the seven deadly sins in Shakespeare: 1. **Pride**. 'Self-love' is called by Parolles 'the most inhibited sin in the canon' (AWW 1.1.145), perhaps because pride is the chief sin of the devil, and the most dangerous of the seven to humans. See **humility, self-love**. 2. **Lust**. Claudio, obviously desperate to save his own life, says of his sister Isabella's fornication with Angelo, 'Sure it is no sin, / Or of the **deadly seven** it is the least' (MM 3.1.3.1.109–10). Incest, one sin of lust, is amusingly called 'a sin to match in my kinred' as Beatrice explains why she would not marry any son of Adam, and especially Benedick (ADO 2.1.64, 61); Malcolm calls Macbeth from that same list of 'every sin / That has a name "Luxurious" and himself 'all "voluptuousness" (MAC 4.3.59–61). 3. **Envy**. King Henry IV worries that it 'mak'st me sin / In envy that my Lord Northumberland / Should be the father to so blest a son' as Hotspur, while his son should be stained by 'riot and dishonour' (1H4 1.1.78–80, 85); we also find the 'sin in envying' in COR (1.1.230). 4. **Avarice**. Malcolm calls Macbeth from that long list of 'every sin / That has a name' 'avaricious' and himself 'stanchless avarice' (MAC 4.3.59–61, 78). Griffith also speaks of avarice when he calls Wolsey 'unsatisfied in getting / (Which was a sin), yet in bestowing, madam, / He was most princely' (H8 4.2.55–7).

Faults called 'sins' but coming from neither traditional list include the following items: 1. Breaking an oath, or being 'forsworn'. Tempted to help Bassanio choose the right casket, Portia names being forsworn rather than dishonoring her father as a 'sin': 'I could teach you / How to choose right, but then I am forsworn. / So will I never be, so may you miss me, / But if you do, you'll make me wish a sin, / That I had been forsworn' (MV 3.2.10–14). The Princess in LLL also argues that no amount of rationalization will keep Navarre's vow-breaking from being a sin: 'Tis **deadly** sin to keep that oath, my lord, / And sin to break it' (LLL 2.1.105–6; cf. LLL 2.1.106; 4.3.113; 4.3.175). 2. Malice. King Henry VI calls 'malice' 'a great and grievous sin', presumably because it offends against the virtue of **forgiveness** (1H6 3.1.128). 3. Ambition. When Surrey calls a falling Cardinal Wolsey's 'ambition, / Thou scarlet sin', 'scarlet' could be associated with bloodshed, but also with the scarlet gowns of conspiring **cardinals** (H8 3.2.254–9). Wolsey also advises his faithful servant: 'Cromwell, I charge thee, fling away ambition! / By that sin fell the **angels**' (H8 3.2.440–1). Lucifer's prideful anger that he was displaced by Christ led to the **revolt** in heaven. 4. Wealth. The 'sin but to be rich' (JN 2.1.594) must refer either to Christ's words in the Sermon on the Mount, 'it is hard for a rich man to enter the kingdom of heaven' (Matt. 19.23; see also Mark 10.24–5), or to the story of **Dives** (the 'rich man') and the beggar Lazarus (Luke 16.19–31). 5. Mockery. Portia intriguingly says that she knows 'it is a sin to be a mocker' (MV 1.2.57) just before she nervously mocks her first five suitors. Rosaline joins precept and practice a little more sincerely when she says of the poor actors, 'I dare not call them fools' (LLL 5.2.371). In Matt. 5.22, Christ warns against such disdainful pride, 'whosoever shall say Thou fool, shall be in danger of hell fire'. 6. **Intemperance**. Malcolm includes 'boundless intemperance' in his long list of 'every sin / That has a name' (MAC 4.3.66), drawing upon both classical and Christian lists of **vices** (and virtues). 7. Disobedience. The 'sin against obedience' (CYM 2.3.111–12) is prominent enough for there to be a homily against disobedience in *Certain Sermons*. Juliet pretends to repent of dishonouring her father when she says 'I have learnt me to repent the sin / Of disobedient opposition' (ROM 4.2.17–18). Innovation, probably meaning insurrection, is similarly described in STM as 'a sin / Which oft th' apostle did forewarn us of, urging obedience to authority' (STM II.C 93–4). 8. **Despair**. When Romeo threatens suicide, Friar Lawrence responds 'O deadly sin! O rude unthankfulness!' (ROM 2.3.44; 1.5.58–9; 3.3.24), referring in a compressed way to the despair of God's grace which would lead to the sin of suicide.

There are many more general uses of 'sin', and some obviously mirror formulaic expressions, like Hubert's distinction between the familiar 'thought, word, and deed' as 'act, consent, and sin of thought' (JN 4.3.135). Jessica twists 'the sins of the father are to be laid upon the children' to 'the sins of my mother should be visited upon me' (MV 3.5.10–14; cf. JN 2.1.179–82). The biblical cadence of Bevis' 'Then is sin cut down like an ox, and iniquity's throat cut like a calf' (2H6 4.2.26–7) suggests not only the prophetic sound of Jeremiah or Amos but also the syntax of contemporary Puritan satire. Margaret's 'Sin, death, and hell have set their marks on him' (R3 1.3.292), invokes the traditional allegory of the same hellish Trinity that Milton dramatises in PL (2. 760ff.). Richard III's 'sin will pluck on sin' (R3 4.2.63–4), like Macbeth's 'I am in blood / Stepp'd in so far that, should I wade no more, / Returning were as tedious as go o'er' (MAC 3.4.135–7), suggests the idea of desperation in evil, the arrogance of the reprobate that he has done deeds that even God could not forgive. This attitude is opposed in a line like 'The blackest sin is clear'd with **absolution**' (LUC 354).

Among the figurative references to sin, Claudio asks Hero's father Leonato, as though he were a priest, for whatever 'penance your invention / Can lay upon my sin' (ADO 5.1.273–4). Sin is personified in 'Poison and treason are the hands of sin' (PER 1.1.139). '[F]lattery is the bellows blows up sin' depicts it metaphorically as the fire of pride (PER 1.2.39–41). Sin is also personified as someone who sits in the 'shady cell' of 'Opportunity', 'to seize the souls that wander by him' (LUC 876, 881–2). 'The time will come, that foul sin, gathering head, / Shall break into corruption' (2H4 3.1.76–7; R2 5.1.58–9) twice identically compare sin to a pus-filled boil about to burst. Feste links sin and folly when he defends both his profession and its patched garments, 'Any thing that's mended is but patch'd; virtue that transgresses is but patch'd with sin, and sin that **amends** is but patch'd with virtue' (TN 1.5.47–9). To Feste, we are all imperfect, patched. Some, like Olivia, comes to smile at that folly, and therefore begin to 'mend' (TN 1.5.74). Others, like Malvolio, literally ill-will in a play subtitled 'What You Will', refuses to admit his own follies and ends as a result both isolated and revengeful. Even Feste's reach sometimes exceeds his grasp.

Romeo playfully but also reverently uses 'sin' as a metaphor for their improper touching and kissing in his first verbal exchange with Juliet (ROM 1.5.93–110). There **Pilgrim**, **profane**, **palmer**, **trespass**, and **purged** all help develop the metaphor:

> ROM.   Thus from my lips, by thine, my sin is purg'd.
> JUL.   Then have my lips the sin that they have took.
> ROM.   Sin from my lips? O trespass sweetly urg'd!
>   Give me my sin again.
>
> (ROM 1.5.107–10)

(C) The Commandments occur in Ex. 20.1–17, and are quoted in *BCP*, 248–9. On the publishing of the Ten Commandments in churches, see Hooper (1843), 1: 274; and Parker (1853), 133. Bradford, however, laments that 'The commandments of God are continually, in the ears of all people, read openly in the churches, yea, written upon the walls, so that all men know them; yet is there none amendment' (1848), 1: 9. See also Andrewes, 3: 150, 151, 153; 2: 10, 11, 284; 5: 400. For two rich discussions of the seven deadly sins, and 'remedies' against them, see Loarte (trans. Brinkley, 1596–97), 176–245, and Vaux (1590b), *sigs*. e8ᵛ–f8ʳ. Cf. Tyndale, complaining of the exploitative remedies of 'Some papists' (1: 271). In 'Of the Distinction of Sins' (*ST* II.1.72), Aquinas divides sins variously as spiritual and carnal (Art. 2), sins against God, self, and neighbour (Art. 4), sins mortal and venial (Art. 5), sins of commission and omission (Art. 6), and 'Sins of Thought, Word, and Deed' (Art. 7). Aquinas also speaks 'Of Original Sin' (*ST* II.1.82–3). For his entire discussion of sin, see *ST* II.1.71–89. On sins of 'thought, word, and deed', see also 'general confession', *BCP*, 259. Holden and

Waith discuss the represented style of Puritan moral disapproval. See 'Sin', *New-CathEncy*, 13: 234–45; 'Sin', *OxfordEncyRef*, 4: 61–5. See also **sins, absolution, penance, baptism, redeem, indulgence, deadly, mortal, repent, folly, wickedness, damnation**.

SIN² *v.*
Do wrong; commit an offence.

Angelo calls his forbidden lust for Isabella 'to sin in loving virtue' (MM 2.2.182). Miranda says of the fifth commandment, 'I should sin / To think but nobly of my grandmother' (TMP 1.2.118), and Northumberland says of the ninth, 'he doth sin that doth belie the dead' (2H4 1.1.98).

SIN-ABSOLVER
Someone like a priest capable of granting remission of the consequences of sin.

Romeo calls the Friar 'a divine, a ghostly confessor, / A sin-absolver, and my friend profess'd' (ROM 3.3.49–50). See **absolution, absolv'd**.

SIN-CONCEIVING
Bearing sinful children rather than thinking sinful thoughts.

When Constance berates Queen Elinor, King John's mother and Prince Arthur's grandmother, for having a 'sin-conceiving womb' (JN 2.1.182), the insult derives not from the idea of original sin but because in her mind 'God hath made her sin and her the plague / On this removed issue' (JN 2.1.185–6). She believes that both the father John and the grandmother Elinor are scourges, sinful agents sent by God to be Arthur's plagues.

SINFUL
Characterised by or full of sin.

Shakespeare's most obviously religious usage occurs in SON 146.1, where the soul is 'poor' because it is 'the centre of my sinful earth'. Bolingbroke charges Richard's friends Bushy and Green with 'your sinful hours' that have 'Made a divorce betwixt his queen and him' (R2 3.1.11–12). More amusingly, Hal once calls Falstaff 'thou globe of sinful continents' for his greatness in sinning (2H4 2.4.285).

SING¹
Chant a religious service, as of a priest.

The Priest in HAM declines to 'sing a requiem and such rest to her [Ophelia] / As to peace-parted souls', saying that it 'would profane the service of the dead' to do so (HAM 5.1.236–8; cf. TMP 2.2.43–4).

SING²
(A) Engage in congregational or individual religious song, as in singing psalms.
(B) The quasi-classical Hymen says 'a wedlock-hymn we sing' (AYL 5.4.137) of the unconventional marriage rite that concludes AYL. Falstaff recalls the

association during the Reformation between some Reformed groups and psalm-singing when he says 'I would I were a weaver, I could sing psalms' (1H4 2.4.133). (C) Donne favours singing in church, once claiming, '**Howl**ing is the noyse of hell, singing the voyce of heaven' (7: 70; see also 7: 51). Hooker says in defending '*Magnificat, Benedictus, and Nunc dimittis*', 'They are songes which concerne us so much more then the songes of David, as the **gospel**l toucheth us more then the **Law**e, the newe testament then the old' (V.40.1).

SING[3] *fig.*
For escort or direct.

Horatio hopes or prays at Hamlet's death, 'flights of angels sing thee to thy rest!' (HAM 5.2.360).

SINGULARITY
(A) Normally eccentric individuality, but in the usage of dissenters like the Puritans, it could refer to their unique moral and religious scrupulousness (*OED* 7.a).

(B) The 'kind of Puritan' Malvolio is tricked with the handwritten advice, 'Put thyself into the trick of singularity'. Then, when the revellers' trap is sprung, he repeats the phrase to Olivia's total bewilderment (TN 2.5.151–2; 3.4.71).

(C) See Forrest (1974), 259–64, on 'Malvolio and Puritan "Singularity" '.

SINS
(A) The plural noun form 'sins' often invokes moral and theological paradigms as well as liturgical formulas.

(B) 'Heaven forgive my sins at the day of judgement!' (WIV 3.3.212) is a good example from the Welch Parson Evans. Cassio says a drunken 'God forgive us our sins!' to Iago (OTH 2.3.112). 'O, forgive me my sins' (TMP 3.2.130) is Trinculo's frightened response to Ariel's mysterious and frightening appearance. The dying words of the pious and naive King Henry VI are 'O God forgive my sins, and pardon thee!' (3H6 5.6.60). The just-forgiven Gloucester, who has stabbed him, responds with a characteristic 'Down, down to hell, and say I sent thee thither' (3H6 5.6.67). When Othello warns Desdemona just before her death at his judgemental but misjudging hands, 'think on thy sins', he sounds like a priest shriving his parishioner (OTH 5.2.40). Such traditional lists as the seven deadly sins and the Ten Commandments are sometimes invoked by merely saying the plural noun, as when Julia upbraids Proteus that inconstancy 'makes him run through all th' sins' (TGV 5.4.112). Henry VIII's Queen Katherine puns on a similar formula when she calls the two Cardinals who have advised her quietly to accept the divorce 'But **cardinal** sins and hollow hearts' (H8 3.1.104).

(C) For this same range of references in the theologians, see Tyndale, 1: 249, 260; Jewel (1845–50), 1: 1104; Becon, 3: 618; Latimer (1844–45), 1: 212; 2.239; Rogers (1854), 214–17; Vaux (1590b), *sig.* a6ʳ; Donne, 9: 408; 5: 81; and Andrewes, 1: 113. See also **indulgence**.

SISTER, SISTERHOOD

A female member of a religious order or sisterhood; the condition of belonging to a group of nuns or sisters. Because Luther so strongly opposed celibacy among priests and nuns, this word was charged with unusual energy during the Reformation. See **nun**.

In MND, Duke Theseus offers Hermia a forbidding though not a completely negative picture of the celibate sister's life. If she decides not to marry her father's choice, she can either 'die the death' or 'endure the livery of a nun, / For aye to be in shady cloister mew'd, / To live a barren sister all your life, / Chaunting faint hymns to the cold, fruitless moon' (MND 1.1.65, 70–3). Such a 'maiden pilgrimage' may be 'thrice blessed', but the alternative, marriage with children, is 'earthlier happy', the life of the convent a 'withering on the virgin thorn' (MND 74–8). In LC the speaker similarly praises 'a nun' as a 'sister sanctified, of holiest note', who would remove herself from a rich life at court and 'spend her living in eternal love', but like Theseus he also complains of such a choice, 'The scars of battle scapeth by the flight, / And makes her absence valiant, not her might' (LC 232–45).

Isabella is a novice so committed to the notoriously severe regulations of 'the sisterhood' of 'the votarists of Saint Clare' (MM 1.4.5) that she asks for 'a more strict restraint / Upon the sisterhood' (MM 1.4.1–5). But though she is 'in probation of a sisterhood' (MM 5.1.72), she is also 'the sister of one Claudio' (MM 5.1.69); indeed, most of the other twenty uses of 'sister' in the play refer literally to her relationship to Claudio and not her relationship to St Clare. Thus, when her desperate and frightened brother asks her to lay down her virginity for his life and she declines, 'More than our brother is our chastity' (MM 2.4.185), we see how complicated Shakespeare has made her sisterhood in the play. Phrases like 'Better it were a brother died at once, / Than that a sister, by redeeming him, / Should die for ever' (MM 2.4.106–8) is another good example of this tension between her conflicting identities. The Duke finally helps her forgive both Claudio and Angelo, but what she, or the audience, finally make of his marriage proposal is a guess that must be informed by some sense of the controversies surrounding celibacy and marriage among the religious, as well as our predilections about genre and gender.

Celia uses 'sisterhood' more lightly when she jokes about what Rosalind too enthusiastically calls the 'sanctity' of Orlando's love for her: 'A nun of winter's sisterhood kisses not more religiously, the very ice of chastity is in them' (AYL 3.4.13–17). Friar Lawrence also desperately proposes after Romeo's suicide that Juliet 'dispose of thee / Among a sisterhood of holy nuns' (ROM 5.3.156–7). He may mean a temporary refuge or a permanent home.

(C) See *NewCathEncy*, 'Nuns', 10: 575; 'Monasticism', 9: 1032–48; and *Oxford-EncyRef*, 'Nuns', 3: 158–60; 'Monasticism', 3: 78–83; and 'Marriage', 3: 18–23.

SKIES, SKY

Sometimes referring directly or indirectly to the abode of God or the gods.

Lucrece consigns 'My soul and body to the skies and ground' (LUC 1199), distinguishing between heaven as a place for the departed soul and earth as a place for its body. When Kent proclaims that 'The wrathful skies / Gallow the very wanderers of the dark, / And make them keep their caves' (LR 3.2.43–5), he may refer merely to a terrible storm, but 'wrathful' implies a terrifying, judgemental consciousness behind the raging storm.

The singular 'sky', though more often referring to the natural than the supernatural canopy, can also imply the abode of the gods and of departed souls, as when the hidden Berowne says 'Like a demigod here sit I in the sky, / And wretched fools' secrets heedfully o'er-eye' (LLL 4.3.77–8). When Pyramus dies with the words 'Now am I dead, / Now am I fled, / My soul is in the sky' (MND 5.1.303), he also speaks (prematurely to be sure) of going to heaven. Queen Margaret hopes that heaven will listen sympathetically to her vindictive cursing: 'I will not think but they ascend the sky, / And there awake God's gentle-sleeping peace' (R3 1.3.286–7). Richard III is momentarily afraid of divine vengeance when he says, 'The sky doth frown and low'r upon our army', but his natural scepticism quickly reasserts itself with 'Why, what is that to me / More than to Richmond? For the self-same **heaven** / That frowns on me looks sadly upon him' (R3 5.3.283–7). Edgar's promise to 'outface / The winds and persecutions of the skies' inevitably implies some sense of unfair divine manipulation of the elements; this anticipates both Lear's angry confrontation with the 'servile ministers' of the heavens later during the storm on the heath, and Gloucester's still later assertion in his blindness of absolute theological despair: 'As flies to wanton boys are we to th' **gods**, / They kill us for their sport' (LR 2.3.12; 3.2.21; 4.1.36–7).

SOLE(S)
The bottom of a shoe; sometimes associated through punning with 'soul'.

Gratiano advises Shylock, who is sharpening his knife on the sole of his shoe, 'Not on thy sole, but on thy soul, harsh Jew, / Thou mak'st thy knife keen' (MV 4.1.123–4). The cobbler in JC similarly says that he might use his trade 'with a safe conscience' because he is 'a mender of bad soles' (JC 1.1.12–13). Launce similarly puns when he says of a pair of shoes, 'This left shoe is my mother, . . . it hath the worser sole' (TGV 2.3.16–17).

SOLEMNITY
The performance of a solemn ritual, often a marriage.

'Our solemnity' in JN refers clearly to 'the rites of marriage [which] shall be solemniz'd' (JN 2.1.555, 539) to cement a temporary peace between England and France. In contrast, Duke Theseus's reference to his marriage with Hippolyta as 'the night / Of our solemnities' (MND 1.1.10–11), combines the performance of a religious ritual and the completion of a contract with the entertainment and the rites of lovemaking that will follow the service. 'A fortnight hold we this solemnity, / In nightly revels and new jollity' refers almost exclusively to the secular celebrations that will follow the wedding (MND 4.1.134; cf. 5.1.69–70).

SOLEMNIZ'D

Made legal and/or holy through the performance of the rites of marriage.

Portia promises her suitor the Prince of Aragon 'If you choose right wherein I am contain'd, / Straight shall our nuptial rites be solemniz'd' (MV 2.9.5–6); Rosalind distinguishes similarly between 'the contract of her marriage and the day it is solemniz'd' (AYL 3.2.314–15). See also JN 2.1.538–9; 1H6 5.3.168; and TMP 5.1.309–10.

SOLICIT

This can mean to pray for.

Thus the narrator speaks of Tarquin's 'having solicited th' eternal power / That his foul thoughts might compass his fair fair', 'As if the heavens should countenance his sin'. Shakespeare underlines the paradox of praying to ravish a good woman with 'So from himself impiety hath wrought, / That for his prey to pray he doth begin' (LUC 341–6). Othello also speaks of prayer when he advises the Desdemona whom he has wrongly condemned and is about to execute, 'If you bethink yourself of any crime / Unreconcil'd as yet to heaven and grace, / Solicit for it straight' (OTH 5.2.26–8).

SOLICITOR

(A) One who intervenes on behalf of; intercessor. The Virgin Mary is sometimes called solicitor, just as Christ is the 'advocate with the father' (1 John 2.1) on behalf of human souls on Judgement Day.

(B) When Desdemona describes herself as Cassio's 'solicitor' (OTH 3.3.27), she may cast herself in the Marian role of intercessor with the sternly judgemental Othello; she may also merely be styling herself Cassio's legal representative.

(C) See Milward (1987), 83–4, 91, on such suggestive words. See **advocation**.

SOLOMON

(A) The Old Testament lawgiver and wise man (2 Chron. 9.22).

(B) In LLL, Solomon is listed by Armado as one of the victims of love, despite his proverbial wisdom: 'yet was Salomon so seduced, and he had a very good wit' (LLL 1.2.174–5). In 1 Kings 11.1 and 4, we are told both that 'King Solomon loved many strange women' in his later life, and that 'when Solomon was old, . . . his wives turned away his heart after other gods'. Later in the same play his proverbial wisdom also informs the improbability, 'To see . . . profound Salomon to tune a jig' (LLL 4.3.165–6). Interestingly, King David did once dance a jig, at least in the English translation, in his joy over recovering the Ark (1 Chron. 15.29; 2 Sam. 6.13–16).

(C) Donne says of this jig, and more, 'David's wife, when he had danced (as she thought) undecently before the Ark, spoke freely enough' (4: 317). On this same dancing, see Donne, 10: 190. Donne also calls Solomon 'excessive in the love of women' and analyses his 'appliableness to women', which 'brought him to that sacriledge', i.e. the 'other gods' of 1 Kings 11.4 (1: 237).

SON
(A) Can refer either to Jesus the Son of God, or to the Prodigal Son of biblical parable.
(B) Autolycus makes up his own story of a man who, after a chequered life, 'compass'd a **motion** of the Prodigal Son, and married a tinker's wife' (WT 4.3.96–7). John of Gaunt refers to Christ's tomb as 'the **sepulchre** in stubborn Jewry / Of the world's ransom, blessed Mary's Son' (R2 2.1.55–6).
(C) See **Mary, prodigal, ransom, Christ**.

SORCERER, SORCERESS, SORCERY
(A) People who were thought to use the dark arts to manipulate human events and probe forbidden mysteries and the arts they practised. The designation can be used to rationalise both defeat and the need for regime change, but it usually stems as well from some actual evidence of the practice of magic.
(B) Antipholus of Syracuse merely explains away his own confusion when he asserts that Ephesus is full of 'dark-working sorcerers that change the mind' (ERR 1.2.99; 4.3.11, 66), but there are several traditions associating **Ephesus** with the dark arts; an incompetent conjurer later performs an **exorcism** on the other Antipholus (ERR 4.4.55–7). The magician Prospero claims that the 'damned witch Sycorax' whom he has dispossessed was guilty of 'mischiefs manifold and sorceries terrible' (TMP 1.2.263–4), but her dispossessed son Caliban also says of Prospero, 'I say by sorcery he got this isle; / From me he got it' (TMP 3.2.52–3). The English general Talbot describes his defeat at the hands of Joan of Arc as 'Contriv'd by art and baleful sorcery' (1H6 2.1.15); his ally Talbot also calls her 'that witch, that damned sorceress' (1H6 3.2.38); Exeter too speaks of the 'subtle-witted French / Conjurers and sorcerers' (1H6 1.1.26) who must have resorted to black magic to kill King Henry V. Only when Joan is shown conjuring devils later in the play (1H6 5.3.2–24) do we realise that these earlier comments are not merely a demonizing of both a woman and the French or a rationalizing away of the unthinkable.
(C) Acts 19.13 associates Ephesus with exorcists or 'conjurers'. Vaux includes sorcerers among those committing *'deadly sinne'* (1590a), *sigs.* G7ᵛ–G8ʳ. Hooper negatively associates 'the conjuration or sorcery' with 'priests, that bless water, wax, bone, bread, ashes, candles' (1843), 1:308. Kermode (1969), xlvii–li; and Sisson (1958) both defend Prospero's sorcery as good magic, good art. Saccio (1977), 87, ascribes Henry V's death to dysentery.

SORROW
(A) A feeling of sadness or regret or its physical manifestation or representation.
(B) Usually this is not a word with religious associations in Shakespeare, but when Cleomines tells Leontes that he has 'done enough, and have perform'd / A saint-like sorrow', indeed 'paid down / More penitence than done trespass' (WT 5.1.1–4), he must be describing both a narrative and an iconographic tradition of depicting the anguish as well as the compassion of the saints. It is possible that Anne Boleyn's 'be perk'd up in a glist'ring grief / And wear a golden sorrow' (H8

2.3.21–2) describes the halo on the grieving and/or penitent saint, though here she is first lamenting with her oxymorons the dangers and the instability she would face if she were to be crowned Henry's queen.

(C) Jewel says of the glorious sorrow of the persecuted saints of the (Protestant) Church: '[L]ook back into the times of persecution, and behold the boldness and constancy of the saints of God. . . . They armed their hearts with the comfort of God's word; thereby were they able to resist in the evil day. They were faithful until death; therefore God gave them a crown of glory' (1845–50), 4: 1172. Donne associates a personal sense of sorrow with spiritual health: 'Blessed am I in the sense of my sins, and in the sorrow for them, but blessed therefore, because this sorrow leads me to my reconciliation to God, and the consolation of his Spirit' (3: 270).

SOUL[1]

(A) When spoken of the living, 'soul' often refers both to an individual's conscience and to its accumulated record of virtuous and vicious thoughts, words and deeds which will be counted at the Last Judgement and determine future joy or misery. This usage therefore sometimes overlaps with soul as the immortal part (*OED sb.* 9), 'the spiritual part of man considered in its moral aspect or in relation to God and His precepts'. Macbeth's comment to Macduff before their final, fatal battle, 'my soul is too much charg'd / With blood of thine already' (MAC 5.8.5–6) names both conscience and the immortal soul accountable at judgement.

In both OTH and HAM, 'soul' refers at first merely to personality, tendencies of the mind or heart; increasingly, however, it means the eternal spirit of the living person that will be subject after death to judgement and its rewards and punishments. In the first half of HAM, only Hamlet's paradoxical assurance that he is spiritually safe from the ghost, even if it is a 'goblin damn'd', carries this spiritual meaning ('and for my soul, what can it do to that, / Being a thing immortal as itself?' – HAM 1.4.40, 66–7). But once 'The Mousetrap' is sprung, Claudius immediately calls himself a 'limed soul, that, struggling to be free / Art more engag'd!' (HAM 3.3.68). Hamlet resolves not to kill his uncle during this prayer, 'in the purging of his soul, / When he is fit and season'd for his passage', but when he is 'about some act / That has no relish of salvation in't' (HAM 3.3.85–6, 91–2). His fantasy is to 'trip him, that his heels may kick at heaven, / And that his soul may be as damn'd and black / As hell, whereto it goes' (HAM 3.3.93–5). 'Soul' also obviously means conscience, the record of a person's moral behaviour, during Hamlet's scene in Gertrude's chamber. After his shriving assault about the sinfulness of her marriage to Claudius, she finally concedes to Hamlet, 'Thou turn'st my eyes into my very soul' (HAM 3.4.89).

In OTH, with the exception of Cassio's drunk and generic 'there be souls must be sav'd, and there be souls must not be sav'd' (OTH 2.3.103–4), 'soul' is also at first merely personality, spunk even. However, Iago's assessment of Othello, 'His soul is so enfetter'd to her love', speaks directly to a spiritual enslavement to

Desdemona that would lead Othello 'to renounce his **baptism**, / All **seal**s and **symbol**s of redeemed sin' (OTH 2.3.343–5). Othello's 'Perdition catch my soul / But I do love thee! and when I love thee not, / Chaos is come again' (OTH 3.3.90–2) seems to confirm Iago's demonic hope, even as '**perdition**' suggests the punishments of hell. Emilia underlines her anger at Iago's slander with 'If he say so, may his **pernicious** soul / Rot half a grain a day!' (OTH 5.2.155–6). Othello will soon asks Iago, 'that **demi-devil**' as he calls him, 'Why he hath thus ensnar'd my soul and body?' (OTH 5.2.301–2). Claudius's vulnerable soul is similarly described as 'limed', caught as a bird in sticky substance, bird-lime. The soul in these exchanges is far from free; indeed, reminiscent of Luther's idea of the bondage of the will, it is like an animal easily trapped in wrongdoings and brutally punished for them.

'Soul' can also refer in the histories to a spiritual work in progress. Mowbray asks Gaunt for forgiveness for 'A trespass that doth vex my grieved soul', adding, 'But ere I last receiv'd the sacrament / I did confess it, and exactly begg'd / Your Grace's pardon, and I hope I had it' (R2 1.1.138–41). Bolingbroke's 'O, God, defend my soul from such deep sin!' (R2 1.1.187), like his lament over the wished-for news of Richard II's death ('Lords, I protest my soul is full of woe / That blood should sprinkle me to make me grow' – R2 5.6.45–6), may be religious posturing, but it is clearly religious. When Buckingham describes Richard III 'praying, to enrich his watchful soul' (R3 3.7.77) we, if not the gullible Mayor and Citizens of London, see the even more obvious hypocrisy. But after the fearful visitation of the eleven ghosts of his victims, three of whom explicitly say 'Let me sit heavy on thy soul to-morrow' (R3 5.3.118, 131, 139), Richard is moved to admit that 'shadows to-night / Have strook more terror to the soul of Richard / Than can the substance of ten thousand soldiers' (R3 5.3.216–18). The moment vividly fulfills Margaret's early curse against Richard, 'The **worm** of conscience still begnaw thy soul!' (R3 1.3.221). Falstaff tries to persuade Pistol to lend him money by reminding him that he has lied for him in the past, for which 'I am damn'd in hell', adding, 'think'st thou I'll endanger my soul gratis?' (WIV 2.2. 10, 15–16). In H5 on the night before Agincourt, the young king and his reluctant soldiers discuss the king's responsibility for the souls of his subjects who die fighting for him, and Hal at least concludes, against their opinion, that 'every subject's soul is his own' (H5 4.1.177).

In the comedies the spiritual drama of the living soul is most vividly present in MM. The phrase 'a stubborn soul' (MM 5.1.480) describes the reprobate Barnadine as someone who through either spiritual sloth or deeply ingrained habits of sinfulness declines to repent before he dies. Isabella also asks Angelo to allow more time for her sinful brother to prepare himself spiritually before executing him: 'When, I beseech you? That in his reprieve, / Longer or shorter, he may be so fitted / That his soul sicken not' (MM 2.4.39–41). Her 'Sir, believe this, / I had rather give up my body than my soul' also misunderstands Angelo's proposition as one of saintly rather than sexual sacrifice. Angelo's nervous response makes this clear: 'I talk not of your soul; our compell'd **sins** / Stand more for number than for **accompt**' (MM 2.4.55–8). Antonio's early slur against Shylock, 'An evil soul producing holy witness / Is like a villain with a smiling cheek, / A goodly apple rotten at the heart. / O, what a goodly outside falsehood hath!' (MV 1.3.99–102), suggests his opinion of Shylock's spiritual reprobation, as does Gratiano's later taunt about Shylock's eager sharpening of his knife against the sole of his shoe, 'Not on thy sole, but on thy soul, harsh Jew, / Thou mak'st thy knife keen' (MV 4.1.123–4). However, Shylock expresses his own concern about judgement when he responds to Portia's pleas that he be merciful with 'Shall I lay perjury upon my soul?' (MV 4.1.229).

(C) Of the soul as conscience, moral capacity, see Donne, 4: 82–3; Tyndale, 1: 330. Of the stain or the sickness of the soul as a repository of sins, see Andrewes, 3: 347; Donne, 2: 158. Luther calls the will 'a prisoner at the mercy of the devil' (LW 32: 92), 'enslaved rather than . . . free' (LW 33: 108); his spiritual mentor Augustine asks of the fallen soul, 'Who can doubt that his is a penal state?' (Augustine [1953], III.xviii.51 [p. 201]). Both Luther and Augustine are referring in speaking of the bondage of the will to such Pauline passages as 2 Tim. 2 and Rom. 7.18–19: 'The good that I would I do not, but the evil which I would not, that I do.' Donne speaks similarly of Romans 7.14, 'I am carnall, sold unto sinne' as 'that Captivitie, to which Adam hath enthralled him, . . . Original sinne' (7: 78–9). On the question of the bondage of the will in HAM and OTH, see Battenhouse (1969), 247–8; Hunter (1976), 126; Hunt (1996); and Hassel (1994a, 616–19, and 2001a). See also **will**[1].

SOUL[2]

(A) The spiritual part surviving after death and capable of experiencing misery or joy in a future state (*OED sb.* 10.a).

(B) This distinctive usage is most common in the English histories. The Bishop of Carlisle describes Mowbray's spiritual commitment to the Crusades when he says he fought 'For Jesu Christ in glorious Christian field' and finally died in Venice, where he 'gave / His body to that pleasant country's earth, / And his pure soul unto his captain Christ, / Under whose colours he had fought so long' (R2 4.1.93–100). Green says when Bolingbroke condemns him to death, 'My comfort is, that heaven will take our souls, / And plague injustice with the pains of hell' (R2 3.1.33–4), and Richard II as he dies treacherously at the hands of Bolingbroke's henchman Exton, 'Mount, mount, my soul! thy seat is up on high, / Whilst my gross flesh sinks downward, here to die' (R2 5.5.111–12). Falstaff says of one of the diseased prostitutes 'she's in hell already, and burns poor souls' (2H4 2.4.338–9), presumably with the torments of some venereal disease. Richard III pretends both piety and compassion when he says that he loves his brother Clarence so much that he will kill him: 'Go tread the path that thou shalt ne'er return: / Simple plain Clarence, I do love thee so / That I will shortly send thy soul to heaven, / If heaven will take the present at our hands' (R3 1.1.117–20). King Henry V once describes his formal acts of piety for his father's political crimes, including 'I have built / Two chauntries, where the sad and solemn priests / Still sing for Richard's soul' (H5 4.1.300–2).

Feste uses the belief that the soul survives death to prove Olivia a fool for excessively mourning her brother's death. His point is that she could only do so if she thought his soul damned:

> FESTE.   I think his soul is in hell, madonna.
> OLIVIA.   I know his soul is in heaven, fool.
> FESTE.   The more fool, madonna, to mourn for your brother's soul, being in heaven.
>   (TN 1.5.68–71)

Dogberry's famous malapropism, 'they should suffer salvation, body and soul' (ADO 3.3.3) stems from the same idea. Julia compares a reunion with her beloved with an eternal soul's going to heaven: 'And there I'll rest, as after much turmoil / A blessed soul doth in Elysium' (TGV 2.7.37–8). Lear similarly refers to Cordelia as 'a soul in bliss', thinking it strange that he should see her at all since he considers himself in purgatory or hell, 'bound upon a wheel of fire' (LR 4.7.45–6). On a much darker note, Othello, knowing that he has wrongly killed Desdemona, imagines them both in a **Last Judgement** tableaux, she in the place of the usually intercessory Virgin, he appealing to her for mercy. But Othello cannot imagine such transcendent forgiving: 'when we shall meet at **compt**, / This look of thine will hurl my soul from heaven, / And **fiends** will snatch at it' (OTH 5.2.273–5). He expects the severest **judgement** at the end of the play: 'Whip me, ye **devils**, / From the possession of this **heavenly** sight! Blow me about in winds! Roast me in **sulphur**! / Wash me in steep-down gulfs of liquid fire' (OTH 5.2.277–80).

The soul and the body are traditionally only in uneasy alliance in Shakespeare. In death they often perform a sort of farewell dance. In life their steps together are even more awkward. Prince Henry says of his father's coming death that like a swan he 'chaunts a doleful hymn to his own death, / And from the organ-pipe of frailty sings / His soul and body to their lasting rest' (JN 5.4.46–8; 5.7.22–4). Anne Boleyn also speaks of the 'panging / Of soul and body's severing' (H8 2.3.15–16). Melune too understands the need of meditation at death to 'part this body and my soul / With contemplation and devout desires' (JN 5.4.47–8). Toby Belch speaks of soul and body as a marriage inevitably dissolved by death when he describes Sir Andrew's fearsome skills at duelling to Viola, 'Souls and bodies he hath divorc'd three' (TN 3.4.237). In SON 146 the soul in life is 'poor' because it is 'the center of my sinful earth'. Only if it can become the master of a body that is declining in importance 'live . . . upon thy servant's loss', will it be restored to health (SON 146. 1, 9). In SON 151 the same conflict leads the speaker to lament: 'I do betray / My nobler part to my gross body's treason; / My soul doth tell my body that he may / Triumph in love' (SON 151. 5–8).

(C) See also *OED sb.* soul 2 and *OED sb.* spirit 11, where spirit is defined as that which is not body. Of the immortal soul versus the mortal body, see Andrewes, 2: 347; 2: 92–3; 5: 266–7; Donne, 8: 62; 2: 63; Bullinger, 1: 175; and Tyndale, 1: 236; 7: 322. Huttar (1968) looks at 'soul' as used in SON 146, as does West (1974). Liston (1985) discusses a reference to 'soul' in HAM.

SOUL[3]

The ghost of the deceased who returns to haunt the living. This is *OED sb.* 12: 'the disembodied spirit of a (deceased) person, regarded as a separate entity, and as invested with some amount of form and personality'.

'Souls' is used as 'ghosts' by both the spirits themselves and their perceivers in R3. Richard hears two such ghosts say 'Thy nephews' souls bid thee despair and die!' and later tells Ratcliffe 'Methought the souls of all that I had murther'd / Came to my tent, and every one did threat / To-morrow's vengeance on the head of Richard' (R3 5.3.149, 204–6). See also **ghost**.

SOUL[4]

In miscellaneous formulaic uses, the distinction between **soul**[1] and **soul**[2] is sometimes more difficult to determine. A phrase like 'pless my soul' or even 'Jeshu pless my soul' (WIV 3.1.11, 16), filtered in this case through Parson Evans' Welch accent, is very common in Shakespeare, and often used casually. Oaths like 'On my soul' and 'By my soul' (as in ADO 4.1.146; 5.1.275; and MV 5.1.209, 247) are other common emphasisers, religious in origin but seldom conveying theological self-consciousness when they are uttered. Proteus refers to the hyperbole of such utterances, at least in a romantic sphere, as 'twenty thousand soul-confirming oaths' (TGV 2.6.16). 'God rest his soul' (as in MV 2.2.71–2) is often similarly superficial. When Ophelia's song ends 'God 'a' mercy on his soul', then adds 'And of all Christians' souls, I pray God' (HAM 4.5.199–200), we know in contrast that she senses some religious import. Similarly, when Antonio offers to bond himself again for Bassanio and says 'My soul upon the forfeit' (MV 5.1.252), he also seems serious (if hyperbolic) about placing his eternal soul up as a kind of spiritual collateral against Bassanio's honesty. When the Second Lord says in AWW that a certain coward will, for 'base fear, offer to betray you, and deliver all the intelligence in his power against you, and that with the divine forfeit of his soul upon oath' (AWW 3.6.30–2), his cynicism nevertheless takes seriously the spiritual bankruptcy of swearing falsely on one's eternal soul.

SOUL-CURER

Someone whose job it is to minister to sick souls, like a curate.

The Host refers to Parson Evans and the French physician Caius as 'Gallia and Gaul, French and Welch, soul-curer and body-curer' (WIV 3.1.97–8).

SOUL-KILLING

Destroying the soul, causing damnation.

Antipholus of Syracuse, disoriented and afraid in Ephesus, speaks of the town as full of 'Soul-killing witches that deform the body' (ERR 1.2.100).

SPARROW

(A) The sparrow has come to signify in the Christian tradition God's concern for even the most insignificant of his creatures, in part from Matt. 10.29, 'Are not two sparrows sold for a farthing, and one of them shall not fall to the ground without your father'.

(B) In AYL the pious old Adam prays, 'He that doth the ravens feed, / Yea, providently caters for the sparrow, / Be comfort to my age!' (AYL 2.3.43–5). Hamlet echoes the same hope when he tells Horatio after his miraculous escape from Claudius's plot against his life, 'There is special providence in the fall of a sparrow' (HAM 5.2.219–20).

(C) Donne says of such biblical verses, 'God exercises another manner of Providence upon man, then upon other creatures. . . . *For yee are of more value then many sparrows,* says Christ there of every man' (9: 74). See also Coverdale (1846), 2: 49; Andrewes, 4: 326; and Shaheen (1999), 219, 261.

SPIRIT (also sometimes **sprite**)

Since Donne finds even among theologians 'a slacknesse, a supinenesse, in consideration of the divers significations of this word *Spirit,* [which] hath occasioned divers errours, when the word hath been intended in one sense, and taken in another' (5: 59), it should come as no surprise that Shakespeare's usage is also sometimes imprecise. In fact, Shakespeare not only tolerates this complexity and imprecision but often also exploits it.

SPIRIT[1]

(A) 'A supernatural, incorporeal, rational being or personality, usually regarded as imperceptible at ordinary times to the human senses, but capable of becoming visible at pleasure, and frequently conceived as troublesome, terrifying, or hostile to mankind' (*OED sb.* 3.a). The evil members of this group, fallen angels, demons, devils and the like, can be commanded by certain mortals, including magi, witches and conjurers, though the devil Mephastophilis implies that if they come, they come of their own will. The good ones, good angels and saints presumably, come not through conjuring but through invocation, prayer, or again of their own volition. This vast and disparate group also includes 'spirits of another sort' (MND 3.2.388), the Pucks and Ariels of (and not of) the world; these, however, reside outside the religious sphere.

(B) Of those spirits who can be conjured, the priest John Hume tells the Duchess of Gloucester that 'Margery Jordan, the cunning witch' and 'Roger Bolingbrook, the conjurer', have promised to conjure 'A spirit rais'd from depth of under ground' (2H6 1.2.75–9). Glendower boasts of a similar conjuring: 'I can call spirits from the vasty deep'. Hotspur, realist in supernatural if not political matters, demurs: 'Why, so can I, or so can any man, / But will they come when you do call for them?' (1H4 3.1.52–4). Joan of Arc has recourse to 'ancient incantations', 'charming spells and periapts' to conjure up 'choice spirits that admonish me / And give me signs of future accidents'. Like Macbeth, she knows that these 'speedy helpers . . . are substitutes / Under the lordly Monarch of the North', evil spirits that serve the devil (1H6 5.3.27, 2–7). She further calls them 'familiar spirits, that are cull'd / Out of the powerful regions under earth', and reveals in her incantation that she has had frequent recourse to them, though they finally fail her (1H6 5.3.10–11). 'Wicked spirits' in both 1H6 (5.4.42) and 2H6 (2.1.170) are clearly spirits one might conjure 'from under ground'. Lady Macbeth also conjures 'you spirits / That tend on mortal thoughts' to 'unsex me here' (MAC 5.1.40–1). All are associated with the demonic, having to do with 'witches and with conjurers' (2H6 2.1.168). See **sorcerer**, **sorcery**.

Beyond conjuring, 'spirits of light' can be both good **angels** and fallen angels, devils or the **devil** himself. 2 Cor. 11.14 tells us that '**Satan** himself is transformed into an angel of light'. Thus when Berowne wants to explain that the ladies have successfully tempted the lords because they resemble angels, he says, 'Devils soonest tempt, resembling spirits of light' (LLL 4.3.253). Apparently these dis-embodied angelic 'spirits' can be vengeful as well as alluring, as when Albany (in the pre-Christian LR) responds to the horror of Gloucester's blinding with the assumption that humanity will go wild 'If that the heavens do not their visible spirits / Send quickly down to tame these vild offenses' (LR 4.2.46–7). Because Edgar disguised as Poor Tom begins to name many devils, especially 'the foul fiend', in the same scene, we might assume that the Fool thrice calls him there a 'spirit' because he thinks him to be a devil too. 'Come not in here, nuncle', he says to Lear, 'here's a spirit', and then, 'A spirit, a spirit! he says his name's poor Tom' (LR 3.4.39–43, 46, 52, 80, 115, etc.).

Befitting both spirits and an age which could still in some ways believe in them, even still discuss them seriously, some of the usage is extremely hard to pin down. 'Methinks in thee some blessed spirit doth speak' (AWW 2.1.175), the King's hopeful words to a Helena who has offered to cure him, seems to express the wish that an angel or a saint is speaking through her (**spirit**[1]); at the same time it could say that her speaking reveals in her a blessed spirit (**spirit**[3]). Similarly, when Paulina wishes 'A better guiding spirit!' (WT 2.3.126–7) for a Perdita denied by Leontes she means both a better guardian angel (**spirit**[1]) and a better mind and will than her father's (**spirit**[3]). Later in the same scene, Antigonus, who must expose the child to the elements, also prays, 'Some powerful spirit instruct the kites and ravens / To be thy nurses!' (WT 2.3.186–7). This could be a prayer either to a god, a saint or an angel (**spirit**[1]), or to the ghost of the departed Hermione (**spirit**[2]), whom he thinks dead: 'I have heard (but not believ'd) the spirits o' th' dead / May walk again. If such thing be, thy mother / Appear'd to me last night' (WT 3.3.16–18). There are similar examples of this complexity in the discussion of HAM under **spirit**[2].

(C) Mephastophilis tells Faustus in *Dr. Faustus* (1990), 12, 'I came now hither of mine owne accord'. Andrewes calls 'angels' 'Spirits; – Glorious Spirits; – Heavenly Spirits; – Immortal Spirits' (1: 4). Johnson (1997), 689–95, discusses 'spirits' in TMP.

SPIRIT[2] (also SPRITE)

(A) A person's ghost is sometimes called a 'sprite' or 'spirit' because of its identification with the immortal soul (*OED sb.* 2.a), either in torment or in bliss. Sometimes in Shakespeare 'spirit' refers more to the ghost, the appearance, than to the soul; sometimes it refers exclusively to the soul; sometimes it means both at once.

(B) Puck speaks of midnight as 'the time of night / That the graves, all gaping wide, / Every one lets forth his sprite, / In the Church-way paths to glide' (MND 5.1.379–82); Macduff cries out upon discovering Duncan's murdered body, 'Malcolm! Banquo! / As from your graves rise up, and walk like sprites, / To countenance this horror!' (MAC 2.3.78–80). HAM is brilliant in its exploitation of the tensions implicit in these shifting boundaries of spirit, ghost and devil. Hamlet calls the ghost of his father a 'blessed spirit or a goblin damn'd' (HAM 1.4.40) and later says, 'The spirit that I have seen / May be a dev'l, and the dev'l hath power / T' assume a pleasing shape' (HAM 2.2.598–600). Is this presence a 'spirit', whether he is his father's ghost or a devil assuming that form? Or is there a distinction in Hamlet's grammar between 'spirit', his father's ghost, and 'dev'l', the demonic imposter? This ghost is called a 'spirit' several times in the play, once by the guard, twice by Horatio, twice again by Hamlet ('my father's spirit – in arms'; 'rest, rest, perturbed spirit'), and once by the ghost himself ('I am thy father's spirit') (HAM 1.1.161, 171; 1.4.6; 1.2.254; 1.5.182, 189). Old Hamlet is also called 'ghost' four times in his scene with young Hamlet, twice 'poor ghost' and once 'honest ghost' by Hamlet and once merely 'ghost' by Horatio (HAM 1.5.4, 96, 125, 138). 'Ghost' is always used in the *s.d.* in HAM, even though 'spirit' is used almost three times more often to refer to this figure in the text.

Brutus twice refers to Caesar's ghost as a spirit (JC 4.3.288, 5.3.95–6), but one of these references seems to designate more the indirect influence of Caesar's murder on the conspirators than the direct action of his literal ghost: 'Thy spirit walks abroad, and turns our swords / In our own proper entrails' (JC 5.3.95–6). When Leontes says that if he remarried, Hermione's 'sainted spirit' would 'Again possess her corpse, and on this stage / . . . appear soul-vex'd' (WT 5.1.57–9), he clearly speaks of the angry returning ghosts in revenge plays. He explains in the process his sense at least, if not also Shakespeare's, of the connection between the word 'spirit' and the word 'ghost'. The spirit is the soul of the deceased; the ghost is its manifestation in the discarded body she has chosen once again to inhabit. Hermione's 'spirit', however, unlike Old Hamlet's, is 'sainted', and so clearly abides in heaven and not in hell or purgatory. When the narrator describes Lucrece, about to kill herself, as someone whose 'contrite sighs unto the clouds bequeathed / Her winged sprite' (LUC 1727–8), her winged sprite is her immortal soul.

(C) 'Spirit' as **ghost** is closely connected to the controversy over **purgatory**. The Protestant Bullinger, for example, says with more of an ear for logic than for popular belief and psychological need (3: 400), 'The last post, wherewith they underprop their purgatory, lest it should fail, is the appearing of spirits'. He then cites Deut. 18, Isa. 8 and Luke 16 to show 'that blessed souls are not sent of God unto us to teach us any thing. Who, I pray you, would give ear to wicked and condemned souls? [which] are of no weight, but most deceivable and full of lying?' (3: 401). Sandys similarly claims that 'The gospel hath chased away walking spirits' (1841), 60. Despite such assertions, Shakespeare still has Puck describe as 'Damned spirits all' the 'ghosts, wand'ring here and there', who must 'Troop home to churchyards' at dawn (MND 3.2.380–2); Hamlet also listens, albeit cautiously, to his father's ghost (HAM 1.4.40–2; 2.2.598–603); and Leontes imagines Hermione's as a 'sainted spirit' which might 'possess her corpse' and walk the stage *(WT* 5.1.57–9). Greenblatt (2001), 200–4, considers the appearance of Hermione's 'spirit' to Antigonus as both ghostlike and dreamlike, then suggests some of the religious dimensions of her coming back to life at the end of the play.

SPIRIT[3]

(A) Spiritual essence; directing inclination or nature (*OED sb.* 8.a).

(B) 'Methinks in thee some blessed spirit doth speak' (AWW 2.1.175) could mean that Helena's speaking reveals her own blessed spirit, or that some supernatural spirit (**spirit**[1]) is speaking through her; similarly, Paulina may wish Perdita a strong mind or a more competent guardian angel when she says, 'Jove send her / A better guiding spirit!' (WT 2.3.126–7).

(C) On 'spirit' as the human soul; see Andrewes, 5: 427; 3: 273–4.

SPIRIT[4]

(A) The Holy Spirit (*OED sb.* 6.b).

(B) It is possible that when Westmoreland says that the 'white investments' of the clergy 'figure innocence, / The dove, and very blessed spirit of peace' (2H4 4.2.45–6), he speaks (from Matt. 3.16 – 'the spirit of God descending like a dove') of the Holy Spirit as well as merely meaning peaceable. Bishops of the time customarily wore white vestments.

(C) For Andrewes on the Holy Spirit, see 3: 128, 207, 383; 2: 347. On readings of this line in 2H4, see Humphries, ed. (1966), 181n, citing Hoby (1701) and Shaaber, ed. (1940), 283n.

SPIRIT[5] *fig.*

Mercutio offers 'To raise a spirit in his mistress' circle', meaning apparently an erection rather than a conjuration (ROM 2.1.24), though the conjuration of spirits empowers his sexual metaphor. The Poet says that Timon's unwise generosity, which has here attracted a jeweller, a merchant, a painter, and this poet, reveals the 'Magic of bounty! all these spirits thy power / Hath conjur'd to attend' (TIM 1.1.6–7). The Chorus in H5 apologises for 'The flat unraised spirits that hath dar'd / On this unworthy scaffold to bring forth / So great an object' as Harry of England (H5 Pr. 8–11). Prospero similarly calls the actors of the Masque of Ceres, 'Spirits, which by mine art / I have from their confines call'd to enact / My present fancies' (TMP 4.1.120–2). Since Shakespeare can use 'spirits' as a metaphor for actors who are impersonating human beings but also for beings conjured by a magician, Prospero's literal magic is so evocative of Shakespeare's metaphoric magic that it is hard to distinguish them.

SPIRITUAL[1]

(A) Religious (rather than secular).

(B) Henry VIII wishes Cardinal Wolsey's 'contemplation were above the earth, /

And fix'd on spiritual object', but fears 'His thinkings are below the moon, not worth / His serious considering' (H8 3.2.130–5). His words may be 'full of heavenly stuff', but his 'earthly audit' has stolen too much time from his 'spiritual leisure' (H8 3.2.136–41). Wolsey finally agrees with his sovereign's audit of his spiritual life: 'Had I but serv'd my God with half the zeal / I serv'd my king, He would not in mine age / Have left me naked to mine enemies' (H8 3.2 455–7). With 'Thou art reverent / Touching thy spiritual function, not thy life', 'Unreverent Gloucester' insults the Bishop of Winchester before another King (1H6 3.1.49–50) by distinguishing between his religious office, which is reverent, and his life, which is not. Queen Katherine makes a similar complaint to Cardinal Wolsey when she says 'You tender more your person's honor than / Your high profession spiritual' (H8 2.4.116–17). Finally, 'Our spiritual convocation' (H5 1.1.76) is the Archbishop of Canterbury's way of referring to a deliberating assembly of clergy.

(C) Becon speaks of 'the spiritual magistrate, I mean the minister of God's word' (2: 318).

SPIRITUAL[2]

Coming from a spirit, or an oracle.

In WT Leontes's 'spiritual counsel' (2.1.186) refers to the advice of the oracle, which he promises to follow but actually ignores.

SPIRITUALITY

(A) Members of the spiritual community.

(B) The Archbishop of Canterbury encourages Henry V to pursue his 'right' in France, 'In aid whereof we of the spirituality / Will raise your Highness such a mighty sum / As never did the clergy at one time / Bring in to any of your ancestors' (H5 1.2.132–5).

(C) Both Tyndale, 1: 180, and Cranmer (1846), 2: 73, illustrate this usage of 'the spirituality'.

SPOON

Gifts commonly given to commemorate baptisms, usually in sets of twelve (RIV, 1060n) and decorated with images of Christ's Apostles. Also, long spoons are utensils associated more than once in Shakespeare with eating with the devil (as in ERR 4.3.63–4), presumably because of their protection from the heat.

Henry VIII jokes with Archbishop Cranmer, a man of modest means but considerable talents, that he is reluctant to sponsor the Princess Elizabeth in baptism because he cannot afford to give her the baptismal spoons associated with that role: 'Come, come, my lord, you'd spare your spoons'. He then promises Cranmer two more 'noble partners' (H8 5.2.201–2) to share the expense. The Porter's Man also makes a wisecrack about the wild christening party that ensues begetting 'a fry of fornication', which will in turn 'beget a thousand' Christians, creating a huge market for christening spoons (H8 5.3.36–9). See **pork** for a similar joke.

STEEPLE
The spire of a church.
Given how many ancient steeples still seem to be standing in England today, it is interesting how often steeples are threatened with destruction in Shakespeare. The First Fisherman in PER describes whales so ravenous that they 'never leave gaping till they swallow'd the whole parish, church, steeples, bells, and all', then 'cast bells, steeple, church, and parish up again' (PER 2.1.33–4, 42–3). Hotspur describes a nature so sick with 'a kind of colic' that it 'Shakes the old beldame earth, and topples down / Steeples and moss-grown towers' (1H4 3.1.31–2). Lear calls upon the 'cataracts and hurricanoes' to 'spout / Till you have drench'd our steeples' (LR 3.2.2–3). Speed's 'O jest unseen, inscrutable; invisible, / As a nose on a man's face or a weathercock on a steeple' (TGV 2.1.135–6) compares two familiar protuberances to an overly obvious jest.

STEVEN, SAINT
(A) St Stephen, an early deacon, probably a Hellenistic Jew, and the first Christian martyr, stoned to death *c.* 35. Feast Day: 26 December.
(B) Though TIT takes place in Imperial Rome, its Clown once gives the Emperor of Rome the oddly Christian-sounding greeting, 'God and Saint Steven give you godden' (TIT 4.4.42–3). He also swears just later 'by' **lady** (TIT 4.4.48).
(C) Farmer (1978), 361–2; Baring-Gould (1914), 15: 296–9.

STIGMATIC
Since a *stigmata* is a supernatural mark of some kind, a stigmatic is one who bears such a mark, like Cain or St Anthony.
  Clifford calls the hunchbacked Richard of Gloucester a 'foul stigmatic' (2H6 5.1.214), and Queen Margaret says of his various deformities, 'Sin, death and hell have set their mark on him, / And all their ministers attend on him' (R3 1.3.292–3). She also calls him 'a foul misshapen stigmatic, / Mark'd by the destinies to be avoided' (3H6 2.2.136–7).

STREW
Scatter or spread.
  One could have 'strew'd repentant ashes on his head' (JN 4.1.110), if metaphor can be believed, but the literal meaning of Arthur's usage here derives from a glowing poker that has become ash-colored as it cools, and will therefore no longer serve to put out Arthur's eyes.

STUDY
(A) This could refer to both the contemplation and the scholarship that were sometimes associated with the monastic life, especially when 'study' and 'fast' are combined.
(B) Angelo is associated with this discipline, at least by analogy, when Lucio describes him to Isabella as someone who 'doth rebate and blunt his natural edge / With profits of the mind: study and fast' (MM 1.4.60–1). The vow of the

lords in LLL is similarly associated by analogy with a life of monastic retreat when Berowne summarises their vows 'Not to see ladies, study, fast, not sleep', and later 'To fast, to study, and to see no woman' (LLL 1.1.48; 4.3.288). This traditional linkage of study and fasting also informs such jests as 'to study where I well may dine, . . . Or study where to meet some mistress fine, . . . Or . . . Study to break it, and not break my troth' (LLL 1.1.61, 63, 66). On the other hand, when the King of Navarre calls 'Things hid and barr'd . . . from common sense' 'study's godlike recompense' (LLL 1.1.57–8), there is something Faustian rather than religious in his desire.

(C) In Scene 5, when Mephastophilis rewards Dr Faustus for signing away his soul by allowing him to 'aske what thou wilt', Faustus immediately asks about such hidden things as the location of hell, even its existence, learning in the process more than he bargains for (ll. 118–40).

SUBSTITUTE

(A) Once in Shakespeare this signifies the idea that a king is God's **minister**, His representative on earth.

(B) Gaunt explains to the Duchess of Gloucester that he must refuse to avenge her husband's death on King Richard II because 'God's is the quarrel, for God's substitute, / His deputy anointed in His sight, / Hath caus'd his death, the which if wrongfully, / Let heaven revenge, for I may never lift / An angry arm against His minister' (R2 1.2.37–41).

(C) Shaheen (1999), 364–6, tells us that the Tudors particularly stressed this theme, using Rom. 13.4 as its chief authority: 'For he is the minister of God; . . . for he beareth not the sword for nought: for he is the minister of God to take vengeance on him that doth evil.' Shaheen adds that Lily's widely known *Grammar* (1549), *sig.* C5r, and the second part of the 'Sermon of Obedience' (1968r), 73–5, also support this idea.

SULPHUR

Probably because of the noxious sulphurous fumes which sometimes belch out of volcanoes like Vesuvius and Aetna, and therefore apparently from the bowels of the earth, the smell of sulphur was associated with hell's **flames**. This sulphurous smell was also associated with lightning, and therefore with God the **Thunderer**.

Hamlet's father's ghost seems therefore to have come from either **hell** or **purgatory** when he describes the place to which he must soon return: 'My hour is almost come / When I to sulph'rous and tormenting flames / Must render up myself' (HAM 1.5.2–4). Othello also makes this olfactory association when he asks,

> Whip me, ye devils,
> From the possession of this heavenly sight!
> Blow me about in winds! roast me in sulphur!
> Wash me in steep-down gulfs of liquid fire!
> (OTH 5.2.277–80)

Extrapolating from the idea that hell, and therefore Satan's bowels, could lie at the centre of the earth and explain its sulphurous smell, Lear conflates hell and rampant sexuality: 'there's hell, there's darkness, / There is the sulphurous pit, burning, scalding, /Stench, consumption' (LR 4.6.127–9).

Pericles shows us that the smell of sulphur is also associated with God and his thunderbolts when he prays in the midst of a great storm to 'The god of this great vast' to 'still / Thy deaf'ning, dreadful thunders, gently quench / Thy nimble, sulphurous flashes' (PER 3.1.1–6). The resolutely Christian novice Isabella also associates 'thy sharp and sulphurous bolt' in distinguishing a usually 'Merciful heaven' from 'man, proud man' (MM 2.2.115–17). But usually, as in COR (5.3.152) and CYM (5.4.115), the god who is associated with this sulphurous bolt is classical, not Christian.

SUMMONERS

(A) Officers who call the accused to appear in an ecclesiastical or secular court.

(B) When Lear, speaking of the 'Close pent-up guilts' which the fearful thunder and lightning would force open in any conscience, orders them to 'cry / These dreadful summoners grace' (LR 3.2.57–9), he uses this word metaphorically.

(C) See BEV, 1194n; Arden KL, 103n. Plummer (1995), 3–4, 31–5, summarises discussions of Chaucer's Summoner, including his role in Chaucer's 'bitter satire on clerical abuse'.

SUNDAY

(A) Usually the Christian sabbath, a day of worship, and therefore a day which carries various religious and quasi-religious associations; also a holiday from work.

(B) In half of its eleven occurrences in Shakespeare, 'Sunday' is named as the day on which Kate and Petruchio will be married: 'kiss me, Kate, we will be married a' Sunday' (SHR 2.1.298, 299, 322, 324, 393, 395). That Sunday was a traditional day of rest from work is made clear when Marcellus remarks about the frenzied work of the shipbuilders in Denmark, 'whose sore task / Does not divide the Sunday from the week' (HAM 1.1.75–6). Hotspur describes as 'velvet guards and Sunday-citizens' people who have put on their best behaviour along with their best clothes, people too refined to use 'A good mouth-filling oath' (1H4 3.1.253–6). Benedick associates such Sunday constraints with the emasculation of marriage: 'and thou wilt needs thrust thy neck into a yoke, wear the print of it, and sigh away Sundays' (ADO 1.1.200–3). It is interesting how many of these references posit Sunday as a day of constraint, a day of emasculation, a woman's day rather than a man's.

(C) 'Remember that thou keep holy the Sabbath day' is of course one of the Ten Commandments (*BCP*, 249). Hatchett (1980), 429, tells us that the Puritans resisted the Reformed tradition of having weddings on Sundays.

SUPERNAL
Heavenly or divine.

When King Philip of France responds to King John's challenge of his authority to champion Arthur as the rightful heir to the crown of England, he says it comes from God, 'that supernal judge that stirs good thoughts / In any breast of strong authority' (JN 2.1.112–13).

SUPERNATURAL
(A) Beyond the natural, spoken of both miraculous events and non-human agents. Donne calls 'the Subject of supernaturall philosophy, Divinity' (9: 51), claims that 'in a regenerate man, all is Metaphysicall, supernaturall' (9: 230), and says that the 'Resurrection is not a conclusion out of naturall **Reason**, but it is an article of supernaturall **Faith**' (7: 95).
(B) Lafew, discussing the King's apparently miraculous recovery at Helena's hands, says to Bertram and Parolles:

> They say miracles are past, and we have our philosophical persons, to make modern and familiar, things supernatural and causeless. Hence it is that we make trifles of terrors, ensconcing ourselves into seeming knowledge, when we should submit ourselves to an unknown fear.
>
> (AWW 2.3.1–6)

In Lafew's irony, 'causeless' means without demonstrable cause. Macbeth describes the witches' prophecy as a 'supernatural soliciting' that 'Cannot be ill; cannot be good' (MAC 1.3.130–1). His agreement to their supernatural contract leads him, a man originally endowed with adequate moral and theological understanding, indeed 'full of the milk of human kindness' (MAC 1.5.17, 1.7.1–31), to 'cancel and tear to pieces that great bond' (MAC 3.2.49), with God, his king, his friend, and his own nature, until he can finally only postulate a universe 'signifying nothing' (MAC 5.5.28).
(C) As C. S. Lewis explains (1978), 47–8, miracles are by definition events that defy natural explanation, though they do not always go against natural laws.

SUPERSTITION (SUPERSTITIOUS)
(A) The word a sceptic, or a rival, would use to describe something another group or person believes. Early Reformers frequently use 'superstition' to criticise the worship and doctrine of the Roman Church, and the more extreme Reformers later make similar claims against the Church of England, provoking defences from such later Church of England apologists as Hooker, Andrewes and Donne that would have sounded Catholic a generation earlier.
(B) Because both early and later Reformers in England tried to prohibit kneeling to statues and praying to saints and other intercessors as forms of idolatry, Perdita's request that the onlookers not disapprove if she kneel and pray to the statue of her mother Hermione cuts close to the bone of Reformation disputes about forms of religious worship: 'do not say, 'tis superstition, that / I kneel, and

then implore her blessing' (WT 5.3.43–4). Queen Katherine of Aragon, notorious for her piety and her love of God, makes it clear that she is also using 'superstitious' as a synonym for 'idolatrous' when she says of her faithfulness to and respect for her husband,

> Have I with all my full affections
> Still met the King? lov'd him next heav'n? obey'd him?
> Been, out of fondness, superstitious to him?
> Almost forgot my pray'rs to content him?
>
> (H8 3.1.129–32)

Pericles challenges the Sailor's belief that dropping the (apparently) dead body of Pericles' Queen Thaisa overboard will still the storm by saying 'That's your superstition' (PER 3.1.51). The word is used in other classical plays to express disapproval of the heeding of dreams and other omens (see JC 2.1.195; TRO 5.3.79; and WT 3.3.40). Dionyza also calls Cleon superstitious in PER (4.3.49) because he is afraid of the judgement of the gods.

(C) See Grindal (1843), 136–40; Bullinger, 4: 502; Fulke (1843), 1: 218; Latimer (1844–45), 1: 70; and Jewel (1845–50), 3: 351 for early Reformers' comments about the 'superstitious' Roman uses of crosses and crossing, shrift, beads, bells, bishops, candles and confession. Donne defends the Church of England fifty years later against such continuing complaints even while embracing the earlier Reformed position: 'I doe not intend, that we should decline all such things, as had been superstitiously abused, in a superstitious Church ... [rather than appreciate] the good use which is made of them in ours. That because pictures have been adored, we do not abhor a picture; Nor sit at the Sacrament, because Idolatry hath been committed in kneeling' (8: 331). Hooker similarly defends the Church of England's practice against what he calls 'pretenders of Reformation' who claim 'our prayers, our sacramentes, our fastes, our tymes and places of publique meetinge together for the worship and service of God, our mariages, our burials, our functions, elections and ordinations ecclesiasticall, allmost whatsoever wee doe in the exercise of our religion accordinge to lawes for that purpose established, all thinges are some waie or other thought faltie, all thinges stained with superstition' (V.4.1). Aquinas (*ST* II.2.92) and Augustine (1958, II.20.30), both speak of idolatry, excessive or inappropriate worship, as superstitious. Mason (1997) argues that Shakespeare unsettlingly juxtaposes superstition and scepticism in R3.

SURPLICE

(A) This loose white vestment worn over the tunic or cassock in religious dress came into use during the eleventh century. Compared to the more elaborate ecclesiastical vestments like the belt, the cope, the stole and the chasuble, the surplice is usually cut of humble cloth, but it was still Roman, and therefore controversial, especially in its more elaborate forms. In considering '**Attire** belonging to the service of God', and especially 'whether the surplice be a fit garment to be used in the service of God', Hooker speaks repeatedly of the 'white garment' associated with the celebration of the Eucharist as one of the 'garmentes of holines', and resists the Puritans in 'Theire allegations . . . *that this popish apparell, the surplice especiallie hath bene by papistes abominablie abused; . . . a monument of Idolatrie*' (V. 29.1–4; V. 30.1).

(B) '[T]he priest in surplice white' is a neutral usage in PHT (13). Defending plain speaking, the Clown in AWW says more caustically, 'Though honesty be no puritan, yet it will do no hurt; it will wear the surplice of humility over the black gown of a big heart' (AWW 1.3.93–5). He seems to associate the Puritans' true pride, their 'big heart', with their black gowns, and their false humility with their opposition to the white surplice that covers it.

(C) Grindal says that 'Ministers are required to wear commonly a long gown, a square cap, and a kind of tippet over the neck hanging from either shoulder, and falling down almost to the heels. In public prayers and every sacred administration, besides this ordinary dress, the ecclesiastical discipline requires the ministers to wear a linen garment, called, by a new appelation, a *surplice*' (1843), 339. Nicolson (2003), 35–6, 43, 53, often mentions the Puritan opposition to the surplice and the **cross**. See also Bradshaw (2002), 'Vestments', 'Clerical Vestments'; *OxfordEncyRef*, 1: 366–71; and *NewCathEncy*, 'Surplice', 13: 821, and 'Clerical Dress', 3: 947–8.

SWEAR
See **'zounds**.

SWORD
(A) This weapon is associated by metonymy with battle, by iconography with the execution of divine and human justice, by shape with the cross, biblically with the ploughshare ('turning swords into ploughshares' – Isa. 2.4) and by spelling with the 'Word'. There is also the biblical metaphor that calls God's word a sword (as in Eph. 6.17).

(B) The sword's symbolism of authority deputed from God is explicit when the Duke in MM says of earthly judges like himself or his deputy Angelo, 'He who the sword of heaven will bear / Should be as holy as severe' (MM 3.2.261–2). Isabella refers to the same idea earlier when she advises Angelo to use 'the deputed sword' with 'grace' and 'mercy' rather than mere justice (MM 2.2.60, 62–3). A newly crowned King Henry V surprises the Lord Chief Justice by praising his integrity and keeping him in office: 'You are right justice, and you weigh this well, / Therefore still bear the balance and the sword' (2H4 5.2.102–3). He then hands the Lord Chief Justice

> Th' unstained sword that you have us'd to bear,
> With this remembrance, that you use the same
> With the like bold, just, and impartial spirit
> As you have done 'gainst me.
>
> (2H4 5.2.114–17)

Hal draws here on both the secular and the religious iconography of Justice (and sometimes Christ) carrying both the sword and the scales, which stand for judging fairly and executing justice decisively. The judgemental Othello also recalls the iconography of Justice when he observes of the still-sleeping Desdemona that her 'balmy breath . . . dost almost persuade / Justice to break her sword!' (OTH 5.2.16–17). Since Othello is wrong, this imagery marks his ironic misjudgement of both himself and his wife.

'Turning the word to sword' (2H4 4.2.10) is an orthographic pun that derives from the close spelling of the two words and their expected opposition in meaning. As its speaker, Prince Hal's brother Prince John, makes clear, the pun works because the Word, the Bible, has often been used to inspire and authorise the sword, war, even though it also preaches forgiveness and forbearance. Prince John tells the Archbishop of York, churchman but also rebel leader, that he would rather hear

> Your exposition on the holy text
> Than now to see you here an iron man, talking,
> Cheering a rout of rebels with your drum,
> Turning the word to sword, and life to death.
> (2H4 4.2.7–10)

Shallow similarly teases the angry Parson Evans just before a threatened duel: 'What? the sword and the word? Do you study them both, Master Parson?' (WIV 3.1.44–5).

Richard II's comment that he stops the duel between Mowbray and Bolingbroke because 'our eyes do hate the dire aspect / Of civil wounds plough'd up with neighbors' sword' (R2 1.3.127–8) reverses the biblical injunction (from Isa. 2.4), which prescribes turning swords into ploughshares. It also complicates it with metaphor, since bodies will be ploughed up in this violence, not the earth.

Because the sword is shaped in the form of the cross, it could be raised for protection against evil spirits as well as more mortal enemies. This usage probably informs Antipholus of Syracuse's quip about the retreating opponents, who include the Courtesan whom he tried to exorcise and also called both 'witch' and 'Sathan' (ERR 4.3.48, 67, 79): 'I see these witches are afraid of swords' (ERR 4.4.147), especially if the actor has raised his sword protectively, like a cross, in the earlier confrontations. There is also of course a simpler joke here about their cowardice.

(C) For an illustration of Christ holding both the sword and the scale at judgement, see Harbison (1976), fig. 85, and of Christ and the sword, figs. 73, 76, 115, 125, 126. Dessen (1969) argues that the violence in HAM overcomes the religious potential of the cross formed by the sword-hilts. Kaplan (1971), notes that Pistol's oath of 'sword' is a corruption of 'God's word'. On the traditional iconography of **Michael** and the sword of **justice**, see Sheingorn (1985), 22; Emmerson (1985), 89, and Harbison (1976), 127–32. On the scales of judgement, see Sheingorn

(1985), 21–6, 42–3, and Harbison (1976), 64, 145. For some Last Judgement art in the vicinity of Stratford in Shakespeare's time, see Davidson and Alexander (1985), 36–40, 69–72, 138–42, and figs. 12, 28 and 29.

'SWOUNDS
Contraction for Christ's or God's wounds. See **'zounds**.

SYMBOL
Something used for or regarded as representing something else; a material object representing something spiritual.

Shakespeare's one usage of this word is not literary but religious. Iago tells himself that Othello's 'soul is so enfetter'd' to Desdemona's love that she could 'win the Moor, were't to renounce his baptism, / All seals and symbols of **redeemed** sin' (OTH 2.3.343–5). He names the sacrament of **baptism**, but his 'all' might also include the bread and wine of communion, the **oil** of the last **unction**, and the **sign** of the **cross**.

SYNAGOGUE
(A) The place of Jewish worship.
(B) Shylock is most compellingly human when, after his 'Hath not a Jew hands' speech and his revelation of his deep love for Leah his wife, which he expresses through the turquoise ring, he directs his friend, 'Go, Tubal, and meet me at our synagogue; go, good Tubal, at our synagogue, Tubal' (MV 3.1.59–73, 120–3, 129–30).
(C) The Reformers are generally respectful when they refer to this Jewish place of worship (e.g. Donne, 2: 217–18; 10: 164; Bullinger, 4: 4; Jewel (1845–50), 2: 942; a few, however, cannot resist alliteratively calling Roman Catholic churches something like 'the synagogues of Satan'. See, for example, Becon, 2: 65; 3: 401; Bale (1849), 282.

TAINT¹ *sb. fig.*
An immoral discolouring (*OED sb.* 1 *Taint* C.1.a, 2.a).

Viola, disguised as a man, includes 'lying, vainness, babbling, drunkenness', but especially 'ingratitude' in the 'taint of vice whose strong corruption / Inhabits our frail blood' (TN 3.4.354–7). Malcolm, having just pretended to be both lustful and avaricious in order to test Macduff's honesty, reverses his story by saying '[I] here abjure / The taints and blames I laid upon myself' (MAC 4.3.123–4). In the first case the noun 'taint' is associated with both inborn follies and vices; in the second, it refers to two of the seven deadly sins.

TAINT² *v.*
To infect, contaminate, or corrupt morally.

The ghost advises Hamlet 'Taint not thy mind' (HAM 1.5.85) in executing revenge. Here the word can have psychological as well as moral dimensions because Hamlet verges on madness as well as sinfulness in response to his father's 'dread command' (HAM 3.4.108).

TAINTED *adj.*
Contaminated morally.

When Bertram describes Parolles as 'A very tainted fellow, and full of wickedness' (AWW 3.2.87), he illustrates and defines this usage. In a similar key but at a higher volume, Joan of Arc calls her English accusers 'polluted with your lusts, / Stain'd with the guiltless blood of innocents, / Corrupt and tainted with a thousand vices' (1H6 5.4.43–5).

TARTAR¹ *sb.*
The Central Asian races, and their descendants like the Mongols and the Turks, that overran Eastern Europe in the Middle Ages (*OED sb.*² 1). Also used generically for pagans and savages (*OED sb.* 3).

Using 'Tartar' racially, Lysander refers to the darker Hermia, whom he once loved, as a 'tawny Tartar' (MND 3.2.263). In the same play Puck refers to these warlike peoples when he promises Oberon that he will return 'Swifter than arrow from the Tartar's bow' (MND 3.2.101). When the witches in MAC pitch 'nose of Turk and Tartar's lips' into their racially charged 'hellbroth' (MAC 4.1.29), they reveal that Turk and Tartar could be superficially distinguished as well as identified in the Renaissance. On a note more of emotional than physiological difference, Helena says that the King owes her such 'gratitude' that even were his a 'flinty Tartar's bosom' he would 'answer thanks' (AWW 4.4.6–8). Referring similarly to the 'brassy bosoms and rough hearts of flints, / From stubborn Turks, and Tartars never train'd / To offices of tender courtesy', the Duke tries unsuccessfully to persuade an equally obdurate Shylock to give a 'gentle answer' of 'commiseration' and not justice for Antonio (MV 4.1.30–4).

TARTAR[2] *adj.*
(A) For Tartarus, the pagan hell; also used at times for the Christian hell. Tartarus was the sunless region under Hades where the Titans were imprisoned; limbo, on the other hand, was to Catholics a place between hell and heaven for unbaptised infants and the good people who died before the coming of Christ.
(B) Dromio of Syracuse conflates these two hells when he says of his master in jail that he is 'in Tartar limbo, worse than hell'; he also describes his master's jailor as a 'devil in an everlasting garment' who 'before the judgment carries poor souls to hell' (ERR 4.2.32–3, 40, 46). Toby's enthusiasm for Maria's plan to gull Malvolio leads him to the casual promise that he would follow her 'to the gates of Tartar, thou most excellent devil of wit' (TN 2.5.205–6). His 'devil' makes this Tartarus hell, not some castle in eastern Europe or western Asia. That Tartarus could be more seriously associated with a Christian hell is clear when Henry V expresses his disappointment that Cambridge has betrayed him: 'If that same demon that hath gull'd thee thus / Should with his lion gait walk the whole world, / He might return to vasty Tartar back, / And tell the legions, "I can never win / A soul so easy as that Englishman's" ' (H5 2.2.121–5).
(C) Battenhouse (1951), 190, makes the useful point that 'the purgatory of the Ancients, or their hell, or their vague afterworld, hades' are all 'Hell from a Christian point of view'.

TEMPERANCE *sb.* **TEMPERATELY** *adv.*
(A) A moderation or self-restraint in words, emotions or actions. This and **fortitude** were the two of the four cardinal virtues of antiquity most readily appropriated into various Christian schemes.
(B) An example in the classical plays is the Roman Proculeius' impossible request of Cleopatra, who is surely the pattern of all intemperance, 'O temperance, lady' as she laments Antony's death (ANT 5.2.48). Escalus more accurately describes the Christian Duke as 'a gentleman of all temperance' (MM 3.2.237). On the other hand, the often intemperate Hamlet tries to convince his mother of his sanity by telling her 'My pulse as yours doth temperately keep time' (HAM

3.4.140). He also urges the actors to 'acquire and beget a temperance' over 'the whirlwind of your passion' (HAM 3.2.6–7) when he cannot control his own.

(C) See *ST* II.2.141–70; Atkinson (1995), 836–7, 881–2; Roberti (1962), 1209–10; Becker and Becker (2001), 1693–9; *NewCathEncy*, 13: 985–7. Hunt (1995) argues that Shakespeare makes the gaining of temperance a major theme in AYL.

TEMPLE[1]

(A) A place of both classical and Christian worship in Shakespeare's usage.

(B) 'The temple of great Jupiter' is the place where peace will be ratified between the Romans and the Britains (CYM 5.5.482–3). 'Apollo's temple' is located at 'sacred Delphos', where the oracle will determine Hermione's guilt or innocence (WT 2.1.183). 'Smoke the temple with our sacrifices' (CYM 5.5.398) refers to pre-Christian religious rites. The many references to the 'temple' in MND (2.1.238; 4.1.180, 197; 4.2.15) also probably describe Greek places of worship, since the setting is in Athens several centuries before Christ; however, the setting there is not so clearly just Athenian, since the fairies, and certainly the labourers, are more English than Greek.

'Temple' can also be a Christian church in Shakespeare. It is in Christian Messina where 'Claudio enrag'd; swore he would meet her as he was appointed next morning at the temple, and there, before the whole **congregation**, shame her with what he saw o'ernight, and send her home again without a husband' (ADO 3.3.159–63). A Catholic friar tries to conduct the marriage ceremony. Portia's 'first, forward to the temple', spoken to Morocco (MV 2.1.43), must also refer to a Christian place of worship in Belmont, since the opposition of Christian versus Jew is so prominent throughout the play. Duncan refers naively to 'the temple-haunting martlet' that evidences that 'heaven's breath / Smells wooingly' in the castle in which he is about to be sacrilegiously murdered (MAC 1.6.4–6). In the histories, the English Talbot promises to 'erect a tomb' to Salisbury within the 'chiefest temple' of Orleans (1H6 2.2.12–13), but 'temple' refers as often to the residence complexes of the Knights Templars of the twelfth and thirteenth centuries, and to their successors, the Inns of Court, as it does to religious buildings (as in 1H4 3.3.199; 1H6 2.4.3, 125).

(C) Donne discusses early Christian usage: '[I]n the very beginning of the Primitive Church, to depart from the custome, and language, and phrase of the *Jews*, and *Gentiles*, as farre as they could, they did much to abstain from this name of *Temple*, and of *Priest*, so that till *Ireneus time, some hundred eighty years after Christ*, we shall not so often find those words, *Temple*, or *Priest*, yet when that danger was overcome, when the Christian Church, and doctrine was established, from that time downward, all the *Fathers* did freely, and safely call the Church the *Temple*' (2: 221–2). See also Calfhill (1846), 233; Becon, 2: 65; Pilkington (1842), 261.

TEMPLE[2] *fig.*

(A) The metaphoric temple of the body is a recurrent religious metaphor which possibly derives from 1 Cor. 3.16: 'Know ye not that ye are the temple of God, and that the Spirit of God dwelleth in you?' Complaining of moral abuse, Andrewes says, 'Our bodies, . . . are far from Temples; rather *prostibula* than *Templa*, brothel-houses, brokers' shops, wine-casks, or I wot not what, rather than Temples. Or if Temples, Temples the wrong way, of Ceres, Bacchus, Venus' (2: 361).

(B) Miranda's exultant 'There's nothing ill can dwell in such a temple' (TMP 1.2.458) and Lucrece's despairing 'Her sacred temple spotted, spoil'd, corrupted' (LUC 1172) are two good examples of this usage. The ravisher Tarquin similarly describes Lucrece after the rape as one whose 'soul's fair temple is defaced' (LUC 719; cf. HAM 1.3.12–14). Macduff grieves over the murdered body of King Duncan: 'Most **sacrilegious** murther hath broke ope / The Lord's **anointed** temple, and stole thence / The life o' th' building' (MAC 2.3.67–9). Here the religious components are all spelled out; it is a sacrilege to deface the temple of the Lord, especially when holy building and human life are made one in the anointed body of God's deputy, the king.

(C) See also Donne, 6: 347; Becon, 3: 608. George Herbert, of course, also calls his collection of devotional poems *The Temple* (1975).

TEMPT, TEMPTATION, TEMPTER

(A) To induce someone to do wrong (*v.*), the inducing inclination to do wrong (*sb.*), or the inducer (*sb.*). Though of course temptation is not exclusive to Christian or even religious experience, it receives a lot of attention during the Christian era, so much so that 'the Tempter' is a common epithet for Satan. However, Donne, like Shakespeare, often stresses the individual's own role in his or her temptation: 'To admit, to invite, to tempt tentations, and occasions of sin, and so to put our selves to the hazard of a spiritual perishing; to give fire to concupiscencies with licentious Meditations, either of sinful pleasures past, or of that which we have then in our purpose and pursuit; to fewel this fire with meats of curiosity and provocation; to blow this fire with lascivious discourses' (5: 228).

(B) Shakespeare often dramatises an intricate blend of the human and the demonic in discussions of temptation within the plays. Angelo wonders about himself and Isabella, 'The tempter or the tempted, who sins most?' (MM 2.2.163); when Angelo concedes, 'nor doth she tempt; but it is I' (MM 2.2.164), he blames himself. On the other hand, he also assigns the temptation to the devil rather than his own heart: 'O cunning enemy, that to catch a saint, / With saints dost bait thy hook! Most dangerous / Is that temptation that doth goad us on / To sin in loving virtue' (MM 2.2.179–82). The roles of human and divine tempter are also richly combined in R3, especially when Queen Elizabeth resists Richard's plea for her daughter's hand with, 'Shall I be tempted of the devil thus?' and he responds, 'Ay, if the devil tempt thee to do good' (R3 4.4.418–19). She may take the name quite literally; at the same time she is, like many other characters in the play who associate 'tempt', 'tempted' and 'devil' with Richard, merely calling him evil (R3 4.2.34–5; 1.4.12–13). Similarly, Richard's response may reflect the condescending glee he takes in this assignation, or concede that he is the devil's man. Horatio's question, 'What if it tempt you toward the flood, my lord', that is towards suicide, suggests that the ghost might be demonic (HAM 1.4.66–7). On the other hand, Hamlet's 'Let the bloat king tempt you again to bed' (HAM 3.4.182) posits Claudius as a mortal tempter.

When Lancelot Gobbo considers whether or not to leave the service of the Jew Shylock for the Christian Bassanio, he is surprised that it is 'the fiend' who 'tempts' him to run away from the Jew, 'My conscience [which] says "No" ' (MV 2.2.2–7):

> To be rul'd by my conscience, I should stay with the Jew my master, who (God bless the mark) is a kind of devil; and to run away from the Jew, I should be rul'd by the fiend, who, saving your reverence, is the devil himself. Certainly the Jew is the very devil incarnation, and in my conscience, my conscience is but a kind of hard conscience, to offer to counsel me to stay with the Jew.
>
> (MV 2.2.22–30)

His confusion amuses us, but it also manifests the moral complexity of the whole play. Troilus, afraid of Cressida's sexual infidelity, refers to 'a still and dumb-discoursive devil, / That tempts most cunningly' (TRO 4.4 90–1). Because of the pre-Christian setting, it is difficult to tell whether this tempter is personified or merely names the personal inclination to do wrong.

Iago uses his assertion that Desdemona and Cassio could have lain 'naked in bed', 'and not mean harm' (OTH 4.1.5) to provoke from his usually unsophisticated General a very sophisticated theological response that combines self-tempting, the devil's tempting, and something more, a forbidden tempting of heaven's protection: 'It is hypocrisy against the devil. / They that mean virtuously, and yet do so, / The devil their virtue tempts, and they tempt heaven' (OTH 4.1.5–8). Theologically, one should not put oneself unnecessarily in the way of temptation. That tempts heaven in the way that Christ was tempted by the devil to tempt heaven, by casting himself from the heights of the temple in order to make God save him, thereby proving his divinity.

(C) See Matt 4.7: 'Thou shalt not tempt the Lord thy God' (and cf. Luke 4.12 and Deut. 6.16). Donne says of our tempting ourselves, '[W]e can direct *tentations* upon our selves. . . . A woman of tentation, . . . shee paints, she curls, she sings, she gazes, and is gazed upon; There's an arrow shot *at randon*; shee aim'd at no particular mark; And thou puttest thy self within shot, and meetest the arrow; Thou soughtest the tentation, the tentation sought not thee' (2: 57). Von Rosador (1986) looks at how temptation operates in MAC.

TEXT

(A) Holy writ.

(B) Bassanio, looking at the three caskets, reasons, 'In religion, / What damned error but some sober brow / Will bless it, and approve it with a text' (MV 3.2.77–80). He is speaking of the annoying tendency of heretics to find their textual support in holy writ. John of Lancaster complains to the rebel leader the

Archbishop of York that he would rather hear 'Your exposition on the holy text' (2H4 4.2.7) than see him on the field of battle. Finally, when Nathaniel tells Holofernes, 'society, saith the text, is the happiness of life' (LLL 4.2.161–2), he could be referring to Gen. 2.18 or a passage in the Service for Holy Matrimony (*BCP*, 291), both of which say essentially that marriage is ordained for 'mutual society, help, and comfort'.

(C) This usage of 'text' is very common in Donne (as in 2: 213; 7: 365; 5: 48) and Andrewes (4: 44; 2: 232), whose sermons are often close readings of biblical texts. See BEV, 52n; Shaheen (1999), 130.

THANK

(A) Express gratitude to God.

(B) Mistress Quickly's and Justice Slender's 'I thank heaven' (WIV 1.4.130; 3.4.58) are followed in one case by 'I praise **heaven** for it' and 'All is in His hands above' (WIV 1.4.144; 141) and in the other by Slender's 'I give heaven praise' (WIV 3.4.59). This religious cluster suggests a habitual, possibly Puritan, manner of speaking and thinking. That Slender and Mistress Quickly could hardly be farther from the **Puritan** mould is part of the joke. Rosalind's caustic advice to Phebe to 'thank heaven, fasting, for a good man's love' (AYL 3.5.58) humorously combines the religious disciplines of **prayer** and **fasting**. Falstaff calls Mistress Quickly 'a thing to thank God on'. When she responds, 'I am no thing to thank God on' (1H4 3.3.117–18), we see her taking the phrase literally enough to picture a client uttering his godly thanks while astride her. Shylock's 'I thank God, I thank God' about Antonio's 'ill luck, ill luck' (MV 3.1.102, 99) is a much more sinister example of this usage in the comedies. For even more casual uses of 'Thank God', see TMP 1.2.175; MM 2.1.72; ADO 1.1.130–2; 3.3.30; LLL 1.2.164–5; AYL 3.3.38–41; 5.1.24.

There is less of this usage in the histories (but see 2H6 2.1.105; 4.2.105). The best examples are Richard of Gloucester's outrageously hypocritical, 'I thank my God for my humility' and his sarcastic response to his mother's despairing 'Art thou my son?', 'Ay I thank God, my father, and yourself' (R3 2.1.73; 4.4.155–6). The statute of 1606 forbidding profanity in plays may partly explain the absence of the phrase 'Thank God' in the tragedies with Christian settings. Shakespeare shows some sensitivity to the setting of the pre-Christian Roman and Greek plays by changing the phrase to 'thank gods' or 'thank heavens' rather than 'thank God' or 'thank heaven'. Examples include 'thank the heavens, lord' (TRO 2.3.240); 'We thank the gods' and 'I thank the gods' (COR 1.9.8; 2.1.121); and 'thank the holy gods' (PER 5.1.198).

(C) For an eloquent prompt of such thankfulness, see Andrewes, 4: 339–40. See also **Oldcastle** and **iteration**.

THANKED

'God be thank'd', 'Heaven be thank'd', etc., is another formula for the casual expression of thanksgiving.

Richard III's cynical 'God be thank'd, there is no need of me' (R3 3.7.165) uses a hypocritical piety to fool the citizens. The exposed traitor Cambridge's 'God be thanked for prevention' (H5 2.2.158) is also hard to credit, since he speaks of his own aborted plot to assassinate his friend, King Henry V. Benedick criticises Claudio's flippant response to the charge that he has slandered Hero, 'You break jests as braggards do their blades, which, God be thank'd, hurt not' (ADO 5.1.186–8).

THANKFUL

Full of thanks to God or the gods.

When Enobarbus responds to Antony's news that his wife Fulvia is dead, 'Why, sir, give the gods a thankful sacrifice' (ANT 1.2.161), his ironic usage correctly honours both the Roman tradition of thankful sacrifice to the gods and the plural form of the noun.

THANKS *sb.*

Gratefulness.

As with 'thank', 'thanks', 'thanked' and 'thankful', phrases like 'give thanks' and 'give God thanks' are fairly common and usually casual in Shakespeare. They are twice humorously associated with false **humility**. Dogberry advises the Watch about his good looks, 'give God thanks, and make no boast of it' (ADO 3.3.19–20). Jaques's similarly boasts of his mind rather than his body: 'I think of as many matters as [Duke Senior], but I give heaven thanks, and make no boast of them' (AYL 2.5.35–7; cf. TMP 1.1.21–6; JN 1.1.83). Henry VIII knows that it is political flattery when Gardiner, now Bishop of Westminster, says, 'Dread sovereign, how much are we bound to heaven / In daily thanks, that gave us such a prince' (H8 5.2.149–50), but he still forgives him his slights to Cranmer, and tries to reconcile them.

THANKSGIVING

(A) Prayer of gratitude, often associated with meals. According to *Preces Privatae* (1564), 'the Acts of Thanksgiving in Eating shall always be concluded by these short prayers', ending '*pacem nobis donet perpetuum. Amen*'.

(B) A Gentleman in MM says, 'There's not a soldier of us all, that in the thanksgiving before meat, do relish the petition well that prays for peace' (MM 1.2.14–16).

(C) *Preces Privatae* (1564), *sig.* Gg6, is cited in Eccles, *Variorum MM*, 22n.

THUNDER

This awesome weather phenomenon was once commonly associated with the gods. Thor is the thunderer of the North; Jove is the classical thunderer named in Shakespeare. Donne reveals that the Christian God can also be heard 'in the voice of Thunder' (10: 109–110): 'How often does God speake, and nobody heares the voyce? He speaks in his Canon, in Thunder' (6: 217). Bullinger also warns that 'terrible threatenings and sharp revengement of God's just judgment are thundered from heaven against us transgressors' (1: 252).

In both Christian and pre-Christian settings in Shakespeare, the dread of thunder is associated with the idea that it manifests heaven's anger and administers deserved retribution. When Macbeth resolves to kill Macduff to quiet his 'pale-hearted fear', 'And sleep in spite of thunder' (MAC 4.1.82–6), he suggests that he worries about more than human reprisal. The Christian convert Othello also asks about the divine punishment he thinks Iago deserves in terms of thunder: 'Are there no stones in heaven / But what serves for the thunder?' (OTH 5.2.234–5). When the Christian novice Isabella compares Angelo's abusive severity in the administration of justice to 'thunder[ing] / As Jove himself does' (MM 2.2.110–11), she shows the fluidity of such classical and Christian references.

Thunder is often associated with divine cautioning and divine retribution in the pre-Christian LR. The sceptic Edmund is just manipulating his father when he says of Edgar, 'I told him, the revengive gods / 'Gainst parricides did all the thunder bend' (LR 2.1.45–6). Cordelia speaks more reverently of Jove's 'deep dread-bolted thunder' (LR 4.7.32). Kent too associates the 'horrid thunder' of the night with the 'wrathful skies' (LR 3.2.43–6). On the heath, in the midst of the storm within and the storm without, Lear, 'contending with the fretful elements' (LR 3.1.4), reveals a richer set of beliefs and misconceptions. He desperately hopes that some power in the universe can through such cataclysmic events as 'all-shaking thunder' purge nature of its annoying imperfections, especially 'all germains spill at once / That makes ingrateful man' (LR 3.2.6–9). Thunder is also an instrument of judgement to Lear, and therefore a supernatural prompt to fear if not also to repentance:

> Let the great gods,
> That keep this dreadful pudder o'er our heads,
> Find out their enemies now. Tremble, thou wretch
> That hast within thee undivulged crimes
> Unwhipt of justice! Hide thee, thou bloody hand;
> Thou perjur'd, and thou simular of virtue
> That art incestuous! Caitiff, to pieces shake,
> That under covert and convenient seeming
> Has practic'd on man's life! Close pent-up guilts,
> Rive your concealing continents, and cry
> These dreadful summoners grace. I am a man
> More sinn'd against than sinning.
>   (LR 3.2.49–60)

In contrast to the Christian Macbeth who hopes to still the judgemental voice of thunder (MAC 4.1.86), the pagan Lear tries to raise its volume. After more humbling, Lear merely asks Poor Tom 'What is the cause of thunder?' (LR 3.4.155). Such questions are informed by classical and Christian presuppositions that connect thunder with the righteous wrath of God; but because tragedies are not sermons in thunder-stones, their answers are elusive.

THUNDER-BEARER
An epithet for Jove.

Lear, trying unsuccessfully to control his anger, says to Goneril, 'Let shame come when it will, I will not call it. / I did not bid the thunder-bearer shoot, / Nor tell tales of thee to high-judging Jove. / Mend when thou canst, be better at thy leisure' (LR 2.4.226–9). By the time he says 'the **thunder** would not peace at my bidding' (LR 4.6.102), Lear has come to question both the moral universe and his own titanic powers to influence it, but such religious beliefs inevitably inform the play.

THUNDER-DARTER
This epithet for Jove the thunderer is used flippantly by Thersites to underline the 'short-arm'd ignorance' (TRO 2.3.10–14) of the Greeks, which would obviously deter them from throwing their lightning very far or very well.

TITHE¹ *sb.*
(A) Tenth; this is the proportion of one's income or wealth prescribed in both Lev. 27.30–2 and Deut. 14.22–6 as the proper annual gift to the Church. Donne says in one place, '*God* takes a tenth part of our goods, in *Tythes*' (4: 366), but reveals that by 1620 'payment of Tythes is growne matter of controversie' (3: 206). In an agrarian economy, the tithe is often a tenth of the commodity rather than a tenth of its monetary value. Shakespeare had, incidentally, business interests in tithing, having purchased some of its rights and duties, which included the maintenance of a parish vicar.
(B) The Duke tells Mariana that they have a lot to do before they can spring the bed-trick on Lucio, and reap its rewards by saying, 'Come, let us go, / Our corn's to reap, for yet our tithe's to sow' (MM 4.1.74–5). They haven't even sown the seed yet; it will therefore be a good while before they can reap the harvest, and count out a tithe for the Church. When Sir Thomas More says of his quick rise to high office, 'I in my father's life / To take prerogative and tithe of knees / From elder kinsmen' (STM 3.9–10), he speaks metaphorically of the tithe as a required gesture of reverence.
(C) See *ST* II.2.87.2, where Aquinas cites Gen. 28.22 in defending the giving of 'Tithes of all Things'. Hooker, V.448–63, also discusses the biblical responsibility of tithing, locating its authority in Gen. 28.20. See also Cross and Livingstone (1997), 1626. On Shakespeare's purchase of a lease of 'tithes of corn, grain, blade, and hay' in and around Stratford in 1605, see Schoenbaum (1977), 246–7.

TITHE² *v.*
To enforce such giving to the Church.

King John tells the papal legate Pandulph that because the Pope's is a 'usurp'd authority', 'no Italian priest / Shall tithe or toll in our dominions' (JN 3.1.160, 153–4).

TITHE-PIG
One of those commodities given as a tithe.

One of Mercutio's fantasies about Queen Mab has her coming 'with a tithe-pig's tail / Tickling a parson's nose as 'a lies asleep, / Then he dreams of another **benefice**' (ROM 1.4.79–81). The Parson dreams of a position where the gift of money might be more common than the gift of a pig.

TOKEN
(A) Usually just a confirming, an identifying, or an authenticating mark, but in a religious sense, an event serving to demonstrate divine power or authority (*OED sb.* 4).
(B) In the 'golden set' of the sun on the evening before his battle with Richard III, Richmond finds 'token of a goodly day to-morrow' (R3 5.3.19–21). Because 'token' can have this specifically theological meaning, it reinforces Richmond's assertion of good cause (R3 5.3.240). More sinister divine tokens, like 'cross blue lightning', are discussed by Casca:

> It is the part of men to fear and tremble
> When the most mighty gods by tokens send
> Such dreadful heralds to astonish us.
> (JC 1.3.50, 54–6)

When Berowne calls the love tokens that the ladies are wearing 'the Lord's tokens', he uses a popular phrase for marks of the plague to describe the plague of love: 'They are infected, in their hearts it lies; / They have the plague, and caught it of your eyes' (LLL 5.2.420–3).
(C) Sandys speaks of 'the signs and tokens going before the coming of Christ to judgement', citing Joel 2.10, 31; Rev. 4.12,13; and Matt. 24.29 as biblical examples (1841), 356–7.

TOLEDO
A cathedral town in central Spain, near Madrid.

Cardinal Wolsey is said in H8 to have supported the separation of King Henry VIII and Queen Katherine to spite Emperor Charles V, Katherine's nephew, 'For not bestowing on him at his asking / The archbishopric of Toledo' (H8 2.1.162–4).

TOLL
Levy taxes, as on parishioners (*OED v.*3 1).

When King John tells the Pope's representative Pandulph 'No Italian priest / Shall tithe or toll in our dominions' (JN 3.1.153–4) he is possibly distinguishing the one-off toll from the yearly tithe.

TOLLING
Ringing, as of church bells.

Northumberland compares ringing church bells to 'the first bringer of unwelcome news', whose 'tongue / Sounds ever after as a sullen bell, / Remem-b'red tolling a departing friend' (2H4 1.1.100–3).

TORMENT[1] *sb.*

The punishments of the damned (*OED sb.* 2.b).

Clarence dreams that a ghost, 'Dabbl'd in blood', 'shriek'd out aloud', 'Seize on him Furies, take him unto torment!' (R3 1.4.54–7). Technically, of course, this is a mythological rather than a religious reference, since the Furies were female divinities who punished crimes at the instigation of their victims, but after Dante there is considerable Christian and classical overlapping. An angel, 'a legion of foul fiends', and Charon also figure into this culturally panoramic dream (R3 1.4.46, 53, 58). Prospero compares Ariel's imprisonment in the oak to 'a torment / To lay upon the damn'd' (TMP 1.2.289–90).

TORMENT[2] *v.*

Inflict such punishment upon the damned.

An extremely angry Clifford uses the verb in a simile describing his burning desire for revenge:

> The sight of any of the house of York
> Is as a fury to torment my soul;
> And till I root out their accursed line,
> And leave not one alive, I live in hell.
> (3H6 1.3.30–3)

Similarly, Richard of Gloucester first describes the world 'but hell' until 'this head / Be round impaled with a glorious crown' (3H6 3.2.168–71), then uses both **torment**[1] and **torment**[2] to describe this hellish state: '[I] Torment myself to catch the English crown; / And from that torment will I free myself' (3H6 3.2.179–80).

TORMENTING

Delivering the torments of hell.

The 'sulph'rous and tormenting flames' (HAM 1.5.2–4) which old Hamlet's ghost must suffer are either those of hell or of **purgatory**; the problem is that neither Hamlet nor the audience can be sure which place it is.

TORTURE

Can like '**torment**' be used to describe hell's pains, or those of purgatory. Milton describes hell as a place of 'torture without end' in *PL* 1.67. Often *fig.*

'This torture should be roar'd in dismal hell' (ROM 3.2.44) is Juliet's first response to what she thinks is the news that Romeo has killed himself. Romeo figuratively calls the news of his banishment 'purgatory, torture, hell itself' (ROM 3.3.17–18). To the Friar's hopeless attempt to convince him that the banishment is 'dear mercy, and thou seest it not', Romeo similarly responds, 'Tis torture, and not mercy. Heaven is here / Where Juliet lives' (ROM 3.3.28–30). Hubert also protests his innocence of Prince Arthur's death, 'Let hell want pains enough to torture me. / I left him well' (JN 4.3.135–9). In a moment of comic exaggeration, Pistol associates tortures with hell in his fustian curse of Mistress Quickly: 'I'll see her damn'd first, to Pluto's damned lake, by this hand, to th' infernal deep, with Erebus and tortures vile also' (2H4 2.4.156–8). His mangled classical and Christian reference to Quickly's damnation includes Pluto as the god of the underworld and Erebus as the place-name.

TRANSCENDENCE
Something beyond human or earthly limitations.

Though their discussion is tinged with cynicism, Lafew, Parolles and Bertram discuss the miraculous recovery of the king at Helena's hands as 'great power, great transcendence', and gloss it as 'the very hand of heaven' in 'a most weak and debile minister' (AWW 2.3.1, 17–18, 30–34). The ballad they quote calls this miracle 'A showing of a heavenly effect in an earthly actor' (AWW 2.3.23–4).

TRANSGRESS'D
(A) Did wrong. Rom. 5.14 speaks of 'Adam's transgression'.
(B) Benedick's comment about Beatrice, 'I would not marry her, though she were endow'd with all that Adam had left him before he transgress'd' (ADO 2.1.250–2), is Shakespeare's only religious usage.
(C) For parallel usage, see Andrewes, 2: 150; 5: 450; Donne, 9: 257; 2: 58–9; and Becon, 3: 605.

TREASURY
A place which protects things of great value. From Luke 12.34, 'Where your treasure is, there will your heart be also', the word can describe a storeplace of spiritual valuables.

When a naive King Henry VI hears only 'The treasury of everlasting joy' in Gloucester's 'Were it not good your grace could fly to heaven?' (2H6 2.1.13–18), it is clear that he has missed the homicidal ambition that lies just beneath the surface of the words.

TRESPASS
A wrongdoing (*sb.*); doing wrong (*v.*). Like 'transgression', 'trespass' is a word more exclusively religious today than it was in the Renaissance. The most familiar formulation is in the Lord's Prayer: 'Forgive us our trespasses, as we forgive those who trespass against us.'

In Shakespeare the strictly religious usage is hard to isolate from the more general reference to wrongdoing. Clearly, when Mowbray speaks to Gaunt of 'A trespass that doth vex my grieved **soul**', and then adds, 'But ere I last receiv'd the **sacrament** / I did confess it, and exactly begg'd / Your Grace's **pardon**, and I hope I had it' (R2 1.1.138–41), there are too many religious words surrounding 'trespass' for the word not to resonate theologically. This is equally true when

Cleomines tells Leontes of his long, deep **penitence** for Hermione's death, 'Sir, you have done enough, and have perform'd / A **saint-like sorrow**. No fault could you make / Which you have not **redeem'd**; indeed paid down / More penitence than done trespass' (WT 5.1.1–4). Since the exchange between Romeo and Juliet is a sonnet driven by religious metaphors of **pilgrims**, **devotion**, **palmers** and **prayer**, and since Hamlet has spent most of the bedroom scene **shriving** his mother, priest-like, for her sexual attachment to Claudius, Romeo's 'Sin from my lips? O trespass sweetly urg'd! Give me my sin again!' and Hamlet's 'That not your trespass but my madness speaks' (ROM 1.5.109; HAM 3.4.146) also feel like religious usage.

TRESPASSES, BOOK OF
(A) The book (from Rev. 20.12) in which all of an individual's sins were recorded for the Last Judgement. This could refer both literally and metaphorically to the conscience. Sandys says, 'The **books** shall be laid wide open in the sight of all **flesh**; the book of God, and the book of man's **conscience**; the book of his **law**, and the book of our life. It shall be examined in the one, what God hath commanded; in the other it shall be testified how man hath obeyed: in the one, what works of mercy he hath required at our hands; in the other, what fruits of merciless affection the ground of our stony hearts hath yielded. And according to the evidence both of the one and of the other, the eternal and irrevocable sentence shall pass from the mouth of God' (1841), 367.
(B) Somewhat anachronistically in pre-Christian Athens, one of the supplicants in TNK tells Theseus that if he grants her wish, 'This good deed / Shall raze you out o' th' book of trespasses / All you are set down there' (TNK 1.1.32–4).
(C) See also Donne, 9: 408.

TRIPLE CROWN
See **crown**.

TROTH
Pledge or promise. In the wedding ceremony the couple plights troth; in other words, they promise to keep their promise; they pledge faithfulness or truthfulness. Even contemporary definitions of the *v.* 'plight' reveal its almost exclusive connection either to keeping the promise to marry or the promise to be faithful in marriage. See **troth-plight**.
   Lysander's attempt to persuade Hermia to sleep with him in the forest clearly uses 'troth' as a noun for engagement to be married: 'One turf shall serve as pillow for us both, / One heart, one bed, two bosoms, and one troth' (MND 2.2.41–2). Hermia, less sure than Anne Hathaway about sex before marriage, gently demurs, to which Lysander responds, not varying his line much, that they are essentially one already: 'Two bosoms interchained with an oath, / So then two bosoms and a single troth' (MND 2.2.49–50). She remains unpersuaded (MND 2.2.58–9). On the other hand, when Posthumus calls himself 'The loyall'st husband that did e'er plight troth' (CYM 1.1.96), he is clearly if also ironically

describing himself to his wife Imogen as someone already married, and loyal to his vows.

Because Anne Boleyn so often says 'By my troth' in swearing to the Old Lady that she is not interested in marrying King Henry VIII, she finally replies, 'Yes, troth and troth. You would not be a queen?' (H8 2.3.23, 33, 34). All these 'troths' protest too much to be believed; they also call attention to the prior pledge to Queen Katherine, one she is even now encouraging Henry to break. Emilia swears 'By my troth', that is, by her wedding vows, that she would willingly cuckold her husband if it would make him a king: 'Who would not make her husband a cuckold to make him a monarch?' (OTH 4.3.70–7).

TROTH-PLIGHT

The statement of the pledge of fidelity during the wedding ceremony (*OED sb.* 1 – 'a solemn promise . . . *esp.* of marriage') or the promise to become married in the future (*OED sb.* 2 – 'Engaged, . . . affianced'). Near the end of the wedding ceremony, the man says 'and thereto I plight thee my troth' (pledge thee my word), and the woman 'and thereto I give thee my troth'. Soon thereafter the Priest concludes the ceremony with 'Those whom God hath joined together, let no man put asunder' (*BCP*, 293).

When Leontes says of the Hermione he considers unfaithful, 'My wife's a hobby-horse, deserves a name / As rank as any flax-wench that puts to / Before her troth-plight' (WT 1.2.276–8), either meaning could apply, though putting-to sexually before even an engagement might be considered a severer fault than merely having sex with the affianced before the formal vows of marriage. When Leontes (in a happier moment) later introduces Florizel to Hermione as 'This' your son-in law, / And son unto the King [Polixenes], whom heavens directing / Is troth-plight to your daughter' (WT 5.3.149–51), 'troth-plight' probably means married, else 'son-in-law' would make little literal sense. Camillo, having earlier advised Florizel to flee to Sicily, where he may 'Enjoy your mistress' and 'marry her' (WT 4.4.530), subsequently refers to Perdita as the wife of a prince with 'your fair princess' and 'your fresh princess'. He calls her at the same time, and without embarrassment, 'the partner of your bed' (WT 4.4.544–7, 551). When Bardolph concedes the justice of Nym's anger that Nell Quickly has married Pistol, 'troth-plight' must mean betrothed and not married: 'It is certain, corporal, that he is married to Nell Quickly, and certainly she did you wrong, for you were troth-plight to her' (H5 2.1.17–19).

TRUMPET

(A) There is a common assumption, from 1 Cor. 15.52 as well as many references from Rev. 8–11, that at the general day of judgement, doomsday, 'the trumpet shall sound, and the dead shall be raised incorruptible, and we shall be changed'. Latimer says of the damned in this drama, 'They shall be cast out in the last day into everlasting fire, when the trumpet shall blow, and the angels shall come and gather all *offendicula* ["the offenders of this world"] from amongst the elect of God' (1844–45), 2: 190–1.

(B) Juliet says in characteristic hyperbole that if 'Romeo [is] slaughter'd' and 'Tybalt . . . dead', 'Then, dreadful trumpet, sound the general doom, / For who is living, if those two are gone?' (ROM 3.2.65, 67–8). The Priest in HAM refers to the same idea when he says of Ophelia's 'doubtful' death and niggardly burial rites, 'but that great command o'ersways the order, / She should in ground unsanctified been lod'g / Till the last trumpet' (HAM 5.1.228–30). So does Young Clifford when, as hyperbolically as Juliet, he bemoans his father's death: 'Now let the general trumpet blow his blast' (2H6 5.2.43).

(C) See also Andrewes, 5: 146. For an illustration of angels blowing trumpets at Judgement, see Harbison (1976), figs. 125, 126, 71, 72.

TRUMPET-TONGUED

(A) Angels, especially those like Gabriel who heralded great events, were associated iconographically with trumpets. 'Blow, Gabriel, Blow' reveals in its continued popularity the persistence of this legend. The New Testament often depicts **angels** blowing trumpets, as in Rev. 8.2, 6: 'Then the seven angels, which had the seven trumpets, prepared themselves to blow their trumpets'.

(B) As Macbeth considers with a still-fully-functioning moral consciousness the consequences, here and hereafter, of killing Duncan, one of 'the pauser[s]' that occurs to his memory, his reason, and his imagination is this image of angelic trumpeting: 'his virtues / Will plead like angels, trumpet-tongued, against / The deep **damnation** of his taking-off' (MAC 1.7.18–20).

(C) Donne says of this voice of God's judgement, 'Yet thou must heare this voice of the Archangell in the Trumpet of God. The Trumpet of God is his loudest Instrument' (4: 71). See Shaheen (1999), 626. Cf. Matt. 24.31.

TRUTH

(A) Verity. Andrewes reminds us that during his hearing of the case against Christ, Pilate directs the question to Christ (in John 18.38), '*Quid est veritas?*', 'What is truth?' Unfortunately, 'when he had asked it another thing took him in the head and up he rose and went his way before Christ could tell him what it was. Such is our seeking for the most part. Some idle question cast, some table-talk moved; some *Quid est veritas* and go on our way' (1: 312).

(B) In Shakespeare's religious usage, truth is sometimes associated with God and opposed to the devil; it is also opposed to 'superstition' and once or twice associated with words like 'religious', 'holy' and 'heavenly' (H8 4.2.74; 5.4.28). 'So help you truth and God' (R2 1.3.183), King Richard's oath-keeping formula to Mowbray and Bolingbroke, implies both that truth and God are distinct and that they are aligned. If one, there would be no need to say both, though Richard is known for his redundancy; if two, one valuing earthly esteem and one heavenly, they are nevertheless not necessarily opposed. On the other hand, when Hotspur confronts Glendower for reciting all the miraculous events that heralded his birth, and possibly for believing them too, he says, twice, 'tell truth and shame the devil' (1H4 3.1.58, 61). Here the devil and truth are as surely in opposition as truth and God are aligned in Richard's formula. A similar connection between truth and holiness, falsehood and the devil, occurs when Helena, complaining that Lysander is lying about his love for her but calling it truth, says, 'When truth kills truth, O devilish-holy fray!' (MND 3.2.129). Even in his moral and epistemological decline, Macbeth can say 'I . . . begin / To doubt th' equivocation of the fiend, / That lies like truth' (MAC 5.5.41–3). The most explicit connections between 'truth' and 'religious' occurs when Queen Katherine says of her friend Griffith's honest description of Cardinal Wolsey's piety in death, 'Whom I most hated living, thou hast made me, / With thy religious truth and modesty, / Now in his ashes honor. Peace be with him!' (H8 4.2.73–5).

(C) Donne, trying to reconcile differences in biblical interpretation, says of competing Catholic and Protestant truth-claims, 'Where divers senses arise, and all true, (that is, that none of them oppose the truth) let truth agree them. But what is Truth? God; and what is God? Charity; Therefore let Charity reconcile such differences' (9: 94–5). See also *ST* II.2.109; Vaux (1590a), *sig.* A6ᵛ; Bale (1849), 436. Satan is Milton's 'false dissembler' (*PL* 3.681).

TUNED

(A) In harmony and concert. This can be used in reference to the **harmony** of the spheres, which signifies the divinely orchestrated orderliness of the created universe.

(B) When Cleopatra looks after his death for a hyperbole to describe Antony's greatness, she finds among others 'his voice was propertied / As all the tuned spheres' (ANT 5.2.83–4). The oxymoron 'Melodious discord, heavenly tune harsh sounding' (VEN 431), Venus' response to the sound of a 'no' coming from Adonis's desirable lips, also derives from this symbol of universal harmony, though her 'heavenly' is obviously sensual rather than spiritual.

(C) See Davies, *Orchestra* (1975), 87–126, 357–76, for a rich representation of many of the correspondences between literal and figurative harmony.

TURK

(A) One of the 'infidels' traditionally opposed to Christian powers and values. Becon's is a characteristic condemnation: 'Consider how grievously and without all mercy the people of Christ in many places be most cruelly invaded, handled, led captive, miserably entreated, imprisoned, slain, murdered, and all their goods spoiled, brent, and taken away of that most spiteful and Nero-like tyrant the great Turk, that mortal enemy of Christ's religion, that destroyer of the christian faith, that perverter of all good order, that adversary of all godliness and pure innocency' (1: 239). Even modeling charity, Becon can say, 'A preacher of the Lord's word is bound to do good unto all men; not only to such as be of the household of faith, but also to Turks, Jews, Saracens, and such other miscreants' (1: 22). Such comments reveal the anxiety of the Christian West about Ottoman expansion into Europe in the last half of the sixteenth century.

(B) It is thus not surprising that when Othello tries to think of an outrageous other who deserved death as much as he does for killing Desdemona, 'a malignant and a turban'd Turk' is the image that comes to his mind (OTH 5.2.353–6).

Othello similarly says of the brawl in which Cassio wounds Montano just after a heaven-sent storm has dispersed the threatening Turkish fleet, 'Are we turn'd Turks, and to ourselves do that / Which heaven hath forbid the Ottomites?' (OTH 2.3.170–1). Rosalind pretends to find scorn in Phebe's love-letter to her with 'Why, she defies me, / Like Turk to Christian', embodying their timeless military and religious confrontation (AYL 4.3.32–3). When Iago tells Desdemona, 'Nay it is true, or else I am a Turk' (OTH 2.1.114), he could as easily have said 'Saracen', 'Jew' or 'Ethiope', much as Benedick says of his new conversion to love for Beatrice, after having professed faithlessness in women, 'If I do not love her, I am a Jew' (ADO 2.3.263). 'Turk', like 'Jew', means 'liar' to them. In HAM 'turn Turk with me' (HAM 3.2.276) means going bad, becoming a renegade or a non-believer. Because she has fallen in love with Benedick after vowing never to love a man, Margaret similarly calls Beatrice one who has 'turn'd Turk', shown apostasy after professing disdain (ADO 3.4.57).

When Lafew says of the churlish lords who would rather not marry Helena, 'Do all they deny her? And they were sons of mine, I'd have them whipt, or I would send them to th' Turk to make eunuchs of' (AWW 2.3.86–8), he refers accurately to the very real fear of Christians captured by the Turks, in raids or in battles, that they would be castrated and sometimes made eunuchs.

(C) See also Donne, 4: 206; 10: 143; Tyndale, 2: 104; Jewel (1845–50), 2: 1036–7. Archbishop Rowan Williams (2002), ch. 5, speaks from a very modern perspective of the tenacity and oversimplification of such ethnic and religious branding, then and now. On the treatment of male Christians captured in Islamic lands, see Malieckal (2002); and on early modern English and Venetian fears of Turks and black Moors, see Malieckal (1999). Vitkus (1997) also discusses the way Turks were seen in Europe, and the anxiety they inspired.

TURLYGOD

OED sb. tirl 1 & 2 has for 'tirl' a wheel of some kind and an act of twirling.

When Edgar mysteriously calls himself 'Poor Turlygod! poor Tom!' (LR 2.3.20) as he resolves to disguise himself as a bedlam beggar, he could use the word to express his self-abandonment to a wild and whirling world of lost identity and changing rules, one not apparently governed by anything just or comprehensible.

UNANEL'D *adj.*

(A) 'Anele' means to administer one of the last rites of the Catholic Church, extreme unction, which is the application of holy oil to the head of the dying. 'Unanel'd' therefore refers to dying without having received this rite.

(B) The ghost of Hamlet's father implies that he is in purgatory 'for a certain term' when he says that he was killed while sleeping, and therefore

> Cut off even in the blossoms of my sin,
> **Unhous'led**, disappointed, unanel'd,
> No **reck'ning** made, but sent to my **account**
> With all my **imperfections** on my head.
> (HAM 1.5.10, 76–9)

(C) See *ST* Suppl. 29–33. Calfhill questions the efficacy and need of this sacrament (1846), 244; More (quoted in Tyndale, 1: 276), defends it as having 'an express promise in the epistle of St James, where he biddeth that if any be sick, he shall induce the priests to come and pray for him and anoint him with oil'.

UNCHARITABLY

Lacking generosity or love. Because 'charity' is according to St Paul the greatest of the three great Christian theological virtues, the others being faith and hope (1 Cor. 13.13), some uses of the word (or here, its opposite), invite religious associations. Charity can refer to love of persons and to love of God; it can also refer to the good acts stemming from that love.

Buckingham, trying to silence her curses and prayers, tells Queen Margaret, 'Peace, peace, for shame! if not, for **charity**', provoking the response,

> Urge neither charity nor shame to me.
> Uncharitably with me have you dealt,

> And shamefully my hopes, by you, are butcher'd.
> My charity is outrage, life my shame
>
> (R3 1.3.272–6)

Margaret, who has been notoriously deficient in love of God or her enemies for most of four plays, suggests here that the only charity left to her is to comfort her lost ones by shaming, frightening and cursing their murderers.

UNCLEAN

(A) Sinful, sometimes with a particularly religious slant that can include echoes of represented Puritan usage. When Becon speaks of the 'vain idols [of the Roman Catholics, which] . . . do not adorn, but deform; not polite but pollute; not deck, but infect, the temples of the Christians, and make them of the churches of God the synagogues of Satan; of houses of prayer, the vile cages of all filthy and unclean birds' (2: 65), he sounds in his expansive euphuism like the outraged moral eloquence of the Puritans that Prince Hal and Falstaff parody in 1.2 and 2.4 of 1H4. A represented Puritan, Ananias, speaks similarly in Jonson's *The Alchemist* of the 'cage of unclean birds' residing at the alchemist's house (1974), 5.3.47.

(B) When Elbow the constable refers to 'fornication, adultery, and all uncleanliness there' in Pompey's brothel (MM 2.1.81), he associates the word with sexual transgressions; his style also sounds very much like that of the represented Puritan. The Puritan-like Angelo's oxymoron 'sweet uncleanness' embodies his own complex blend of lust and moral severity (MM 2.4.54). When Rosalind speaks of putting 'good meat into an unclean dish' (AYL 3.3.36), she is probably speaking only of good hygiene, but the words do suggest the Old Testament dietary laws that might be found in Exodus or Leviticus.

(C) See *Certaine Sermons*, pp. 78–89, for the sermons 'against whoredome and uncleannesse'. Poole (1995) speaks of such 'staging of Puritanism' in 1H4.

UNCTION

(A) The action of anointing the sick or the dying in the Catholic rite is called extreme unction (*OED* 1.b); alternately, prayer is said for someone who is in danger of death (see *OED adj.* extreme 3). Vaux describes 'Extreme unction or anoyling' as 'a Sacrament, wherein the sicke persone (by holy Oyle & and wordes of [C]hrist) are relieved, that more happily they may departe out of this world, & also that their bodies may be restored to health, if it be expedient' (1590a) *sigs.* H5^v–H6^v.

(B) Hamlet uses the word metaphorically when he criticises his mother for failing to heed his moral advice: 'Mother, for love of grace, / Lay not that flattering unction to your soul, / That not your trespass but my madness speaks' (HAM 3.4.144–6). Obviously, both 'for love of grace' and 'trespass' add to the religious environment.

(C) Vaux continues, 'The mater is oyle olive **halowed** by a Bishop, wherewith the sick is anoyled upon the eyes, eares, mouth, nose, hands, & feete. A man is anoyled upon the reines of the bake, and a woman upon the belly: by cause concupiscence reigneth most in those partes. . . . The effect of the Sacrament of annoyling is, to put away and purge veniall sinne commited by mispeding of our senses, & to **purge** and put away sinnes forgotten' (1590a), *sigs.* H5ᵛ–H6ᵛ. See **unanel'd**.

UNDERSTANDING *sb., adj.*
(A) Augustine refers to understanding, **memory** and **will** as the 'trinity' of moral faculties. The Jesuit Puente says 'that the Understanding may forme a true, proper, and entire conceipt of the thing that it meditateth, and may remaine . . . persuaded to receive, and to embrace those truths that it hath meditated, to propound them to the Will, and to move it therby to exercise its Actions' (1619), 1: 3–4.
(B) The clearest example of the religious usage of 'understanding' in Shakespeare occurs when Claudius complains that Hamlet's excessive grief for his dead father 'is a course / Of impious stubbornness':

> It shows a will most incorrect to heaven,
> A heart unfortified, or mind impatient,
> An understanding simple and unschooled
> For what we know must be.
> (HAM 1.2.94–8)

When the young King Henry V warns his advisor the Archbishop of Canterbury to give him godly advice about his rights to France, his use of 'understanding' stresses its prominent role in a moral universe:

> And God forbid, my dear and faithful lord,
> That you should fashion, wrest, or bow your reading
> Or nicely charge your understanding soul
> With opening titles miscreate.
> (H5 1.2.13–16)

(C) For a rich discussion of the place of memory, understanding and will in the Catholic meditative tradition, see Martz (1962), *esp.* pt. 1. See also Augustine (2002), X.11.18; Aquinas, *ST* I.79.6–7. See also **reason**.

UNFAITHFUL
Those who lack religious faith.
Shakespeare uses the word metaphorically when Rosalind tells Orlando that she will number him among 'the gross band of the unfaithful' (AYL 4.1.195) if he breaks his promise to meet her later. See **faithless**.

UNFORTIFIED
Without **fortitude**, one of the cardinal virtues appropriated from the Aristotelian scheme, and therefore as often moral as religious in usage.
Claudius calls Hamlet's 'heart unfortified' (HAM 1.2.96) in his lengthy grief

for his father. Surrounding words like 'impious', 'a will most incorrect to heaven', and 'a fault to heaven' (HAM 1.2.94–5, 101) convince us that his criticism has a religious edge.

UNGODLY
Though the theologians use it for wicked and irreligious persons and acts, in Shakespeare 'ungodly' is usually a casual way of referring to an unfortunate time.

When Constance complains to King Philip of France that he has betrayed her interests in making peace with King John, she calls it an 'ungodly day' (JN 3.1.109). It is only when she twice calls on the 'heavens' to avenge 'these perjur'd kings' that we wonder if she means not just a day against her own interest but one when the wishes of God were ignored or resisted.

UNGRACIOUS
Usually merely socially impolite; in a few instances the surrounding words encourage the religious reading, 'without grace', meaning divorced from God's favour or forgiveness.

Thus in TN Olivia's calling Toby Belch an 'Ungracious wretch, / Fit for the mountains and the barbarous caves, / Where manners ne'er were preach'd!' (TN 4.1.47–9) probably refers merely to his lack of social graces. On the other hand, York's reprimand to the rebellious Bolingbroke, 'Grace me no grace, nor uncle me no uncle. / I am no traitor's uncle, and that word "grace" / In an ungracious mouth is but profane' (R2 2.3.87–9), is pointedly religious, especially with the thrice-repeated 'grace' and the added 'profane'. When Hal, playing his father, criticises Falstaff, playing Prince Hal, 'Swearest thou, ungracious boy?' (1H4 2.4.445), the reference is both social and religious. Hal has been behaving out-rageously with Falstaff, but it is Falstaff's blasphemous ' 'Sblood' that provokes the specific criticism of his swearing (1H4 2.4.443). Ophelia's usage to Laertes is similar: 'Do not, as some ungracious pastors do, / Show me the steep and thorny way to heaven, / Whiles . . . / Himself the primrose path of dalliance treads, / And reaks not his own rede' (HAM 1.3.47–51). King Edward criticises himself for failing to countermand the order on his brother's life, 'But for my brother not a man would speak, / Nor I (ungracious) speak unto myself / For him, poor soul' (R3 2.1.127–9). Only when he adds, 'O God! I fear thy justice will take hold / On me and you, and mine and yours, for this' (R3 2.1.132–3), do we know that he is thinking of this failure in religious as well as familial terms. When Iden promises to bury the slain rebel Jack Cade upon a dunghill, 'And there cut off thy most ungracious head' (2H6 4.10.82), Cade is called 'monstrous' because he has led a rebellion against the king; 'ungracious', 'damned wretch' and 'I might thrust thy soul to hell' (2H6 4.10.66, 77, 79), add to the religious layering. See **gracious**.

UNHALLOWED[1]
Without saintliness or reverence; unholy.

When the kind but not always wise Escalus calls the disguised Duke an 'unreverend and unhallowed friar' (MM 5.1.305), his point is that a person dressed in religious garb should behave in a religious way. Paradoxically, the Duke is literally 'unhallowed' since he is only disguised as a friar, not officially ordained (**unhallowed**³). Warwick clearly if also cynically distinguishes between a 'state holy or unhallow'd' (1H6 3.1.59). See **hallowed**.

UNHALLOWED²
Blasphemous, sacrilegious.

Since Paris thinks that Romeo is about to desecrate something sacred, Juliet's Capulet tomb, instead of worshipping Thanatos there, he challenges him to 'Stop thy unhallowed toil, vile Montague!' (ROM 5.3.54). 'Unhallowed' primarily means unspeakably evil each time it is applied to the ravishing Tarquin (LUC 192, 392, 552), though the fact that Lucrece is called 'divine' and 'a shrine' in the first passage (LUC 193–4), 'blessed' and 'holy-thoughted' (LUC 383–4) in the second, and 'pure piety' (LUC 542) in the third suggests that 'unhallowed' was at least part of a metaphoric system in which her great virtue is ennobled by association with holiness, and his crime defined as sacrilege.

UNHALLOWED³
Unblessed; not marked by religious observance.

'Unhallowed' clearly means 'unblessed', not spoken of or observed with thankful reverence, when King Henry VI says to the cured blind man Simpcox, 'Poor soul, God's goodness hath been great to thee. / Let never day nor night unhallowed pass, / But still remember what the Lord hath done' (2H6 2.1.81–3). Unfortunately, the miracle is exposed as a sham.

UNHALLOWED⁴
Not Christian; not baptised.

Though 'Unhallowed dam' and 'unhallowed slave' in TIT (5.2.190; 5.3.14) are insults as general as 'son of a bitch', Gratiano's 'unhallowed dam' (MV 4.1.136) is a slur against his Jewish mother and his Jewish heritage.

UNHOLY
Unlike 'unhallow'd', 'unholy' is usually a general insult with only the peripheral religious nuance of without sanctity, piety or holiness.

Polonius probably describes Hamlet's courtship of Ophelia as 'unholy' (HAM 1.3.129–31) to justify the 'sanctified' and 'pious' he also uses to describe its hypocrisy. Whereas the reference to Fortune's 'unholy service' (PER 4.4.50) could set a belief in chance against a belief in providence, it more likely laments the fact that Pericles and Marina will be subjected to mishaps beyond their control, and perhaps beyond all control. Silvia calls her forced marriage with Thurio an 'unholy match' (TGV 4.3.30).

UNHOUSL'D
(A) Without having received communion. The archaic 'housel' is the *sb.* for the Eucharist or the *v.* for administering the Eucharist, from OE húsl (*OED sb. & v.*).

The Reformer Cooper, speaking against 'the common use of your private mass', says 'it is to be wished that people were so devout, as they would daily receive their housel (for so ye term it): and yet is not the priest to be letted to receive, when the people will not dispose themselves unto it' (1850), 85.

(B) The ghost of Hamlet's father blames his purgatorial 'torment' on a death so sudden that he died deprived of both the Eucharist and Extreme Unction, 'Unhous'led' and 'unanel'd', and was thus 'sent to my account / With all my imperfections on my head' (HAM 1.5.77–9).

(C) More also speaks of 'the holy howsyll, the sacrament of the altar' (quoted in Tyndale, 3: 96n).

UNPREPARED

Not spiritually readied for death.

Othello, about to execute Desdemona for her imagined infidelity with Cassio, advises her almost like a priest to confess her crime and pray for mercy: 'If you bethink yourself of any crime / Unreconcil'd as yet to heaven and grace, / Solicit for it straight' (OTH 5.2.27–8). To her understandably perplexed response, 'Alack my lord, what may you mean by that?' he adds, growing more impatient, 'Well do it, and be brief, I will walk by. / I would not kill thy unprepared spirit, / No, heaven forfend, I would not kill thy soul' (OTH 5.2.29–32). Then he loses all control and stifles her without a prayer. See **prepared**.

UNREVEREND (also 'unreverent')

This usually refers either to personal disrespect or outrageous immaturity, but it can more specifically describe disrespect for a divine or a divinely appointed person, a father, a magistrate, a king.

When Tranio uses 'unreverend' to describe the outrageous way Petruchio has dressed himself for his marriage to Kate, 'See not your bride in these unreverent robes' (SHR 3.2.112), he describes clothing which would dishonour both the bride and the ceremony. Escalus's 'thou unreverend and unhallowed friar' (MM 5.1.305) likewise refers to both the failure of the Friar to behave with the dignity appropriate to his religious office and clothing and to the slander he is said to have uttered against the Duke. The charge and counter-charge of Gloucester and the Bishop of Winchester explicitly combine this mixture of political and religious irreverence:

> WINCHESTER. Unreverent Gloucester!
> GLOUCESTER.   Thou art reverent
> Touching thy spiritual function, not thy life.
>
>   (1H6 3.1.49–50)

See also **reverend**.

UNSANCTIFIED

Unblessed; sometimes just evil, without redeeming qualities.

We infer that King Claudius must have countermanded the usual practice of denying suicides burial in holy ground when the priest in HAM says that because Ophelia's 'death was doubtful', 'She should in ground unsanctified been lodg'd / Till the last trumpet' (HAM 5.1.227–9). Lady Macduff's defiant comment to the murderers that Macduff is, 'I hope, in no place so unsanctified / Where such as thou mayst find him' (MAC 4.2.81–2) is, in contrast, mostly about the murderers' total abandonment to evil. See **sanctified**.

UNTHANKFULNESS

(A) A lack of gratitude to God. Donne says of this sin, 'If you have called a man unthankfull, you have called him by all the ill names that are: for this complicated, this manifold, this pregnant vice, *Ingratitude*, the holy language, the *Hebrew*, lacks a word' (7: 420–1).

(B) Twice in Shakespeare this lack of appreciation is directly associated with theological despair and the consequent threat of suicide. The Friar claims that Romeo's refusal to accept his banishment with patience is 'deadly sin!' and 'rude unthankfulness' (ROM 3.3.24), calling his later threat of suicide 'doing damned hate upon thyself' and railing on 'the heaven and the earth' (ROM 3.3.118–19). To Queen Elizabeth's similar threat to kill herself, 'I'll join with black despair against my soul, / And to myself become an enemy', the Duchess of York immediately cries 'rude impatience'. Elizabeth's son Dorset agrees: 'God is much displeas'd / That you take with unthankfulness his doing', calling her despair and her complaints being 'opposite with heaven' (R3 2.2.36–8, 89–90, 94).

(C) See also Andrewes, 5: 31; Sandys (1841), 156; Becon, 1: 185; and *ST* II.2.106–7.

USE, USURER, USURY

(A) Lending money for interest and the person who does so. Because this was a practice technically forbidden to Christians during the Middle Ages and the Renaissance, but permitted to Jews, the same anger that borrowers have always felt when they demonize banks and bankers was further honed by religious difference.

(B) Though the common medieval and Renaissance association of usury and Jews lurks in the margin of Shakespeare's usage of these terms, only once is it explicit. Shylock forces us to associate Antonio's insults with both his usury and his religion, and it is not clear that Antonio distinguishes them either: 'You call me misbeliever, cut-throat dog, / And spet upon my Jewish gaberdine, / And all for use of that which is mine own' (MV 1.3.111–13; cf. MV 3.1.47–8). However, a non-Jew, the Catholic Bishop of Westminster, is called 'a most pernicious usurer', presumably because he so persistently extorts money from his English parishioners for the use of Rome (1H6 3.1.17).

The common association between usury and miserliness informs two other references. The Friar criticises Romeo's outrageous expressions of despair by arguing that if he kills himself he will be no better a steward of his own gifts than a usurer who does not put money to its best use, that is, in acts of Christian charity: 'thy shape, thy love, thy wit, / Which like a usurer abound'st in all / And usest

none in that true use indeed / Which should bedeck thy shape, thy love, thy wit'
(ROM 3.3.122–5). In the sonnets, a lover's failure to spend Nature's generous
gift to him by loving someone else and leaving children makes him similarly a
'beauteous niggard' and a 'profitless usurer' (SON 4.5, 7). The idea that usury
was an unnatural breeding, money generating more money, lies behind Antonio's charge, 'Or is your gold and silver ewes and rams?' to which Shylock
responds, 'I cannot tell, I make it breed as fast' (MV 1.3.95–8). Antonio also
complains that Shylock should not make 'A breed for barren metal of his friend'
(MV 1.3.134), that is, not practice usury on a friend. All this probably stems from
Deut. 23.20, 'unto a stranger thou mayest lend upon usury', to which Sandys says,
'The Jews even till this day will not lend upon usury among themselves, but lend
freely to their brethren and without gain' (1841), 231. Ironically, this passage
celebrates Jewish charity, not Jewish miserliness.

(C) See also Donne, 6: 82; 1: 209; Jewel (1845–50), 2: 853; Latimer (1844–45),
1:303; Grindal mentions 'the statute made in the thirty-seventh year of the reign
of King Henry the Eighth, for Reformation of usury, and revived by an act made
in the thirteenth year of the reign of the Queen's Majesty' (1843), 172. For Jacob
and the parti-coloured lambs, see Gen. 30.32–43. Warren Smith (1964) argues
that Shylock is a villain because he is a usurer, not because he is a Jew. Mischo
(1995) suggests connections between usury and Christian charity in the
procreation sonnets, and Siegel (1962) that usury was one of the popular
perceptions of both Puritans and Jews. See Sokol and Sokol (2000), 387–93.

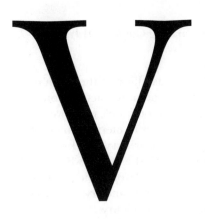

VAIN

Useless because merely worldly; proud (*OED adj.* 1.b).

Like '**vainglory**', 'vain' is usually a psychological rather than a theological word in Shakespeare. Cardinal Wolsey, fallen from power, reveals the traditional religious usage when he laments in his valedictory speech, 'Vain pomp and glory of this world, I hate ye!' (H8 3.2.365). In this same speech Wolsey also associates 'My high-blown pride' with the fall of Lucifer (H8 3.2.361, 371).

VAINGLORY

(A) Traditionally one of the words for **pride**, the greatest of the seven deadly sins.

(B) Shakespeare usually employs this word psychologically rather than theologically. However, when Henry VIII's pious Queen Katherine of Aragon describes herself as 'A woman (I dare say without vainglory) / Never yet branded with suspicion', she uses the word with religious nuance. As a religious woman, she believes that defending her reputation is more important than avoiding a messy trial and quietly agreeing to a divorce from King Henry VIII; as a woman of the world, she also knows that defending herself in this cause will seem to manifest a very un-Christian pride (H8 3.1.127–8, 113–17).

(C) See (under fortitude) *ST* II.2.132. Becon, 1: 448–9, cites at least twenty biblical passages 'Against Pride, or Vain Glory'. See **vain** and **vanity**[1].

VALENTINE, SAINT

(A) Third-century Roman Christian martyr. The association of St Valentine's Day (14 February) with couples and courtship is apparently a calendrical and ornithological coincidence relating to the resumed mating of birds around the middle of February.

(B) Ophelia, mad and lovelorn, sings 'To-morrow is Saint Valentine's Day' during her conversation with Claudius and Gertrude (HAM 4.5.48).

(C) Farmer (1978), 388; Baring-Gould (1914), 2:296–7.

VANITY[1]; VAINNESS

(A) Self-glorious pride', the deadliest of the seven deadly sins. Sandys preaches, 'This vanity staineth our best and purest actions; our prayer, when we pray that we may be seen and thought holy; our alms, when we give that we may have a praise; our fasting, when we use it either to merit unto ourselves, or thereby to seem devout unto others; our preaching, when we seek our own commendation, when we study not so much to please God as men, when much learning puffeth us up, when we take a pride in our picked words and pleasant utterance, when we rejoice with Herod to hear the people shout and cry, "The voice of a God" ' (1841), 102–3.
(B) The Chorus assures us that Henry V's decision not to carry 'His bruised helmet and his bended sword' with him on his triumphal procession into London after the victory at Agincourt shows him 'free from vainness and self-glorious pride' (H5 5pr. 20). The explanation that 'He forbids it', 'Giving full trophy, signal, and ostent / Quite from himself to God' (H5 5pr. 19–22) roots this intrusive editorial firmly in Christian soil. Such an explicit reference helps us see the more subtle cluster of religious and quasi-religious references to vanity in the H4 plays and in H5. Buckingham describes the 'two clergymen!' who flank Richard in his hypocritical show of pious unworldliness as 'Two props of virtue for a Christian prince, / To stay him from the fall of vanity' (R3 3.7.92–7). Viola's protestation that she hates 'lying, vainness, babbling, drunkenness, / Or any taint of vice whose strong corruption / Inhabits our frail blood' (TN 3.4.355–7) is a religious reference if we concede that 'our frail blood' refers to the common idea of human fallenness as well as merely her assumed role as a man. See **pride**, **vainglory**, and **humility**.
(C) The *Te Deum* which King Henry V orders to be sung after the Battle of Agincourt similarly ascribes all glory to God.

VANITY[2]

Spiritual frivolity.

Prince Hal once calls Falstaff 'that vanity in years' (1H4 2.4.454). Hal also says over the apparently dead Falstaff, 'O, I should have a heavy miss of thee / If I were much in love with vanity!' (1H4 5.4.105–6). Here most clearly Falstaff is the embodiment of the vanity of the world which Hal is forsaking, literally in himself, allegorically in this passing friendship. Falstaff's 'Hal, I prithee trouble me no more with vanity' (1H4 1.2.82) reveals the topsy-turvydom of the pot-bellied embodiment of vanity, both self-love and superficiality, calling the princely kettle black. Prince Hal's father King Henry IV shows how completely he has misunderstood his son's only apparent frivolity when he says of his succession, 'Up, vanity! / Down, royal state!' (2H4 4.5.119–20). Hotspur also underestimates his rival's complexity and his danger as well when he says just before Hal kills him in single combat: 'I can no longer brook thy vanities' (1H4 5.4.74). Hal proclaims after his father's death and Hotspur's, and not incidentally just before he will banish Falstaff,

> The tide of blood in me
> Hath proudly flow'd in vanity till now;
> Now it doth turn and ebb back to the sea,
> Where it shall mingle with the state of floods,
> And flow henceforth in formal majesty.

(2H4 5.2 129–33)

The Archbishop of Canterbury testifies in H5 that he has been as good as his word: 'The breath no sooner left his father's body, / But that his wildness, mortified in him, / Seem'd to die too' (H5 1.1.25–7); the admiring French Constable bears witness to the same Reformation when he tells the French court, 'You shall find his vanities forespent / Were but the outside of the Roman Brutus' (H5 2.4.36–7).

VANITY[3]

(A) The emblematic representation of this vice as well as the vice itself. The death of greatness or pride is among the most common symbols of vanity, witness Hamlet's reflection in the graveyard on the presumptuousness of the 'politician', the 'courtier', 'my Lord Such-a-one', 'my Lady Worm', 'the skull of a lawyer', and finally, both 'Alexander' and 'Imperious Caesar, dead and turn'd to clay' (HAM 5.2.78, 82–6, 88, 99, 208–9, 213).

(B) Falstaff shows his complete misunderstanding of the common iconography of vanity when he says over the corpse of the fallen Sir Walter Blount, 'Here's no vanity' (1H4 5.3.33).

(C) The Bridgeman Art Library database in Grove Art Online includes an 'Allegory of Vanity' by Antonio Pereda y Salgado (1611–78) from the Galleria degli Uffizi, Florence that includes a globe, a skull, a pistol, armour, jewellery and money among its images of vanity.

VEILED

A nun in a religious community who wears a shoulder-length covering of the face can be described as 'veiled'. Indeed 'to take the veil' is to become a **nun** (*OED sb.* veil 1.b).

Orsino says of Olivia's mourning rites for her brother that 'like a cloistress she will veiled walk' (TN 1.1.25–7).

VENGE

God can be said to 'venge' a wrong when he strikes down an offender in **righteous anger**.

Jachimo reveals the bare bones of this classical and Christian commonplace when he speaks of the 'office of the gods to venge it' (CYM 1.6.92); the 'it' in this case is his slander that Posthumus has been unfaithful to Imogen. Albany applauds the death of Cornwall as an act of divine retribution: 'This shows you are above, / You justicers, that these our nether crimes / So speedily can venge!' (LR 4.2.78–80).

VENGEANCE

(A) Because the Judaeo-Christian God is often said to have threatened vengeance, as in 'Vengeance is mine' (as in Deut. 32.35; Prov. 6.34; Isa. 34.8; Jer. 50.28; Rom. 12.19; Heb. 10.30), the word is often associated with God's **wrath** and the Day of **Judgement**. Sandys says of this, 'God hath appointed a day hereafter to **judge** the world with that **justice** which shall give unto every man according to that which he hath done, be it good or evil, and which shall render vengeance unto them that know not God, but **rest** unto such as now are troubled for his sake' (1841), 353. Of course, the concept of divine vengeance is not unknown in the classical world, and so it appears in Shakespeare's classical as well as his Christian plays. The calls for divine vengeance in Shakespeare as often manifest personal animosity as the disinterested conviction of divine wrath.

(B) Lear reveals a sense of personal victimization that assumes cosmic proportions when he commands that 'All the stor'd vengeances of heaven fall / On [Goneril's] ingrateful top' (LR 2.4.162). Regan's insensitive, even atheistic, corrective is 'O the blest Gods' (LR 2.4.168). Paulina shares Lear's expectation of the Gods, or at least of Apollo, when she laments just after Hermione's reported death, 'The sweet'st, dear'st creature's dead, and vengeance for't / Not dropp'd down yet' (WT 3.2.201).

Calls for divine vengeance are also not infrequent in the Christian settings of the English histories. The papal **legate** Pandulph says that the people will so abhor King John for his atrocities that they will find in every natural event signs of God's displeasure, 'Plainly denouncing vengeance upon John' (JN 3.4.153–9). Whether John of Gaunt actually believes his own expedient piece of theology, or simply doesn't want to kill King Richard II, he plainly defers to divine vengeance against the wishes of Woodstock's wife: 'Put we our quarrel to the will of heaven, / Who, when they see the hour's ripe on earth, / Will rain hot vengeance on offenders' heads' (R2 1.2.6–8). King Henry IV subsequently tells his wayward son Prince Hal that his misdeeds manifest God's 'secret doom' for his own political misdeeds, and that 'the hot vengeance, and the rod of heaven' will 'punish my mistreadings' (1H4 3.2.4–11). Whatever the king's personal and political motives, his speech clearly articulates the mysterious theology of divinely appointed vengeance. Interestingly, he reverses here the biblical motif of the misdeeds of the father being visited upon the son (as in Ex. 20.5; Num. 14.18).

(C) See also Vaux (1590a), *sig.* I8[r]; Hooper (1852), 2: 37–8, and *ST* II.2.108. For the difference between Christian and pagan vengeance in TIT, see Broude (1979). Lepley (1983) suggests that vengeance is legitimated in COR. Desai (1993) argues Hamlet is a 'minister' of God's and of state vengeance. Keyishian (1995) also writes on vengeance in the plays. See **revenge**.

VENIAL

(A) Light or pardonable, often distinguished from **deadly** or **mortal** when describing sins. According to Vaux, the venial sin lacks the malice towards another that characterises mortal sin; it also lacks the mortal sin's contempt of God in conscious evil (1590a), *sigs.* G7[v]-H1[r]. To Catholics, venial sins risk temporal punishment in this life or in purgatory; mortal sins risk eternal punishment in hell.

(B) Iago tells Othello that if Desdemona merely lay 'naked with her friend in bed / An hour, or more, not meaning any harm' she may have committed only a 'venial slip'. However, the 'But' which follows, in 'But if I give my wife a hand-kerchief' (OTH 4.1.2–10), implies that the one 'slip' Iago thinks he can use to prove her infidelity, the gift of the handkerchief, is a mortal slip, and thus one that the judgemental Othello can never forgive.

(C) See *ST* III.87, 'Of the Remission of Venial Sin', and *ST* II.1.88, 'of venial and mortal sin'. For several Protestant complaints about venial and mortal sins and Catholic doctrines about **penance**, **purgatory**, good **works**, **holy water**, and sacred **ceremonies**, see Pilkington (1842), 527, and Rogers (1854), 216–17, 180, 299; see also Komonchak (1987), 961–2.

VESTAL

A virgin dedicated to the Roman goddess Vesta was called a vestal virgin; thus a vestal is a woman committed to a life of chastity.

At least once Shakespeare connects this classical commitment to the chastity of nuns in Christian holy orders. Venus, trying to shame Adonis into making love, calls those women committed to formal vows of chastity 'Love-lacking vestals and self-loving nuns' (VEN 752).

VESTMENTS

(A) Religious clothing.

(B) Timon, obviously describing pagan rather than Christian priests, urges Alcibiades not to be deterred in his wholesale slaughter of Athenians by 'sight of priests in holy vestments bleeding' (TIM 4.3.126).

(C) See **surplice**, **robe**, **gown**.

VICAR

(A) A vicar can be a minor officiant in the Church of England, someone per-forming the offices of a rector in his absence, or of a priest in a very small parish; a vicar can also be someone very important in the Roman Catholic Church, as, for example, the Pope's representative or the Pope himself, who could be called the Vicar of Christ.

(B) In Shakespeare, the vicar is always the relatively unimportant churchman, someone like 'Oliver Martext, the vicar of the next village', not a 'good priest' but one who will join Touchstone and Audrey in marriage as badly as a poor carpenter joins green and seasoned wood in a wainscot that will only 'warp, warp' (AYL 3.3.43, 85–9). In contrast, Fenton assumes that a 'vicar' can marry him and the 'fair Anne Page' successfully, 'give our hearts united ceremony' (WIV 4.6.9, 48–51). Gremio, describing the madcap marriage of Petruchio and Kate, uses 'priest' and 'vicar' to describe the same man, unless the vicar had to step in to finish the ceremony because Petruchio had given the priest 'such a cuff' that he could not recover (SHR 3.2.158–68).

(C) See Grindal (1843), 159; Vaux (1590a), *sig.* A7^v.

VICE^1 *n.* Sin.

Donne speaks of 'these two vices ... two principall enemies, the two chiefe corrupters of mankinde; pride to be the principall spiritual sin, and lust, the principall that works upon the body' (9: 377). Latimer calls 'Envy ... a foul and abominable vice, ... more directly against charity than any other sin is' (1844–45), 2: 8.

The usage of 'vice' for 'sin' is usually straightforward, especially in Shakespeare's comedies and histories (see ERR 3.2.12; MM 4.2.112; and LLL 5.2.349). '[T]his vice' in MM 2.2.5 is Claudio's lust or fornication with Juliet (see also MM 2.4.116; 3.1.137; 3.2.99); in TN 2.3.153, the 'vice' is Malvolio's pride. In the histories we hear of 'this vice of lying' (2H4 3.2.304), and 'that vice' of pride (H5 3.6.152), and Richard III's proud confession of his own 'deep vice' (R3 2.2.28).

Greater rhetorical and moral complexity sometimes characterises this usage, as when Troilus warns Hector of his 'vice of mercy' (TRO 5.3.37), presumably meaning that he should be more ruthless with his enemies. The Friar could be describing both his own ill-fated intervention and Romeo and Juliet's eventual suicides when he says that 'virtue itself turns vice, being misapplied, / And vice sometime by action dignified' (ROM 2.3.21–2). Hamlet feels obliged to apologise to his mother for his aggressive moral advice: 'Virtue itself of vice must pardon beg' (HAM 3.4.154). When Iago laments that he is a 'wretched fool, / That lov'st to make thine honesty a vice' (OTH 3.3.375–6), he reminds us with his paradox that he persistently uses the appearance of honesty to destroy the honest. Finally, York rejects King Henry IV's offer not to execute his rebellious son because of 'thy abundant goodness': 'So shall my virtue be his vice's bawd' (R2 5.3.65–7). Such paradoxes suggest many things, including both sin's deceptive power and the occasional inadequacy of traditional morality to contain or categorise it. See also **sin**.

VICE^2 *sb.*

(A) A 'Vice' is also one of the leading characters of the morality plays, the clever **tempter** who sometimes abuses the **devil** with his wooden sword, but who also tries to destroy human goodness. Calfhill's 'Answer to the Treatise of the Cross' compares the priest at the 'holy **Mass**' to 'the Vice ... come from the **Altar**' (210). This figure, sometimes called **Iniquity**, represented all of the vices.

(B) In TN, Feste compares his dealings with Malvolio to the Vice's dealings with the devil: 'Like to the old Vice, / ..., / Who with dagger of lath, / In his rage and his wrath, / Cries, ah, ha! To the devil'; then he explicitly identifies his quarry, Malvolio, with the Vice's 'goodman devil' (TN 4.2.124–31). Falstaff calls Justice Shallow 'this Vice's dagger' because he is as skinny as lathing, so 'starv'd', that 'when 'a was naked, he was for all the world like a fork'd redish' or a 'mandrake' (2H4 3.2.304, 310–11, 315, 319). When Prince Hal calls Falstaff 'that reverent Vice' (1H4 2.4.453), he is styling him an unusually fat version of the same dramatic figure. Richard III exults in his own similarity to 'the formal Vice, Iniquity', who is known to 'moralise two meanings in one word' and thus rhetorically deceive his innocent quarry (R3 3.1.82–3). When Hamlet calls Claudius 'a Vice of kings' to Gertrude, he may suggest that he is a composite of vices, but he may also be calling him a grotesque, comic version of evil who is more a thief than a king, indeed a 'cutpurse of the empire and the rule, / That from the shelf the precious diadem stole, / And put it in his pocket'. That would fit in with Hamlet's estimation that Claudius is 'a slave that is not twentieth part the **tithe** / Of your precedent lord' (HAM 3.4.97–101).

(C) Bevington (1962), 9–11, 79–83, 121–3, discusses the dominant role of the Vice figure in plays like *Three Laws* (1538) and *Mankind* (*c.* 1471). Hamill (1974) argues from 'a vice of kings' (HAM 3.4.98) that Claudius is imaged as a Vice figure.

VICE³ *Fig.*
Among the many metaphors for vice in Shakespeare are vice as a plant that is sometimes weeded and sometimes cultivated (MM 3.2.270); vice as the 'canker' that 'the sweetest buds doth love' (SON 70.7); vice as a crack in a wall that can be patched, 'daub'd . . . with show of virtue' (R3 3.5.29); and the vices as something deeply engraved or 'grafted' into one person (MAC 4.3.51). 'Vice repeated' is compared by Pericles to 'the wand'ring wind', which 'Blows dust in others' eyes, to spread itself' (PER 1.1.96–7); vice is also a prostitute (R2 5.3.67) who needs a bawd to do her business. Lear compares 'small vices' to the naked skin that would show through 'tatter'd clothes', but be hidden by 'Robes and furr'd gowns' (LR 4.6.164–5).

VIGIL
The evening before a feast day. Cranmer laments of 'vigils, otherwise called watchings, [which] remained in the calendars upon certain saints' evens, because in old times the people watched all those nights' (1846), 2: 175.

Henry V, during his inspiring St Crispian's Day speech before the Battle of Agincourt, tells his troops, 'He that shall see this day, and live old age, / Will yearly on the vigil feast his neighbors, / And say, "To-morrow is Saint Crispian" ' (H5 4.3.44–6).

VILLAINY
Usually referring to treacherous acts, like Iago's successful slander of Desdemona (OTH 5.2.190–3), 'villainy' is also used in Shakespeare to describe the postlapsarian world, the time after the fall of Adam and Eve.

Falstaff, excusing himself once again, asks Prince Hal how he can be held accountable in this fallen world if Adam and Eve disobeyed God while they still lived in Paradise: 'Thou knowest in the state of innocency Adam fell, and what should poor Jack Falstaff do in the days of villainy?' (1H4 3.3.164–6).

VIRGIN

Christ's mother, the Blessed Virgin Mary, is commonly addressed 'Ave virgo', 'Hail, Virgin', in the religious lyrics – a phrase that is often associated in those poems and in the various prayers to Mary with Gabriel's equally familiar greeting to her from Luke 1.28: 'Ave gratia plena', 'Hail, full of grace'.

Such associations may partly explain Isabella's offence when Lucio greets her with a similar if also more cynical 'Hail virgin, if you be' (MM 1.4.16). She says, 'You do **blaspheme** the good, in mocking me' (MM 1.4.38). See **madonna**.

VIRTUOUS

Having one good quality as well as a general goodness.

Occasionally Shakespeare's usage of 'virtue' is explicitly religious. Nerissa's 'Your father was ever virtuous' is quickly connected with 'and holy men at their death have good inspiration' (MV 1.2.27–8). Joan of Arc calls herself near her death 'virtuous and holy, chosen of above', though she is about to lie, 'I never had to do with wicked spirits' (1H6 5.4.39–42). Suffolk is doubly deceitful when he describes Margaret of Anjou to her potential husband the young King Henry VI as having 'humble lowliness of mind' and 'virtuous chaste intents', especially since she later lustfully and irreligiously calls that same Suffolk her 'alderliefest sovereign', whether 'In courtly company, or at my beads' (2H6 1.1.27–8). Somewhat less ambiguously, the ghost of her pious King blesses Richmond before the Battle of Bosworth Field, 'Virtuous and holy, be thou conqueror' (R3 5.3.128). Richard of Gloucester, warming to the task of manipulative religious hypocrisy, calls it 'A virtuous and Christian-like conclusion – / To pray for them that have done scathe to us' (R3 1.3.315–16).

VISION

(A) A supernaturally sent message, dream, insight or prophecy.

(B) Joan of Arc clearly describes her motivating vision in religious terms: 'God's mother deigned to appear to me', 'in a vision full of majesty' (1H6 1.2.78–81). The Bastard of Orleance confirms that this is 'a vision sent to her from heaven', and that she is 'Ordained . . . to . . . drive the English forth the bounds of France' (1H6 1.2.52–4). Bottom describes his 'most rare vision' in Pauline terms: 'The eye of man hath not heard, the ear of man hath not seen' (MND 4.1.211–12; cf. 1 Cor. 2.9). Here Shakespeare associates the word 'vision' not only with dreams but also through allusion with religious insight and mystical experience.

Of darker things, Macbeth refers to the 'dagger which I see before me' as a 'fatal vision', and wonders if it is 'sensible to feeling as to sight' (MAC 2.1.36). It is never made clear whether this is merely hallucinatory, 'a dagger of the mind . . . proceeding from the heat-oppressed brain' (MAC 2.1.38–9) or an actual supernatural event. Hamlet refers with similar psychological, moral and epistemological uncertainty to the ghost of his father as 'this vision here' (HAM 1.5.137). Even if it is objectively real, 'an honest ghost' it might be 'a dev'l', which 'abuses me to damn me' (HAM 1.5.138; 2.2.599–603). His mother calls him 'mad' (HAM 3.4.105) when he sees it in her chamber, but others have witnessed the ghost (see

HAM 1.1.20–175). Lady Macbeth similarly tells Macbeth 'you look but on a stool' (MAC 3.4.67) when he claims to have seen Banquo's ghost.

(C) On the Pauline context of Bottom's dream, see Rashbrook (1952), 49; Cox (1969), 140; Vos (1966), 114; Greenfield (1968), 236–44; Battenhouse (1975), 32–53; Bryant (1961), Hassel (1980), 52–8; on the substance of its shadows, see also Young (1966), 115–26. For discussions of Hamlet's ghost, see **ghost**. West (1968), ch. 5, discusses 'Night's Black Agents in Macbeth'; and Diehl (1983) discusses the link between physical and moral vision in MAC. Garber (1974), 59–61, defines 'vision' as it is used in MND.

VOTARY, VOTARESS, VOTARIST
Someone male, female, or either, bound by vows to a religious order; a devoted worshipper of God.

Isabella refers clearly to this religious meaning in a Christian context when she asks Francisca the nun for 'a more strict restraint / Upon the sisterhood, the votarists of Saint Clare' (MM 1.4.4–5). In a classical context, the Chorus Gower tells us of Pericles's lost queen, 'at Ephesus, / Unto Diana there's a votaress' (PER 4. Cho. 4).

The word can also be used metaphorically for someone devoted to 'fond desire' or 'love' (TGV 1.1.52; 3.2.58; SON 154.5). The lords of LLL are twice called votarists for their ill-advised and ultimately ill-kept vows 'not to see ladies, study, fast, not sleep' (LLL 2.1.37; 4.2.137; 1.1.48). In fact, when the Princess calls them 'vow-fellows' (LLL 2.1.38) she helps us define 'votarist' etymologically, since the words all stem from the Latin *vovēre*, to vow.

VOW¹
Religiously sworn promise.

King Philip of France asks the papal legate Pandulph how he would dissolve the 'religious strength of sacred vows' (JN 3.1.229) that have recently joined the kingdoms and the rulers of England and France, saying that they would 'jest with heaven' (JN 3.1.242) if they broke them. Pandulph reminds him that since he has sworn to be 'the champion of our Church', this political vow makes 'faith an enemy to faith': 'O let thy vow / First made to heaven, first be to heaven perform'd' (JN 3.1.263–7). Somewhat incongruously, Salisbury later emphasises the religious seriousness of his own vow of revenge by comparing it to incense, a 'breathing to his breathless excellence / The incense of a vow, a holy vow' (JN 4.3.66–7). Hamlet is called a 'prodigal' by Polonius for trying to trick Ophelia with 'almost all the holy vows of heaven' (HAM 1.3.114). Sincere and insincere vows are further sanctified in Shakespeare by their association with 'God' (1H4 4.3.60; 3H6 2.3.29; R3 1.4.206; TIT 5.1.81); 'knees' or kneeling (2H6 1.3.199; 3H6 2.3.29); 'heaven' and 'heavenly' (3H6 1.1.24; TIT 1.1.474; LLL 5.2.356); the 'soul' (3H6 2.3.34); and someone's 'reverent tomb' (TIT 2.3.296). We especially shudder when we hear Iago swear 'In the due reverence of a sacred vow' (OTH 3.3.461–2) when he kneels to dedicate himself to Othello's cause against Cassio and Desdemona.

VOW²

(A) A liturgically prescribed promise, as during the service of marriage or ordination.

(B) For marrying Claudius so soon after his father's death, or for unnamed and perhaps unknown crimes and misdemeanours, Hamlet accuses his mother of making her 'marriage vows as false as dicers' oaths' (HAM 3.4.44–5).

(C) The Catholic Persons says of the onset of the Reformation that Martin Luther 'lefte his religion, cast away his habite, broke his vowes, married a nonne, and by litle and litle began to preache straunge new doctrines, especiallye tending to al libertie and carnalitie' (1581), *sig.* A8.

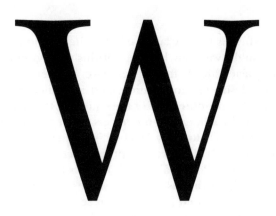

WALKING-STAFF

The religious 'palmer' or pilgrim was often depicted as carrying a walking-staff.

As Richard II, contemplating his deposition, enumerates the symbols of kingship that he will have to trade for symbols of the penitential and monastic life to come, he includes 'My sceptre for a palmer's walking-staff' (R2 3.3.147–8, 151).

WASH

(A) Clean, literally, or symbolically. Pontius **Pilate** washed his hands of the blood of Christ (see Matt 27.24) as a symbolic declaration of his own guiltlessness in Christ's death. Since the gesture so obviously did not clear him in the judgement of history, it has come to signify unconvincing assertions of guiltlessness. Because Herod ordered the slaughter of all the young children of Israel in a futile attempt to thwart prophecies that he would be succeeded by a messiah born of the seed of **Abraham** (as in Matt. 2.16), Herod-like hands are those so grotesquely stained with innocent blood that they cannot be cleansed.

(B) During his deposition scene Richard II compares himself to Christ and his subjects to Pilate:

> Though some of you, with Pilate, wash your hands,
> Showing an outward pity, yet you Pilates
> Have here deliver'd me to my sour cross,
> And water cannot wash away your sin.
> (R2 4.1.239–42)

Richard's chief opponent, Bolingbroke, also inadvertently compares himself to Herod as he unconvincingly claims judicial or executive authority to either try or execute Richard's friends Bushy and Green: '[Y]et, to wash your blood / From off my hands, here in the view of men, / I will unfold some causes of your deaths'

(R2 3.1.5–7). After he has killed Clarence in R3, the second murderer says 'How fain, like Pilate, would I wash my hands / Of this most grievous murther!' (R3 1.4.272–3). Uncharacteristically for Shakespeare, neither analogy is very good. Apparently Pilate's desire for an ablution, and its futility, caught the popular imagination so well that the other half of the equation, the refusal not only to kill but even to authorise the killing, was not necessary for the allusion to work.

When Macbeth responds to Lady Macbeth's urging that he 'wash this filthy witness from your hand', 'Will all great Neptune's ocean wash this blood / Clean from my hand? No' (MAC 2.2.44, 57–8), his literally bloodstained hands suggest Herod's perpetually bloody hands in the mysteries, in religious art, even in the popular *santons* that represented (and still represent) this figure. Herod may also lurk behind Bolingbroke's promises to undertake a 'voyage to the Holy Land, / To wash this blood off from my guilty hand' (R2 5.6.49–50).

Henry wishes that 'every soldier in the wars [should] do as every sick man in his bed, wash every mote out of his conscience; and dying so, death is to him advantage' (H5 4.1.178–80).

(C) Hassel (2001b) discusses the presence in MAC of the Herod figure of religious art and of the morality plays. See **prepar'd**.

WATCHFUL

Spiritually alert; aware of spiritual consequences. Tyndale says of spiritual preparedness, 'Watch, . . . as a man should watch a tower or a castle. We must remember that the snares of the devil are infinite and innumerable, and that every moment arise new temptations, and that in all places meet us fresh occasions; against which we must prepare ourselves and turn to God . . . for without him we can do nought' (1: 92).

Buckingham cynically describes Richard to the Mayor and the Citizens as 'meditating with two deep divines; / Not sleeping, to engross his idle body, / But praying, to enrich his watchful soul' (R3 3.7.75–7). Richmond is more sincere when he prays to God before the Battle of Bosworth Field, 'Make us thy ministers of chastisement, / That we may praise thee in the victory! / To thee I do commend my watchful soul' (R3 5.3.113–15). See also **vigil**.

WATER

Sometimes associated in Shakespeare with spiritual cleansing; also part of a diet associated with fasting.

'Go get some water, and wash this filthy witness from your hands'; and 'A little water clears us of this deed', Lady Macbeth's two literal references to cleansing water, might have reverberated with irony in MAC because she seems so oblivious to water's deeper symbolic currents. The second provokes Macbeth's more knowing response, 'all great Neptune's ocean will not **wash** this blood / Clean from my hand' (MAC 2.2.43–4, 57–8, 64). When the King assigns Costard the 'sentence', 'Thou shalt fast a week with bran and water' for seeing a woman against their vows, Costard thinks of this as a religious reference: 'I had rather pray a month with mutton and porridge' (LLL 1.1.300–3). See **fast**, **pray** and **holy water**.

WATER HOLY – see **HOLY WATER**

WEAVER

(A) Immigrants from the Low Countries were often both weavers and Puritans, or at least dissenters, and they brought their traditions of psalm singing with them to England.

(B) Falstaff makes fun of this tradition when he says 'I would I were a weaver, I could sing psalms, or any thing' (1H4 2.4.133). His alter-ego in TN, Sir Toby Belch, also refers to this tradition when he says of his friends' very secular singing at Twelfth Night, 'Shall we rouse the night-owl in a catch that will draw three souls out of one weaver?' (TN 2.3.58–9). The 'weaver' they arouse, Malvolio, is no night-owl, but he is called later in the same scene a 'kind of Puritan' (TN 2.3.139).

(C) See BEV, 779n; RIV, 451n; Shaheen (1999), 414. Poole (1995), 66, connects Falstaff with the weavers and their Puritan psalm singing.

WHITE-FRIARS

(A) A Carmelite friary in London.

(B) After having just told the Lady Anne that he would bury the corpse of her father-in-law King Henry VI 'at Chertsey monast'ry', Richard of Gloucester orders the gentlemen to take it 'to White-friars' (R3 1.2.214, 226). Actually, Holinshed reports that Henry's corpse rested at Black-Friars before it was conveyed to Chertsey.

(C) See Hosley (1968), 218.

WHITSUN

(A) Whitsunday, the seventh Sunday after Easter, is a festival celebrating the descent of the Holy Spirit to the disciples of Christ on the day of Pentecost. Originally white robes might have been worn on that day, hence the 'whit'.

(B) Shakespeare's two references, to 'Whitsun pastorals' (WT 4.4.134) and 'a Whitsun morris-dance' (H5 2.4.25), evoke only secular traditions of the calendrical occasion.

(C) Donne preaches many Whitsunday sermons (as in 6: 114–31; 8: 253–69; 9: 232–49). See also *Certaine Sermons*, 2nd tome, pp. 206–17, for the sermons of 'the comming downe of the holy Ghost, and the manifold gifts of the same. *For Whitsunday.*'

WICKED[1] *adj.*

(A) Evil, not holy, as of damned or demonic doers or doings.

(B) Paulina is afraid that if she makes the statue of Hermione move, Leontes will think she is 'assisted / By wicked powers' (WT 5.3.91). In HAM, if the Ghost's 'intent' is that he 'Abuses me to damn me', then it is similarly 'wicked' rather than 'charitable' (HAM 2.2.603; 1.4.42). The witches presumably call Macbeth 'something wicked' before he sees their apparitions because he has to their delight become something damned, chosen evil alternatives knowing them to be 'strong themselves in ill', and chosen as well to suppress good impulses because they '[keep] me pale' (MAC 2.1.50; 4.1.45; 3.2.55; 3.2.50). All are marks of **mortal** sin. Iago's 'wicked lie' (OTH 5.2.181) is also presumably not only destructive of life, sinful, but also destructive of eternal bliss, his own and Othello's (OTH 5.2.276–80). Touchstone advises the simple shepherd Corin, 'if thou never wast at court, thou never saw'st good manners; if thou never saw'st good manners, then thy manners must be wicked, and wickedness is sin, and sin is damnation' (AYL 3.2.40–3). This may be odd logic, but its basis is theological.

(C) Donne says of Satan that 'the most collective name that is given him in all Scriptures [is] . . . *The wicked one*; One that is all wickednesse, and one that is the wickednesse of all' (9: 400).

WICKED² *sb.*

(A) The sinful; either persons who do wickedness or those who do not conform to someone else's ideas of piety and worship. To Donne, '*The wicked*' is 'not hee that hath fallen into some particular sinnes, though great, [but] he that runnes headlong into all wayes of wickedness' (9: 400).

(B) Falstaff's claim that Hal had made him 'little better than one of the wicked' takes on some religious meaning, especially when he says just earlier that Hal is 'able to corrupt a **saint**' (1H4 1.2.91, 94–5), presumably himself. Adding, 'I'll be damn'd for never a king's son in Christendom' (1H4 1.2.95, 97), Falstaff caps off his moral and religious excursion by connecting the 'wicked' with the fallen, and thus with damnation. Falstaff also says in defence of the slight fault of drinking too much sherry, 'If sack and sugar be a fault, God help the wicked' (1H4 2.4.470–71). Of his insults against Prince Hal, Falstaff rationalises, 'I disprais'd him before the wicked, that the wicked might not fall in love with thee'. But Hal is not buying: 'is thine hostess here of the wicked? or is thy boy of the wicked? or honest Bardolph, whose zeal burns in his nose, of the wicked?' (2H4 2.4.319–21; 328–30).

(C) As Shaheen says (1999), 439, 'the wicked', a common phrase from Scripture (Prov. 3.33, 4.14, 4.19, etc.), is frequently appropriated into Puritan discourse against non-Puritans. The usage is also common in theological discourse, as in Loarte (trans. Brinkley, 1596–97), 86; Jewel (1845–50), 2: 943. In *Bartholomew Fair*, Jonson helps brand both Dame Purecraft and Zeal of the Land Busy as Puritans by their overuse of 'the wicked', and 'wicked' (1963), 5.5.57; 4.6.107; see also 1.6.13, 35; 3.6.80. Poole (1995), 67, also connects Falstaff's use of 'the wicked' with Puritan usage.

WILL¹

(A) Will is the capacity to make and act upon moral choice (*OED sb.* 6). The Jesuit Puente says that the third part of 'Mentall praier' 'is, with the freedom of our will to draw forth sundry Affections, or vertuous Actes, conformable to that which the Understanding hath meditated, . . . as Hatred of our selves; Sorrowe for our Sinnes; Confusion of our owne misery: Love of God; Trust in his mercye, . . . desire to obtaine true vertues; effectuall purposes to doe good

workes, and to . . . amend our life; resignation of our selves to the Will of God'
(1619; 1: 4). The theological profile of this word is raised by its central place in
the Reformation debate about grace and works. If Aquinas thought that we could
by an exertion of the will obey the Law of God, and therefore in a sense save
ourselves by our good works (as in *ST* I.82–3.1.1 – 'I answer that man has free
will'), Augustine was as convinced that we could not, that the will was bound by
the other fallen moral faculties (*On the Trinity* [2002], X.11), and Augustine was
as much Luther's mentor as Aquinas was Erasmus'.

(B) Iago's famous speech urging Roderigo to control his self-destructive
impulses has been called Pelagian (see **garden**) because of its assertion of the
absolute power of the human will, and its inevitable corollary, the strength of
moral powers like **reason**:

> Virtue? A fig! 'tis in ourselves that we are thus or thus. Our bodies are our gardens, to
> the which our wills are gardeners. . . . If the beam of our lives had not one scale of
> reason to poise another of sensuality, the blood and baseness of our natures would
> conduct us to most prepost'rous conclusions. But we have reason to cool our raging
> motions, our carnal stings, our unbitted lusts.
>
> (OTH 1.3.319–30)

Despite this pronouncement, Iago is so bound by sexual jealousy that he destroys
himself in the process of destroying Desdemona and Othello; he also knows of
this bondage well enough to have based his plan against them on his belief that
Othello's 'soul is so enfetter'd to her love' that he would for her love 'renounce
his **baptism**, / All **seals** and **symbols** of redeemed sin' (OTH 2.3.343–5). Though
the reference is more elusive, Macbeth's excuse to Banquo for not having had
time enough to prepare for Duncan's coming, 'Our will became the servant to
defect, / Which else should free have wrought' (MAC 2.1.18–19), echoes the
same set of issues. Because we are fallen, our will is always subject to defect. The
Friar in ROM also describes free will gone wrong when he complains of Romeo's
'rude unthankfulness' (ROM 3.3.24), his outcries of despair and his threats of
suicide, that there are 'in man as well as herbs' 'grace and rude will'. The Friar
adds of this fallen will, 'And where the worser is predominant, / Full soon the
canker death eats up that plant' (ROM 2.3.28–30).

Ironically, when Hamlet complains about the bondage of his will, he is confused in the opposite way, annoyed that his conscience keeps him from doing
whatever he wills, that is, whatever he wants to do, however dangerous such
desires are to him here and hereafter. First, he says as he considers either committing suicide or killing Claudius that 'the dread of something after death'
'puzzles the will' (HAM 3.1.77–9). Later he complains that though 'I have cause,
and will, and strength, and means / To do't', that is, to kill Claudius, he is
deterred by some 'craven scruple / Of thinking too precisely on th' event'. He
even calls this moral reason or understanding 'but one part wisdom / And ever
three parts coward' (HAM 4.4.40–6). Hamlet complains more than once that
'the native hue of resolution / Is sicklied o'er with the pale cast of thought'

(HAM 3.1.80–1). The paradox is that Hamlet's reason may be functioning properly in controlling his will, refusing to condone an act that might be damnable. But though the object of his revenge, Claudius, has earlier complained that Hamlet has 'a will most incorrect to heaven' (HAM 1.2.95), he also concedes during his attempted prayer of repentance that his own soul is 'limed' (HAM 3.3.68).

Lysander also confusedly articulates a tension between will and **reason** when he awakens in the forest to find that he has suddenly fallen out of love with Hermia and into love with Helena. Three times in a row he asserts against what we have seen in the play that his reason has led him to this change; the third time he names the will as its wayward opposite. If 'The will of man is by his reason sway'd; / And reason says you are the worthier maid', he must let 'Reason [become] the marshal to my will' and follow Helena (MND 2.2.115–20). The comedy lies in his perverse misunderstanding of himself, the experience, the reason, and the will. Lysander's mind has been changed by a Puckishly engineered love potion; reason has nothing to do with it.

The subtitle of Shakespeare's 'Twelfth Night', or 'What You Will' can just mean 'or whatever name you choose for the play'; it can also suggest that Twelfth Night, the culminating night of Christmas revelry, is a time when anything goes. But Twelfth Night is also the eve of Epiphany, a festival like the Christmas season itself closely associated with the twinned motifs of enlightenment and **humility**. Toby Belch and his drunken mates stand for the "what you will" of misrule, the 'rude will' of doing whatever they want to do. Further, in the midst of characters like Olivia, Orsino and Toby who are coming to be humbled and therefore enlightened, Malvolio, 'sick of self-love' (TN 1.5 90–1), will not be cured, will not smile at his **folly**, will not forgive. Malvolio's name in Italian literally breaks down into *mal voglio*, ill-will. In TN characters of good will humbly accept their imperfections and rejoice in their common membership in a community of imperfection; the ill-willing of self-love keeps Malvolio from such a redeeming humility.

(C) On the question of the freedom of the will in the moral process, see also Aquinas, *ST* I.79.6; ST II.1.19. On the rich exchange between Luther and Erasmus on the bondage versus the freedom of the will, see Trinkaus (1999). Donne, speaking of these difficult and explosive issues with characteristic moderation, says 'In the heat of disputation, and argument, and to make things straight, [the disputants] bent them too much on the other hand, . . . as in S. *Augustines* disputations against the Pelagians, who over-advanced the free will of man, and the Manicheans, who . . . annihilated the free will of man, we shall find sometimes occasions to doubt whether [Augustine was] not transported sometimes with vehemency against his present adversary' (7: 203). See also 'Free Will', *OxfordEncyRef*, 2: 141–6; *NewCathEncy*, 6: 89–95. On the question of the bondage of the will in HAM and OTH, see Battenhouse (1969), 247–8, 380–423; Hunter (1976), chs. 5 and 6; Hunt (1996); and Hassel (1994a), 616–19. Mallette (1994) argues that HAM expresses a moderate, non-Calvinistic view of free will. On the place of memory, understanding and will in the Catholic meditative tradition, see Martz (1962), *esp.* pt. 1. On the puzzled will and the fallen reason in TN and MND, see Hassel (1980), chs. 3 and 6. On good-will and ill-will in TN, see Lewalski (1965). See also **soul**[1], **snares**, **garden**.

WILL[2]

(A) Wish or desire, spoken of God's providential design. 'Thy will be done' is a familiar phrase from The Lord's Prayer; its echoes become prominent parts of some passages in Shakespeare.

(B) King Henry VI's 'God's will be done' (2H6 3.1.86) is the clearest reference. More interesting, however, is Bolingbroke's sarcastic and envious retort to Richard II's pronouncement of his banishment, 'Your will be done' (R2 1.3.144). It is less clear if polytheistic references like 'The wills above be done' (TMP 1.1.67) and 'Their sacred wills be done' (WT 3.3.7) also echo the words of this prayer. Characters in Shakespeare refer fairly often, and sometimes not too happily, to 'the will of heaven' (R2 1.2.6).

'God's will' can also be used as an oath which casually underlines the sincerity of the speaker, as when King Henry V chastises the fearful Westmoreland before the Battle of Agincourt, 'God's will, I pray thee wish not one man more.' Westmoreland later replies 'God's will, my liege, would you and I alone, / Without more help, could fight this royal battle!' (H5 4.3.23, 74–5). An angrier example occurs when Warwick challenges Somerset, 'Now, by God's will, thou wrong'st him' (1H6 2.4.82). See also ROM 3.3.76.

(C) See *ST* I.19, on 'The Will of God'.

WINCHESTER

Another of the cathedrals in England.

'Bishop of Winchester' is King Henry VIII's formal name for his secretary Gardiner, a man he promoted to the Bishopric but later reprimands for both flattery and cruelty (H8 5.2.158–9, 164). His alternate title, 'Lord of Winchester' (H8 5.2.93, 108–9; H8 5.2.204) often marks a disrespect that accompanies his fall from power. Henry Beauford begins 1H6 as 'Bishop of Winchester' but soon becomes 'Cardinal of Winchester' (1H6 1.3.19). In 2H6 he remains a thorn in his great-nephew King Henry VI's side, and is called twice by him 'uncle of Winchester' (2H6 1.1.56, 68).

WITCH[1]

(A) Though 'witch' can as it does today merely serve as a general word of disapproval, it can also refer in Shakespeare's time to a woman who has devoted herself to evil and black magic, and therefore to the devil.

(B) The three witches in Macbeth are called 'juggling' and 'equivocati[ng]' 'fiends' by Macbeth, as well as 'devil[s]' and by Banquo 'the instruments of darkness' (MAC 1.3.107; 5.8.19; 5.5.42; 1.3.124). Oddly, though the three witches are named in stage directions throughout MAC, the words 'witch', 'witch's', and 'witchcraft' are each mentioned only once in the play proper (MAC 1.3.6; 4.1.23; 2.1.51). Sycorax, Caliban's mother in TMP, is called 'that damn'd witch' (TMP

1.2.263). Though the 'witch' Antipholus of Syracuse tries to conjure away is actually only a courtesan, she has already been called 'Sathan', 'Mistress Sathan', 'the devil', 'the devil's dam', a 'fiend', a 'devil', and a 'sorceress' in this hyperbolic scene (ERR 4.3.48–51, 63–6, 71, 76). Antipholus feared from the start that Ephesus was a place famous for witchcraft, 'Soul-killing witches that deform the body' (ERR 1.2.100). Joan of Arc is almost as often called 'witch' by the Englishman Talbot (as in *IH6* 1.5.6, 21; 3.2.38). Though this is in part a demonizing response to her amazing success against his English troops, Joan does later confirm his charges when she conjures 'familiar spirits' (1H6 5.3). Talbot also threatens to 'conjure' her, and calls her '**devil** or **devil's dam**', '**hell**', 'strumpet', and '**damned sorceress**' (1H6 1.5.5–12, 21–2; 3.2.38; 5.3.34). Richard of Gloucester plays the witch card more cynically when he accuses two female rivals of deforming his arm into 'a blasted sapling, wither'd up': 'this is Edward's wife, that monstrous witch, / Consorted with that harlot, strumpet Shore, / That by their witchcraft thus have marked me' (R3 3.4.69–72). There are similar charges of witchcraft against female political opponents in 2H6 (as in 1.2.75–6 and 2.3.7), though again some of these accused, Marjory Jordan and Roger Bolingbrook, actually practise witchcraft and conjuring.

(C) For biblical injunctions against both witchcraft and enchantments, see Ex. 22.18 and Lev. 19.26. Donne associates a belief or trust in witchcraft not only with a desperate dependence on devils, but also the Catholic belief in the intercession of saints and angels: 'Trust not in flesh, but in spirituall things, That wee neither bend our hopes downeward, to infernall spirits, to seeke help in Witches; nor mis-carry it upward, to seeke it in Saints, or Angels, but fix it in him, ... our blessed, and gracious, and powerfull God' (6: 295–6); he also includes 'Witchcraft' among the 'sinnes ... that are Contracts with the *Devil*' (6: 197). Donne (citing 1 Sam. 28.3–25) uses the story of Saul to show that witches are wrong for counsel (2: 343). Donne also offers this unusually compassionate analogy between desperate women and desperate Catholic parishioners: '[I]f there be a broken woman, a woman loaden with sin, as the Apostle speaks (2 Tim. 3.6), and thereby dejected into an inordinate melancholy, (for such a melancholy as makes Witches, makes Papists too), ... she be thereby as apt to change Religions now, as Loves before, and as weary of this God, as of that man' (4: 108). See also Perkins's *Discourse of the Damned Art of Witchcraft* (1613); King James's *Daemonologie* (1603); and the letter from John Jewel in 1559 (in *Zurich Letters* [1842], 1: 44). See **witchcraft**.

WITCH[2]
A male witch or wizard.

Jachimo uses the word metaphorically to describe the personal magnetism of the man Posthumus as 'such a holy witch / That he enchants societies into him; / Half all men's hearts are his' (CYM 1.6.166–8). The word does not seem to offend his wife Imogen here, but it is a strange sort of compliment, dangerous and ambiguous.

WITCHCRAFT

(A) A group of witches, the practice of witches, including sorcery (its synonym in Gal. 5.20), or a metaphorical reference about romantic enchantment.

(B) Banquo may refer to either a group of witches or their ritual practices when he speaks of midnight as a time when 'witchcraft celebrates / Pale Hecat's off'rings' (MAC 2.1.51–2). Brabantio claims that Othello could not have successfully won Desdemona's heart 'sans witchcraft'; Othello quickly denies the literal charge with a metaphor: telling Desdemona of his own extraordinary adventures 'only is the witchcraft I have us'd' (OTH 1.3.64, 169). When King John calls the selling of indulgences a 'juggling witchcraft' used to 'Purchase corrupted pardon of a man' (JN 3.1.162–71), his usage poises between the literal and the metaphoric, the mere trickery of con men versus the promise of supernatural soliciting.

(C) The King James Bible reads Gal. 5.20 as 'sorcery' and the *Geneva Bible* as 'witchcraft'. Kaula (1966) looks at witchcraft in OTH. For the parallels between sexual transgression and witchcraft in OTH, see Gutierrez (1991). Grinnell (1997) argues that the discourse of witchcraft in R3 hides political tools, and Rosenfield (2002) that WT aligns witchcraft with healing and rebirth. See also West (1984), West (1939), ch. 8, and 'Witchcraft', *NewCathEncy*, 14: 977–9; *OxfordEncyRef*, 4: 277–82.

WITTENBERG

(A) Luther's university in Central East Germany, and the site of many of his Reformation writings and lectures.

(B) It is mentioned four times in close succession that Hamlet and Horatio are students at Wittenberg (HAM 1.2.113, 119, 164, 168).

(C) See Waddington (1989), Hassel (1994a, b) and Frye (1984) on possible Lutheran dimensions of Hamlet and his play. See also 'Wittenberg', *OxfordEncyRef*, 4: 282–6; *NewCathEncy*, 14: 983.

WIZARD

A male witch who conjures or exorcises demons.

Antipholus of Ephesus calls the aggressive but blundering conjurer Pinch a 'doting wizard' for invoking all the saints to 'conjure' 'Sathan, hous'd within this man' out of Antipholus (ERR 4.4.54, 58). 'The wizard' Somerset 'Hath made . . . famous in his death' is the conjurer Roger Bolingbrook, who raised the spirit who prophesied that Somerset should avoid castles. Richard cynically recalls this prophecy after he kills Somerset 'underneath an alehouse' paltry sign, / The Castle in Saint Albans, Somerset' (2H6 5.2.67–9; 1.4.34–5). Finally, Clarence laments that his brother King Edward IV 'hearkens after prophecies and dreams', 'And says a wizard told him that by G / His issue disinherited should be' (R3 1.1.54–8). Ironically, the G is correct despite Clarence's scepticism; it just happens to refer to his brother Richard of Gloucester instead of George Clarence.

WORD[1]

(A) Scripture, the Word of God. Because **Scripture** (rather than tradition) was so often the touchstone of the more extreme Reformers in disputed matters of religious belief and practice, as well as the locus of disputes about translations into the vernacular, the Word of God assumed great prominence in controversial exchanges. Donne reasserts the literalness of the word 'Scripture' in arguing its centrality to doctrinal debate: '[T]his manifestation of his Will, must be permanent, it must be *written*, there must be a *Scripture*, . . . [if] from that Word of God, all Articles of our Beliefe are to bee drawne' (3: 358); the Recusant Sander complains of the Reformers' use of biblical authority, 'Did they not by that colour ["the sincere word of God"] overthrow monasteries, Churches, **altars**, **images** of **Saintes**, and mine owne image and **crosse**? Did they not denie the **sacrifice** of the **Masse**, praing for the dead, and such like auncient usages, only for pretence of the **word** of God?' (1565), *sig*. PPpp2ʳ.

(B) As Richard II considers his ruined life and his kingship, he tries to console himself with 'thoughts of things divine'. The problem is that as soon as he does so, he finds these thoughts 'intermix'd / With scruples', and complains that they 'set the word itself against the word'. We know that he is talking about Scripture when he quickly specifies two biblical examples: ' "Come, little ones", and then again, "It is as hard to come as for a camel / To thread the postern of a small needle's eye" ' (R2 5.5.12–17). Mark 10.14 reads, 'Suffer the little children to come unto me', and Mark 10.24–5, 'It is easier for a camel to go through the eye of a needle than for a rich man to enter into the kingdom of God.' Richard finds the two passages so contradictory that they discourage his further seeking of religious comfort. See **needle's eye**.

(C) For the importance of recognizing what version of the Bible Shakespeare would have known best, see Noble (1935), 58–89, and Shaheen (1998 and 2000). Shaheen (1987) discusses how Shakespeare acquired his knowledge of the Bible. Marx (2000) examines the influence of the Bible on Shakespeare; Shuger (1994) discusses the English Bibles of the Reformation. Barnaby and Wry (1998) read MM as a cautionary tale about the use of biblical rhetoric in political contexts. See **sword** for a punning use of **word**[1].

WORD[2]

'Holy word' can refer to liturgical formulations, or to sincere vows.

'Holy words' must mean liturgical words when Romeo tells Friar Lawrence, 'Amen, amen!' 'Do thou but close our hands with holy words' (ROM 2.6.1–2, 6). Hamlet speaks of the same ritual when he calls his mother's marriage with Claudius 'such a deed / As from the body of contraction plucks / The very soul, and sweet religion makes / A rhapsody of words' (HAM 3.4.46–8); obviously he feels that she has broken the contract.

WORK, WORKS

(A) Acts; especially in Christian thought, acts manifesting **faith** or **grace**.

(B) Though Shakespeare often plays with the opposition of grace and **merit**, he does not usually verbally juxtapose its parallel, faith or grace versus works. Helena may be thinking of the distinction between faith and works, however, when she persuades the reluctant King to accept her offered miraculous cure by reminding him that 'He that of greatest works is finisher / Oft does them by the weakest minister' (AWW 2.1.136–7), adding that it is 'presumption in us when / The help of heaven we count the act of men' (AWW 2.1.151–2). Her point is that he would be accepting God's grace in her cure rather than Helena's works, her 'endeavours', which she calls 'Inspired merit', 'The greatest grace leading grace' (AWW 2.1.148, 160). Malcolm similarly says of Edward the Confessor's 'most miraculous work' of healing, 'How he solicits heaven, / Himself best knows'; Malcolm does know that 'sundry blessings hang about his throne / That speak him full of grace' (MAC 4.3.146–50, 158–9). The Lord similarly says that the alliance which will overthrow Macbeth and free Scotland from his tyranny will be joined by 'Him above / To ratify the work' (MAC 3.6.32–3).

(C) Donne the preacher offers a metaphysical poet's attempt at compromise when he describes the Epistle of Paul to the Romans, the one that all parties cite in the dispute about grace and works, as 'this precious ring, being made of that golden Doctrine, That Justification is by faith, . . . enameled with that beautifull Doctrine of good works too, in which enameled Ring, as a precious stone set in the midst thereof, there is set, the glorious Doctrine of our Election, by Gods eternall Predestination' (3: 377). See also *Certaine Sermons*, pp. 30–9, for the 'Sermon of Good workes annexed unto Faith'; Andrewes, 5: 282–5; and 'Justification', *OxfordEncyRef*, 2: 360–8.

WORLD[1]

(A) A fallen place, and therefore a location of sinfulness and suffering (*OED sb.* 4.d). 'The sins of the world' can therefore refer to all human sinfulness, as in the *Agnus Dei* in the Gloria: 'O Lord God, Lamb of God, Son of the Father, that takest away the sins of the world, have mercy upon us.'

(B) Falstaff tries to argue for the world instead of against it when he warns Prince Hal, 'Banish plump Jack, and banish all the world' (1H4 2.4.479–80). When Lady Macduff, about to be killed or worse by Macbeth's henchmen, despairs of being saved with 'I am in this earthly world – where to do harm / Is often laudable, to do good sometime / Accounted dangerous folly' (MAC 4.2.75–7), she distinguishes between the fallen morality of this world and the moral perfection of the next. Hamlet makes a similar point and a similar distinction when he laments 'How weary, stale, flat, and unprofitable / Seem to me all the uses of this world!' – then names some of these wrongs 'unrighteous', 'wicked' and 'incestuous' (HAM 1.2.133–5). The unusually religious King Henry VI similarly asks, 'Would I were dead, if God's good will were so; / For what is in this world but grief and woe?' This prefaces a long list of the unworldly pursuits he would enjoy were he merely 'a homely swain' (3H6 2.5.19–22); it also distinguishes both between this world of woe and the next of bliss, and between the world of kingship and the fields and streams of pastoral retreat.

(C) For the *Agnus Dei*, see *BCP*, 265; for a discussion of 'the world's ransom' (as in R2 2.1.55–6; WT 5.2.14–15), see **ransom**.

WORLD²

(A) In a cosmological or theological sense, 'this world' (*OED sb.* 1.a) is often distinguished from the next (*OED sb.* 1.d), which might be either heaven or hell. (B) Macbeth's fearsome if also impotent vow to 'let the frame of things disjoint, both the worlds suffer, / Ere we will eat our meal in fear, and sleep / In the affliction of these terrible dreams / That shake us nightly' (MAC 3.2.16–19), refers to both of these worlds, here and hereafter. So does Laertes when he promises to kill Hamlet whatever the consequences: 'I dare damnation. To this point I stand, / That both the worlds I give to negligence, / Let come what comes' (HAM 4.5.134–6). '**Pendant** world' and '**lower** world' (MM 3.1.125; TMP 3.3.54) refer both cosmologically and theologically to this world's relationship to **heaven**.

(C) Donne clearly distinguishes between this world and the world hereafter when he says, '*Peace* in this world, is a pretious *Earnest*, and a faire and lovely *Type* of the everlasting **peace** of the world to come: And warre in this world, is a shrewd and fearefull *Embleme* of the **everlasting** discord and tumult, and **torment** of the world to come' (4: 182–3). For this world and the next, see Donne, 3: 188. For 'Christian world' (AWW 4.4.2) see **Christian**.

WORLD³

(A) The 'world' can also refer to 'worldly' or material pursuits, especially but not exclusively sinful pursuits as opposed to heavenly or spiritual ones (*OED sb.* 2). These compose the first part of the formula 'the world, the flesh and the devil'. That formula is sometimes implied in Shakespeare's usage, but the actual triad is never explicitly named, as it is, for example, in Donne's 'For thus I leave the world, the flesh, the devil' (1971, Holy Sonnet 6.14); or 'Lest the world, flesh, yea Devil putt thee out' (1971, Holy Sonnet 17.14).

(B) The worldly Cardinal Wolsey, stripped of his power, says in a moment of spiritual honesty, 'Vain pomp and glory of this world, I hate ye! / I feel my heart new-open'd' (H8 3.2.365–6). Isabella combines the meanings of **world²** and **world³** when she admonishes the Duke to trust her 'as thou believ'st / There is another comfort than this world' (MM 5.1.48–9). A true believer, she seems to say, would be naturally inclined to distrust illusory worldly rewards. The Duke also uses some combination of **world²** and **world³** when he says to the reprobate Barnadine, who has refused to prepare himself spiritually for death, that he is 'said to have a stubborn soul / That apprehends no further than this world, / And squar'st thy life according' (MM 5.1.480–2).

(C) Donne says, 'The sight, and the Contemplation of God, and our present benefits by him, and our future interest in him, must make us blinde to the world so, as that we look upon no face, no pleasure, no knowledge, with such an Affection, such an Ambition, such a Devotion, as upon God, and the wayes to him' (6: 215).

WORLDLY

(A) Concerned with the things of the world, the material or the temporal as opposed to the heavenly, the eternal, and the spiritual. Becon advises 'that on the seventh day we rest from all worldly and bodily business, labours, and works, that we may the more freely serve the Lord our God, and consider the things which appertain unto the salvation of our souls' (2: 80).

(B) When Richard II says with a mixture of hope and desperation, 'The breath of worldly men cannot depose / The deputy elected by the Lord' (R2 3.2.56–7), he distinguishes between people merely pursuing their own personal interests on the political stage and those operating under God's authority and protection. Responding to the bad news of his defecting troops, Richard II pretends to be immune to the bad news: 'The worst is worldly loss thou canst unfold' (R2 3.2.94). As he lies dying, his usurper Bolingbroke, now King Henry IV, makes a similar distinction to his son: 'My worldly business makes a period' (2H4 4.5.230). Buckingham describes Richard of Gloucester to the Mayor and the Citizens who want him to become king as 'Divinely bent to meditation, / And in no worldly suits would he be mov'd'. Following phrases like 'holy **exercise**', '**meditation**', '**praying**', and '**watchful soul**' (R3 3.7.62–3, 73–7) reveal how firmly the worldly and the **spiritual** are being opposed here.

(C) Donne, 3:117; 8: 98–9, speaks of the heaven that '*Mahomet* hath proposed to his followers, a heaven that should abound with worldly delights'. Tyndale, 2: 288, complains of 'the Pope that devised all these fashions, to corrupt the prelates with abundance of worldly pleasures'.

WORLD-WITHOUT-END

(A) The phrase appears in the *Prayer Book* as the formulaic conclusion of many collects like that for Whitsunday (*BCP*, 168–9), and in other prayers like the *Jubilate Deo* in Morning Prayer (*BCP*, 58; Ps. 100): 'World without end. Amen.' It also comes just after the sacrament is received during Holy Communion (*BCP*, 265).

(B) In both LLL 5.2.789 and SON 57.5 we find reference to a 'world-without-end bargain'. In the former case the Princess declines to accept the King's proposal of marriage until he has undergone a **penance** that will prove both his truthfulness and his ability to keep his vows. In the sonnet, 'world-without-end hour' seems to refer rather to a sensual satisfaction that will never come in this Petrarchan world of eternal frustration and pursuit.

(C) See *BCP*, 339, 336. Interestingly, none of the prayers for the marriage ceremony ends with this phrase.

WORM[1]

Because worms are so closely associated with the decomposition of the human body in the grave, they are frequently named in passages considering human mortality and the short-sighted human privileging of **body** over **soul**.

SON 146 speaks directly about the underfed soul and the overfed body when it asks, 'Shall worms, inheritors of this excess, / Eat up thy charge? Is this the body's end?' and ends with the explicitly religious advice: 'Within be fed, without be rich no more: / So shalt thou feed on Death, that feeds on men, / And Death once dead, there's no more dying then' (SON 146.7, 12–14). The inscription on the golden casket begins, 'All that glisters is not gold', and ends, 'Gilded tombs do worms infold' (MV 2.7.65–9). The vanity of the world and the brevity of human life is twice more articulated in terms of worms, once when Richard II says upon hearing of the defection of most of his troops, 'Let's talk of graves, of worms and epitaphs' (R2 3.2.145), and once when Prince Hal, having just defeated the gallant Hotspur in single combat, finishes Hotspur's dying sentence on himself, 'Percy, thou art dust, / And food for –' with 'For worms, brave Percy' (1H4 5.4.87). For other examples of this commonplace in Shakespeare see R3 4.4.386; H8 4.2.126; SON 71.4; SON 74.10.

WORM[2] *fig.*

(A) Because the worm can be imagined as gnawing away slowly but persistently, it also became a **symbol** of gnawing spiritual anxiety. Donne asks, 'what confection of gnawing worms, of gnashing teeth, of howling cries, of scalding brimstone, of palpable darknesse, can be so, so insupportable, so inexpressible, so inimaginable, as the curse and malediction of God?' (7: 367). Donne also speaks of 'plowing, and weeding, and worming a conscience' (2: 107).

(B) 'The worm of conscience still begnaw thy soul' is among the most vivid of Margaret's curses for Richard (R3 1.3.221). Benedick also mentions 'Don Worm (his conscience)' in nervously praising himself before Beatrice (ADO 5.2.84).

(C) The Geneva gloss to the 'worme' of Isaiah 66.24 reads, 'a continual torment of conscience, which shall ever gnawe them' (*fol.* 305ᵛ). The Cambridge Puritan Perkins says 'Of the estate of the Reprobates in hell': 'Hereupon is the punishment of those that are condemned, called Hel fire, a worme, weeping, and gnashing of teeth, utter darknesse, &c.' (1597a), 209 (ch. 57). See also Mark 9.44–6. Curiously, a worm of conscience is recorded among the physical properties of the Coventry players. See Craig (1957), 101, on the 'Two Worms of Conscience'. Mason (1994) traces Queen Margaret's 'Christian worm' in R3 back to Chrysostom. Ogawa (1997), 194–200, discusses worms in HAM.

WORMS

(A) Luther defended his 95 theses on 17–18 April 1521, at the Diet of Worms. A 'diet' was a formal assembly of councillors of the Holy Roman Empire, and Worms, a port on the Rhine in southwestern Germany. Tyndale, Luther's famous English disciple, proudly says that 'Martin offered at Worms, before the emperor and all the lords of Germany, to abide by his book and to dispute' (3: 185–6).

(B) Shakespeare may have expected some of his audience to hear the indirect reference to Luther's Diet of Worms in Hamlet's macabre joke to Claudius, 'Your worm is your only emperor for diet' and his tasteless reference to Polonius' corpse, 'a certain convocation of politic worms are e'en at him' (HAM

4.3.19–21). We are often reminded in the play that Hamlet and Horatio were students at **Wittenberg**, Luther's university.

(C) See NV HAM, 3: 318n. Wilson, ed. HAM (1954), 220n.

WORMWOOD

(A) A bitter herb used to wean children from the nipples of their mothers, as a purgative for worms, and as a protection against mice. Wormwood is also a symbol of biblical origin of something so bitter to the soul that it would effect remorse. Deut. 29.18 reads: 'lest there should not be among you a root that beareth gall and wormwood'. The *Geneva Bible*'s gloss to that passage describes 'such sinne, as the bitter frute thereof might choke & destroye you' (*fol.* 94).

(B) When Hamlet says 'Wormwood, wormwood' about the Player-Queen's protestations of eternal fidelity to her dying husband, he is speaking of course of the bitter taste her promises might raise in his mother Gertrude's mouth, since she has in Hamlet's mind remarried Claudius too quickly. Since he uses 'The **Mouse-trap**' play to 'catch the conscience of the king' (HAM 3.2.237; 2.3.605), Hamlet may also be imaging himself here as an exterminator, and wormwood as the vermifuge that will destroy his quarry Claudius.

(C) Donne once says, 'When God offers the Booke, which is the Register of our sinnes to our Consciences, or the Decree of his Judgements to our understanding, or to our sense, it is writ in gall and wormwood, and in the bitternesse of sorrow' (9: 408); elsewhere he asks, 'what extraction of Wormwood can be so bitter, . . . so insupportable, so inexpressible, so in-imaginable, as the curse and malediction of God?' (7: 367). See also Prov. 5.4, Jer. 9.15 and 23.15, and Amos 5.7. The *OED* discusses wormwood as a vermifuge (*OED sb.* wormwood 1 and *OED* vermifuge 1). Hockey (1965) notes that the word comments on both disease and cure. Hassel (1993) reconstructs various Renaissance understandings of wormwood that might operate in HAM.

WORSHIP

(A) Though 'your worship' is usually a secular phrase of **reverent** greeting in Shakespeare, the verb refers to the activity associated with a church **service**. When 'worship' is used metaphorically, pertaining to extreme **devotion** to a master or a woman, a person rather than a god, false, improper **worship**, **idolatry**, is often the point of the reference. Because the forms of worship were among the most prominent issues in the Reformation, the word sometimes evokes Protestant–Catholic and Protestant–Protestant tensions. Donne associates idolatrous worship with Catholicism when he speaks of 'a *Rome* of **superstition** and Idolatry' (1: 245); he also calls the Reformation in England 'the death of Idolatry in this Land' (4: 92), and 'charge[es] [Rome] with *Idolatry*, in the *peoples practise* . . . in the greatest mystery of all their **Religion**, in the *Adoration* of the **Sacrament**' (3: 132).

(B) Proteus directly questions the appropriateness of Valentine's worship of Silvia, 'Was this the idol that you worship so?' He also calls her 'heavenly saint' and 'divine' (TGV 2.4.144–7). Then after Valentine promises to adore her picture if she will give it to him, Silvia also warns him about idolatry: 'I am very loath to be your idol, sir', 'To worship shadows and adore false shapes' (TGV 4.2.128, 30). 'Idol', 'worship' and 'adore' all suggest that this sort of worship is as potentially sacrilegious to some Reformers as bowing to candles and altars and asking intercession of the saints and the Virgin. To Prospero's offer of 'pardon' if he will change, Caliban responds,

> Ay, that I will; and I'll be wise hereafter,
> And seek for grace. What a thrice-double ass
> Was I to take this drunkard for a god,
> And worship this dull fool!
>
> (TMP 5.1.295–8)

Paradoxically, his seeking for grace from Prospero suggests that he has been cured of the idolatry of one man, only to begin worshipping another. An odder but in some ways also a clearer case is that of the Dauphin's early worship of Joan of Arc. Comparing her to **Mahomet**, to '**Helen**, the mother of great **Constantine**', and to **Saint Philip**'s daughters, he asks, 'How may I **reverently** worship thee enough?' (1H6 1.2.140–5).

(C) On false worship as idolatry, see also Grindal (1843), 140; Latimer (1844–45), 1: 497; Fulke (1843), 1: 212. On idolatry and the exaggerated praise of Petrarchan poetry, see Roche (1989), *esp.* ch. 8.

WRATH[1]

(A) Anger. The wrath of God is a complex theological issue in a Christian world that speaks almost equally of **justice** and **mercy**, punishment and **forgiveness**. Calvin goes to some lengths to soften the implications of this concept in his own stern theology. It was the fear of God's wrath, combined with an increasing emphasis on human imperfection near the onset of the Reformation in Germany, that allowed Luther's doctrine of justification by grace alone to take such a foothold. Paradoxically, a similar fear of Christ's severity at **Judgement** had led to the increasing importance of the Virgin Mary and the saints as intercessory figures in the Catholic tradition.

(B) 'By penitence th' Eternal's wrath's appeas'd' (TGV 5.4.81) explicitly combines the theology of God's wrath and its appeasement through sacrament or spiritual discipline. Valentine says it in forgiving Proteus, and he acknowledges in the process that his forgiveness mirrors that of heaven: 'Who by repentance is not satisfied / Is nor of heaven nor earth, for these are pleas'd' (TGV 5.4.79–80). Clarence, chastened to repentance by his fearsome dream, prays to a similar god of wrath and mercy,

> O God! if my deep pray'rs cannot appease thee,
> But thou wilt be aveng'd on my misdeeds,
> Yet execute thy wrath in me alone!
> O, spare my guiltless wife, and my poor children.
>
> (R3 1.4.69–72)

At the end of the same play Richmond asks this vengeful but righteous God to arm his soldiers: 'Put in their hands thy bruising irons of wrath' (R3 5.3.110). Richmond fashions himself in that passage God's '**captain**' and his troops God's '**minister**s of chastisement' (R3 5.3.108, 113). King John also claims to be 'God's wrathful agent' (JN 2.1.87). The Countess in AWW worries that her son Bertram will not escape eternal wrath unless Helena, whom he has forsaken, or possibly the Virgin Mary herself, mother of all intercessory figures, intercedes for him with God:

> He cannot thrive,
> Unless her prayers, whom heaven delights to hear
> And loves to grant, reprieve him from the wrath
> Of greatest justice.
>
> (AWW 3.4.26–9)

(C) Of 'God's wrath at judgement', see Andrewes: 'God afflicteth some in mercy, and others in wrath. God is not wroth but with sin, nor grievously wroth but with grievous sin' (2: 149); of God's wrath and 'the damnation of hell', he says, 'Ire and fire are but one thing' (1: 426). See also Calvin (1561), *fols.* 259ᵛ; 62–3, 67–70; Calvin (1958), 2: 146; Calvin (1952), 259; Calvin, (1950), 188; Walker (1608), 244–7, 307–9; and Marbeck (1581), 845–6. For a range of views on 'the mystery of godliness' in R3, see Frey (1976), 96–7; Wilders (1978), 58; French (1974), 313–24; Hunter (1976), 68; and Hassel (1987), 114–16. See also Morris (1972), ch. 11, on 'The Justice of God'.

WRATH²

(A) Human (and demonic) ire, one of the seven deadly sins. Vaux calls human 'Wrath . . . an inordinate desire of revengement' (1590b, *sig.* f3).

(B) Though 'wrath' is often admired as an impressive feature of military valour in Shakespeare, or an effective device of intimidation (as in TGV 5.4.127; WT 2.3.139; JN 3.1.340), the word can also be used pejoratively. Thus Feste describes 'the old Vice' of the morality plays as carrying 'a dagger of lath, / In his rage and his wrath' (TN 4.2.124–7); Clifford calls the rebellious and deformed Richard of Gloucester a 'heap of wrath, foul indigested lump' (2H6 5.1.158); and Queen Margaret says of his father Richard Plantagenet early in the next play, 'Wrath makes him deaf' (3H6 1.4.53). Perhaps most pointedly, Gloucester's brother King Edward laments that no one dissuaded him from ordering his brother Clarence's murder, 'Who sued to me for him? Who (in my wrath) / Kneel'd [at] my feet and bid me be advis'd? / Who spoke of brotherhood? Who spoke of love?' (R3 2.1.107–9). 'The devil wrath' in OTH 2.3.297 also seems to be one of the seven deadly sins rather than the Devil's own inadvertently dutiful enactment of the just wrath of God. Its companion in that line is 'the devil drunkenness'; the pair have just led Cassio to his downfall.

(C) Becon warns (from the Lord's Prayer – 'Forgive us our trespasses, as we forgive them that trespass against us') that if we do not 'forgive our offenders;

then it is a most sure sign, that our sins are not forgiven, but that the hot wrath and fierce vengeance of God abideth still upon us, and that we remain in a most damnable state' (2: 183). He is not alone in this opinion. On the remedies against wrath, see Loarte (trans. Brinkley, 1596–97), 225–38. Levin (1977) suggests that Falstaff embodies a mock wrath and Hotspur a true one in 1H4.

WRIT

(A) The phrase 'holy writ' refers to the Scriptures, or to a passage from them.
(B) Iago is apparently correct about Othello when he says of the damning hand-kerchief: 'Trifles light as air / Are to the jealous confirmations strong / As proofs of holy writ' (OTH 3.3.322–4); Richard III brags about his deception in similar terms:

> But then I sigh, and, with a piece of Scripture,
> Tell them that God bids us do good for evil:
> And thus I clothe my naked villainy
> With odd old ends stol'n forth of holy writ.
> (R3 1.3.333–7)

(C) Donne uses 'the generall name of Scripture, and Holy Writ' identically (7: 385). See *OED sb.* 1.c.

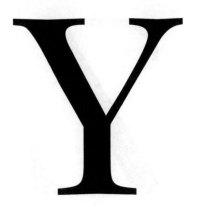

YORK

'York' in Shakespeare is not the great minster begun in 1220 and finished in 1470 but the powerful churchmen, Bishops, Archbishops and Cardinals, associated with York by name.

In 3H6, Warwick the Kingmaker instructs the Lord of Somerset to 'See that forthwith Duke Edward be convey'd / Unto my brother, Archbishop of York'; in the following scene, Edward's Queen Elizabeth, no friend of Warwick's now that he has deserted the Yorkist cause, also identifies 'the Bishop of York' as 'Fell Warwick's brother' (3H6 4.3.52–3; 4.4.11–12). This is George Neville, a prominent politician and ecclesiastic who was named Chancellor of England in 1460 and again in 1470. In H8, 'the right reverend Cardinal of York' (H8 1.1.51; cf. 2.2.105) is no less a political force than Wolsey, who is also twice called 'Lord of York' (H8 2.2.121; 3.1.62). See also 1H4 3.2.118–20; 2H4 4.1.225.

ZEAL

Sometimes deep personal conviction, or the rigorous observance of religious duties; sometimes the outlandish expression of religious extremism. Donne once warns the religious controversialists, 'Fix your meditations upon Christ Jesus so, as he is now at the right hand of his Father in heaven, and entangle not your selves so with controversies about his body, as to lose reall charity, for imaginary zeale' (9: 77–8). On the other hand, Donne also concedes appropriate zeal, the **blessed** madness of true religious **devotion**, as when he says that even 'our blessed Saviour himself did some such act of vehement zeal, as that his very friends thought him *mad*' and that St Paul 'thought his *madnesse* justifiable too; *If we be besides our selves, it is for God* (2. Cor. 5.13). . . . S. *Paul* was mad for love; S. *Paul* did, and we doe take into our contemplation, the beauty of a Christian soul . . . and we are mad for the love of this soul' (10: 125).

Buckingham pretends to think he is interrupting Richard of Gloucester's religious devotions when he says 'pardon us the interruption / Of thy devotion and right Christian zeal' (R3 3.7.102–3). The ironic description of Cardinal Wolsey's enthusiasm for his work combines religious and political meanings: 'How holily he works in all his business! / And with what zeal!' (H8 2.2.22–3). After Wolsey falls from power and reverts to a genuine spiritual life, he also uses the word 'zeal' to describe both secular and religious passions: 'Had I but serv'd my God with half the zeal / I serv'd my king, He would not in mine age / Have left me naked to mine enemies' (H8 3.2.455–7). Though the speaker is using irony, religious and political zeal also are combined when King Philip of France is described as 'France, whose armor conscience buckled on, / Whom zeal and charity brought to the field / As God's own soldier' (JN 2.1.564–6).

Because the secular vow of the four lords in LLL 'Not to see ladies, study, fast, not sleep' (LLL 1.1.48) has some analogies to a monastic vow, the word 'zeal' is used more than once in ironic reference to its inevitable failure. The King, having overheard both Dumaine and Longaville protest a forbidden romantic love, uses both 'faith' and 'zeal' in his gleeful anticipation of their humiliating exposure: 'What will Berowne say when that he shall hear / Faith infringed, which such zeal did swear?' (LLL 4.3.143–4). The King's taunting 'What zeal, what fury, hath inspir'd thee now?' (LLL 4.3.225) is similar. The Servant also describes Perdita's extraordinary beauty with words of extreme religious **devotion**: 'This is a creature, / Would she begin a **sect**, might quench the zeal / Of all **professors** else, make proselytes / Of who she but bid follow' (WT 5.1.106–9). Loaded words like 'zeal', **'profess'** and **'profession'** as witnessing, and **'sect'** might all evoke Reformation tensions. Prince Hal's description of Bardolph as someone 'whose zeal burns in his nose', and his resultant scepticism about Falstaff's claim that he is 'of the **wicked**' (2H4 2.4.329–30) also appropriates some of this religious argot.

ZEALOUS

'Characterised by religious fervour', or deeply committed to any cause or person.

When Richard of Gloucester (in the scene in which he and Buckingham are trying to convince the Mayor and the Citizens of Richard's piety and his lack of interest in the crown) says 'When holy and devout religious men / Are at their beads, 'tis much to draw them thence, / So sweet is zealous contemplation' (R3 3.7.92–4), the zeal he refers to is religious, if also hypocritical. With a nice combination of romantic and religious fervour, Helena prays for blessings on an undeserving Bertram whilst committing herself to a religious pilgrimage: 'Bless him at home in peace, whilst I from far / His name with zealous fervour sanctify' (AWW 3.4.10–11). The romantic more clearly predominates over the religious when the lover of SON 27.6 promises that his thoughts 'Intend a zealous pilgrimage to thee'.

'ZOUNDS

(A) A mild blasphemy referring like **''sblood'** to Christ's wounds on the cross. Sometimes also spelled ' 'swounds'. When Buckingham, pretending exasperation at Richard's pretended reluctance to take the throne, says ' 'Zounds, I'll entreat no more', Richard pretends to be offended by this blasphemy: 'O, do not swear, my Lord of Buckingham' (R3 3.7.219–20).

(B) Like ' 'sblood', ' 'zounds' is often innocuous in Shakespeare, but sometimes pregnant with associative meaning. Iago's close relationship to the irreverent vice figure of the miracles and moralities requires him to blaspheme with gleeful frequency. But his ' 'Zounds, sir, y' are robb'd. . . . Even now, now, very now, an old black ram / Is tupping your white ewe', like its companion in the same scene, ' 'Zounds, sir, you are one of those that will not serve God, if the devil bid you' (OTH 1.1.86–9, 108–9), suggest that the 'profane' in Brabantio's 'What profane wretch art thou?' (OTH 1.4.114) refers to the religious as well as the social impropriety of such words. ' 'Zounds' in the play is also repeatedly associated with the threat of wounding. Cassio, admittedly drunk, pursues Roderigo (to wound him) with ' 'Zounds, you rogue, you rascal'. Montano, stabbed and bleeding in this quarrel, says, ' 'Zounds, I bleed still, I am hurt to th' death'. Even the General Othello uses this blasphemy to threaten violence: ' 'Zounds, if I stir, / Or do but lift this arm, the best of you / Shall sink in my rebuke' (OTH 2.3.145, 164, 207–9; see also OTH 2.3.145; 3.3.154; 3.4.98). Hamlet's 'Hah, ' 'swounds, I should take it; for it cannot be / But I am pigeon-liver'd, and lack gall / To make oppression bitter, or ere this / I should' a' fatted all the region kites / With this slave's offal' (HAM 2.2.576–80) ironically swears by Christ's wounds in the context of desiring to inflict equally grievous ones upon Claudius. The Murderers in R3 also use ' 'zounds' twice during their debate with Clarence about his execution (R3 1.4. 125, 145–6).

Like ' **'Swounds**', ' 'Zounds' is a frequent guest in 1H4. Hotspur associates the little curse with his own promise to support Mortimer even if it means that he will sacrifice his own blood in the process: ' 'Zounds, I will speak of him, and let my soul / Want mercy if I do not join with him. / Yea, on his part I'll empty all these veins, / And shed my dear blood drop by drop in the dust' (1H4 1.3.131–4). ' 'Zounds' twice more punctuates Hotspur's foolhardy if also gallant courage (1H4 2.3.22–3; 4.1.17). Its fustian exaggeration ironically connects Hotspur's sacrificial wounds and Christ's. Falstaff's many ' 'Zounds', in contrast, usually punctuate his cowardice and his girth rather than his courage, as when he says ' 'Zounds, will they not rob us?' (1H4 2.2.65) in response to Hal's description of the couriers of the King's money. Poins's ' 'Zounds, ye fat paunch, and ye call me coward by the Lord, I'll stab thee' again threatens swordplay (1H4 2.4.142–6). Poins's 'By the Lord' further underlines the blasphemy (1H4 2.4.145). At the end of the play Falstaff says a cowardly ' 'Zounds' over the fallen body of Hotspur; says again ' 'Zounds, I am afraid of this gunpowder Percy, though he be dead', then adds ' 'Zounds': 'How if he should counterfeit too, and rise? By my faith, I am afraid he would prove the better counterfeit' (1H4 5.4.121–4). The counterfeit death and apparent rebirth of Falstaff and the actual death and feared resurrection of Hotspur are connected by these reiterated blasphemies on ' 'Sblood' and ' 'Zounds' to the ironic, 'counterfeit' relationship of both of these deaths and rebirths to Christ's. See also 1H4 1.2.90–103; 2.1.79–82.

(C) See *Certaine Sermons*, pp. 45–51, for the sermons 'Against Swearing and Perjury'. Taylor (1993), 55, argues that despite their frequent appearances in some of Shakespeare's plays, ' 'swounds' and ' 'zounds' were systematically eliminated from several Folio texts for which we have Quarto precedents, including ROM and R3.

Primary Bibliography

A. *Miscellaneous Works*

The Agony and the Betrayal, in *York Plays*, ed. Lucy Toulmin Smith, New York: Russell and Russell, repr. 1963.

Alciatus, Andreas, *Emblems in Translation*, ed. Peter M. Daly, Toronto: University of Toronto Press, 1985.

Allen, William, *A Defense and Declaration of the Catholike Churchies Doctrine, touching purgatory . . .*, Antwerp: John Latins, 1565; STC 371.

Andrewes, Lancelot, *Ninety-Six Sermons*, 1843, New York: AMS Press, repr. 1967. [Andrewes].

Aquinas, Thomas, St, *Summa Theologica*, trans. Fathers of the English Dominican Province, 3 vols, New York: Benziger Brothers, 1947–48; [*ST*].

Augustine, St, *Basic Writings of*, ed. Whitney J. Oates, 2 vols, New York: Random House, 1948.

Augustine, St, *The City of God*, trans. Marcus Dods, New York: Modern Library, 1950.

Augustine, St, *On Free Will in Earlier Writings*, sel. and trans. John H.S. Burleigh, Philadelphia, PA: Westminster Press, 1953.

Augustine, St, *On Christian Doctrine*, ed. and trans. D. W. Robertson, Jr, New York: The Liberal Arts Press, 1958.

Augustine, St, *On the Trinity*, ed. Gareth B. Matthews, trans. Stephen McKenna, Cambridge: University Press, 2002.

A Bestiary for Saint Jerome, ed. Herbert Friedmann, Washington, DC: Smithsonian Institution Press, 1980.

The Book of Common Prayer 1559: The Elizabethan Prayer Book, ed. John E. Booty, Charlottesville, VA: The University Press of Virginia, 1976.

A Breefe Collection Concerning the Love of God . . ., Anon, Douay: Laurence Kellam, 1603; STC 5554.

Calvin, John, *Institutes of the Christian Religion*, trans. Thomas Norton, London: Reinolde [W]olfe & Richarde Harison, 1561.

Calvin, John, *The Mystery of Godliness and other Selected Sermons*, Grand Rapids, MI: William B. Eerdmans, repr. 1950.

Calvin, John, *Sermons from Job*, trans. Leroy Nixon, Grand Rapids, MI: William B. Eerdmans, 1952.

Calvin, John, *Tracts and Treatises on the Doctrine and Worship of the Church*, trans. Henry Beveridge, ed. Thomas F. Torrance, 3 vols, Grand Rapids, MI: William B. Eerdmans, 1958.

Certaine Sermons or Homilies appointed to be read in Churches, In the Time of the late Queen Elizabeth, a facimile repr. of the 1623 edn, ed. Mary Ellen Rickey and

Thomas B. Stroup, Gainesville: Scholars' Facimiles & Reprints, 1968; [*Certaine Sermons*].

Two Coventry Corpus Christi Plays, ed. Hardin Craig, London: Oxford University Press, 1957; EETS, E.S. 87.

Davies, Sir John, 'Orchestra', in *The Poems of Sir John Davies*, ed. Robert Krueger, Oxford: Clarendon Press, 1975.

Donne, John, *The Sermons of John Donne*, ed. George R. Potter and Evelyn M. Simpson, Berkeley, CA: University of California Press, 1953–62. [Donne].

Donne, John, *The Anniversaries*, ed. Frank Manley, Baltimore, MD: Johns Hopkins Press, 1963.

Donne, John, *The Complete English Poems*, ed. A. J. Smith, London: Penguin Books, 1971.

Donne, John, *Biathanatos*, ed. Ernest W. Sullivan II, Newark: University of Delaware Press, 1984.

The English Hexapla, ed. J. Martin Augustin Scholz, London: S. Bagster, 1841.

Erasmus, Desiderius, *Opus Epistolarum Des. Erasmi Roterodami*, ed. P. S. and H. M. Allen, 12 vols, Oxford: Clarendon Press, 1906–58.

Erasmus, Desiderius, *The Praise of Folie*, trans. Sir Thomas Chaloner, London: Oxford University Press, 1965, (1509 orig.); EETS no. 257.

Erasmus, Desiderius, *Controversies*, ed. J. K. Sowards, trans. Peter Macardle and Clarence H. Miller, in *Collected Works of Erasmus*, vol. 6, Toronto: University of Toronto Press, 1999.

Erasmus, Desiderius, *Controversies*, ed. Charles Trinkaus, trans. Peter Macardle and Clarence H. Miller, in *Collected Works of Erasmus*, vol. 7, Toronto: University of Toronto Press, 1999.

Florio, John, *Queen Anna's New World of Words, or Dictionarie of the Italian and English Tongues*, London: Melch. Bradwood, 1611.

Foxe, John, *Acts and Monuments . . .*, London: Company of the Stationers, 1641 (8th repr. of the 1563 original).

The Geneva Bible, a facsimile of the 1560 edition, intro. Lloyd E. Berry, Madison, WI: University of Wisconsin Press, 1969.

Granada, Fr. Lewis de, *Of Prayer, and Meditation . . .*, trans. Richard Hopkins, Paris: Thomas Brumeau, 1582; STC (2nd edn) 16907.

Granada, Fr Lewis de, *Memoriall of a Christian Life*, [trans. Richard Hopkins], Rouen: George L'oyselet, 1586.

Granada, Fr Lewis de, *A Spiritual Doctrine, Conteining a Rule To live wel, with divers Praiers and Meditations*, [trans. Richard Gibbons], Louen: Laurence Kellam, 1599.

Herbert, George, *The English Poems of George Herbert*, ed. C. A. Patrides, London: J. M. Dent & Sons, 1974.

Heywood, Thomas, *The Hierarchie of the Blessed Angels*, London: Adam Islip, 1635.

Hooker, Richard, *Of the Laws of Ecclesiastical Polity*, Preface; Books 1 to IV, ed. George Edelin, Cambridge, MA: Harvard University Press, 1977; (Repr. of the London edn: John Windet, 1593); (the Folger Library Edition of the Works of Richard Hooker, W. Speed Hill, General Editor); [Hooker I, II, III or IV].

Hooker, Richard, *Of the Laws of Ecclesiastical Polity*, Book V, ed. W. Speed Hill, Cambridge, MA: Harvard University Press, 1977; (Repr. of the London edn: John Windet, 1597); (The Folger Library Edition of the Works of Richard Hooker, W. Speed Hill, General Editor); [Hooker V].

Hooker, Richard, *Of the Laws of Ecclesiastical Polity*, Books VI, VII, VIII, ed. P. G. Stanwood, Cambridge, MA: Harvard University Press, 1981; (Repr. of the London edn: J. Best, 1662); (the Folger Library Edition of the Works of Richard Hooker, W. Speed Hill, General Editor); [Hooker VI, VII or VIII].

James I, King, *Daemonologie*, London: William Cotton and Will. Aspley, 1603; STC (2nd edn) 14365.5.

Jonson, Ben, *Bartholomew Fair*, ed. Eugene Waith, New Haven, CT: Yale University Press, 1963.

Jonson, Ben, *The Devil is an Ass*, in *Ben Jonson's Plays*, ed. Felix Schelling, vol. 1, London: Everyman's Library, 1970

Jonson, Ben, *The Alchemist*, ed. Alvin Kernan, New Haven, CT: Yale University Press, 1974.

Lily, William and John Colet, *A Short Introduction of Grammar*, [1549], Menston: Scolar Press, repr. 1970; STC 15611.

Loarte, Jasper, *The Exercise of a Christian Life*, [trans. Stephen Brinkley, 1596–97]; STC 16642.

Luther, Martin, 'Defense and Explanation of all the Articles, 1521', in *Career of the Reformer II*, ed. George W. Forell, vol. 32, in *Luther's Works* (*LW*), 55 vols, St Louis, MO: Concordia Press, 1955–86; [*LW* 32].

Luther, Martin, *Lectures on Galatians*, ed. Walter A. Hansen, vol. 26 in *Luther's Works* (*LW*), 55 vols, St Louis, MO: Concordia Press, 1955–86; [*LW* 26].

Luther, Martin, *Lectures on Romans*, ed. Hilton C. Oswald, vol. 25 in *Luther's Works* (*LW*), 55 vols, St Louis, MO: Concordia Press, 1955–86; [*LW* 25].

Luther, Martin, *On the Bondage of the Will*, in *Career of the Reformer III*, ed. Philip S. Watson, vol. 33 in *Luther's Works* (*LW*), 55 vols, St Louis, MO: Concordia Press, 1955–86; [*LW* 33].

Luther, Martin, *Sermons on the Gospel of John*, ed. Jaroslav Pelikan, vols. 22 and 23, in *Luther's Works* (*LW*), 55 vols, St Louis, MO: Concordia Press, 1955–86; [*LW* 22 and *LW* 23].

Machiavelli, Niccolo, *The arte of warre*, trans. Peter Whitehorne, London, 1560; STC 17164.

Marbeck, John, *A booke of notes and common places*, London: Thomas East, 1581; STC 17299.

Marbeck, John, *The Work of John Marbeck*, ed. R. A. Lever, Oxford: The Sutton Courtenay Press, 1978.

Marlowe, Christopher, *Dr. Faustus*, ed. Roma Gill, Oxford: Clarendon Press, 1990.

Marlowe, Christopher, *The Jew of Malta*, ed. Roma Gill, Oxford: Clarendon Press, 1995.

Marvell, Andrew, 'To His Coy Mistress', in *The Metaphysical Poets*, rev. edn, ed. Helen Gardner, Middlesex: Penguin Books, 1966.

Milton, John, *The Complete Poetical Works*, ed. Douglas Bush, Boston: Houghton Mifflin, 1965.

The Mirrour of Mans Salvacioun, ed. Avril Henry, Aldershot: Scolar Press, repr. 1986.

The Mirror of Salvation, ed. Albert Labriola and John W. Smelz, Duquesne: Duquesne University Press, repr. 2002.

More, Sir Thomas, *The Dialogue Concerning Tyndale*, ed. W. E. Campbell, in *The English Works of Sir Thomas More*, 2 vols, London: Eyre and Spottiswood, 1927.

The New Testament Octapa, ed. Luther A. Weigle, New York: Thomas Nelson, 1962.

Perkins, William, *The Foundation of Christian Religion*, 2nd edn, [London]: Thomas Orwin, 1591; STC 19710.

Perkins, William, *A Golden Chain, or The Description of Theologie, containing the order of the causes of Salvation and Damnation, according to Gods word*, 2nd edn, trans. R. H., Cambridge: John Legate, 1597a; STC 19663.

Perkins, William, *A Graine of Musterd-Seed* [Anr. edn], London: Felix Kingston, 1597b. STC 19724.6.

Perkins, William, *The workes of that famous and worthie minister of Christ . . . M. W. Perkins*, [Cambridge]: John Legate, [1608]; STC 19649.

Perkins, William, *A Discourse on the Damned Art of Witchcraft*, [Cambridge]: Cantrel Legge, 1610; STC 19698.

Perkins, William, *The Work of William Perkins*, ed. Ian Breward, Abingdon, England: Sutton Courtenay Press, 1970.

Persons, Robert, *A Brief Censure . . .*, Doway: John Lyon, 1581; STC 19393.

Persons, Robert, [N. D.], *A Review of Ten Publike Disputations*, [St Omer], 1604b; STC 19414. [Also reproduced in facsimile in vol. 306 of the series *English Recusant Literature 1558–1640*, ed. D. M. Rogers, Ilkley, Yorkshire: The Scolar Press, 1976].

Persons, Robert, [R. P.], *The Summarie of the Christian exercises*, Rouen, 1582, STC 19353. [Called *Christian Directorie* in the 1585 edn.]

Persons, Robert, [N. D.], *A Treatise of Three Conversions of England from Paganisme to Christian Religion*, [St Omer], 1603; STC 19416.

Persons, Robert, [N. D.], *A Treatise of Three Conversions of England from Paganisme to Christian Religion*, [the second part, mistitled 'The Third Part], [St Omer], 1604a; STC 19416.

Persons, Robert, [N. D.], *A Treatise of Three Conversions of England from Paganisme to Christian Religion*, is also reproduced in facsimile in vols. 304–6 of the series *English Recusant Literature 1558–1640*, ed. D. M. Rogers, Ilkley, Yorkshire: The Scolar Press, 1976; vol. 1: 1603; vols. 2 and 3: 1606.

Pole, Cardinal, *A Treatie of Justification*, [trans. Sir Thomas Copley], Lovanni: [John Fowler], 1569; STC 20088.

Preces Privatae, Londini: Gulielmus Seres, 1573; STC 20380.

Puente, Luis de la, *Meditations upon the Mysteries of our Holie Faith, with the Practice of Mental Prayer*, trans. John Heigham, S. Omers: [C. Boscard] 1619; STC 20486.

Rastell, John, *A confutation of a sermon produced by M. Jewel*, Antwerp: Aegid. Diest, 1564; STC 20726.

Rastell, John, *The Third Booke, . . . that it is time to BEWARE OF M. JEWEL*, Antwerp: Joannis Fouleri, 1566; STC 20729a.

Rowley, Samuel, *When You See Me, You Know Me. Or the famous Chronicle Historie of King Henry the Eight*, London: Nath. Butter, 1632; STC (2nd edn) 21420.

Salkeld, John, *A Treatise of Angels*, London: Nathaniel Butter, 1613; STC (2nd edn) 21621.

Saunder [Sander], Nicolas, *The supper of our Lord*, Louanii: [John Fowler], 1565; STC 21694.

Saunder [Sander], Nicolas, *Treatise of the images of Christ a. of his Saints*, Louvain: J. Fowler, 1567; STC 21696.

Scot, Reginald, *The Discoverie of Witchcraft*, London: William Brome, 1584; STC (2nd edn) 21864.

Shacklock, Richard, *The Hachet of Heresie*, Antwerp: Aeg. Diest, 1565; STC 13888.

Southern, A. C., *Elizabethan Recusant Prose 1559–82*, London: Sands & Co., 1950.

Spenser, Edmund, *The Poetical Works of Edmund Spenser*, ed. J. C. Smith and E. De Selincourt, London: Oxford University Press, 1926.

Sternhold, Thomas and John Hopkins, coll., *The whole booke of Psalmes, collected into English metre*, London: John Windet, 1600; STC (2nd edn) 2500.5.

Sutcliffe, Matthew, *The practice, proceedings, and lawes of armes*, London: Christopher Barker, 1593; STC (2nd edn) 23468.

Trapp, John, A., *A commentary upon all the books of the New Testament*, London: R. W. [Robert White], 1656.

Travels Through France and Italy (1647–49), ed. Luigi Monga, Geneve: Slatkine, 1987.

Tyndale, William, *Tyndale's New Testament*, ed. David Daniell, New Haven, CT: Yale University Press, 1989.

Vaughan, Henry, *The Complete Poetry of Henry Vaughan*, ed. French Fogle, New York: New York University Press, 1965.

Vaux, Laurence, *A Catechisme or Christian Doctrine necessarie for Children and ignorante people . . . with an other later addition of instruction of the laudable Ceremonies used in the Catholike Church*, [Rouen: G. L'Oyselet,] 1590a; STC (2nd edn) 24627a.

Vaux, Laurence, *A Brief Fourme of Confession, Instructing all Christian folke how to co[n]fesse their sinnes, & so to dispose themselves, that they may enjoy the benefite of true Penance, dooing the woorthy fruites therof, according to the use of Christs Catholique Church*, [Rouen: G. L'Oyselet,] 1590b; STC (2nd edn) 24627a.

Voraigne, Jaques, *The Golden Legend*, trans. Granger Ryan and Helmut Ripperger, New York: Longmans, 1941; (first trans. Caxton 1485).

Walker, Ralph, *A learned and profitable treatise of Gods providence*, London: Felix Kyngston, 1608; STC (2nd edn) 24963.

Whitney, Geffrey, *A Choice of Emblemes*, ed. Henry Green, New York: Benjamin Blom, repr. 1967.

Whitney, Geffrey, *A Choice of Emblemes*, Leyden, 1586.

Wither, George, *A Collection of Emblemes, Ancient and Modern*, intro. Rosemary Freeman, Columbia: University of South Carolina Press, 1975.

B. *Works cited from the 'The Parker Society . . . for the publication of the works of the fathers and early writers of the reformed English church', [Cambridge: University Press, 1841–55].*

Bale, John, *Select Works of John Bale, D.D., Bishop of Ossory: Containing the Examinations of Lord Cobham, William Thorpe, and Anne Askewe, and The Image of Both Churches*, ed. Rev. Henry Christmas, Cambridge: The University Press, 1849.

Becon, Thomas, *The Early Works of Thomas Becon, S.T.P., Chaplain to Archbishop Cranmer, Prebendary of Canterbury, &c.: Being the Treatises Published by Him in the Reign of King Henry VIII*, ed. Rev. John Ayre, Cambridge: The University Press, 1843; [Becon 1].

Becon, Thomas, *The Catechism of Thomas Becon, S.T.P., Chaplain to Archbishop Cranmer, Prebendary of Canterbury, &c.: With Other Pieces Written by Him in the Reign of King Edward the Sixth*, ed. Rev. John Ayre, Cambridge: The University Press, 1844; [Becon 2].

Becon, Thomas, *Prayers and Other Pieces of Thomas Becon, S.T.P., Chaplain to Archbishop Cranmer, Prebendary of Canterbury, &c.*, ed. Rev. John Ayre, Cambridge: The University Press, 1844; [Becon 3].

Bradford, John, *The Writings of John Bradford, M.A., Fellow of Pembroke Hall, Cambridge, and Prebendary of St. Paul's, Martyr, 1555: Containing Sermons, Meditations, Examinations, &c.*, ed. Aubrey Townsend, Cambridge: The University Press, 1848; [Bradford 1].

Bradford, John, *The Writings of John Bradford, M.A., Fellow of Pembroke Hall, Cambridge, and Prebendary of St. Paul's, Martyr, 1555: Containing Letters, Treatises, Remains*, ed. Aubrey Townsend, Cambridge: The University Press, 1853; [Bradford 2].

Bullinger, Henry, *The Decades of Henry Bullinger, Minister of the Church of Zurich, Translated by H.L.: The First and Second Decades*, ed. Rev. Thomas Harding, Cambridge: The University Press, 1849; [Bullinger 1].

Bullinger, Henry, *The Decades of Henry Bullinger, Minister of the Church of Zurich, Translated by H.L.: The Third Decade*, ed. Rev. Thomas Harding, Cambridge: The University Press, 1850; [Bullinger 2].

Bullinger, Henry, *The Decades of Henry Bullinger, Minister of the Church of Zurich, Translated by H.L.: The Fourth Decade*, ed. Rev. Thomas Harding, Cambridge: The University Press, 1851; [Bullinger 3].

Bullinger, Henry, *The Decades of Henry Bullinger, Minister of the Church of Zurich, Translated by H.L.: The Fifth Decade*, ed. Rev. Thomas Harding, Cambridge: The University Press, 1852; [Bullinger 4].

Calfhill, James, *An Answer to John Martiall's Treatise of the Cross, by James Calfhill, D.D., Dean of Bocking, Archdeacon of Colchester, and Bishop Elect of Worcester*, ed. Rev. Richard Gibbings, Cambridge: The University Press, 1846.

Cooper, Thomas, *An Answer in Defence of the Truth Against the Apology of Private Mass, by T. Cooper, Afterwards Bishop, First of Lincoln, and then of Winchester, Published in 1562*, ed. Rev. William Goode, Cambridge: The University Press, 1850.

Coverdale, Myles, *Writings and Translations of Myles Coverdale, Bishop of Exeter*, ed. Rev. George Pearson, Cambridge: The University Press, 1844; [Coverdale 1].

Coverdale, Myles, *Remains of Myles Coverdale, Bishop of Exeter*, ed. Rev. George Pearson, Cambridge: The University Press, 1846; [Coverdale 2].

Cranmer, Thomas, *Writings and Disputations of Thomas Cranmer, Archbishop of Canterbury, Martyr, 1556, Relative to the Sacrament of the Lord's Supper*, ed. Rev. John Edmund Cox, Cambridge: The University Press, 1844; [Cranmer 1].

Cranmer, Thomas, *Miscellaneous Writings and Letters of Thomas Cranmer, Archbishop of Canterbury, Martyr, 1556*, ed. Rev. John Edmund Cox, Cambridge: The University Press, 1846; [Cranmer 2].

Fulke, William, *A Defence of the Sincere and True Translations of the Holy Scriptures into the English Tongue against the Cavils of Gregory Martin, by William Fulke, D.D., Master of Pembroke Hall, Cambridge*, ed. Rev. Charles Henry Hartshorne, Cambridge: The University Press, 1843; [Fulke 1].

Fulke, William, *Stapleton's Fortress Overthrown. A Rejoinder to Martiall's Reply. A Discovery of the Dangerous Rock of the Popish Church Commended by Sanders, by William Fulke, D.D., Master of Pembroke Hall, Cambridge*, ed. Rev. Richard Gibbings, Cambridge: The University Press, 1848; [Fulke 2].

Fulke, William, *The Text of the New Testament of Jesus Christ*, London: 1589.

Gough, Henry, *A General Index to the Publications of the Parker Society*, Cambridge: The University Press, 1855.

Grindal, Edmund, *The Remains of Edmund Grindall, D.D., Successively Bishop of London, and Archbishop of York and Canterbury*, ed. Rev. William Nicholson, Cambridge: The University Press, 1843.

Hooper, John, *Early Writings of John Hooper, D.D., Lord Bishop of Gloucester and Worcester, Martyr, 1555*, ed. Rev. Samuel Carr, Cambridge: The University Press, 1843; [Hooper 1].

Hooper, John, *Later Writings of Bishop Hooper, Together with His Letters and Other Pieces*, ed. Rev. Charles Nevinson, Cambridge: The University Press, 1852; [Hooper 2].

Hutchinson, Roger, *The Works of Roger Hutchinson, Fellow of St. John's College, Cambridge, and afterwards of Eton College, A.D. 1550*, ed. John Bruce, Cambridge: The University Press, 1842.

Jewel, John, *The Works of John Jewel, Bishop of Salisbury: The First Portion*, ed. Rev. John Ayre, Cambridge: The University Press, 1845; [Jewel 1].

Jewel, John, *The Works of John Jewel, Bishop of Salisbury: The Second Portion*, ed. Rev. John Ayre, Cambridge: The University Press, 1847; [Jewel 2].

Jewel, John, *The Works of John Jewel, Bishop of Salisbury: The Third Portion*, ed. Rev. John Ayre, Cambridge: The University Press, 1848; [Jewel 3].

Jewel, John, *The Works of John Jewel, Bishop of Salisbury: The Fourth Portion*, ed. Rev. John Ayre, Cambridge: The University Press, 1850; [Jewel 4].

Latimer, Hugh, *Sermons of Hugh Latimer, Sometime Bishop of Worcester, Martyr, 1555*, ed. Rev. George Elwes Corrie, Cambridge: The University Press, 1844; [Latimer 1].

Latimer, Hugh, *Sermons and Remains of Hugh Latimer, Sometime Bishop of Worcester, Martyr, 1555*, ed. Rev. George Elwes Corrie, Cambridge: The University Press, 1845; [Latimer 2].

413

Liturgical Services: Liturgies and Occasional Forms of Prayer Set Forth in the Reign of Queen Elizabeth, ed. William Keatinge Clay, Cambridge: The University Press, 1847.

The Two Liturgies, A.D. 1549, and A.D. 1552: With Other Documents Set Forth by Authority in the Reign of King Edward VI, ed. Joseph Ketley, Cambridge: The University Press, 1844.

Norden, John, *A Progress of Piety, Whose Jesses Lead into the Harbour of Heavenly Heart's Ease*, Cambridge: The University Press, 1847.

Nowell, Alexander, *A Catechism Written in Latin By Alexander Nowell, Dean of St. Paul's: Together with The Same Catechism Translated into English by Thomas Norton*, ed. G. E. Corrie, Cambridge: The University Press, 1853.

Nowell, Alexander, *A Catechisme or First Instruction and Learning of Christian Religion*, 1570, trans. Thomas Norton, New York: Scholars' Facimiles and Reprints, 1975.

Parker, Matthew, *Correspondence of Matthew Parker, D.D., Archbishop of Canterbury*, ed. John Bruce, Cambridge: The University Press, 1853.

Philpot, John, *The Examinations and Writings of John Philpot, B.C.L., Archdeacon of Winchester, Martry, 1555*, ed. Rev. Robert Eden, Cambridge: The University Press, 1842.

Pilkington, James, *The Works of James Pilkington, B.D., Lord Bishop of Durham*, ed. Rev. James Scholefield, Cambridge: The University Press, 1842.

Private Prayers Put Forth by Authority during The Reign of Queen Elizabeth, ed. William Keatinge Clay, Cambridge: The University Press, 1851.

Ridley, Nicholas, *The Works of Nicholas Ridley, D.D., Sometime Lord Bishop of London, Martyr, 1555*, ed. Rev. Henry Christmas, Cambridge: The University Press, 1841.

Rogers, Thomas, *The Catholic Doctrine of The Church of England, An Exposition of the Thirty-Nine Articles, by Thomas Rogers, A.M., Chaplain to Archbishop Bancroft*, ed. Rev. J. J. S. Perowne, Cambridge: The University Press, 1854.

Sandys, Edwin, *The Sermons of Edwin Sandys, D.D., Successively Bishop of Worcester and London, and Archbishop of York; To Which Are Added Some Miscellaneous Pieces, by The Same Author*, ed. Rev. John Ayre, Cambridge: The University Press, 1841.

Tyndale, William, *Doctrinal Treatises and Introduction to Different Portions of The Holy Scriptures, by William Tyndale, Martyr, 1536*, ed. Rev. Henry Walter, Cambridge: The University Press, 1848; [Tyndale 1].

Tyndale, William, *Expositions and Notes on Sundry Portions of The Holy Scriptures, Together with The Practice of Prelates, by William Tyndale, Martyr, 1536*, ed. Rev. Henry Walter, Cambridge: The University Press, 1849; [Tyndale 2].

Tyndale, William, *An Answer to Sir Thomas More's Dialogue, The Supper of the Lord After the True Meaning of John VI and 1 Cor. XI; and WM. Tracy's Testament Expounded, by William Tyndale, Martyr, 1536*, ed. Rev. Henry Walter, Cambridge: The University Press, 1850; [Tyndale 3].

Whitaker, William, *A Disputation on Holy Scripture, Against the Papists, Especially Bellarmine and Stapleton, by William Whitaker, D.D., Regius Professor of Divinity, and Master of St. John's College, in The University of Cambridge*, ed. Rev. William Fitzgerald, Cambridge: The University Press, 1849.

Whitgift, John, *The Works of John Whitgift, D.D., Master of Trinity College, Dean of Lincoln, &c. Afterwards Successively Bishop of Worcester and Archbishop of Canterbury: The First Portion,* ed. Rev. John Ayre, Cambridge: The University Press, 1851; [Whitgift 1].

Whitgift, John, *The Works of John Whitgift, D.D., Master of Trinity College, Dean of Lincoln, &c. Afterwards Successively Bishop of Worcester and Archbishop of Canterbury: The Second Portion,* ed. Rev. John Ayre, Cambridge: The University Press, 1852; [Whitgift 2].

Whitgift, John, *The Works of John Whitgift, D.D., Master of Trinity College, Dean of Lincoln, &c. Afterwards Successively Bishop of Worcester and Archbishop of Canterbury: The Third Portion,* ed. Rev. John Ayre, Cambridge: The University Press, 1853; [Whitgift 3].

The Zurich Letters, Comprising The Correspondence of Several English Bishops and Others, With Some of the Helvetian Reformers, During the Early Part of The Reign of Queen Elizabeth, transl. and ed. Robinson Hastings, Cambridge: The University Press, 1842; [Zurich 1].

The Zurich Letters (Second Series), Comprising The Correspondence of Several English Bishops and Others, With Some of the Helvetian Reformers, During the Reign of Queen Elizabeth, transl. and ed. Robinson Hastings, Cambridge: The University Press, 1845; [Zurich 2].

C. *Editions of Shakespeare*

1. *Complete Editions*

William Shakespeare: The Complete Works (The Complete Pelican Shakespeare), ed. Alfred Harbage, Baltimore, MD: Penguin Books, 1969; [PEL]

The Riverside Shakespeare, ed. G. Blakemore Evans, 2nd edn, Boston: Houghton Mifflin, 1997; [RIV]

The Complete Works of Shakespeare, ed. David Bevington, 4th edn, New York: HarperCollins, 1992; [BEV]

William Shakespeare: The Complete Works, ed. Stanley Wells and Gary Taylor, Oxford: Clarendon Press, 1986.

2. *Individual Editions*

Berdan, John M. and Tucker Brooke, eds, *The Life of King Henry the Eighth,* New Haven, CT: Yale University Press, 1925.

Cairncross, Andrew S., ed., *The First Part of King Henry VI (Arden Shakespeare),* London: Methuen & Co., 1962.

Cairncross, Andrew S., ed., *The Second Part of King Henry VI,* rev. edn *(Arden Shakespeare),* Cambridge: Methuen & Co., 1962.

Eccles, Mark, *Measure for Measure,* in *A New Variorum Edition of Shakespeare,* New York: Modern Language Association of America, 1980.

Foakes, R. A., ed., *Henry VIII*, 3rd edn, rev., *(Arden Shakespeare)*, London: Methuen & Co., 1957.

Furness, Horace Howard, ed., *Hamlet*, in *A New Variorum Edition of Shakespeare*, 2 vols, Philadelphia, PA: J. B. Lippincott, 1877.

Furness, Horace Howard, *King Lear*, in *A New Variorum Edition of Shakespeare*, Philadelphia, PA: J. B. Lippincott, 1880.

Furness, Horace Howard, *The Tragedy of Richard the Third*, in *A New Variorum Edition of Shakespeare*, Philadelphia, PA: J. B. Lippencott, 1909.

Furness, Horace Howard, *Twelfth Night*, in *A New Variorum Edition of Shakespeare*, Philadelphia, PA: J. B. Lippencott, 1901.

Furness, Horace Howard, Jr, ed., *The Tragedie of Coriolanus*, in *A New Variorum Edition of Shakespeare*, Philadelphia, PA: J. B. Lippencott, 1928.

Hammond, Antony, ed., *King Richard III (Arden Shakespeare)*, London: Methuen & Co., 1981.

Hemingway, Samuel Burdett, ed., *Henry the Fourth Part I*, in *A New Variorum Edition of Shakespeare*, Philadelphia, PA: J. B. Lippincott, 1936.

Honigman, E. A. J., ed., *King John (Arden Shakespeare)*, 4th edn, rev., Cambridge, MA: Harvard University Press, 1954.

Kermode, Frank, ed., *The Tempest (Arden Shakespeare)*, London: Methuen, 1969.

Lothian, J. M. and T. W. Craik, eds, *Twelfth Night (Arden Shakespeare)*, London: Methuen & Co., 1975.

Maxwell, J. C., ed., *King Henry the Eighth*, Cambridge: The University Press, 1962.

Muir, Kenneth, ed., *King Lear (Arden Shakespeare)*, 9th edn, London: Methuen & Co., 1975.

Parker, R. B., ed., *The Tragedy of Coriolanus*, Oxford: Clarendon Press, 1994.

Wilson, John Dover, ed., *Hamlet*, Cambridge: The University Press, 1954.

Secondary Bibliography

Aberbach, D., 'The Job motif in *King Lear*', *Notes and Queries* 26 (1979): 129–32.

Adamson, W. D., 'Unpinned or undone? Desdemona's critics and the problem of sexual innocence', *Shakespeare Studies* 13 (1980): 169–86.

Adelman, Janet, 'Her father's blood: Race, conversion, and nation in *The Merchant of Venice*', *Representations* 81 (2003): 4–30.

Alexander, Nigel, 'Hamlet and the art of memory', *Notes and Queries* 15 (1968): 137–9.

Alston, Margaret, 'Iconoclasm in England: Official and clandestine', in *Iconoclasm vs. Art and Drama*, ed. Clifford Davidson and Ann Eljenholm Nichols, Kalamazoo: Medieval Institute, 1989.

Anderson, Linda, *A Kind of Wild Justice: Revenge in Shakespeare's Comedies*, Newark: University of Delaware Press, 1987.

Armstrong, William A., 'Torch, cauldron and taper: Light and darkness in *Macbeth*', in *Poetry and Drama, 1570–1700: Essays in Honour of Harold F. Brooks*, ed. Anthony Coleman and Antony Hammond, London: Methuen, 1981.

Asp, Carolyn, 'Shakespeare's Paulina and the *Consolatio* tradition', *Shakespeare Studies* 11 (1978): 145–58.

Atkinson, David J., ed., *New Dictionary of Christian Ethics and Pastoral Theology*, Downers Grove and Leicester: Intervarsity Press, 1995.

Attwater, Donald, *The Penguin Dictionary of Saints*, Baltimore, MD: Penguin, 1965.

Austen, Glyn, 'Ephesus restored: Sacramentalism and redemption in *The Comedy of Errors*', *Literature and Theology* 1 (1987): 54–69.

Baines, Barbara J., 'Assaying the power of chastity in *Measure for Measure*', *SEL* 30 (1990): 283–301.

Baker, J. H., 'The English law of sanctuary', *Ecclesiastical Law Journal* 2 (1990): 8–13.

Baker, J. Wayne, '*Sola Fide, Sola Gratia*: The battle for Luther in seventeenth century England', *Sixteenth Century Journal* 16 (1985): 115.

Baldo, Jonathan, 'Wars of memory in *Henry V*', *Shakespeare Quarterly* 47 (1996): 132–59.

Baldwin, T. W., *On the Compositional Genetics of The Comedy of Errors*, Urbana, IL: University of Illinois Press, 1965.

Barber, C. L., *Shakespeare's Festive Comedy*, Cleveland and New York: Meridian Books, 1967.

Baring-Gould, S., *The Lives of the Saints*, 16 vols, rev. edn, Edinburgh: John Grant, 1914.

Barish, Jonas, *Ben Jonson and the Language of Prose Comedy*, Cambridge, MA: Harvard University Press, 1960.

Barnaby, Andrew and Joan Wry, 'Authorised versions: *Measure for Measure* and the politics of bibical translation', *Renaissance Quarterly* 51 (1998): 1225–54.

Barnes, A. D., 'Kent's "Holy Cords": A biblical allusion in *King Lear* II.ii.74–76', *English Language Notes* 22 (1984): 20–2.

Bate, Jonathan, 'Shakespeare's foolosophy', in *Shakespeare Performed: Essays in Honor of R. A. Foakes*, ed. Grace Ioppolo, Newark: University of Delaware Press, 2000.

Battenhouse, Roy W., 'The Ghost in Hamlet: A Catholic "lynchpin"?', *Studies in Philology* 48 (1951): 161–92.

Battenhouse, Roy W., *Shakespearean Tragedy: Its Art and Its Christian Premises*, Bloomington, IN: Indiana University Press, 1969.

Battenhouse, Roy W., 'Falstaff as Parodist and Perhaps Holy Fool', *PMLA* 90 (1975): 32–52.

Battenhouse, Roy W., 'Religion in *King John*: Shakespeare's view', *Connotations* 1 (1991): 140–9.

Battenhouse, Roy W., *Shakespeare's Christian Dimension*, Bloomington, IN: University of Indiana Press, 1994.

Beauregard, David N., ' "Inspired merit": Shakespeare's theology of grace in *All's Well That Ends Well*', *Renascence* 51 (1999): 218–39.

Becker, Lawrence C. and Charlotte B. Becker, *Encyclopedia of Ethics*, 2nd edn, 3 vols, New York and London: Routledge, 2001.

Belsey, Catherine, 'The serpent in the garden: Shakespeare, marriage, and material culture', *Seventeenth Century* 11 (1996): 1–20.

Bentley, James, *The Way of Saint James*, London: Pavilion, 1992.

Berninghausen, Thomas F., 'Banishing Cain: The gardening metaphor in *Richard II* and the Genesis myth of the origin of history', *Essays in Literature* 14 (1987): 27–38.

Bevington, David, *From Mankind to Marlowe*, Cambridge, MA: Harvard University Press, 1962.

Bevington, David, ' "More Needs She the Divine Than the Physician": The limitations of medicine in Shakespeare's late plays', in *'Divers Toyes Mengled': Essays on Medieval and Renaissance Culture*, ed. Michel Bitot and Roberta Mullini, Tours: University Francois Rabelais, 1996.

Bevington, David and Milla Riggio, ' "What revels are in hand?" Marriage celebrations and patronage of the arts in Renaissance England', in *Shakespeare and Theatrical Patronage in Early Modern England*, ed. Paul Whitfield White and Suzanne R. Westfall, Cambridge: Cambridge University Press, 2002.

Bevington, David and Paula Sheingorn, 'Alle this was token Domysday to Drede', in *Homo, Memento Finis*, intro. David Bevington, Kalamazoo: Medieval Institute Publications, 1985.

Bicks, Caroline, 'Backsliding at Ephesus: Shakespeare's Diana and the churching of women', in *Pericles: Critical Essays*, ed. David Skeele, New York: Garland, 2000.

Binns, J. W., 'Shakespeare's Latin citations: The editorial problem', *Shakespeare Survey* 35 (1982): 119–28.

Black, James, 'Henry IV's pilgrimage', *Shakespeare Quarterly* 34 (1983): 18–26.

Bland, D. S., ' "Get thee to a Nunnery": A comment', *Notes and Queries* 12 (1965): 332.

Blick, Fred, 'Shakespeare's musical sonnets: Numbers 8, 128, and Pythagoras', *The Upstart Crow* 19 (1999): 152–68.

Blincoe, Noel, 'Is Gertrude an adulteress?' *ANQ* 10 (1997): 18–24.

Bloom, Harold, *Ruin the Sacred Truths: Poetry and Belief from the Bible to the Present*, Cambridge, MA: Harvard University Press, 1989.

Boehrer, Bruce Thomas, 'Bestial buggery in *A Midsummer Night's Dream*', in *The Production of English Renaissance Culture*, ed. David Lee Miller, Sharon O'Dair and Harold Weber, Ithaca: Cornell University Press, 1994.

Book of Saints, Benedictine Monks, St Augustine's Abbey, Ramsgate, 5th edn, London: Adam and Charles Black, 1966.

Box, Terry, 'Shakespeare's *Romeo and Juliet*', *Explicator* 47 (1988): 4–5.

Bradshaw, Paul F., ed., *The New SCM Dictionary of Liturgy and Worship*, London: SCM Press, 2002.

Brandon, S. G. F., ed., *A Dictionary of Comparative Religion*, New York: Charles Scribner's Sons, 1970.

Bremer, Francis J., ed., *Puritanism*, Boston: Massachusetts Historical Society, 1993.

Brenner, Gerry, 'Shakespeare's politically ambitious Friar', *Shakespeare Studies* 13 (1980): 47–58.

Bristol, Michael D., 'Lenten butchery: Legitimation crisis in *Coriolanus*', in *Shakespeare Reproduced: The Text in History and Ideology*, ed. Jean E. Howard and Marion F. O'Connor, New York: Methuen, 1987.

Brockbank, Philip, 'Blood and wine: Tragic ritual from Aeschylus to Soyinka', *Shakespeare Survey* 36 (1983): 11–19.

Broude, Ronald, 'Four forms of vengeance in *Titus Andronicus*', *Journal of English and German Philology* 78 (1979): 494–507.

Brownlow, F. W., *Shakespeare, Harsnet, and the Devils of Denham*, Newark: University of Delaware Press, 1993.

Bryant, J. A. Jr, *Hippolyta's View*, Lexington, KT: University of Kentucky Press, 1961.

Bryant, James C., 'The problematic Friar in *Romeo and Juliet*', *English Studies* 55 (1974): 340–50.

Bullough, Geoffrey, *Narrative and Dramatic Sources of Shakespeare*, 8 vols, London: Routledge and Kegan Paul, 1957–75.

Burgoyne, Sidney C., 'Cardinal Pandulph and the "Curse of Rome" ', *College Literature* 4 (1977): 232–40.

Butler, F. G., 'Vestures and gestures of humility: *Coriolanus* Acts II and III', *English Studies in South Africa* 25 (1982): 79–108.

Butler, F. G., 'Erasmus and the deaths of Cordelia and Lear', *English Studies* 73 (1992): 10–21.

Caiger-Smith, A., *English Medieval Mural Paintings*, Oxford: Clarendon Press, 1963.

Calderwood, James L., *Shakespeare and the Denial of Death*, Amherst, MA: University of Massachusetts Press, 1987.

Campbell, O. J. and Edward G. Quinn, eds, *The Reader's Encyclopedia of Shakespeare*, New York: Thomas Y. Crowell, 1966.

Campbell, W. E., *Erasmus, Tyndale, and More*, Milwaukee: Bruce Publishing, n.d.

Candido, Joseph, '*Henry V's Non Nobis*', *Notes and Queries* 50 (2003): 42–3.

Canfield, J. Douglas, *Word as Bond in English Literature from the Middle Ages to the Restoration*, Philadelphia, PA: University of Pennsylvania Press, 1989.

Carnall, Geoffrey, 'Shakespeare's Richard III and St Paul', *Shakespeare Quarterly* 14 (1963): 186–8.

Carroll, William C., *Fat King, Lean Beggar: Representations of Poverty in the Age of Shakespeare*, Ithaca: Cornell University Press, 1996.

Carson, Neil, 'Shakespeare and the dramatic image', in *Mirror Up to Shakespeare: Essays in Honour of G. R. Hibbard*, ed. J. C. Gray, Toronto: University of Toronto Press, 1984.

Cassirer, Ernst, *The Individual and the Cosmos in Renaissance Philosophy*, New York: Harper & Row, 1963.

Cassola, Arnold, 'On the meaning of "Enciel'd" in *Measure for Measure*', *English Language Notes* 27 (1990): 22–7.

Cefalu, Paul A., ' "Damned custom . . . habits devil": Shakespeare's *Hamlet*, anti-dualism, and the early modern philosophy of mind', *ELH* 67 (2000): 399–431.

Chamberlain, Stephanie, 'Defrocking ecclesiastical authority: *Measure for Measure* and the struggle for matrimonial reform in early modern England', *Ben Jonson Journal* 7 (2000): 115–28.

Clark, Sandra, *The Elizabethan Pamphleteers: Popular Moralistic Pamphlets 1580–1640*, Rutherford: Fairleigh Dickinson University Press, 1983.

Clark, Willene B., ed. and trans., *The Medieval Book of Birds; Hugh of Fouilloy's Avarium*, Binghamton: Medieval and Renaissance Texts and Studies, 1992.

Cohen, D. M., 'The Jew and Shylock', *Shakespeare Quarterly* 31 (1980): 53–63.

Cohen, D. M., 'Shylock and the idea of the Jew', in *Jewish Presences in English Literature*, ed. Derek Cohen and Deborah Heller, Montreal: McGill-Queen's University Press, 1990.

Colley, Scott, 'Richard III and Herod', *Shakespeare Quarterly* 37 (1986): 451–8.

Collinson, Patrick, *The Elizabethan Puritan Movement*, Berkeley, CA: University of California Press, 1967.

Collinson, Patrick, *English Puritanism*, rev. edn, London: The Historical Society, 1987.

Cook, Ann Jennalie, *Making a Match: Courtship in Shakespeare and His Society*, Princeton, NJ: Princeton University Press, 1991.

Cox, Catherine, ' "Horn-pypes and funeralls": Suggestions of hope in Shakespeare's tragedies', in *The Work of Dissimilitude: Essays from the Sixth Citadel Conference on Medieval and Renaissance Literature*, ed. David G. Allen and Robert A. White, Newark: University of Delaware Press, 1992.

Cox, Catherine, 'Neither Gentile nor Jew: Performative subjectivity in *The Merchant of Venice*', *Exemplaria* 12 (2000): 359–83.

Cox, Harvey, *The Feast of Fools*, Cambridge, MA: Harvard University Press, 1969.

Cox, John D., 'The medieval background of *Measure for Measure*', *Modern Philology* 81 (1983): 1–13.

Cox, John D., 'Devils and power in Marlowe and Shakespeare', *Yearbook of English Studies* 23 (1993): 46–64.

Cox, John D., 'Stage devilry in two King's Men Plays of 1606', *Modern Language Review* 93 (1998): 934–47.

Craig, Hardin, ed., *Two Coventry Corpus Christi Plays*, London: Oxford University Press, 1957.

Cressy, David, *Bonfires and Bells*, Berkeley and Los Angeles, CA: University of California Press, 1989.

Cross, F. L. and E. L. Livingstone, eds, *The Oxford Dictionary of the Christian Church*, Oxford: Oxford University Press, 1997.

Cubeta, Paul M., 'Falstaff and the art of dying', *SEL* 27 (1987): 197–211.

Cunningham, Dolora, 'Repentance and the art of living well', *Ashland Studies in Shakespeare*, Ashland: Oregon Shakespeare Festival, 1955.

Curry, Walter Clyde, *The Demonic Metaphysics of Macbeth*, New York: Haskell House, 1968.

Dachslager, Earl, ' "The stock of Barabbas": Shakespeare's unfaithful villains', *The Upstart Crow* 6 (1986): 8–21.

Daley, A. Stuart, 'Calling and Commonwealth in *As You Like It*: A late Elizabethan political play', *The Upstart Crow* 14 (1994): 28–46.

Davidson, Clifford, '*Anthony and Cleopatra*: Circe, Venus, and the Whore of Babylon', *Bucknell Review* 25 (1980): 31–55.

Davidson, Clifford, 'The anti-visual prejudice', in *Iconoclasm vs. Art and Drama*, ed. Clifford Davidson and Ann Eljenholm Nichols, Kalamazoo: Medieval Institute, 1989.

Davidson, Clifford and Jennifer Alexander, *The Early Art of Coventry, Stratford-Upon-Avon, Warwick, and Lesser Sites in Warwickshire*, Kalamazoo: Medieval Institute Publications, 1985.

Davidson, Gustav, *A Dictionary of Angels, Including the Fallen Angels*, New York: Free Press [1967].

Davies, Horton, *Worship and Theology in England*, Princeton, NJ: Princeton University Press, 1970.

Davies, Horton and Marie Hélène Davies, *Holy Days and Holidays*, Lewisburg: Bucknell University Press, 1982.

Dawson, R. MacG., 'But why Enobarbus?' *Notes and Queries* 34 (1987): 216–17.

Dean, Paul, 'Shakespeare's causes', *Cahiers Elisabethains* 36 (1989): 25–35.

Dean, Paul, 'The afterlife of *Hamlet*', *English Studies* 83 (2002): 519–26.

De Grazia, Margreta, 'The ideology of superfluous things: *King Lear* as period piece', in *Shakespeare's Tragedies*, ed. Susan Zimmerman, New York: St Martin's, 1998.

Delaney, John J., *Dictionary of Saints*, New York: Doubleday, 1980.

Dent, R. W., 'Hamlet: scourge and minister', *Shakespeare Quarterly* 29 (1978): 82–4.

Desai, R. W., 'Hamlet as "The minister of God to take vengeance" ', *English Language Notes* 31 (1993): 22–7.

Dessen, Alan C., 'Hamlet's poisoned sword: A study in dramatic imagery', *Shakespeare Studies* 5 (1969): 53–69.

Dessen, Alan C., 'The Elizabethan stage-Jew and Christian example', *Modern Language Quarterly* 35 (1974): 231–45.

Devereux, James A., 'The last temptation of Shakespeare: The sonnets and despair', *Renaissance Papers* (1979): 29–38.

Diehl, Huston, 'Horrid image, sorry sight, fatal vision: The visual rhetoric of *Macbeth*', *Shakespeare Studies* 16 (1983): 191–203.

Diehl, Huston, *Staging Reform, Reforming the Stage: Protestantism and Popular Theater in Early Modern England*, Ithaca, NY, and London: Cornell University Press, 1997.

Diehl, Huston, ' "Infinite Space": Representation and reformation in *Measure for Measure*', *Shakespeare Quarterly* 49 (1998): 393–410.

Doebler, John, 'The play within the play: the *Muscipula Diaboli* in *Hamlet*', *Shakespeare Quarterly* 23 (1972), 162–9.

Doob, Penelope B. R., *Nebuchadnezzar's Children*, New Haven, CT, and London: Yale University Press, 1974.

Durston, Christopher and Jacqueline Eales, eds, *The Culture of English Puritanism, 1560–1700*, London: Macmillan, 1996.

Easting, Robert, 'Johnson's note on "Aroint thee, witch!" ' *Notes and Queries* 35 (1988): 480–2.

Edelman, Charles, 'Which is the Jew that Shakespeare knew?: Shylock on the Elizabethan stage', *Shakespeare Survey* 52 (1999): 99–106.

Edelman, Charles, *Shakespeare's Military Language: A Dictionary*, London: Athlone Press, 2000.

Edgerton, William L., 'Shakespeare and the "Needle's Eye"', *Modern Language Notes* 66 (1951): 549–50.

Eliade, Mircea, ed., *The Encyclopedia of Religion*, 16 vols, New York: Macmillan, 1987.

Elton, William R., *King Lear and the Gods*, San Marino: Huntington Library, 1966.

Emmerson, Richard Kenneth, 'Nowe ys common this daye', *Homo, Memento Finis*, intro. David Bevington, Kalamazoo: Medieval Institute Publications, 1985.

Encyclopaedia Britannica, 14th edn, London, 1929.

Engel, William E., *Mapping Mortality: The Persistence of Memory and Melancholy in Early Modern England*, Amherst, MA: University of Massachusetts Press, 1995.

Engel, William E., *Death and Drama in Renaissance England*, Oxford: Oxford University Press, 2002.

Evans, G. Blakemore, 'Dogberry and Job', *Notes and Queries* 37 (1990): 183.

Evans, John X., 'Erasmian folly and Shakespeare's *King Lear*: A study in humanist intertextuality', *Moreana* 27 (1990): 3–23.

Farmer, David Hugh, *The Oxford Dictionary of Saints*, Oxford: Clarendon, 1978.

Farrell, Kirby, 'Self-effacement and autonomy in Shakespeare', *Shakespeare Studies* 16 (1983): 75–99.

Farrell, Kirby, 'Prophetic behavior in Shakespeare's histories', *Shakespeare Studies* 19 (1987): 17–40.

Farrell, Kirby, *Play, Death, and Heroism in Shakespeare*, Chapel Hill, NC: University of North Carolina Press, 1989.

Flachmann, Michael, 'Fitted for death: *Measure for Measure* and the *Contemplatio Mortis*', *English Literary Renaissance* 22 (1992): 222–41

Fleissner, Robert F., 'The "Nothing" element in *King Lear*', *Shakespeare Quarterly* 13 (1962): 67–70.

Fleissner, Robert F., 'A clue to the "Base Judean" in *Othello*', *Notes and Queries* 28 (1981): 137–8.

Fleissner, Robert F., 'Love's lost in *Othello*: What "the Base Indian" is founded on', *English Studies* 76 (1995): 140–2.

Forrest, James F., 'Malvolio and Puritan "singularity" ', *English Language Notes* 11 (1974): 259–64.

Freedman, Barbara, 'Egeon's doubt: Self-division and self-redemption in *The Comedy of Errors*', *English Literary Renaissance* 10 (1980): 360–83.

Freinkel, Lisa, 'Shakespeare and the theology of will', *Graven Images* 2 (1995): 31–47.

French, A. L., 'Hamlet's nunnery', *English Studies* 48 (1967): 141–5.

French, A. L., 'The mills of God and Shakespeare's early history plays', *English Studies* 55 (1974): 313–24.

Frey, David L., *The First Tetralogy*, The Hague: Mouton, 1976.

Frye, Roland Mushat, 'Ladies, gentlemen, and skulls: *Hamlet* and the iconographic traditions', *Shakespeare Quarterly* 30 (1979): 15–28.

Frye, Roland Mushat, *The Renaissance Hamlet*, Princeton, NJ: Princeton University Press, 1984.

Garber, Marjorie, *Dream in Shakespeare: From Metaphor to Metamorphosis*, New Haven, CT: Yale University Press, 1974.

Garber, Marjorie, 'Remember me: *Memento Mori* figures in Shakespeare's plays', *Renaissance Drama* 12 (1981): 3–25.

Garber, Marjorie, ' "What's past is prologue": Temporality and prophecy in Shakespeare's history plays', in *Renaissance Genres: Essays on Theory, History, and Interpretation*, ed. Barbara Kiefer Lewalski, Cambridge, MA: Harvard University Press, 1986.

Garner, Shirley Nelson, 'Male bonding and the myth of women's deception in Shakespeare's plays', in *Shakespeare's Personality*, ed. Norman H. Holland, Sidney Homan and Bernard J. Paris, Berkeley, CA: University of California Press, 1989.

Gash, Anthony, 'Shakespeare, carnival and the sacred: *The Winter's Tale* and *Measure for Measure*', in *Shakespeare and Carnival: After Bakhtin*, ed. Ronald Knowles, Houndmills: Macmillan, 1998.

George, C. H. and Katherine George, *The Protestant Mind of the English Reformation (1570–1640)*, Princeton, NJ: Princeton University Press, 1961.

Ghose, Indira, 'Licence to laugh: Festive laughter in *Twelfth Night*', in *A History of English Laughter*, ed. Manfred Pfister, Amsterdam: Rodopi, 2002.

Gillespie, Stuart, *Shakespeare's Books: A Dictionary of Shakespeare's Sources*, London: Athlone, 2001.

Girard, René, 'Hamlet's dull revenge', in *Literary Theory/Renaissance Texts*, ed. Patricia Parker and David Quint, Baltimore, MD: Johns Hopkins, 1986.

Girard, René, 'Collective violence and sacrifice in *Julius Caesar*', in *New Casebooks: Julius Caesar*, ed. Richard Wilson, New York: Palgrave, 2002.

Go, Kenji, ' "I am that I am" in Shakespeare's Sonnet 121 and 1 Corinthians 15:10', *Notes and Queries* 49 (2002): 241–2.

Grant, Michael, *Herod the Great*, London: Weidenfeld & Nicolson, 1971.

Greenblatt, Stephen, 'Shakespeare and the exorcists', in *Shakespeare and the Question of Theory*, ed. Patricia Parker and Geoffrey Hartman, New York: Methuen, 1985.

Greenblatt, Stephen, 'The eating of the soul', *Representations* 48 (1994): 97–116.

Greenblatt, Stephen, *Hamlet in Purgatory*, Princeton, NJ: Princeton University Press, 2001.

Greenfield, Thelma N., '*A Midsummer Night's Dream* and *The Praise of Folly*', *Journal of Comparative Literature* 20 (1968): 236–44.

Grimal, Pierre, ed., *The Dictionary of Classical Mythology*, trans. A. R. Maxwell-Hyslop, Oxford: Basil Blackwell, 1986.

Grinnell, Richard W., 'Witchcraft and the theater in *Richard III*', *The Upstart Crow* 17 (1997): 66–77.

Guilfoyle, Cherrell, '*Mactacio Desdemonae*: Medieval scenic form in the last scene of *Othello*', *Comparative Drama* 19 (1985–86): 305–20.

Guillory, John, ' "To please the wiser sort": Violence and philosophy in *Hamlet*', in *Historicism, Psychoanalysis, and Early Modern Culture*, ed. Carla Massio and Douglas Trevor, New York: Routledge, 2000.

Gurr, Andrew, *Playgoing in Shakespeare's London*, 2nd edn, Cambridge: Cambridge University Press, 1996.

Gutierrez, Nancy A., 'An allusion to "India" and pearls', *Shakespeare Quarterly* 36 (1985): 220.

Gutierrez, Nancy A., 'Witchcraft and adultery in *Othello*: Strategies of subversion', in *Playing with Gender: A Renaissance Pursuit*, ed. Jean R. Brink *et al.*, Urbana, IL: University of Illinois Press, 1991.

Gutierrez, Nancy A., 'Double standard in the flesh: Gender, fasting, and power in English renaissance drama', in *Disorderly Eaters: Texts in Self-Empowerment*, ed. Lilian R. Furst and Peter W. Graham, University Park, PA: Pennsylvania State University Press, 1992.

Hager, Alan, ' "The teeth of emulation": Failed sacrifice in Shakespeare's *Julius Caesar*', *The Upstart Crow* 8 (1988): 54–68.

Hall, Basil, 'The early rise and gradual decline of Lutheranism in England', *Reform and Reformation: England and the Continent c1500–c1750*, ed. Derek Baker, Oxford: Basil Blackwell, 1979.

Hallett, Charles A. and Elaine S. Hallett, *The Revenger's Madness: A Study of Revenge Tragedy Motifs*, Lincoln, NE: University of Nebraska Press, 1980.

Hamill, Paul, 'Death's lively image: The emblematic significance of the closet scene in *Hamlet*', *Texas Studies in Literature and Language* 16 (1974): 249–62.

Hamilton, A. C., *The Spenser Encyclopedia*, Toronto: University of Toronto Press, 1990.

Hamilton, Donna, 'Some romance sources for King Lear', *Studies in Philology* 71 (1974): 173–91.

Hamilton, Donna, *Shakespeare and the Politics of Protestant England*, Lexington, MA: University Press of Kentucky, 1992.

Hamlin, William M., *The Image of America in Montaigne, Spenser, and Shakespeare*, New York: St Martin's, 1995.

Hankins, John E., ' "The penalty of Adam": *As You Like It*, II.i.5', in *Shakespearean Essays*, ed. Alwin Thaler and Norman Sanders, Knoxville, TN: University of Tennessee Press, 1964.

Harbison, Craig, *The Last Judgment in Sixteenth Century Europe*, New York: Garland, 1976.

Harford, George and Morley Stevenson, eds, *The Prayer Book Dictionary*, London: Sir Isaac Pitman and Sons, 1912.

Harper-Hill, Christopher, 'John and the Church of Rome', in *King John: New Interpretations*, ed. S. D. Church, Woodbridge: The Boydell Press, 1999.

Harris, Jonathan Gil, ' "Look not big, nor stamp, nor stare": Acting up in *The Taming of the Shrew* and the Coventry Herod plays', *Comparative Drama* 34 (2000–01): 365–98.

Hassel, R. Chris, Jr, 'Donne's *Ignatius His Conclave* and the new astronomy', *Modern Philology* 68 (1971a): 329–37.

Hassel, R. Chris, Jr, 'Saint Paul and Shakespeare's romantic comedies', *Thought* 43 (1971b): 371–88.

Hassel, R. Chris, Jr, 'Love versus charity in *Love's Labour Lost*', *Shakespeare Studies* 10 (1977): 17–41.

Hassel, R. Chris, Jr, *Renaissance Drama and the English Church Year*, Lincoln, NE: University of Nebraska Press, 1979.

Hassel, R. Chris, Jr, *Faith and Folly in Shakespeare's Romantic Comedies*, Athens, GA: University of Georgia Press, 1980.

Hassel, R. Chris, Jr, 'Last words and last things: St John, apocalypse, and eschatology in *Richard III*', *Shakespeare Studies* 18 (1986): 25–40.

Hassel, R. Chris, Jr, *Songs of Death: Performance, Interpretation, and the Text of Richard III*, Lincoln, NE: University of Nebraska Press, 1987.

Hassel, R. Chris, Jr, ' "Wormwood, Wormwood" ', *Deutsche Shakespeare Gesellschaft West* (1993): 150–62.

Hassel, R. Chris, Jr, 'Hamlet's "Too, too solid flesh" ', *The Sixteenth Century Journal* 25 (1994a): 609–22.

Hassel, R. Chris, Jr, ' "How infinite in faculties": Hamlet's confusion of God and man', *Literature and Theology* 8 (June 1994b), 127–39.

Hassel, R. Chris, Jr, 'Shakespeare's "removed mysteries" ', *Connotations* 7 (1997/1998): 355–67.

Hassel, R. Chris, Jr, 'Mouse and mousetrap in *Hamlet*', *Shakespeare Jahrbuch* 135 (1999): 77–92.

Hassel, R. Chris, Jr, 'Intercession, detraction, and just judgment in Othello', *Comparative Drama* 35 (2001a): 43–68.

Hassel, R. Chris, Jr, ' "No boasting like a fool"? Macbeth and Herod', *Studies in Philology* 98 (2001b): 205–24.

Hassel, R. Chris, Jr, 'Hamlet's Puritan style', *Religion and the Arts* 7–1/2 (2003): 103–28.

Hatchett, Marion J., *Commentary on the American Prayer Book*, New York: Seabury Press, 1980.

Hawkes, Terence, *Shakespeare and the Reason*, New York: Humanities Press, 1965.

Healy, Thomas, 'History of judgment in *Henry VIII*', in *Shakespeare's Late Plays: New Readings*, ed. Jennifer Richards and James Knowles, Edinburgh: Edinburgh University Press, 1999.

Henry, Carl F. H., ed., *Baker's Dictionary of Christian Ethics*, Grand Rapids, MI: Baker Book House, 1973.

Hill, Christopher, *Society and Puritanism in Pre-Revolutionary England*, New York: Schoken, 1964.

Hillman, David, 'The inside story', in *Historicism, Psychoanalysis, and Early Modern Culture*, ed. Carla Mazzio and Douglas Trevor, New York: Routledge, 2000.

Hitt, Jack, *Off The Road*, New York: Simon & Schuster, 1994.

Hockey, Dorothy C., ' "Wormwood, Wormwood!" ', *English Language Notes* 2 (1965): 174–7.

Hogan, Patrick C., 'Othello, racism, and despair', *CLA Journal* 41 (1998): 431–51.

Holden, William, *Anti-Puritan Satire*, New Haven, CT: Yale University Press, 1954.

Holdsworth, R. V., ' "Nunnery" in *Hamlet* and Middleton', *Notes and Queries* 40 (1993): 192–3.

Holmer, Joan Ozark, 'Othello's threnos: "Arabian trees" and "Indian" versus "Judean" ', *Shakespeare Studies* 13 (1980): 145–67.

Holmer, Joan Ozark, ' "When Jacob graz'd his uncle Laban's sheep": A new source for *The Merchant of Venice*', *Shakespeare Quarterly* 36 (1985): 64–5.

Honigmann, E. A. J., 'Sir John Oldcastle, Shakespeare's martyr', in *'Fanned and Winnowed Opinions': Shakespearean Essays Presented to Harold Jenkins*, ed. John W. Mahon and Thomas A. Pendleton, London: Methuen, 1987.

Hopkins, Lisa, *The Shakespearean Marriage: Merry Wives and Heavy Husbands*, Houndsmills: Macmillan, 1998.

Hosley, Richard, ed., *Shakespeare's Holinshed*, New York: Capricorn Books, 1968.

Hotine, Margaret, '*Richard III* and *Macbeth* – Studies in Tudor Tyranny?', *Notes and Queries* 38 (1991): 480–6.

Hull, Suzanne W., *Chaste, Silent & Obedient: English Books for Women*, San Marino: Huntington Library, 1982.

Hunt, Maurice, 'Malvolio, Viola, and the question of instrumentality: Defining providence in *Twelfth Night*', *Studies in Philology* 90 (1993): 277–97.

Hunt, Maurice, 'Wrestling for temperance: *As You Like It* and the *Faerie Queene*, Book II', *Allegorica* 16 (1995): 31–46.

Hunt, Maurice, 'Predestination and the heresy of merit in *Othello*', *Comparative Drama* 30 (1996): 346–76.

Hunter, Robert G., *Shakespeare and the Comedy of Forgiveness*, New York: Columbia University Press, 1965.

Hunter, Robert G., *Shakespeare and the Mystery of God's Judgments*, Athens, GA: University of Georgia Press, 1976.

Huttar, Charles A., 'The Christian basis of Shakespeare's Sonnet 146', *Shakespeare Quarterly* 19 (1968): 355–65.

Ingram, R. W., ' "The true concord of well-tuned sounds": Shakespeare and music', *Review of National Literatures* 3 (1972): 138–62.

Isaac, Dan, 'The worth of a Jew's eye: Reflections of the Talmud in *The Merchant of Venice*', *Maarav* 8 (1992): 349–74.

Jackson, Samuel Macauley, ed., *The New Schaff-Herzog Encyclopedia of Religious Knowledge*, New York and London: Funk and Wagnalls, 1910.

Jacobs, Henry E., 'Prophecy and ideology in Shakespeare's *Richard III*', *South Atlantic Review* 51 (1986): 3–17.

Jeffrey, David Lyle, ed., *A Dictionary of Biblical Tradition in English Literature*, Grand Rapids, MI: William B. Eerdmans, 1992.

Johnson, Nora, 'Body and spirit, stage and sexuality in *The Tempest*', *ELH* 64 (1997): 683–701.

Johnston, Arthur, 'The Player's speech in *Hamlet*', *Shakespeare Quarterly* 13 (1962): 21–30.

Jonassen, Frederick B., 'The meaning of Falstaff's allusion to the Jack-a-Lent in *The Merry Wives of Windsor*', *Studies in Philology* 88 (1991): 46–68.

Jorgensen, Paul A., *Lear's Self-Discovery*, Berkeley, CA: University of California Press, 1967.

Jorgensen, Paul A., 'A formative Shakespearean legacy: Elizabethan views of God, fortune, and war', *PMLA* 90 (1975): 222–33.

Josipovici, Gabriel, 'A tale of a heel and a hip', *Comparative Criticism* 21 (1999): 21–34.

Kaiser, Walter Jacob, *Praisers of Folly*, Cambridge, MA: Harvard University Press, 1963.

Kamps, Ivo, ' "I love you madly, I love you to death": Erotomania and Liebestod in *Romeo and Juliet*', in *Approaches to Teaching Shakespeare's Romeo and Juliet*, ed. Maurice Hunt, New York: Modern Language Association, 2000.

Kaplan, Joel H., 'Pistol's "Oath": *Henry V*, II.i.101', *Shakespeare Quarterly* 22 (1971): 399–400.

Kastan, David Scott, 'Killed with hard opinions: Oldcastle, Falstaff, and the reformed text of *1 Henry IV*', in *Textual Formations and Reformations*, ed. Laurie E. Maguire and Thomas L. Berger, Newark: University of Delaware Press, 1998.

Kaufman, Peter Iver, *Prayer, Despair, and Drama: Elizabethan Introspection*, Urbana, IL: University of Illinois Press, 1996.

Kaula, David, 'Othello possessed: Notes on Shakespeare's use of magic and witchcraft', *Shakespeare Studies* 2 (1966): 112–32.

Kaula, David, ' "Mad idolatry" in Shakespeare's *Troilus and Cressida*', *Texas Studies in Literature and Language* 15 (1973): 25–38.

Kaula, David, '*Hamlet* and the image of both churches', *SEL* 24 (1984): 241–55.

Keefer, Michael H., 'Accommodation and synecdoche: Calvin's God in *King Lear*', *Shakespeare Studies* 20 (1987): 147–68.

Kehler, Dorothea, ' "So jest with heaven": Deity in *King John*', in *King John: New Perspectives*, ed. Deborah T. Curren-Aquino, Newark: University of Delaware Press, 1989.

Keyishian, Harry, *The Shapes of Revenge: Victimization, Vengeance, and Vindictiveness in Shakespeare*, Atlantic Highlands: Humanities, 1995.

Kiefer, Frederick, ' "Written troubles of the brain": Lady Macbeth's conscience', in *Reading and Writing in Shakespeare*, ed. David M. Bergeron, Newark: University of Delaware Press, 1996.

Kiessling, Nicholas K., '*The Winter's Tale*, II.iii.103–7: An allusion to the hag-incubus', *Shakespeare Quarterly* 28 (1977): 93–5.

Kinney, Arthur F., 'Shakespeare's *Comedy of Errors* and the nature of kinds', *Studies in Philology* 85 (1988): 29–52.

Kinney, Arthur F., *Lies Like Truth: Shakespeare, Macbeth, and the Cultural Moment*, Detroit: Wayne State University Press, 2001.

Klause, John, 'Politics, heresy, and martyrdom in Shakespeare's Sonnet 124 and *Titus Andronicus*', in *Shakespeare's Sonnets: Critical Essays*, ed. James Schiffer, New York: Garland, 1999.

Knapp, Jeffrey, 'Preachers and players in Shakespeare's England', *Representations* 44 (1993): 29–59.

Koch, Mark., 'The shaking of the superflux: *King Lear*, charity, value, and the tyranny of equivalence', *The Upstart Crow* 10 (1990): 86–100.

Kolin, Philip C., *The Elizabethan Stage Doctor as a Dramatic Convention*, Salzburg: Universität Salzburg, 1975.

Komonchak, Joseph A., Mary Collins and Dermot A. Lane, eds, *The New Dictionary of Theology*, Wilmington: Michael Glazier, 1987.

Kronenfeld, Judy, ' "So distribution should undo excess, and each man have enough": Shakespeare's *King Lear* – Anabaptist egalitarianism, Anglican charity, both, neither?' *ELH* 59 (1992): 755–84.

Kronenfeld, Judy, *King Lear and the Naked Truth: Rethinking the Language of Religion and Resistance*, Durham: Duke University Press, 1998.

Lake, Peter, *Moderate Puritans and the Elizabethan Church*, Cambridge: University Press, 1982.

Lambert, Malcolm, *Franciscan Poverty; The Doctrine of the Absolute Poverty of Christ and the Apostles in the Franciscan Order 1210–1323*, London: SPCK, 1961.

Lancashire, Anne, 'The emblematic castle in Shakespeare and Middleton', in *Mirror Up to Shakespeare*, ed. J. C. Gray, Toronto: University of Toronto Press, 1984.

Lang, Jovian P., OFM, *Dictionary of the Liturgy*, New York: Catholic Book Publishing, 1989.

Laroque, François, 'Shakespeare's "Battle of Carnival and Lent": The Falstaff scenes reconsidered (*1 and 2 Henry IV*)', in *Shakespeare and Carnival: After Bakhtin*, ed. Ronald Knowles, Houndsmills: Macmillan, 1998.

Lascelles, Mary, '*King Lear* and Doomsday', *Shakespeare Survey* 26 (1973): 69–79.

Lemercier, Sophie, 'The supernatural and the representation of justice in Shakespeare's theatre', *European Studies* (2001): 105–16.

Lepley, Jean, 'Should Rome burn? The morality of vengeance in *Coriolanus* (and beyond)', *Soundings* 66 (1983): 404–21.

Levin, Harry, 'Interrogation, doubt, irony: Thesis, anthesis, synthesis', *The Question of Hamlet*, New York: Oxford University Press, 1959.

Levin, Joel, 'The measure of law and equity: Tolerance in Shakespeare's Vienna', in *Law and Literature Perspectives*, ed. Bruce L. Rockwood and Roberta Kevelson, New York: Peter Lang, 1996.

Levin, Lawrence L., 'Hotspur, Falstaff, and the emblem of wrath in *1 Henry IV*, *Shakespeare Studies* 10 (1977): 43–65.

Levin, Richard, 'The Indian/Iudean crux in *Othello*', *Shakespeare Quarterly* 33 (1982): 60–7.

Levin, Richard, 'More nuns and nunneries and Hamlet's speech to Ophelia', *Notes and Queries* 41 (1994): 41–2.

Levin, Richard, 'Shakespeare's weddings (and other rites)', *Shakespeare Newsletter* 52 (2002): 63–4.

Levy, Eric, 'The mind of man in *Hamlet*', *Renascence* 54 (2002): 219–33.

Lewalski, Barbara K., 'Biblical allusion and allegory in *The Merchant of Venice*', *Shakespeare Quarterly* 13 (1962): 327–43.

Lewalski, Barbara K., 'Thematic patterns in *Twelfth Night*', *Shakespeare Studies* 1 (1965): 327–43.

Lewalski, Barbara K., *Protestant Poetics and the Seventeenth Century Religious Lyric*, Princeton, NJ: Princeton University Press, 1979.

Lewis, C. S., *The Dawn Treader*, New York: Macmillan, 1952.

Lewis, C. S., *The Allegory of Love, a Study in Medieval Tradition*, Oxford: Oxford University Press, 1973 (first publ. 1936).

Lewis, C. S., *Miracles*, New York: Macmillan, 1978.

Lim, Walter S., 'Knowledge and belief in *The Winter's Tale*', *SEL* 41 (2001): 317–34.

Lindley, David, 'The stubbornness of Barnadine: Justice and mercy in *Measure for Measure*', *The Shakespeare Yearbook* 7 (1996): 333–51.

Liston, William, 'Laertes' advice to Ophelia in *Hamlet*, I.iii.12–4', *College Literature* 12 (1985): 1987–89.

Little, Arthur L., Jr, *Shakespeare Jungle Fever: National-Imperial Re-Visions of Race, Rape, and Sacrifice*, Stanford, CA: Stanford University Press, 2000.

Loomis, Catherine, 'Othello's "entire and perfect Chrysolite": A reply', *Notes and Queries* 46 (1999): 238–9.

Low, Anthony, 'Hamlet and the Ghost of Purgatory: Intimations of Killing the Father', *English Literary Renaissance* 29 (1999): 443–67.

Lukacher, Ned, *Demonic Figures: Shakespeare and the Question of Conscience*, Ithaca: Cornell University Press, 1994.

Lupton, Julia Reinhard, 'Afterlives of the saints: Hagiography in *Measure for Measure*', *Exemplaria* 2 (1990): 375–401.

Lupton, Julia Reinhard, 'Othello circumcised: Shakespeare and the Pauline discourse of nations', *Representations* 57 (1997): 73–89.

Lupton, Julia Reinhard, 'Exegesis, mimesis, and the future of humanism in *The Merchant of Venice*', *Religion and Literature* 32 (2000): 123–39.

Luxon, Thomas H., 'A second Daniel: The Jew and the 'True Jew' in *The Merchant of Venice*', *Early Modern Literary Studies* 4.3 (January 1999): 3.1–37.

McAlindon, Tom, 'Pilgrims of Grace: *Henry IV* historicised', *Shakespeare Survey* 48 (1995): 69–84.

McAlindon, Tom, 'The discourse of prayer in *The Tempest*', *SEL* 41 (2001): 335–55.

McCoy, Richard, 'Love's martyrs: Shakespeare's "Phoenix and Turtle" and the sacrificial sonnets', in *Religion and Culture in Renaissance England*, ed. Claire McEachern and Debora Shuger, Cambridge: Cambridge University Press, 1997.

McCoy, Richard, ' "Look upon me, sir": Relationships in *King Lear*', *Representations* 81 (2003): 46–60.

MacCulloch, Thomas, *Thomas Cranmer: A Life*, New Haven, CT: Yale University Press, 1996.

Macdonald, Roland R., '*Meaure for Measure*: The flesh made word', *SEL* 30 (1990): 265–82.

McEachern, Claire, 'Figures of fidelity: Believing in *King Lear*', *Modern Philology* 98 (2000): 211–30.

McFeely, Maureen Connolly, ' "This day my sister should the cloister enter": The convent as refuge in *Measure for Measure*', in *Subjects on the World's Stage: Essays on British Literature of the Middle Ages and the Renaissance*, ed. David C. Allen and Robert A. White, Newark: University of Delaware Press, 1995.

McGee, Arthur R., '*Macbeth* and the Furies', *Shakespeare Survey* 19 (1966): 55–67.

McGrath, Alister E., *Reformation Thought: An Introduction*, 3rd edn., Oxford: Blackwell Publishers Ltd, 2001.

MacKenzie, Clayton G., 'Renaissance emblems of death and Shakespeare's *King John*', *English Studies* 79 (1998): 425–9.

Mack, Maynard, 'The world of Hamlet', *The Yale Review* 41 (1952): 502–23.

Mack, Maynard, *King Lear in Our Time*, Berkeley, CA: University of California Press, 1965.

McLean, Susan, 'Prodigal sons and daughters: Transgression and forgiveness in *The Merchant of Venice*', *Papers on Language and Literature* 32 (1996): 45–62.

McMullan, Gordon, ' "Swimming on bladders": The dialogics of Reformation in Shakespeare and Fletcher's *Henry VIII*', in *Shakespeare and Carnival: After Bakhtin*, ed. Ronald Knowles, London: Macmillan, 1998.

Maguin, Jean Marie, 'Rise and fall of the King of Darkness', in *French Essays on Shakespeare and His Contemporaries: 'What Would France with Us?'*, ed. Jean Marie Maguin and Michele Willems, Newark: University of Delaware Press, 1995.

Malieckal, Bindu, ' "Bondslaves and pagans shall our statesmen be": Moors, Turks, and Venetians in *Othello*', *Shakespeare Yearbook* 10 (1999): 162–89.

Malieckal, Bindu, ' "Wanton irreligious madness": Conversion and castration in Massinger's *The Renegado*', *Essays in Arts and Sciences* 31 (2002): 25–43.

Mallette, Richard, 'From gyves to graces: *Hamlet* and free will', *Journal of English and German Philology* 93 (1994): 336–55.

Mallette, Richard, *Spenser and the Discourses of Reformation England*, Lincoln, NE: University of Nebraska Press, 1997.

Malloch, A. E. and Frank L. Huntley, 'Some notes on equivocation', *PMLA* 81 (1966): 145–6.

Maslen, Elizabeth, 'Yorick's place in *Hamlet*', *Essays and Studies* 36 (1983): 1–13.

Manley, Frank, ed., *John Donne: The Anniversaries*, Baltimore, MD: Johns Hopkins Press, 1963.

March, Jenny, *Cassell Dictionary of Classical Mythology*, London: Cassell, 1998.

Marshall, Cynthia, 'Dualism and the hope of reunion in *The Winter's Tale*', *Soundings* 69 (1986): 294–309.

Marshall, Cynthia, *Last Things and Last Plays: Shakespearean Eschatology*, Carbondale, IL: Southern Illinois University Press, 1991.

Martin, Randall, 'Catholic Ephesians in *Henry IV, Part Two*', *Notes and Queries* 49 (2002): 225–6.

Martz, Louis, *The Poetry of Meditation*, New Haven, CT: Yale University Press, 1962.

Marx, Steven, 'Holy War in *Henry V*', *Shakespeare Survey* 48 (1995): 85–97.

Marx, Steven, *Shakespeare and the Bible*, Oxford: Oxford University Press, 2000.

Mason, Shirley Carr, 'Queen Margaret's Christian worm of conscience', *Notes and Queries* 41 (1994): 32–3.

Mason, Shirley Carr, ' "Foul wrinkled witch": Superstition and scepticism in Shakespeare's Margaret of Anjou', *Cahiers Elisabethains* 52 (1997): 25–37.

Matheson, Mark, '*Hamlet* and "A matter tender and dangerous" ', *Shakespeare Quarterly* 46 (1995): 383–97.

Matthews, Richard, 'Edmund's redemption in *King Lear*', *Shakespeare Quarterly* 26 (1975): 25–9.

Maxwell, J. C., 'Helena's pilgrimage', *Review of English Studies* 20 (1969): 189–92.

Mazzaro, Jerome, 'Madness and memory: Shakespeare's *Hamlet* and *King Lear*', *Comparative Drama* 19 (1985): 97–116.

Mazzaro, Jerome, 'Shakespeare's "Books of memory": *1 and 2 Henry VI*', *Comparative Drama* 35 (2001–02): 393–414.

Meagher, Paul Kevin, ed., *Encyclopedic Dictionary of Religion*, 3 vols, Washington: Corpus Publications, 1979.

Metzger, Bruce M. and Michael D., Coogan, eds, *The Oxford Companion to the Bible*, Oxford: Oxford University Press, 1993.

Metzger, Mary Janell, ' "Now by my hood, a gentle and no Jew": Jessica, *The Merchant of Venice*, and the discourse of early modern English Identity', *PMLA* 113 (1998): 52–63.

Mills, A. D., ed., *A Dictionary of English Place Names*, Oxford: Oxford University Press, 1991.

Milward, Peter, *Shakespeare's Religious Background*, Bloomington, IN: Indiana University Press, 1973.

Milward, Peter, *Religious Controversies of the Elizabethan Age*, Lincoln, NE: University of Nebraska Press, 1977.

Milward, Peter, *Religious Controversies of the Jacobean Age*, Lincoln, NE: University of Nebraska Press, 1978.

Milward, Peter, *Biblical Influences in Shakespeare's Great Tragedies*, Bloomington, IN: Indiana University Press, 1987.

Milward, Peter, 'More on "the base Judean" ', *Notes and Queries* 36 (1989): 329–31.

Mischo, John B., ' "That use is not forbidden usury": Shakespeare's procreation sonnets and the problem of usury', in *Subjects on the World's Stage: Essays on British Literature of the Middle Ages and the Renaissance*, ed. David C. Allen and Robert A. White, Newark: University of Delaware Press, 1995.

Moisan, Thomas, 'Interlinear trysting and "household stuff": The Latin lesson and the domestication of learning in *The Taming of the Shrew*', *Shakespeare Studies* 23 (1995): 100–19.

Monta, Susannah Brietz, ' "Thou fall'st a blessed martyr": Shakespeare's *Henry VIII* and the Polemics of Conscience', *English Literary Renaissance* 30 (2000): 262–83.

Morris, Harry, '*Hamlet* as a *Memento Mori* poem', *PMLA* 85 (1970): 1035–40.

Morris, Harry, *Shakespeare's God*, New York: St Martin's Press, 1972.

Morris, Harry, 'Prince Hal: Apostle to the Gentiles', *CLIO* 7 (1978): 227–46.

Morris, Harry, *Last Things in Shakespeare*, Tallahassee, FL: Florida State University Press, 1985.

Morris, Harry, 'The judgment theme in *The Merchant of Venice*', *Renascence* 39 (1986): 292–311.

Morse, William R., 'Shakespearean self-knowledge: The synthesizing imagination and the limits of reason', in *Drama and Philosophy*, ed. James Redmond, Cambridge: Cambridge University Press, 1990.

Moschovakis, Nicholas R., ' "Irreligious piety" and Christian history: Persecution as pagan anachronism in *Titus Andronicus*', *Shakespeare Quarterly* 53 (2002): 460–86.

Muir, Kenneth, 'Samuel Harsnett and *King Lear*', *Review of English Studies*, n.s. 2 (1951): 11–21.

Mullins, Edwin, *The Pilgrimage to Santiago*, New York: Taplinger, 1974.

Murray, W. A., 'Why was Duncan's blood golden?' *Shakespeare Survey* 19 (1966): 34–44.

Nathan, Norman, ' "Abram", not "Abraham", in *The Merchant of Venice*', *Notes and Queries* 17 (1970): 127–8.

Nathan, Norman, 'Iago, Iachimo, Jaques, Jaques de Boys, Jaquenetta, St Jaques, and Jacob', *Names* 35 (1987): 235–7.

Neill, Michael, 'Remembrance and revenge: *Hamlet, Macbeth* and *The Tempest*', in *Jonson and Shakespeare*, ed. Ian Donaldson, Atlantic Highlands, NJ: Humanities, 1983.

Neillands, Rob, *The Road to Compostela*, Wiltshire: Moorlands, 1985.

Nelson, Timothy G. A., 'The fool as clergyman (and vice-versa): An essay on Shakespearean comedy', in *Jonson and Shakespeare*, ed. Ian Donaldson, Atlantic Highlands, NJ: Humanities, 1983.

New Catholic Encyclopedia, ed. William J. McDonald, San Francisco: McGraw-Hill, 1967.

Nicolson, Adam, *God's Secretaries*, New York: HarperCollins, 2003.

Noble, Richmond, *Shakespeare's Biblical Knowledge*, New York: Macmillan, 1935.

Nosworthy, James M., '*Macbeth, Doctor Faustus*, and the juggling fiends', in *Mirror Up to Shakespeare: Essays in Honour of G. R. Hibbard*, ed. J. C. Gray, Toronto: University of Toronto Press, 1984.

Nuttall, A. D., *Timon of Athens*, Twayne's New Critical Introductions to Shakespeare, Boston: Twayne, 1989.

O'Connor, Michael, 'The Rosary', *Theotokos: A Theological Encyclopedia of the Blessed Virgin Mary*, rev. edn, Wilmington: M. Glazier, 1983.

Ogawa, Yasuhiro, 'Grinning death's-head: *Hamlet* and the vision of the grotesque', in *The Grotesque in Art and Literature*, ed. James Luther Adams and Wilson Yates, Grand Rapids, MI: Eerdmans, 1997.

O'Meara, John, ' "And I will kill thee / And love thee after": Othello's "sacrifice" as dialectic of faith', *English Language Notes* 28 (1990): 35–42.

The Oxford Encyclopedia of the Reformation, ed. Hans J. Hillerbrand, 4 vols, New York: Oxford University Press, 1996.

The Oxford English Dictionary, 2nd edn., prepared by J. A. Simpson and E. S. C. Weiner, 20 vols, Oxford: Clarendon Press, 1989.

Oz, Avraham, 'Nation and place in Shakespeare: The case of Jerusalem as a national desire in early modern English drama', in *Post-Colonial Shakespeares*, ed. Ania Loomba and Martin Orkin, London: Routledge, 1998.

Ozment, Steven, ed., *Reformation Europe: A Guide to Research*, St Louis: Center for Reformation Research, 1982.

Pack, Robert, *The Long View: Essays on the Discipline of Hope and Poetic Craft*, Amherst, MA: University of Massachusetts Press, 1991.

Palmer, Barbara D., *The Early Art of the West Riding of Yorkshire*, Kalamazoo: Medieval Institute Publications, 1990.

Parker, Barbara L., *A Precious Seeing: Love and Reason in Shakespeare's Plays*, New York: New York University Press, 1987.

Parker, Barbara L., 'The Whore of Babylon and Shakespeare's *Julius Caesar*', *SEL* 35 (1995): 251–69.

Parten, Anne, 'Masculine adultery and feminine rejoinders in Shakespeare, Dekker and Sharpham', *Mosaic* 17.1 (1984): 9–18.

Partridge, Eric, *Shakespeare's Bawdy*, London: Routledge, 1968.

Pastoor, Charles, 'The subversion of prodigal son comedy in *The Merchant of Venice*', *Renascence* 53 (2000): 3–22.

Paxson, James J., 'Shakespeare's medieval devils and Joan La Pucelle in *I Henry VI*', in *Henry VI: Critical Essays*, ed. Thomas A. Pendleton, New York: Routledge, 2001.

Pinciss, Gerald M., *Forbidden Matter: Religion in the Drama of Shakespeare and His Contemporaries*, Newark: University of Delaware Press, 2000.

Pineas, Ranier, *Thomas More and Tudor Polemics*, Bloomington, IN: Indiana University Press, 1968.

Plant, Sarah, 'Shakespeare's Lucrece as chaste bee', *Cahiers Elisabethains* 49 (1996): 51–7.

Platt, Peter G., *Reason Diminished: Shakespeare and the Marvellous*, Lincoln, NE: University of Nebraska Press, 1997.

Plummer, John F., ed., *A Variorum Edition of . . . The Summoner's Tale*, Norman and London: University of Oklahoma Press, 1995.

Poisson, Rodney, 'Othello's "base Indian": A better source for the allusion', *Shakespeare Quarterly* 26 (1975): 462–6.

Poole, Kristen, 'Saints alive! Falstaff, Martin Marprelate, and the staging of Puritanism', *Shakespeare Quarterly* 46 (1995): 47–75.

Price, Simon and Emily Kearnes, ed., *The Oxford Dictionary of Classical Myth and Religion*, Oxford: Oxford University Press, 2003.

Prosser, Eleanor, *Hamlet and Revenge*, 2nd edn., Stanford, CA: Stanford University Press, 1971.

Ramsey, Paul, '*Othello*: The logic of damnation', *The Upstart Crow* 1 (1978): 24–35.

Ranald, Margaret Loftus, ' "As marriage binds, and blood breaks": English marriage and Shakespeare', *Shakespeare Quarterly* 30 (1979): 68–81.

Rappaport, Gideon, '*Hamlet*: Revenge and readiness', *The Upstart Crow* 7 (1987): 80–95.

Rashbrook, R. P., 'Shakespeare and the Bible', *Notes and Queries* 197 (1952): 49–50.

Reed, Robert Rentoul, Jr, *Crime and God's Judgement in Shakespeare*, Lexington, MA: University Press of Kentucky, 1984.

Reynolds, Simon, 'The lawful name of marrying contracts and strategems in *The Merry Wives of Windsor*', *The Shakespeare Yearbook* 7 (1996): 313–14.

Ribner, Irvin, 'Shakespeare, Christianity, and the problem of belief', *The Centennial Review* 8 (1964): 99–108.

Richards, Bernard, '*Hamlet* and the theatre of memory', *Notes and Queries* 35 (1988): 53.

Richards, Michael R., 'Hamlet – divine physician', *The Upstart Crow* 1 (1978): 53–63.

Richmond, Hugh, 'Shakespeare's Navarre', *Huntington Library Quarterly* 42 (1979): 193–216.

Roberti, Francesco Cardinal, ed., *Dictionary of Moral Theology*, trans. Henry J. Yannone, Westminster: Newman Press, 1962.

Roberts, Jeanne Addison, 'Shades of the triple Hecate in Shakespeare', *Proceedings of the PMR Conference: Annual Publication of the International Patristic, Mediaeval, and Renaissance Conference* 12–13 (1987–88): 47–66.

Roberts, John W., *A Critical Anthology of English Recusant Devotional Prose, 1558–1603*, Pittsburg: Duquesne University Press, 1966.

Roche, Thomas P., *Petrarch and the English Sonnet Sequences*, New York: AMS Press, 1989.

Rose, Mark, 'Conjuring Caesar: Ceremony, history, and authority in 1599', *English Literary Renaissance* 19 (1989): 291–304.

Rosenfield, Kirstie Gulick, 'Nursing nothing: Witchcraft and female sexuality in *The Winter's Tale*', *Mosaic* 35 (2002): 95–112.

Rosenheim, Judith, 'The stoic meaning of the Friar in *Measure for Measure*', *Shakespeare Studies* 15 (1982): 171–215.

Saccio, Peter, *Shakespeare's English Kings*, New York: Oxford University Press, 1977.

Salingar, Leo, 'Memory in Shakespeare', *Cahiers Elisabethains* 45 (1994): 59–64.

Schoenbaum, Samuel, *William Shakespeare: A Compact Documentary Life*, Oxford: Oxford University Press, 1977.

Scolnicov, Hanna, 'Chastity, prostitution and pornography in *Measure for Measure*', *Shakespeare Jahrbuch* 134 (1998): 68–81.

Scott, William O., 'Macbeth's – and our – self-equivocations', *Shakespeare Quarterly* 37 (1986): 160–74.

Scott, William O., 'Self-Undoing paradox, scepticism, and Lear's abdication', in *Drama and Philosophy*, ed. James Redmond, Cambridge: Cambridge University Press, 1990.

Scoufos, Alice Lyle, *Shakespeare's Typological Satire: A Study of the Falstaff–Oldcastle Problem*, Athens, GA: Ohio University Press, 1979.

Scoufos, Alice Lyle, 'The *Paradiso Terrestre* and the testing of love in *As You Like It*', *Shakespeare Studies* 14 (1981): 215–27.

Sears, Lloyd C., *Shakespeare's Philosophy of Evil*, North Quincy: Christopher Publishing, 1974.

Sexton, Joyce H., ' "Rooted love": Metaphors for baptism in *All's Well That Ends Well*', *Christianity and Literature* 43 (1994): 261–87.

Shaheen, Naseeb, ' "Like the base Judean" ', *Shakespeare Quarterly* 31 (1980): 93–5.

Shaheen, Naseeb, 'Shakespeare's knowledge of the Bible – how acquired', *Shakespeare Studies* 20 (1987): 201–14.

Shaheen, Naseeb, 'Shylock's "Abram" in *The Merchant of Venice*', *Notes and Queries* 38 (1991): 56–7.

Shaheen, Naseeb, 'Shakespeare, the Psalter, and the Vulgate in *Henry V*', *Shakespeare Quarterly* 43 (1992): 71–2.

Shaheen, Naseeb, 'Shakespeare and the Authorised Version', *Notes and Queries* 45 (1998): 343–5.

Shaheen, Naseeb, *Biblical References in Shakespeare's Plays*, Newark: University of Delaware Press, 1999.

Shaheen, Naseeb, 'Shakespeare and the Bible', *Notes and Queries* 47 (2000): 94–7.

Shannon, Laurie J., 'Emilia's argument: Friendship and "human title" in *The Two Noble Kinsmen*', *ELH* 64 (1997): 657–82.

Shapiro, James, *Shakespeare and the Jews*, New York: Columbia University Press, 1996.

Sheingorn, Paula, 'For God is such a doomsman', *Homo, Memento Finis*, intro. David Bevington, Kalamazoo: Medieval Institute Publications, 1985.

Shirley, Frances A., *Swearing and Perjury in Shakespeare's Plays*, London: George Allen and Unwin, 1979.

Shuger, Debora Kuller, *Habits of Thought in the English Renaissance: Religion, Politics, and the Dominant Culture*, Berkeley, CA: University of California Press, 1990.

Shuger, Debora Kuller, *The Renaissance Bible: Scholarship, Sacrifice, and Subjectivity*, Berkeley, CA: University of California Press, 1994.

Shuger, Debora Kuller, *Political Theologies in Shakespeare's England: The Sacred and the State in Measure for Measure*, New York: Palgrave, 2001.

Siegel, Paul N., 'Christianity and the religion of love in *Romeo and Juliet*', *Shakespeare Quarterly* 12 (1961): 371–92.

Siegel, Paul N., 'Shylock the Puritan', *Columbia University Forum* 5 (1962): 16.

Simonds, Peggy Muñoz, 'The marriage topos in *Cymbeline*: Shakespeare's variations on a classical theme', *English Literary Renaissance* 19 (1989a): 94–117.

Simonds, Peggy Muñoz, 'Sacred and sexual motifs in *All's Well That Ends Well*', *Renaissance Quarterly* 42 (1989b): 33–59.

Simonds, Peggy Muñoz, *Myth, Emblem, and Music in Shakespeare's Cymbeline: An Iconographic Reconstruction*, Newark: University of Delaware Press, 1992.

Simmons, Joseph L., *Shakespeare's Pagan World: The Roman Tragedies*, Charlottesville, VA: University Press of Virginia, 1973.

Sinfield, Alan, 'Hamlet's special providence', *Shakespeare Survey* 33 (1980): 89–97.

Sisson, C. J., 'The magic of Prospero', *Shakespeare Survey* 11 (1958): 74–6.

Slights, Camille Wells, 'The conscience of the king: *Henry VIII* and the reformed conscience', *Philological Quarterly* 80 (2001): 27–55.

Smidt, Kristian, 'Spirits, ghosts and gods in Shakespeare', *English Studies* 77 (1996): 422–38.

Smith, Irwin, *Shakespeare's Blackfriars Playhouse: Its History and Its Design*, New York: New York University Press, 1964.

Smith, Jonathan Z., ed., *The HarperCollins Dictionary of Religion*, San Francisco: Harper, 1995.

Smith, Warren D., 'Shakespeare's Shylock', *Shakespeare Quarterly* 15.3 (1964): 193–9.

Snyder, Susan, '*King Lear* and the prodigal son', *Shakespeare Quarterly* 17 (1966): 361–9.

Sokol, B. J. and Mary Sokol, *Shakespeare's Legal Language: A Dictionary*, London: Athlone Press, 2000.

Spencer, Janet M., 'Violence and the sacred: Holy fragments, Shakespeare, and the postmodern', *Christianity and Literature* 50 (2001): 613–29.

Spevack, Marvin, *The Harvard Concordance to Shakespeare*, Harvard, MA: Harvard University Press, 1973.

Spinrad, Phoebe S., '*Measure for Measure* and the art of not dying', *Texas Studies in Literature and Language* 26 (1984): 74–93.

Starr, G. A., 'Caesar's just cause', *Shakespeare Quarterly* 17 (1966): 77–9.

Stein, Arnold, *John Donne's Lyrics: The Eloquence of Action*, Minneapolis, MN: University of Minnesota Press, 1963.

Stockard, Emily E., ' "Transposed to form and dignity": Christian folly and the subversion of hierarchy in *A Midsummer Night's Dream*', *Religion and Literature* 29 (1997): 1–20.

Stott, G. St John, 'The need for Banquo's ghost', *Notes and Queries* 39 (1992): 334–6.

Streete, Adrian, 'Charity and law in *Love's Labour Lost*: A Calvinist analogue?', *Notes and Queries* 49 (2002): 224–5.

Stritmatter, Roger, 'A new biblical source for Shakespeare's concept of "All see-ing heaven" ', *Notes and Queries* 46 (1999): 207–9.

Stritmatter, Roger, 'By providence divine: Shakespeare's awareness of some Geneva marginal notes of I Samuel', *Notes and Queries* 47 (2000a): 97–100.

Stritmatter, Roger, ' "Old" and "new" law in *The Merchant of Venice*. A note on the source of Shylock's mortality in Deuteronomy 15', *Notes and Queries* 47 (2000b): 70–2.

Stump, Donald V., '*Hamlet*, Cain and Abel, and the pattern of divine providence', *Renaissance Papers* (1985): 27–38.

Targoff, Ramie, 'The performance of prayer: Sincerity and theatricality in early modern England', *Representations* 60 (1997): 49–69.

Targoff, Ramie, ' "Dirty" amens: Devotion, applause, and consent in *Richard III*', *Renaissance Drama* 31 (2002): 31–61.

Taylor, Gary and John Jowett, *Shakespeare Reshaped*, Oxford: Clarendon Press, 1993.

Taylor, Michael, ' "Here is a thing too young for such a place": Innocence in *Pericles*', *ARIEL* 13 (1982a): 3–19.

Taylor, Michael, 'Innocence in *The Winter's Tale*', *Shakespeare Studies* 15 (1982b): 227–42.

Thatcher, David, 'Antigonus' dream in *The Winter's Tale*', *The Upstart Crow* 13 (1993): 130–42.

Thatcher, David, 'Mercy and "natural guiltiness" in *Measure for Measure*', *Texas Studies in Literature and Language* 37 (1995): 264–84.

Thatcher, David, 'The uncomfortable "Friar" in *Measure for Measure*', *Shakespeare Jahrbuch* 132 (1996): 114–27.

Thomas, Gordon K., 'Speaking of reason to the Danes', *The Upstart Crow* 1 (1978): 69–73.

Tiffany, Grace, 'Calvinist grace in Shakespeare's romances: Upending tragedy', *Christianity and Literature* 49 (2000): 421–45.

Tilley, Morris Palmer, *A Dictionary of the Proverbs in England in the Sixteenth and Seventeenth Centuries*, Ann Arbor, MI: University of Michigan Press, 1950.

Tillyard, E. M. W., *The Elizabethan World Picture*, New York: Macmillan, 1944.

Todd, Margo, ed., *Reformation to Revolution*, London: Routledge, 1995.

Tristram, Philippa, 'Strange images of death', *Leeds Studies in English* 14 (1983): 196–211.

Tuchman, Barbara Wertheim, *A Distant Mirror: The Calamitous Fourteenth Century*, New York: Knopf, 1978.

Tufts, Carol Strongin, 'Shakespeare's conception of moral order in *Macbeth*', *Renascence* 50 (1998): 169–82.

Van Beek, Martin, *An Inquiry Into Puritan Vocabulary*, Gröningen: Wolters-Noordhoff, 1969.

Vanita, Ruth, 'Mariological memory in *The Winter's Tale* and *Henry VIII*', *SEL* 40 (2000): 311–37.

Van Tassel, David E., 'Clarence, Claudio, and Hamlet: "The dread of something after death"', *Renaissance and Reformation* 7 (1983): 48–62.

Velie, Alan R., *Shakespeare's Repentance Plays: The Search for an Adequate Form*, Rutherford: Fairleigh Dickinson University Press, 1972.

Vitkus, Daniel J., 'Turning Turk in *Othello*: The conversion and damnation of the Moor', *Shakespeare Quarterly* 48 (1997): 145–76.

von Rosador, Kurt Tetzeli, ' "Supernatural soliciting": Temptation and imagination in *Doctor Faustus* and *Macbeth*', in *Shakespeare and His Contemporaries: Essays in Comparision*, ed. E.A.J. Honigmann, Manchester: Manchester University Press, 1986.

von Rosador, Kurt Tetzeli, 'Presented nakedness in *King Lear*', *Archiv für das Studium der Neueren Sprachen und Literaturen* 228 (1991): 26–40.

Vos, Nelvin, *The Drama of Comedy: Victim and Victor*, Richmond, Va.: John Knox Press, 1966.

Voss, Paul J., ' "My ghostly Father": Teaching the Friar in *Romeo and Juliet*', in *Approaches to Teaching Shakespeare's Romeo and Juliet*, ed. Maurice Hunt, New York: Modern Language Association of America, 2000.

Waddington, Raymond B., 'Lutheran Hamlet', *English Language Notes* 27 (1989): 27–42.

Waddington, Raymond B., ' "All in all": Shakespeare, Milton, Donne and the soul-in-body topos', *English Literary Renaissance* 20 (1990): 40–68.

Walker, Lewis, *Shakespeare and the Classical Tradition: An Annotated Bibliography*, New York: Routledge, 2002.

Walker, Williston, *A History of the Christian Church*, rev. edn., New York: Scribner's, 1959.

Wasserman, Jerry, ' "And every one have need of other": Bond and relationship in *King Lear*', *Mosaic* 9 (1976): 15–30.

Waswo, Richard, 'Damnation, Protestant style: *Macbeth*, *Faustus*, and Christian tragedy', *Journal of Medieval and Renaissance Studies* 4 (1974): 63–99.

Waters, D. Douglas, 'Shakespeare and the "Mistress-Missa" tradition in *King Henry VIII*', *Shakespeare Quarterly* 24 (1973): 459–62.

Watson, J. R., *The English Hymn*, Oxford: Clarendon, 1997.

Watson, Robert N., 'Giving up the ghost in a world of decay: *Hamlet*, revenge, and denial', *Renaissance Drama* 21 (1990): 199–223.

Watson, Robert N., *Death as Annihilation in the English Renaissance*, Berkeley, CA: University of California Press, 1994.

Watson, Robert N., '*Othello* as Protestant propaganda', in *Religion and Culture in Renaissance England*, ed. Claire McEachern and Debora Shuger, Cambridge: Cambridge University Press, 1997.

Watson, Robert N., '*Othello* as Reformation tragedy', in *In the Company of Shakespeare: Essays on English Renaissance Literature in Honor of G. Blakemore Evans*, Madison, WI: Fairleigh Dickinson University Press, 2002.

Wayne, Valerie, 'Historical differences: Misogyny and *Othello*', in *The Matter of Difference: Materialist Feminist Criticism of Shakespeare*, ed. Valerie Wayne, Ithaca: Cornell University Press, 1991.

Weedin, E. K. Jr., 'Love's Reason in *Othello*', *SEL* 15 (1975): 293–308.

Wegemer, Gerard, 'Henry VIII on trial: Confronting malice and conscience in Shakespeare's *All Is True*', *Renascence* 52 (2000): 111–30.

Weigel, Luther A., *The English New Testament from Tyndale to the Revised Standard Version*, New York and Nashville, TN: Abingdon-Cokesbury Press, 1949.

Weitz, Morris, '*Hamlet*: Philosophy the Intruder', in *Shakespeare, Philosophy, and Literature: Essays*, ed. Morris Weitz and Margaret Collins Weitz, New York: Peter Lang, 1995.

Wengert, Timothy J., *Human Freedom, Human Righteousness*, New York: Oxford University Press, 1998.

Wenzel, Siegfried, 'The wisdom of the fool', in *The Wisdom of Poetry: Essays in Early English Literature in Honor of Morton W. Bloomfield*, ed. Larry Dean Benson and Siegfried Wenzel, Kalamazoo: Medieval Institute Publications, 1982.

West, Michael, 'The internal dialogue of Shakespeare's Sonnet 146', *Shakespeare Quarterly* 25 (1974): 109–22.

West, Robert H., *The Invisible World: A Study of Pneumatology in Elizabethan Drama*, Athens, GA: University of Georgia Press, 1939.

West, Robert H., *Shakespeare and the Outer Mystery*, Lexington, KT: University of Kentucky Press, 1968.

West, Robert H., *Reginald Scot and Renaissance Writings on Witchcraft*, Boston: Twayne Publishers, 1984.

Whall, Helen M., 'Divining Paul in Shakespeare's comedies', *Hellas* 7 (1996): 29–37.

Whitaker, Virgil Keeble, *Shakespeare's Use of Learning*, San Marino: Huntington Library, 1953 (1969 printing).

White, Paul Whitfield, *Theatre and Reformation: Protestantism, Patronage, and Playing in Tudor England*, Cambridge: University Press, 1993.

Whitehead, Frank, 'The Gods in *King Lear*', *Essays in Criticism* 42 (1992): 196–220.

Wickham, Glynne, 'Hell-Castle and its door-keeper', *Shakespeare Survey* (1966): 68–74.

Wiggers, G. F., *An Historical Presentation of Augustianism and Pelagianism*, trans. Ralph Emerson, Andover: Gould, Newman & Saxton, 1840.

Wilders, John, *The Lost Garden*, Towota, NY: Rowman and Littlefield, 1978.

Wilks, John S., 'The discourse of reason: Justice and the erroneous conscience in *Hamlet*', *Shakespeare Studies* 18 (1986): 117–44.

Williams, George Walton, 'Petitionary prayer in *King Lear*', *South Atlantic Quarterly* 85 (1986): 360–73.

Williams, Gordon, *A Glossary of Shakespeare's Sexual Language*, London: Athlone, 1997.

Williams, Mary C., 'Much ado about chastity in *Much Ado About Nothing*', *Renaissance Papers* (1984): 37–45.

Williams, Rowan, *Writing in the Dust*, Grand Rapids, MI, and Cambridge, MA: William B. Eerdmans, 2002.

Willis, Deborah, 'The monarch and the sacred: Shakespeare and the ceremony for the healing of the King's Evil', in *True Rites and Maimed Rites: Ritual and*

Anti-Ritual in Shakespeare and His Age, ed. Linda Woodbridge and Edward Berry, Urbana, IL: University of Illinois Press, 1992.

Yaffe, Martin D., *Shylock and the Jewish Question*, Baltimore, MD: Johns Hopkins University Press, 1997.

Young, Bruce, 'Shakespearian tragedy in a Renaissance context: *King Lear* and Hooker's *Of the Laws of Ecclesiastical Polity*', in *Approaches to Teaching Shakespeare's King Lear*, New York: Modern Language Association, 1986.

Young, Bruce, 'Parental blessings in Shakespeare's plays', *Studies in Philology* 89 (1992a): 179–210.

Young, Bruce, 'Ritual as an instrument of grace: Parental blessings in *Richard III*, *All's Well That Ends Well*, and *The Winter's Tale*', in *True Rites and Maimed Rites*, ed. Linda Woodbridge and Edward Berry, Urbana, IL: University of Illinois Press, 1992b.

Young, David, *Something of Great Constancy*, New Haven, CT: Yale University Press, 1966.

Zamir, Tzachi, 'Upon one bank and shoal of time: Literature, nihilism, and moral philosophy', *New Literary History* 31 (2000): 529–51.

Index of Shakespeare's Works

All's Well That Ends Well adore, altar, amend, blessing, blood[1], catechism, chastity, cloister, compt, crimes, damned[2], darkness, devil[6], evil[2], evils, exorcist, faith[2], feast[1], folly, fool, Saint Francis, Furies, God, goddess, gossip, gown, hellish, holy[2], humility, idolatry, Saint Jaques, kneel, limbo, miracle, Nebuchadnezzar, nun, organ, pancake, Papist, penitent, pilgrim, Poysam, prayers, Puritan, rector, reliques, reprieve, ring[1], rite, sacrament, Saint[1], sainted, sanctify[1], sanctimony[1], Shrove Tuesday, sin[1], soul[4], spirit[1&3], supernatural, surplice, tainted, Tartar[1], transcendence, Turk, work, world[2], wrath[1], writ, zealous

Antony and Cleopatra accident, deities, demon, determin'd, divine[4], fast, goddess, gods, hell, Herod, Jewry, priest, sacrifice[1], temperance, thankful

As You Like It Adam, answer[2], bell[1], bread, catechism, chapel[1], chastity, christen[1], damnation[1], damned[2], deifies, devil[1], Egypt, faith[4], fasting, fool, God, godhead, hedge-priest, holy[1&2], homily, hymn, Jove, Judas[1], Latin, made[1], maker, married, Martext, monastic, mortal[1], nature, neighbourly, nun, observance, painted, parish, parishioners, patience, penalty, praised, priest, providently, purgation, ravens, religion[5], religious[1], Roman, sacred, sanctify[2], sanctity, save[3], sermon[1], sing[2], sisterhood, solemniz'd, sparrow, thank, thanks, Turk, unclean, unfaithful, vicar, wicked[1]

The Comedy of Errors abbess, abbey, Adam, angel[2], apparell'd, beads, bless[4], blessed (blest)[3], blessing, blood[3], charitable, conjure, cross[2], damn, deliver, devil[1], Ephesus, evil[3], fast, feast[1], flood[2], God, gossip, heaven[1&4], holy[1], judgement[1], lash, light, limbo, lust, Noah, paradise, Pentecost, possessed, pray, priory, privilege, prodigal, Sathan, sin[1], sorceress, soul-killing, sword, Tartar[2], vice[1], witch[1], wizard

Coriolanus churchyard, deity[3], fast, godded, goddess, gods, mysteries, petition, priest, requite, Roman, sacrifice[1], save[3], sin[1], sulphur, thank

Cymbeline angel[1], benediction, blessed (blest)[4], cherubin, conscience, covet, deity[1], devil[4], dew, divine[1&2], Elysium, exorciser, fall[3], godhead, godly[1], gods, hell, holy[2], hope, impious[2], religion[3], Roman, sacrifice[1], sacrilegious, Scripture, self-slaughter, shrine, sin[1], sulphur, temple[1], troth, venge, water holy, witch[2]

Hamlet Abel, abstinence, account, Adam, affection, angel[1&2], apprehend, audit, believe, bell[1], below, bestial, blessing, bodkin, Cain, canon, canonised, cause, celebrate, ceremony, chapel, chastity, Charity Saint, chaunts, choler, Christian[2], churchyard, clay, confess[1], conscience, crimes, cross[2], curse[3], damn, damnation[1], damned[3], desert, desperation, devotion[1], diet, dirge, disappointed, divine[1], divinity[2], doomsday, dreadful, dust, earth[3], eternal[1], eternity[1], even-Christen, Everlasting[2], evil[1], fast, fault, flames, flesh[3&4], forgive, garden, ghost[1], Gis, glass, God, God-a-mercy, godly[1], grace[1], hallowed, haunt, heathen, heaven[2], heavenly[1], hell, Herod, howl, immortal[1], imperfections, impious[1], Israel, jaw-bone, Jephthah, lash, lauds, lenten, love[1], made[1], make, marriage, mass, memory, merit, minister[2], mote, murder, nature, nunn'ry, obedient, obsequious, obsequy, obstinate, occulted, offence, ordinant, organ, orisons, ostentation, pagan, pastor, Saint Patrick, pelican, philosophy, pious[1], powers, pray, prayer[1], priest, prison-house, profane, providence[1], pure, purged, purging, quintessence, reason, reckoning,

441

reform, religion[4], repent, repentance, requiem, rest[1&2], revenge, revengeful, rite, rood, rue, sacred, salvation, sanctify[2], sanctuarize, save[2&3], Saviour, scourge[2], Scripture, self-slaughter, sexton, shriving, sing[1&3], soul[1&4], sparrow, spirit[2], sulphur, Sunday, taint[2], temperance, temperately, tempt, tormenting, trespass, trumpet, Turk, unanel'd, unction, understanding, unfortified, ungracious, unholy, unhousl'd, unsanctified, Saint Valentine, vanity[3], vice[1&2], vision, vow[1&2], wicked[1], will[1], Wittenburg, word[2], world[1&2], Worms, wormwood, 'zounds

Henry IV, Part I acknowledge, Adam, advantage, all-hallown, altar, amendment, angel[2], anthem, archbishop, archdeacon, banes, bishop, bless[1], blessed (blest)[1], catechism, cause, choler, Christ, christen[2], cross[1], damnable[2], damned[2], darkness, death[1], death's-head, devil[1&4], Dives, doomsday, dust, envy, fault, feet, fish, flesh[1], forgive, Friday, God, God's body, Hallowmas, haunt, Hebrew, hell, holy[1], Holy-rood day, image, Iniquity, innocency, iteration, Jerusalem[1], Jesu, Jesus, kine, laud, Lazarus, light, Martlemas, *memento mori*, merit, Michaelmas, nail'd, Saint Nicholas, offerings, Oldcastle, pagan, painted, pardon, Paul's, pharaoh, pilgrim, pontifical, prayers, praying, prelate, Psalms, reverend, robe, rod, sacrifice[4], Saint[1], salvation, Satan, save[1&3], 'sblood, scourged, sepulchre[1], shadow, Shrewsbury, sign[1], sin[1], sing[2], spirit[1], steeple, Sunday, temple[1], thank, truth, unclean, ungracious, vanity[2&3], vengeance, vice[2], villainy, vow[1], weaver, wicked[2], world[1], worm[1], York, 'zounds

Henry IV, Part 2 affection, Saint Albons, angel[2], anthem, archbishop, ashes, balm, bell[1], bishop, book[3], Cain, candle, cause, covet, death[1&2], death's-head, divine[3], Ephesus, Erebus, flesh[1&3], fool, forgive, gluttony, goddaughter, gossip, holy[1], howl, ill[2], immortal[1], infernal, investments, Japhet, Jerusalem[1], Jesu, Jesus, Job, Jove, justice, laud, lechery, Lent, light, Martlemas, martyr, minister[1], Oldcastle, Paul's, peace[1], Pluto, prodigal, Psalmist, reverence, ring[2], rood, sanctify[1&3], save[1], seal, sect[2], Shrovetide, sin[1&2], sinful, soul[2], spirit[4], sword, text, toll, tolling, torture, understanding, vanity[2], vice[1&2], wicked[2], worldly, York, zeal

Henry V Abraham, acquit, Adam, Almighty[2], almshouses, amen[2], angel[1&2], appeal, arm, Babylon, balm, baptism, beadsman, Belzebub, blessed (blest)[5], book[2], Canterbury, cause, celestial, ceremony, chantry, Cheshu, Chrish, Christian[2], christom, clergy, confess[1], contrite, convocation, covetousness, Saint Crispin, damnation[1], damned[3], Saint Davy, demon, Saint Denis, Deum, devil[1&2], diable, divinity[1], Elysium, faith[4], fall[1], fault, feast[2], fiends, flames, Saint George, God, goddess, grace[3], heavenly[1], hell, Herod, howl, idolatry, ill[1], impious[1], incarnate, Jeshu, Jewry, Jove, latter day, mass, miracle, mortified, nick, *non nobis*, Numbers, Book of, offences, pardon, patience, pax, piety, praised, prayers, press, pride, priest, pure, reckoning, religiously, revolt, right[1], rightful, rite, robe, Roman, sacred, sacrifice[4], Saint[1], save[1], seigneur, self-love, sin[1], soul[1&2], spirit[5], spiritual[1], spirituality, Tartar[2], thanked, unction, vanity[1&2], vice[1], vigil, wash, Whitsun, will[2]

Henry VI, Part 1 Abel, altar, ban, bell[1], blessed (blest)[2&3], blood, Cain, calling, cardinal[1], celestial, Christian[2], church[1], Constantine, Damascus, death[2], Deborah, Saint Denis, devil[1], dove, dreadful, faith[1&3], feast[2], fiend[1], flesh[3], Saint George, ghost[1], God's Mother, Goliah, hag, Hecate, Saint Katherine, King of kings, Lady, legate, lord, lowliness, Mahomet, marriage, Saint Martin, memory, mercy, minister[2], miracle, miscreant, Saint Philip, Pope, preach, prelate, privilege, procession, professors, prophet[1], religion[3], religious[1], reverent, reverently, righteous, ring[2], sacrament, sacred, saint[2], Sampson, scourge[2], sin[1], solemniz'd, sorcerer, sorcery, spirit[1], spiritual[1], tainted, temple[1], unhallowed[1], unreverent, use, virtuous, vision, will[2], Winchester, witch[1], worship

Henry VI, Part 2 adjudg'd, Saint Albons, Almighty, angry, apostle, appeal, Ave-Maries, ban, beadle, beads, bell[1], bishop, blaspheming, blessed (blest)[2&3], book[1&2], breastplate, canonised, cardinal[1], cathedral, choir[2], Christ, church[1], churchman, clergy, clerk[1], college, commandments, conjure, crown[1&2], darkness, departed, devotion[2], Elysium, envy, eternal[1], everlasting[1], exorcisms, garden, Saint George, God's Mother, hag, hell, image, impious[1], Jesus, joys, judge[2], judgement[1], Lent, light, made[2], Saint Magnus, minister[2],

ostentation, painted, penance, peopled, perjury, Saint Peter, Pharaoh, prayers, predestinate, pride, pure, redemption, religious[1], revenge, reverence, ring[2], rite, sanctuary[4], sexton, sin[1], Solomon, soul[2&4], Sunday, temple[1], thank, thanked, thanks, transgressed, Turk, worm[2]

Othello above, accident, accomptant, advocation, affection, affliction, amen[1], amend, angel[1], baptism, barbarian, beneath, bestial, bless[3], blessed (blest)[1], castigation, catechise, cause, cherubin, circumcised, compt, confess[1], curse[3], damn, demi-devil, devil[1,3,4&5], diablo, divine[2&4], divinity[3], eternal[1], evil[2], faith[5], fall[2], feet, fiends, fiery, forgive, garden, gardener, God, godliness[1], haunt, heathen, heaven[1], heavenly[2], hell, Indian, judge[1], justice, kneel, By'r Lady, light, lord, lust, made[1], married, mercy, mortal[2], obey, offence, pagan, Palestine, pearl, perdition, pernicious, Saint Peter, powers, prayer[1&3], profane, purgatory, redeem, renounce, reprobance, requite, reverence, sacrifice[1], sanctify[4], sanctimony[2], save[1], soul[1&2], seals, sect[2], self-slaughter, serpent, shrift, sin[1], sins, solicit, solicitor, soul[2], sulphur, sword, symbol, tempt, thunder, troth, Turk, unprepared, venial, vice[1], villainy, vow[1], wicked[1], will[1], witchcraft, wrath[2], writ, 'zounds

The Passionate Pilgrim ban, bell[1], descant[1], saint[5]
Pericles altar, belfry, bell[1], beneath, chastity, conscience, deliver, divinity[1], fasting-days, feast[2], fish, flesh[2], God, goddess, godly[1], gods, hallowed, marriage, martyr, miracle, music, oblations, parish, powers, preach, priest, Puritan, requite, sanctity, sexton, sin[1], steeple, sulphur, superstition, thank, unholy, vice[3], votaress
The Phoenix and the Turtle anthem, priest, requiem, surplice

The Rape of Lucrece absolution, conscience, eternity[1], hell, impious[1], incense, lust, pilgrimage, reprobate, ring[2], sacred, saint[6], saint-like, self-slaughter, shrine, sin[1], skies, spirit (sprite)[2], temple[2], unhallowed[2]
Richard II Abel, Abraham, Adam, all hail, almsman, angel[1], anointed, answer[1], archbishop, ashes, balm, beads, beadsmen, bishop, blessed (blest)[2], blood[2&3], book[3], Cain, camel, Canterbury, Carlisle, cause, Christ, Christian[2], clergyman, clerk[1], cloister, confess[1], cross[3&4], damned[2], death[2], demi-paradise, deputy, despair, divine[3&4], earth[2], Eden, Eve, faith[3], fall[1], flesh[2&3], fool, forfend, garden, Saint George, ghost[1], glass, God, Golgotha, grace[1&3], Hallowmass, haunt, heaven[1], hell, high, hope, image, infidels, Jesu, Jewry, Judas[1], King of kings, Saint Lambert's day, lower, made[2], make, Mary, Master, minister[2], mirror, miscreant, needle's eye, never-quenching, pagan, painted, palmer, pardon, pelican, penitence, Pilate, pray, priest, prophet[1&2], pure, ransom, redemption, religious[1], reverence, reverent, right[1&3], rightful, rue, sacrament, sacred, sacrifice[1], saint[4], Saracens, save[3], sepulchre[1&2], serpent, sign[1], sin[1], sinful, son, soul[1&2], substitute, sword, trespass, truth, ungracious, vengeance, vice[1&3], walking-staff, wash, will[2], word[1], world[1], worldly, worm[1]
Richard III Abraham, abodements, accident, all-ending day, all-seeing, All-Seer, All-Souls, amen[2], amend, angel[1&2], anoint, apostle, appease, beads, begnaw, bestial, bishop, bless[1], blessed (blest)[2&4], body, book[1], cacodemon, cardinal[1], cause, chaplain, charitable, Chertsey, Christian[2], churchman, clergyman, conjoin, conscience, contemplation, curse[2], damnable[1], deity[1], descant[1&2], despair, destiny, determin'd, devil[3], devotion[1], divine[2,4&5], doctor, doomsday, dreadful, earth[3], enemy[2], eternal[3], evil[2], exercise, Exeter, faith[5], faithful, fiends, fool, friar, Furies, Saint George, ghost[1&2], godfather, God, God's Mother, gossip, grace[1&3], gracious[1], hag, haunt, heaven[1&2], hell, hellish, high, holy[1], hope, howl, humility, image, importune, infidels, Iniquity, Jesu, joys, judgement[1], just, King of kings, law, legions, lord, marry, meditation, meek, mercy, minister[2], monastery, mortal[1], murder, nun, ordinance, patience, Saint Paul, Paul's, pew-fellow, Pilate, praised, pray, prayer[4], prayers, praying[1&2], prepar'd, privilege, prophecy, prophesy, Redeemer, religious[1], remorse, repent, revenge, reverend, right[1&2], ring[1], rood, Sabbath, sacrament, saint[1,2&6], sanctuary[2], save[1&3], scourge[2], Scripture, shadow, shriek, shrift,

Venus and Adonis answer[4], anthem, choir[2], damned[3], Elysium, eternal[3], lust, nun, self-love, tuned, vestal

The Winter's Tale amend, angry, benediction, bless[1&4], blessing, book[3], celebrate, celestial, chaunts, churchyard, damnable[2], divine[1], doctrine, evil[2], fasting, God, godly[2], gods, gossip, hallowed, heavens, heretic, ill-doing, innocence, miracle, motion, naked, oracle, penitent, peril, piety, powers, prayer[1], priest, prodigal, professors, Psalms, Puritan, ransom, rosemary, sacred, sainted, saint-like, sanctity, seal, sect[2], she-angel, shriek, son, sorrow, spirit[1,2&3], spiritual[2], superstition, temple[1], trespass, troth-plight, usurer, vengeance, Whitsun, wicked[1], will[2], wrath, zeal

General Index

This is a selective index both to Shakespeare's characters and to the authors or titles included in the primary bibliography. There are also a few miscellaneous references. When more than 40 references to a character have occurred, the reader is referred to the Index of Shakespeare's Works for the pertinent play(s).

449